THE TAX LAW OF CHARITABLE GIVING

Bruce R. Hopkins

JOHN WILEY & SONS
New York • Chichester • Brisbane • Singapore • Toronto

SUBSCRIPTION NOTICE

This text is printed on acid-free paper.

This publication is designed to provide accurate and authoritative information in regard to the subject matter covered. It is sold with the understanding that the publisher is not engaged in rendering legal, accounting, or other professional services. If legal advice or other expert assistance is required, the services of a competent professional person should be sought.

Library of Congress Cataloging-in-Publication Data:
Hopkins, Bruce R.
    The tax law of charitable giving / Bruce R. Hopkins.
        p.   cm.—(Nonprofit law, finance, and management series)
    Includes index.
    ISBN 0-471-55527-4 (cloth : acid-free paper)
    1. Income tax—United States Deductions—Charitable contributions.   2. Inheritance and transfer tax—Deductions—Law and legislation—United States.   3. Charitable uses, trusts, and foundations—United States.   4. Corporations—Charitable contributions—Law and legislation—United States.   I. Title. II. Series.
    KF6388.H63   1993
    343.7305′2668—dc20   92-44924
    [347.30352668]

Printed in the United States of America
10 9 8 7 6 5 4 3 2

This book is dedicated to

John J. Schwartz

who has worked tirelessly and selflessly in the realm of philanthropy and charitable giving for the good of others for nearly fifty years. I have been privileged to know Jack over the second half of his meritorious and distinguished career, and have never ceased to be impressed, if not awed, by the scope and significance of Jack's professional work, and the elegance with which he does it. Jack once paid me the highest compliment of my life (I will not embarrass either one of us by revealing it here), so it is the least I can do to repay his kind words and good deeds by associating Jack with a book on charitable giving.

About the Author

Bruce R. Hopkins is a lawyer with the Washington, D.C., law firm of Powers, Pyles & Sutter where he specializes in the representation of nonprofit organizations. He has served as Chair of the Committee on Exempt Organizations, American Bar Association; Chair, Section of Taxation, National Association of College and University Attorneys; and President, Planned Giving Study Group of Greater Washington, D.C. He was accorded the Assistant Commissioner's (IRS) Award in 1984. He also teaches a course on nonprofit organizations at The George Washington University National Law Center.

Mr. Hopkins is the series editor of Wiley's Nonprofit Law, Finance, and Management Series. In addition to *The Law of Tax-Exempt Organizations, Sixth Edition*, he is the author of *Charity, Advocacy, and the Law, The Law of Fund-Raising*, and *Starting and Managing a Nonprofit Organization: A Legal Guide*, all published by John Wiley and Sons, Inc. He also writes *The Nonprofit Counsel*, a monthly newsletter, also published by Wiley.

Mr. Hopkins earned his J.D. and LL.M. degrees at The George Washington University and his B.A. at the University of Michigan.

Preface

This book, *The Tax Law of Charitable Giving*, has been on my mind for a long time. It has been written, in parts, many times over the years, with the manuscript pages ending up accumulating dust in some forgotten storage box. As has been the case in other contexts, it took some gentle prodding by Jeffrey Brown and Marla Bobowick at John Wiley & Sons, Inc., to get me going on a contemporary version of the book once again.

It is not that I did not want to write this book; that is certainly not the case. In fact, I have long dreamed of—does it sound too immodest to say it?—a trilogy. This reflects nearly two and one-half decades of law practice, where I have come to see the law uniquely affecting nonprofit organizations as falling into one of three areas: the law of tax-exempt organizations, the law of fund-raising, and the law of charitable giving. The books on the first two of these three subjects have been written; the time had come to begin (or re-begin) the third.

Still, I found my writing time diverted to other subjects (such as the book on advocacy by charitable organizations and the law); postponement continued to be the order of the day.

While writing supplements to the tax-exempt organizations and fund-raising books, I found myself wanting to write supplements for a book on the law of charitable giving. This is because of the swirl of developments in the law taking place in all three arenas. The problem, however, was obvious: One cannot supplement a book that does not exist—or only exists in one's mind.

So, I set about to write this book. I do not mean to imply that I wrote it just so I could write supplements for it. I wrote it because I continued to be impressed by the volume of law being generated in this field, and I wanted readers to have a book that explained the basics and new developments in a complete and comprehensive manner. Moreover, I wanted the book to sketch the law in this area as clearly as is reasonably possible (and, in some instances, it really is not very clear at all). The law on the subject is becoming more intricate, and those who need to keep up with the law in this field deserve a single place to go to find both the fundamentals and recent developments.

Like the other books that I have been privileged to write, this will be supplemented annually. Thus, this book (like the others) are ongoing, alive projects. I believe this book has captured the basics; the supplements will keep them current.

It may well be that the wait to write this book has been propitious. As it is finalized, Washington and the nation is watching a new presidential administration and a substantially changed Congress. Tax policy changes are around the corner and tax legislation in 1993 is as inevitable as these things get. The legislation that would have been the Revenue Act of 1992—and which contained many provisions directly affecting the law of charitable giving—was vetoed. Some of its contents of import to charitable organizations are certain to appear in new laws.

The courts are active in this field, as is the Internal Revenue Service. So there is no dearth of law in this field.

This book captures the state of the law of charitable giving as of the close of 1992. Much more law is unavoidable, keeping this field alive and sometimes confusing. The book is offered as a vehicle to survey the law and minimize the confusion.

As I have stated before, I cannot but thank John Wiley & Sons, Inc., for their support and confidence over the years. I am very proud of the Wiley Nonprofit Law, Finance and Management Series, and the company's commitment to quality publications in those fields. Wiley is making a very unique contribution to the generation and distribution of knowledge in these fields, and I am honored to be a part of this effort. Thanks go again to those that deserve it the most: Jeff Brown and Marla Bobowick (their "gentle" proddings notwithstanding).

My thanks to Michael E. Murphree and Carole S. George, both Washington, D.C. lawyers in private practice, for contributing chapters 2, 8, 18, 19, and 20.

BRUCE R. HOPKINS

Washington, D.C.
December 1992

Contents

Part I

Charitable Giving Law:
An Introduction

1

Introduction To Charitable Giving

This book concerns the law of charitable giving. For the most part, this law consists of federal tax law requirements, although state law is often a factor as well. The law of charitable giving frequently interrelates with the laws concerning tax-exempt status and public charity/private foundation classification of charitable organizations.

§ 1.1 INTRODUCTION TO THE CHARITABLE DEDUCTION

The "charitable contribution" is the subject of extensive law. On the face of it, this is a rather simple matter, requiring merely a "gift" and a "charitable" recipient. While these elements are crucial (and are discussed throughout these pages), they by no means comprise the whole of the subject. Far more is involved in determining the charitable contribution deduction.

There are, in fact, several charitable contribution deductions in American law, including three at the federal level: one for the income tax, one for the estate tax, and one for the gift tax. Most states have at least one form of charitable deduction, as do many counties and cities.

The principal charitable contribution deduction is the one that is part of the federal income tax system. A charitable contribution actually paid during a tax year is allowable as a deduction in computing taxable income for federal income tax purposes. This deduction is allowable irrespective of either the method of accounting employed or the date on which the contribution may have been pledged.

The federal income tax charitable contribution deduction is available to both individuals and corporations. In both instances, the amount deductible may be dependent upon a variety of conditions and limitations. These elements of the law of charitable giving are the subject of much of this book. The federal gift and estate tax charitable contribution deductions are discussed in Chapter 8.

An income tax charitable deduction can be available for gifts of money and of property. This deduction can also be available with respect to outright transfers of money or property to charity, as well as to transfers of partial interests in property. This is the subject of Part III of the book. A gift of a partial interest in property is often known as "planned giving"—the subject that comprises Part IX.

Aside from the law underlying the charitable deduction itself, there are several other aspects of law that can bear on the availability of the deduction. These elements of law, discussed in Part VI, include receipt, recordkeeping, reporting, and disclosure requirements. Also involved, and discussed in Part VI, is the battery of laws regulating the fund-raising process.

There is much additional law that relates to charitable giving and that is outside the scope of this book. However, as this book is part of a series on nonprofit organizations, there are books on the law governing charitable organizations as such, the law comprising regulation of the charitable fund-raising process, tax and financial planning for charitable organizations, the fund-raising process itself, and the accounting rules for charitable organizations.

Prior to review of the laws specifically applicable to charitable giving, it is necessary to understand something of the body of federal tax law concerning tax exemption for charitable organizations and the history underlying this aspect of the law.

§ 1.2 DEFINING "TAX-EXEMPT ORGANIZATIONS"

A "tax-exempt organization" is a unique entity. Almost always, it is a nonprofit organization.[1] The concept of a "nonprofit organization" is

[1]The term "nonprofit" organization is used throughout, rather than the term "not-for-profit." The latter term is used, such as in the federal tax setting, to describe activities (rather than organizations), the expenses of which do not qualify for the business expense deduction (Internal Revenue Code of 1986 section ("§") 183). Throughout this book, the Internal Revenue Code of 1986 is cited as the "IRC."

A companion book by the author provides a summary of the body of law concerning tax-exempt organizations as such (*The Law of Tax-Exempt Organizations*. New York: John Wiley & Sons, Inc., 6th ed. 1992).

usually a matter of state law, while the concept of a "tax-exempt organization" is principally a matter of the federal tax law.

The so-called "nonprofit sector" of United States society has never been totally comfortable with this name. Over the years, it has been called, among other titles, the "philanthropic sector," "private sector," "voluntary sector," "third sector," and "independent sector." In a sense, none of these appellations is appropriate.[2]

The idea of "sectors" of United States society has bred the thought that, in the largest sense, there are three of them. The institutions of society within the United States are generally classified as governmental, for-profit, or nonprofit entities. Governmental entities are the branches, departments, agencies, and bureaus of the federal, state, and local governments. For-profit entities comprise the business sector of this society. Nonprofit organizations constitute, as noted, what is frequently termed the "third sector," the "voluntary sector," the "private sector," or the "independent sector" of United States society. Even these terms are sometimes confusing; for example, the term "private sector" has been applied to both the for-profit and nonprofit sectors.

The rules concerning the creation of nonprofit organizations are essentially a subject for state laws. While a few nonprofit organizations are chartered by the U.S. Congress, most are incorporated or otherwise formed under state law. There is a substantial difference between nonprofit and tax-exempt organizations. While almost all tax-exempt organizations are nonprofit organizations, there are types of nonprofit organizations that are not tax-exempt. There is considerable confusion in United States society as to what the term "nonprofit" means—it does not mean that the organization cannot earn a "profit" (excess of revenue over expenses). The essential difference between a nonprofit organization and a for-profit organization is found in the so-called "private inurement doctrine."[3] Most nonprofit organizations are subject to this doctrine.

---

[2]A discussion of these sectors appears in Ferris and Graddy, "Fading Distinctions among the Nonprofit, Government, and For-Profit Sectors," Chapter 8, Hodgkinson, Lyman, and associates, *The Future of the Nonprofit Sector* (San Francisco: Jossey-Bass, 1989). An argument that the sector should be called the "first sector" is advanced in Young, "Beyond Tax Exemption: A Focus on Organizational Performance Versus Legal Status," Chapter 11, Hodgkinson, Lyman, and associates, *id.*

[3]See Chapter 4 § 4.

The concept of a nonprofit organization is best understood through a comparison with a for-profit organization.

In many respects, the characteristics of the two categories of organizations are identical; both require a legal form, have a board of directors and officers, pay compensation, face essentially the same expenses, are able to receive a profit, make investments, and produce goods and/or services.

However, a for-profit entity has owners—those who hold the equity in the enterprise, such as stockholders of a corporation. The for-profit organization is operated for the benefit of its owners; the profits of the enterprise are passed through to them, such as the payment of dividends on shares of stock. This is what is meant by the term "for-profit" organization; it is one that is intended to generate a profit for its owners. The transfer of the profits from the organization to its owners is considered the inurement of net earnings to the owners in their private capacity.

But, unlike the for-profit entity, the nonprofit organization generally is not permitted to distribute its profits (net earnings) to those who control and/or financially support it; a nonprofit organization usually does not have any owners (equity holders).[4] Consequently, the private inurement doctrine is the substantive dividing line that differentiates, for law purposes, nonprofit organizations and for-profit organizations.

Thus, both nonprofit organizations and for-profit organizations are able to generate a profit; the distinction between the two entities pivots on what is done with this profit.[5] The for-profit organization endeavors to produce a profit for what one commentator called its "residual claimants."[6] The nonprofit organization usually seeks to make that profit work for some end that is beneficial to society.

The private inurement doctrine is applicable to nearly all types of

---

[4] A few states allow nonprofit organizations to issue stock; this is done for control purposes only, in that the stock does not carry with it any rights to dividends.

[5] One commentator has stated that charitable and other nonprofit organizations "are not restricted in the amount of profit they may make; restrictions apply only to what they may do with the profits" (Weisbrod, "The Complexities of Income Generation for Nonprofits," Chapter 7, Hodgkinson, Lyman, and associates, *id.*, n. 2).

[6] Norwitz, "'The Metaphysics of Time': A Radical Corporate Vision," 46 *Bus. Law.* (No. 2) 377 (Feb. 1991).

tax-exempt organizations. However, it is most pronounced with respect to charitable organizations.[7] By contrast, in some types of nonprofit (and tax-exempt) organizations, private benefit is the exempt purpose and function; this is the case, for example, with employee benefit trusts and social clubs.[8]

As this chapter indicates thus far, there are subsets and subsubsets within the nonprofit sector. Tax-exempt organizations are subsets of nonprofit organizations. Charitable organizations (using the broad definition)[9] are subsets of tax-exempt organizations. Charitable organizations (in the narrow sense) are subsets of charitable organizations (in the broader sense of that term).[10]

These elements of the nonprofit sector may be visualized as a series of concentric circles, as shown on page 8.

For a variety of reasons, the organizations comprising the nation's independent sector have been granted exemption from federal and state taxation and, in some instances, have been accorded the status of entities contributions to which are tax deductible under federal and state tax law. Federal, state, and usually local law provide exemptions from income tax for (and, where appropriate, deductibility of contributions to) a wide variety of organizations, including churches, colleges, universities, health care providers, various chari-

[7]The federal law of tax exemption for charitable organizations requires that each of these entities be organized and operated so that "no part of . . . [its] net earnings . . . inures to the benefit of any private shareholder or individual" (IRC § 501(c)(3)).
[8]IRC §§ 501(c)(9), (17), and (20) (employee benefit trusts), and IRC § 501(c)(7) (social clubs). The various categories of tax-exempt organizations and the accompanying Internal Revenue Code sections are summarized in § 9, *infra*.
[9]This broad definition carries with it the connotation of "philanthropy" (e.g., Van Til, "Defining Philanthropy," Chapter 2, Van Til and associates, *Critical Issues in American Philanthropy* (San Francisco: Jossey-Bass, 1990). Also Payton, *Philanthropy: Voluntary Action for the Public Good* (New York: Macmillan Pub. Co. 1988); O'Connell, *Philanthropy in Action* (New York: The Foundation Center, 1987).
[10]The complexity of the federal tax law is such that the charitable sector (using the term in its broadest sense) is also divided into two segments: charitable organizations that are considered "private" (private foundations) and charitable organizations that are considered "public" (all charitable organizations other than those that are considered "private"); these nonprivate charities are frequently referred to as "public charities." See Chapter 4 § 3.

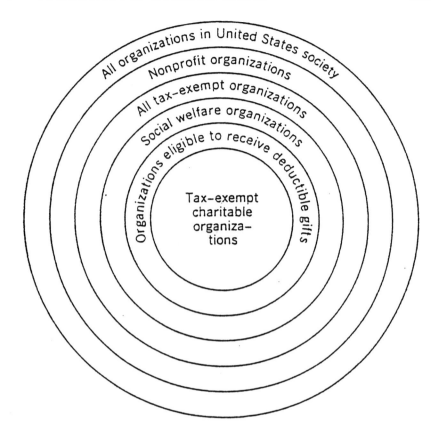

ties, civic leagues, labor unions, trade associations, social clubs, political organizations, veterans' groups, fraternal organizations, and certain cooperatives. Yet, despite the longevity of most of these exemptions, the underlying rationale for them is vague and varying. Nonetheless, the rationales for exemption appear to be long-standing public policy, inherent tax theory, and unique and specific reasons giving rise to a particular tax provision.

§ 1.3 HISTORICAL CONSIDERATIONS

James J. McGovern, Associate Chief Counsel (Employee Benefits and Exempt Organizations), Office of Chief Counsel, Internal Revenue Service, has correctly observed[11] that the various categories of tax-exempt organizations (described in Internal Revenue Code of

[11]McGovern, "The Exemption Provisions of Subchapter F," 29 *Tax Lawyer* 523 (1976).

1986[12] §§ 501, 521, 526, 527, and 528) "are not the result of any planned legislative scheme" but were "enacted over a period of eighty years by a variety of legislators for a variety of reasons."[13]

Mr. McGovern pointed out that, prior to 1894, all customs and other tax legislation enacted by Congress specified the entities subject to taxation. Thus, until that date, tax "exemption" existed by virtue of statutory omission. However, when the income tax of 1894 imposed a flat two percent rate on corporate income, Congress was required to face the task of defining the appropriate subjects of tax exemption. Consequently, section 32 of the Tariff Act of 1894 provided exemption for nonprofit charitable, religious, and educational organizations, fraternal beneficiary societies, certain mutual savings banks, and certain mutual insurance companies. Although the 1894 Act succumbed to a constitutional challenge, the Sixteenth Amendment subsequently was ratified and the Revenue Act of 1913 and comparable measures subsequently were enacted, permanently establishing the principles of progressive taxation and tax exemption.

Mr. McGovern concluded that there were three basic considerations underlying the concept of tax exemption, particularly for charitable entities. The first of these considerations was "heritage"; he wrote that the "history of mankind reflects that our early legislators were not setting precedent by exempting religious or charitable organizations."[14] The second of these considerations was "morality"; he noted that "[l]egislative history clearly indicates, for example, that Congress has generally been willing to exempt the income of organizations formed for the mutual benefit of members so long as they are primarily financed by such members"[15] (this is a restatement of the inherent tax theory underlying exemption, discussed below). As a prime example of a tax exemption based on "policy" grounds, Mr. McGovern cited a senator in 1894 pleading the case for exemption of mutual savings banks:

> Argument ought not to be necessary to sustain the proposition that mutual savings banks should be absolutely exempt from any income taxation.
>
> They represent the savings of the poor; they are not established for

[12]Title 26, United States Code.
[13]McGovern, *supra*, n. 11, at 524.
[14]*Id.* at 527.
[15]*Id.*

ordinary business purposes; the earnings—aside from those necessary for legitimate expenses—belong to the depositors, and are paid to them from time to time in the shape of interest or dividends; they ordinarily have no capital stock, and the managers are simply the agents or trustees of the depositors.

. . . This Government cannot afford to permit the savings of the poor to be taxed through a Federal income tax. It would be the crowning infamy of this bill.[16]

He cites "special interest legislation" as the third consideration underlying the concept of exemption.

In the conclusion of this analysis, McGovern wrote that "[w]hile it is clear, in retrospect, that many of the [exemption] provisions have long outlived their historic justification, it is also clear in contemporary application that many of them continue to play a very crucial role in the law of tax-exempt organizations."[17]

§ 1.4   PUBLIC POLICY AND NATIONAL HERITAGE

The public policy rationale for exempting organizations from tax is best illustrated by the category of organizations described in IRC § 501(c)(3), namely, charitable, educational, religious, scientific, literary and similar entities, and, to a lesser extent, the "social welfare" organization, exempted by virtue of IRC § 501(c)(4). The federal tax exemption for charitable and other organizations may be traced to the origins of the income tax,[18] although most of the committee reports accompanying the 1913 act and subsequent revenue acts are silent on the reasons for initiating and continuing the exemption. One may nevertheless safely venture that the exemption for charitable organizations in the federal tax statutes is largely an extension of comparable practice throughout the whole of history. Presumably,

---

[16] 26 Cong. Rec. 6622 (1894).

[17] McGovern, *supra*, n. 11, at 547. Other overviews of the various tax exemption provisions appear in Hansmann, "The Rationale for Exempting Nonprofit Organizations from Corporate Income Taxation," 91 *Yale L. J.* 69 (1981); and Bittker and Rahdert, "The Exemption of Nonprofit Organizations from Federal Income Taxation," 85 *Yale L. J.* 299 (1976).

[18] 38 Stat. 166. The income tax charitable contribution deduction originated in the 1894 statute (28 Stat. 556, § 32) that was declared unconstitutional in *Pollock* v. *Farmers' Loan and Trust Co.*, 157 U.S. 429 (1895), overruled on other grounds in *State of South Carolina* v. *Baker*, 485 U.S. 505 (1988).

Congress simply believed that these organizations should not be taxed and found the proposition sufficiently obvious as to not warrant extensive explanation. Some clues may be found in the definition of "charitable" activities in the income tax regulations,[19] in which is included purposes such as the relief of the poor, advancement of education or science, erection or maintenance of public buildings, and lessening of the burdens of government. Clearly then, the exemption for charitable organizations is a derivative of the concept that they perform functions which, in the organizations' absence, government would have to perform; therefore, government is willing to forego the tax revenues it would otherwise receive in return for the public services rendered by charitable organizations.

Since the founding of the United States and beforehand in the colonial period, tax exemption—particularly with respect to religious organizations—was common.[20] The churches were openly and uniformly spared taxation.[21] This practice has been sustained throughout the nation's history—not only at the federal but at the state and local levels, most significantly with property taxation.[22] The U.S. Supreme Court, in upholding the constitutionality of the religious tax exemption, observed that "[t]he State has an affirmative policy that considers these groups as beneficial and stabilizing influences in community life and finds this classification [exemption] useful, desirable, and in the public interest."[23]

The U.S. Supreme Court early concluded that the foregoing rationalization was the basis for the federal tax exemption for charitable entities. In 1924, the Court noted that "[e]vidently the exemption is made in recognition of the benefit which the public derives from corporate activities of the class named, and is intended to aid them when not conducted for private gain."[24]

A U.S. court of appeals has observed, with respect to the exemption for charitable organizations, that "[o]ne stated reason for a de-

[19] Income Tax Regulations ("Reg.") § 1.501(c)(3)-1(d)(2).
[20] Cobb, *The Rise of Religious Liberty in America* 482–528 (1902); Lecky, *History of European Morals* (1868).
[21] Torpey, *Judicial Doctrines of Religious Rights in America* 171 (1948).
[22] *Trustees of the First Methodist Episcopal Church* v. *City of Atlanta*, 76 Ga. 181 (1886); *Trinity Church* v. *City of Boston*, 118 Mass. 164 (1875).
[23] *Walz* v. *Tax Commission*, 397 U. S. 664, 673 (1970).
[24] *Trinidad* v. *Sagrada Orden de Predicadores de la Provincia del Santisimo Rosario de Filipinas*, 263 U.S. 578, 581 (1924).

duction or exemption of this kind is that the favored entity performs a public service and benefits the public or relieves it of a burden which otherwise belongs to it."[25] One of the rare congressional pronouncements on this subject is further evidence of the public policy rationale. In its committee report accompanying the Revenue Act of 1938, the House Ways and Means Committee stated:

> The exemption from taxation of money or property devoted to charitable and other purposes is based upon the theory that the government is compensated for the loss of revenue by its relief from financial burden which would otherwise have to be met by appropriations from public funds, and by the benefits resulting from the promotion of the general welfare.[26]

One federal court observed that the reason for the charitable contribution deduction has "historically been that by doing so, the Government relieves itself of the burden of meeting public needs which in the absence of charitable activity would fall on the shoulders of the Government."[27]

Other aspects of the public policy rationale are reflected in caselaw and the literature. Charitable organizations are regarded as fostering voluntarism and pluralism in the American social order.[28] That is, society is regarded as benefiting not only from the application of private wealth to specific purposes in the public interest but also from the variety of choices made by individual philanthropists as to which activities to further.[29] This decentralized choicemaking is arguably more efficient and responsive to public needs than the cumbersome and less flexible allocation process of government administration.[30]

The principle of pluralism was stated by John Stuart Mill, in *On Liberty* (1859), as follows:

---

[25] *St. Louis Union Trust Company* v. *United States*, 374 F.2d 427, 432 (8th Cir. 1967). Also *Duffy* v. *Birmingham*, 190 F.2d 738, 740 (8th Cir. 1951).

[26] H. Rep. No. 1860, 75th Cong., 3d Sess. (1939), at 19.

[27] *McGlotten* v. *Connally*, 338 F. Supp. 448, 456 (D.D.C. 1972).

[28] *Green* v. *Connally*, 330 F. Supp. 1150, 1162 (D.D.C. 1971), aff'd sub. nom., *Coit v. Green*, 404 U.S. 997 (1971).

[29] Rabin, "Charitable Trusts and Charitable Deductions," 41 *N.Y.U.L. Rev.* 912, 920–925 (1966).

[30] Saks, "The Role of Philanthropy: An Institutional View," 46 *Va. L. Rev.* 516 (1960).

In many cases, though individuals may not do the particular thing so well, on the average, as the officers of government, it is nevertheless desirable that it should be done by them, rather than by the government, as a means to their own mental education—a mode of strengthening their active faculties, exercising their judgment, and giving them a familiar knowledge of the subjects with which they are thus left to deal. This is a principal, though not the sole, recommendation of jury trial (in cases not political); of free and popular local and municipal institutions; of the conduct of industrial and philanthropic enterprises by voluntary associations. These are not questions of liberty, and are connected with that subject only by remote tendencies; but they are questions of development . . . The management of purely local businesses by the localities, and of the great enterprises of industry by the union of those who voluntarily supply the pecuniary means, is further recommended by all the advantages which have been set forth in this Essay as belonging to individuality of development, and diversity of modes of action. Government operations tend to be everywhere alike. With individuals and voluntary associations, on the contrary, there are varied experiments, and endless diversity of experience. What the State can usefully do is to make itself a central depository, and active circulator and diffuser, of the experience resulting from many trials. Its business is to enable each experimentalist to benefit by the experiments of others; instead of tolerating no experiments but its own.

This same theme was echoed by the then-Secretary of the Treasury George P. Shultz, in testimony before the House Committee on Ways and Means in 1973, when he observed:

These organizations ["voluntary charities, which depend heavily on gifts and bequests"] are an important influence for diversity and a bulwark against over-reliance on big government. The tax privileges extended to these institutions were purged of abuse in 1969 and we believe the existing deductions for charitable gifts and bequests are an appropriate way to encourage those institutions. We believe the public accepts them as fair.[31]

The principle of voluntarism in the United States was expressed by Norman Fink, while Vice President for Development, Columbia University, as follows:

Voluntarism has been responsible for the creation and maintenance of churches, schools, colleges, universities, laboratories, hospitals, li-

[31] "Proposals for Tax Change," Department of the Treasury, April 30, 1973, at 72.

braries, museums, and the performing arts; voluntarism has given rise to the private and public health and welfare systems and many other functions and services that are now an integral part of the American civilization. In no other country has private philanthropy become so vital a part of the national culture or so effective an instrument in prodding government to closer attention to social needs.[32]

Charitable organizations, maintained by tax exemption and nurtured by the ability to attract deductible contributions, are reflective of the American philosophy that all policy-making should not be reposed in the governmental sector. "Philanthropy," wrote one jurist,

> is the very possibility of doing something different than government can do, of creating an institution free to make choices government cannot—even seemingly arbitrary ones—without having to provide a justification that will be examined in a court of law, which stimulates much private giving and interest.[33]

The public policy rationale for tax exemption (particularly for charitable organizations) was reexamined and reaffirmed by the Commission on Private Philanthropy and Public Needs in its findings and recommendations in 1975."[34] The Commission observed:

> Few aspects of American society are more characteristically, more famously American than the nation's array of voluntary organizations, and the support in both time and money that is given to them by its citizens. Our country has been decisively different in this regard, historian Daniel Boorstin observes, "from the beginning." As the country was settled, "communities existed before governments were there to care for public needs." The result, Boorstin says, was that "voluntary collaborative activities" were set up to provide basic social services. Government followed later.
>
> The practice of attending to community needs outside of government has profoundly shaped American society and its institutional framework. While in most other countries, major social institutions such as universities, hospitals, schools, libraries, museums and social welfare agencies are state-run and state-funded, in the United States many of

[32] Fink, "Taxation and Philanthropy—A 1976 Perspective," 3 *J. Coll. & Univ. L.* 1, 6–7 (1975).
[33] Friendly, "The Dartmouth College Case and the Public-Private Penumbra," 12 *Texas Q.* (2d Supp.) 141, 171 (1969).
[34] *Giving in America—Toward A Stronger Voluntary Sector* (1975). All quotations in this book from the Commission's report are used by permission.

the same organizations are privately controlled and voluntarily supported. The institutional landscape of America is, in fact, teeming with nongovernmental, noncommercial organizations, all the way from some of the world's leading educational and cultural institutions to local garden clubs, from politically powerful national associations to block associations—literally millions of groups in all. This vast and varied array is, and has long been widely recognized as part of the very fabric of American life. It reflects a national belief in the philosophy of pluralism and in the profound importance to society of individual initiative.

Underpinning the virtual omnipresence of voluntary organizations, and a form of individual initiative in its own right, is the practice—in the case of many Americans, the deeply ingrained habit—of philanthropy, of private giving, which provides the resource base for voluntary organizations.

These two interrelated elements, then, are sizable forces in American society, far larger than in any other country. And they have contributed immeasurably to this country's social and scientific progress. On the ledger of recent contributions are such diverse advances as the creation of noncommercial "public" television, the development of environmental, consumerist and demographic consciousness, community-oriented museum programs, the protecting of land and landmarks from the often heedless rush of "progress." The list is endless and still growing; both the number and deeds of voluntary organizations are increasing. "Americans are forever forming associations," wrote de Tocqueville. They still are: tens of thousands of environmental organizations have sprung up in the last few years alone. Private giving is growing, too, at least in current dollar amounts.[35]

This public policy rationale likewise largely underpins the exemption for social welfare organizations contained in IRC § 501(c)(4). The social welfare organization exemption also originated in 1913 and the income tax regulations include the promotion of social welfare within the definition of "charitable."[36] However, gifts to social welfare organizations are generally not deductible as charitable contributions, because these entities are not "charitable" in nature.

The public policy rationale also relates to other categories of tax-exempt organizations. For example, while charitable and social welfare organizations operate to promote the general welfare, trade associations and other forms of business leagues act to promote the welfare of the business and industrial community. Thus, exemption

---

[35]*Id.* at 9–10.
[36]Reg. § 1.501(c)(3)-1(d)(2).

from federal income tax is accorded "business leagues" under IRC
§ 501(c)(6), presumably on the theory that a healthy business climate
advances the public welfare.[37]

Exemption from taxation for certain types of nonprofit organizations is a principle that is larger than the Internal Revenue Code.
Citizens combating problems and reaching solutions on a collective
basis—in "association"—is inherent in the very nature of the American societal structure. Nonprofit associations are traditional in the
United States, and their role and responsibility are not diminished in
modern society. Rather, some contend that the need for the efforts of
nonprofit organizations is greater today than previously, in view of
the growing complexity and inefficiency of government. To tax associations and other nonprofit entities would be to flatly repudiate and
contravene this doctrine, which is so much a part of the nation's
heritage.

This view of nonprofit "associations" operating in the United States
has been the most eloquently stated by Alexis de Tocqueville. He,
too, espoused the principle of pluralism, as expressed in his *Democ-
racy in America*:

> Feelings and opinions are recruited, the heart is enlarged, and the
> human mind is developed only by the reciprocal influence of men
> upon one another. I have shown that these influences are almost null
> in democratic countries; they must therefore be artificially created,
> and this can only be accomplished by associations. . . . A government
> can no more be competent to keep alive and to renew the circulation
> of opinions and feelings among a great people than to manage all the
> speculations of productive industry. No sooner does a government
> attempt to go beyond its political sphere and to enter upon this new
> track than it exercises, even unintentionally, an insupportable tyranny;
> for a government can only dictate strict rules, the opinions which it
> favors are rigidly enforced, and it is never easy to discriminate be-
> tween its advice and its commands. Worse still will be the case if the
> government really believes itself interested in preventing all circula-
> tion of ideas: it will then stand motionless and oppressed by the
> heaviness of voluntary torpor. Governments, therefore, should not be
> the only active powers; associations ought, in democratic nations, to
> stand in lieu of those powerful private individuals whom the equality
> of conditions has swept away.

But de Tocqueville's classic formulation on this subject came in his
portrayal of the use by Americans of "public associations" in civil life:

[37]*Retail Credit Association of Minneapolis* v. *United States*, 30 F. Supp. 855
(D. Minn. 1938).

Americans of all ages, all conditions, and all dispositions constantly form associations. They have not only commercial and manufacturing companies, in which all take part, but associations of a thousand other kinds, religious, moral, serious, futile, general or restricted, enormous or diminutive. The Americans make associations to give entertainments, to found seminaries, to build inns, to construct churches, to diffuse books, to send missionaries to the antipodes; in this manner they found hospitals, prisons, and schools. If it is proposed to inculcate some truth or to foster some feeling by the encouragement of a great example, they form a society. Wherever at the head of some new undertaking you see the government in France, or a man of rank in England, in the United States you will be sure to find an association.

One of the modern-day exponents of the role and value of the independent sector in the United States is John W. Gardner, former Secretary of Health, Education, and Welfare, founder of Common Cause, and one of the founders of Independent Sector. Mr. Gardner has written extensively on the subject of the necessity for and significance of the nation's nonprofit sector. He wrote that "[t]he area of our national life encompassed by the deduction for religious, scientific, educational, and charitable organizations lies at the very heart of our intellectual and spiritual strivings as a people, at the very heart of our feeling about one another and about our joint life."[38] He added that "[t]he private pursuit of public purpose is an honored tradition in American life"[39] and believed that "[a]ll elements in the private sector should unite to maintain a tax policy that preserves our pluralism."[40] Likewise, Robert J. Henle, formerly president of Georgetown University and presently a professor at St. Louis University, wrote of how "[t]he not-for-profit, private sector promotes the free initiative of citizens and gives them an opportunity on a nonpolitical basis to join together to promote the welfare of their fellow citizens or the public purpose to which they are attracted."[41]

It is not possible, in a book of this nature, to fully capture the philosophical underpinnings of the independent sector. Yet, this task has been accomplished by Brian O'Connell, President of Independent Sector.[42] In a foreword to Mr. O'Connell's work, John W.

[38] Gardner, "Bureaucracy vs. The Private Sector," 212 *Current* 17–18 (May 1979).
[39] *Id.* at 17.
[40] *Id.* at 18.
[41] Henle, "The Survival of Not-for-Profit, Private Institutions," *America* 252 (October 23, 1976).
[42] O'Connell, *America's Voluntary Spirit* (New York: The Foundation Center, 1983).

Gardner stated this basic truth: "All Americans interact with voluntary or nonprofit agencies and activities regularly, although they are often unaware of this fact."[43] Still, the educational process must continue, for as Mr. Gardner wrote: "The sector enhances our creativity, enlivens our communities, nurtures individual responsibility, stirs life at the grassroots, and reminds us that we were born free."[44] Mr. O'Connell's collection includes thoughts from sources as diverse as Max Lerner (". . . the associative impulse is strong in American life; no other civilization can show as many secret fraternal orders, businessmen's 'service clubs,' trade and occupational associations, social clubs, garden clubs, women's clubs, church clubs, theater groups, political and reform associations, veterans' groups, ethnic societies, and other clusterings of trivial or substantial importance"[45]), Daniel J. Boorstin (". . . in America, even in modern times, communities existed before governments were here to care for public needs"[46]), Merle Curti (". . . voluntary association with others in common causes has been thought to be strikingly characteristic of American life"[47]), John W. Gardner ("For many countries . . . monolithic central support of all educational, scientific, and charitable activities would be regarded as normal. . . [b]ut for the United States it would mean the end of a great tradition"[48]), Richard C. Cornuell ("We have been unique because another sector, clearly distinct from the other two, has, in the past, borne a heavy load of public responsibility"[49]), John D. Rockefeller 3rd ("The third sector is . . . the seedbed for organized efforts to deal with social problems"[50]), Waldemar A. Neilsen (". . . the ultimate contribution of the Third Sector to our national life—namely what it does to ensure the continuing responsiveness, creativity and self-renewal of our democratic society"[51]), Richard W. Lyman (". . . an array of its [the independent sector's] virtues that is by now fairly familiar: its contributions to pluralism and diversity, its tendency to enable individuals to participate in civic life in ways that

[43]*Id.* at xi.
[44]*Id.* at xv.
[45]*Id.* at 81.
[46]*Id.* at 131 (emphasis in the original).
[47]*Id.* at 162.
[48]*Id.* at 256.
[49]*Id.* at 278.
[50]*Id.* at 356.
[51]*Id.* at 368.

make sense to them and help to combat that corrosive feeling of powerlessness that is among the dread social diseases of our era, its encouragement of innovation and its capacity to act as a check on the inadequacies of government"[52]), and himself ("The problems of contemporary society are more complex, the solutions more involved and the satisfactions more obscure, but the basic ingredients are still the caring and the resolve to make things better"[53]).

Consequently, it is erroneous to regard tax exemption or the charitable contribution deduction as anything other than a reflection of this larger doctrine. Congress is not merely "giving" eligible nonprofit organizations any "benefits"; the exemption from taxation or charitable deduction is not a "loophole," a "preference," or a "subsidy"—it is not really an "indirect appropriation." Rather, the various Internal Revenue Code provisions comprising the tax exemption system exist basically as a reflection of the affirmative policy of American government to not inhibit by taxation the beneficial activities of qualified tax-exempt organizations acting in community and other public interests. (At the same time, it must be conceded that there is no constitutional law protection for tax exemption and the charitable contribution deduction, and thus that Congress is essentially free to structure these rules as it wishes.)

§ 1.5 INHERENT TAX THEORY

Aside from considerations of public policy, there exists an inherent tax theory for tax exemption. The essence of this rationale is that the receipt of what otherwise might be deemed income by a tax-exempt organization is not a taxable event, in that the organization is merely a convenience or means to an end, a vehicle whereby those participating may receive and expend money in much the same way as they would if the money was expended by them individually.

---

[52]*Id.* at 371.
[53]*Id.* at 408. A companion book by the author addresses this point in additional detail, and traces the origins and development of a hypothetical charitable organization to illustrate the applicability of various federal and state laws concerning nonprofit organizations (*Starting and Managing a Nonprofit Organization: A Legal Guide* (New York: John Wiley & Sons, Inc., 1989)). This hypothetical organization is also treated in Blazek, *Tax Planning and Compliance for Tax-Exempt Organizations* (New York: John Wiley & Sons, Inc., 2nd edition, 1993).

This rationale chiefly underlies the exemption for certain social clubs, which enable individuals to pool their resources for the purpose of provision of recreation and pleasure more effectively than can be done on an individual basis. This tax rationale was summarized by one federal court as follows:

> Congress has determined that in a situation where individuals have banded together to provide recreational facilities on a mutual basis, it would be conceptually erroneous to impose a tax on the organization as a separate entity. The funds exempted are received only from the members and any "profit" which results from overcharging for the use of the facilities still belongs to the same members. No income of the sort usually taxed has been generated; the money has simply been shifted from one pocket to another, both within the same pair of pants.[54]

This rationale has also been reflected in congressional committee reports.[55] It was most recently invoked by Congress when enacting the specific tax exemption for homeowners' associations. Thus the Senate Finance Committee observed:

> Since homeowners' associations generally allow individual homeowners to act together in order to maintain and improve the area in which they live, the committee believes it is not appropriate to tax the revenues of an association of homeowners who act together if an individual homeowner acting alone would not be taxed on the same activity.[56]

This rationale, however, operates only where "public" money is not unduly utilized for private gain.[57]

The inherent tax theory also serves as the rationale for the tax exemption for political organizations. Thus, the legislative history underlying this tax exemption states that these organizations should be treated as tax-exempt organizations "since political activity (includ-

[54]*McGlotten* v. *Connally, supra*, n. 27 at 458.
[55]H. Rep No. 91-413, at 48, 91st Cong., 1st Sess. (1969); S. Rep. No. 91-552, at 71, 91st Cong., 1st Sess. (1969). A similar rationale for the income tax exemption of churches has been advanced (Bittker, "Churches, Taxes, and the Constitution," 78 *Yale L. J.* 1285 (1969)).
[56]S. Rep. No. 94-938, 94th Cong., 2d Sess. (1976), at 394.
[57]*West Side Tennis Club* v. *Commissioner*, 111 F.2d 6 (2d Cir. 1940), cert. den., 311 U.S. 674 (1940).

ing the financing of political activity) as such is not a trade or business which is appropriately subject to tax."[58]

§ 1.6   FREEDOM OF ASSOCIATION

Tax exemption for nonprofit membership organizations may be viewed as a manifestation of the constitutionally protected right of association accorded the members of these organizations. There are two types of "freedoms of association." One type—termed the "freedom of intimate association"—is the traditional type of protected association derived from the right of personal liberty. The other type—the "freedom of expressive association"—is a function of the right of free speech protected by the First Amendment to the U.S. Constitution.

By application of the doctrine of freedom of intimate association, the formation and preservation of certain types of highly personal relationships are afforded a substantial measure of sanctuary from unjustified interference by government.[59] These personal bonds are considered to foster diversity and advance personal liberty.[60] In assessing the extent of constraints on the authority of government to interfere with this freedom, a court must make a determination of where the objective characteristics of the relationship, which is created where an individual enters into a particular association, are located on a spectrum from the most intimate to the most attenuated of personal relationships.[61] Relevant factors will include size, purpose, policies, selectivity, and congeniality.[62]

The freedom to engage in group effort is guarateed under the

---

[58]S. Rep. No. 93-1357, 93d Cong., 2d Sess. (1974), at 26.

[59]*Pierce* v. *Society of Sisters*, 268 U.S. 510 (1925); *Meyer* v. *Nebraska*, 262 U.S. 390 (1923).

[60]*Zablocki* v. *Redhail*, 434 U.S. 374 (1978); *Quilloin* v. *Walcott*, 434 U.S. 246 (1978); *Smith* v. *Organization of Foster Families*, 431 U.S. 816 (1977); *Carey* v. *Population Services International*, 431 U.S. 678 (1977); *Moore* v. *East Cleveland*, 431 U.S. 494 (1977); *Cleveland Board of Education* v. *LaFleur*, 414 U.S. 632 (1974); *Wisconsin* v. *Yoder*, 406 U.S. 205 (1973); *Stanley* v. *Illinois*, 405 U.S. 645 (1972); *Stanley* v. *Georgia*, 394 U.S. 557 (1969); *Griswold* v. *Connecticut*, 381 U.S. 479 (1965); and *Olmstead* v. *United States*, 277 U.S. 438 (1928).

[61]*Runyon* v. *McCrary*, 427 U.S. 160 (1976).

[62]*Roberts* v. *United States Jaycees*, 468 U.S. 609 (1984).

doctrine of freedom of expressive association and is viewed as a way of advancing political, social, economic, educational, religious, and cultural ends.[64] Government, however, has the ability to infringe on this right where compelling state interests, unrelated to the suppression of ideas and that cannot be achieved through means significantly less restrictive of associational freedoms, are served.[65]

These two associational freedoms have recently been the subject of a U.S. Supreme Court analysis concerning an organization's right to exclude women from its voting membership.[66] The Court found that the organization involved and its chapters were too large and unselective to find shelter under the doctrine of freedom of intimate association. While the Court also conceded that the "[f]reedom of association therefore plainly presupposes a freedom not to associate," it concluded that the governmental interest in eradicating gender-based discrimination is superior to the associational rights of the organization's male members.[67] In general, the Court held that to tolerate this form of discrimination would be to deny "society the benefits of wide participation in political, economic, and cultural life."[68]

§ 1.7 OTHER RATIONALES

By no means, however, can each provision of the Internal Revenue Code exempting a category of organizations from tax be neatly correlated with one or more of the above-discussed rationales.

Some of the federal tax exemptions were enacted in the spirit of being merely declaratory of or to further then-existing law. The

[63]*Rent Control Coalition for Fair Housing* v. *Berkeley,* 454 U.S. 290 (1981).
[64]*NAACP* v. *Claiborne Hardware Co.,* 458 U.S. 886 (1982); *Larson* v. *Valente,* 456 U.S. 228 (1982); *In re Primus,* 436 U.S. 412 (1978); and *Abood* v. *Detroit Board of Education,* 431 U.S. 209 (1997).
[65]*Brown* v. *Socialist Workers '74 Campaign Comm.,* 459 U.S. 87 (1982); *Democratic Party* v. *Wisconsin,* 450 U.S. 107 (1981); *Buckley* v. *Valeo,* 424 U.S. 1 (1976); *Cousins* v. *Wigoda,* 419 U.S. 477 (1975); *American Party* v. *White,* 415 U.S. 767 (1974); *NAACP* v. *Button,* 371 U.S. 415 (1963); *Shelton* v. *Tucker,* 364 U.S. 486 (1960), and *NAACP* v. *Alabama,* 347 U.S. 449 (1958).
[66]*Roberts* v. *United States Jaycees, supra* n. 62.
[67]*Id.* at 622–629.
[68]*Id.* at 625. In general, Linder, "Freedom of Association After *Roberts* v. *United States Jaycees*," 82 *Mich. L. Rev.* (No. 8) 1878 (1984).

House Ways and Means Committee, in legislating a forerunner to the provision that exempts certain voluntary employees' beneficiary associations, commented that these associations "are common today [1928] and it appears desirable to provide specifically for their exemption from ordinary corporation tax."[69] The exemption for nonprofit cemetery companies was enacted to parallel existing state and local property tax exemption.[70] The exemption for farmers' cooperatives has been characterized as part of the federal government's posture of supporting agriculture.[71] The provision exempting certain U.S. corporate instrumentalities was declaratory of the exemption simultaneously provided for the particular enabling statute.[72] The provision providing tax exemption for multiparent title-holding organizations is the result of the refusal of the IRS to grant tax-exempt status to title-holding corporations that have more than one unrelated tax-exempt parent entity.

Some tax-exempt organization provsions are by-products of other legislative efforts, such as the provision exempting professional football leagues, which was enacted as part of the legislation effecting the merger between the National Football League and the American Football League. The most common example of this phenemenon frequently arises in the employee benefits field, where principal changes in the law in that area have an impact on the law of tax-exempt organizations, such as the law concerning voluntary employees' beneficiary associations, supplemental unemployment benefit trusts, group legal services plans, Black Lung Benefits Trusts, and multiemployer pension plan trusts.

Other federal tax exemption provisions may be traced to an effort to achieve a particular, stated objective. These provisions tend to be of more recent vintage, testimony to the fact of a more complex Internal Revenue Code. Thus, the tax exemption for veterans' organizations as enacted to create a category of organizations entitled to use a particular exemption from the unrelated business income tax. Similarly, the exemption for college and university investment vehicles is the result of Congress's effort to preserve the exempt status of

---

[69] H. Rep. No. 72, 78th Cong., lst Sess. (1928), at 17.
[70] Lapin, "The Golden Hills and Meadows of the Tax-Exempt Cemetery," 44 *Taxes* 744, 746–748 (1966).
[71] Comment, 27 *Iowa L. Rev.* 128, 151–155 (1941).
[72] H. Rep. No. 704, 73rd Cong., 2d Sess. (1934), at 21–25.

a particular common investment fund in the face of a determination by the IRS to the contrary.[73]

All of the foregoing rationales for tax-exempt organizations have been described in philosophical, historical, political, policy, or technical tax terms. Yet another approach to an understanding of exempt organizations can be found in economic theory.

Principles of economics are essentially founded on the laws of supply (production) and demand (consumption). Using the foregoing analyses, exempt organizations appear to have arisen in response to the pressures of the supply side, namely, the need for the goods and services provided, and the force of pluralistic institutions and organizations in society. But others view tax-exempt organizations as responses to sets of social needs that can be described in demand-side economic terms, a "positive theory of consumer demand."[74]

According to the demand-side analysis, consumers in many contexts prefer to deal with nonprofit, tax-exempt organizations in purchasing goods and services. The reason for this is that a nonprofit organization has a "legal commitment to devote its entire earnings to the production of services,"[75] while for-profit organizations have a great incentive to raise prices and cut quality. Generally, it is too difficult for consumers to monitor these forces. This means that consumers have a greater basis for trusting tax-exempt organizations to provide the services—a restatement, in a way, of the fiduciary concept. Thus, the consumer, pursuant to this analysis, "needs an organization that he can trust, and the non-profit, because of the legal constraints under which it must operate, is likely to serve that function better than its for-profit counterpart."[76]

This phenomenon has been described as "market failure" as far as for-profit organizations are concerned, in that, in certain circumstances, the market is unable to police the producers by means of

---

[73] In general, Symposium, "Federal Taxation and Charitable Organizations," 39 *Law and Contemp. Probs.* 1 (1975); Symposium, "Non-Profit Organizations' Impact on U.S. Society," 19 *Clev. St. L. Rev.* 207 (1970); Note, "Tax Exemption: Firmly Rooted," 41 *Notre Dame Lawyer* 695 (1966); Webster, "Certain inconsistencies and discrimination in the taxation of exempt organizations," 21 *J. Tax.* 102 (1964).

[74] Hansmann, "The Role of Nonprofit Enterprise," 89 *Yale Law J.* 835, 896 (1980).

[75] *Id.* at 844.

[76] *Id.* at 847.

ordinary contractual devices."[77] This, in turn, has been described as "contract failure," which occurs where "consumers may be incapable of accurately evaluating the goods promised or delivered" and "market competition may well provide insufficient discipline for a profit-seeking producer."[78] Hence, according to this theory, the consuming public selects the nonprofit organization, which operates without the profit motive and offers the consumer the "trust element" that the for-profit organizations cannot always provide.

However, although the economic demand-side theory is fascinating and undoubtedly contains much truth, it probably overstates the aspect of consumer demand and downplays historical realities, tax considerations, and human frailties. The nonprofit organization antedates the for-profit corporation and many of today's tax-exempt organizations may be nonprofit because their forebears started out as such. And the forces of pluralism of institutions and organizations continue to shape much of the contemporary independent sector.

§ 1.8   STATISTICAL PROFILE OF SECTOR

Over the years, there have been many efforts to analyze and portray the independent sector in statistical terms. One of the most significant of these undertakings, conducted jointly by the Survey Research Center at the University of Michigan and the U.S. Census Bureau, was published in 1975 as part of the findings of the Commission on Private Philanthropy and Public Needs.[79] The data compiled for the Commission's use were for 1973, which showed charitable giving by individuals to amount to about $26 billion and the value of volunteer work as another $26 billion.[80]

Other Commission findings were that college graduates give six times as much on the average as do those with high school educations, small town residents give more than city dwellers, the married give more than the single, and the old give more than the young.

---

[77] *Id.* at 845.
[78] *Id.* at 843.
[79] Note 34, *supra.*
[80] A survey by The Gallup Organization, Inc., released in 1981, indicates that 31 percent of Americans engage in some volunteer service on a regular, active basis and that 52 percent of American adults and about the same proportion of teenagers volunteered over a one-year period.

The "giving of time was also found to correlate closely with the giving of money; the contributor of one is likely to be a contributor of the other."[81]

The most recent attempt to comprehensively profile the contemporary independent sector of the United States principally utilized data for 1984.[82] This analysis, in estimating the dimensions of the sector within the context of the entire American economy, concluded that, of total national income ($3.144 trillion), the independent sector's share was 5.6 percent, as contrasted with the for-profit sector's share of 79.3 percent and the government's share of 14.5 percent. Of the earnings from work ($2.169 trillion) generated by Americans in 1984, the independent sector accounted for 7.2 percent, while the for-profit sector accounted for 75.3 percent and the governmental sector 16.8 percent. Of the total number of entities in the United States in 1984 (19.4 millon), the independent sector accounted for 4.2 percent, the business sector about 94 percent, and the governmental sector less than 1 percent. Current operating expenditures for all nonprofit organizations (not just those comprising the independent sector) in 1984 were $209.8 billion. Although the independent sector grew faster than other sectors of the U.S. economy throughout the 1970s, by 1984 the independent sector was declining by comparison to the other two sectors on most national indicators.

According to this analysis, the total sources of funds for the independent sector in 1984 were dues, fees, and other charges (37.8 percent), contributions (26.9 percent), government (26.9 percent), and other receipts (including investment income) (8.4 percent). During this year, about 80 percent of the funds was used for current operations, with 5.7 percent expended for construction and capital improvements. Of the total expenditures for current operations ($201.5 billon), 52 percent was for health, 24 percent for education and research, nearly 10 percent for social services, 8.5 percent for religion, and 3 percent for civic and social purposes. In 1984, the total full-time employment equivalent of volunteers (5 million in the

[81] *Giving in America—Toward A Stronger Voluntary Sector, supra,* n. 40, at 13–14.
[82] Hodgkinson and Weitzman, *Dimensions of the Independent Sector* (2d ed. 1986). For purposes of this analysis, the term "independent sector" was defined to constitute only IRC § 501(c)(3) organizations (352,884 IRS-recognized organizations plus 338,244 churches and the like) and IRC § 501(c)(4) organizations (130,344 organizations).

independent sector) had an assigned value of $80 billion, representing 24 percent of total sources of support. The proportion of total employment represented by the independent sector was 7.1 percent in 1984; 67.3 percent of these employees were female and nearly 14 percent were black.

Private charitable contributions in 1984 totaled $73 billion, representing 32.7 percent of operating expenditures (as contrasted with 70.6 percent in 1955) and 2.4 percent of national income. Most of these gifts came from living persons (82.8 percent), with the balance from bequests (6.7 percent), private foundations (5.3 percent), and business corporations (5.2 percent). In 1984, 89 percent of Americans made charitable contributions, with an average gift of $640, 39 percent of the donors giving at least 2 percent of their incomes, and 70 percent of the gifts to religious organizations. Persons with household incomes of $50,000 or more, while accounting for 13 percent of the nation's households, made 37 percent of total individual contributions in 1984. In 1983, private foundations granted $4.5 billion for charitable ends, while corporate contributions totaled $3.8 billion in 1984.

This analysis also profiled the independent sector, in terms of trends in funding and expenditures, by subsector, namely, health services; education and research; religious organizations; civic, social, and fraternal organizations; arts and culture; foundations; and legal services. Of the total annual funds received by the independent sector in 1984 ($253.5 billion), health services (primarily hospitals) accounted for one-half; education and research, 23 percent; religion, nearly 12 percent; social services, 8 percent; civic, social, and fraternal organizations, nearly 3 percent; and arts and culture, and foundations (including international activities), about 2.5 percent each. For this purpose, support included private contributions; dues, fees, and like charges; government funds; and endowment funds. The health services subsector received 48 percent of its 1984 support from the private sector, 35 percent from government, and 8 percent from contributions. The comparable percentages for education and research were 53, 17, and 14.5 percent; social services, 12.6, 44, and 37 percent; civic, social, and fraternal, 13, 50, and 30 percent; and arts and culture, 10, 13 and 66.7 percent. The percentage of funds used by the subsectors for current operating expenditures in 1984 was health services, over 80 percent; education and research, also over 80 percent; religious organizations, 59 percent; social service organizations, 93 percent; civic, social, and fraternal organizations, 95 percent; legal services, 100 percent; and arts and culture, 49 percent.

Of the 94.5 million nonagricultural employees in the United States in 1984, 7.2 million were employees of nonprofit organizations; of these, 6.7 were employed in the independent sector. Total wages and salaries in the independent sector in 1984 were $90.6 billion. The health services subsector was responsible for 46.7 percent of this employment; education and research, 22 percent; religion, 9.7 percent; civic, social, and fraternal, 5 percent; and arts and culture, 1.5 percent.

Other 1984 data on the health services subsector show that it then represented 52 percent of the independent sector's total current operating expenditures; of these expenditures, 88 percent were by hospitals (3,539 institutions); 5.3 percent of these expenditures were by nursing and personal care facilities; 6.5 percent of these expenditures were by the outpatient care and allied services component of the subsector; and the estimated value of volunteer time for the subsector was $8 billion. The education and research subsector included 27,694 private elementary, secondary, and special schools, and 1,803 private colleges (1983 data), and 1,338 libraries and information centers, and 1,946 educational and scientific research organizations (1982 data); independent colleges and universities accounted for nearly 52 percent of this subsector's total operating expenditures; and the estimated value of volunteer time for this subsector was $6.1 billion. There were 52,571 social service organizations in 1982; individual and family services consumed 26 percent of this subsector's operating expenditures; job training and related services represented 10 percent of this subsector's operating expenditures; residential care amounted to 20 percent of this subsector's operating expenditures; and the estimated value of volunteer time for this subsector was $17 billion. In 1984, there were approximately 4,200 entities, such as public radio and television broadcasting organizations, and nonprofit theaters, symphony orchestras, operas and dance companies, museums, and botanical and zoological gardens, that attracted volunteer time with an estimated value of about $2.5 billion. Otherwise, in 1982, there were 24,261 private foundations; 35,457 civic, social, and fraternal organizations; and 1,302 legal services organizations; there were an estimated 338,000 religious organizations in 1983.

Total revenue for charitable organizations (other than private foundations) was $196.3 billion in 1982. Contributions and program revenue combined provided 84 percent of this amount.

According to the American Association of Fund-Raising Counsel Trust for Philanthropy, which annually publishes a survey of charitable giving, the level of charitable giving in 1985 was a record $79.84 billion.[83] (Charitable giving in 1984 was reported to be $74.25 billion and $66.82 billion for 1983.) Living individuals provided 82.7 percent of this giving in 1985 ($66.06 billion), with bequests yielding 6.5 percent ($5.18 billion), private foundations 5.4 percent ($4.3 billion), and corporations another 5.4 percent. This nearly $80 billion was allocated to more than 300,000 tax-exempt organizations and institutions as follows: 47.2 percent ($37.73 billion) for religion, 14.1 percent ($11.25 billion) for hospitals and other health purposes, 13.8 percent ($11.05 billion) for education, 10.7 percent ($8.56 billion) for social services, 6.4 percent ($5.09 billion) for the arts and humanities, 2.8 percent ($2.24 billion) for civic and public causes, and 4.9 percent ($3.92 billion) for other purposes. In 1985, giving as a portion of personal income reached 2.01 percent, the highest such level in sixteen years. The increase in corporate contributions (over 13 percent in relation to 1984) was the highest of any of the donor groups. That double-digit jump was among the highest ever recorded for year-to-year corporate philanthropy.

Five years later, this data reflected considerable growth in charitable giving in the United States. The level of charitable giving in 1990 was $117.47 billion.[84] Of this amount, $98.6 billion was from living individuals, $7.64 billion was from estates, $7.23 billion was from private foundations, and $6 billion was from corporations. Of this $117.47 billion, $63.31 billion was contributed in connection with religion, $12.41 billion to education, $11.82 billion for human services, $9.9 billion to health, $7.89 billion for arts and humanities, $4.92 billion for public/society benefit organizations, $2.29 billion for the environment and wildlife, $2.22 billion for international affairs, and $2.69 billion for undesignated purposes.

Total giving to charity in the United States in 1992 rose to $124.77 billion.[85] Individuals contributed $103.13 billion, giving from estates was $7.78 billion, grants from private foundations totaled $7.76 billion, and contributions by corporations reached $6.1 billion.

Of this $124.77 billion, $67.59 billion was given for religious purposes, $13.28 billion was given for educational purposes, $10.61 billion was given to human service organizations, $9.68 billion was given for health purposes, $8.81 billion was given for the arts and

[83]*Giving USA* (1986).
[84]*Giving USA* (1992).
[85]*Id.*

humanities, $4.93 billion was given to public/society benefit organizations, $2.59 billion was donated for international affairs, $2.54 was given to environment and wildlife organizations, and the remaining $4.74 billion was for undesignated purposes.[86]

As the Commission on Private Philanthropy and Public Needs observed, the "arithmetic of the nonprofit sector finds much of its significance in less quantifiable and even less precise dimensions—in the human measurements of who is served, who is affected by nonprofit groups and activities." The Commission added:

> In some sense, everybody is: the contributions of voluntary organizations to broadscale social and scientific advances have been widely and frequently extolled. Charitable groups were in the forefront of ridding society of child labor, abolitionist groups in tearing down the institution of slavery, civic-minded groups in purging the spoils system from public office. The benefits of nonprofit scientific and technological research include the great reduction of scourges such as tuberculosis and polio, malaria, typhus, influenza, rabies, yaws, bilharziasis, syphilis and amoebic dysentery. These are among the myriad products of the nonprofit sector that have at least indirectly affected all Americans and much of the rest of the world besides.

> Perhaps the nonprofit activity that most directly touches the lives of most Americans today is noncommercial "public" television. A bare concept twenty-five years ago, its development was underwritten mainly by foundations. Today it comprises a network of some 240 stations valued at billions of dollars, is increasingly supported by small, "subscriber" contributions and has broadened and enriched a medium that occupies hours of the average American's day.

> More particularly benefited by voluntary organizations are the one quarter of all college and university students who attend private institutions of higher education. For hundreds of millions of Americans, private community hospitals, accounting for half of all hospitals in the United States, have been, as one Commission study puts it, "the primary site for handling the most dramatic of human experiences—birth, death, and the alleviation of personal suffering." In this secular age, too, it is worth noting that the largest category in the nonprofit

[86] A study for Independent Sector by the Gallup Organization, Inc., revealed that the typical household in the United States gave $649 in charitable contributions in 1991, compared to $806 in 1990. This average figure is the lowest in the five years that the survey has been conducted. The poll was off 2,600 individuals. The shortfall was blamed primarily on the nation's economic recession and the adverse publicity concerning the United Way of America.

sector is still very large indeed, that nearly two out of three Americans belong to and evidently find comfort and inspiration in the nation's hundreds of thousands of religious organizations. All told, it would be hard to imagine American life without voluntary nonprofit organizations and associations, so entwined are they in the very fabric of our society, from massive national organizations to the local Girl Scouts, the parent-teachers association or the bottle recycling group.[87]

According to the records of the Internal Revenue Service,[88] there are, as of 1990, 1,024,766 entities on its Master File of Tax-Exempt Organizations and Businesses.[89] These are 9 United States instrumentalities (IRC § 501(c)(1)), 6,278 title-holding companies (IRC § 501(c)(2)), 489,882 charitable organizations (IRC § 501(c)(3)),[90] 142,473 social welfare organizations (IRC § 501(c)(4)), 71,653 labor and agricultural organizations (IRC § 501(c)(5)), 65,896 business leagues (IRC § 501(c)(6)), 62,723 social clubs (IRC § 501(c)(7)), 100,321 fraternal beneficiary societies (IRC § 501(c)(8)), 14,210 voluntary employees' beneficiary societies (IRC § 501(c)(9)), 18,350 domestic fraternal beneficiary societies (IRC § 501(c)(10)), 10 teachers' retirement funds (IRC § 501(c)(11)), 5,873 benevolent life insurance associations (IRC § 501(c)(12)), 8,565 cemetery companies (IRC § 501(c)(13)), 6,352 credit unions (IRC § 501(c)(14)), 1,137 mutual insurance companies (IRC § 501(c)(15)), 19 crop operations finance corporations (IRC § 501(c)(16)), 667 supplemental unemployment benefit trusts (IRC § 501(c)(17)), 8 employee-funded pension trusts (IRC § 501(c)(18)), 27,460 war veterans' organizations (IRC § 501(c)(19)), 197 group legal services organizations (IRC § 501(c)(20)), 22 black lung benefits trusts (IRC § 501(c)(21)), no multiemployer pension trusts (IRC § 501(c)(22)), 2 veterans' organizations founded prior to 1880 (IRC § 501(c)(23)), no exempt trusts described in § 4049 of the Employee Retirement Income Security Act (IRC

[87] *Giving in America—Toward A Stronger Voluntary Sector*, *supra*, n. 34, at 34–38.

[88] Hereinafter the "IRS."

[89] IRS, *Highlights 1990* (Department of the U.S. Treasury, Pub. 1265 (1991), at 38 (Table 25)).

[90] This figure does not include churches, conventions and associations of churches, integrated auxiliaries of churches, subordinate units of churches, and organizations covered under a group exemption, inasmuch as these entities do not have to file an application for recognition of tax exemption (*id.* at 47, notes for Table 25).

§ 501(c)(24)), 107 title-holding companies for multiple beneficiaries (IRC § 501(c)(25), 94 religious and apostolic organizations (IRC § 501(d)), 76 cooperative hospital service organizations (IRC § 501(e)), one cooperative service organization of educational institutions (IRC § 501(f)), 9 child care organizations (IRC § 501(k)), and 2,372 farmers' cooperatives (IRC § 521).

During 1990, the IRS recognized the tax-exempt status of 29,780 charitable (IRC § 501(c)(3)) organizations.[91] It denied 464 of these applications and took other administrative action (in instances where the applicant withdrew the application or the applicant failed to furnish the required information) in 10,129 other instances.

The same numbers for social welfare organizations are 2,116, 46, and 845. For trade associations and similar entities, the numbers are 2,347, 48, and 527. For social clubs, the numbers are 1,298, 51, and 594. And, for voluntary employees' beneficiary associations, the numbers are 1,338, 3, and 409.

During 1990, the IRS examined the returns of 491,100 tax-exempt organizations, utilizing the services of 16,205 revenue agents.[92] The numbers of information returns (Form 990 and the like) examined by the IRS include the following: charitable organizations other than private foundations (3,240), private foundations (1,278), social welfare organizations (624), labor and agricultural organizations (638), business leagues (953), social clubs (916), all other IRC § 501(c) organizations (904), and farmers' cooperatives (266).[93]

Throughout 1990, the IRS examined the returns of 324 political organizations, the unrelated business income tax returns of 3,013 organizations, and the employment tax returns of 3,792 tax-exempt organizations.[94]

§ 1.9 CATEGORIES OF TAX-EXEMPT ORGANIZATIONS

There are several categories of tax-exempt organizations under the federal income tax law. Most of these are the subject of IRC § 501(c). As one court observed, this section "generally consists of narrowly defined categories of exemption," which "are replete with rigid re-

---

[91] *Id.* at 38 (Table 26).
[92] *Id.* at 28 (Table 11).
[93] *Id.* at 46 (notes for Table 11).
[94] *Id.*

quirements which a putatively exempt organization must demonstrate it meets."[95]

The most well known of the types of tax-exempt organizations are the "charitable" entitles described in IRC § 501(c)(3). These organizations, and giving to them, are the subjects of this book.

Closely related to the charitable organization in many respects is the "social welfare organization" that is described in IRC § 501(c)(4).

Another grouping of tax-exempt organizations under federal tax law is the general membership organization, such as the "business league," "chamber of commerce," and "board of trade" (IRC § 501(c)(6)), labor, agricultural, and horticultural groups (IRC § 501(c)(5)), "local association of employees" (IRC § 501(c)(4)), "social club" (IRC § 501(c)(7)), and homeowners' association (IRC § 528). Charitable and social welfare organizations, however, may also be membership organizations.

There are a variety of fraternal and veterans' organizations that qualify for federal income tax exemption. These are the fraternal beneficiary association that use a lodge system and provide membership benefits (IRC § 501(c)(8)), the domestic fraternal society that uses a lodge system but does not provide membership benefits (IRC § 501(c)(10)), the veterans' organization (IRC § 501(c)(19)), and the pre-1880 veterans' trust (IRC § 501(c)(23)).

Federal tax law provides exemption for a variety of employee benefit organizations. These are the "voluntary employees' beneficiary association" (IRC § 501(c)(9)), the "group legal service organization" (IRC § 501(c)(20)), the "black lung benefits trust" (IRC § 501(c)(21)) and Chapter 32 § 6), and the "multi-employer pension plan trust" (IRC § 501(c)(22)). Within this category also are the miscellaneous benefit trusts, namely, the "local teachers' retirement fund association" (IRC § 501(c)(11)), the "supplemental unemployment benefit trust" (IRC § 501(c)(17)), and the pre-June 25, 1959, pension trust (IRC § 501(c)(18)).

Another group of tax-exempt organizations is the mutual or cooperative companies. These are represented by the "local benevolent life insurance association," the "mutual ditch or irrigation company" and "like organizations" (IRC § 501(c)(12)), the "mutual insurance company" (IRC § 501(c)(15)), the "cemetery company" (IRC

---

[95] *Knights of Columbus Building Association of Stamford, Connecticut, Inc.* v. *United States*, 88-1 U.S.T.C. ¶ 9336 (D. Conn. 1988).

§ 501(c)(13)), credit unions (IRC § 501(c)(14)), the "cooperative service organizations" (IRC § 501(e) and (f)), the "crop financing organization" (IRC § 501(c)(16)), the "farmers' cooperative" (IRC § 521), and the "shipowners' protection and indemnity association" (IRC § 526).

The balance of the types of tax-exempt organizations do not readily lend themselves to classification, except as an enumeration of entities other than the foregoing. These are the instrumentalities of the United States (IRC § 501(c)(1)), "title-holding corporation" (IRC § 501(c)(2) and (25)), and "political organization" (IRC § 527).

§ 1.10   THE TAX POLICY CONTEXT

As discussed at the outset of this chapter, there are basically four federal tax law incentives for charitable giving: the charitable contribution deductions used in determining income, gift, and estate taxation, and the tax exemption for qualified charitable organizations. It is necessary to place these incentives in an overall tax policy context, so as to fully understand their workings and consequences, see the impact of tax law changes on these incentives, and predict their future.

Federal tax policy in the United States today is replete with fundamental contradictions, including:

- simplification v. fairness
- revenue needs v. sensible laws
- revenue goals v. behavior goals
- progressivity v. regressivity

Sadly, one of the principal forces for change in tax policy and structure these days is the need for more tax revenue. This need is installing in the tax law a variety of provisions that, while they may not make sense from a pure tax philosophy standpoint, raise revenue. Likewise, there are concepts that should be part of federal tax law, but are not, because they "cost" revenue.

There is no revelation in the observation that the United States tax policy-making system is politicized. For the most part, there is nothing wrong with this; indeed, in an open society, politics and taxes are inescapably intertwined. But sometimes proposed tax law revisions are exploited for purposes of mere posturing. Two cases in point emerge from the 1990 tax law-making struggle. Did the White House push for a capital gains tax reduction largely to satisfy a constituency? Did the Democrats in Congress advocate a surtax on millionaires principally to embarrass the Republicans? Another, more recent, example was the proposal from the Chairman of the House Committee on Ways and Means for a surtax to fund U.S. military operations in the Persian Gulf. Was that an illustration of sound tax policy, or was it an attempt, for political reasons, to highlight the cost of that war?

Makers of tax policy frequently tout, often in a political setting, objectives such as "fairness" and "simplicity." But these objectives are often in conflict. Frequently, "fairness" can only be achieved by means of "complexity." Complexity stems from having to write laws that make distinctions between taxpayers in varying circumstances, to achieve equity. The citizens of the United states live in an intricate, complex society; it should not be surprising that the U.S. tax laws reflect this intricacy.

For example, the U.S. tax law generally dictates that all "income" be taxed. For most taxpayers, income is revenue in the form of salary, wages, interest, dividends, and the like. But is "capital gain" (net earnings derived from the sale of assets) a form of "income"? That is, should these two forms of revenue be taxed the same?

One's answer to these questions depends on one's resolution of another contradiction. There are those who say that the sole purpose of the tax law is to raise revenue. In contrast, there are those who believe it is appropriate to use the tax laws to induce behavior. The capital gains debate again serves as a good illustration. It is "simpler" to tax capital gain as ordinary income. However, a preference in tax treatment of capital gain may induce more investment in capital assets, which would have positive consequences for the overall state of the economy. A tax law distinction between capital gain and ordinary income flies in the face of "simplicity," but the consequential "complexity" may produce desired behavior for the good of the country.

Other examples of this point abound. The federal tax law would be simpler without the home mortgage interest deduction, but that feature of the law is believed to further a national policy of encouraging home ownership. What about the individual retirement account deduction, child care credit, credit for the elderly or disabled, exclusion of municipal bond interest, and the like?

However, while the foregoing illustrations may justify "complexity" over "simplicity," they sometimes do not serve the objective of "fairness." For example, some may perceive higher taxation of interest and dividends, and a correspondingly lower-tax preference for capital gains, as "unfair." This is an illustration of tax law used to motivate individuals' behavior. Likewise, recently enacted taxes on liquor and tobacco have been called "sin" taxes; these taxes are certainly in place to generate revenue but they may also reduce what some regard as inappropriate behavior. Will new, higher taxes on gasoline prompt fuel conservation?

As noted, "fairness" in the tax law is usually achieved by "complexity," which means adding to the tax law features called "exceptions," "deductions," "exemptions," "credits," and so forth. This is one reason the tax law differentiates between "gross income" and "adjusted gross income." For example, one who earns a salary but pays out a portion of it as alimony, which is taxable to the divorced spouse, is merely the conduit of the amount paid to the former spouse and thus is allowed to subtract the payment from gross income in computing adjusted gross income. "Fairness" dictates this deduction, even though it adds an element of "complexity" to the tax law.

Not all deductions can be justified on the basis of pure fairness, however. The deductions that once were in the law, employed in moving the taxpayer from adjusted gross income to taxable income, for the payment of consumer interest and sales taxes, were in the law as a means of reducing the tax burdens on the middle class, rather than as a means of achieving some inherent notion of "fairness." Sometimes the motive behind deductions is a blend of assistance to the middle class and fairness, such as the mortgage interest deduction. These motives underlie the proposal to offer some type of credit or deduction for payments of college tuition.

Other discordant elements permeate the tax law. One of these elements is "progressivity." This goal flies directly in the face of the goal of "simplicity." "Progressivity," however, is closely related to "fairness," in that it proposes the payment of taxes in relation to the taxpayer's ability to pay. Thus, the principal of "progressivity" has it that the wealthier the taxpayer, the more he, she, or it (organization) should pay in taxes. This objective, which is perceived by many as "fair," is achieved by a progression of marginal tax rates, or brackets, which become applicable as the taxpayer earns more. The conflict here, of course, is that the greater the number of tax rates, designed to induce "fairness," the greater the complexity of the tax law and, correspondingly, the greater the inducement for the sophisticated taxpayer to attempt to reduce taxes for a particular year.

For example, a common viewpoint is that a "fair" tax system would cause taxpayers to pay as taxes a certain set percentage of their gross income. This approach, termed a "flat tax," is the ultimate in tax law simplicity. Yet, this approach blatantly contradicts the concepts of "fairness" and "progressivity," because the flat tax does not take into account such important life experiences as high medical expenses, casualty losses, retirement planning, and the like.

Congress bowed to pressures for a flat tax in 1986. Although a pure flat tax was not enacted, the tax exposure of individuals was substantially flattened by a reduction in the tax rates and a repeal or reduction of many deductions. The 1986 revisions were not enacted to generate revenue, but to achieve fairness and simplicity: the 1986 law reduced the number of marginal tax rates to two.

However, in the subsequent years, Congress adopted the view that the 1986 tax changes had contributed to the federal deficit, and therefore "cost" the federal government tax revenues. "Simplicity" became too expensive. So, when the tax legislation in 1990 was enacted, a third tax bracket was a feature. Thus, an element of complexity was added to produce revenue.

Today, there are three tax brackets: 15, 28, and 31 percent. Two tax brackets are "simpler" but they are not "fair" and not at all "progressive." (Of course, two tax brackets are more progressive and "fairer" than one.) Three tax brackets may be "fairer" and more "progressive," but they are not a feature of the tax law that promotes "simplicity."

The changes in the tax law in 1990 are instructive of these points. All other aspects of the tax law being equal, tax counselors advise pushing deductions into the current tax year and deferring income to the next. This approach is based on current tax savings in relation to the time value of money. However, as 1990 was drawing to a close, tax planners for the well-to-do emphasized the use of deductions in 1991 and the incurrence of income in 1990, because the top tax rate in 1990 was 28 percent (disregarding the bubble) and in 1991 became 31 percent. Obviously, then, a deduction generally was "worth more" in 1991 and income was taxed at a lower rate in 1990.

At this point, simplicity and perhaps fairness were sacrificed to the strategy of tax planning. Indeed, "tax planning" usually multiplies complexity. So, someone in the maximum tax bracket of 28 percent in 1990 and 31.9 percent in 1991 struggled to direct income into 1990 (where it was taxed at a lower rate) and to postpone deductions to 1991 (where they became "worth" more). This type of advice is predicated on the presumption (usually accurate) that tax law changes behavior.

The charitable contribution deduction, particularly the one that is part of the income tax, is not based on thoughts of simplicity or fairness. To some degree, it is a behavior-causing provision, in that it stimulates gifts to charity. The charitable contribution deduction has not been deliberately created to produce complexity, although that is a result.

The charitable contribution deduction is in the federal tax law because of the belief of Congress that the services provided by charitable organizations are valuable to society and that the existence of these organizations is inherently a significant part of the American social order. This underlying rationale for the law has been discussed above.[96]

Advocates of the charitable contribution deduction should face the reality of tax policy formulation and confront the issues head on. Rather than defend the law in terms of simplicity or fairness, they must accept the reality of complexity. They must defend their position on one basis: the deduction is a reflection of and is in furtherance of the American way of life. The charitable contribution deduction is a manifestation of a free society—it is based on the view that many of society's problems can be solved by means other than the intervention of government. But individuals cannot effectively act alone in this regard; they must act collectively, either through government agencies or nonprofit organizations. The American bias, based upon distrust of the state, is to favor the latter.

The charitable contribution deduction, as well as the tax exemption for charitable organizations, is based on this philosophical premise. Taxation of charity is literally un-American.

For a variety of reasons, however, principally the fact that in the early 1990s the emphasis is on deficit reduction, the tax preferences for charity are being challenged. Some argue that the charitable contribution deduction is merely a "subsidy" to the donor that is provided by all others in the taxpaying population, in that, absent the charitable deduction, more funds would flow to the U.S. Treasury. Others say that the "cost of giving" is unfairly less for the wealthy; for example, a taxpayer in the 31 percent bracket who contributes $1.00 to charity only economically parts with 69 cents, while a donor in the 15 percent bracket has a cost of giving of 85 cents of every dollar.

Few advocates of tax law change assert that the tax preferences for charity should be repealed. From the standpoint of the exemption,

---

[96] See § 4, *supra.*

this is understandable, since gifts are not income in any event. Moreover, simple politics prevents legislators from advocating wholesale repeal of the tax preferences for charity.

However, incremental reduction of these preferences is occurring, and organized philanthropy is having difficulty thwarting these developments. The mainstay of organized philanthropy—the income tax charitable contribution deduction—may be slipping away. It is falling to the pressures caused by the drive for more tax revenues and the push for the elusive goals of "fairness" and "simplicity." It must be remembered that there are only two ways to increase net tax revenues: raise rates, or repeal or reduce tax preferences.

This stark fact of tax policy should greatly concern organized philanthropy. Significant tax rate increases are, of course, politically unpopular. At the same time, significant spending cuts are unlikely. Thus, future revenue increases will be wrought in part from the repeal and/or reduction of so-called "tax preferences." This approach is not only politically sound but also resonates with the elusive goals of fairness and simplicity.

Organized philanthropy has been adversely affected whenever tax legislation is passed; for the reaons given, it is likely this process will continue.

There is still another conflict in current tax policy. A tax provision that exists to induce behavior carries a preference for someone—as there is a stick, so there is a carrot. This phenomenon can be seen in the ongoing fight over a capital gains tax preference. The same is true with the charitable contribution deduction. Is it designed to preserve and further the "American way" or is it a loophole for the wealthy? There are ample proponents on both sides of this issue.

There is a major problem here for philanthropy. The striving for more tax revenue at the federal level, and the drive for simplicity and fairness, are leading to the elimination of itemized deductions. Aside from the old standby of business deductions, the only ones left of any consequence are the mortgage interest deduction and the charitable contribution deduction. The pressures for a flatter tax are enormous; these deductions will likely be eroded, at least in part, as the consequence of these pressures, absent strong resistance from the charitable community. The reality is that organized philanthropy is going to have to coexist with these conflicting policies—at least until a time when the intense demand for increased federal revenue has subsided. How it manages to do that will have much to say about the shape of tomorrow's charitable contribution deductions.

2

The United States Tax System—An Overview

by Michael E. Murphree

The law in the United States concerning charitable giving is essentially federal income tax law. The federal law of charitable giving is inextricably intertwined with nearly all aspects of the federal law of income taxation, so much so that a full understanding of the law of charitable giving cannot be obtained without comprehension of the overall tax structure of which it is a part. This chapter provides an overview of that structure, as a setting for the tax law subjects that are integral to the law of charitable giving.

The United States income tax system has grown into a comprehensive and complex body of statutory law, regulatory law, and case law. However, within this labyrinth of tax law is a basic structure and framework. Forming a part of this basic structure and framework are important concepts and terms which govern and guide one's course through the income tax system. This basic structure, and the concepts and terms that make up this system, are examined and discussed in this chapter.

The U.S. income tax is a tax upon the receipt of "income." The tax is imposed upon certain entities which are in receipt of income, and is computed and assessed on an annual basis. These taxpaying entities generally file annual returns with the IRS which report income and other items used in the computation of the income tax.

§ 2.1 INCOME

Since the federal income tax is a tax imposed upon income, what is or is not income is a matter of major concern. The term income connotes an element of profit—receipt of money or property as a result of some enterprise. This is distinguishable from wealth, which is previously accumulated money or property.

The concept of what is or is not income initially seems straightforward and simple. When one performs labor, one typically receives compensation in the form of wages or salary. One may also receive goods, which are commonly considered as payment "in kind." Both forms of payment are income, as a return for services rendered.

When one invests money or capital, one typically receives interest, dividends, rent, or a similar return as a result of the investment. One could also receive property as a return on one's investment. These forms of payment are income, as a return on the investment.

But some forms of payment do not fit so neatly within these concepts of income or profit. An award of compensatory damages and punitive damages in a civil action raises interesting questions. Compensatory damages repay a victim for a loss suffered by payment of dollars of value relative to the loss sustained. The victim is being made whole for a loss, not receiving some sort of profit from his or her labor or capital. Punitive damages—money awarded to a victim as a punishment to the wrongdoer—are also not the result of some profitable endeavor of labor or capital.

An item of income is considered, for tax purposes, to first be an item of "gross income."

The federal tax law contemplates, in addition to the generation of gross income, persons who are the recipients of the income and who will pay a tax on it. These persons are as follows:

- individuals
- corporations
- trusts
- estates

The ways of determining gross income and the rates for taxing it differ, but these persons are taxpayers: those human beings and legally fictional entities that are obligated to pay the federal income tax.

§ 2.2   GROSS INCOME

The term "gross income" is defined in the Internal Revenue Code as "all income from whatever source derived."[1] The statutory definition

[1] IRC § 61.

of gross income has been broadly defined by the Supreme Court to include within its reach all "undeniable accessions to wealth, clearly realized, and over which the taxpayer has complete dominion."[2] The Court made it clear in this opinion that such accessions to wealth are income regardless of their source, and regardless of any attached label as to its nature. Under this broad definition, a gain (accession to wealth) that is clearly realized, regardless of label or source, is gross income.

Gross income includes, among other items:

- alimony
- bartering income
- business income
- cancellation of indebtedness income
- dividends
- gains
- gambling winnings
- interest
- pensions and annuities
- rental income
- royalties
- tips, wages, and salaries

Many other items of compensation or gain can be identified within the sweeping definition of gross income.[3]

Defining and computing gross income is the initial step in the process of computing and determining tax on income.

§ 2.3 EXCLUSIONS FROM INCOME

Although the definition of gross income is broad, Congress has seen fit to exclude certain items of income from its reach.[4] Items specifically excluded from gross income by statute are referred to as "exclu-

---

[2]*Commissioner v. Glenshaw Glass Co.*, 348 U.S. 426 (1955).
[3]IRC §§ 71-90.
[4]IRC §§ 101-135.

sions" and are not included in arriving at the total gross income figure, for tax purposes, for a taxpayer.

Examples of exclusions include:

- accident and health insurance proceeds
- employer provided meals and lodging
- gifts and inheritances
- housing allowances for clergy
- interest on state and local bonds
- life insurance proceeds
- military allowances
- veterans' benefits
- welfare and public assistance benefits
- workers' compensation benefits

Excluding certain income items from the scope of gross income is the second step in computing and determining tax on income.

§ 2.4   ADJUSTED GROSS INCOME

The term "adjusted gross income" is defined as gross income less certain expenses.[5] The business expense deductions discussed below are allowed as deductions from gross income to arrive at adjusted gross income.

Outlays that may be subtracted from gross income to determine adjusted gross income include the following:

- alimony payments
- allowable moving expenses
- certain business expenses

Making adjustments to gross income by deducting certain amounts to arrive at adjusted gross income is the third step in computing and determining tax on income.

The reason for adjusted gross income is to provide a fair basis for the allowance of non-economic personal expense deductions. Thus,

----

[5]IRC § 62(a).

adjusted gross income is gross income after adjusting for the economic costs of generating revenue to the taxpayer.

§ 2.5 DEDUCTIONS

(a) Business Expense Deductions

"Deductions" are expense items incurred in the production of gross income which are allowed to be deducted or subtracted from gross income to arrive at an adjusted gross income figure. Deductions are a reflection of the fact that there are inherent costs associated with the production of income, and that these costs are neither uniform nor equally born by all taxpayers. Equal amounts of gross income (revenue) may have different costs of production (expense). Therefore, to arrive at a fair base upon which to impose an income tax, deductions are allowed to cover the costs associated with the production of a given amount of income. As a result of the business deductions allowed by the federal tax law, income tax is imposed on the net economic gain, not the total gross gain.

For example, assume two taxpayers have received equal amounts of gross income and have equal adjustments. Each taxpayer is an air courier company. They each have a gross income of $100,000, representing their revenue for the year. Taxpayer A has a fleet of modern, fuel efficient planes. During the year, Taxpayer A burned $10,000 of fuel. The fuel expense is a cost of doing business and is a deduction from gross income. The adjusted gross income of Taxpayer A for the year is $90,000. Taxpayer B however, has a fleet of old, inefficient, fuel-hungry planes. During the same year Taxpayer B burned $40,000 of fuel. The adjusted gross income of Taxpayer B for the year is $60,000. Although each taxpayer has generated the same amount of revenue for the year, they had different costs of doing business in earning the revenue. Therefore, to arrive at a fair base upon which to tax the income of each taxpayer, deductions are allowed to cover the differing costs of generating revenue.

Deductions against income are allowed for costs associated with profit-seeking (business or investment) activities that generate income. Personal, living, or family expenses are not profit-seeking expenses and are not allowed as deductions.[6] Furthermore, business

---

[6]IRC § 262.

expense deductions are generally limited to those outlays that are: ordinary and necessary, current, and incurred for business reasons.[7]

The federal tax law sets forth a number of allowable deductions, including depreciation[8] and loss[9] deductions.

(b) Personal Expense Deductions

As noted in the preceding section, deductions from the federal income tax are generally limited to expenses associated with the cost of carrying on a trade or business. These costs represent the economic cost of generating revenue. The net result from the deductions is economic gain or income. Representing personal consumption, and not the economic cost of doing business, personal expenses are not generally allowed as deductions from income.

Although the purpose of the income tax scheme is to tax economic profit or gain, the law permits a number of personal expense deductions that have no bearing on economic gain. There are a number of policy reasons underlying these personal deductions. Casualty[10] and medical[11] deductions are allowed for expenses that may be unanticipated and/or unduly burdensome. Charitable[12] deductions are allowed to encourage and promote philanthropic endeavors. Home mortgage interest[13] deductions are allowed as a form of tax subsidy for borrowers who use capital to purchase homes. State and local tax[14] deductions are allowed as a means of offsetting or reducing the cumulative and burdensome impact of multiple taxing authorities. These personal expense deductions are allowed for social policy reasons, rather than for the costs associated with producing economic gain.

Personal expense deductions (itemized deductions in lieu of the standard deduction) are deducted from adjusted gross income to arrive at taxable income as the fourth step in computing and determining tax on income.

[7]IRC §§ 162(a), 212.
[8]IRC §§ 167, 168.
[9]IRC § 165.
[10]IRC § 165(c)(3).
[11]IRC § 213(a).
[12]IRC § 170(a).
[13]IRC § 163(a).
[14]IRC § 164.

§ 2.6　STANDARD DEDUCTION

Individual taxpayers, when appropriate, itemize their allowable personal expenses as their personal deduction from adjusted gross income. As an election in lieu of itemization, individual taxpayers are permitted to utilize a "standard deduction."[15] This was introduced into the federal tax law as a means for allowing taxpayers to take a personal deduction without the need for record-keeping to support the personal expenses.

The standard deduction (in lieu of personal itemized expense deductions) is deducted from adjusted gross income to arrive at taxable income as an alternative fourth step in computing and determining tax on income.

§ 2.7　TAXABLE INCOME

"Taxable Income" is defined by the federal tax law.[16] For taxpayers taking itemized deductions (I.D.), taxable income is defined as gross income minus the deductions allowed by the federal tax law other than the standard deduction. For taxpayers electing the standard deduction, taxable income is defined as adjusted gross income (A.G.I.) minus the taxpayer's standard deduction (S.D.) and personal or dependent exemption (P/D E). Mathematically, the formula is:

$$A.G.I. - ((I.D. \text{ or } S.D.) + P/D\ E) = \text{Taxable Income}$$

Taxable income is the base figure upon which the federal income tax is imposed.

(a)　Personal Exemption

Every individual taxpayer is entitled to deduct from adjusted gross income an amount allowed as a personal exemption (unless that taxpayer can be claimed as a dependent by another taxpayer). This personal exemption is allowable for individual taxpayers, and not other taxpaying entities. Individuals filing joint tax returns with their spouses can take two personal exemptions, one for themselves and one for their spouse.

---

[15] IRC § 63(c).
[16] IRC § 63.

In 1991, individual taxpayers were allowed to deduct $2,150 (an amount adjusted annually for inflation) for their personal exemption.[17]

(b) Dependent Exemption

In addition to deducting an amount from adjusted gross income as a personal exemption, individual taxpayers can deduct the same $2,150 amount in 1991 as a dependency deduction. Where a five part test is met ((1) member of household or relationship test; (2) citizenship test; (3) joint return test; (4) gross income test; (5) support test) by the taxpayer, a deduction is allowable for a dependent.

§ 2.8 TAXABLE ENTITIES

The entities subject to the imposition of a federal income tax are, as noted, corporations,[18] individuals,[19] estates,[20] and trusts.[21] Due to the nature of the income tax system, there is an anomaly created by the taxation of corporate entities. Corporations are fictional entities which are owned by their stockholders. Income received by a corporation is subject to an income tax. Where the corporation pays out its income in the form of dividends to individual stockholders, the income is again subject to tax at the individual level. This results in a double income tax, first at the corporate level, then again at the individual level.

To alleviate this burden, certain corporations that meet special statutory criteria are not taxed at the corporate level, but only at the individual level. These qualifying corporations are known as S corporations and are treated in much the same way as partnerships.

Business entities such as partnerships and sole proprietorships, while separate legal entities, are not separate taxable entities. Income received by partnerships is reported on the partnership level, but the income tax is imposed on each individual partner on the partner's share of partnership income. Income received by sole proprietorships is taxed to the individual proprietor generating the income.

[17] IRC §§ 151-152.
[18] IRC § 11.
[19] IRC § 1.
[20] *Id.*
[21] *Id.*

(a) Individuals

One category of taxpaying entity is the "individual." Individuals are living, natural persons, not fictional creatures.

(b) Corporations

A "corporation" is a legal creature, existing as an entity of state law. The hallmark of a corporation is that it usually shields and insulates persons (individuals) from legal liability that may arise during the course of its existence and operation.

As noted above, corporations are generally owned by individual taxpaying shareholders, and are themselves taxpaying entities. This results in two layers of income taxation.

(c) Estates

Another category of taxpaying entity is the "estate." An estate is recognized as a legally separate person, separate from the individual who, by death, created it. Estates are the legal creation that encompasses all the property and rights belonging to a deceased individual, or "decedent."

(d) Trusts

"Trusts" are also creatures of law. A trust is a legal entity created by state law and encompassing property transferred to it (known as the trust "res") by the trust's creator/donor (known as the "grantor" of the trust) for the benefit of some one or some thing (known as the trust "beneficiary"). A trust may be created during the life of a grantor, (an *inter vivos* trust), or upon the death of a grantor, (a testamentary trust).

(e) Associations

Other business entities or organizations that do not meet the definition or criteria of a corporation will not be separately taxed. Instead, the taxable income they receive will be taxable to the individuals that form or compose the organization. These types of organizations that are not corporations are generically referred to as "associations."

Even though an organization is not considered to be a corporation for purposes of state law, it may be deemed a corporation for purposes of federal income tax law.[22] Typically, organizations would like to be deemed associations to avoid taxation, while the government would like them to be considered separate taxable entities. An organizational test is employed to determine whether an entity is considered, for income tax purposes, a taxable corporation or a non-taxable association.[23] The test seeks to determine whether the entity in question more closely resembles (resemblance test) the characteristics of a corporation, or a non-corporate association.[24] Such an entity may not be an individual, a corporation, an estate, or a trust under state law. However, the entity may be deemed a taxable corporation if it more closely resembles a corporation than an association for purposes of federal tax law.

This demonstrates an important aspect of federal income tax law: substance, not form, usually governs and controls federal income tax questions.

§ 2.9 ANNUAL ACCOUNTING PERIOD (TAXABLE YEAR)

The income tax imposed on entities is reported and taxed on an annual basis for an "annual accounting period" or taxable year.[25] All of an entity's income is therefore allocated to the appropriate taxable year.

There are two methods of reporting or accounting for income on an annual basis. The first is the "calendar year" method.[26] A calendar year is, as its name implies, a period of twelve consecutive months that corresponds to a calendar year. It begins on January 1 and ends on December 31. Individuals are typically calendar year taxpayers. The second method is the "fiscal year."[27] This annual period is any other twelve-month period beginning on the first day of a calendar month and ending on the last day of the twelfth calendar month for that period. As an example, a twelve-month period beginning on November 1 in the current year and ending October 31 of the following year is a fiscal year.

---

[22] IRC § 7701 defines a corporation to include associations.
[23] Reg. § 301.7701-2(a)(1).
[24] *Morrissey et. al. v. Commissioner*, 296 U.S. 344 (1935).
[25] IRC § 441.
[26] IRC § 441(d).
[27] IRC § 441(e).

§ 2.10 ACCOUNTING METHOD

Closely related to the annual accounting period (the taxable year in which income is received or allocated) is the taxpayer's method or basis of calculating when the entity receives income. This is referred to as a taxpayer's "accounting method."[28] The particular accounting method used to determine when an entity receives income will necessarily affect the year to which the income is allocated. Once again there are two methods: the "cash receipts and disbursement"[29] method and the "accrual"[30] method.

Under the cash receipts and disbursements method, income (and expense) is recognized to the taxpayer when cash is received (income) or paid out (expense). In the accrual method, income (and expense) is recognized when a right to receive income or an obligation for an expense arises.

§ 2.11 TIMING

Because income is taxed on an annual basis, "timing" is important. Timing concerns the question of allocation, that is, determining to which taxable year an income or expense item is allocated. The receipt of income in a particular tax year can have a significant impact on an entity's tax burden. A taxpayer can, and may wish to, accelerate or postpone the receipt of income in any particular year so as to minimize tax.

Timing is directly related to the annual accounting period and method of accounting of a taxpayer. The timing implications of each are apparent when one views a simple transaction. An individual taxpayer is entitled to receive the sum of $500 immediately upon the completion of a contract. The taxpayer completes the contract on December 20 of Year 1, but does not receive the cash payment until January 15 of Year 2, several weeks later.

(a) Timing and Accounting Method

Under the cash method of accounting, the taxpayer recognizes receipt of the income on January 15, when it is actually received.

---

[28] IRC § 446.
[29] IRC § 446(c)(1).
[30] IRC § 446(c)(2).

Under the accrual method, the taxpayer recognizes the income on December 20 since the right to receive the income arose upon the completion of the contract, not when the payment was actually received.

(b)   Timing and Annual Accounting Period (Tax Year)

Assuming a calendar year taxpayer, the method of accounting will affect the tax year to which the $500 income is allocated and taxed. The income in the example is allocated to Tax Year 2 under the cash method of accounting, but Tax Year 1 under the accrual method.

If a fiscal year beginning November 1 and ending October 31 is assumed, the $500 income would fall within the same taxable year under either method of accounting.

As can be seen from this simple example, timing differences in the taxpayer's annual accounting period and method of accounting can have significant tax consequences.

§ 2.12   PROPERTY

As noted at the beginning of this chapter, the federal income tax system is designed to tax income, not wealth. Recall that income is generally viewed as the current receipt or realization of money or property as an economic profit or gain (accession to wealth), while wealth, is previously earned and accumulated money or property.

Income can take a number of forms. It can be in the form of a medium of exchange, the most common medium being currency. Dollars, francs, pounds, rubles, yen and the like are each forms of currency used by nations as their economic medium of exchange. One may receive money (currency) in exchange for goods or services. But noncurrency mediums of exchange also exist for providing goods and services in the economy. One may receive property, or labor, as compensation in exchange for the provision of goods or services. These noncurrency receipts are just as much income or accessions to wealth (economic gain) as are the receipts of currency (money). These forms of non-monetary or non-currency income are barter income and are taxable as income.

All property of every kind can be allocated into one of two categories. The first category of property is known as real property, and the second is known as personal property.

(a) Real Property

"Real property" is land. Real property includes not just the physical land, but things that are naturally or artificially attached or annexed to the physical land. A tree is a natural attachment to the land, and a building is an artificial attachment.

One major characteristic of real property, as distinguished from other forms of property, is its permanence, its immobile nature. Real property, and things attached to it, are permanently affixed in place. Land, and things attached to it, is not movable.

Another major characteristic of real property is that it has a real, tangible, physical manifestation. It can be seen and touched.

(b) Personal Property

"Personal property" can be defined by exclusion. It is all property that is not real property. Personal property includes a realm of items. Personal property is itself divided into two major categories: tangible and intangible personal property.

(c) Tangible Personal Property

"Tangible personal property" is physical property that is capable of being seen and touched. It has substance. Unlike real property, which is immovable land, personal property is movable.

Some examples of tangible personal property are:

- automobiles
- furniture
- jewelry
- animals

(d) Intangible Personal Property

"Intangible personal property" is personal property which is incapable of being seen or touched. It is not perceptible by human senses. It is neither physical land nor other physical property. Intangible personal property is usually evidenced by a form of documentation.

Intangible personal property can take many forms. The most common type of intangible personal property is a security, such as a stock or bond, which is evidenced by a stock certificate or bond instrument. It can be a right under a contract. By virtue of the law governing relationships between parties to a contract, one party may have the right to some performance by another party. That right is not manifested in any physical form. However, the right arises and exists in law. It has value to the party seeking performance, and the right to performance (or the economic value of the performance) can be enforced through a legal action. The right to performance in a contract, therefore, is intangible personal property.

Good will in a business is another example of intangible personal property. The reputation and customer loyalty that people associate with the name of a business is a valuable, and protectable, business asset. However, customer good will is not manifested in anything physical. It is the imperceptible and intangible good feelings and loyalties people have and associate with a business concern.

§ 2.13   INVENTORY

"Inventory," for income tax purposes, is generally considered to be the taxpayer's stock in trade. It is the sum total of items, raw materials, or finished goods held by the taxpayer for production of income in the trade or business. Inventory is usually held by a corporation, rather than an individual.

Inventory represents a part of the cost of the goods sold in a business, and therefore is a component of expense to be deducted from gross income to more clearly reflect economic gain or profit to the taxpayer. Because the inventory of a taxpayer is dynamic, constantly changing as goods are sold and new inventory added to stock, means and methods for identifying and valuing the constantly changing stock in trade must be employed. Because income tax is assessed on an annual basis, the means and methods used must account for yearly change in inventories.

(a)   Valuation and Identification of Inventory

The main reason for utilizing inventories is to match costs of doing business with the revenues generated thereby. As more directly stated in the federal tax law, it is to clearly reflect income. Indeed, the federal tax law requires that inventories be used where it is necessary to clearly determine a taxpayer's income.[31]

[31] IRC § 471.

A simple example will show the importance of inventories in measuring income. In this illustration, a taxpaying business has an inventory of five items. Each item cost the business $20. Three of the items in the inventory were sold. Each item was sold for $30. The three sales generated a total revenue to the business of $90 (3 × $30 = $90). Since the three inventory items cost the business $20, the total cost of the goods sold was $60 (3 × $20 = $60). The revenue of $90 less the cost of goods sold of $60 results in a net income of $30. The $30 represents the economic gain after taking into account the cost of the inventory sold.

Now suppose the items of inventory had different costs:

1. $20
2. $22
3. $25
4. $27
5. $30

If three items were sold for the same $30, how would one measure the value of the cost of the goods sold so as to get a true measure of economic profit? If items one, two and three were sold, their cost would be $67 with a resulting net income of $23 ($90 − $67 = $23). If items three, four and five were sold, their cost would be $82 with a net income of only $8 ($90 − $82 = $8). If one were able to individually identify each item sold, one could accurately match the item with its cost and get a clear picture of income; if not, it would be impossible to get a clear reflection of income. Although it may be possible to track and account for a very small inventory of items, the task becomes impractical as the inventory grows, and as the inventory of goods turns over during the taxable year.

To deal with this problem of valuation, two methods are utilized. The first is the "cost" method. It measures the value of an item of inventory on the basis of its actual cost. The second is the "cost or market" method. It measures the cost of inventory items based upon their cost or fair market value, whichever is lower.

The valuation methods are used in conjunction with methods of tracking or identifying the items of inventory. Two tracking methods are used. The first method is the "First-In, First-Out" (FIFO) method, which assumes that the items of inventory that are first acquired are the items that are first sold. Either the "cost" or the "cost or market" method of valuation may be used. The different valuation methods have an effect on the amount of income that is deemed to be received by the taxpayer in its yearly accounting period. In periods of inflation or rising market prices, income (profits) tends to be greater while in periods of deflation or a falling market, income (profits) tends to be less when "cost" is used rather than "cost or market" valuation.

Last-In, First-Out (LIFO)[32] is the second method for tracking inventories. It assumes that the items of inventory last purchased are the first sold. Under LIFO, only the "cost" method of valuation is permitted.[33] Since the most recently purchased items of inventory are the first items sold, the effects of inflation (rising market prices) or deflation (falling market prices) are minimized. The effect of price increases or decreases tend to be less dramatic than those utilizing the FIFO method.

Obviously, the choice of method of tracking inventories (FIFO or LIFO) and the method for their valuation ("cost" or "cost or market") can have a significant impact on the income (profit or loss) picture of a taxpayer.

§ 2.14 GAIN

In discussing what is income for tax purposes, the U.S. Supreme Court[34] noted that accessions to wealth, clearly realized, and within the control or dominion of the taxpayer, are income. An accession to wealth is an increase or addition to wealth. In other words, a taxpayer gains something as an addition to his wealth by an accession. These gains through accessions to wealth are income.

The concept of gain is clear in the service context. One performs services and receives a wage or salary. If one is an employee, one's wage or salary is an economic gain in wealth of the taxpayer. Personal expenses, but not real economic expenses, are incurred in the production of this income. Gross income and adjusted gross income are basically the same. If one performs personal services as a business person, one may have a number of costs associated with its production. Since a cost is incurred in producing income, the total

---

[32]Method permitted under IRC § 472.
[33]IRC § 472(b)(2).
[34]Noted in *Commissioner* v. *Glenshaw Glass Co.*, *supra*, n. 2.

revenue earned is not a true measure of accession to wealth. The costs incurred are deducted to arrive at a better measure of economic gain. Therefore, business expenses are deducted from the gross income to arrive at adjusted gross income. This adjusted gross income is a clearer measure of the economic gain of a business person's personal services.

Gains can arise with respect to property as well. When one sells property, one typically receives money in exchange. This is frequently referred to as liquidating an asset.

Liquidity refers to the ease with which an asset can be used as a medium of exchange in the economy. Since money is the medium of exchange, it is perfectly liquid. On the other hand, assets like land are not typically used in the market as a medium of exchange. One usually sells, or liquidates, an asset like land for its equivalent value in money. Money is then used for other transactions in the economy. In selling an asset, one is merely changing the form of one's holding. Money is substituted for the asset.

For the most part, all assets (property) have value, even if the value is little or nominal. The value is generally considered to be the "fair market value," or what a willing purchaser is prepared to pay to a willing seller in a fair market in an arm's length (free from undue familiarity) transaction. A fair market is an open market, one not controlled by either the buyer or seller. The price for goods is determined not by the parties, but by the economics of the marketplace. The law of supply and demand operates freely to set the value of all assets in the market. As supply rises or falls, the cost of the good rises and falls in relation thereto. As the demand rises and falls, the cost of the good likewise rises and falls in relation thereto.

The method used to arrive at the value of an asset is called valuation. It attempts to ascertain the fair market value for an asset. The value is usually determined in one of two ways. The first method is the cost, or actual, method of valuation. The value of an asset is considered to be the amount it costs a purchaser to buy the asset. This method purports to measure the actual or true value of the asset. The second method is appraisal. An appraisal is an estimate of the value of an asset. It attempts to ascertain an asset's fair market value by making an assessment of various factors that a buyer and seller look to in making an exchange. The relative supply and demand, the cost of comparable goods, etc. are used to estimate an asset's value.

The actual cost of an asset may not be the same as its appraised value. Also, the fair market value of an asset may be different from both the cost and appraised value of an asset. A purchaser may get a bargain sale and pay an amount below that of the market. Likewise, a seller may get a windfall by selling an asset for more than its value in the market. Also, the buyer and seller may conspire to fix a price which is not a fair value. Such economic dislocations are normal in an imperfect and real market place.

For the most part, in "arm's length" transactions between parties that are not related, the actual selling price for an asset is considered to be its cost. Also, where an appraisal is made in good faith, it is considered to be representative of the asset's fair market value.

(a) Basis

The importance of valuation has to do with the measure of the amount of gain derived on the sale or disposition of an asset. Just as gross income is not, without reduction for costs of production, a clear reflection of economic gain, neither is the total amount realized by the seller on the sale of an asset. The total amount realized on a sale also reflects a return of the initial investment (the cost) in the asset. The return of the cost paid for an asset is not an accession to wealth, but merely a return of previously accumulated and invested wealth. Likewise, costs to improve or enhance the asset are invested and returned as part of the purchase price. Therefore, a mechanism must be used to apportion out those costs invested in the asset and returned by the sales proceeds, and those sales proceeds that represent an economic gain to the seller.

"Basis" is the term that refers to the investment in property. The mechanism for apportioning out investments in an asset are the general basis rules found in the federal tax law.[35] The tax basis for an investment in property is usually the cost of the asset.[36]

However, property that is acquired from a decedent has a "stepped-up" rather than a cost basis.[37] The person acquiring property from a decedent has a basis equal to the fair market value of the property at the date of the decedent's death (or, if elected, under the alternate valuation date[38]). Any gain in the value of the decedent's asset during the decedent's lifetime will be deemed a nontaxable part

[35] IRC §§ 1011-1023.
[36] IRC § 1012.
[37] IRC § 1014.
[38] IRC § 2032.

of the recipient taxpayer's investment in the property when it is sold.

Property that is acquired by gift has a "carry-over" rather than a cost basis.[39] The person who receives a gift of property has the same basis in the property as that of the donor of the property. The basis is "carried over" to the new owner of the property, hence the term. Any gain in value of the gifted property in the hands of the donor will be taxable to the recipient when it is sold. However, the recipient can take advantage of the cost basis of the donor, rather than having a zero cost basis as a result of the gift.

(b) Adjusted Basis

Just as gross income must be adjusted by business expense deductions to reflect the true economic gain of the taxpayer, so too must basis be adjusted to reflect true economic gain (or loss) in the disposition of property.

In determining gain or loss, the federal tax law provides that basis in property be adjusted.[40] Generally, basis is adjusted[41] for:

- expenditures
- receipts
- losses
- or other items properly chargeable to capital account (but no adjustments for certain taxes[42] or other carrying charges and circulation expenditures[43])

Basis is also adjusted under the general rule for the following items to the extent the allowable items resulted in a reduction of tax:

- exhaustion
- wear and tear
- obsolescence
- amortization
- depletion

[39] IRC § 1015.
[40] IRC § 1011 provides that basis be adjusted as provided in IRC § 1016.
[41] IRC § 1016.
[42] IRC § 266 taxes.
[43] IRC § 173.

The federal tax law provides a number of other basis adjustments that are not relevant to an overview of income taxation.[44]

(c) Determination of Gain

Upon a "sale or other disposition of property," gain (or loss) is computed as the "amount realized" from such sale or disposition of the property less the adjusted basis[45] in the property.[46] Expressed mathematically, the formula is:

$$\text{Gain (or Loss)} = \text{Amount Realized} - \text{Adjusted Basis}$$

The amount realized on the sale or disposition is the sum of any money received plus the fair market value of any property received in the transaction.[47]

(d) Realization

In order for there to be a gain, there must be a realization of income. A U.S. Supreme Court opinion[48] requires that accessions to wealth must be clearly realized in order for there to be income subject to income taxation.

Economically, gain (or loss) is dynamic, occurring over a period of time. The fair market value of property fluctuates constantly. Property may gain or lose value during the entire time it is owned. Such increase or decrease in fair market value represents the economic gain or loss associated with the ownership of the property over time.

Furthermore, economic gain (or loss) can be real or nominal over time. Real gain (or loss) is the actual increase (or decrease) in value of the asset over time. Nominal gain (or loss) is the relative increase (or decrease) in value of the asset over time.

To understand the difference between real and nominal value, one must consider the economic price factor of inflation or deflation in the market. Over time, prices in the marketplace change, possibly reflecting differences in value associated with certain assets. This is

[44]IRC § 1016.
[45]IRC § 1011.
[46]IRC § 1001(a).
[47]IRC § 1001(b).
[48]*Commissioner* v. *Glenshaw Glass Co.*, *supra*, n. 2.

real change. Change may also occur in the value of money. If money becomes less valuable (or if the supply of money increases), the value of an asset in relation to money correspondingly changes. If the real value of an item of property remains constant, but the relative value of money becomes less, the item will cost more since the value of money has declined. This is a phenomenon typical of an inflationary period. Prices for a commodity rise, even though its real value to consumers remains unchanged. The price change is a nominal increase due to the change in value of money, while the underlying real value of the commodity remains constant.

(e) Appreciation

"Appreciation" is a term that refers to the increase in the value of property. As the above discussion makes clear, appreciation (the increase in value of property) is composed of two elements, real and nominal changes in the value of property. One element, real appreciation, reflects the true increase in economic value of the property. The other, nominal appreciation, reflects the relative effect of the change in the value of money, not the change in value of the property.

Over time, then, the value (and accessions to wealth) of property of a taxpayer may change. Coupled with that is the fact that the federal income tax system utilizes an annual accounting period for purposes of accounting and taxing income. Each year, a taxpayer may have an increase or decrease in wealth due to the real or nominal change in the value of property held by the taxpayer.

Although changes in value do occur over time, and can be measured annually, the income tax system does not attempt to track, measure, and tax economic gain (or loss) annually. Instead, gain (or loss) is accounted only where there is the occurrence of some transactional event, a sale or exchange or other disposition of property. The tax on gains (or losses), then, is a transactional tax, and not an economic tax.

"Realization" denotes the transactional event giving rise to gain (or loss) for income tax purposes. The event is a sale or exchange or disposition of property. An event giving rise to realization occurs when property is sold for money, where property is exchanged for other property, or where property is given in exchange for the satisfaction of some contractual obligation. A contractual obligation is a valuable property right; its exchange—the satisfaction of a contract right—for other property is a transactional disposition within the contemplation and reach of the gain provisions of the federal tax law.

Questions do arise as to whether a particular event or transaction is a realization of income, and as to when (in which taxable year) the realization event occurred.

(f)   Recognition

Once taxable gain is realized, the next step is to determine whether such taxable gain will be recognized and subject to income taxation. Under the federal tax law, the general rule is that "the entire amount of gain or loss . . . on the sale or exchange of property shall be recognized."[49] "Recognition" is the process of taking gain into account for income tax purposes. The gain is recognized and subject to current taxation, unless a deferral is permitted.

Under the federal tax law, the deferral of realized gain (or loss) is termed "non-recognition." For various policy reasons, Congress has granted a deferral into the future of a currently realized gain. The federal tax law contains a number of non-recognition provisions.[50] The most well known non-recognition provisions are:

Like Kind Exchanges.[51]   Non-recognition is allowed (with some exceptions, and under certain conditions) for exchanges of property held for investment, or property used in a trade or business, where such property is exchanged only for property of a like kind to be similarly held for investment, or used in the trade or business. The idea is that gain should not be recognized and taxed in a transaction where the character of the property remains essentially unchanged. Property is considered to be essentially unchanged if property of a like kind is substituted in its place.

Stock Exchanges.[52]   Corporations do not recognize gain on the receipt of money or property acquired in exchange for stock in the corporation. Since stock represents the economic cost of investment by stockholder-owners in the corporation, and not economic revenues, it would be unfair to tax such shareholder basis in the corporate business entity.

Involuntary Conversions.[53]   Where property is involuntarily or

[49] IRC § 1001(c).
[50] IRC §§ 1031-1042.
[51] IRC § 1031.
[52] IRC § 1032.
[53] IRC § 1033.

compulsorily converted—through destruction, theft, seizure, condemnation (or threat thereof), and the like—into similar or related property, gain is not recognized. It is considered unfair to impose a taxable gain on a taxpayer suffering an unintended and involuntary conversion of property.

Rollover of Gain in Residence.[54] Where, under the federal tax rules,[55] homeowners sell their old principal residence, and reinvest the sales proceeds in a new home within two years before and two years after the sale, no gain is recognized except to the extent the adjusted sales price[56] of the old residence exceeds the purchase cost of the new residence. Congress wishes to promote trading-up in home ownership, and encourages this practice by deferring gain in the sale and repurchase of homes.

Congress has also chosen to discourage or penalize certain realization transactions. To accomplish this, losses are not recognized and are, therefore, unavailable to offset other taxable income of the taxpayer. An example are straddles of personal property, especially stocks. The federal tax law denies a taxpayer the recognition of a loss to the extent the loss exceeds unrecognized gain.[57] The abuse policed by the section is whipsawing of the federal treasury. It is unfair to defer (not recognize currently) taxable gain on one part of a straddle transaction, and yet recognize a current loss on another part to offset income and further reduce current tax liability.

§ 2.15 TAX TREATMENT OF INCOME

Under current tax law, income (a taxpayer's taxable income) is subject to progressive taxation. That is, income is taxed at higher marginal rates as the level of a taxpayer's income rises. The "marginal rate" of taxation refers to a taxpayer's rate of taxation within a defined range of income, such as from zero to $1,000. The range of income (zero to $1,000, for example) is termed an income tax "bracket." A lower marginal rate of taxation is imposed on low income brackets, while higher marginal rates of taxation are imposed on high income brackets. The "effective rate" of taxation is the average tax rate over the range of income subject to the differing marginal rates.

Tax rates for individual taxpayers are divided into four categories:

[54] IRC § 1034.
[55] IRC § 1034.
[56] Defined in IRC § 1034(b).
[57] IRC § 1092.

single, married filing jointly, married filing separately, and head of household. The rate of tax on each category is different. There are also separate tax rates for corporations and estates.

To illustrate the concept of progressive tax rates, the rate for single individuals for 1992 was:

Income tax bracket	Percentage tax rate
$0 but not over $21,450	15%
Over $21,450 but not over $51,900	28%
Over $51,900	31%

The marginal rate of taxation at the lowest bracket level is 15 percent. The marginal rate rises to 28 percent and then 31 percent. The rate of tax becomes progressively more as income rises.

A similar tax rate exists for corporations. The tax rate in 1992 for domestic corporations was:

Income tax bracket	Percentage tax rate
Not over $50,000	15%
Over $50,000 but not over $75,000	25%
Over $75,000	34%

As with individuals, the marginal tax imposed increases as income rises. However, with respect to corporations, the benefit of progressive rates (lower levels of income taxed at marginally lower rates) is phased out as taxable corporate income exceeds $100,000. An additional 5 percent tax is imposed on income exceeding $100,000, up to $11,750 in additional tax. The net effect is that, for corporations with income exceeding $350,000, the marginal and effective tax rates equal a flat tax of 34 percent on all levels of income.

Prior to the 1986 tax changes, there were a greater number of tax brackets with a wider range in tax rates. For individuals, the marginal rates started at 11 percent and rose to a maximum of 50 percent (a range of 39 percentage points). Today, the brackets are compressed to three levels ranging from 15 percent to 33 percent (a range of only 16 percentage points). The significance of this is that, for the highest marginal rate taxpayers, deductions and exclusions have greatly reduced value. Since every dollar of income has a corresponding tax, every dollar excluded from tax has a tax savings. A dollar that escapes tax (by deduction or exclusion) at the 50 percent rate saves the taxpayer 50 cents on the dollar, or one-half. Today, that tax savings is only one-third, or 33 cents on the dollar. Tax planning and tax controversies concerning current exclusions or deductions have become less profitable, or less valuable, to higher income taxpayers.

§ 2.16 CAPITAL ASSETS, GAINS, AND LOSSES

(a) Capital Assets

"Capital assets" are defined by the federal tax law as property held by the taxpayer, whether or not connected to the taxpayer's trade or business.[58] The law specifically excludes from consideration as capital assets the following:

- inventory
- stock in trade
- depreciable business property
- real business property
- copyrights and other artistic works (within certain guidelines)
- trade or business receivables
- government publications (within certain guidelines)

Despite the seemingly broad definition of a capital asset, and the limited exceptions, the term has been construed to mean investment property which tends to appreciate in value over time. Indeed, the Supreme Court[59] held that property seemingly within the statutory definition of a capital asset may be excluded therefrom where the property is an integral part of the taxpayer's business, and is not truly investment property.

(b) Capital Gains and Losses

Historically, income has been divided into two major categories: ordinary income and capital gains income. "Ordinary income" refers to the typical or ordinary receipt of income—wages and salaries, rents,

[58]IRC § 1221.
[59]*Corn Products Refining* Co. v. *Commissioner*, 350 U.S. 46 (1955).

dividends, interest and the like. "Capital gain" income, on the other hand, refers to income generated by capital assets.

Ordinary income receives ordinary income tax treatment. That is, the normal tax rates are applied to ordinary income. Capital gains income, however, has historically been given preferential tax treatment. Until the 1986 Tax Reform Act, taxpayers other than corporations were allowed an exclusion of 60 percent of all net long-term capital gains.[60] In other words, only 40 percent of net long-term capital gains were included in taxable income. With only 40 percent subject to tax, at the maximum marginal rate of 50 percent for individuals, the effective tax rate on net long-term capital gains was 20 percent. Unlike deductions, saving the taxpayer only 50 percent, or 50 cents on the dollar, net long-term capital gains were extremely valuable. Conversion of the income into long-term capital gains at the maximum marginal rate of 50 percent reduced tax to 20 percent. Taxpayers could save not just 50 cents, but 80 cents, on every dollar.

Corporations under the old law also benefited from net long-term capital gains treatment. Under the former federal tax law,[61] a corporation could chose to be taxed at the alternative rate of 28 percent. Where corporate income exceeded $50,000, the marginal tax rates ranged from 30 percent to 46 percent. Therefore, it would be beneficial to a corporation to choose to be taxed at the alternative rate of 28 percent on its net long-term capital gains. The 28 percent alternative rate has been eliminated. For corporate income over $50,000, the marginal rates have been reduced to a range of 25 percent and then 34 percent.

The benefits associated with compression of the tax brackets and reduced marginal tax rates were not without cost. Indeed, one of the more favored tax preferences available to taxpayers was eliminated as a result of the overall tax breaks granted to taxpayers by the 1986 act. Individual taxpayers are no longer allowed a 60 percent deduction for long-term capital gains. Similarly, corporations no longer have the alternative tax of 28 percent for long-term capital gains.

However, the capital gains provision of the federal tax law remains in place. Congress chose to retain the capital gains structure in place to facilitate reinstatement of a rate differential for capital gains should tax rates be increased in the future.

The capital gains structure is still important for a number of rea-

[60] IRC § 1202 (repealed by § 301(a), of the Tax Reform Act of 1986).
[61] IRC § 1201(a).

sons. Capital gains are important in computation of charitable deductions. Further, although all capital gains are treated alike and taxed at ordinary rates, capital losses are not. Capital losses can only be used to offset capital gains, and up to only $3,000 of ordinary income. Ordinary losses by contrast can offset all income. Capital asset status is also important in that it affects the amount of gain recognized on a transaction. Ordinary gains are fully taxable, while capital gains allow for a recovery of basis and only taxes the excess as a gain.

(c)   Long- and Short-Term Capital Gains and Losses

Gains and losses from capital assets are classified as either long- or short-term. The "term" refers to the period of time a capital asset has been held by the taxpayer. The Internal Revenue Code[62] provides rules for determining the length of time capital assets have been held.

Long-term capital gains and losses means gains or losses from capital assets held for more than one year.[63] Short-term capital gains and losses means gains or losses from capital assets held for not more than one year.[64] Special netting rules apply to these capital gains and losses.[65]

§ 2.17   CARRYOVERS

The federal income tax is imposed annually. The unit of measure is the taxable year, or annual accounting period, for a taxpayer. Each tax year is construed to be a discrete and separate period. In one case[66] the taxpayer had a net operating loss for its taxable year and sought to carry over the loss to another year to offset income. The Supreme Court denied the taxpayer's effort and reinforced the strict concept of a discrete taxable year.

To overcome the result in this case, and the harsh effects of denial of an offset in other years of a current net operating loss, Congress changed the federal tax law.[67] Generally, a "carry back" of net operat-

---

[62] IRC § 1223.
[63] IRC § 1222(3), (4).
[64] IRC § 1222(1), (2).
[65] IRC § 1222.
[66] *Burnet* v. *Sanford & Brooks Co.*, 282 U.S. 359 (1931).
[67] IRC § 172.

ing losses to the previous three taxable years is permitted.[68] Likewise, a "carryover" to the following fifteen years is generally allowed.[69]

Special rules apply to capital losses.[70] For corporate taxpayers, a carry back of three years and a carryover of five years is generally permitted for net capital losses.[71] Other taxpayers are generally allowed a carryover to the next tax year of:

- the excess of net short-term capital losses over net long-term capital gains, treated as a net short-term capital loss in the succeeding year
- the excess of net long-term capital losses over net short-term capital gains, treated as a long-term capital loss in the succeeding year

§ 2.18   ALTERNATIVE MINIMUM TAX

In the past, certain high income taxpayers were able to greatly reduce their income tax liability due to their receipt of exempt or preferred income. To curb this perceived abuse, Congress adopted an "alternative minimum tax" to assure that taxpayers with tax preference income pay at least a minimum amount of tax. Under the federal minimum tax law[72], corporate taxpayers are subject to a 20 percent tax and non-corporate taxpayers are subject to a 24 percent tax on defined tax preferences. The items of tax preference subject to the special tax are:

- amount by which depletion deduction exceeds adjusted basis
- amount by which excess intangible drilling costs exceeds 65 percent of net income from oil, gas, and geothermal property
- certain private activity bond tax-exempt interest
- appreciated capital gain property claimed as charitable deduction, but not tangible personal property
- excess of accelerated over straight-line depreciation for property placed in service prior to 1987

[68] IRC § 172.
[69] IRC § 172.
[70] IRC § 1212.
[71] Net capital loss defined in IRC § 1222(10).
[72] IRC §§ 55-59.

- excess of accelerated over straight-line depreciation on most leased personal property placed in service by personal holding companies and non-corporate taxpayers prior to 1987
- excess of accelerated over normal amortization for most pollution control facilities placed in service before 1987
- excess of accelerated over straight-line depreciation on certain property placed in service by personal holding companies and non-corporate taxpayers prior to 1987
- excess of accelerated over straight-line depreciation on certain real property placed in service by taxpayers prior to 1987

In addition to the items of tax preference, the alternative minimum tax rules require that certain adjustments be made to selected tax items. Certain adjustments are made for:

- depreciation
- mining exploration and development costs
- long-term contracts
- alternative tax net operating loss deduction
- pollution control facilities
- installment method of accounting
- alternative tax energy preference deduction

Certain other adjustments are made for non-corporate taxpayers:

- alternative tax itemized deductions
- personal exemptions and standard deduction
- circulation, research, and experimental expenses
- incentive stock options
- passive farm tax shelter losses
- other passive business activity losses

Other adjustments are made for corporate taxpayers:

- adjusted current earnings
- merchant marine capital construction funds
- Blue Cross/Blue Shield organizations

Calculating the alternative minimum tax due is a multi-step process. The taxpayer first adds "regular taxable income" (RTI) to the amount of "tax preference items" (TPI) to obtain an "alternative minimum taxable income" (AMTI). Second, the taxpayer reduces his or her alternative minimum taxable income (AMTI) by an "exemption" (Exmpt). The resulting amount is multiplied by the "alternative minimum tax rate" (AMT Rate), and then reduced by any available "alternative minimum tax foreign tax credit" (AMTFTC). The result is a "tentative minimum tax" (TMT). The taxpayer's regular tax is then subtracted from the tentative minimum tax (TMT) to yield a minimum tax that is imposed in addition to the regular tax.

Mathematically, the process for computing the alternative minimum tax is:

$$RTI + TPI = \text{Alternative Minimum Taxable Income}$$

$$((AMTI - Exmpt) \times AMT\ Rate) - AMTFTC = \text{Tentative Minimum Tax}$$

$$TMT - \text{Regular Tax} = \text{Minimum Tax}$$

The resulting minimum tax is an additional tax liability resulting from adding back certain tax preferences that reduced the initial tax liability of the taxpayer.

(a) Capital Expenditures

Not all expenses are currently deductible to taxpayers. Where an asset is expected to have a useful life that will extend substantially beyond the current taxable year, the federal tax law denies a deduction and requires capitalization of the expenditure.[73] The underlying concept of this rule is that it would be unfair to permit a taxpayer to receive the benefit of a current deduction for an asset that will provide economic utility over a period of years. Examples of assets with long useful lives are:

- land
- buildings
- plants and equipment
- patents
- goodwill

---

[73] IRC § 263.

The cost of these types of assets must be capitalized rather than fully deductible in the tax year of acquisition.

§ 2.19   DEPRECIATION

One method for recovering the capital invested in long-lived assets is depreciation. A "depreciation" deduction is allowed for the reasonable exhaustion, wear and tear, and obsolescence of property held for investment or used in the trade or business.[74] Generally, an amount of the purchase price is deducted each year as a portion of the total acquisition cost. The total depreciation, and the period of depreciation, are meant to roughly equal the value of the asset over its useful life. Some assets are depreciated over a period that is shorter than their expected life.[75] This accelerated depreciation is designed to encourage investment in certain assets.

As an example, an asset is purchased for $100. It has an expected useful life of five years. At the end of its useful life, it is expected to have no remaining value, not even salvage value. Under the straight-line method of depreciation, an equal amount is to be deducted each year over the life of the asset. In other words, depreciation is ratable. Here, $20 is deducted each year for five years.

(a)   Depreciation Recapture

The depreciation recapture rules in the federal tax law are designed to prevent the conversion of ordinary income into capital gain income. The significance of recapture was more apparent under the prior tax law when net long-term capital gains enjoyed a substantial tax advantage. Unlike ordinary gains, which were fully taxable, net long-term capital gains enjoyed a 40 percent tax deduction. Only 60 percent of net long-term capital gains were subject to tax. Taxpayers holding depreciable capital assets soon discovered that they could enjoy a double tax advantage. They could first offset current ordinary income with depreciation deductions. Later, when the capital asset was sold, the gain would be a capital gain. Even though the previous depreciation deductions lowered the basis of the asset, thereby increasing the taxable gain, only 60 percent of the gain would be

[74]IRC § 167.
[75]IRC § 168.

taxed. The net effect was that any depreciation which offset ordinary income in an earlier year would now be converted into a capital gain subject to preferential tax treatment.

To combat this, the federal tax law was changed to require taxpayers to recapture prior depreciation deductions and convert what might otherwise be capital gains back into ordinary income.

The federal tax law contains a number of provisions that accomplish recapture. The most important provisions are the recapture of depreciation on real property and on personal property.

§ 2.20 TAX CREDITS

Deductions against income have the effect of a tax savings. Depending on the marginal rate of a taxpayer, every dollar of a deduction results in a tax savings of the amount of tax at the marginal rate. A 33 percent taxpayer will save 33 cents in taxes for every dollar of a deduction. A 15 percent taxpayer, by contrast, will save only 15 cents in taxes for every dollar of a deduction. Deductions are, therefore, worth more to high bracket taxpayers than to low bracket taxpayers.

To alter this consequence, tax "credits" are sometimes substituted for tax deductions. A tax credit is a dollar-or-dollar credit against income tax imposed. Because each dollar of credit offsets a dollar of tax, the tax savings is 100 percent. Further, the value of tax savings is equal for all taxpayers, regardless of marginal tax rate. Therefore, high level income taxpayers receive the same value for their tax credits as do low income taxpayers.

§ 2.21 FOREIGN TAX CREDITS

Sometimes, U.S. citizens and corporations are taxed by foreign governments on income taxable by the United States. To offset or minimize the impact of such a double tax burden, federal tax law provides a tax credit, subject to a limitation,[76] for income taxes paid to foreign countries.[77] The limitation is designed to prevent taxpayers from using the foreign tax credits to offset or reduce U.S. tax on income from U.S. sources.

The foreign tax credit limitation is computed using the "overall

[76] IRC § 904.
[77] IRC §§ 901-908.

method."[78] Under this method, the maximum foreign tax credit allowed is found by dividing "foreign source taxable income" (FSTI) by "worldwide taxable income" (WTI), and multiplying the result by the taxpayer's U.S. tax. Stated mathematically, the formula is:

(FSTI / WTI) × U.S. Tax = Maximum Foreign Tax Credit

For example, a taxpayer has a worldwide taxable income of $100,000. From country A, taxpayer has $30,000 of taxable income. From country B, taxpayer has $20,000 of taxable income. Taxpayer's U.S. tax is $25,000. The maximum foreign tax credit available to taxpayer is $12,500: (($30,000 + $20,000) / $100,000) × $25,000 = $12,500.

The above is a general and abbreviated outline of the foreign tax credit rules. A number of other important rules, outside the scope of this book, also apply in this area.

[78] IRC § 904(a).

Part II

Charitable Giving Law:
The Basics

3

The Concept of Planned Giving

Any analysis of the law of charitable giving would be inadequate without substantial attention to the various forms of "planned giving." At the same time, there is more to the law of charitable giving than planned giving. The purpose of this chapter is to place the concept of planned giving in its appropriate context. The chapters of Parts II and III can be read with this concept in perspective. The details of planned giving are the subject of Part IV.

Planned giving has, over the years, been made to seem deeply mysterious and very complicated, with the result that managers of many charitable organizations, and those who assist them in the fundraising process, are fearful of it. Most charitable organizations think about planned giving from time to time but many of these put off implementing a planned giving program to another day—a tomorrow that never comes.

This chapter summarizes the concept of planned giving and introduces its basic forms. As noted, the details associated with each of the planned giving techniques are discussed in Part IV of this book.

§ 3.1 INTRODUCTION

Donors and the charitable organizations they support commonly expect gifts to be in the form of outright transfers of money or property. For both parties, a gift is usually a unilateral transaction, in a financial sense, with the donor parting with the contribution and the donee charitable organization acquiring it. The advantages to the donor in these instances are confined to the resulting charitable contribution deduction and the emotional enhancement derived from the making of the gift.

There are, however, forms of charitable giving that provide far greater financial and tax advantages to the donor. This type of giving is frequently referred to as "planned giving" and sometimes "deferred giving."

It is somewhat difficult to create a "bright line" (that is, clearly delineating) test for differentiating between planned gifts and other charitable gifts. Of course, small and modest outright gifts of money or property do not qualify as planned gifts. Beyond that, opinions differ. Some assert that any gifts made by means of a will are planned gifts; others disagree. Some believe that gifts of insurance policies are planned gifts; others say they are not. Wherever the line is drawn, it can be said that a planned gift is a charitable gift that is integrated with the donor's overall financial (including estate) plans.

§ 3.2   APPRECIATED PROPERTY GIFTS

Returning to the above generalizations, the impulse donor is one who makes an outright gift of a small amount of money. The interest donor is much more likely than an impulse donor to make a gift using property. The integrated donor is more likely to make a contribution of property than one of money.

One of the chief principles underlying the advantages of charitable contributions of securities, real estate, and other property is that the deductible amount is generally equal to the full fair market value of the property at the time of the gift.[1] This means that the amount of appreciation in the property (the amount exceeding the donor's basis), which would be taxed as capital gain if sold, escapes regular income taxation. (As discussed in Chapter 10, there may be some alternative minimum tax complications.) For this favorable result to occur, the property must constitute long-term capital gain property.[2] It is also worth mentioning that percentage limitations apply regarding the extent of annual gift deductibility (principally depending upon whether the donee is a public charity or a private foundation[3]; on the carryover rules concerning the deductibility of excess gift amounts[4]; and on special rules that apply in computing the deduction for gifts of tangible personal and other forms of property[5]).

[1] See Chapter 6 § 2.
[2] See the discussion of this term in Chapters 2 § 14 and 10 § 1.
[3] See Chapter 4 § 3.
[4] See Chapter 7.
[5] See Chapter 6.

Consequently, the key to wise charitable giving is to give property that is long-term capital gain property and that has substantially appreciated in value. The greater the appreciation, the greater the charitable deduction and other income tax savings. The appreciated property gift is, therefore, a fundamental concept of planned giving.

§ 3.3 PLANNED GIFTS—THE CORE CONCEPTS

There are two basic types of planned gifts. One type utilizes a will, whereby the gift is derived from a decedent's estate (as a bequest or devise). The other type involves a gift made during the donor's lifetime, using a trust or other agreement.

On many occasions, these gifts are called "deferred gifts," because the actual receipt of the contribution by the charity is deferred until the happening of some event (usually the donor's death). But the term "deferred giving" has fallen out of favor, as some donors gain (to the chagrin of the gift-seeking charity) the impression that it is their tax benefits that are being deferred.

A planned gift usually is a contribution of a donor's interest in money or an item of property, rather than an outright gift of the entirety of the money or property. (The word "usually" is used because gifts using insurance do not neatly fit this definition and because some treat an outright gift of property through an estate as a planned gift.) Technically, this is a gift of a "partial interest" in property. Thus, planned giving usually is partial interest giving. Further, an item of property has within it two "interests." One is an "income interest" and the other is a "remainder interest."

The income interest within an item of property is a function of the income generated by the property. A person may be entitled to all of the income from a property or some portion of the income—for example, income equal to six percent of the fair market value of the property, even though the property is producing income at the rate of nine percent. This person is said to have the (or an) income interest in the property. Two or more persons (such as husband and wife) may have income interests in the same item of property and these interests may be held concurrently or consecutively. An income interest is capable of being accorded a present value at the time the interest is created.

The remainder interest within an item of property is the projected value of the property, or the property produced by reinvestment, at some future date. That is, the remainder interest in property is an amount equal to the then value of the property (or its offspring) when it is to be received at a subsequent point in time. As an illustration, if A gives B a portfolio of securities, telling B that he or she can hold the securities for a period of ten years and have the income from the portfolio during that time, following which the securities must be returned to A, B has the income interest in the securities and A has the remainder interest. Thus, while A has made a gift to B of the income interest, A has retained the remainder interest in the property. In planned giving, usually the donor (here, A) retains the income interest and the charitable organization involved is the donee of the remainder interest.

These interests are measured by the value of the property, the age of the donor(s), and the period of time that the income interests will exist. The actual computation is usually made by means of actuarial tables promulgated by the Department of the Treasury.

An income interest or a remainder interest in property may, then, be contributed to charity. However, it is infrequent that a deduction is available for a charitable gift of an income interest in property. By contrast, the charitable contribution of a remainder interest in an item of property will—assuming all of the technical requirements are met—give rise to a (frequently sizable) charitable contribution deduction.

When a gift of a remainder interest in property to a charitable organization is made, the charity usually will not acquire title to that remainder interest until the income interests have expired. Nonetheless, the donor receives the charitable deduction for the tax year in which the remainder interest in the property for the recipient charity is established. When a gift of an income interest in property to a charity is made, the charity acquires that interest immediately and retains it until such time (sometimes measured by a term of years) as the remainder interest commences. Again, any resulting charitable deduction is available for the tax year in which the income interest in the property for the charity is established.

Basically, the federal tax law requires that a planned gift be made by means of a trust if a charitable deduction is to be available. The trust used to facilitate a planned gift is known as a "split-interest trust" because the trust is the mechanism for satisfying the requirements with respect to the income and remainder interests.[6] That is, the trust is the medium for splitting the property into its two component interests. Split-interest trusts are charitable remainder trusts,

[6]IRC § 4947(a)(2).

pooled income funds, and charitable lead trusts (explained below). It should be added that there are some exceptions to the general requirement for use of a split-interest trust in planned giving. The principal one is the charitable gift annuity, which uses a contract rather than a trust. Individuals may give a remainder interest in their personal residence or farm to charity and receive a charitable deduction without utilizing a trust.[7] Further, a contribution of an undivided portion of one's entire interest in property is not regarded as a contribution of a partial interest in property.[8]

Still, a person contemplating a planned gift to a charitable organization will usually do so by means of a split-interest trust. Charitable giving can result in many financial advantages to the donor where one or more of the planned gift techniques are utilized, particularly when appreciated property (such as securities or real estate) is used.

A donor, although desirous of supporting a particular charitable organization, may be unwilling or unable to fully part with property, either because of a present or perceived need for the income that the property provides and/or because of the capital gains taxes that would be experienced if the property was sold. The planned gift is likely to be the answer in this situation, because the donor may satisfy his or her charitable desires and yet continue to receive income, perhaps on an enhanced basis, from the property. Moreover, the donor receives a charitable contribution deduction for the gift of the remainder interest, which will reduce or eliminate the tax on the income from the gift property. Also, there is no regular income tax on the capital gain inherent in the property (although, as noted, there may be some alternative minimum tax consequences). Further, if the gift property is not generating sufficient income, the trustee of the split-interest trust may dispose of the property and reinvest the proceeds in more productive property, which will enable the donor to receive more income from the property than was the case prior to the making of the gift.

§ 3.4 CHARITABLE REMAINDER TRUSTS

The most widespread form of planned giving involves a split-interest trust known as the "charitable remainder trust."[9] The term is nearly

---

[7]IRC § 170(f)(3)(B)(i). See Chapter 14 § 2.
[8]IRC § 170(f)(3)(B)(ii). See Chapter 14 § 3.
[9]The charitable remainder trust is the subject of Chapter 11.

self-explanatory: the entity is a trust, in which has been created a remainder interest that is destined for one or more charitable organizations. Each charitable remainder trust arrangement is specifically designed for the particular circumstances of the donor(s), with the remainder interest in the gift property designated for one or more charitable organizations.

One or more income interests are also created in a charitable remainder trust; thus, the charitable remainder trust is a split-interest trust.

(a) General Rules

A qualified charitable remainder trust must provide for a specified distribution of income, at least annually, to one or more beneficiaries (at least one of which is not a charitable organization) for life or for a term of no more than twenty years, with an irrevocable remainder interest to be held for the benefit of, or paid over to, the charitable organization.[10] These beneficiaries are the holders of the income interests and the charitable organization has the remainder interest; these interests are defined with particularity in the charitable remainder trust agreement.

The manner in which the income interests in a charitable remainder trust are ascertained is dependent upon whether the trust is a "charitable remainder annuity trust" or a "charitable remainder unitrust." In the case of the charitable remainder annuity trust, the income payments are in the form of a fixed amount (hence the word "annuity"). In the case of the charitable remainder unitrust, the income payments are in the form of an amount equal to a fixed percentage of the fair market value of the assets in the trust.

The charitable remainder annuity trust provides the advantage of a fixed return. The charitable remainder unitrust becomes attractive in the face of inflation, since the amount paid out is a function of the annual measurement of the value of the trust's assets.

Where the annuity interest or unitrust interest is payable over a term of years, any "person" (including an individual, corporation, trust, or partnership) can be a beneficiary. However, where the term is for someone's life, only an individual (or a charity) can be a beneficiary. If these rules are not followed, the charitable deduction

[10]IRC § 664.

will not be allowed, or will be allowed only if state law causes immediate acceleration of the remainder interest.

All categories of charitable organizations—both public charities and private foundations[11] are eligible to be remainder beneficiaries of as many charitable remainder trusts as they can muster. However, the allowability of the charitable deduction will vary as respects the type of charitable organization that is the donee, due to the percentage limitations.[12]

Usually, a bank or similar financial institution serves as the trustee of a charitable remainder trust. These institutions should have the capacity to administer the trust, make appropriate investments, and timely adhere to all income distribution and reporting requirements. It is common, however, for the charitable organization that is the remainder beneficiary to act as trustee. If the donor or a related person is named the trustee, the "grantor trust" rules may apply, with the gain from the sale by the trust of appreciated property taxed to the donor.[13]

Conventionally, once the income interest expires, the assets in a charitable remainder trust are distributed to the charitable organization that is the remainder beneficiary. However, the assets (or a portion of them) may be retained in the trust. If a retention occurs, the trust will be classified as a private foundation, unless it can sidestep those rules.

(b) Charitable Remainder Annuity Trusts

One basic type of charitable remainder trust is, as noted, the charitable remainder annuity trust.

(i) Specific Rules

Where an annuity trust is utilized, the donor (or other income beneficiary or beneficiaries) annually receives income in the form of a fixed amount, called a "sum certain." This stated dollar amount is the same either as to each recipient or as to the total amount payable for each year of the payment period. The amount may be expressed as a

---

[11] See Chapter 4 § 3.
[12] See Chapter 7.
[13] IRC §§ 671-677.

fraction or a percentage of the initial net fair market value of the property irrevocably passing in trust.

A federal income tax charitable deduction is available for the creation of a remainder interest for a charity by means of a charitable remainder annuity trust where seven basic criteria are satisfied:

- The trust must be structured to pay an annuity to or for the use of one or more noncharitable beneficiaries;
- Each noncharitable beneficiary must be alive at the time the trust is established;
- The annuity must be equal to at least five percent of the initial net fair market value of the gift property;
- The annuity must be payable at least annually;
- The annuity must be payable either for a term of years (up to twenty) or for the life of the noncharitable beneficiary (or beneficiaries);
- The trust cannot pay any amounts, other than the annuities, to or for the use of any person other than the charitable organization that is the remainder beneficiary;
- The remainder interest created by the trust must be transferred to or for the use of the charitable organization(s) involved or retained by the trust for such use.

There are other requirements, but these are the crucial ones.

A donor cannot make any additional contributions to a charitable remainder trust. However, a donor may create as many charitable remainder annuity trusts as may be desired.

A trust does not qualify as a charitable remainder annuity trust if any person has the power to alter the amount to be paid to any named person, other than the charitable beneficiary, if that power would cause any person to be treated as the owner of the trust, or any portion of it, under the "grantor trust" rules. The trust may not be subject to a power to invade, alter, amend, or revoke for the beneficial use of a person other than a charitable organization.

According to the IRS, there cannot be a federal income tax charitable deduction for a transfer to a charitable remainder annuity trust where there is greater than a five-percent probability that a noncharitable beneficiary will receive annuity payments to the extent that the trust becomes depleted, therefore leaving nothing for the charity holding the remainder interest.[14]

(ii) Determining the Charitable Deduction

The charitable deduction resulting from a contribution by means of a charitable remainder annuity trust is determined by use of tables promulgated by the Department of the Treasury. (Once that potential deduction is determined, the actual deduction is dependent upon compliance with the general charitable giving rules.) These tables yield a number called a "factor," which when multiplied against the total amount transferred into the trust provides the deductible portion.

Three elements must be taken into account in determining this charitable deduction:

- the age of the income beneficiary (or ages of the income beneficiaries) if the term of the trust is measured by a life (or lives), or the term of the trust, if it is for a stated period of years
- the annuity percentage
- the date or dates during the year when payment to the income beneficiary (or beneficiaries) will be made

As to the first element, it is necessary to know the beneficiary's date of birth, in that the age to use is that closest to his or her birth date.

(c) Charitable Remainder Unitrusts

The other basic type of charitable remainder trust is, as noted, the charitable remainder unitrust.

(i) Specific Rules

Where a unitrust is utilized, the donor (or other income beneficiary or beneficiaries) annually receives income in an amount equal to a fixed percentage of the net fair market value of the trust assets, valued annually (a "unitrust amount"). A percentage is fixed if it is

---

[14]Rev. Rul. 77-374, 1977-2 C.B. 329.

the same either as to each recipient or as to the total percentage payable in each year of the payment period.

A federal income tax charitable deduction is available for the creation of a remainder interest for a charity by means of a charitable remainder unitrust where seven basic criteria are satisfied. (Some of these elements are the same as with respect to a charitable remainder annuity trust, since they are common for all charitable remainder trusts.) These criteria are as follows:

- The trust must be structured to pay a unitrust amount to or for the use of one or more noncharitable beneficiaries;
- Each noncharitable beneficiary must be alive at the time the trust is established;
- The unitrust amount must be equal to at least five percent of the net fair market value of the trust property, valued annually;
- The unitrust amount must be payable at least annually;
- The unitrust amount must be payable either for a term of years (up to twenty) or for the life of the noncharitable beneficiary (or beneficiaries);
- The trust cannot pay any amounts, other than the unitrust amount, to or for the use of any person other than the charitable organization that is the remainder beneficiary;
- The remainder interest created by the trust must be transferred to or for the use of the charitable organization involved or retained by the trust for that use.

A donor can make additional contributions to a charitable remainder unitrust.

A trust does not qualify as a charitable remainder unitrust if any person has the power to alter the amount to be paid to any named person, other than the charitable beneficiary, if that power would cause any person to be treated as the owner of the trust, or any portion of it, under the "grantor trust" rules.

The trust may not be subject to a power to invade, alter, amend, or revoke for the beneficial use of a person other than a charitable organization.

In appropriate circumstances, it may be preferable to use the "income only" type of charitable remainder unitrust. With this trust, the income payments may be only the actual income (if any) of the trust (up to the otherwise required minimum five percent of annual value). Additionally, a unitrust may provide for income payments in subsequent years to constitute or include catch-up payments, so as to bring the income payments over the multi-year period involved to the amounts that would have been paid had the standard fixed percentage approach been used. This type (or these types) of unitrust is advantageous in situations where the income generated by the gift property at the time of the gift is not sufficient to satisfy the general payout requirement, and the makeup option is appropriate where it is anticipated that the income from the property will increase or that the trust will be able to dispose of the property and reinvest the proceeds in more productive assets. Gift property that can be suitable for an income-only charitable remainder unitrust includes raw real estate, yachts, and stamp and coin collections.

(ii)   *Determining the Charitable Deduction*

As is the case with the charitable remainder annuity trust, the federal income tax charitable deduction resulting from a contribution by means of a charitable remainder unitrust is determined by use of Treasury Department tables; likewise, the deductible portion of the transfer is ascertained through the determination and application of a factor.

Four elements of fact must be taken into account in determining this charitable deduction:

- the age of the income beneficiary (or ages of the income beneficiaries) if the term of the trust is measured by a life (or lives) or, the term of the trust, if it is to be for a stated period of years
- the unitrust amount percentage
- the date of valuation of the trust's assets
- the date or dates during the year when payment to the income beneficiary (or beneficiaries) will be made

(d)   Tax Treatment of Distributions

A noncharitable beneficiary of distributions from a charitable remainder trust is taxed on the payments in accordance with the types of revenue experienced by the trust. This tax scheme is represented by four tiers of potential tax treatment, which serve to characterize the amounts paid to income beneficiaries (whether as annuity amounts or unitrust amounts). These tiers are as follows:

- First, the payments are characterized as ordinary income, to the extent the trust has ordinary income for the current year and undistributed ordinary income from prior years.
- Second, the payments are characterized as capital gain, to the extent the trust has any capital gain for the current year and any undistributed capital gain from prior years. This capital gain will be taxed as ordinary income, except that the recipient can first offset long-term capital gain with long-term capital loss and short-term capital gain with short-term capital loss.
- Third, the payments are "other income"—principally, tax-exempt income, such as interest on municipal bonds (see below)—to the extent the trust has any other income for the current year and any undistributed other income from prior years.
- Finally, the payments are characterized as a nontaxable distribution of corpus.

The determination of the character of amounts distributed is made as of the end of the appropriate tax year of the trust. (This tax structure is different from that normally used to characterize distributions from trusts, which causes the payments to proportionately reflect the types of revenue experienced by the trust.)

Thus, the charitable remainder trust rules first force upon the noncharitable beneficiaries the least favorable of tax treatments of their payments. However, this result can be alleviated in the early years by the charitable deduction occasioned by the gift (assuming the donor is the income beneficiary).

(e) Tax Treatment of Charitable Remainder Trusts

Charitable remainder trusts are generally exempt from federal income taxation. However, this tax exemption is lost for any year in which the trust has income that is derived from an activity that is unrelated to the exempt purposes of the charitable organization that has the remainder interest in the gift property.[15] This includes unrelated debt-financed income.

(f) Remainder Trust Agreements

A charitable remainder trust, like any trust, is established upon the execution of a trust agreement. The law contains a battery of strin-

---

[15] See Chapter 4 § 6.

gent requirements that must be strictly adhered to if the trust is to qualify as a charitable remainder trust. Where these requirements are not satisfied, there generally cannot be any charitable deduction for a gift to the trust. There are, however, special rules pursuant to which a charitable remainder trust can be reformed and thus qualify for the charitable deduction. Further, a defective trust cannot be exempt as a charitable remainder trust.

Certain provisions of the private foundation rules are applicable to charitable remainder trusts.[16] A qualified charitable remainder trust must name a specific charitable organization as the (or a) remainder beneficiary. Under appropriate circumstances, a substitute remainder beneficiary may be designated by the donor, a noncharitable beneficiary, or the trustee. The trust instrument must also make provision for an alternative charitable organization remainder beneficiary.

Nearly all of the foregoing requirements of law must be reflected in the trust agreement, if the trust is to constitute a qualified charitable remainder trust.

(g) Gift Tax Aspects

Generally, the federal gift tax charitable deduction rules with respect to charitable remainder trusts are the same as the federal income tax charitable deduction rules.[17] However, a federal gift tax return may be required, although the charitable deduction will preclude the tax.

Where there is a single noncharitable beneficiary of a charitable remainder trust, and that beneficiary is not the donor, the donor has made a potentially taxable gift of the current value of the income interest. (Where the donor is also the sole income beneficiary, there is no gift, inasmuch as the tax law does not recognize the concept of an individual donating to himself or herself.) The $10,000 annual gift tax exclusion ($20,000, in the case of a two-spouse gift) is available, however, as well as the general unified estate and gift tax credit. When the non-donor beneficiary is the donor's spouse, the gift will qualify in full for the unlimited marital deduction.

Where there are two noncharitable beneficiaries of a charitable remainder trust, and one of the beneficiaries is not a donor, the result is a gift to the other beneficiary of the current value of his or her income interest. The value of the gift will depend upon whether

[16]See Chapter 4 § 3.
[17]These rules are discussed in Chapter 8.

the donor or the other beneficiary is the principal beneficiary. Again, the annual gift tax exclusion and the unified credit are available, as is the marital deduction (where the other beneficiary is the donor's spouse).

Care must be exercised with respect to the tax status of the remainder beneficiary. While any charitable organization is an eligible beneficiary for gift tax purposes, the scope of the gift tax definition of charity is narrower.

(h) Estate Tax Aspects

If an individual creates a charitable remainder trust during lifetime and is not an income beneficiary, the value of the gift(s) is added to the donor's taxable estate and any gift tax paid is credited against any estate tax.[18]

Where an individual creates a charitable remainder trust during lifetime and has an income interest in it for any period that does not terminate before his or her death, the value of the trust principal will be included in the estate. Even where the decedent did not retain an income interest, the value of the trust principal will be part of the gross estate if he or she retained a testamentary power to revoke the donee's interest.

Again, the marital deduction is available and the same considerations apply with respect to the charitable donee.

§ 3.5 POOLED INCOME FUNDS

Another planned giving technique is the gift to a "pooled income fund."[19] Like a charitable remainder trust, a pooled income fund is a form of split-interest trust, where a remainder interest is contributed to charity and the income is paid over to noncharitable beneficiaries. However, as the name implies, the pooled income fund involves a pool of gifts rather than gifts from a single source.

(a) General Rules

A donor to a qualified pooled income fund[20] receives a charitable contribution deduction for the gift to a charitable organization of the

---

[18]The federal estate tax rules are discussed in Chapter 8.
[19]The pooled income fund is the subject of Chapter 12.
[20]IRC § 642(c)(5).

remainder interest in the donated property. By the transaction, income interests in one or more noncharitable beneficiaries are created, with the remainder interest in the gift property designated for the charity that maintains the fund.

The pooled income fund basic instrument (trust agreement or declaration of trust) is written to facilitate gifts from an unlimited number of donors; thus, the essential terms of the transaction are established in advance for all participants. That is, there is no tailoring of the terms of the transfer to fit any one donor's particular circumstances (as is the case, for example, with the charitable remainder trust). The pooled income fund is, literally, a pooling of gifts. Such gifts may be of a considerably lesser amount than those to a charitable remainder trust, and are generally confined to cash and readily marketable securities (other than tax-exempt bonds).

A pooled income fund receives gifts from a number of donors, with each donor contributing an irrevocable remainder interest in the gift property to or for the use of an eligible charity. Each donor creates an income interest for the life of one or more beneficiaries, who must be living at the time of the transfer. The properties transferred by the donors must be commingled in the fund (to create the necessary pool).

Each income interest beneficiary must receive income at least once each year, determined by the rate of return earned by the fund for the year. Beneficiaries receive their proportionate share of the fund's income. The income share is based upon the number of units owned by the beneficiary in the fund, and each unit must be based upon the fair market value of the assets when transferred.

Thus, a pooled income fund is essentially an investment vehicle, the funding of which is motivated by charitable intents. The operation of the fund is similar to the operation of a mutual fund. However, there are three important exceptions. First, the capital in a pooled income fund is held by the trustee(s) (which may be, or include, the charity involved) and cannot be sold or redeemed by a donor or an income beneficiary. Second, realized capital gains are reinvested as additions to principal and are not distributed to a donor or an income beneficiary. Third, upon termination of all designated income interests, the full value of the units assigned to an item of gift property are transferred to or retained for the benefit of the charity involved.

A pooled income fund must be maintained by one or more charitable organizations. This maintenance requirement means that the charity must exercise control over the fund; the organization does not have to be the trustee of the fund (although it can be) but must have the power to remove and replace the trustee. An income beneficiary of, or donor to, the fund may not be a trustee. However, a donor may be a trustee or officer of the charitable organization that maintains the fund, provided he or she does not have the general trustee's responsibilities towards the fund.

Unlike the case with respect to other forms of planned giving, only certain categories of charitable organizations may maintain a pooled income fund. Most types of public charities can maintain such a fund, while private foundations and some nonprivate foundations cannot.[21]

For a contribution of a remainder interest to a charitable organization, made by means of a pooled income fund, to be deductible, nine elements (of which some have been described) must be present. These are as follows.:

- The donor must transfer an irrevocable remainder interest in the property.
- The remainder interest must be transferred to or for the use of a charitable organization that is qualified as at least one of the types of public charities.
- The donor must create, by means of the transfer to the fund, an income interest for the life of one or more noncharitable beneficiaries.
- The property that is the subject of the gift must be commingled with property transferred by other donors.
- There must be no investments by the fund in tax-exempt securities.
- The fund must consist only of amounts transferred in compliance with the pooled income fund requirements of law.
- The fund must be maintained by the charitable organization to which the remainder interest is contributed.
- A donor or a beneficiary of an income interest in a pooled income fund cannot be a trustee of the fund.
- The income paid each year to the income beneficiaries is determined by the rate of return earned by the fund for the year.

[21]The distinctions between public and private charities are summarized in Chapter 4 § 3.

The deductible portion of a transfer of property to a pooled income fund is determined by reference to actuarial tables promulgated by the Department of the Treasury.

The same general tax advantages available as the result of gifts to charitable remainder trusts are available for gifts to pooled income funds. This is particularly true when the gift is made using fully marketable and appreciated securities. The pooled income fund transfer may accommodate a smaller amount (value) of securities than a transfer to a remainder trust. However, if fixed income is an important consideration, the charitable remainder annuity trust (see above) or the charitable gift annuity (see below) will be preferable to a gift to a charitable remainder unitrust or pooled income fund.

(b) Valuation and Assignment of Units

A pooled income fund is divided into units, each of which represents an interest in the fund equal in value to each of the other units. The fair market value of the assets of a pooled income fund is frequently determined as of the first business day of each fiscal year and as of the first business day of each of the other three fiscal year quarters.

The value of a unit is determined by dividing the fair market value of the fund's assets on the determination day by the number of outstanding units. Gifts generally will be added to the fund on the next determination day following receipt and the income interest in the gifts will be assigned a number of units determined by dividing the fair market value of the gift on that day by the value of a unit determined on that day. If a donor provides for two or more beneficiaries to receive income with respect to his or her gift concurrently, the units assigned to the income interest in the gift will be allocated proportionately among the concurrent beneficiaries so that they will share the income interest in the gift as specified by the donor.

The charitable organization involved should reserve the right in appropriate circumstances to add gifts to the fund on a day other than a determination day, in which case a special valuation of units will be made on that day.

Once determined, the number of units assigned to the income interest (or share thereof) in a gift will not change, but the value of a unit will change as the value of the fund's assets changes. When principal amounts are severed from the fund and transferred to the charitable organization, the units assigned or allocated thereto will be cancelled.

(c) Distribution of Income

The documents associated with a pooled income fund should make provision for the timing of the distribution of income. For example, if the calendar year is the fiscal period, donors may be notified that distributions of the income of the fund will be made quarterly, on or about the fifteenth day of the month following the close of each calendar quarter, that is, about the 15th of January, April, July, and October, in each year, to income beneficiaries in proportion to their respective income interests. All income must be distributed annually; to the extent that any portion of the income for a taxable year has not been fully distributed by the four above-described quarterly payments, then an additional make-up payment must be made within the first sixty-five days of the taxable year next following.

Each unit outstanding for less than the entire year will be entitled to receive a fractional payment based on the portion of the year for which it was outstanding. Realized and unrealized appreciation or depreciation of principal should not be taken into account in determining income. Therefore, the following items should be treated as principal and not income: (1) gains and losses from the sale, exchange, redemption, or other disposition of investment assets; (2) stock dividends, stock splits, and similar distributions; (3) capital gain dividends of regulated investment companies (mutual funds); (4) liquidating distributions; and (5) any other dividends or distributions not deemed to be taxable as income under the federal tax laws.

The income payable with respect to each unit will depend, of course, on the income earned by the pooled income fund; the charitable organization cannot predict what that income will be.

(d) Determining the Charitable Deduction

As noted earlier, a planned gift is predicated on the fundamental concept that an item of property carries with it an income interest and a remainder interest. Most deductible planned gifts involve a contribution of a remainder interest in property to a charitable organization.

Such is the case with a gift to a charitable organization by means of a pooled income fund. As always, a first step is to determine the fair market value of the property being transferred. Once that is done, the "present value" of the income interest retained or designated by a donor is ascertained. The difference between the property's value and the value of the income interest is the value of the remainder interest. The amount of the charitable deduction occasioned by a transfer of cash or property to a pooled income fund is based upon the value of the remainder interest in the property (that is, the fair market value of the property less the value of the income interest).

The present value of the income interest in property contributed to a pooled income fund is generally dependent upon two elements: the age of the income beneficiary (or beneficiaries) and the rate of return experienced by the pooled income fund. The rate of return used to value the income interest is determined by reference to the highest rate of return experienced by the fund for any of the three years of the fund preceding the year in which the transfer is made. Where a pooled income fund has not been in existence for three years in advance of the year of a gift, a 9 percent rate of return must be presumed.

The Department of the Treasury has developed tables to use in determining the present value of remainder interests in property transferred to pooled income funds. These tables, which are gender neutral, establish factors used with respect to income beneficiaries of various ages and rates of return.

(e) Tax Treatment of Income Distributions and Pooled Income Funds

A beneficiary of income distributions from a pooled income fund is taxed on the payments in accordance with the tax rules that apply to the types of net income experienced and distributed by the fund.

Thus, the tax treatment of distributions to income beneficiaries from pooled income funds is determined in accordance with the standard trust rules. The rules governing the taxation of distributions to income beneficiaries from charitable remainder trusts (which, as noted above, characterize the receipts as ordinary income, capital gain, and/or nontaxable return of capital) are inapplicable to distributions from pooled income funds.

Unlike charitable remainder trusts, pooled income funds are not formally tax-exempt. However, a pooled income fund is allowed a deduction for distributions of income to beneficiaries and for long-term capital gains that have been permanently set aside for charitable purposes. (Therefore, a pooled income fund is taxable on all income, including short-term capital gain, which is not distributable to beneficiaries.) Consequently, a pooled income fund is essentially tax-exempt.

(f) Selection of the Trustee

As noted, a pooled income fund must be maintained by the charitable organization that is the recipient of the remainder interests in the cash or properties contributed. However, while this means that the charitable organization must retain the ability to select the trustee (or trustees) of a pooled income fund, it does not mean that the charitable organization must be the (or a) trustee.

Some charitable organizations designate, in the instrument that creates the pooled income fund, a financial institution as trustee of the fund. This can create a problem if the charitable organization and the financial institution subsequently part ways. A more prudent approach is to enable the charitable organization to name the trustee in a separate agreement and/or to be a co-trustee with the financial institution. In this way, if a new financial institution is selected, the pooled income fund organizational instrument need not be altered.

(g) Pooled Income Fund Governing Instruments

The document by which a pooled income fund is created is either termed a "declaration of trust" or, where there is a basic contractual relationship with a trustee embodied in the document, a "trust agreement." A pooled income fund instrument's provisions must, to ensure the availability of the charitable deductions, be in compliance with the various operating rules. The IRS has issued sample provisions for pooled income fund organizational documents.

A pooled income fund declaration of trust or trust agreement must contain provisions

- requiring that the property transferred to a pooled income fund by each donor be commingled with, and invested or reinvested with, other property transferred to the fund by other donors;
- prohibiting a pooled income fund from accepting or investing in tax-exempt securities;

- probibiting the fund from having, as a trustee, a donor to the fund or a beneficiary (other than the charitable organization that receives the remainder interests) of an income interest in any property transferred to the fund;
- directing the trustee of the pooled income fund to distribute income currently or within the first 65 days following the close of the tax year in which the income is earned;
- stating that the income interest of any designated beneficiary shall either terminate with the last regular payment which was made before the death of the beneficiary or be prorated to the date of his or her death;
- stating that, upon termination of the income interest(s) retained or created by a donor, the amount severed from the fund must either be paid to, or retained for the use of, the designated charity;
- prohibiting the fund from engaging in any act of self-dealing;
- requiring such distributions as are required to enable the fund to satisfy the private foundation mandatory payout requirements;
- prohibiting the fund from retaining any excess business holdings;
- prohibiting the fund from making any jeopardizing investments; and
- prohibiting the fund from making any taxable expenditures.

A pooled income fund life agreement (the document by which the gift is evidenced) must (1) specify at the time of the transfer the particular beneficiary or beneficiaries to whom the income is payable and the share of income distributable to each person so specified, and (2) contain an acknowledgement of the donor that he or she has read the brochure explanatory of the pooled income fund prior to execution of the life income agreement.

Still other provisions may (and generally should) appear in one or both of the pooled income fund instruments. Thus, a pooled income fund declaration of trust, and in many instances the life income agreement, may or should contain one or more of the following provisions: (1) a formal name of the pooled income fund; (2) a statement of the purposes of the fund; (3) a statement of the maintenance requirement; (4) a summary of the general terms and conditions applicable to pooled income fund gifts; (5) authorization of the remainderman of the fund to invest its properties in the fund (see below); (6) a summary of the methods of valuation of the pooled income fund and the dates on which the valuation shall be determined; (7) a summary of the unit plan or other method of evidencing an income interest in the fund; (8) an explanation of the considerations with respect to the timing of the making of a gift to the fund; (9) a statement as to whether the fund is on the cash or accrual method of accounting; (10) a definition of the receipts of the fund that are chargeable to income and to principal; (11) a summary of the procedures for computing and distributing income for the income beneficiaries of the fund; (12) a discussion of the treatment of property in the fund upon termination of the income interest in it; (13) a statement of the identity of, and the powers of, the trustee(s) of the fund; (14) a statement as to whether the fund is to use the calendar year or another fiscal year; (15) a statement as to the ability of amendment of the pooled income fund declaration of trust; and (16) a provision stating that a unit of participation is entitled to share in the income of the fund in a lesser amount than would otherwise be determined under the general unit plan rules, provided that the income otherwise allocable to the unit is paid within the tax year it is received to the charity to or for which the remainder interest is contributed.

(h) Seeding

Generally, the investment practices of a pooled income fund must be in conformance with the conventional charitable trust law requirements. However, although the law states that a fund can include only amounts received from transfers which meet the statutory tests, the charity may combine the assets of the fund with the organization's endowment assets for investment purposes, as long as adequate records are maintained to show the separate nature of the two categories of assets.

A charitable organization may begin operation of its pooled income fund by seeding the fund, in whole or in part, with its own assets. This may have to be done, for example, where the trustee is a financial institution that demands an initial deposit in the fund and there are inadequate gifts at the outset. Thereafter, as gifts come in, the assets can be withdrawn from the fund. Income beneficiaries do not participate in the earnings from non-gift assets in the fund.

§ 3.6 CHARITABLE GIFT ANNUITIES

Another form of planned giving is the "charitable gift annuity."[22]
Unlike the charitable remainder trust and the pooled income fund,
the charitable gift annuity is not based upon use of a split-interest
trust. Rather, the annuity is reflected in an agreement between the
donor and donee, where the donor agrees to make a gift and the
donee agrees, in return, to provide the donor (and/or someone else)
with an annuity.

The donor, in the process of creating a charitable gift annuity, is in
fact engaging in two transactions, albeit with one payment: the
purchase of an annuity and the making of a charitable gift. It is the
latter that gives rise to the charitable deduction. One sum is transferred; the amount in excess of that necessary to purchase the annuity is the charitable gift portion. It is because of the dual nature of
the transaction that the charitable gift annuity transfer constitutes a
"bargain sale."[23]

As with the annuity paid out of a charitable remainder annuity
trust, the annuity resulting from the creation of a charitable gift
annuity arrangement is a fixed amount paid at regular intervals. The
amount paid is dependent upon the age of the beneficiary, determined at the time the contribution is made.

A portion of the annuity paid is tax-free, being a return of capital.
Where appreciated securities are given, there will be capital gain on
the appreciation that is attributable to the value of the annuity. If the
donor is the annuitant (receiver of the annuity), the capital gain can
be reported ratably over the individual's life expectancy. However,
the tax savings occasioned by the charitable contribution deduction
may shelter the capital gain—resulting from the creation of a charitable gift annuity—from taxation.

Because the arrangement is by contract between donor and donee,
all of the assets of the charitable organization are on the line for
ongoing payment of the annuities. (By contrast, with most planned
giving techniques the resources for payment of income are confined
to those in a split-interest trust.) That is why a few states impose a
requirement that charities establish a reserve for the payment of gift

[22] Gifts by means of a charitable gift annuity are the subject of Chapter 13.
[23] See Chapter 9 § 5.

annuities and why many charitable organizations are reluctant to embark upon a gift annuity program. However, charitable organizations that are reluctant to commit to the ongoing payment of annuities can eliminate the risk by reinsuring them.

§ 3.7   CHARITABLE LEAD TRUSTS

The foregoing forms of planned giving have this common element: the donor transfers to a charitable organization the remainder interest in the property, with one or more noncharitable beneficiaries retaining the income interest. However, the reverse may occur—and that is the essence of the "charitable lead trust."[24]

(a)   General Rules

A charitable lead trust is a vehicle by which property transferred to it is apportioned into an income interest and a remainder interest. Like the charitable remainder trust and the pooled income fund, it is a split-interest trust. Pursuant to a charitable lead trust, an income interest in property is contributed to a charitable organization, either for a term of years or for the life of one individual or the lives of more than one individual. The remainder interest in the property is reserved to return, at the expiration of the income interest (the "lead period"), to the donor or some other noncharitable beneficiary or beneficiaries; often the property passes from one generation (the donor's) to another.

The charitable lead trust can be used to accelerate into one year a series of charitable contributions that would otherwise be made annually, with a corresponding single-year deduction for the "bunched" amount of charitable gifts.

In some sets of circumstances, a charitable deduction is available for the transfer of an income interest in property to a charitable organization. There are stringent limitations, however, on the deductible amount of charitable contributions of these income interests.

A charitable lead trust can be funded by a donor or donors during lifetime, as well as by means of transfers from an estate.

The charitable lead trust is frequently used to transfer property from one member of a family to another, usually from one generation to the next. For example, a father may establish a charitable lead

---

[24]Gifts by means of the charitable lead trust are the subject of Chapter 15.

trust, providing income from the trust to a charitable organization for a term of years, with the trust corpus to thereafter pass to his daughter. This type of transfer may be subject to a gift tax, but the actual tax cost of the gift is substantially reduced because of the reduction in the amount transferred to the ultimate beneficiary by the value of the income interest contributed to a charitable organization. If a charitable lead trust is used to shift property to a generation other than the immediate next one, the transfer may be subject to the generation-skipping transfer tax.

The income interest created for a charitable organization by means of a charitable lead trust is defined in one of two ways. The income interest may be stated as a guaranteed annuity or as an annual payment equal to a fixed percentage of the fair market value of the trust property, valued annually. These interests have the same names as in the charitable remainder trust context; the first of these interests is an "annuity interest" and the other is "unitrust interest."

An annuity interest or a unitrust interest in property may, as discussed above, be created by means of a charitable remainder trust. These interests are subject to minimum amounts that must be payable to the income beneficiaries. However, an income interest created by a charitable lead trust is not governed by any minimum or maximum payout requirement.

Also, as discussed, an income interest in property created by means of a charitable remainder trust may be measured by a term of years. The income interest term established by a charitable remainder trust cannot be longer than twenty years. By contrast, there is no restriction in federal law on the length of the term during which the income interest is payable to a charitable organization out of a charitable lead trust.

(b) Income Tax Charitable Deduction (If Any)

A transfer of money or property to a charitable lead trust may or may not result in a current "front end" income tax charitable contribution deduction for the donor.

If certain conditions are met, a charitable deduction will be available for the value of an income interest created by means of a charitable lead trust. These conditions are principally twofold. First, as noted, the income interest must be in the form of an annuity interest or a unitrust interest. Where this is done, the charitable contribution deduction is available for federal income, gift, and estate tax purposes, when the other requirements are satisfied. Second, the donor must be treated as the owner of the income interest, pursuant to the so-called "grantor trust" rules. (This is a federal tax law requirement, with the donor being the "grantor.") This latter requirement means that the income as received by the charitable lead trust is taxed to the donor/grantor (unless municipal bonds are used—see above).

A charitable lead trust may be established in such a fashion that there is no income tax charitable contribution deduction for the income interest involved. Under this approach, the trust is written so that the grantor trust rules are inapplicable; this is accomplished by causing the donor to not be considered the owner of the income interest. The tax consequence of such a charitable lead trust is that the donor forgoes a charitable contribution deduction at the front end but he or she concurrently avoids taxation on the income of the trust for each of the years that the trust is in existence. In this situation, while there is no charitable deduction, there is nonetheless a "deduction" in the sense that the income generated by the property involved is outside the stream of taxable income flowing to the donor.

From an income tax standpoint, the facts and circumstances of each case must be evaluated to ascertain whether a charitable lead trust is appropriate for an individual (or family) and, if so, whether or not the charitable contribution deduction should be utilized. A person with a year of abnormally high income may find considerable advantage in a charitable lead trust that yields a charitable deduction, since that deduction will be of greatest economic advantage in relation to the higher income taxation, and the trust income subsequently attributable to the donor will be taxable in a relatively lower amount. Conversely, the charitable lead trust without the deduction is sometimes utilized in support of a charitable organization by an individual where outright contributions by him or her to the organization cannot be fully deductible because of the percentage limitations on annual charitable contribution deductions.

(c) Valuing the Charitable Deduction

The Department of the Treasury has promulgated tables to use in valuing remainder interests created by charitable remainder trusts, both annuity trusts and unitrusts. These tables are also used to value an income interest that is stated as an annuity or unitrust interest.

(d) Tax Treatment of the Charitable Lead Trust

A qualified charitable remainder trust is an entity that generally is exempt from federal income taxation. However, a charitable lead trust is not exempt from income taxation. Consequently, the tax treatment accorded a charitable lead trust is dependent upon whether or not the "grantor trust" rules are applicable.

If the grantor trust rules are applicable, so that the donor is treated as the owner of the trust, the income of the trust will be taxable to the donor and not to the trust. This means that the trust will not have any income tax liability.

If the grantor trust rules are inapplicable, so that the donor is not treated as the owner of the trust, the income of the trust will be taxable to the trust. In this situation, the charitable lead trust is allowed an unlimited charitable deduction for the payments from it (pursuant to the trust agreement) to the charitable organization that is the income beneficiary.

(e) Testamentary Use of Lead Trusts

Like the other forms of planned giving, a charitable lead trust can be used to benefit a charitable organization out of the assets of a decedent's estate. That is, the income interest thereby created for a charitable organization can be transferred as a charitable bequest by means of such a trust. The remainder interest would be reserved for one or more noncharitable beneficiaries, such as the decedent's heirs.

In this situation, a charitable deduction is available to the estate. Again, the deduction is for the present value of the income interest being transferred to a charitable organization.

When a federal estate tax charitable deduction becomes available, there is no need for anyone to recognize the income of the charitable lead trust. That is, there is no application of the equivalent of the grantor trust rules, whereby an individual is considered the owner of the trust, in this context.

(f) Private Foundation Rules

As is the case with many types of trusts used in the planned giving context, a charitable lead trust, being a split-interest trust, is treated as a private foundation for certain purposes.

In general, the private foundation rules that pertain to a charitable lead trust are those concerning termination of private foundation status, governing instruments requirements, self-dealing, excess business holdings, jeopardizing investments, and taxable expenditures.[25] However, a charitable lead trust is exempt from the excess business holdings and jeopardizing investments rules where the amounts in the trust for which a charitable contribution deduction was allowed (namely, the income interest) have an aggregate value of no more than 60 percent of the total fair market value of all amounts in the trust.

§ 3.8 OTHER FORMS OF PLANNED GIVING

There are, in addition to the above four forms of planned giving, additional forms. These include:

- charitable contributions out of an estate[26]
- charitable contributions of life insurance[27]
- charitable contributions of a life interest in an individual's personal residence or farm[28]

---

[25] See Chapter 4 § 3.

[26] None of these forms requires a split-interest trust for their creation, although split-interest trusts can be created as part of an individual's estate. See Chapter 8.

[27] This form of planned giving is discussed in Chapter 17.

[28] This form of planned giving is discussed in Chapter 14 § 2.

4

The Fundamental Definitions

§ 4.1 MEANING OF "GIFT"

The basic federal law on the subject of the tax aspects of charitable giving is contained in the Internal Revenue Code and in the interpretations of that body of law found in court opinions, Treasury Department and IRS regulations, and IRS public rulings. (Technically not "law," pronouncements by the IRS on this subject may be found in private letter rulings, technical advice memoranda, and general counsel memoranda.) This body of law is quite specific on various aspects of the law of charitable giving, as the pages of this book attest.

Despite this extensive treatment of these aspects of the law, there is an omission in the developed rules concerning charitable giving; the federal law is very scarce on the meaning of the word "gift" or "contribution."[1] This is highly significant, obviously, because there must be a "gift" before there can be a "charitable gift."

(a) General Rules

Integral to the concept of the charitable contribution deduction, then, is the fundamental requirement that money or property transferred to a charitable organization be transferred pursuant to a transaction that constitutes a "gift."[2] Just because money is paid, or

[1] By contrast, most state charitable solicitation statutes contain a definition of the term "gift." See Hopkins, *The Law of Fund-Raising* (John Wiley & Sons, Inc. 1991), at 257–258.
[2] For these purposes, at least, the terms "contribution," "gift," and "donation" have the same meaning.

property is transferred, to a charitable, educational, religious, or like organization, it does not necessarily mean that the payment or transfer is a gift. Consequently, when a university's tuition, a hospital's health care fee, or an association's dues are paid, there is no gift, and thus there is not a charitable deduction for the payment.[3]

Certainly, there is some law, most of it generated by the federal courts, as to what constitutes a gift. (The Internal Revenue Code and the tax regulations are essentially silent on the subject.) Basically, the meaning of the word "gift" has two elements: it is a transfer that is "voluntary" and is motivated by something other than "consideration."[4] The law today places more emphasis on the second element than on the first. Thus, the income tax regulations (promulgated in amplification of the business expense deduction rules) state that a transfer is not a contribution when it is made "with a reasonable expectation of financial return commensurate with the amount of the donation."[5] Instead, this type of payment is a purchase (of a product and/or a service). Thus, the IRS states that a "contribution" is

> A voluntary transfer of money or property that is made with no expectation of procuring financial benefit commensurate with the amount of the transfer.[6]

The IRS follows another principle of law:

> Where consideration in the form of substantial privileges or benefits is received in connection with payments by patrons of fund-raising activities, there is a presumption that the payments are not gifts.[7]

A corollary of these seemingly simple rules is that, as these guidelines reflect, a single transaction can be partially a gift and partially a purchase, so that when a charitable organization is the payee only the gift portion is deductible.[8]

---

[3]E.g., *Channing v. United States*, 4 F. Supp. 33 (D. Mass. 1933), aff'd per curiam, 67 F.2d 986 (1st Cir. 1933), cert. den., 291 U.S. 686 (1934); Rev. Rul. 54-580, 1954-2 C.B. 97.
[4]"Consideration" is something being received (usually, goods and/or services) in return for a payment. Where payments are made to receive something in exchange, the transaction is more in the nature of a contract.
[5]Reg. § 1.162-15(b).
[6]Reg. § 1.170A-1(c)(5).
[7]Rev. Rul. 86-63, 1986-1 C.B. 88.
[8]See Chapter 24.

Years ago, the U.S. Supreme Court observed that a gift is a transfer motivated by "detached or disinterested generosity."[9] Along this same line, the Court referred to a gift as a transfer made "out of affection, respect, admiration, charity or like impulses."[10] (This is the factor frequently referred to as donative intent.[11]) However, the more contemporary definition of the term "gift" concentrates less on what was in the mind of the donor at the time of the gift and more on the circumstances surrounding the transaction, with emphasis on whether the "donor" received anything as a consequence of the "gift." This is because some courts are finding it difficult to determine the subjective intent of the transferor.[12]

Thus, the contemporary law on the point, as reflected in the view of the Supreme Court, is that a "payment of money [or transfer of property] generally cannot constitute a charitable contribution if the contributor expects a substantial benefit in return."[13] This observation was made in the context of an opinion concerning a charitable organization that raised funds for its programs by providing group life, health, accident, and disability insurance policies, underwritten by insurance companies, to its members. Because the members had favorable mortality and morbidity rates, experience rating resulted in substantially lower insurance costs than if the insurance were purchased individually. Since the insurance companies' costs of providing insurance to the group were uniformly lower than the annual premiums paid, the companies paid refunds of the excess ("dividends") to the organization that were used for its charitable pur-

[9]*Commissioner* v. *Duberstein*, 363 U.S. 278, 285 (1960), quoting from *Commissioner* v. *LoBue*, 351 U.S. 243, 246 (1956).

[10]*Robertson* v. *United States*, 343 U.S. 711, 714 (1952).

[11]E.g., *DeJong* v. *Commissioner*, 309 F.2d 373 (9th Cir. 1962), aff'g, 36 T.C. 896 (1961); *Transamerica Corporation* v. *United States*, 254 F. Supp. 504 (N.D. Cal. 1966), aff'g, 392 F.2d 522 (9th Cir. 1968); *Fausner* v. *Commissioner*, 55 T.C. 620 (1971); *Wolfe* v. *Commissioner*, 54 T.C. 1707 (1970); *Howard* v. *Commissioner*, 39 T.C. 833 (1963); and *Crosby Valve & Gage Company*, 46 T.C. 641 (1966), aff'd, 380 F.2d 146 (1st Cir. 1967), cert. den., 389 U.S. 976 (1967).

[12]*Transamerica Corporation* v. *United States*, supra, n. 11; *Crosby Valve & Gage Company* v. *Commissioner*, supra, n. 11; *Wardwell, Estate of* v. *Commissioner*, 301 F.2d 632 (8th Cir. 1962), rev'g, 35 T.C. 443 (1960); *Citizens & Southern National Bank of South Carolina* v. *United States*, 243 F. Supp. 900 (W.D.S.C. 1965); *Marquis* v. *Commissioner*, 49 T.C. 695 (1968); and *Perlmutter* v. *Commissioner*, 45 T.C. 311 (1965).

[13]*United States* v. *American Bar Endowment*, 477 U.S. 105, 116–117 (1986).

poses. Critical to the organization's fund-raising efforts was the fact that it required its members to assign it all dividends as a condition for participating in the insurance program. The organization advised its insured members that each member's share of the dividends, less its administrative costs, constituted a tax-deductible contribution.

However, the U.S. Supreme Court disagreed with that conclusion. It found that none of the "donors" knew that they could have purchased comparable insurance for a lower cost; the Court thus assumed that the value of the insurance provided by the organization at least equaled their premium payments. The Court concluded that these individuals failed to demonstrate that they intentionally gave away more than they received.

The Court wrote: "The *sine qua non* of a charitable contribution is a transfer of money or property without adequate consideration. The taxpayer, therefore, must at a minimum demonstrate that he [or she] purposefully contributed money or property in excess of the value of any benefit he [or she] received in return."[14] Thus, by comparing the cost of similar insurance policies, the Court reached the conclusion that they received full value in response to what they paid in the form of insurance premiums.

Essentially the same rule was subsequently articulated by the Court, when it ruled that an exchange having an "inherently reciprocal nature" is not a gift and thus cannot be a charitable gift, where the recipient is a charity.[15] In this case, the Court considered the character of payments to the Church of Scientology, which provides "auditing" sessions designed to increase members' spiritual awareness and training courses at which participants study the tenets of the faith and seek to attain the qualifications necessary to conduct auditing sessions. The Church, following a "doctrine of exchange," set forth schedules of mandatory fixed prices for auditing and training sessions which vary according to a session's length and level of sophistication.

The payors contended that the payments were charitable contributions. The Court disagreed, holding that the payments were made with an expectation of a quid pro quo in terms of goods or services, which are not deductible. The Court focused on the fact that the Church established fixed prices for the auditing and training sessions, calibrated particular prices to sessions of particular lengths and

[14]*Id.* at 118.
[15]*Hernandez* v. *Commissioner*, 109 S. Ct. 2136, 2144 (1989).

sophistication levels, returned a refund if services went unper-
formed, distributed "account cards" for monitoring prepaid but as-
yet-unclaimed services, and categorically barred the provision of free
services.

Reviewing the legislative history of the charitable contribution deduction, the Court found that "Congress intended to differentiate
between unrequited payments to qualified recipients and payments
made to such recipients in return for goods or services. Only the
former were deemed deductible."[16] In the case, charitable deductions
were not allowed because the payments "were part of a quintessen-
tial *quid pro quo* exchange."[17] In so holding, the Court rejected the
argument that payments to religious organizations should be given
special preference in this regard.[18]

Several years before, the IRS published its position on the point,
holding that the payments for the auditing and training sessions are
comparable to payments of tuition to schools.[19]

A third contemporary opinion from the U.S. Supreme Court on
the point held that funds transferred by parents to their children
while they served as full-time, unpaid missionaries of a church are
not deductible as charitable contributions to or for the use of the
church.[20] This opinion turned on whether the funds transferred to
the accounts of the children were deductible as contributions "for the
use of" the church. In deciding this issue, the Court looked to the
legislative history of this term and concluded that this phraseology
was intended by Congress to convey a meaning similar to the words
"in trust for," so that in selecting the phrase "for the use of" Congress
was referring to donations made in trust or in a similar legal arrangement.[21] The Court added that, while this interpretation "does not
require that the qualified organization take actual possession of the

[16]*Id.* at 2144.
[17]*Id.* at 2145.
[18]Cf. the dissent, *id.* at 2151–2156, which argued that the *quid* was exclusively of spiritual or religious worth and that precedents show that, in
somewhat comparable circumstances, the IRS has a practice of allowing
deductions for fixed payments for religious services.
[19]Rev. Rul. 78-189, 1978-1 C.B. 68. In *Brown* v. *Commissioner*, 62 T.C. 551
(1974), aff'd, 523 F.2d 365 (8th Cir. 1975), it was held that the payments are
not deductible as medical expenses (IRC § 213).
[20]*Davis* v. *United States*, 110 S. Ct. 2014 (1990).
[21]A discussion of gifts "for the use of" a charitable organization is in Chapter
10 § 2.

contribution, it nevertheless reflects that the benefactors must have significant legal rights with respect to the disposition of donated funds.[22]

The Court thus rejected the claim that a charitable deduction should be allowed merely where the charitable organization has "a reasonable opportunity to supervise the use of contributed funds."[23] It observed that the IRS "would face virtually insurmountable administrative difficulties in verifying that any particular expenditure benefited a qualified donee" were a looser interpretation of the phrase utilized. The larger interpretation would, wrote the Court, "create an opportunity for tax evasion that others might be eager to exploit," although the Court was quick to note that "there is no suggestion whatsoever in this case that the transferred funds were used for an improper purpose."[24] The Court also found that the funds were not transferred "in trust for" the church. The money was transferred to the children's personal bank accounts on which they were the sole authorized signatories. No trust or "similar legal arrangement" was created. The children lacked any legal obligation to use the money in accordance with church guidelines, nor did the church have any legal entitlement to the money or a cause of action against missionaries who used their parents' money for purposes not approved by the church. Thus, the charitable deductions were denied.

Notwithstanding these three recent Supreme Court opinions, however, the donative intent doctrine still has its adherents. For example, a court denied an estate tax charitable deduction to an estate because a trust, funded by the estate, from which the gifts were made was modified solely to preserve the estate tax charitable deduction.[25]

In the case, the decedent created a trust, which was funded with interests in real property. This trust had charitable remainder beneficiaries, but the trust did not qualify for the estate tax charitable contribution deduction[26] because it was a defective (for tax purposes) split-interest trust.[27] Following his (the donor's) death, a successor trust was established, with equivalent funding of the income interest beneficiaries outside the trust. The second trust became a wholly

---

[22]*Davis* v. *United States, supra,* n. 20, at 2021.
[23]*Id.* at 2022.
[24]*Id.*
[25]*La Meres, Estate of* v. *Commissioner,* 98 T.C. 294 (1992).
[26]See Chapter 8.
[27]See Chapter 3.

charitable trust and the estate claimed a charitable deduction for the amounts that were paid to the charitable beneficiaries. This process did not constitute a qualifying reformation.[28] The IRS disallowed the charitable deduction claimed by the estate. The Tax Court upheld the disallowance. The court found that the trust "was an attempt to qualify the charitable bequests for the [estate tax charitable] deduction."[29] The court added that "[t]here is no evidence indicating a nontax reason" for the second trust,[30] and disallowed the deduction because the trust "was modified for reasons independent of tax considerations."[31] The court added that, if it ruled to the contrary it would be rendering the reformation procedure superfluous, because the trust could be retroactively amended.

In another donative intent case, a husband and wife granted to a charitable conservancy organization a scenic easement over 167 acres of their 407 acres of property and claimed a $206,900 charitable contribution deduction for the gift.[32] On audit, the IRS disallowed the deduction, claiming, in part, that the donors lacked the requisite "donative intent." The alleged absence of donative intent was based on the assertion that the donors made the gift of the scenic easement for the sole purpose of maintaining their property's value and to receive a tax deduction. The government made much of the fact that the donee conservancy group "recited the estimated tax advantages of a scenic easement conveyance" and that the donors sought reconveyance of the easement once the charitable deduction was disallowed.[33]

The matter went to court, where it was found that the requisite donative intent was present at the time the scenic easement was conveyed. The court said that the federal tax law "permits deductions for *bona fide* gifts notwithstanding the motivations of a taxpayer."[34] The court wrote that, "[i]n order to be entitled to a tax deduction, the taxpayer must not expect a substantial benefit as a *quid pro quo* for the contribution.[35] "However," the court continued, "the charita-

[28] See Chapter 8 § 7.
[29] *La Meres Estate* v. *Commissioner, supra,* n. 25, at 308.
[30] *Id.*
[31] *Id.*
[32] This type of gift is discussed in Chapter 9 § 6.
[33] *McLennan* v. *United States,* 91-2 U.S.T.C. ¶ 50, 447 (Cl. Ct. 1991), at 89, 644.
[34] *Id.*
[35] *Id.*

ble nature of a contribution is not vitiated by receipt of a benefit incidental to the greater public benefit."[36] While generally agreeing with the IRS' construction of the facts, the court found that the decision by the donors to contribute the easement "would invariably encourage other neighboring landowners to impose similar development restrictions on their property."[37] The court also found that the donors believed that the imposition of a conservation easement on their property would diminish the value of the property. Thus, the court, in rejecting the IRS' allegations, ruled that any benefit that inured to the donors from the conveyance "was merely incidental to an important, public spirited, charitable purpose."[38]

Nonetheless, despite all of the foregoing, one federal court of appeals has put this matter rather starkly, succinctly observing that this is a "particularly confused issue of federal taxation."[39] Not content with that, this appellate court went on to portray the existing Internal Revenue Code structure on this subject as "cryptic," with the indictment that "neither Congress nor the courts have offered any very satisfactory definition" of the terms "gift" or "contribution."[40]

(b) Quid Pro Quo Situations

As noted, where the transaction involves consideration, so that the "donor" receives something of value approximate to the amount contributed, there is no "gift." This is because the donor received a quid pro quo in exchange for the gift and thus there is no true "gift" at all. (There are several sets of circumstances where a transfer is partially a gift and partially a sale or exchange, and these circumstances are discussed elsewhere.)[41]

In one case, a manufacturer of sewing machines sold the machines on a discounted basis (bargain sales) to schools and other charitable organizations. The issue was whether the company was entitled to a charitable deduction for the gift element in the transactions. The court formulated the appropriate test as follows:

---

[36] Id.
[37] Id.
[38] Id. at 89, 645.
[39] Miller v. Internal Revenue Service, 829 F.2d 500, 502 (4th Cir. 1987).
[40] Id. at 502.
[41] See Chapter 24.

[I]f the benefits received, or expected to be received, are substantial, and meaning by that, benefits greater than those that inure to the general public from transfers for charitable purposes (which benefits are merely *incidental* to the transfer), then in such case we feel the transferor has received, or expects to receive, a *quid pro quo* sufficient to remove the transfer from the realm of deductibility [as a charitable gift].[42]

In application of this standard, the court differentiated between the discounts allowed to schools and those for other charities. As to the former, the court concluded that the discounts were offered "for the *predominant* purpose of encouraging those institutions to interest and train young women in the art of machine sewing; *thereby* enlarging the future potential market by developing prospective purchasers of home sewing machines and, more particularly . . . [the company's] machines—the brand on which the future buyers learned to sew."[43] Thus, these discounts were held to not be of a charitable nature, with the court convinced that the company's "predominant reason for granting such discounts was other than charitable" in that it "expected a return in the nature of future increased sales."[44] By contrast, as to the bargain sales of sewing machines to charitable organizations other than schools, the court was of the view that "any benefits to be derived from such discounts were merely incidental to the charitable nature of the transfer and, therefore, do not destroy the claimed charitable contribution deduction."[45] The incidental effect of this giving policy was the "development and maintenance of a favorable public image for . . . [the company] in the eyes of those [charitable] organizations and their members."[46]

In another case, a company was denied a charitable contribution deduction for the transfer of land to a high school district, on the ground that the conveyance was made with the expectation that, as a consequence of the construction of public access roads through the property, it would receive substantial benefits in return.[47] Indeed, that is what occurred. The court wrote that the "receipt or expected

[42] *Singer Company* v. *United States*, 449 F.2d 413, 423 (Ct. Cl. 1971) (emphasis in original).
[43] *Id.* at 423.
[44] *Id.* at 424.
[45] *Id.*
[46] *Id.*
[47] *Ottawa Silica* v. *United States*, 699 F.2d 1124 (Fed. Cir. 1983).

receipt of substantial benefits in return for a conveyance precludes a charitable contribution . . . [deduction]."[48] The court found that the company "knew that the construction of a school and the attendant roads on its property would substantially benefit the surrounding land, that it made the conveyance expecting its remaining property to increase in value, and that the expected receipt of these benefits at least partially prompted . . . [the company] to make the conveyance."[49] The court concluded that "this is more than adequate reason to deny . . . [the company] a charitable contribution for its conveyance."[50]

In a similar circumstance, two property owners conveyed a parcel of real estate to a corporation, taking back a note secured by a deed of trust on the property. The next year, these individuals delivered a quitclaim deed for a one-half interest in the note and deed of trust to a school and claimed a charitable deduction for the value of the transfer. Two years later, as part of a settlement, the individuals assigned the note to a creditor. They advised the school of the situation, causing the school to quitclaim its interest in the note and trust to the creditor. The next year, these individuals made a cash payment to the school and claimed a charitable deduction for that payment. The court held that the portion of the gift of money equal to the value of the interest in the note and trust that the school quitclaimed to the creditor was not a gift and thus was not deductible; the excess was found to be a charitable gift.[51] This was the outcome because, had the school not executed the quitclaim, the individuals would have been obligated to pay an additional and comparable sum of money to the creditor. "Under such circumstances," wrote the court, "it can only be concluded that . . . [the individuals] received a benefit of equal value when . . . [the school] executed the quitclaim.[52]

Several other court opinions contain applications of the *quid pro quo* rationale in this setting.[53] This rationale is, of course, that the

---

[48]*Id*. at 1135.
[49]*Id*.
[50]*Id*.
[51]*Considine* v. *Commissioner*, 74 T.C. 955 (1980).
[52]*Id*. at 968.
[53]E.g., *Stubbs* v. *United States*, 428 F.2d 885 (9th Cir. 1970), cert. den., 400 U.S. 1009 (1971); *Jefferson Mills, Inc.* v. *United States*, 367 F.2d 392 (5th Cir. 1966); *Wegner* v. *Lethert*, 67-1 U.S.T.C. ¶ 9229 (D. Minn. 1967); *Allis-*

transferor is receiving goods, services, and/or other benefits of value comparable to the money and/or property transferred and thus the transaction is a purchase rather than a gift.

This rationale is followed by the IRS as well. An illustration of the IRS's application of these rules appears in its guidance concerning the deductibility of payments to a private school where the "donor" is a parent of a child attending the school.[54] Basically, payments of tuition to a school are not deductible as charitable gifts.[55] The general standard in this context is this:

> Whether a transfer of money by a parent to an organization that operates a school is a voluntary transfer that is made with no expectation of obtaining a commensurate benefit depends upon whether a reasonable person, taking all the facts and circumstances of the case into account, would conclude that enrollment in the school was in no manner contingent upon making the payment, that the payment was not made pursuant to a plan (whether express or implied) to convert nondeductible tuition into charitable contributions, and that receipt of the benefit was not otherwise dependent upon the making of the payment.[56]

The IRS generally presumes that these payments are not charitable contributions where one or more of the following factors are present:

- the existence of a contract under which the parent agrees to make a "contribution" and which contains provisions ensuring the admission of the parent's child,

---

Chambers Mfg. Co. v. *United States*, 200 F. Supp. 91 (E.D. Wis. 1961); *Seldin* v. *Commissioner*, 28 T.C.M. 1215 (1969); and *Scheffres* v. *Commissioner*, 28 T.C.M. 234 (1969). Some old cases also are based on this rationale. E.g., *Bogardus* v. *Commissioner*, 302 U.S. 34 (1937); *Channing* v. *United States, supra*, n. 3.

[54] Rev. Rul. 83–104, 1983–2 C.B. 46.

[55] *Oppewal* v. *Commissioner*, 468 F.2d 1000 (1st Cir. 1972); *DeJong* v. *Commissioner, supra*, n. 11. The IRS ruled that payments to a church made in expectation that the church will pay the tuition for the contributors' children at a church-related school are not deductible as charitable gifts (IRS Private Letter Ruling 9004030). By contrast, a contribution to a school was held to qualify as a deductible gift notwithstanding the fact that the donor's grandchild then attended the school (IRS Private Letter Ruling 86080420).

[56] Rev. Rul. 83-104, *supra*, n. 54, at 47.

- a plan allowing parents either to pay tuition or to make "contributions" in exchange for schooling,
- the earmarking of a contribution for the direct benefit of a particular student, or
- the otherwise unexplained denial of admission or readmission to a school of children of parents who are financially able, but who do not contribute to the school.

Moreover, in other cases, although no single factor may be determinative, a combination of several factors may indicate that a payment is not a charitable contribution. In these cases, both "economic and noneconomic pressures placed upon parents" are taken into account.[57] The factors that the IRS will ordinarily take into consideration, but will not limit itself to, are these:

- the absence of a significant tuition charge,
- substantial or unusual pressure to contribute applied to parents of children attending a school,
- contribution appeals made as part of the admissions or enrollment process,
- the absence of significant potential sources of revenue for operating the school other than contributions by parents of children attending the school, and
- other factors suggesting that a contribution policy has been created as a means of avoiding the characterization of payments as tuition.

Nonetheless, the IRS concluded: "However, if a combination of such factors is not present, payments by a parent [to a school attended by a child of the parent] will normally constitute deductible contributions, even if the actual cost of educating the child exceeds the amount of any tuition charged for the child's education."[58]

A comparable issue can arise with seminars, where there is no enrollment or entrance fee. The participants may be given the opportunity to make a contribution to the educational organization conducting the seminar at its conclusion. The organization may suggest, but not require, that participants contribute a specified amount to

[57]*Id.* at 47–48.
[58]*Id.* at 48.

cover the costs incurred by the organization in providing the seminar. A "contribution" of this nature is not a gift and it is not deductible as a charitable contribution.[59]

Likewise, a payment to a home for the elderly or similar institution or organization, where the payor has a dependent parent who is a resident of the home, is generally not a gift.[60] However, an unrestricted contribution to a combined charity fund by a payor in this circumstance is deductible where the fund distributes the contributions to member organizations, which include the home, according to a formula.[61]

Still another example of payments that are for services rendered are those for adoption assistance. Thus, a court has held that a husband and wife were not entitled to a charitable contribution deduction for payments made to a charitable organization that operates an adoption service for placement of a child in their home, in that the payment was an adoption fee rather than a gift.[62] There is (questionable) authority to the contrary, holding that, even though a charitable organization provided adoption services to the "donor," a payment by the donor to the organization following placement of a child is a deductible charitable contribution because the organization was not authorized by law to charge for its adoption services.[63]

Still another illustration of this point arose when the Chief Coun-

---

[59]Rev. Rul. 76-232, 1976-1 C.B. 62. However, if the contribution is in excess of the monetary value of all benefits and privileges received, the amount of the excess would be a deductible charitable gift. See Chapter 4 § 1. Also, under appropriate circumstances, the expenses of attending a seminar may be deductible as a business expense, notwithstanding the fact that the seminar is conducted by a charitable or educational (IRC § 501(c)(3)) organization.

[60]In one instance, a subscription by an individual for a "room endowment" to a charitable nursing home was held to create an enforceable legal obligation by the individual or her estate, and when paid was, for tax purposes, properly deemed a charitable contribution, even though the subscription, which entitled the individual to occupy the room, was paid the day before she was admitted to the home (*Wardwell, Estate of* v. *Commissioner, supra,* n. 12).

[61]Rev. Rul. 80–77, 1980–1 C.B. 56.

[62]*Arceneaux* v. *Commissioner,* 36 T.C.M. 1461 (1977).

[63]*Wegner* v. *Lethert, supra,* n. 53. This opinion is surely in error, for the test is the extent of the value of the services received by the "donor" rather than the cost of providing the services or similar circumstances concerning the "donee."

sel's Office of the IRS ruled that a business corporation's contribution to a charitable organization, designated by an employee of the corporation, is not deductible as a charitable gift by the corporation where the contribution was made under a program to match the employee's contribution to the corporation's political action committee.[64] The reason for the lack of deduction: the corporation received a quid pro quo for the payment to the charity, in the form of a contribution to its political action committee. Typically, a "charity-PAC matching program" (recognized by the Federal Election Commission[65]) allows employees of a business to designate a charitable organization as the recipient of a contribution from the corporate employer. The contribution subsequently made by the corporation was an amount equal to the sum of the contributions that the employees made to the corporation's political action committee during the previous year.[66]

As another illustration of this point, two courts denied contribution status to payments to the United States Olympic Team (a charitable organization), incurred by parents of a figure skater while accompanying her to various international competitions, because the payors were "motivated primarily by concern for their daughter rather than by an interest in the Olympic Team in general."[67] The appellate court said that "a contribution may not be deducted where the expectation of personal benefit is the primary motive."[68]

One of the most well-publicized of these issues was the tax consequences for contributions made in the context of athletic scholarship programs. Although the specific rule in this connection was ultimately provided by Congress,[69] IRS guidelines published in 1986 (which were superseded by the statutory provision), well illustrate the general principle.

[64] IRS General Counsel Memorandum 39877.

[65] Federal Election Committee Advisory Opinion 1989-7.

[66] In a somewhat mysterious application of this principle, the IRS ruled that contributions by certain graduates of a college or university to an historical preservation society would not be deductible by the donors, where the funds donated would be used to preserve the historically valuable characteristics of a building housing a fraternity of which the prospective donors are members (alumni), because of their "personal interest" in the fraternity (IRS Private Letter Rulings 9119011 and 9118012).

[67] *Babilonia* v. *Commissioner*, 681 F.2d 678, 679 (9th Cir. 1982), aff'g, 40 T.C.M. 485 (1980).

[68] *Id.*, 681 F.2d at 679.

[69] IRC § 170(l).

The athletic scholarship program that troubled the IRS the most can be described as follows. An individual pays $300 to an athletic scholarship program maintained by a tax-exempt university, thereby becoming a "member" of the program. The only benefit accorded members is that they are permitted to purchase, for $120, a season ticket to the university's home football games in a designated area in the stadium. Because the games are regularly sold out well in advance, tickets to the games covered by the season ticket would not have been readily available to the "donor" if the "donor" had not made the payment. The $300 membership fee is paid annually and a separate payment is required for each season ticket. The university did not inform its "donors" of the fair market value of the right to purchase a season ticket in the designated area.

The IRS held that, under these circumstances, the right to purchase the season ticket was a "substantial benefit."[70] Because this substantial benefit was afforded the "donor" because of payment of the membership fee, the IRS held that a presumption arose that the $300 reflected the value of the benefit received, so that there was no charitable deduction for the payment. The IRS noted that, assuming the same facts, except that the individual paid $500, the "donor" made a charitable gift of $200.

These guidelines offered a variation of these facts. The facts were the same as the first instance, except that the tickets are made available to members before sale to the general public and that seating in the stadium "reasonably comparable" to that available to the donor as a result of the membership would have been "readily available" to the donor even if the payment had not been made. On these facts, the IRS found the benefit "not substantial," so that the entire $300 was a deductible charitable gift. On another variation, the facts were the same as in the first instance, except that the games are not regularly sold out and seating reasonably comparable to that available to the "donor" as a result of membership would not have been readily available to the "donor" if the payment had not been made. Also, the university reasonably estimated that the fair market value of the right to purchase a season ticket in the designated area of the stadium was $"X" and it advised prospective members that the difference between $300 and $X was a deductible gift. In making that estimate, the university considered the level of de-

[70] Rev. Rul. 86-63, *supra*, n. 7, at 89.

mand for tickets, the general availability of seats, the relative desirability of seats based on their types, locations, and views, and "other relevant factors."[71] Under these circumstances, again, the right to purchase the ticket was a "substantial benefit."[72] And, again, the position of the IRS was that a presumption arose that the $300 reflected the value of the benefit received. However, because of the university's estimate that the fair market value of the benefit was $X, the IRS regarded the amount equal to the difference between $300 and $X as a deductible charitable gift.

In some circumstances, a benefit to a donor will not cause loss of a charitable contribution deduction but instead will cause taxation of gain in addition to a tax deduction. This involves the so-called "step transaction doctrine," which is discussed elsewhere.[73] Nonetheless, it is appropriate to illustrate the point here. In one case, an individual contributed appreciated securities to a charitable organization with the understanding that the charity would liquidate the stock and purchase his yacht with the sales proceeds. The charity completed the transaction; the donor was found to be taxable on the gain realized as the result of liquidation of the stock.[74] The appellate court wrote that "where there is an understanding that a contribution of appreciated property will be utilized by the donee charity for the purpose of purchasing an asset of the contributor, the transaction will be viewed as a matter of tax law as a contribution of the asset—at whatever its then value is—with the charity acting as a conduit of the proceeds from the sale of the stock."[75] The court added: "This makes the taxpayer/putative-donor taxable on the gain of the stock though entitled to deduct the value of the asset given, whatever that value in fact is."[76]

(c) Incidental Benefits

Where a benefit to a donor is "incidental," the benefit will not defeat the charitable deduction. Some instances:

---

[71]*Id.* at 88.
[72]*Id.* at 89.
[73]See Chapter 6 § 8.
[74]*Blake* v. *Commissioner*, 697 F.2d 473 (2d Cir. 1982), aff'g, 42 T.C.M. 1336 (1981).
[75]*Id.*, 697 F.2d at 480.
[76]*Id.*

- A tornado destroyed several homes in a town. The local chapter of the American National Red Cross provided food and temporary shelter to an individual whose home was destroyed. The individual, motivated by gratitude, made a (deductible) contribution to the chapter.[77]

- An individual owned a home in an area served by a volunteer fire department. State or local taxes are not used to support the fire department. The individual made a (deductible) contribution to the volunteer department's annual fund drive.[78]

- An individual's daughter is a member of a local unit of the Girl Scouts of America. The individual made a (deductible) contribution to the Girl Scouts of America.[79]

- Merchants and owners of property in a city made (deductible) contributions to the city to enable it to provide railroad companies with new facilities outside the city in exchange for the railroads' removal of their inner-city facilities and relinquishment of their right of way through the city (even though the merchants and property owners received some benefit from removal of the railroad facilities).[80]

- An organization made (deductible) contributions to a police department to assist the department, as a regular part of its operations, in offering rewards for information leading to the apprehension and conviction of persons engaging in criminal activity within the community in which the organization is located.[81]

- A parent of a murdered individual made a (deductible) contribution of reward money to the police department of a political subdivision for information leading to the conviction of the murderer, with some or all of the money available for public purposes if not needed to pay the award.[82]

[77] Rev. Rul. 80-77, *supra*, n. 61.
[78] *Id.*
[79] *Id.*
[80] Rev. Rul. 67-446, 1967-2 C.B. 119. In this instance, the benefits to the merchants and property owners were considered incidental in comparison to the benefits accruing to the general public. Also Rev. Rul. 79-323, 1979-2 C.B. 106; Rev. Rul. 69-90, 1969-1 C.B. 63.
[81] Rev. Rul. 74-246, 1974-1 C.B. 130.
[82] Rev. Rul. 81-307, 1981-2 C.B. 78. Again (see n. 80, *supra*), the benefit to the donor was deemed incidental in comparison to the benefits accruing to the general public.

The application of rationales other than the *quid pro quo* test in relatively recent years is somewhat surprising, in that Congress, speaking by means of legislative history in 1954, wrote that "gifts" are "contributions which are made with no expectation of a financial return commensurate with the amount of the gift."[83] Thus, it would seem that the *quid pro quo* test should, unquestionably, be the law.

(d) Absence of Value Transferred

In some instances, a federal income tax charitable contribution deduction is denied because nothing of substance or value is transferred to a charitable organization.

For example, in one case, a charitable contribution deduction for the transfer by a corporation of certain film property to the Library of Congress was denied on the ground that what was physically conveyed (principally, negatives on nitrate-base plastic) had little value; the donor claimed a deduction of over $10 million.[84] Also, a motion picture production company retained access to the property and was relieved of storage costs and potential liability, which the court found to undercut the concept of a gift.

In another case, donors of mining claims to charity were held to not be entitled to any charitable deduction because the claims lacked any value.[85] The court found a "total absence of objective support for the value claimed" and that the "donor's" expert witness' testimony involved values that were mere "financial fantasies."[86]

Where situations like this are particularly egregious or otherwise are abusive, the courts have the authority to levy certain penalties.[87]

Another illustration of this situation is the carefully contrived "circular gift." A court case illustrated the point.[88] The transaction in-

---

[83]H. Rep. No. 1337, 83d Cong., 2d Sess. (1954), at A44; S. Rep. No. 1622, 3d Cong., 2d Sess. (1954), at 196. These reports accompanied IRC § 162(b), which provides that a payment cannot be deducted as a business expense (under IRC § 162) where it is properly deductible as a charitable contribution (under IRC § 170) but is not deductible in a tax year because of restrictions such as the percentage limitations (see Chapter 7).

[84]*Transamerica Corporation* v. *United States, supra,* n. 11.

[85]*Parker* v. *Commissioner,* 86 T.C. 547 (1986). Also *Snyder* v. *Commissioner,* 86 T.C. 567 (1986).

[86]*Parker* v. *Commissioner, supra,* n. 85, at 565.

[87]See Chapter 11 § 5.

[88]*Allen* v. *Commissioner,* 91–1 U.S.T.C. ¶ 50,080 (9th Cir. 1991).

volved three related organizations. One was a business league operated in support of small business interests (BL). BL was funded by
an individual (A). A also established, with BL funds, a charitable
organization (CO). A third organization was a for-profit entity (FP),
owned 40 percent by A and 60 percent by BL. Upon application, FP
would loan money to a borrower at a 3 percent interest rate, with no
principal payment due for twenty years. On the day the borrower
received the loan proceeds, he or she would transfer the funds to
CO, along with a small contribution from his or her own funds. The
borrower would then claim a charitable contribution deduction for
the entire amount transferred to CO.

The court found a "cooperative arrangement" among the three
organizations, facilitated by the fact that A was the sole signatory on
the bank accounts of the organizations.[89] The court found the following "circular flow" of funds: (1) CO loaned money to BL on a short-
term basis at a 2 1/2 percent interest rate, (2) BL then lent the
money to FP for a twenty-year term, also at a 2½ percent rate, (3)
FP then lent the funds at a 3 percent interest rate to investors, and
(4) the investors would complete the flow by contributing the funds
to CO.[90] The consequence of this money circle scheme was that the
organizations and the "contributors" improved themselves financially.
With each transaction, FP received a promise of small interest payments and a repayment of principal in twenty years. CO, while
breaking even on the funds "contributed" (since it was the source of
the funds), received a small contribution from an investor's personal
funds with each transaction. Each investor received a large tax benefit from the charitable deduction, a benefit that more than offset the
present value of the interest and principal he or she agreed to pay to
FP. Said the court: "The loser in the whole enterprise was the
federal government, which in effect financed the gains received by
the . . . [three related] organizations and the private investors."[91]

One of the many of these "donors" (the subject of the case) was B.
He borrowed $22,500 from FP; within 20 minutes of the borrowing,
he added $2,500 of his own funds and made a $25,000 "gift" to CO.
The IRS disallowed $22,500 of the claimed charitable deduction and
the matter went to court, where the government prevailed. The
denial of the deduction was based on the lack of economic substance

[89]*Id.* at 87, 325.
[90]*Id.*
[91]*Id.*

underlying the transaction. The court concluded that the three organizations "operated essentially as an integrated whole" with respect
to the loan program.[92] It viewed the three organizations as a "single
unit" that was not enriched by the $22,500 "contribution."[93] The
court observed that the passage of the $22,500 through the three
organizations left each of them in essentially the same position as if
no contribution had been made. Aside from the $2,500 "true" contri-
bution, the court found that the only real economic change at the
close of the transaction was B's obligation to pay funds over the next
twenty years to FP, a result no different than if B had signed a note
to pay CO $22,500 over twenty years. The court observed that this
type of promise to make a contribution in the future does not qualify
for a current charitable contribution.[94]

(e) Donor Recognition

One of the most recent applications of this aspect of the law arose
out of the identification of college athletic events using the name of
the corporate sponsor (such as the conversion of the Cotton Bowl to
the Mobil Cotton Bowl). In 1991, the IRS ruled that the payments
received by the tax-exempt organization that sponsors the Cotton
Bowl were not gifts but were payments for services rendered, in the
nature of advertising.[95] A consequence of this ruling was the publication of so-called "donor recognition guidelines," in proposed form.
The purpose of these guidelines is to enable charitable organizations
to determine whether "recognition" provided to a "donor" is "incidental" (so that the payment qualifies as a gift) or is "substantial" (so
that some or all of the payment is considered a payment for a
service).

   Charitable organizations became concerned about this ruling, since it
has implications far beyond college and university bowl games. The
IRS bowl game ruling raised, once again, the question as to when
the extent of donor recognition renders a payment not a gift. Recognizing this problem, the IRS promulgated proposed guidelines for its
auditing agents to use when conducting examinations of tax-exempt

---

[92]*Id.* at 87, 326.
[93]*Id.*
[94]See the discussion of gifts of notes in Chapter 5.
[95]IRS Technical Advice Memorandum 9147007.

organizations.[96] These guidelines, as the IRS put it, "set forth specific indicators to be considered in making a determination as to whether an organization is engaged in an unrelated trade or business activity."

These guidelines stated that the provision of substantial valuable marketing and other services by a tax-exempt organization in return for its support in the form of funding may constitute unrelated business income. By contrast, this is not the case where there is no expectation that the organization will provide a substantial return benefit.

The IRS agreed that the mere recognition of a corporate contributor as a benefactor normally is incidental to the contribution and not of sufficient value to the contributor to constitute unrelated trade or business. That is, "mere recognition" does not transform the gift into taxable advertising income.

For example, mere recognition occurs where a university names a professorship, where a scholarship or building is named after a benefactor, where an underwriting of a public radio or television program or museum exhibition is acknowledged, or where a contributor to a fund-raising event or a performing arts organization in an accompanying program is listed.

The IRS recognized that "[a]ssociating the name of the sponsor with the name of the exempt organization's event will not, in itself, trigger" the imposition of the unrelated income tax. Rather, said the IRS, "all the facts and circumstances of the relationship between the sponsor and [the] exempt organization must be considered." The IRS stated: "A determination of whether a substantial return benefit is present should include an analysis of: the value of the services provided in exchange for the payment; the terms under which payments and services are rendered; the amount of control that the sponsor exercises over the event; and whether the extent of the organization's exposure of the donor's name constitutes significant promotion."

The IRS noted that it would not apply these guidelines to organizations that are "of a purely local nature," that receive "relatively insignificant" gross revenue from corporate sponsors, and generally operate with significant amounts of volunteer labor. These organizations include youth athletic organizations such as little league baseball and soccer teams, and local theaters and youth orchestras.

As indicated in the ruling concerning bowl association payments,

[96]IRS Ann. 92-15, 1992-5 I.R.B. 51.

the IRS is concerned wherever there is a written contract memorializing the relationship. Thus, the examination guidelines stated that
"the examiner should thoroughly review the corporate sponsorship
contracts/arrangements (either written or oral) to determine whether
the agreement requires the exempt organization to perform any services, including advertising, for the corporate sponsor in return for
revenue." The guidelines advised the examining agent to "[r]equest
any information that will assist you in thoroughly understanding the
corporate sponsorship contracts/arrangements."

Examining agents would be required to "[r]eview copies of minutes of the organization's board of directors or trustees meetings or
any correspondence or other written statements between the exempt
organization, corporate sponsor, or other party relating to the corporate sponsorship contract/arrangement." These agents would be urged
to review films, videotapes, or photographs of the event over the
years to determine the extent to which the corporate sponsor's name
is mentioned or depicted.

If a tax-exempt charitable organization has corporate sponsorships/
arrangements, the IRS examiner would be expected to "review the
agreements to determine whether the organization is performing
substantial services or providing other benefits in return for the
payments received." The factors to be considered by the IRS as
tending to indicate an unrelated trade or business would include:

- whether the corporate sponsorship contract/arrangement requires
  - the corporate sponsor's name or logo to be included in the
    official event title (the bowl game situation),
  - the corporate sponsor's name or logo to be prominently
    placed throughout the stadium, arena, or other site where
    the event is held,
  - the corporate sponsor's name or logo to be printed on mate-
    rials related to the event,
  - the corporate sponsor's name or logo to be placed on partic-
    ipant uniforms or other support personnel uniforms,
  - the corporate sponsor to refer to its sponsorship in adver-
    tisements over the course of the contract,
  - that participants be available to the corporate sponsor for
    personal appearances and endorsements,
  - the tax-exempt organization to arrange for special seating,

accommodations, transportation, and hospitality facilities at the event for corporate sponsor clients or executives.

- whether the corporate sponsorship contract/arrangement requires media coverage of the event.

- whether the corporate sponsorship contract/arrangement provides for promotional arrangements that do more than merely acknowledge the sponsor. The agents are to consider (1) specification of size color and content of sponsorship acknowledgment; (2) listing of corporate sponsor products or services in the acknowledgement.

- whether the payment is contingent upon the tax-exempt organization securing television, radio, or other marketing contracts to provide the sponsor's name logo widespread exposure. Also, the extent, if any, that the payment is based on the television ratings of the event is to be considered.

- whether the contract/arrangement includes extensions or renewals which are contingent upon continued public exposure.

- whether the arrangement can be terminated for failure to provide certain benefits.

- whether the segment of the public expected to see the identifying sponsorship information can reasonably be expected to purchase the sponsor's goods or services.

Concerning sporting events, the IRS examiners would be alerted to the possibility that the entity under audit might raise as a defense the fact that a portion of the sponsorship amount is paid to the participating tax-exempt organizations providing teams. In these situations, said the IRS, the examiner should obtain information from the participating institutions regarding terms and conditions, if any, governing the funds and the ultimate use made of the income. In this regard, the IRS noted, media reports have indicated that funds may be used for travel and other expenses related to attending the event than the regular activities of the participating organization.

The IRS said that examiners should be alert to additional services provided to the corporate sponsor through the same or ancillary contracts. These services would include such items as tickets, travel, and lodging for VIPs, their family members, or the individuals that are guests of the corporate sponsor. Frequently, perquisites such as chauffeur-driven limousines, hospitality suites, and "lavish" receptions are also included, the IRS cautioned.

These guidelines stated that, in determining whether amounts derived by tax-exempt organizations from corporate sponsors are subject to tax on unrelated business income, the examiner should first determine whether all of the technical requirements under the federal tax law are met. The examiner would be advised to examine whether any of the modifications or exceptions to this body of law (such as for rent or royalties) are applicable.

Under this proposal, it is not determinative, for purposes of unrelated business income tax, whether corporate sponsorship payments, where substantial services are required, are treated as contributions or business expenses by the sponsor. Also, under the proposal, IRS agents would be advised that, if there is unrelated business income, they should analyze the overhead, administrative, and other expenses claimed by the tax-exempt organization and review the basis for allocation of the expenditures. Finally, the proposed guidelines would advise IRS examiners that they should document the extent to which the sponsorship income is "accurately and consistently" reported on the organization's annual information return (Form 990) and unrelated business income tax return (Form 990-T).

The IRS held a public hearing, on July 21–23, 1992, on these proposed examination guidelines regarding the treatment of corporate sponsorship income received by tax-exempt organizations conducting public events.[97]

The IRS is concerned that some tax-exempt organizations that conduct "public events" may receive income from corporate sponsors that is income from the sale of advertising, rather than a gift. Advertising income is unrelated business income.[98] This activity is distinguishable from situations where tax-exempt, charitable organizations are merely recognizing the generosity of corporate donors.

The proposed guidelines contained a framework for an analysis of the payments received by exempt organizations from corporate sponsorship arrangements and set forth specific indicators to be considered in making a determination as to whether an organization is engaged in an unrelated trade or business activity.

The IRS believed that this matter raises "important and sensitive" issues under present law with respect to charitable organizations. Thus, it invited public comment on the proposed examination guidelines. After consideration of the comments received, the IRS con-

[97]This hearing was announced by the IRS in Ann. 92-88, 1992-26 I.R.B. 34.
[98]See Chapter 24.

cluded that a public hearing was warranted to further discuss the proposed examination guidelines before they are finalized.

In order to assist the IRS in its consideration of the proposed guidelines, the Service requested that oral comments at the hearing include a discussion of some or all of the following issues:

• Should the audit tolerance provision of the guidelines be replaced with a "safe harbor," which excludes from the examination guidelines (1) those exempt organizations below a specified size, and/or (2) any sponsorship payments which do not exceed a certain dollar amount?

• Should the facts and circumstances approach set forth in the proposed guidelines be replaced with a more mechanical test? If so, what should that test be?

• Should the guidelines list specific factors that are considered as tending only to show mere donor recognition? If so, what are those specific factors? What kinds of benefits are so insubstantial that they are merely "incidental" to the arrangement?

• What are important examples of mere recognition or acknowledgement of corporate contributors?

• What factors indicate that advertising is involved?

• When do identifying references to a corporate sponsor's products, services, or slogans constitute advertising? Is the frequency of these identifying references relevant?

• Should unrelated business income tax liability only arise where sponsorship income is used for advertising services? How should advertising services be defined? Are promotional and marketing services included?

• How should expenses that are not directly related to advertising be treated? Is the allocation rule governing exploitation of exempt activities the appropriate rule to use in sponsorship income cases? If the exploitation method does not apply, what is a reasonable method for allocating items of overhead expenses?

• How should certain expenses, such as payments to third-party exempt organizations, be treated?

• Should the guidelines provide that, under a reasonable allocation method, an exempt organization may use a fragmentation approach to demonstrate that the sponsorship income is partly a contribution or royalty?

In addition, the IRS invited oral comments on any other issue relevant to the question of the treatment of corporate sponsorship income.

Thus, a "gift" or "contribution" is a payment of money or a transfer of property to a charitable organization where the person making the payment or transfer is not receiving anything of consequence, of approximate value, in return. As noted, and as discussed elsewhere,[99] a payment may be part gift and part payment for a service or good.

§ 4.2   MEANING OF "CHARITABLE" ORGANIZATION

At the simplest definitional level, a charitable contribution is a "gift" to a "charitable" organization. The concept of a "gift" has just been explored. Now it is appropriate to consider the meaning of the term "charitable" for purposes of the law of charitable giving.

(a)   Introduction and Summary

The law of "charitable" organizations is essentially the province of the law of tax-exempt organizations.[100] However, there is not absolute parity between the law of tax-exempt organizations and the law of charitable giving on this point. That is, there are organizations that are considered "charitable" for purposes of federal income tax exemption but not for purposes of the federal income tax charitable contribution deduction. Likewise, there are organizations that are considered "charitable" for purposes of the federal charitable deductions that are not "charitable" entities under the tax-exempt organizations rules. This is because federal tax law defines organizations that are charitable ones for charitable deduction purposes in a provision of the Internal Revenue Code that is different from that used for purposes of tax exemption; for charitable giving purposes, the charitable status does not derive from an organization's tax exemption but from its treatment as a charitable donee.

Four Internal Revenue Code sections require highlighting at this point. They are:

1.   The federal income tax exemption for "charitable" organizations is derived from their classification under Internal Revenue Code section 501(c)(3).

2.   The federal income tax charitable contribution deduction rules

[99] *Id.*
[100] See *The Law of Tax-Exempt Organizations*, particularly Part II.

classify eligible charitable donees under Internal Revenue
Code section 170(c); organizations that are described in section 501(c)(3) that are also eligible charitable donees are those
that are described in IRC section 170(c)(2).

3.   The federal gift tax charitable contribution deduction rules
     classify eligible charitable donees under Internal Revenue
     Code section 2522(a).

4.   The federal estate tax charitable contribution deduction rules
     classify eligible charitable donees under Internal Revenue
     Code section 2055(a).

The gift and estate tax rules in this regard are the subject of
Chapter 8. This analysis, then, is confined to the federal income tax
rules.

Nearly every organization that is considered a "charitable" organization for purposes of the federal income tax exemption[101] is considered a "charitable" organization for purposes of the federal income
tax charitable contribution deduction.[102] The only exception to this
rule is the organization that tests for public safety. This organization,
while embraced by the tax exemption rules as a charitable entity, is
omitted from charitable donee status for purposes of the income tax
charitable contribution deduction.[103]

There are, however, certain organizations that cannot qualify for
tax exemption purposes as "charitable" organizations that can qualify,
for purposes of the law of charitable giving, as "charitable" donees.
Nonetheless, these entities are all tax-exempt organizations. They are
the following:

•   a state, a possession of the United States, a political subdivision
    of a state or U.S. possession, the United States, or the District
    of Columbia—but only if the contribution is made for exclu-
    sively public purposes (Internal Revenue Code section
    170(c)(1)).[104]

[101] IRC § 501(c)(3).
[102] IRC § 170(c)(2). The IRS frequently issues rulings on the qualification of
organizations as charitable donees (e.g., IRS Private Letter Ruling 9037021).
[103] The "public safety testing" organization is the subject of *The Law of Tax-
Exempt Organizations*, Chapter 11 § 2.
[104] These entities are not tax-exempt in the sense that they are described in
IRC § 501(c). However, they are very much tax-exempt organizations in the
generic sense of that term. See *The Law of Tax-Exempt Organizations* at
Chapter 7 § 12.

- a post or organization of war veterans, or an auxiliary unit or society of, or trust or foundation for, such a post or organization, that is organized in the United States or any of its possessions and where no part of its earnings inures to the benefit of any private shareholder or individual (Internal Revenue Code section 170(c)(3)).[105]

- a domestic fraternal society, order, or association, operating under the lodge system, but only if the contribution is to be used exclusively for religious, charitable, scientific, literary, or educational purposes, or for the prevention of cruelty to children or animals (Internal Revenue Code section 170(c)(4)).[106]

- a cemetery company owned and operated exclusively for the benefit of its members, or a corporation chartered solely for burial purposes as a cemetery corporation and not permitted by its charter to engage in any business not necessarily incident to that purpose, if the company or corporation is not operated for profit and no part of its net earnings inures to the benefit of any private shareholder or individual (Internal Revenue Code section 170(c)(5)).[107]

In summary, organizations that are tax-exempt pursuant to federal tax law generally find that exemption under Internal Revenue Code

[105]Veterans' organizations generally are tax-exempt by reason of IRC § 501(c) (19). See *The Law of Tax-Exempt Organizations*, Chapter 34 § 10. Some veterans' organizations are tax-exempt by reason of being classified as social welfare organizations under IRC § 501(c)(4) (*id.*, Chapter 28) and some are classified as charitable organizations under IRC § 501(c)(3) (*id.*, Part II).

[106]These organizations are tax-exempt by reason of IRC § 501(c)(8). See *The Law of Tax-Exempt Organizations*, Chapter 34 § 4. This is a category of charitable donee only in the case of contributions by individuals (IRC § 170(c)(4)).

[107]These organizations are tax-exempt by reason of IRC § 501(c)(13). See *The Law of Tax-Exempt Organizations*, Chapter 34 § 6.

Occasionally, the IRS will allow deductibility of a gift, as if it was made to a "charitable" donee, where the recipient is a type of tax-exempt organization that does not itself qualify as a "charitable" donee (see the text accompanied by ns. 104–107, *supra*), as long as the gift is made for a "charitable" purpose. Instances of organizations of this nature include title-holding corporations (tax-exempt by reason of IRC § 501(c)(2); see *The Law of Tax-Exempt Organizations*, Chapter 34 § 2) and business and professional organizations, *id.*, Chapter 29).

section 501(a), by virtue of being listed in section 501(c). Organizations that are charitable donees for federal income tax law purposes have that status under Internal Revenue Code section 170, by virtue of being listed in section 170(c).

(b)   "Charitable" Organizations—Criteria

A summary of the law of "charitable" organizations, for purposes of the law of charitable giving, is difficult because the term "charitable" is used in several ways. This portion of the analysis is confined to a summary of the law pertaining to those organizations that are charitable in the sense that they are also "charitable" organizations for federal tax exemption purposes.[108]

This type of organization is a "charitable donee" if it is

> organized and operated exclusively for religious, charitable, scientific, literary, or educational purposes, or to foster national or international amateur sports competition (but only if no part of its activities involve the provision of athletic facilities or equipment), or for the prevention of cruelty to children or animals.[109]

In addition, the following criteria must be met for an organization to be considered a "charitable donee":

- It is created or organized in the United States or in a possession of the United States, or under the law of the United States, a state, the District of Columbia, or a possession of the United States.[110]
- No part of the organization's net earnings inures to the benefit of any private shareholdeer or individual.[111]
- It does not have as a substantial part of its activities attempts to influence legislation.[112]

---

[108]That is, they are organizations described in IRC § 501(c)(3).
[109]IRC § 170(c)(2)(B).
[110]IRC § 170(c)(2)(A).
[111]IRC § 170(c)(2)(C). The so-called "private inurement doctrine" is discussed in *The Law of Tax-Exempt Organizations*, Chapter 13.
[112]IRC § 170(c)(2)(D). The limitations on attempts to influence legislation by charitable donees is the subject of *The Law of Tax-Exempt Organizations*, Chapter 14. Also, Hopkins, *Charity, Advocacy, and the Law*, Chapters 5 and 8.

- It does not participate in, or intervene in (including the publishing or distributing of statements), any political campaign on behalf of (or in opposition to) any candidate for public office.[113]

There are, therefore, two dimensions to the term "charitable" in this context. One is the definition of the term "charitable" as one of seven categories of "charitable donee" status (as reflected in the above quote). The other is a definition of the term "charitable" that embraces all categories of "charitable donees."

As to the latter definition, the law is clear that the concept of "charity" is an overarching one that encompasses all of the specific categories, such as religion and education. This is because the United States tax law precepts of charity are based on common law standards, which the courts have held must inform the statutory uses of the term. For example, one court observed that "we must look to established [trust] law to determine the meaning of the word 'charitable'."[114] Likewise, the court subsequently wrote that Congress intended to apply these tax rules "to those organizations commonly designated charitable in the law of trusts."[115] Another court noted that "[t]he term 'charitable' is a generic term and includes literary, religious, scientific educational institutions."[116] The U.S. Supreme Court held that "Congress, in order to encourage gifts to religious, educational, and *other charitable objects*, granted the privilege of deducting . . . gifts from gross income."[117]

One of the reasons that the term "charitable" has such an all-inclusive gloss in this definitional setting is that the Supreme Court has held that all organizations that wish to qualify as "charitable" entities—both for tax exemption and charitable donee purposes—must adhere to a "public policy" doctrine. In so doing, the Court

[113]IRC § 170(c)(2)(D). The prohibition on efforts to engage in political campaign activities by charitable donees is the subject of *The Law of Tax-Exempt Organizations*, Chapter 15. Also, Hopkins, *Charity, Advocacy, and the Law*, Chapters 14 and 16.

[114]*Pennsylvania Co. for Insurance on Lives* v. *Helvering*, 66 F.2d 284, 285 (D.C. Cir. 1933).

[115]*International Reform Federation* v. *District Unemployment Board*, 131 F.2d 337, 339 (D.C. Cir. 1942).

[116]*United States* v. *Proprietors of Social Law Library*, 102 F.2d 481, 483 (1st Cir. 1939).

[117]*Helvering* v. *Bliss*, 293 U.S. 144, 147 (1934) (emphasis supplied).

wrote that each of these entities must meet "certain common law standards of charity" and that "[t]he form and history of the charitable exemption and deduction sections of the various income tax acts reveal that Congress was guided by the common law of charitable trusts."[118] The Court said that charitable organizations must "be in harmony with the public interest" and "must not be so at odds with the common community conscience as to undermine any public benefit that might otherwise be conferred."[119] While recognizing the authority of the IRS to determine what is "public policy," the Court held that "a declaration that a given institution is not 'charitable' should be made only where there can be no doubt that the activity involved is contrary to a fundamental public policy."[120] (In the factual setting of the case, the Court concluded that racial discrimination in education is contrary to public policy and that an educational institution that does not conform to this policy is not "charitable.")

These findings were presaged in a Supreme Court observation made over 100 years beforehand: "A charitable use, where neither law nor public policy forbids, may be applied to almost any thing that tends to promote the well-doing and well-being of social man."[121]

Nonetheless, the specific legal meanings of the term "charitable" are to be found in the narrower of the two definitions, which is an amalgam of court opinions, Department of Treasury regulations, and IRS rulings. Other bodies of law, although not as extensive, have evolved from use of the other terms, principally "religious," "educational," and "scientific."

(i) "Charitable" Organizations

There are several ways for an organization to be considered a "charitable" entity for purposes of the law of charitable giving.[122] These include:

- Relief of poverty. This is the most basic and historically founded form of charitable activity. The tax regulations define

---

[118]*Bob Jones University* v. *United States*, 461 U.S. 574, 586, 587–588 (1983).

[119]*Id.* at 591–592.

[120]*Id.* at 592.

[121]*Ould* v. *Washington Hospital for Foundlings*, 95 U.S. 303, 311 (1877). This broad definition of the term "charitable" and the reach of the public policy doctrine is discussed in *The Law of Tax-Exempt Organizations*, Chapter 5.

the term "charitable" to include "[r]elief of the poor and distressed or of the underprivileged."[123] Assistance to the indigent is undoubtedly the most generally understood and accepted form of charitable endeavor.

- Advancement of religion. The scope of this category of "charitable" activity is imprecise, due to the recognition of "religious" activities as a separate basis for tax-exempt status (see below). Organizations that are "charitable" because they advance religion generally are those that support or otherwise assist "religious" organizations.[124]

- Advancement of education. Likewise, the scope of this category of "charitable" activity is imprecise, due to the recognition of "educational" activities as a separate basis for tax-exempt status (see below). Organizations that are "charitable" because they advance education generally are those that support or otherwise assist "educational" organizations.[125]

- Advancement of science. Similarly, the scope of this category of "charitable" activity is imprecise, due to the recognition of "scientific" activities as a separate basis for tax-exempt status (see below). Organizations that are "charitable" because they advance science generally are those that support or otherwise assist "scientific" organizations.[126]

- Lessening of the burdens of government. An organization that is "charitable" is one that lessens the burden of a government, where the governmental unit considers the burden to be among its burdens. Organizations of this type either provide services directly in the context of government activity or provide support to a governmental agency or department.[127]

- Promotion of social welfare. An organization is "charitable" because it promotes "social welfare"; this is one of the broadest categories of charitable organizations. This purpose includes activities such as lessening neighborhood tensions, eliminating

[122]The law underlying these categories is discussed in *The Law of Tax-Exempt Organizations*, Chapter 7.
[123]Reg § 1.501(c)(3)-1(d)(2).
[124]*Id.*
[125]*Id.*
[126]*Id.*
[127]*Id.*

prejudice and discrimination, defending human and civil rights secured by law, and combatting community deterioration and juvenile delinquency.[128]

- Community beautification and maintenance. An organization can be "charitable" by reason of the fact that its purpose is community beautification and maintenance, and the preservation of natural beauty.[129]

- Promotion of health. An organization can be "charitable" because it engages in activities that "promote health."[130] This purpose embraces the establishment and maintenance of hospitals, clinics, homes for the aged, and the like.

- Promotion of the arts. An organization may be "charitable" because it engages in one or more activities that promote the arts. This purpose includes the establishment and maintenance of theaters, the promotion of public appreciation of one of the arts, and the promotion and encouragement of the talent and ability of young artists.[131]

- An organization can be "charitable" by functioning as a "public interest law firm."[132] These firms provide legal representation for important citizen interests that are unrepresented because the cases are not economically feasible for private law firms.

- Local economic development corporations. One of the most recent of the forms of "charitable" organizations is the local economic development corporation, which engages in a variety of activities, including investment in local businesses, housing opportunities, and encouragement of established businesses to open offices and plants in economically depressed areas.[133]

- other categories of "charitable" organizations are these:
  - organizations established to promote environmental conservancy[134]

---

[128] *Id.*

[129] Rev. Rul. 78-85, 1978-1 C.B. 150.

[130] Rev. Rul. 69-545, 1969-2 C.B. 117.

[131] E.g., Rev. Rul. 64-175, 1964-1 (Part 1) C.B. 185; Rev. Rul. 64-174, 1964-1 (Part 1) C.B. 183.

[132] E.g. Rev. Rul. 75-74, 1975-1 C.B. 152.

[133] E.g., Rev. Rul. 81-284, 1981-2 C.B. 130.

[134] E.g., Rev. Rul. 76-204, 1976-1 C.B. 152.

- organizations established to promote patriotism[135]
- organizations that provide care for orphans[136]
- organizations that facilitate student and cultural exchanges[137]
- organizations that promote, advance, and sponsor recreational and amateur sports.[138]
- organizations that maintain public confidence in the legal system.[139]

(ii) "Educational" Organizations

Organizations that are considered "educational" for purposes of the law of charitable giving[140] are:

- formal educational institutions, such as primary, secondary, and post-secondary schools; colleges and universities; early childhood centers; and trade schools.[141] These entities have a regularly scheduled curriculum, a regular faculty, and a regularly enrolled body of students in attendance at the place where the educational activities are regularly carried on.[142]
- other types of "formal" organizations, such as museums, zoos, planetariums, and symphony orchestras.[143]
- organizations that have programs that relate to the instruction or training of the individual for the purpose of improving or developing his or her capabilities.[144] These entities include a wide variety of training organizations, and study and research organizations.
- organizations that have programs that relate to the instruction

[135] E g., Rev. Rul. 78-84, 1978-1 C.B. 150.
[136] E.g., Rev. Rul. 80-200, 1980-2 C.B. 173.
[137] E.g., Rev. Rul. 80-286, 1980-2 C.B. 179.
[138] *Hutchinson Baseball Enterprises, Inc.* v. *Commissioner,* 73 T.C. 144 (1979), aff'd, 696 F.2d 757 (10th Cir. 1982).
[139] *Kentucky Bar Foundation, Inc.* v. *Commissioner,* 78 T.C. 921 (1982).
[140] The law underlying these categories is discussed in *The Law of Tax-Exempt Orgnizations,* Chapter 8.
[141] Reg. § 1.501(c)(3)-1(d)(3)(ii)(1).
[142] IRC § 170(b)(1)(A)(ii).
[143] Reg. § 1.501(c)(3)-1(d)(3)(ii)(4).
[144] Reg. § 1.501(c)(3)-1(d)(3)(i).

of the public on subjects useful to the individual and beneficial to the community.[145] These organizations provide a range of personal services, instruct the public in the field of civic betterment, and (again) engage in study and research.

(iii) "Religious" Organizations

Organizations that are considered "religious" for purposes of the law of charitable giving[146] include:

* churches, synagogues, and similar places of worship[147]
* conventions and associations of churches[148]
* integrated auxiliaries of churches[149]
* church-run organizations, such as schools, hospitals, orphanages, nursing homes, publishing entities' broadcasting entities, and cemeteries
* religious orders
* apostolic groups[150]
* missionary organizations
* bible and tract societies

The courts and the IRS traditionally have been reluctant to rule as to whether an organization is a "church" or the like or a "religious" entity, if only because of concern with constitutional law constraints. However, this reluctance is dissipating, and the IRS and the courts are developing criteria for defining "churches" and other "religious" organizations.

(iv) "Scientific" Organizations

Organizations that are considered "scientific" for purposes of the law of charitable giving[151] include

---

[145]*Id.*

[146]The law underlying these categories is discussed in *The Law of Tax-Exempt Organizations*, Chapter 9.

[147]IRC § 170(b)(1)(A)(i).

[148]*Id.*

[149]*Id.*

[150]IRC § 501(d).

[151]The law underlying these categories is discussed in *The Law of Tax-Exempt Organizations*, Chapter 10.

- organizations that are engaged in scientific research[152]
- organizations that are otherwise operated for the dissemination of scientific knowledge (such as publishing entities)[153]

(v) Other "Charitable" Organizations

There are several other categories of "charitable" organizations:[154]

- literary organizations[155]
- organizations that seek to prevent cruelty to children or animals[156]
- cooperative hospital service organizations[157]
- cooperative educational service organizations[158]
- amateur sports organizations[159]

Consequently, the organizations that are eligible "charitable" donees for purposes of the law of charitable giving are those that are "charitable" in the common law sense (most of which have been rendered "charitable" by statute, regulation, or IRS ruling) and those that have been encompassed by the definition by statute.

§ 4.3 "PUBLIC CHARITIES" AND "PRIVATE FOUNDATIONS"

The federal income tax deduction, or the extent of this deduction, for a contribution of money or property to a charitable organization, is often dependent upon the tax classification of the donee organization. From the perspective of the tax law, not all charitable organizations are regarded the same. In general, the federal tax law categorizes "charitable" organizations that are eligible donees for purposes of the charitable deduction as being one of the following types:

---

[152]Reg. § 1.501(c)(3)-1(d)(1)(i)(c).
[153]*Id.*
[154]The law underlying these categories is discussed in *The Law of Tax-Exempt Organizations*, Chapter 11.
[155]Reg. § 1.501(c)(3)-1(d)(1)(i)(e).
[156]Reg. § 1.501(c)(3)-1(d)(1)(i)(g).
[157]IRC § 501(e).
[158]IRC § 501(f).
[159]IRC § 501(c)(3) and 501(j).

- public charitable organizations
- private charitable organizations ("private foundations")
- A hybrid of the two
- Other eligible donees[160]

The terms "public" and "private," as used in this context, often generate confusion. The term "public" is not used in the sense of a governmental entity (as in a "public" school), nor is the term "private" used in the sense of business activity (as in "private" enterprise) or as the counterpart of a governmental entity (such as a "private" school). Neither term has anything to do with the nature of a charitable organization's board of directors or trustees (as in a "public" board, rather than a "private" one). These terms, used in the charitable giving and tax-exempt organizations settings, relate to how the charitable organization is financially supported.

Charitable organizations are presumed to be private foundations.[161] This presumption is rebuttable (if the facts so warrant) by a showing that the organization qualifies as one of the types of public charitable organizations or as one of the hybrid charitable organizations. Since there is no advantage to being a private foundation, most charitable organizations strive to rebut this presumption, principally to avoid the private foundation rules,[162] to facilitate maximum charitable contribution deductions, and to escape the more burdensome federal reporting obligations of private foundations.[163]

(a) Public Charitable Organizations

Public charitable organizations are the most favored of the categories of charitable organizations for charitable giving purposes. There are essentially four categories of public charitable organizations:

- the "institutions"
- publicly supported organizations (donative entities)
- publicly supported organizations (service provider entities)
- supporting organizations

[160]This reference to "other charitable donees" is to organizations that are the subject of the text accompanying ns. 101–104, *supra.*
[161]IRC § 509(a).
[162]See *The Law of Tax-Exempt Organizations*, Chapters 19–25.
[163]See *The Law of Tax-Exempt Organizations*, Chapter 37 § 4.

(i) The "Institutions"

There are some entities in the category of public charitable organizations that have classification "institution" because they satisfy the requirements of at least one category of "public" institution. These entities are not private foundations, not because of how they are funded, but because of the nature of their operations.

Churches.   A church is a public charitable organization and thus is not a private foundation.[164]

The IRS has formulated a test that it uses to ascertain whether or not an organization qualifies as a "church." The IRS position is that, to be a church for tax purposes, an organization must satisfy at least some of the following criteria: a distinct legal existence, a recognized creed and form of worship, a definite and distinct ecclesiastical government, a formal code of doctrine and discipline, a distinct religious history, a membership not associated with any other church or denomination, a complete organization of ordained ministers ministering to their congregations and selected after completing prescribed courses of study, a literature of its own, established places of worship, regular congregations, regular religious services, schools for the religious instruction of the young, and schools for the preparation of its ministers.[165] The courts are generally adhering to these criteria.[166]

Thus, to avoid private foundation status as a church, the organization must be more than an organization that generally engages in religious activities.[167]

Conventions and Associations of Churches.   A convention or association of churches is a public charitable organization and thus is not a private foundation.[168]

The IRS recognizes that the term "convention or association of churches" has a historical meaning generally referring to a coopera-

---

[164]IRC §§ 170(b)(1)(A)(i) and 509(a)(1).
[165]Internal Revenue Manual § 321.3.
[166]E.g., *American Guidance Foundation, Inc.* v. *United States*, 490 F. Supp. 304 (D.D.C. 1980). Also *St. Martin Evangelical Lutheran Church* v. *South Dakota*, 451 U.S. 772 (1981).
[167]See *The Law of Tax-Exempt Organizations*, Chapters 9 § 3 and 171.
[168]IRC §§ 170(b)(1)(A)(i) and 509(a)(1).

tive undertaking by churches of the same denomination.[169] However, a tax-exempt organization, the membership of which is comprised of churches of different denominations, has been held to qualify as an association of churches.[170]

Integrated Auxiliaries of Churches. An integrated auxiliary of a church is a public charitable organization and thus is not a private foundation.[171]

IRS regulations define an integrated auxiliary of a church as a tax-exempt organization the principal activity of which is exclusively religious and which is controlled by or associated with a church or a convention or association of churches.[172] Under these regulations, integrated auxiliaries of a church include men's and women's fellowship associations, mission societies, theological seminaries, and religious youth organizations. Schools of a general academic or vocational nature, hospitals, orphanages, homes for the elderly, and the like are not considered, by these regulations, to be integrated auxiliaries of churches, even though they have a religious environment or promote the teachings of a church.

While some courts have upheld this approach of the IRS,[173] others have differed.[174]

Educational Institutions. An "educational organization which normally maintains a regular faculty and curriculum and normally has a regularly enrolled body of pupils or students in attendance at the place where its educational activities are regularly carried on" is a public charitable organization and thus is not a private foundation.[175] This type of organization must have as its primary function the presentation of formal instruction.[176]

---

[169] Rev. Rul. 74-224, 1974-1 C.B. 61. Also *Chapman* v. *Commissioner*, 48 T.C. 358 (1967).

[170] *Id.* In general, see *The Law of Tax-Exempt Organizations*, Chapters 9 § 3 and 17 § 1.

[171] IRC §§ 170(b)(1)(A)(i) and 509(a)(1).

[172] Reg. § 1.6033-2(g)(5)

[173] E.g., *Parshall Christian Order* v. *Commissioner*, 45 T.C.M. 488 (1983).

[174] E.g., *Tennessee Baptist Children's Homes, Inc.* v. *United States*, 604 F. Supp. 210 (M.D. Tenn. 1984). In general, see *The Law of Tax-Exempt Organizations*, Chapter 37 § 4.

[175] IRC §§ 170(b)(1)(A)(ii) and 509(a)(1).

[176] Reg. § 1.170A-9(b). Also, Rev. Rul. 78-309, 1978-2 C.B. 123.

It is pursuant to these rules that institutions such as primary, secondary, preparatory and high schools and colleges and universities derive public charitable organization status. These institutions also encompass federal, state, and other public schools which qualify under these rules, although their tax-exempt and public charitable organization status may be derived from their categorization as governmental agencies or instrumentalities.[177] However, an organization cannot achieve public charitable organization status as an operating educational institution where it is engaged in both educational and noneducational activities (for example, a museum operating a school), unless the noneducational activities are merely incidental to the educational activities.[178]

Thus, to avoid private foundation status as an educational institution, the organization must be more than an organization that generally engages in educational activities.[179]

Health Care Institutions.   A hospital is a public charitable organization and thus is not a private foundation.[180]

A hospital is defined, for federal tax purposes, as an "organization the principal purpose or functions of which are the providing of medical or hospital care or medical education or medical research."[181] A hospital must promote the health of a class of persons broad enough to benefit the community and must be operated to serve a public rather than a private interest.[182] The term "hospital" includes federal hospitals, and state, county, and municipal hospitals which are instrumentalities of those governmental units, rehabilitation facilities, outpatient clinics, extended care facilities, community mental health and drug treatment centers, and cooperative hospital service organizations. However, the term does not include convalescent homes, homes for children or the elderly, or institutions the principal purpose or function of which is to train handicapped individuals to

[177] See the text accompanying ns. 196 and 197, *infra.*
[178] Reg. § 1.170A-9(b).
[179] Educational institutions are discussed in greater detail in *The Law of Tax-Exempt Organizations,* Chapter 17 § 1; educational organizations in general are discussed at *id.,* Chapter 8.
[180] IRC §§ 170(b)(1)(A)(iii) and 509(a)(1).
[181] IRC § 170(b)(1)(A)(iii).
[182] *Supra,* n. 130.

pursue a vocation,[183] nor does it include free clinics for animals.[184]

For these purposes, the term "medical care" includes the treatment of any physical or mental disability or condition, whether on an inpatient or outpatient basis, provided the cost of the treatment is deductible[185] by the individual treated.[186]

Thus, to avoid private foundation status as a hospital, the organization must be more than an organization that generally engages in activities that promote health.[187]

Medical Research Organizations. A "medical research organization" is a public charitable organization and thus is not a private foundation.[188] It is an organization "directly engaged in the continuous active conduct of medical research in conjunction with a hospital."[189] The organization need not be formally affiliated with a hospital to be considered primarily engaged in the active conduct of medical research in conjunction with a hospital. However, there must be a joint effort on the part of the research organization and one or more hospitals pursuant to an understanding that the organizations will maintain continuing close cooperation in the active conduct of medical research.[190]

The term "medical research" means the conduct of investigations, experiments, and studies to discover, develop, or verify knowledge relating to the causes, diagnosis, treatment, prevention, or control of physical or mental diseases and impairments of human beings. To qualify, the organization must have the appropriate equipment and professional personnel necessary to carry out its principal function.[191]

---

[183] Reg. § 1.170A-9(c)(1).

[184] Rev. Rul. 74-572, 1974-2 C.B. 82.

[185] IRC § 213.

[186] Reg. § 1.170A-9(c)(1). The rules concerning the tax qualification of hospitals are discussed in *The Law of Tax-Exempt Organizations*, Chapters 7 § 6 and 17 § 1.

[187] Organizations that generally promote health are discussed in *The Law of Tax-Exempt Organizations*, Chapter 7 § 6.

[188] IRC §§ 170(b)(1)(A)(iii) and 509(a)(1).

[189] IRC § 170(b)(1)(A)(iii).

[190] Reg. § 1.170A-9(c)(2)(vii).

[191] Reg. § 1.170A-9(c)(2)(iii).

Medical research encompasses the associated disciplines spanning the biological, social, and behavioral sciences.[192]

Certain Supporting Foundations.   Certain supporting foundations are public charitable organizations and thus are not private foundations. These organizations are "foundations" that provide support for colleges and universities that are administered by governments.[193]

The organization must normally receive a substantial part of its support (exclusive of income received in the exercise or performance of its tax-exempt activities) from the United States or from direct or indirect contributions from the general public. It must be organized and operated exclusively to receive, hold, invest, and administer property and to make expenditures to or for the benefit of a college or university (including a land grant college or university), which itself is a public charitable organization[194] and which is an agency or instrumentality of a state or a political subdivision of a state, or which is owned or operated by a state or political subdivision of a state or by an agency or instrumentality of one or more states or political subdivisions.[195]

Governmental Units.   A governmental unit is a public charitable organization and thus is not a private foundation.[196] This category includes a state, a possession of the United States, or any political subdivision of either of the foregoing, or the United States or the District of Columbia.[197]

(ii) Publicly Supported Organizations—Donative Entities

General Rules.   An organization is not a private foundation if it is a charitable entity which "normally receives a substantial part of its support" (other than income from a tax-exempt function) from a gov-

---

[192]The rules concerning medical research organizations are discussed in *The Law of Tax-Exempt Organizations*, Chapter 17 § 1.

[193]IRC §§ 170(b)(1)(A)(iv) and 509(a)(1).

[194]See the text accompanying ns. 172–176, *supra*.

[195]The rules concerning these supporting foundations are discussed in *The Law of Tax-Exempt Organizations*, Chapter 17 § 1.

[196]IRC §§ 170(b)(1)(A)(v) and 509(a)(1); Reg. § 1.170A-9(d).

[197]IRC § 170(c)(1). The rules concerning governmental units are discussed in *The Law of Tax-Exempt Organizations*, Chapters 7 § 12, 17 § 1, and 34 § 14.

ernmental unit[198] or from direct or indirect contributions from the general public. [199]

The general way for a charitable organization to achieve nonprivate foundation status under these rules is for it to normally derive at least one-third of its support from qualifying public and/or governmental sources. [120] Thus, an organization qualifying as a publicly supported entity under these rules must maintain a support fraction, the denominator of which is total eligible support and the numerator of which is the amount of support from eligible public and/or governmental sources.

For these purposes, the term "support" means amounts received as gifts, grants, contributions, membership fees, net income from unrelated business activities, gross investment income, [201] tax revenues levied for the benefit of the organization and either paid to or expended on behalf of the organization, and the value of services or facilities (exclusive of services or facilities generally furnished to the public without charge) furnished by a governmental unit to the organization without charge. [202] All of the foregoing items are amounts that, if directly or indirectly received by the organization, comprise the denominator of the support fraction.

In computing the eligible amount of public support (the numerator of the support fraction), contributions from individuals, trusts, or corporations constitute public support to the extent that the total amount of contributions from any donor during the computation period does not exceed an amount equal to two percent of the organization's total support for the period. [203] Therefore, the total amount of support by a donor is included in full in the denominator of the support fraction and the amount determined by application of the two percent limitation is included in the numerator of the support fraction. The latter amount is the amount of support in the form of direct or indirect contributions from the general public. Donors who stand in a defined relationship to one another[204] must share a single two percent limitation.

---

[198] See the text accompanying ns. 195 and 196, *supra*.
[199] IRC §§ 170(b)(1)(A)(vi) and 509(a)(1).
[200] Reg. § 1.170A-9(e)(2).
[201] IRC § 509(e).
[202] IRC § 509(d); Reg. § 1.170A-9(e)(7)(i).
[203] Reg. § 1.170A-9(e)(6)(i).
[204] IRC § 4946(a)(1).

However, this two percent limitation does not generally apply to support received from other publicly supported organizations of the donative type, nor to grant support from governmental units. Thus, these types of support are, in their entirety, public support, as "indirect" contributions from the general public.[205] Because a charitable organization can be classified as not being a private foundation pursuant to a categorization other than a donative type publicly supported organization (such as by being one of the "institutions"[206]), and nonetheless meet the requirements of a donative type publicly supported organization [207] the two percent limitation does not apply with respect to contributions from these organizations. For example, financial support from a church is generally considered to be indirect public support in full, since churches derive substantial amounts of their support from the general public, even though their non-private foundation status is derived, as discussed,[208] from their institutional status as churches.[209]

Nonetheless, the two percent limitation will apply with respect to support received from a donative type publicly supported organization or governmental unit if the support represents an amount that was expressly or implicitly earmarked by a donor to the publicly supported organization or unit of government as being for, or for the benefit of, the organization asserting status as a donative type publicly supported organization.[210]

In constructing the support fraction, an organization must exclude from both the numerator and the denominator of the support fraction amounts received from the exercise or performance of its exempt purpose or function and contributions of services for which a charitable deduction is not allowable.[211] However, an organization will not be treated as meeting the support test if it receives almost all of its support from gross receipts from related activities and an insignificant amount of its support from the general public (directly and indirectly) and governmental units.[212] The organization may exclude

---

[205] Reg. § 1.170A-9(e)(6)(i).
[206] See the text accompanying ns. 164–197, *supra*.
[207] Rev. Rul. 76-416, 1976-2 C.B. 57.
[208] See the text accompanying ns. 164–167, *supra*.
[209] Rev. Rul. 78-95, 1978-1 C.B. 71.
[210] Reg. § 1.170A-9(e)(6)(v).
[211] Reg. § 1.170A-9(e)(7)(i).
[212] Reg. § 1.170A-9(e)(7)(ii).

from both the numerator and denominator of the support fraction an amount equal to one or more so-called "unusual grants."[213]

In computing the support fraction, review must be made of the organization's support that is "normally" received. This means that the organization must meet the one-third support test for a period encompassing the four tax years immediately preceding the year involved, on an aggregate basis. Where this is done, the organization will be considered as meeting the one-third support test for its current tax year and for the tax year immediately succeeding its current tax year [214]

"Facts and Circumstances" Test.   Notwithstanding the foregoing general rules, an organization may qualify as a donative type publicly supported organization, where it cannot satisfy the one-third requirement, by meeting a "facts and circumstances" test, as long as the amount normally received from public and/or governmental sources is "substantial."[215] To meet this test, the organization must demonstrate the existence of three elements: (1) the total amount of public and/or governmental support normally received by the organization is at least ten percent of its total support normally received; (2) the organization has a continuous and *bona fide* program for solicitation of funds from the general public, governmental units, or public charitable organizations; and (3) it satisfies all other pertinent facts and circumstances, including the percentage of its support from public and/or governmental sources, the "public" nature of the organization's governing board, the extent to which its facilities or programs are publicly available, its membership dues rates, and whether its activities are likely to appeal to persons having some broad common interest or purpose.[216]

Concerning the governing board factor, the organization's nonprivate foundation status will be enhanced where it has a governing body which represents the interests of the public, rather than the personal or private interests of a limited number of donors. As noted, one of the important elements of this facts and circumstances test is the availability of public facilities or services. Examples of entities meeting this requirement are a museum that holds its build-

[213]Reg. § 1.170A-9(e)(6)(ii). E.g., Rev. Rul. 76-440, 1976-2 C.B. 58.
[214]Reg. § 1.170A-9(e)(4)(i) .
[215]Reg. § 1.170A-9(e)(3).
[216]*Id.*

ing open to the public, a symphony orchestra that gives public performances, a conservation organization that provides educational services to the public through the distribution of educational materials, and a home for the elderly that provides domiciliary or nursing services for members of the general public.[217]

Community Foundations. A community foundation (or community trust) may qualify as a donative type public charitable organization if it attracts, receives, and depends on financial support from the general public on a regular, recurring basis. Community foundations are designed primarily to attract large contributions of a capital or endowment nature from a small number of donors. They are generally identified with a particular community or area and are controlled by a representative group of persons from that community or area. Individual donors relinquish control over the investment and distribution of their contributions and the income derived from the contributions, although donors may designate the purposes for which the assets are to be used, subject to change by the governing body of the community foundation.[218]

(iii)   Publicly Supported Organizations—Service Provider Entities

An organization is not a private foundation if it is a charitable organization that is broadly, publicly supported and thus is responsive to the general public, rather than to the private interests of a limited number of donors or other persons.[219]

For a charitable organization to achieve non-private foundation status under these rules, it must normally receive more than one-third of its support from any combination of (1) gifts, grants, contributions, or membership fees[220] and (2) gross receipts from admissions, sales of merchandise, performance of services, or furnishings of facilities in activities related to its tax-exempt function,[221] as long as the support in either category is from so-called "permitted

---

[217]*Id.*

[218]Reg. § 1.170A-9(e)(10)(i). These rules, concerning all three categories of donative type public charitable organizations, are discussed in *The Law of Tax-Exempt Organizations*, Chapter 17 § 2.

[219]IRC § 509(a)(2); Reg. § 1.509(a)-3(a)(4). Also IRC § 170(b)(1)(A)(viii).

[220]IRC § 509(a)(2)(A)(i).

[221]IRC § 509(a)(2)(A)(ii).

sources." Permitted sources are governmental units,[222] the charitable "institutions,[223] donative type public charitable organizations,[224] and persons other than disqualified persons[225] with respect to the organization. Thus, an organization seeking to qualify under this one-third support test for service provider publicly supported organizations must construct a support fraction, with the amount of support received from these two categories of sources constituting the numerator of the support fraction and the total amount of support received by the organization being the denominator of the support fraction.[226] The organization may exclude from both the numerator and denominator of the support fraction an amount equal to one or more so-called "unusual grants."[227]

There is no limitation on the amount of support which may be taken into account in determining the numerator of the support fraction under these rules concerning gifts, grants, contributions, and membership fees, except that this support must, as noted, come from permitted sources. However, in computing the amount of support received from gross receipts that is allowable toward the one-third requirement, gross receipts from related activities received from any person or from any bureau or similar agency of a governmental unit are includible in any tax year to the extent that the receipts do not exceed the greater of $5,000 or one percent of the organization's support for the year.[228]

The term "support"[229] (in addition to the two categories of "public" support referenced above) means (1) net income from unrelated business activities, (2) gross investment income,[230] (3) tax revenues levied for the benefit of the organization and either paid to or expended on behalf of the organization, and (4) the value of services or facilities (exclusive of services or facilities generally furnished to the public without charge) furnished by a governmental unit to the organization without charge. The term does not include any gain from the disposi-

[222] See the text accompanying ns. 196–197, *supra*.
[223] See the text accompanying ns. 164–195, *supra*.
[224] See the text accompanying ns. 198–218, *supra*.
[225] IRC § 4946. See *The Law of Tax-Exempt Organizations*, Chapter 19.
[226] IRC § 509(a)(2)(A); Reg. § 1.509(a)-3(a)(2).
[227] Reg. § 1.509(a)-3(c)(3).
[228] Reg. § 1.509(a)-3(b)(1).
[229] IRC § 509(d).
[230] IRC § 509(e).

tion of property which would be considered as gain from the sale or exchange of a capital asset, or the value of exemption from any federal, state, or local tax or any similar benefit.[231] These six items of "support" are combined to constitute the denominator of this support fraction.

To avoid private foundation classification under these rules, an organization also must normally receive not more than one-third of its support from the sum of (1) gross investment income,[232] including interest, dividends, payments with respect to securities loans, rents, and royalties, and (2) any excess of the amount of unrelated business taxable income over the amount of the tax on that income.[233] To qualify under this test, an organization must construct a "gross investment income fraction," with the amount of gross investment income received constituting the numerator of the fraction and the total amount of support received being the denominator of the fraction.[234]

These support and investment income tests are computed on the basis of the nature of the organization's "normal" sources of support. An organization is considered as "normally" receiving one-third of its support from permitted sources and not more than one-third of its support from gross investment income for its current tax year and immediately succeeding tax year if, for the four tax years immediately preceding its current tax year, the aggregate amount of support received over the four-year period from permitted sources is more than one-third of its total support and the aggregate amount of support over the four-year period from gross investment income is not more than one-third of its total support.[235]

(iv) Supporting Organizations

Another category of charitable organization that is not a private foundation is the so-called "supporting organization."[236] Organizations which are deemed not to be private foundations because they are

---

[231] IRC § 509(d).
[232] IRC § 509(e).
[233] IRC § 509(a)(2)(B).
[234] Reg. § 1.509(a)-3(a)(3).
[235] Reg. § 1.509(a)-3(c)(1)(i). These rules are discussed in *The Law of Tax-Exempt Organizations*, Chapter 17 § 3.
[236] IRC § 509(a)(3). Also IRC § 170(b)(1)(A)(viii).

supporting organizations are those organizations which are not themselves one of the public institutions[237] or a publicly supported organization[238] but are sufficiently related to organizations that are public or publicly supported entities so that the requisite degree of public control and involvement is considered present.[239]

A supporting organization must be organized, and at all times thereafter operated, exclusively for the benefit of, to perform the functions of, or to carry out the purposes of one or more public charitable organizations.[240] A supporting organization must be operated, supervised, or controlled by or in connection with one or more public charitable organizations.[241] Thus, the relationship between the supporting and supported organizations must be one of three types: (1) "operated, supervised, or controlled by," (2) "supervised or controlled in connection with," or (3) "operated in connection with."[242]

The distinguishing feature of the relationship between a supporting organization and one or more supported public charitable organizations encompassed by the phrase "operated, supervised, or controlled by" is the presence of a substantial degree of direction by one or more public charitable organizations over the policies, programs, and activities of the supporting organization—a relationship comparable to that of a parent and subsidiary.[243] The distinguishing feature of the relationship between a supporting organization and one or more supported public charitable organizations encompassed by the phrase "supervised or controlled in connection with" is the presence of common supervision or control by the persons supervising or controlling both the supporting organization and the supported public charitable organization (or organizations), to ensure that the supporting organization is responsive to the needs and requirements of the supported organization.[244] The distinguishing feature of the relationship between a supporting organization and one or more supported public charitable organizations encompassed by the phrase "operated in connection with" is that the supporting organization is responsive

---

[237] See the text accompanying ns. 164–197, *supra.*
[238] See the text accompanying ns. 198–235, *supra.*
[239] Reg. § 1.509(a)-4(a)(5).
[240] IRC § 509(a)(3)(A); Reg. § 1.509(a)-4(a)(2).
[241] IRC § 509(a)(3)(B).
[242] Reg. §§ 1.509(a)-4(a)(3), 1.509(a)-4(f)(2).
[243] Reg. §§ 1.509(a)-4(f)(4), 1.509(a)-4(g)(1)(i).
[244] Reg. §§ 1.509(a)-4(f)(4), 1.509(a)-4(h)(1).

to and significantly involved in the operations of the supported public charitable organization.[245]

The supporting organization must engage solely in activities which
support or benefit the supported organization.[246] These activities may
include making payments to or for the use of, or providing services
or facilities for, individual members of the charitable class benefited
by the supported organization. The supporting organization need not
pay over its income to the supported organization but may carry on
an independent program or activity which supports or benefits the
supported organization. A supporting organization may also engage in
fund-raising activities, such as solicitations, dinners, and unrelated
trade or business activities, to raise funds for the supported organization or for permissible beneficiaries.[247]

A supporting organization can be created to support and benefit
one or more tax-exempt social welfare organizations,[248] labor or agricultural organizations,[249] or business leagues (trade, business, or professional associations),[250] as long as the supported organization (or
organizations) meets the one-third support test of the rules concerning the service provider type of publicly supported organization.[251]

A supporting organization must not be controlled directly or indirectly by one or more disqualified persons (other than foundation
managers), excluding public charitable organizations.[252]

(b) Other Organizations That Are
Not Private Foundations

There are three other categories of "charitable" organizations[253] that
are treated as entities other than "private foundations" for purposes
of the law of charitable giving. These are the following:

[245]Reg. § 1.509(a)-4(f)(4).
[246]Reg. § 1.509(a)-4(e)(1), (2).
[247]Reg. § 1.509(a)-4(e)(2).
[248]That is, organizations that are tax-exempt by reason of IRC § 501(c)(4).
See *The Law of Tax Exempt Organizations*, Chapter 28.
[249]That is, organizations that are tax-exempt by reason of IRC § 501(c)(5).
See *The Law of Tax-Exempt Organizations*, Chapter 31.
[250]That is, organizations that are tax-exempt by reason of IRC § 501(c)(6).
See *The Law of Tax-Exempt Organizations*, Chapter 29.
[251]IRC § 509(a)(3), last sentence; Reg. § 1.509(a)-4(k).
[252]IRC § 509(a)(3)(C); Reg. § 1.509(a)-4(a)(4). These rules are discussed in
The Law of Tax-Exempt Organizations, Chapter 17 § 5.
[253]That is, organizations that are described in IRC § 501(c)(3).

- Private operating foundations.[254] This type of private foundation is an organization that would be a "standard" private foundation but for the fact that most of its earnings and much of its assets are devoted directly to the conduct of its charitable activities.[255]
- "Conduit" foundations.[256] This type of private foundation timely makes qualifying distributions (usually, grants[257]) that are treated as distributions out of corpus, in an amount equal in value to all contributions received in the year involved, whether as cash or property.[258]
- "Common fund" foundations.[259] This type of private foundation is one that pools contributions received in a common fund but allows donors to retain the right to designate annually the organizations to which the income attributable to the contributions is given and to direct the organizations to which the corpus of the contributions is eventually to be given.[260]

(c) Private Foundations

A private foundation, then, is a "charitable" organization[261] that is not one of the foregoing types of charitable organizations. It is essentially a charitable organization that is funded from one source (usually, one individual, family, or corporation), that receives its ongoing funding from investment income (rather than a consistent flow of charitable contributions), and that makes grants for charitable purposes to other persons rather than conducts its own programs.

§ 4.4 THE UNRELATED BUSINESS INCOME RULES

The unrelated business income rules that are applicable to charitable and other tax-exempt organizations were enacted in 1950 and were significantly enhanced in 1969.[262]

---

[254] IRC §§ 170(b)(1)(A)(vii) and 170(b)(1)(E)(i).
[255] IRC § 4942(j)(3). The rules concerning private operating foundations are discussed in *The Law of Tax-Exempt Organizations*, Chapter 18 § 1.
[256] IRC §§ 170(b)(1)(A)(vii) and 170(b)(1)(E)(ii).
[257] See *The Law of Tax-Exempt Organizations*, Chapter 21.
[258] The rules concerning conduit foundations are discussed in *The Law of Tax-Exempt Organizations*, Chapter 18 § 2.
[259] IRC §§ 170(b)(1)(A)(vii) and 170(b)(1)(E)(iii).
[260] The rules concerning common fund foundations are discussed in *The Law of Tax-Exempt Organizations*, Chapter 18 § 3.
[261] That is, an organization described in IRC § 501(c)(3).
[262] IRC §§ 511–514.

The objective of these rules is to prevent unfair competition between tax-exempt organizations and for-profit, commercial enterprises.[263] The rules are intended to place the unrelated business activities of a tax-exempt organization on the same tax basis as the non-exempt business with which it competes.

(a)   Introduction

Prior to enactment of the unrelated income rules, the federal law embodied the "destination of income" test.[264] Pursuant to this standard, the law merely required that the net profits of organizations be used in furtherance of exempt purposes. That is, the test did not consider the source of the profits, thereby tolerating forms of unfair competition.

Thus, in adopting and expanding these rules, Congress has not prohibited commercial ventures by nonprofit organizations. Rather, it struck a balance, as the U.S. Supreme Court characterized the matter, between "its two objectives of encouraging benevolent enterprise and restraining unfair competition."[265]

Essentially, for an activity of a tax-exempt organization to be subject to tax, four tests must be satisfied, in that the activity must

- constitute a "trade or business,"
- be "regularly carried on,"
- not be "substantially related" to the tax-exempt purposes of the organization, and
- not be specifically exempted (or have the income from the activity specifically exempted) from taxation.[266]

Nearly all types of tax-exempt organizations are subject to the unrelated income rules, including charitable organizations.[267] The unrelated income rules are also applicable "in the case of any college or university which is an agency or instrumentality of any government

---

[263] Reg. § 1.513-1(b).

[264] The test is discussed in *The Law of Tax-Exempt Organizations*, Chapter 39.

[265] *United States v. American College of Physicians*, 475 U.S. 834 (1986).

[266] Reg. § 1.513-1(a).

[267] IRC § 511(a)(2)(A).

or any political subdivision thereof, or which is owned or operated by a government or any political subdivision thereof, or by any agency or instrumentality of one or more governments or political subdivisions," as well as "in the case of any corporation wholly owned by one or more such colleges and universities."[268]

To be tax-exempt, an organization must be organized and operated primarily for exempt purposes.[269] The federal tax law allows an exempt organization to engage in a certain amount of activity unrelated to its exempt purposes.[270] Where the organization derives net income from one or more unrelated business activities, known as "unrelated business taxable income," it is subject to tax on that income. An organization's tax exemption will be revoked if an inappropriate portion of its activities is not in furtherance of an exempt purpose.[271]

Business activities may preclude initial qualification of an otherwise exempt organization as a charitable or other entity. This would occur through its failure to satisfy the "operational test," which looks to see whether the organization is being operated principally for exempt purposes.[272] Likewise, an organization will not meet the "organizational test" if its articles of organization empower it, as more than an insubstantial part of its activities, to carry on activities that are not in furtherance of its exempt purpose [273]

(b) "Trade or Business" Defined

For purposes of the federal tax rules, the term "trade or business," in this setting, includes "any activity which is carried on for the production of income from the sale of goods or the performance of services."[274] Accordingly, most activities which would constitute a trade or business under basic tax law principles[275] are considered a trade or business for purposes of the unrelated trade or business rules.[276]

This definition of "trade or business" is very encompassing and

[268]IRC § 511(a)(2)(B).
[269]See *The Law of Tax Exempt Organizations*, Chapter 6 § 1.
[270]E.g., Reg. § 1.501(c)(3)-1(e)(1).
[271]E.g., Reg. § 1.501(c)(3)-1(c)(1).
[272]See *The Law of Tax-Exempt Organizations*, Chapter 6 § 2.
[273]*Ibid*, Chapter 6 § 1.
[274]IRC § 513(c).
[275]IRC § 162.
[276]Reg. § 1.513-1(b).

embraces nearly every activity of a tax-exempt organization. Absent a specific exemption (see below), only investment activities generally escape this classification.

In this sense, every tax-exempt organization should be viewed as a bundle of activities, each of which is a trade or business. Thus, the IRS is empowered to examine each of the activities in the bundle in search of unrelated business endeavor. As Congress chose to state the principle, "an activity does not lose identity as a trade or business merely because it is carried on within a larger aggregate of similar activities or within a larger complex of other endeavors which may, or may not, be related to the exempt purposes of the organization."[277] This is known as the "fragmentation rule."

Congress also enacted a rule which states that, "[w]here an activity carried on for profit constitutes an unrelated trade or business, no part of such trade or business shall be excluded from such classification merely because it does not result in profit."[278]

(c) "Regularly Carried On"

To be considered an unrelated trade or business, an activity of a tax-exempt organization must be "regularly carried on by it."[279]

Income from an activity of a tax-exempt organization is considered taxable only when, assuming the other criteria are satisfied, the activity is regularly carried on, as distinguished from sporadic or infrequent commercial transactions.[280] The factors which determine whether an activity is regularly carried on are the frequency and continuity of the activities and the manner in which the activities are pursued.[281]

These factors must be evaluated in light of the purpose of the unrelated business income tax to place tax-exempt organizations' business activities upon the same tax basis as their non-exempt business competitors. Thus, specific business activities of a tax-exempt organization will generally "be deemed 'regularly carried on' if they manifest a frequency and continuity, and are pursued in a manner

[277] IRC § 513(c).
[278] Id.
[279] IRC § 513(c).
[280] Reg. § 513-1(c).
[281] Reg. § 1.513-1(c)(1).

generally similar to comparable commercial activities of nonexempt organizations."[282]

Where income-producing activities are performed by commercial organizations on a year-round basis, the performance of these activities for a period of only a few weeks does not constitute the regular carrying on of a trade or business.[283] Similarly, occasional or annual income-producing activities, such as fund-raising events, do not constitute a business regularly carried on. However, the conduct of year-round business activities, such as parking lot rental, for one day each week would constitute the regular carrying on of a business.[284] Where commercial entities normally undertake income-producing activities on a seasonal basis, the conduct of the activities by a tax-exempt organization during a significant portion of the season is deemed the regular conduct of that activity.[285]

A trade or business is regularly carried on if the attributes of the activity are similar to the commercial activities of nonexempt organizations.[286]

(d) Concept of "Unrelated" Business

The term "unrelated trade or business" is defined to mean "any trade or business the conduct of which is not substantially related (aside from the need of such organization for income or funds or the use it makes of the profits derived) to the exercise or performance by such organization of its charitable, educational, or other purpose or function constituting the basis for its exemption."[287]

Thus, a regularly conducted trade or business is subject to tax, unless it is substantially related to the accomplishment of the organization's exempt purpose.[288] To be substantially related, the activity must have a substantial causal relationship to the achievement of an exempt purpose.[289] The fact that an asset is essential to the conduct of an organization's exempt activities does not shield the commercial income from taxation where that income was produced by that as-

[282] Id.
[283] Reg. § 1.513-1(c)(2)(i).
[284] Id.
[285] Id.
[286] Reg. § 1.513-1(c).
[287] IRC § 513(a).
[288] Reg. § 1.513-1(a).
[289] Reg. § 1.513-1(d)(2).

set.[290] The income-producing activities must still meet the causal relationship test if the income is not to be subject to tax.[291] This issue arises when an organization owns a facility or other assets that are put to dual use. For example, the operation of an auditorium as an ordinary motion picture theater for public entertainment in the evening would be treated as an unrelated activity even though the theater is used exclusively for tax-exempt purposes during regular hours.[292]

A related concept is that activities should not be conducted on a scale larger than is reasonably necessary for the performance of the exempt functions.[293] Those activities in excess of the needs of exempt functions constitute the conduct of an unrelated business.[294]

(e) "Unrelated Business Taxable Income"

As indicated, to be subject to the unrelated income rules, an activity must satisfy four tests. The first three of these tests is built into the definition of the term "unrelated business taxable income."

That term is defined as "the gross income derived by any organization from any unrelated trade or business . . . regularly carried on by it, less the deductions allowed . . . [under federal tax law] which are directly connected with the carrying on of such trade or business."[295]

Both this gross income and allowable deductions are computed in conformance with the "modifications" discussed below.

Tax-exempt organizations are subject to tax on their unrelated business taxable income at the regular corporate tax rates or at individual rates if the organization is not incorporated.[296]

(f) Exempted Activities

Certain business activities conducted by tax-exempt organizations are exempt from unrelated business taxation. These include the following:

[290] Reg. § 1.513-1(d).
[291] Reg. § 1.513-1(d)(2).
[292] Id.
[293] Reg. § 1.513-1(d)(3).
[294] Id.
[295] IRC § 512(a)(1).
[296] IRC § 511.

- a trade or business "in which substantially all the work in carrying on such trade or business is performed for the organization without compensation."[297]

- a trade or business which is carried on by the organization "primarily for the convenience of its members, students, patients, officers, or employees."[298] This exemption is available only to organizations that are "charitable" entities[299] or are governmental colleges and universities.[300]

- a trade or business "which is the selling of merchandise, substantially all of which has been received by the organization as gifts or contributions."[301]

- "qualified public entertainment activities."[302] This type of activity is "any entertainment or recreational activity of a kind traditionally conducted at fairs or expositions promoting agricultural and educational purposes, including, but not limited to, any activity one of the purposes of which is to attract the public to fairs or expositions or to promote the breeding of animals or the development of products or equipment."[303] This exemption is available only to charitable, social welfare, labor, and agricultural organizations.[304]

- "qualified convention and trade show activities."[305] This type of activity is "any activity of a kind traditionally conducted at conventions, annual meetings, or trade shows, including, but not limited to, any activity one of the purposes of which is to attract persons in an industry generally (without regard to membership in the sponsoring organization) as well as members of the public to the show for the purpose of displaying industry products or to stimulate interest in, and demand for, industry

[297] IRC § 513(a)(1).
[298] IRC § 513(a)(2).
[299] That is, organizations that are described in IRC § 501(c)(3).
[300] That is, are institutions described in IRC § 511(a)(2)(B).
[301] IRC § 513(a)(3).
[302] IRC § 513(d).
[303] IRC § 513(d)(2)(A).
[304] That is, organizations described in IRC §§ 501(c)(3), (4), or (5), respectively. Social welfare organizations are the subject of *The Law of Tax-Exempt Organizations*, Chapter 28, and labor and agricultural organizations are the subject of *ibid*, Chapter 31.
[305] IRC § 513(d).

products or services, or to educate persons engaged in the industry in the development of new products and services or new rules and regulations affecting the industry."[306] This exemption is available only to charitable, social welfare, labor, and agricultural organizations, and business leagues.[307]

- in the case of a charitable hospital, the furnishing of certain cooperative services to one or more small hospitals under certain circumstances.[308]

- the conduct of certain bingo games.[309]

- in the case of charitable and veterans' organizations, contributions to which are deductible for federal income tax purposes,[310] activities relating to the distribution of low cost articles if the distribution of the articles is incidental to the solicitation of charitable contributions.[311]

- in the case of charitable and veterans' organizations, contributions to which are deductible for federal income tax purposes, any trade or business consisting of (1) exchanging with another of these organizations, names and addresses of donors to or members of the organization, or (2) renting the names and addresses to another of these organizations.[312]

(g) Exempted Income

Certain types of income are exempt from the unrelated income tax.[313]

Because the unrelated business rules apply to active business conducted by tax-exempt organizations, most types of "passive" income are exempt from taxation. This exemption generally covers income such as dividends, interest, payments with respect to securities loans, annuities, royalties, most rents, capital gains, and gains on the lapse or termination of options written by the organization.[314]

[306] IRC § 513(d)(3)(A).
[307] That is, organizations described in IRC §§ 501(c)(3), (4), (5), or (6), respectively. Business leagues are the subject of *The Law of Tax-Exempt Organizations*, Chapter 29.
[308] IRC § 513(e).
[309] IRC § 513(f).
[310] See 2, *supra*.
[311] IRC § 513(h)(1)(A).
[312] IRC § 513(h)(1)(B).
[313] IRC § 512(b).
[314] IRC §§ 512(b)(1), (2), (3), and (5).

However, the unrelated debt-financed income rules override the general exception for passive income.[315] Also, interest, annuities, royalties, and rents derived from a controlled corporation may be taxable.[316] It should be noted that there are (three) exceptions pertaining to research income.[317] There is a specific deduction, of $1,000,[318] for any type of unrelated business income.

§ 4.5 FACTORS AFFECTING DEDUCTIBILITY OF CHARITABLE GIFTS

There are several factors that affect the deductibility of charitable gifts:

- The transaction must be a "gift."[319]
- The recipient of the gift must be a "charitable" organization.[320]
- The year of the gift.
- The subject of the gift, whether money or property.
- If the gift is of property, the nature of the property that is contributed, such as
  - Long-term capital gain property
  - Short-term capital gain property
  - Ordinary income property
  - Inventory.
- If the gift is of property, the value of the property contributed.[321]
- The public charity/private foundation status of the charitable recipient.[322]
- The nature of the recipient if it is an organization other than a public charitable organization or a private foundation.

---

[315] IRC §§ 512(b)(4) and 514. The unrelated debt-financed income rules are the subject of *The Law of Tax-Exempt Organizations*, Chapter 43.
[316] IRC § 512(b)(13).
[317] IRC § 512(b)(7), (8), and (9).
[318] IRC § 512(b)(12).
[319] See § 1, *supra*.
[320] See § 2, *supra*.
[321] See Chapter 11 § 1.
[322] See § 3, *supra*.

- The use to which the contributed property is put, such as unrelated use of tangible personal property,[323] or specific charitable uses, for example, the rules concerning gifts of inventory.[324]
- The nature of the interest in the money or property contributed, that is, whether the gift is of an outright interest or a partial interest.[325]
- Compliance with the record-keeping, reporting, and other substantiation requirements.[326]

Each charitable contribution can be tested against the above criteria in determining its deductibility for federal income tax purposes.

[323] See Chapter 6 § 6.
[324] See Chapter 9 § 4.
[325] See Chapter 3 and Part IV.
[326] See Chapter 23.

5

Timing of Charitable Deductions

The general rule is that a federal income tax charitable contribution deduction arises at the time of, and for the year in which, the deduction is actually paid.[1] A significant exception to this rule is the body of law concerning the tax deductibility of contributions carried over to a year subsequent to the one in which the gift was made; in this situation, the contribution is actually paid in one year but the allowable charitable deduction arises in, and is treated for tax purposes as paid in, another year.[2] The mere making of a pledge will not result in an income tax charitable deduction.[3] Of course, a mere intent to make a charitable gift does not generate a contribution deduction.[4]

The matter of the timing of a federal income tax charitable contribution deduction concerns the tax year for which the gift is deductible. To determine this year, the federal tax law follows the concept of "title"; that is, the contribution is for the year in which title to the item that is the subject of the gift passes from the donor to the donee. Title to property generally passes when all of the rights to and interests in the property have been properly transferred.

[1]IRC § 170(a)(1); Reg. § 1.170A-1(a)(1). Also *Christensen* v. *Commissioner*, 40 T.C. 563 (1963).
[2]See Chapter 7.
[3]Reg. § 1.170A-1(a)(1). Also Rev. Rul. 75-348, 1975-2 C.B. 75; Rev. Rul. 55-410, 1955-1 C.B. 297; and *Mann* v. *Commissioner*, 35 F.2d 873 (Ct. App. D.C. 1929).
[4]*Glynn* v. *Commissioner*, 76 T.C. 116 (1981), aff'd in unpublished opinion (1st Cir. 1982).

The element that is critical to the passage of title in an item of property is "delivery," for delivery is the way title in property is actually transferred from one person to another.[5] Consequently, a charitable contribution deduction generally comes into being on the date the gift property is delivered by the donor to the charitable donee.[6] This general rule assumes a number of elements, including the following:

- The absence of a condition (to occur either before or after the transfer) that defeats, or will defeat, the clear passage of title to the donee,[7] unless
  - The condition is so remote as to be negligible,[8] or
  - The condition is one that entails a legitimate restriction on the donee's use of the gift property (such as a confining of the use of the gift for scholarship purposes or for the acquisition of a building for use by the charitable donee in its charitable activities).
- Compliance with the substantiation requirements.[9]

When the mails are used, the United States Postal Service is

---

[5]E.g., Rev. Rul. 69-93, 1969-1 C.B. 139 (holding that title to real estate is transferred on the date that the "deed passed," not on the previous date when the parties executed a contract for the sale of the property). The Tax Court of the United States has held that a sale of land occurred when the "title was finally approved and the deed of conveyance was signed passing title and the right of possession to the vendee . . ." *Wurtsbaugh v. Commissioner*, 8 T.C. 183, 189 (1947)."

[6]Reg. § 1.170A-1(b), which states that "[o]rdinarily, a contribution is made at the time delivery is effected."

[7]The subject of conditional gifts is addressed in Chapter 10 § 3.

[8]Reg. § 1.170A-1(e), which states: "If as of the date of a gift a transfer for charitable purposes is dependent upon the performance of some act or the happening of a precedent event in order that it might become effective, no deduction is allowable unless the possibility that the charitable transfer will not become effective is so remote as to be negligible. If an interest in property passes to, or is vested in, charity on the date of the gift and the interest would be defeated by the subsequent performance of some act or the happening of some event, the possibility of occurrence of which appears on the date of the gift to be so remote as to be negligible, the deduction is allowable."

[9]See Chapter 22.

considered the agent of the recipient. Thus, when a contribution is mailed, the date of gift is usually the date the item is placed in the U.S. mail system.

The concept of delivery, however, does not necessarily mean that the donee must take actual physical possession of the property before a gift of the property becomes deductible. Title may pass when the charitable donee has the right or entitlement to possession of the property; one court wrote that "the donee simply must have the right to interrupt the donor's possession and the right to have physical possession of the property during each year following the donation . . ."[10] This can involve forms of "constructive delivery," but the donor must give up custody, control, and management of the property; otherwise, the gift transaction is not "complete."[11]

§ 5.1   GIFTS OF MONEY—IN GENERAL

A charitable contribution of U.S. currency is deductible for the year in which the money is mailed or otherwise delivered to the charitable donee. This rule pertains to situations where the gift is made in cash, rather than by check. Of course, the "title" to the money passes at the time the ownership of the currency changes hands. Actions indicating intent to make a gift of money, such as instructions to a bookkeeper, are insufficient; the deduction arises in the year of actual payment.[12]

§ 5.2   GIFTS OF MONEY BY CHECK

Gifts of money are usually made by means of a check, if only as a matter of record-keeping. In this context, the above general rules

[10]*Winokur* v. *Commissioner*, 90 T.C. 733, 740 (1988).
[11]E.g., *LaGarde* v. *Commissioner*, 76-1 U.S.T.C. ¶ 9248 (N.D. Ala. 1975); *Mellon* v. *Commissioner*, 36 B.T.A. 977 (1937). Also *Murphy* v. *Commissioner*, 61 T.C.M. 2935 (1991). Instances where the "donor" retained too much dominion and control over the property that was the subject of the gift are in *Woods* v. *Commissioner*, 58 T.C.M. 673 (1989), aff'd in unpublished opinion (6th Cir. 1991); *Stjernholm* v. *Commissioner*, 58 T.C.M. 389 (1989), aff'd in unpublished opinion (10th Cir. 1991); and *Roughen* v. *Commissioner*, 54 T.C.M. 510 (1987).
[12]*Nehring* v. *Commissioner*, 131 F.2d 790 (7th Cir. 1942). Also *Jordan* v. *United States*, 297 F. Supp. 1326 (W.D. Okl. 1969).

apply. That is, title to the funds passes, and thus a charitable gift is made, at the time the check is mailed or otherwise delivered to the charitable donee.[13] This rule also applies where the gift is made using a third-party check. However, in addition to the assumptions noted above, this rule assumes that the check evidencing the contribution clears the bank involved in due course.[14] Thus, a "gift" of a bad check is no gift at all.

Therefore, charitable gifts by check made at year end may be deductible for the year in which the check was written, even though the check evidencing the gift does not clear the account involved until early in the subsequent year.

Nonetheless, the general rules concerning gifts apply. Thus, the IRS has written that "a gift is not consummated by the mere delivery of the donor's own check or note. The gift of a check does not become complete until it is paid, certified, or accepted by the drawee, or is negotiated for value to a third person."[15] For example, in one instance, where the checks were written immediately prior to an individual's death, there were inadequate funds in the account, and the checks were not presented for payment until approximately eight months after death, the value of the non-charitable gift of the checks was held by the IRS to be includible in the decedent's estate.[16]

A charitable gift involving a postdated check becomes deductible as of the date of the check, assuming all other requirements are satisfied.[17] A check involving a charitable gift that has not cleared the bank involved prior to the death of the donor gives rise to a federal

[13]Reg. § 1.170A-1(b). Also *Witt, Estate of* v. *Fahs*, 160 F. Supp. 521 (S.D. Fla. 1956); and *Spiegel, Estate of* v. *Commissioner*, 12 T.C. 524 (1949).

[14]The IRS has written that a charitable contribution in the form of a check is deductible in the tax year in which the check was delivered "provided the check is honored and paid and there are no restrictions as to time and manner of payment thereof" (Rev. Rul. 54-465, 1954-2 C.B. 93).

[15]Rev. Rul. 67-376, 1967-2 C.B. 351.

[16]IRS Private Letter Ruling 8706011.

[17]*Griffin* v. *Commissioner*, 49 T.C. 253 (1967), where the Tax Court wrote: "A postdated check is not a check immediately payable but is a promise to pay on the date shown. It is not a promise to pay presently and does not mature until the day of its date, after which it is payable on demand the same as if it had not been issued until that date although it is, as in the case of a promissory note, a negotiable instrument from the time issued" (at 261).

income tax charitable contribution deduction as of the time the check was delivered to the donee.[18]

A postdated check is essentially a promissory note; the rules concerning gifts by promissory notes are discussed below.

§ 5.3   GIFTS OF MONEY BY CREDIT CARD

An income tax charitable contribution can be made, and be deductible, by means of a credit card. When a gift is made using a bank-based credit card, the contribution is deductible for the year the donor charges the gift on the account (rather than for the year when the account including the charged amount is paid).[19] In reaching this conclusion, the IRS concluded that the credit card holder, by using the card to make the contribution, became immediately indebted to a third party (the bank) in such a way that the cardholder could not thereafter prevent the charitable organization from receiving payment. This is because the credit card draft received by the charitable organization from the credit card holder is immediately creditable by the bank to the organization's account as if it were a check.

In this regard, the IRS analogized this situation to that where a charitable contribution is made using borrowed funds. The IRS reasoned as follows: "Since the cardholder's use of the credit card creates the cardholder's own debt to a third party, the use of a bank credit card to make a charitable contribution is equivalent to the use of borrowed funds to make a contribution."[20] The general rule is that, when a deductible payment is made with borrowed money, the deduction is not postponed until the year in which the borrowed money is repaid.[21] These expenses must be deducted in the year they are paid and not when the loans are repaid.

---

[18]*Spiegel, Estate* of v. *Commissioner, supra,* n. 13. Consequently, these funds should not be in the donor's estate for estate tax purposes (*Belcher, Estate of* v. *Commissioner,* 83 T.C. 227 (1984)). However, this rule does not apply with respect to gifts by check written to non-charitable donees (*McCarthy* v. *United States,* 86-2 U.S.T.C. ¶ 13,700 (7th Cir. 1986)).

[19]Rev. Rul. 78-38, 1978-1 C.B. 67. This ruling revoked Rev. Rul. 71-216, 1971-1 C.B. 96, which held that a person making a contribution to a qualified charitable organization by a charge to a bank credit card is entitled to a charitable contribution deduction for the amount contributed in the tax year the donor paid the amount to the bank.

[20]Rev. Rul. 78-38, *supra,* n. 19, at 68.

[21]*Granan* v. *Commissioner,* 55 T.C. 753 (1971).

Gifts by means of a bank credit card are to be distinguished from gifts by means of a promissory note and the like (see below). The issuance of a promissory note (or debenture bond) represents a mere promise to pay at some future date and delivery of the note (or bond) to a charitable organization is not a requisite "payment."[22]

§ 5.4 GIFTS OF MONEY BY TELEPHONE

An income tax charitable contribution can be made, and be deductible, by means of the telephone. This can occur through use of a "pay by phone" account maintained at a financial institution. When the gift is made by transfer from this type of account, which the donor has initiated by telephone, the deduction arises on the date the financial institution makes the payment to the charitable organization.[23] In this instance, the financial institution is acting as the agent of the donor.[24]

§ 5.5 GIFTS OF SECURITIES

There are some items of property as to which the law has constructed a formal system for the transfer of title. This is the case in connection with stocks, bonds, and other securities (which are forms of intangible personal property). A security usually is evidenced by a certificate, and title to the underlying security can be transferred by an endorsement on the certificate, indicating transfer of the security from one person to another. Transfers of securities are usually effected by brokers.

Thus, a person may make a contribution of a security to a charitable organization, and create a federal income tax contribution deduction, where the endorsed certificate evidencing the security is delivered to the charitable organization. Delivery can also be accomplished by such a transfer to an agent of the charitable donee.

Where the certificate is mailed, the deduction arises as of the date on which the certificate was mailed. Where the certificate is delivered to the corporation that issued the security or to a broker acting on behalf of the donor, for purposes of arranging for transfer of title to the security to the charitable donee, the charitable deduction will

---

[22] Rev. Rul. 78-38, *supra*, n. 19.
[23] Rev. Rul. 80-335, 1980-2 C.B. 170.
[24] E.g., *Commissioner* v. *Bradley*, 56 F.2d 728 (6th Cir. 1932).

come into being on the date the transfer of the security is formally recorded by the issuing corporation.[25] However, when the certificate is delivered to a broker representing the charitable donee, the deduction arises as of the date of delivery.[26] Mere notation on the records of the transferee charitable organization of a contribution of securities is not sufficient to cause effective transfer of title.[27]

A court case illustrates some of the intricacies of these rules. An individual decided to contribute some stock to several charities, wanting to make these gifts before a payment of money for some of the shares pursuant to a tender offer and before accrual of the right to dividend income from the shares. The donor sent a letter to a trust company withdrawing the stock from a trust and requesting delivery of the stock to a bank. On the same day, the donor wrote to the bank identifying the charitable donees. Further, on the same day, the donees were sent a memorandum directing them to instruct the bank as to the disposition of the stock (that is, whether the donees wanted to accept the tender offer or retain the stock). The final offer was made about one week later, with the actual transfer of the shares on the corporation's books made approximately one month following the sending of the letters and memorandum by the donor. In the interim, dividends were declared; they were sent to the charities by the bank. The donor claimed a charitable deduction for the gifts of the securities and did not report the dividends as income.

The IRS concluded that the donor had control of the stock when it was sold and therefore attributed the capital gain on the sale of the securities to the donor. The dividend income was also found to be gross income to the donor. The issues were litigated, with the donor prevailing. The court found that the donor established a voluntary trust for the donees, using an independent party (the bank) as trustee. This, said the court, effectively removed any potential for the exercise of control by the donor "despite the failure to accomplish titular transfer on the corporate books."[28] The federal income

---

[25]Reg. § 1.170A-1(b). Of course, in applying this rule, it must be shown that the intermediate transferee is, in fact, an agent of the donor; e.g., *Sawade, Estate of* v. *Commissioner*, 795 F.2d 45 (8th Cir. 1986); *Greer* v. *Commissioner*, 70 T.C. 294 (1978), aff'd (on another issue), 634 F.2d 1044 (6th Cir. 1980); and *Londen* v. *Commissioner*, 45 T.C. 106 (1965).

[26]E.g., *Morrison* v. *Commissioner*, 53 T.C.M. 251 (1987).

[27]*McCall* v. *United States*, 72-1 U.S.T.C. ¶ 9263 (D.S.C. 1972).

[28]*Richardson* v. *Commissioner*, 49 T.C.M. 67, 73 (1984).

tax regulation on the point[29] was held to be inapplicable inasmuch as delivery was neither to the donor's agent nor to the issuing corporation or its agent. Thus, delivery was held to be effected upon tender of the stock by the bank to the offeror, which was prior to the stock sale dates and the dividend declaration date. The consequence of all this was that the donor was held to have the charitable deduction for the gifts of the stock, and not to have any capital gain and dividend income tax liability.

§ 5.6   GIFTS OF A COPYRIGHT INTEREST

Another item of intangible personal property that, to be transferred, must be passed in a formal manner, is a copyright interest. A determination as to whether a properly completed transfer of a copyright interest occurred is essentially governed by state law but only after certain federal law restrictions are satisfied.[30] The federal requirements involve a written transfer instrument signed by the donor as owner.[31] A copyright certificate is issued; however, possession of the certificate does not constitute ownership of the copyright itself.[32]

In one instance, an individual physically presented a copyright certificate, reflecting a book that was generating royalties, to a charitable organization, in an attempt to make a charitable gift. There was no executed written transfer instrument and no formal action was taken by the recipient organization to formally transfer the copyright to it. A court held that, "[t]herefore, standing alone, . . . [the individual's] physical presentation of the copyright certificate to . . . [the charitable organization], although accomplished with much ceremony, was insufficient to transfer a legal interest in the copyright" to the charity; "[t]his invalid transfer," the court continued, "does not begin to qualify as a deductible charitable contribution."[33]

[29] See n. 25, *supra.*

[30] *Kingsrow Enterprises, Inc.* v. *Metromedia, Inc.*, 397 F. Supp. 879 (S.D. N.Y. 1975).

[31] 17 U.S.C. § 28 (1976).

[32] The copyright "is not transferred by mere physical delivery, or other acquisition, of the certificate" (*Kingsrow Enterprises, Inc.* v. *Metromedia, Inc., supra,* n. 30, at 881).

[33] *Smith* v. *Commissioner,* 42 T.C.M. 431, 437-438 (1981).

§ 5.7   GIFTS BY MEANS OF NOTES

The making of a note, promising to pay money and/or transfer property to a charitable organization, and delivery of the note to the charity, does not create a charitable contribution deduction. This is because a mere promise to pay does not effect transfer of title to the property.[34] Of course, when the money and/or property is actually transferred to the charitable donee, in satisfaction of the requirements of the note, an income tax charitable contribution deduction results.[35] (A promissory note is an item of intangible personal property.)

These distinctions are based on the requirement that a charitable deduction is available only in the year the contribution is actually paid.[36] Delivery of a note is not payment of the amount it represents.[37]

A note in these circumstances may bear interest, or purport to bear interest. The tax consequences of the payment of the interest are dependent upon the enforceability of the note. Where the note is enforceable, the payment of interest on the note is deductible as an interest expense; if the note is not enforceable, the additional amounts paid are not interest for tax purposes, but are deductible as charitable contributions.[38]

§ 5.8   GIFTS OF TANGIBLE PERSONAL PROPERTY

A person may make deductible gifts of tangible personal property to a charitable organization. Items of tangible personal property include works of art, furniture, automobiles, and clothing.

Usually, there is no formal system in law for the recording and

---

[34]Rev. Rul. 78-38, *supra*, n. 19. This rule assumes that the notes represent bona fide debt (e.g., *Lippmann* v. *Commissioner*, 52 T.C. 130 (1969)).

[35]Rev. Rul. 68-174, 1968-1 C.B. 81. Also *O'Neil* v. *United States*, 82-1 U.S.T.C. ¶ 9209 (E.D. Cal. 1982), aff'd without opinion, (9th Cir. 1982); *Guren* v. *Commissioner*, 66 T.C. 118 (1976); and *Petty* v. *Commissioner*, 40 T.C. 521 (1963).

[36]See the text accompanying n. 1, *supra*. Also *Story III* v. *Commissioner*, 38 T.C. 936 (1962); and *Andrus* v. *Burnet*, 50 F.2d 332 (D.C. Ct. App. 1931).

[37]See Chapter 4 § 1(d).

[38]Rev. Rul. 68-174, *supra*, n. 35.

transfer of an item of tangible personal property. (The obvious exception, of course, is the title requirements involving motor vehicles.) However, in appropriate circumstances, title transfer of tangible personal property to a charitable organization can be evidenced by the making of a deed of gift.

§ 5.9 GIFTS OF REAL PORPERTY

A person may make a contribution of real property to a charitable organization and receive an income tax charitable deduction. There is, of course, a formal system in law for the recording and transfer of title to parcels of real estate; transfers of real property are generally effected by means of deeds.

As to the timing of the deduction, the contribution deduction for a gift of real property generally comes into being on the date the donor delivers a deed to the property to the charitable donee.[39] Recording of the deed is not necessary to make the transfer complete.[40]

A charitable contribution deduction for a transfer of mortgaged land to a charitable organization by a partnership was denied by a court because the property was subject to a special warranty deed. Under state law, the donor partnership remained liable on the outstanding mortgage. The deed imposed an obligation on the grantor to protect the grantee against adverse claims which may impair the grantee's title to the land. Thus, the court held that the warranty was merely a promise to make payments in the future, with a charitable deduction available when the payments are actually made.[41]

§ 5.10 GIFTS BY LETTERS OF CREDIT

A charitable contribution made by means of an irrevocable banker's letter of credit is the subject of the charitable deduction as of the

---

[39] E.g., *Dyer v. Commissioner*, 58 T.C.M. 1321 (1990); *Brotzler v. Commissioner*, 44 T.C.M. 1478 (1982); *Guest v. Commissioner*, 77 T.C. 9 (1981); *Alioto v. Commissioner*, 40 T.C.M. 1147 (1980); *Dodge, Jr. v. Commissioner*, 27 T.C.M. 1170 (1968); and *Johnson v. United States*, 280 F. Supp. 412 (S.D.N.Y. 1967).

[40] *Douglas v. Commissioner*, 58 T.C.M. 563 (1989).

[41] *Tidler v. Commissioner*, 53 T.C.M. 934 (1987).

date the letter of credit was established. This is because an irrevocable letter of credit from a bank is the equivalent of money.[42]

In one instance, an individual established an irrevocable banker's letter of credit in favor of a charitable organization. The letter of credit was for an aggregate amount of $150,000, payable by drafts drawn by the charity. The entire $150,000 was distributed to the charitable organization in four amounts, one in the year the letter of credit was established and the other three in the subsequent year. The IRS ruled that the entire $150,000 was deductible by this individual for the year in which the letter of credit was established, because the full amount was made available without restriction to the charitable organization. The fact that the charity only withdrew a portion of the amount available during the first year was held to be immaterial, because the charitable organization could have withdrawn the entire amount.[43]

§ 5.11   GIFTS OF OPTIONS

A person may own an item of property and create an option by which another person may purchase the property at a certain price at or during a certain time. An option may be created for or transferred to a charitable organization. However, there is no federal income tax charitable contribution deduction for the transfer of an option to a charitable organization. Rather, the charitable deduction arises at the time the option is exercised by the charitable donee.[44]

Thus, the transfer to a charitable organization of an option by the option writer is similar to the transfer of a note or pledge by the maker (see above). In the note situation, there is a promise to pay money at a future date; in the pledge situation, there is a promise to pay money or transfer some other property, or to do both, at a future date. In the option situation, there is a promise to sell property at a future date.

§ 5.12   GIFTS BY CORPORATIONS

The foregoing rules apply with respect to gifts by both individual and corporate donors. Thus, the general rule that a federal income tax

[42]*Watson* v. *Commissioner*, 69 T.C. 544 (1978), aff'd, 613 F.2d 594 (5th Cir. 1980).
[43]IRS Private Letter Ruling 8420002.
[44]Rev. Rul. 82-197, 1982-2 C.B. 72; Rev. Rul. 78-181, 1978-1 C.B. 261.

charitable contribution deduction arises at the time of, and for the year in which, the deduction is paid is equally applicable to individual and corporate donors.

However, a corporation that reports its taxable income using the accrual method of accounting may, at its election, deduct contributions paid within 2½ months after the close of its tax year, as long as

- the board of directors of the corporation authorized the making of a charitable contribution during the tax year, and
- the charitable contribution is made after the close of the tax year of the corporation and within the 2½ month period.[45]

This election must be made at the time the return for the tax year is filed, by reporting the contribution on the return. There must be attached to the return when filed a written declaration that the resolution authorizing the contribution was adopted by the board of directors during the tax year involved and the declaration must be verified by a statement signed by an officer authorized to sign the return that it is made under penalties of perjury. There must also be attached to the return when filed a copy of the resolution of the board of directors authorizing the contribution.[46]

To satisfy this rule, contributions of property need not be segregated by year and there is no requirement that the donees be identified at the time the resolution is adopted.[47]

[45]IRC § 170(a)(2); Reg. § 1.170A 11(b). Illustrations of this rule appear in IRS Private Letter Rulings 8618051 and 7802001.
[46]Reg. § 1.170A-11(b)(2). In *Chase v. Commissioner*, 19 T.C.M. 234 (1960), and *Wood-Mosaic Company v. United States*, 160 F. Supp. 63 (W.D. Ky. 1958), charitable deductions were denied because there was no evidence that the corporations authorized the contributions during the tax years involved.
[47]IRS Private Letter Ruling 7802001.

Part III

Charitable Giving in General

6

Gifts of Money and Property

The purpose of this chapter is to summarize the federal tax law concerning the determination of the income tax charitable deduction for contributions of money or property, where the donor is not retaining or creating any interest in the item being transferred. The calculation of this deduction must be made under these rules before application of the general percentage limitations, which are the subject of Chapter 7. Contributions of money or property, where the donor is creating an interest in the item being transferred, are the subject of Part IV.

§ 6.1 GIFTS OF MONEY

An individual or corporation may make a contribution of money — usually United States currency—to a charitable organization. This deduction is based on the amount of funds being transferred.

Example 6.1

X, an individual, makes a contribution of $1,000 to a charitable organization during calendar year 1994. Consequently, X has a federal income tax charitable contribution deduction based on the $1,000 for that year.

A gift of money in the form of currency of a country other than the United States (such as a contribution of a coin collection) may be treated as a gift of property.

When a contribution is made in the form of money, there is not a problem of valuation, as there can be in connection with contributions of property. Gifts of money, nonetheless, are subject to the substantiation requirements.[1]

§ 6.2   GIFTS OF PROPERTY—GENERAL CONSIDERATIONS

The law of charitable giving becomes far more complex in the case of a donor who makes a contribution of property, rather than a contribution of money.

At the outset, a determination must be made as to the value of the property.[2] This value is known as the "fair market value" of the property. The process of valuing property for these purposes is discussed in Chapter 10 § 1.

In many instances, the federal income tax charitable contribution deduction for contributions of property is based upon the fair market value of that property. However, there may be instances where that value must be reduced for purposes of computing the charitable deduction. Generally, when this reduction in the deduction is required, the amount that is deductible is the amount equal to the donor's basis in the property. The deduction reduction rules are discussed below.[3]

Since the deduction for a gift of property is often based on the fair market value of the property, a donor can be benefitted where the property has increased in value since the date on which the donor acquired the property. The property is said to have "appreciated" in value, and property in this circumstance is known as "appreciated property." Where certain requirements are satisfied, a donor is entitled to a charitable deduction based on the full fair market value of the property.

This rule—allowance of the charitable deduction based on full value of an item of property—is one of the rules in the tax law that is most beneficial to donors. This is particularly the case when it is considered that the donor in this circumstance is not required to recognize any gain on the transfer.[4] The gain is the amount that

---

[1]See Chapter 23.

[2]Reg. § 1.170A-1(c)(1).

[3]An exception is the rule concerning corporate gifts of inventory, where the charitable deduction may be as much as twice basis (see Chapter 9 § 4).

[4]E.g., *Campbell* v. *Prothro*, 209 F.2d 331 (5th Cir. 1954); *White* v. *Brodrick*, 104 F. Supp. 213 (D. Kan. 1952). The IRS agrees with this conclusion. E.g.,

would have been recognized had the donor sold the property; it is sometimes referred to as the "appreciation element."

The ability of a donor to have a charitable deduction based upon the fair market value of the property and not recognize gain on the appreciation element in the property is viewed by some as an unwarranted benefit to donors and a violation of tax policy. Indeed, in some instances, recognition of gain is required.[5] Moreover, the rule applying the alternative minimum tax in this setting is designed, in part, to counteract this benefit. (This alternative minimum tax rule is discussed in Chapter 10 § 6. In essence, it requires the appreciation element in a gift of appreciated property to be treated as an item of tax preference for purposes of computing the alternative minimum tax; the charitable deduction is thus confined to an amount equal to the basis in the property.)

Likewise, a loss is not recognized when an item of property is contributed to a charity. In this circumstance, the donor should sell the property, experience the loss, and contribute the sales proceeds to charity. (By contrast, the donor of appreciated property is usually best advised to contribute the property to a charitable organization, rather than sell the property and donate the after-tax proceeds to the charity.)

The ability of a donor to have a charitable deduction, for a contribution of property, based upon the fair market value of the property is dependent upon several factors. Chief among these are the following:

- the nature of the property contributed,
- the tax classification of the charitable donee, and
- the use to which the charitable donee puts the property.

As to the first of these factors, the federal tax law categorizes items of property as follows:

Rev. Rul. 55-531, 1955-2 C.B. 520; Rev. Rul. 55-275, 1955-1 C.B. 295; and Rev. Rul. 55-138, 1955-1 C.B. 223, modified by Rev. Rul. 68-69, 1968-1 C.B. 80.

[5]The most common example of this is the rule in connection with bargain sales (see Chapter 9 § 5). Another instance would be gifts of property that is subject to debt (see Chapter 9 § 3).

- long-term capital gain property,
- short-term capital gain property, and
- ordinary income property.

(These terms are discussed and defined in Chapter 2.)

As to the second of these factors, the federal tax law classifies entities as to which deductible charitable contributions can be made as follows:

- public charitable organizations,
- private foundations,
- governmental bodies, and
- other types of tax-exempt organizations (such as veterans' organizations).

(These terms are discussed and defined in Chapter 4 § 3.)

As to the third of these factors, the federal tax law divides the use to which a charitable organization puts donated property as follows:

- a use that is related to the donee organization's tax-exempt purpose ("related use"), or
- a use that is not related to the donee organization's tax-exempt purpose ("unrelated use").

The rules concerning unrelated business activities are summarized in Chapter 4 § 4.

The extent to which a contribution of property is deductible for federal income tax purposes is dependent upon the interplay of these three factors, plus:

- the value of the property (see Chapter 10 § 1),
- the percentage limitations (see Chapter 7), and
- compliance with the substantiation rules (see Chapter 23).

§ 6.3 GIFTS OF LONG-TERM CAPITAL GAIN PROPERTY—GENERAL CONSIDERATIONS

Where a donor makes a contribution of "long-term capital gain property" to a public charitable organization, the charitable deduction is generally based on the full fair market value of the property. There generally is no need for the donor to recognize the capital gain element. This rule is also generally applicable where the donee is a governmental entity.

The rule is not applicable where the donee is a charitable organization other than a public charitable organization. In that instance, the charitable deduction is confined to the basis of the donor in the property.[6]

§ 6.4   GIFTS OF ORDINARY INCOME PROPERTY

The federal tax law places limitations on the deductibility of property which, if sold, would give rise to gain that is not long-term capital gain. This type of property, which is termed "ordinary income property," includes "short-term capital gain property."

Federal tax law provides a rule requiring the modification of what would otherwise be the charitable deduction for a contribution of property that is ordinary income property.

(a)   "Ordinary Income Property" Defined

The categories of property for charitable giving purposes are discussed elsewhere.[7] Recall, however, that ordinary income property is property that has appreciated in value, any portion of the gain on which would give rise to ordinary income (or short-term capital gain) if the property had been sold by the donor at its fair market value at the time of the charitable gift. Ordinary income is income that is not long-term capital gain. For these purposes, ordinary income and short-term capital gain are regarded as the same.

Thus, ordinary income property is property that, if sold at its fair market value by the donor at the time of its contribution to a charitable organization, would generate a gain that is not long-term capital gain.[8]

Examples of ordinary income property are

- property held by the donor primarily for sale to customers in the ordinary course of a trade or business (inventory[9]);

[6]See § 5, *infra.*
[7]See Chapter 2.
[8]Reg. § 1.170A-4(b)(1).
[9]See Chapters 2 and 9 § 4.

- a capital asset held for a period of time that is less than the period required to cause the property to become long-term capital gain property (short-term capital gain property);
- a work of art created by the donor;
- a manuscript created by the donor;
- letters and memoranda prepared by or for the donor;
- stock acquired in a non-taxable transaction which, if sold, would generate ordinary income;[10]
- stock in a so-called "collapsible corporation" which, if sold, would generate ordinary income;[11]
- stock in certain foreign corporations which, if sold, would generate ordinary income.[12] and
- property used in a trade or business,[13] treated as a capital asset, where gain would have been recognized, upon sale of the property by the donor at its fair market value at the time of the contribution, as ordinary income by reason of the application of recapture rules.[14]

The term "ordinary income property" does not include an income interest in respect of which a federal income tax charitable contribution deduction is allowed.[15]

(b) Deduction Reduction Rule

Often, as noted, the rule for the deduction arising from a gift of property to a charitable organization is that the amount of the deduction is equal to the amount of the fair market value of the property at the time of the gift.[16] However, in the case of a charitable gift of

---

[10]This is stock that is described in IRC § 306(a). This type of stock is known as "section 306 stock." The IRS applied this deduction reduction rule in the case of a charitable gift of section 306 stock in Private Letter Ruling 8930001.

[11]IRC § 341.

[12]IRC § 1248.

[13]IRC § 1231(b).

[14]IRC § 170(e)(1), last sentence; Reg. § 1.170A-4(c)(4). The recapture rules are the subject of IRC §§ 617(d)(1), 1245(a), 1250(a), 1252(a), and 1254(a).

[15]Reg. § 1.170A-4(b)(1). See Chapter 16.

[16]IRC § 170(a).

ordinary income property, the amount of the charitable contribution for the gift of the property must be reduced by the amount of gain which would have been recognized as gain which is not long-term capital gain if the property had been sold by the donor at its fair market value, determined at the time of the contribution to the charitable organization.[17] The amount of gain that is taken into account in making this reduction is sometimes termed the "ordinary income element."

Consequently, this deduction reduction rule basically means that a donor's deduction for a contribution of an item of ordinary income property to a charitable organization is confined to the donor's basis in the property. The amount that is deductible is the fair market value of the property, reduced by the amount that is equal to the ordinary income element.

This rule applies

- irrespective of whether the donor is an individual or a corporation;
- irrespective of the tax classification of the charitable organization that is the donee (for example, public or private charity);
- irrespective of whether the charitable contribution is made "to" or "for the use of" a charitable organization;[18] and
- to a gift of ordinary income property prior to application of the appropriate percentage limitation(s).[19]

Example 6.2

A is an individual. On June 15, 1994, A contributed to a charitable organization shares of stock having a fair market value of $5,000. A acquired the stock on March 1, 1994, for the purchase price of $3,000. A's charitable deduction, computed to the extent of this deduction reduction rule, was $3,000. The amount of this deduction was equal to A's basis in the stock. More technically, A was required to reduce the potential charitable deduction ($5,000) by the ordinary income element ($2,000). This result was required because A did not hold the stock long enough for the shares to become long-term capital gain property rather than short-term capital gain property.

---

[17] IRC § 170(e)(1)(A); Reg. § 1.170A-4(a)(1).
[18] See Chapter 11 § 2.
[19] As to the latter of these three points, see Chapter 5.

Example 6.3

B is an individual. B contributed, to a charitable organization, intangible property to which certain recapture rules[20] apply. The property had a fair market value of $60,000 and an adjusted basis of $10,000. If the property had been sold by B at its fair market value at the time of the contribution, $20,000 of the gain of $50,000 ($60,000 − $10,000) would have been treated as ordinary income (because of the recapture rule) and the remainder ($30,000) would have been long-term capital gain. B's contribution of $60,000 had to be reduced by $20,000.[21]

Example 6.4

C is a corporation, in the business of selling appliances. C contributed certain appliances, having a fair market value of $25,000, to a charitable organization in 1994. C acquired these appliances in 1993 for $15,000. C's charitable deduction, computed to the extent of this deduction reduction rule, was $15,000. (If C had donated these appliances for the benefit of the ill or the needy, or infants, a greater charitable contribution deduction may have been available.)[22]

(c) Special Rules of Inapplicability

This deduction reduction rule does not apply to reduce the amount of the charitable contribution where, by reason of the transfer of the contributed property, ordinary income or capital gain is recognized by the donor in the same tax year in which the contribution is made.[23] Thus, if recognition of the income or gain occurs in the same tax year in which the contribution is made, this rule is inapplicable where income or gain is recognized upon

- the transfer of an installment obligation to a charitable organization;[24]

[20] IRC § 1245.
[21] Reg. § 1.170A-4(d), Example (2).
[22] See Chapter 9 § 4.
[23] Reg. § 1.170A-4(a), last paragraph.

- the transfer of an obligation issued at a discount to a charitable organization;[25] or
- the assignment of income to a charitable organization.[26]

Also, this deduction rule does not apply to a charitable contribution by a nonresident alien individual or a foreign corporation of property, the sale or other disposition of which within the United States would have resulted in gain that is not effectively connected with the conduct of a trade or business in the United States.[27]

§ 6.5 CERTAIN GIFTS OF CAPITAL GAIN PROPERTY

In general, contributions of long-term capital gain property to public charitable organizations are deductible, with the federal income tax charitable contribution deduction computed on the basis of the fair market value of the property.[28]

However, where contributions are made to a charitable organization that is not a public charitable organization, a deduction reduction rule applies. However, this rule does not apply to

- a private operating foundation;
- a pass-through foundation; or
- a common fund foundation.[29]

(a) Deduction Reduction

This deduction reduction rule states: When a charitable gift of capital gain property is made, the amount of the charitable deduction that

---

[24] IRC § 453(d).

[25] IRC § 454(b).

[26] Reg. § 1.170A-4(a), last paragraph.

[27] Reg. § 1.170A-4(c)(5), last sentence. This type of gain is the subject of IRC §§ 871(a) or 881.

[28] See §§ 2 and 3, *supra*.

[29] IRC § 170(e)(1)(B)(ii), by cross-reference to the three types of private foundations referenced in IRC § 170(b)(1)(E). The law concerning these three entities is discussed in Chapter 4 § 3.

would otherwise be determined must be reduced by the amount of gain which would have been long-term capital gain if the property contributed had been sold by the donor at its fair market value, determined at the time of the contribution, where the gift is to or for the use of a private foundation (with the above three exceptions).[30]

In these circumstances, where the contributed property is capital gain property the charitable deduction that would otherwise be determined must be reduced by the amount of the unrealized appreciation in value. The charitable deduction under these rules is confined to the basis in the property.

Example 6.5

X owned a painting that he purchased for $25,000 and that had a value of $50,000. In X's hands, the property was long-term capital gain property. X contributed this painting to a private nonoperating foundation. X's charitable deduction computed under this rule was $25,000. However, if the painting had been donated to a private operating foundation, the charitable deduction (to the extent of this rule) would have been $50,000.

This rule applies

- irrespective of whether the donor is an individual or a corporation;
- irrespective of whether the charitable contribution is made "to" or "for the use of" a charitable organization;[31] and
- to a gift of property prior to application of the appropriate percentage limitation(s).[32]

An exception to this deduction reduction rule is that it does not apply in the case of a contribution of so-called "qualified appreciated stock."[33] (That is, where this exception is applicable, the charitable deduction for a contribution of stock to a private foundation is based on the fair market value of the stock at the time of the gift.)

Basically, the term "qualified appreciated stock" means any stock

---

[30] IRC § 170(e)(1)(B)(ii); Reg. § 1.170A-4(b)(2)(i).
[31] See Chapter 11 § 2.
[32] As to the latter of these three points, see Chapter 5.
[33] IRC § 170(e)(5)(A).

- for which (as of the date of the contribution) market quotations are readily available on an established securities market, and
- that is capital gain property.[34]

However, the term "qualified appreciated stock" does not include any stock of a corporation contributed by a donor to a private foundation to the extent that the amount of stock contributed (including prior gifts of the stock by the donor) exceeds ten percent (in value) of all of the outstanding stock of the corporation.[35] In making this calculation, an individual must take into account all contributions made by any member of his or her family.[36]

This exception is scheduled to expire so that it does not apply with respect to contributions made after December 31, 1994.[37]

§ 6.6 GIFTS OF PROPERTY FOR UNRELATED USE

Another special rule involving the calculation of the charitable deduction potentially applies when a donor makes a contribution of tangible personal property to a charitable organization.

(a) General Rule

The special rule is this: When a charitable gift of tangible personal property is made, the amount of the charitable deduction that would otherwise be determined must be reduced by the amount of gain which would have been long-term capital gain if the property contributed had been sold by the donor at its fair market value, determined at the time of the contribution, where the use by the donee is unrelated to its tax-exempt purpose.[38] This rule also applies where the donee is a governmental unit, where the use to which the con-

---

[34] IRC § 170(e)(5)(B).

[35] IRC § 170(e)(5)(C)(i).

[36] IRC § 170(e)(5)(C)(ii). The term "member of the family" has the same meaning as that referenced in IRC § 267(c)(2), which is that the "family" of an individual "include[s] only his [or her] brothers and sisters (whether by the whole or half blood), spouse, ancestors, and lineal descendants" (IRC § 267(e)(4)).

[37] IRC § 170(e)(5)(D).

[38] IRC § 170(e)(1)(B)(i); Reg. § 1.170A-4(b)(2)(ii).

tributed property is put is for a purpose other than an exclusively public purpose.[39]

In these circumstances, where the contributed property is capital gain property the charitable deduction that would otherwise be determined must be reduced by the amount of the unrealized appreciation in value.[40]

This rule applies

- irrespective of whether the donor is an individual or a corporation;
- irrespective of the tax classification of the charitable organization that is the donee (for example, public or private charity);
- irrespective of whether the charitable contribution is made "to" or "for the use of" a charitable organization;[41] and
- to a gift of tangible personal property prior to application of the appropriate percentage limitation(s).[42]

Where tangible personal property is put to a related use by the recipient charitable organization, the charitable deduction is based on the fair market value of the property (that is, there is no deduction for the capital gain element).

(b) Unrelated Use

The term "unrelated use" means a use of an item of contributed property

- by a charitable organization which is not related to the purpose or function constituting the basis of the tax exemption for the charitable organization, or
- by a governmental unit which is for a purpose other than an exclusively public purpose.[43]

---

[39] *Id.*

[40] For this purpose, a fixture which is intended to be severed from real property is treated as tangible personal property (Reg. § 1.170A-4(b)(2), last sentence).

[41] See Chapter 11 § 2.

[42] As to the latter of these four points, see Chapter 7.

[43] Reg. § 1.170A-4(b)(3)(i). See Chapter 4 § 4.

Example 6.6

X owned a painting that he purchased for $25,000 and that had a value of $50,000. In X's hands, the property was long-term capital gain property. X contributed this painting to an educational institution, which used the painting for educational purposes by placing it in its library for display and study by art students. Since this use was a related use, X's charitable deduction computed under this rule was $50,000.[44]

If a charitable donee sells an item of tangible personal property donated to it, this deduction reduction rule is triggered, because sale of the property is not a related use of the property. Thus, donors of tangible personal property should exercise caution when contemplating a gift of the property, particularly when the donor knows the property is going to be promptly sold (such as a gift to support an auction).

Example 6.7

This example is based on the facts of Example 6.6. However, instead of the educational uses made of the painting, the educational institution decided to promptly sell the painting, with the proceeds of sale used by the institution for educational purposes, This use of the property was an unrelated use and X's charitable deduction computed under this rule was $25,000 ($50,000 reduced by the long-term capital gain element of $25,000). This is the case even though the proceeds of the sale were put to a related use.

If furnishings contributed to a charitable organization are used by it in its offices and buildings in the course of carrying out its functions, the use of the property is not an unrelated use. If a set or collection of items of tangible personal property is contributed to a charitable organization or governmental unit, the use of the set or collection is not an unrelated use if the donee sells or otherwise disposes of only an insubstantial portion of the set or collection. The use by a trust of tangible personal property contributed to it for the benefit of a charitable organization is an unrelated use if the use by

---

[44] *Id.*

the trust is one which would have been unrelated if made by the charitable organization.[45]

A donor who makes a charitable contribution of tangible personal property to or for the use of a charitable organization or governmental unit may treat the property as not being put to an unrelated use by the donee if

- the donor establishes that the property is not in fact put to an unrelated use by the donee,[46] or
- at the time of the contribution or at the time the contribution is treated as made, it is reasonable to anticipate that the property will not be put to an unrelated use by the donee.[47]

In the case of a contribution of tangible personal property to or for the use of a museum, if the object donated is of a general type normally retained by the museum or other museums for museum purposes, it is considered reasonable for the donor to anticipate, unless the donor has actual knowledge to the contrary, that the object will not be put to an unrelated use by the donee, whether or not the object is later sold or exchanged by the donee.[48]

§ 6.7   VARIATIONS IN APPLYING PROPERTY RULES

The rules contained in this section of the chapter and the previous sections may be illustrated by the following example:

Example 6.8

On July 1, 1994, C, an individual, made the following charitable contributions, all of which were to a public charitable organization, PC, except in the case of stock to a private foundation, PF:

Continued

---

[45]*Id.* The last of these rules is of particular importance in the context of planned giving, where property contributed is often given to a trust, such as a charitable remainder trust (see Chapter 12).

[46]Reg. § 1.170A-4(b)(3)(ii)(a).

[47]Reg. § 1.170A-4(b)(3)(ii)(b).

[48]*Id.*

Example 6.8 Continued

Property	Fair Market Value	Adjusted Basis	Recognized Gain if Sold
Ordinary income property	$50,000	$35,000	$15,000
Property which, if sold, would produce long-term capital gain			
(1) Stock that is a capital asset, contributed to			
(i) PC	25,000	21,000	4,000
(ii) PF	15,000	10,000	5,000
(2) Tangible personal property that is a capital asset, put to unrelated use by PC ...	12,000	6,000	6,000
Total	$102,000	$72,000	$30,000

Example 6.9

After making the necessary reductions required by the above rules, the amount of charitable contributions allowed (before application of the general percentage limitations[49]) was as follows:

Property	Fair Market Value	Reduction	Contribution Allowed
Ordinary income property	$50,000	$15,000	$35,000
Property which, if sold, would produce long-term capital gain			
(1) Stock contributed to			
(i) PC	25,000	-0-	25,000
(ii) PF	15,000	5,000	10,000
(2) Tangible personal property	12,000	6,000	6,000
Total	$102,000	$26,000	$76,000[50]

[49]See Chapter 5.
[50]This example is based on Reg. § 1.170A-4(d), Example (1)(a) and (b).

Example 6.10

This example is based on the facts in Example 6.9, except that C is a corporation. The amount of charitable contributions allowed (before application of the general percentage limitations) would have been as follows:

Property	Fair Market Value	Reduction	Contribution Allowed
Ordinary income property	$50,000	$15,000	$35,000
Property which, if sold, would produce long-term capital gain			
(1) Stock contributed to			
(i) PC	25,000	-0-	25,000
(ii) PF	15,000	5,000	10,000
(2) Tangible personal			
property	12,000	6,000	6,000
Total	$102,000	$26,000	$76,000[51]

---

§ 6.8   THE "STEP TRANSACTION" RULE

Throughout this chapter, the general rule has been that a contribution of appreciated capital gain property to a public charitable organization is deductible on the basis of the fair market value of the property.[52]

However, if the donee charitable organization sells the property soon after the contribution is made, the donor may be placed in the position of having to recognize, for federal income tax purposes, the capital gain element. This can happen where, under the facts and circumstances surrounding the gift, the donee was obligated to sell the gift property to a purchaser that was prearranged by the donor. In this situation, the IRS will attempt to regard the transaction as a

---

[51] This example is based on Reg. § 1.170A-4(d), Example (1)(c).
[52] See § 2, *supra*.

sale of the property by the "donor" to the third-party purchaser and a gift of the sales proceeds to the charitable organization.[53]

This is an application of the so-called "step transaction" doctrine, where two (or more) ostensibly independent transactions (here, the gift and subsequent sale) are consolidated for tax purposes.

§ 6.9 CHARITABLE PLEDGES

The making of a pledge does not give rise to a federal income tax charitable contribution deduction. The deduction that is occasioned, such as it may be, is determined as of the time the pledge is satisfied.[54]

The enforceability of a pledge is a matter of state law. Some states require the existence of consideration as a prerequisite to the existence of an enforceable pledge, while other states will enforce a pledge on broader, social grounds.

[53]E.g., *Martin* v. *Machiz*, 251 F. Supp.381 (D. Md. 1966); and *Magnolia Development Corporation* v. *Commissioner*, 19 T.C.M. 934 (1960).
[54]Rev. Rul. 55-410, 1955-1 C.B. 297.

7

The Percentage Limitations

The deductibility, pursuant to federal income tax law, of a contribution to a charitable organization can be dependent upon several factors.[1] Two of these factors are the following:

- the nature of the item (money[2] or property) that is the subject of the gift, and
- the federal tax law classification of the charitable organization that is the recipient of the gift.

These two elements are manifested in various limitations, expressed as percentages, imposed on both individual and corporate donors.[3]

§ 7.1 INTRODUCTION AND OVERVIEW

One of the elements in determining the extent of deductibility of a charitable gift is the nature of the item contributed. This subject is treated more fully in Chapter 2, but it is noted here that the federal income tax law basically distinguishes between gifts of money and gifts of property. As to the latter, the law differentiates between the following categories of property:

[1] See Chapter 4 § 5.
[2] The term "money" (synonymous with "cash") is used throughout this book to refer to United States currency. If the gift is of currency of another country, it may be treated as "property."
[3] These limitations may operate to prevent a donor from deducting, in any one year, the entirety of the value of a charitable gift. There was once an "unlimited" federal income tax charitable contribution deduction but that has been phased out of the law.

- long-term capital gain property,
- ordinary income property, or
- short-term capital gain property.

These terms describe categories of property on the basis of the tax categorization of the revenue that would result upon sale of the property. For example, "long-term capital gain property" is property that, if sold, would generate long-term capital gain. Because these terms use the word "gain," it is usually understood that these properties have appreciated in value (so-called "appreciated property") and thus would produce a gain upon their sale. Long-term capital gain property is often referred to as "capital gain property" and that is the case throughout this text.[4]

For these purposes, contributions of ordinary income property and short-term capital gain property are generally treated, for charitable deduction purposes, the same as gifts of money. Thus, the tax rules that reference the deductibility of gifts of "money" are generally also applicable to gifts of property that, if sold, would give rise to ordinary income or to short-term capital gain.

The other of these two elements is the federal tax law classification of the charitable donee. (This factor is applicable only in the case of giving by individuals.) That is, the law in this context basically differentiates between gifts to public charitable organizations and gifts to private foundations and certain other tax-exempt organizations. Although this subject is discussed in Chapter 4, it is appropriate to note that the term "public charitable organization" is used to refer to a charitable organization[5] that is not a private foundation. The principal types of public charitable organizations are churches, schools, colleges, universities, hospitals, a variety of publicly supported charitable organizations, and supporting organizations.

The deductibility of gifts by individuals involves several sets, and sometimes combinations, of percentage limitations. The percentages that are applicable to individuals are applied to an individual donor's "contribution base."[6]

The essence of this chapter is the following:

---

[4]The federal income tax regulations utilize the term "30-percent capital gain property" (Reg. § 1.170A-8(d)(3)).

[5]That is, an organization that is tax-exempt under IRC § 501(a) by reason of being described in IRC § 501(c)(3).

[6]See § 2, *infra*.

- An individual's contribution base essentially is the same as his or her adjusted gross income.[7]

- An individual's federal income tax charitable contribution deduction for a tax year is subject to limitations of 50, 30, and/or 20 percent of the individual's contribution base.

- The maximum federal income tax charitable contribution deduction for a tax year for an individual is 50 percent of his or her contribution base.

- An individual's federal income tax charitable contribution deduction for a tax year cannot exceed an amount equal to 50 percent of his or her contribution base where the gift (or gifts) is of money (and/or ordinary income property and/or short-term capital gain property) and the charitable recipient is a public charitable organization.

- In general, an individual's federal income tax charitable contribution deduction for a tax year cannot exceed an amount equal to 30 percent of his or her contribution base where the gift is of capital gain property that has appreciated in value and the charitable recipient is a public charitable organization

- An individual donor *can* elect to have a 50 percent limitation apply, where the gift is of capital gain property that has appreciated in value and the charitable recipient is a public charitable organization, by reducing the deduction by the amount of the appreciation element.

- An individual's federal income tax charitable contribution deduction for a tax year cannot exceed an amount equal to 30 percent of his or her contribution base where the gift (or gifts) is of money and the charitable recipient is an entity other than a public charitable organization.

- An individual's federal income tax charitable contribution deduction for a tax year cannot exceed an amount equal to 20 percent of his or her contribution base where the gift is of capital gain property that has appreciated in value and the charitable recipient is an entity other than a public charitable organization.

- These limitations are blended where the individual donor contributes more than one type of item (money or property) in a

---

[7]The concept of "adjusted gross income" is discussed in Chapter 2.

tax year and/or gives to more than one type of charitable organization in a tax year.

- Each of these percentage limitations rules allows for contributions in excess of the limitations to be carried forward and deducted over the subsequent five years, in order of time.
- If a husband and wife file a joint return, the deduction for charitable contributions is the aggregate of the contributions made by the spouses and the percentage limitations are based on the aggregate contribution base of the spouses.
- The charitable contribution deduction for a corporation for a tax year is subject to a limitation of 10 percent of the corporation's pre-tax net income.
- There are no percentage limitations applicable in the estate tax or gift tax charitable contribution deduction context.[8]

There are two other limitation rules that are the subject of Chapter 6 but warrant mention at this point so that they can be correlated with the information in this chapter.

- Where an individual makes a contribution of an item of tangible personal property, that has appreciated in value, to a public charitable organization, where the public charity does not use the property for a purpose that is related to its tax-exempt purposes,[9] the donor must reduce the deduction by the entirety of the capital gain element.
- Where an individual makes a contribution of an item of appreciated property to a charitable organization that is not a public charitable organization, the donor must reduce the deduction by all of the capital gain element.

§ 7.2   INDIVIDUAL'S "CONTRIBUTION BASE" AND CORPORATION'S "TAXABLE INCOME"

The percentage limitations used in ascertaining the deductibility of charitable gifts are applied, in the case of individuals, to an amount equal to the donor's "contribution base."[10] The term "contribution

[8]See Chapter 8.
[9]See Chapter 4 § 4.
[10]IRC § 170(b)(1)(F).

base" means the individual's adjusted gross income,[11] computed without regard to any net operating loss carryback[12] to the tax year.[13] For most individuals, the amounts comprising the contribution base and adjusted gross income are the same.

The concept of a contribution base is not applicable with respect to contributions by corporations. Rather, the percentage limitation is applicable to a corporation's "taxable income." However, this taxable income is determined without regard to the charitable deduction rules, rules providing special deductions for corporations[14] any net operating loss carryback to the tax year,[15] and any capital loss carryback to the tax year.[16]

§ 7.3   THE PERCENTAGE LIMITATIONS: AN OVERVIEW

Because of the intricacies of these percentage limitation rules, an overview of them is appropriate. Each of these rules are discussed fully in subsequent sections of this chapter.

(a)   General Rules

An individual's federal income tax charitable contribution deduction for a tax year is subject to limitations of 50, 30, and/or 20 percent of the individual's contribution base.[17] The limitation or limitations that are applicable depend upon the tax classification of the charitable organization that is the donee and the nature of the item (money or property) that is contributed. However, irrespective of the combination of charities and gifts, an individual's income tax charitable deduction for a tax year cannot exceed an amount equal to 50 percent of his or her contribution base. If a husband and wife file a joint return, the deduction for charitable contributions is the aggregate of the contributions made by the spouses and the percentage limitations are based on the aggregate contribution of the spouses.[18]

---

[11] IRC § 62. See Chapter 2.
[12] IRC § 172.
[13] Reg. § 1.170A-8(e).
[14] IRC §§ 241-247, 249-250.
[15] IRC § 172.
[16] IRC § 1212(a)(1).
[17] Reg. § 1.170A-8(a)(1).
[18] Reg. § 1.170A-8(a)(1). See § 15, *infra*.

The percentage limitation (or limitations) that is applicable will depend, in part, on whether the charitable recipient is "public" or "private," as discussed in Chapter 4.

Contributions of money to public charitable organizations, in a tax year, are deductible in an amount not in excess of 50 percent of the individual donor's contribution base for that year.[19] The 50 percent limitation is also applicable with respect to gifts of tangible personal property that have been reduced by the capital gain element because the property was put to an unrelated use by the donee charitable organization.[20]

There is a 30 percent limitation, which is applicable where the contribution (or contributions) is to one or more public charitable organizations and the gift or gifts is of capital gain property.[21] This rule is applicable with respect to gifts that do not have to be reduced by the amount of the appreciation element inherent in the property.[22] Where a special election is made, contributions of capital gain property may be subject to the 50 percent limitation rather than the 30 percent limitation.[23]

In general, contributions of money to private foundations (and/or certain other donees, such as veterans' organizations and fraternal organizations), in a tax year, are deductible in an amount not in excess of 30 percent of the individual donor's contribution base for that year.[24] However, if it is lesser, the limitation is an amount equal to the excess of 50 percent of the donor's contribution base for the year over the amount of charitable contributions that are allowable under the 50 percent limitation.[25]

Contributions of capital gain property to private foundations and certain other donee organizations are usually subject to a 20 percent limitation.[26]

[19] IRC § 170(b)(1)(A); Reg. § 1.170A-8(b). See § 4, *infra.*
[20] IRC § 170(b)(1)(C)(i).
[21] *Id.* See § 5, *infra.*
[22] See Chapter 6.
[23] IRC § 170(b)(1)(C)(iii). See § 6, *infra.*
[24] IRC § 170(b)(1)(B)(i). See § 7, *infra.*
[25] IRC § 170(b)(1)(B)(ii).
[26] IRC § 170(b)(1)(D)(i). See § 11, *infra.*

(b) Carryover Rules

Donors of gifts that exceed the applicable percentage limitation or limitations are entitled to carry the excess amounts forward, for purposes of deduction over the succeeding five years, in order of time. The carryover rules apply to

- individuals, in relation to the 50 percent limitation,[27]
- individuals, in relation to the 30 percent limitation, concerning gifts of capital gain property,[28]
- individuals, in relation to the general 30 percent limitation,[29]
- individuals, in relation to the 20 percent limitation,[30] and
- corporations.[31]

The carryover rules apply with respect to contributions made during a tax year in excess of the applicable percentage limitation even though the donor elects to utilize the standard deduction[32] for that year instead of itemizing the deductions allowable in computing taxable income for that year.[33]

The carryover provisions do not apply to contributions made out of an estate. The provisions do not apply to a trust unless it is a private foundation which is allowed[34] a charitable deduction subject to the provisions applicable to individuals.[35]

§ 7.4 THE 50 PERCENT LIMITATION

(a) General Rules

The maximum federal income tax charitable contribution deduction for a tax year for an individual is 50 percent of the individual's contribution base.

---

[27] IRC § 170(d)(1).
[28] IRC § 170(b)(1)(C)(ii).
[29] IRC § 170(b)(1)(B), last sentence.
[30] IRC § 170(b)(1)(D)(ii).
[31] IRC § 170(d)(2).
[32] See Chapter 2.
[33] Reg. § 1.170A-10(a)(2).
[34] Reg. § 1.642(c)-4.
[35] Reg. § 1.170A-10(a)(3).

An individual's charitable contributions made during a tax year to one or more public charitable organizations, where the subject of the gift is money, are deductible to the extent that the contributions in the aggregate do not exceed 50 percent of the individual's contribution base for the tax year.[36] Under the tax rules concerning charitable giving, a tax year in which a gift is made is termed a "contribution year."[37]

This limitation is applicable with respect to gifts to public and publicly supported charitable organizations, private operating foundations, governmental units, and certain special types of foundations.[38]

A contribution to a charitable organization that is not a public charitable organization does not qualify for the 50 percent limitation, notwithstanding the fact that the organization makes the contribution available to a public charitable organization.[39]

These rules are illustrated by the following two examples (in these, and in all other examples concerning individuals in this chapter, the individual donor (or donors) reports his or her income to the IRS on a calendar year basis).

Example 7.1

A had, for 1994, a contribution base of $100,000. During 1994, she made charitable contributions of money to a church, a university, and a hospital (each of which is a public charitable organization), totaling $45,000, and made no other charitable gifts in 1994. A was allowed a federal income tax charitable contribution deduction for 1994 for the $45,000. (Her maximum allowable deductible giving for 1994 was $50,000, that is, 50% of $100,000.)

Example 7.2

H and W (husband and wife) had, for 1994, a contribution base of $150,000. During 1994, H made charitable contributions of money to a hospital, totalling $30,000; during that contribution year, W made charitable contributions of money to a school, totalling $40,000. Nei-

Continued

---

[36] IRC § 170(b)(1)(A); Reg. § 1.170A-8(b).
[37] E.g., Reg. § 1.170A-8(d)(2)(ii).
[38] IRC § 170(c)(1), (2). See Chapter 4 § 3.
[39] Reg. § 1.170A-8(b).

Example 7.2 Continued

ther *H* nor *W* made any other charitable gifts in 1994. Filing jointly, *H* and *W* were able to properly claim a charitable contribution deduction of $70,000 for 1994. (Their maximum allowable deductible charitable giving for 1994 was $75,000, that is, 50% of $150,000.)

As discussed elsewhere,[40] where an individual makes a contribution of an item of tangible personal property, that has appreciated in value, to a public charitable organization, where the public charity does not use the property for a purpose that is related to its tax-exempt purposes, the donor must reduce the deduction by all of the capital gain element.[41] (The "capital gain element" is the portion of the proceeds, had the property been sold, that would have been long-term capital gain.) Once the (potentially) deductible amount is determined under this rule, the amount is then subjected, for purposes of determining the actual charitable contribution deduction, to the 50 percent limitation.[42]

Also, as discussed below,[43] there is a special rule whereby the charitable contribution deduction for a gift of capital gain property is subject to the 50 percent limitation rather than a 30 percent limitation (to which the deduction for gifts of that type of property are generally subject).

There are, then, five instances in which a charitable contribution deduction may be limited by the 50 percent limitation:

- gifts of money,
- gifts of ordinary income property (property the sale of which would produce ordinary income),
- gifts of short-term capital gain property (property the sale of which would produce short-term capital gain),
- gifts of capital gain property where the charitable deduction was reduced by the amount of the capital gain element because the charitable donee put the property to an unrelated use,[44] and

---

[40] See Chapter 6 § 6.
[41] IRC § 170(e)(1)(B)(i).
[42] IRC § 170(b)(1)(C)(i).
[43] See § 6, *infra.*
[44] See Chapter 4 § 4.

- gifts of capital gain property where a special election is made.

(b) Carryover Rules

In general, the excess of

The amount of the charitable contribution or contributions of money made by an individual in a contribution year to one or more public charitable organizations,

divided by

50 percent of his or her contribution base for the contribution year,

is treated as a charitable contribution paid by him or her to a public charitable organization, subject to the 50 percent limitation, in each of the five tax years immediately succeeding the contribution year in order of time.[45] Thus, for federal income tax purposes, an amount paid to a charitable organization in one year is, when the carryover rules are applied, treated as "paid" to a charitable organization in a subsequent year.

These rules may be illustrated by the following two examples:

Example 7.3

The facts are the same as in Example 7.1, except that A made charitable contributions of money to public charitable organizations totaling $55,000. She was allowed a charitable contribution deduction for 1994 of $50,000 (50% of $100,000) and the balance of $5,000 was carried forward, to be used in the subsequent five years, beginning in 1995.

Example 7.4

H and W had a contribution base for 1994 of $50,000 and for 1995 of $40,000, and filed a joint tax return for both years. In 1994, H and W made a charitable contribution of money in the amount of $27,000

Continued

---

[45]IRC § 170(d)(1); Reg. § 1.170A-10(b)(1).

Example 7.4 Continued

to PC (a public charitable organization). In 1995, they made a charitable contribution in money of $15,000 to PC. They were able to prop-
erly claim a charitable contribution deduction of $25,000 in 1994
(50% of $50,000) and the excess of $2,000 ($27,000 − $25,000) constituted a charitable contribution carryover which was subsequently
treated by them as a charitable contribution paid by them to a public
charitable organization in each of the five succeeding tax years in
order of time. Since 50 percent of their contribution base for 1995
($20,000) exceeded the charitable contribution of $15,000 made by
them in 1995 to PC (computed without regard to the carryover rules),
the 1994 carryover amount of $2,000 was treated as paid to a public
charitable organization in 1995. Thus, H and W had a $17,000 federal
income tax charitable contribution deduction for 1995.

In applying these rules, the amount of the excess contributions
which are to be treated as paid in any one of the five tax years
immediately succeeding the contribution year to a public charitable
organization may not exceed the lesser of the following three
amounts:

- The amount by which 50 percent of the donor's contribution
  base for the succeeding tax year involved exceeds the sum of
  - The charitable contributions actually made (computed with-
    out regard to the carryover rules) by the donor in the year
    to public charitable organizations, and
  - The charitable contributions, other than contributions of
    capital gain property to which the 30 percent limitation
    applies,[46] made to public charitable organizations in years
    preceding the contribution year which, pursuant to the carry-
    over rules, are treated as having been paid to a public
    charitable organization in the succeeding tax year involved.
- In the case of the first tax year succeeding the contribution
  year, the amount of the excess charitable contribution in the
  contribution year.
- In the case of the second, third, fourth, and fifth tax years
  succeeding the contribution year, the portion of the excess
  charitable contribution in the contribution year which has not

[46]See § 5, *infra.*

been treated as paid to a public charitable organization in a year intervening between the contribution year and the succeeding year involved.

If a donor, in any one of the five tax years succeeding a contribution year, elects to utilize the standard deduction instead of itemizing deductions allowable in computing taxable income, there must be treated as paid (but not allowable as a deduction) for the year of the election the lesser of these three amounts.[47] This rule applies because the standard deduction is deemed to include the charitable contribution deduction (for the taxpayer who does not itemize his or her tax deductions); absent this rule, a taxpayer would, in effect, receive a double deduction for a charitable contribution.

These rules may be illustrated by the following three examples, which show, on a more technical basis, how these rules operate.

Example 7.5

B had a contribution base for 1994 of $20,000 and for 1995 of $30,000. In 1994, B contributed $12,000 in money to PC, a public charitable organization; in 1995, B contributed $13,500 in money to PC. B was able to properly claim a charitable contribution deduction of $10,000 (50% of $20,000) for 1994 and the excess of $2,000 ($12,000 − $10,000) constituted a charitable contribution carryover which was treated as a charitable contribution paid by B to a public charitable organization in the five tax years immediately succeeding 1994 in order of time. B was able to claim a charitable contribution deduction of $15,000 (50% of $30,000) in 1995. This $15,000 consisted of the $13,500 contribution to PC in 1995 and $1,500 of the $2,000 carried over from 1994. The $15,000 contribution treated as paid in 1995 was computed as follows:

1994 excess contributions $2,000

50% of B's contribution base for 1995 .... $15,000

Less:
Contributions actually made in
1995 to a public charitable
organization $13,500

Continued

---

[47] Reg. § 1.170A-10(b)(2).

Example 7.5 Continued

Contributions made to public
charitable organizations in years
prior to 1994 treated as having
been paid in 1995   0

$13,500

Balance $1,500

Amount of 1994 excess charitable gift treated as paid in 1995: the lesser of $2,000 (1994 excess contributions) or $1,500 (excess of 50% of contribution base for 1995 ($15,000) over the sum of the contributions to a public charitable organization actually made in 1995 ($13,500) and the contributions to public charitable organizations made in years prior to 1994 treated as having been paid in 1995 ($0), which is $13,500). Thus, $1,500 of the contribution made by B in 1994 is treated, for tax purposes, as having been paid in 1995. The remaining $500 was carried forward for possible use in 1996, depending upon B's other tax circumstances.

If the excess contributions made by B in 1994 had been $1,000 instead of $2,000, the amount of the 1994 excess contributions treated as paid in 1995 would have been $1,000 rather than $1,500. In this situation, there would not be any carryover for 1996.[48]

Example 7.6

This example is based on the facts of Example 7.5. B had a contribution base for 1995 of $10,000 and for 1996 of $20,000. With respect to 1995, B elected to not itemize his deductions and to utilize the standard deduction in computing his taxable income. B's contributions to public charitable organizations in 1995 were $300 in money. With respect to 1996, B itemized his deductions, which included a $5,000 contribution of money to C. B's deductions for 1995 were not increased by reason of the $500 available as a charitable contribution carryover from 1993 (excess contributions made in 1993 of $2,000, less the amount of the excess treated as paid in 1994 of $1,500), inasmuch as B elected to use the standard deduction in 1995. How-

Continued

---

[48]Reg. § 1.170A-10(b)(2), Example (1).

Example 7.6 Continued

ever, for purposes of determining the amount of the excess charitable contributions made in 1993 which was available as a carryover to 1996, B was required to treat the $500 as a charitable contribution paid in 1995—the lesser of $500 or $4,700 (50% of contribution base of $5,000 over contributions actually made in 1995 to public charitable organizations of $300). Therefore, even though the $5,000 contribution by B in 1996 to C did not amount to 50 percent of B's contribution base for 1996 (50% of $20,000), B was able to claim a charitable contribution deduction of only the $5,000 actually paid in 1996, since the entire excess charitable contribution made in 1993 ($2,000) was treated as paid in 1994 ($1,500) and in 1995 ($500).[49]

Example 7.7

The following facts apply with respect to D who itemized her deductions in computing taxable income for each of the following years:

	1993	1994	1995	1996	1997
Contribution base	$10,000	$7,000	$15,000	$10,000	$9,000
Contributions of cash to public charitable organzations (no other contributions)	6,000	4,400	8,000	3,000	1,500
Allowable charitable contribution deductions (computed without regard to carryover of contributions)	5,000	3,500	7,500	5,000	4,500
Excess contributions for tax year to be treated as paid in five succeeding tax years ...	1,000	900	500	0	0

Since D's contributions in 1996 and 1997 to public charitable organizations were less than 50 percent of her contribution base for those years, the excess contributions for 1993, 1994, and 1995 were treated as having been paid to public charitable organizations in 1996 and 1997 as follows:

Continued

---

[49] Reg. § 1.170A-10(b)(2), Example (2).

Example 7.7 Continued

1996

Contribution year	Total Excess	Less: Amount treated as paid in year prior to 1966	Available charitable contributions carryovers
1993	$1,000	0	$1,000
1994	900	0	900
1995	500	0	500
Total			$2,400

50 percent of D's contribution base for 1996 . . . . $5,000

Less: Charitable contributions made in 1996 to public
    charitable organizations 3,000
                         $2,000

Amount of excess contributions treated as paid in 1996—lesser of $2,400 (available carryovers to 1996) or $2,000 (excess of 50% of contribution base ($5,000) over contributions actually made in 1996 to public charitable organizations ($3,000) $2,000

1997

Contribution year	Total Excess	Less: Amount treated as paid in year prior to 1966	Available charitable contributions carryovers
1993	$1,000	$1,000	0
1994	900	900	0
1995	500	100	$ 400
1996	0	0	0
Total			$ 400

50 percent of D's contribution base for 1997 . . . . $4,500

Less: Charitable contributions made in 1997 to public
    charitable organizations 1,500
                         $3,000

Amount of excess contributions treated as paid in 1997—lesser of $400 (available carryovers to 1997) or $3,000 (excess of 50% of contribution base ($5,500) over contributions actually made in 1997 to public charitable organizations ($1,500) . . . . $ 400[50]

---

[50] Reg. § 1.170A-10(b)(2), Example (3).

§ 7.5   THE 30 PERCENT LIMITATION FOR GIFTS OF CERTAIN PROPERTY

(a)   General Rules

A 30 percent limitation applies with respect to charitable contributions of certain property that has appreciated in value since the time of the acquisition of the property by the donor, where the recipient is a public charitable organization.[51] Thus, even though the donee is a public charitable organization, the percentage limitation in this context is 30 percent, not 50 percent.[52]

To be subjected to treatment under this 30 percent limitation, an item of property must satisfy three requirements:

- The property must be a capital asset.[53]
- If the property were sold by the donor at its fair market value at the time of the contribution, the sale would result in the recognition of gain, all or any portion of which would be long-term capital gain.
- The circumstances are not such that the amount of the contribution need be reduced by the appreciation element inherent in the capital gain property.[54]

Property that qualifies for this 30 percent limitation is, as noted, referred to throughout this text as "capital gain property."[55]

The fair market value of an item of capital gain property is used in calculating the value of the deduction, although the actual deduction for a contribution year may be less as the result of this (or other) limitation.

In general, then, an individual may deduct charitable contribu-

---

[51] IRC § 170(b)(1)(C)(i); Reg. § 1.170A-8(d)(1).
[52] As noted (see the text accompanying n. 42, *supra*), this 30 percent limitation does not apply with respect to gifts of certain tangible personal property.
[53] See Chapter 2. A property that is used in a trade or business (IRC § 1231(b)) is treated as a capital asset.
[54] See Chapter 6 §§ 5, 6.
[55] IRC § 170(b)(1)(C)(iv); Reg. § 1.170A-8(d)(3).

tions of capital gain property made during a tax year to any public charitable organization to the extent that the contributions in the aggregate do not exceed 30 percent of the donor's contribution base.[56]

Example 7.8

This example may be compared to Example 7.1. A had, for 1994, a contribution base of $100,000. During 1994, she made charitable contributions using securities that had appreciated in value, to $45,000, since she acquired them (and were capital gain property), to a church, a university, and a hospital (each of which is a public charitable organization). A was allowed a federal income tax charitable contribution deduction for 1994 of $30,000 (30% of $100,000), rather than $45,000 (A's deduction in Example 7.1).

However, the full 30 percent limitation may not always apply; the allowable amount for a contribution year may be less. This is because contributions of money to public charitable organizations, and their percentage limitations, have to be taken into account first.[57] In this process, the value of the capital gain property contributed to public charitable organizations that must be used is the full fair market value, not the amount limited by the 30 percent rule.[58]

The federal income tax law thus establishes an order of priority, as between categories of gifts to public charitable organizations, which can determine the deductibility of charitable gifts. The federal income tax law favors giving of money to public charitable organizations, rather than the giving of property to these charitable organizations. Therefore, when computing current or carried-forward charitable deductions, contributions of money to public charitable organizations are, as noted, considered first.

This rule is illustrated by the following example:

---

[56] IRC § 170(b)(1)(C)(i); Reg. § 1.170A-8(d)(1).
[57] *Id.* One category of gifts that is not considered in this regard is contributions of capital gain property to charitable organizations that are not public charitable organizations (see § 11, *infra*).
[58] IRC § 170(b)(1)(B)(ii); Reg. § 1.170A-8(c)(2)(ii).

Example 7.9

C, an individual, had a contribution base for 1994 of $100,000. During that year, C made a gift of capital gain property to PC, a public charitable organization, in the amount of $10,000. During that year, C also contributed $45,000 in money to PC. C's federal income tax charitable contribution deduction for 1994 was $50,000 (50% of $100,000), consisting of the $45,000 of money and $5,000 of the gift of property. Thus, even though the value of the capital gain property, taken alone, was less than 30 percent of C's contribution base, only a portion of it ($5,000) was deductible for 1994 income tax purposes.

(b) Carryover Rules

Subject to certain conditions and limitations, the excess of

> The amount of the charitable contributions of capital gain property subject to the 30 percent limitation made by an individual in a contribution year to public charitable organizations,

divided by

> 30 percent of his or her contribution base for the contribution year,

is treated as a charitable contribution of capital gain property, subject to this 30 percent limitation, paid by him or her to a public charitable organization in each of the five tax years immediately succeeding the contribution year in order of time.[59] Also, any charitable contribution of capital gain property subject to the 30 percent limitation which is carried over to these years under the general carryover rules[60] is treated as though it were a carryover of capital gain property under the special carryover rules[61] concerning this type of property.[62]

In applying these rules, the amount of the excess contributions which are to be treated as paid in any one of the five tax years

---

[59] IRC § 170(b)(1)(C)(ii); Reg. § 1.170A-8(c)(1).
[60] See text accompanying n. 92, *infra*.
[61] IRC § 170(b)(1)(C)(ii).
[62] Reg. § 1.170A-10(c)(1).

immediately succeeding the contribution year to a public charitable organization may not exceed the lesser of the following four amounts:

- the amount by which 30 percent of the donor's contribution base for the succeeding tax year involved exceeds the sum of
  - the charitable contributions of capital gain property made (computed without regard to the carryover rules) by the donor in the year to public charitable organizations, and
  - the charitable contributions of capital gain property made to public charitable organizations in years preceding the contribution year which, pursuant to the contribution rules, are treated as having been paid to a public charitable organization in the succeeding tax year involved.

- the amount by which 50 percent of the donor's contribution base for the succeeding tax year involved exceeds the sum of
  - the charitable contributions made (computed without regard to the carryover rules) by the donor in the year to public charitable organizations,
  - the charitable contributions of capital gain property made to public charitable organizations in years preceding the contribution year which, pursuant to the carryover rules, are treated as having been paid to a public charitable organization in the succeeding year involved, and
  - the charitable contributions, other than contributions of capital gain property, made to public charitable organizations which, pursuant to the general carryover rules, are treated as having been paid to a public charitable organization in the succeeding year involved.

- in the case of the first tax year succeeding the contribution year, the amount of the excess charitable contribution of capital gain property in the contribution year.

- in the case of the second, third, fourth, and fifth tax years succeeding the contribution year, the portion of the excess charitable contribution of capital gain property in the contribution year which has not been treated as paid to a public charitable organization in a year intervening between the contribution year and the succeeding tax year involved.

For purposes of applying the first and second of these amounts, the amount of charitable contributions of capital gain property actually made in a year succeeding the contribution year is determined by first applying the 30 percent limitation.

If a donor, in any one of the four tax years succeeding a contribution year, elects to utilize the standard deduction instead of itemizing the deductions allowable in computing taxable income, there must be treated as paid (but not allowable as a deduction), in the year the standard deduction is used, the lesser of the above four amounts.[63]

§ 7.6 THE ELECTABLE 50 PERCENT LIMITATION

The federal tax law provides an opportunity for an individual donor to elect application of the 50 percent limitation where the 30 percent limitation would otherwise apply. That is, an individual donor may elect for any tax year to reduce his or her potential federal income tax charitable contribution deduction, occasioned by the gift or gifts of capital gain property to charity made during the tax year, by the amount of what would have been long-term capital gain had the property been sold, in exchange for use of the 50 percent limitation.[64] This election may be made with respect to contributions of capital gain property carried over to the tax year involved even though the donor has not made any contribution of capital gain property in the year. If this election is made, the 30 percent limitation[65] and the carryover rules with respect to it[66] are inapplicable to the contributions made during the year.[67] This means that the 50 percent limitation applies.

Of course, in deciding whether to make this election, an individual must determine whether the 50 percent limitation or the 30 percent limitation is most suitable for him or her (or both) under the circumstances. A principal factor is usually the extent to which the property has appreciated in value; this election can be preferable where the property has not appreciated much in value. Another factor is whether the donor is seeking the maximum charitable contribution

---

[63] Reg. § 1.170A-10(c)(2). The rationale for this rule is discussed in the text following n. 47, *supra*.
[64] IRC § 170(b)(1)(C)(iii); Reg. § 1.170A-8(d)(2).
[65] IRC § 170(b)(1)(C)(i).
[66] IRC § 170(b)(1)(C)(ii).
[67] Reg. § 1.170A-8(d)(2)(i)(a).

deduction for a contribution year. Since capital gain property generally is deductible using the fair market value of the property, the 30 percent limitation can operate to reduce what would otherwise be a larger charitable contribution deduction if the 50 percent limitation applied. This election enables a donor to calculate the deduction by using the fair market value of the property rather than simply the basis in the property.[68] This rule may be illustrated by the following example:

Example 7.10

M had a contribution base for 1994 of $100,000. During that year, M made a gift of capital gain property having a fair market value of $45,000 to PC, a public charitable organization. M's basis in this property was $38,000. She made no other charitable gifts during 1994. M was advised that, if she did not make the election, her charitable contribution deduction for 1994 would be $30,000 (30% of $100,000), with a carryover of $15,000 ($45,000 − $30,000). However, she was also advised that, if she made the election, her charitable contribution deduction for 1994 would be $38,000 ($45,000 less the capital gain element of $7,000). Being particularly concerned with her tax liability for 1994, M made this election so she could have a $38,000 (rather than a $30,000) charitable deduction for that year. She thus knowingly abandoned the $15,000 carryover that would have been potentially used in computing her tax liability for 1995.

If there are carryovers to a tax year of charitable contributions of capital gain property made in preceding, qualifying tax years (subject to the 30 percent limitation), the amount of the contributions in each preceding year must be revised as if this deduction reduction rule had applied to them in the preceding year[69] and must be carried over to the tax year and succeeding years as contributions of property other than capital gain property. The percentage limitations for the preceding tax year and for any tax years intervening between that year and the year of the election are not redetermined and the

---

[68]This method of reducing the charitable deduction is the same as that required with respect to gifts of capital gain property to charitable organizations that are not public charitable organizations (see Chapter 6 § 5) and for gifts of tangible personal property that are not used for related exempt purposes by the charitable donee (see Chapter 6 § 6).
[69]Reg. § 1.170A-8(d)(2)(i)(b).

amount of any charitable deduction allowed for the years with respect to the charitable contributions of capital gain property in the preceding year is not redetermined. However, the amount of the charitable deduction so allowed in the preceding tax year must be subtracted from the reduced amount of the charitable contributions made in that year (that is, the capital gain element must be subtracted) in order to determine the excess amount which is carried over from that year. If the amount of the deduction so allowed in the preceding tax year equals or exceeds the reduced amount of the charitable contributions, there may not be any carryover from that year to the year of the election.[70]

This election may be made for each tax year in which a charitable contribution of capital gain property is made or to which the charitable deduction is carried over under the rules of the 30 percent limitation.[71] If there are also carryovers, under the general rules concerning carryovers of excess contributions,[72] to the year of the election by reason of this election for a previous tax year, these carryovers may not be redetermined by reason of the subsequent election.[73] However, when the election is made, it must apply with respect to all contributions of capital gain property made to public charitable organizations during the contribution year.[74]

These rules may be illustrated by the following two examples:

Example 7.11

H had a contribution base for 1994 of $100,000 and for 1995 of $120,000. In 1994, H made a contribution of capital gain property to a public charitable organization, PC, having a fair market value of $40,000 and a basis of $25,000. In 1995, H made a contribution of capital gain property to PC having a fair market value of $50,000 and a basis of $45,000. H did not make any other charitable gifts during those years. H did not make the election for 1994. Therefore, H properly claimed a charitable contribution deduction for that year in the amount of $30,000 (30% of $100,000) and carried forward the amount of $10,000 ($40,000 − $30,000).

Continued

---

[70] *Id.*
[71] See the text accompanying n. 59, *supra.*
[72] See the text accompanying n. 45, *supra.*
[73] Reg. § 1.170A-8(d)(2)(i)(c).
[74] IRC § 170(b)(1)(C)(iii); Reg. § 1.170A-8(d)(2).

Example 7.11 Continued

H elected to have the 50 percent limitation apply to his contribution of $50,000 in 1995. Accordingly, H was required to recompute his carryover from 1994 as if the deduction reduction rule had applied to his contribution of capital gain property in that year.

If the deduction reduction rule had applied in 1994 to H's contribution of capital gain property, the amount of H's contribution for these purposes would have been reduced from $40,000 to $25,000, the reduction of the $15,000 being all of the gain ($40,000 − $25,000) which would have been long-term capital gain had H sold the property at its fair market value at the time of its contribution in 1994. Accordingly, by taking this election into account, H did not have a recomputed carryover to 1995 because the $25,000 was fully deductible in 1994 (H's maximum charitable deduction in that year was $30,000 (30% of $100,000)). However, H's charitable contribution deduction of $30,000 allowed for 1994 did not have to be recomputed by reason of this election.

Pursuant to the election for 1995, the contribution of capital gain property for that year was reduced from $50,000 to $45,000, the reduction of $5,000 being all of the gain of $5,000 ($50,000 − $45,000) which would have been long-term capital gain had H sold the property at its fair market value at the time of its contribution in 1995.

Accordingly, H was allowed a charitable contribution deduction for 1995 of $45,000, rather than of $36,000 (30% of $120 000) had the election not been made.

Example 7.12

In 1994, A made a charitable contribution to a church of capital gain property having a fair market value of $60,000 and an adjusted basis of $10,000. A's contribution base for 1994 was $50,000 and A did not make any other charitable contributions in that year. A did not elect for 1994 to have the deduction reduction rule apply to the contribution. A was allowed, under the 30 percent limitation, a charitable contribution deduction for 1994 of $15,000 (30% of $50,000). Under the carryover rules for capital gain property,[75] A was allowed a carryover to 1995 of $45,000 ($60,000 − $15,000) for his contribution of this capital gain property.

Continued

---

[75]See the text accompanying n. 59, *supra*.

Example 7.12 Continued

In 1995, A made a charitable contribution to a church of capital gain property having a fair market value of $11,000 and an adjusted basis of $10,000. A's contribution base for 1995 was $60,000 and he did not make any other charitable contributions in that year. He elected for 1995 to have the election apply to his contribution of $11,000 in that year and to his carryover of $45,000 from 1994. Accordingly, A was required to recompute his carryover from 1994 as if the deduction reduction rule had applied to his contribution of capital gain property in that year.

If the deduction reduction rule had applied in 1994 to A's contribution of capital gain property, the amount of A's contribution for these purposes would have been reduced from $60,000 to $10,000, the reduction of the $50,000 being all of the gain ($60,000 − $10,000) which would have been long-term capital gain had A sold the property at its fair market value at the time of its contribution in 1994. Accordingly, by taking this election into account, A did not have a recomputed carryover to 1995 in connection with his contribution of capital gain property in 1994 because the $10,000 was fully deducted in 1994 (A's maximum charitable deduction in that year was $15,000 (30% of $50,000)). However, A's charitable contribution deduction of $15,000 allowed for 1994 did not have to be recomputed by reason of this election.

Pursuant to the election for 1995, the contribution of capital gain property for that year was reduced from $11,000 to $10,000, the reduction of $1,000 being all of the gain of $1,000 ($11,000 − $10,000) which would have been long-term capital gain had A sold the property at its fair market value at the time of its contribution in 1995.

Accordingly, A was allowed a charitable contribution deduction for 1995 of $11,000[76]

This example also illustrates a circumstance where the election is inappropriate. In the example, A did not need to make the election in 1995 to cause all of the $11,000 gift to be deductible in that year, because the maximum amount of allowable giving was $18,000 (30% of $60,000). Worse, in making the election, A lost the economic effect of the $45,000 carryforward to 1994.

If a husband and wife file a joint federal income tax return for a year in which a charitable contribution is made and one of the spouses makes this election in a later year when he or she files a

---

[76]Reg. § 1.170A-8(f), Example (9).

separate return, or if a spouse dies after a contribution year for which a joint return is filed, any excess contribution of capital gain property which is carried over to the election year from the contribution year must be allocated between the husband and wife as provided under the rules concerning carryovers of excess contributions.[77] If a husband and wife file separate returns in a contribution year, any election in a later year when a joint return is filed is applicable to any excess contributions of capital gain property of either individual carried over from the contribution year to the election year. This is also the case where two individuals become married and file a joint return. A remarried individual who filed a joint return with his or her former spouse for a contribution year and thereafter filed a joint return with his or her present spouse must treat the carryover to the election year as provided under the rules[78] concerning carryovers of excess contributions.[79]

This election is made by attaching to the federal income tax return for the year of the election a statement indicating that the election is being made. Preferably, the statement will make reference to the appropriate section of the Internal Revenue Code[80] and, ideally, of the regulations.[81] If there is a carryover to the tax year of any charitable contributions of capital gain property from a previous tax year or years, the statement must show the recomputation[82] of the carryover, setting forth sufficient information with respect to the previous tax year or any intervening year to show the basis of the recomputation. The statement must indicate the district director of the IRS, or the director of the internal revenue service center, with whom the return for the previous tax year or years was filed, the name or names in which the return or returns were filed, and whether each of the returns was a joint return or a separate return.[83]

This election cannot be made retroactively. In the principal case on the point, the donors calculated their charitable deduction for a significant gift of property (which was highly appreciated in value) by making this election. This act produced a charitable deduction for

[77] Reg. § 170A-10(d)(4)(i), (iii).
[78] Reg. § 1.170A-10(d)(4)(ii).
[79] Reg. § 1.170A-8(d)(ii).
[80] IRC § 170(b)(1)(C)(iii).
[81] Reg. § 1.170A-8(d)(2)(i).
[82] Reg. §§ 1.170A-8(d)(2), 1.170A-4.
[83] Reg. § 1.170A-8(d)(2)(iii).

the year of the gift and for two subsequent years. Two years later, the donors recalculated their charitable deduction stemming from the gift and filed amended returns using the 30 percent limitation. This approach gave them a smaller deduction in the year of the gift and the two following years but it produced a charitable contribution deduction in each of the next three tax years. Litigation was launched when the IRS disallowed the deductions for the most recent three years.

One of the arguments advanced by the donors was the thought that they never made a valid election to use the 50 percent limitation, so that they were not bound by that initial decision. But the court held that the election was valid, holding that no particular words are required and that adequate notice as to the election was provided to the IRS.[84] The other argument was that this election is revocable. Persuaded by the government's argument that irrevocability is required to avoid burdensome uncertainties in the administration of the revenue laws, the court held that the donors were bound by their election in the year of the gift. The court observed that "where . . . the taxpayer's initial election later becomes, through hindsight, less financially advantageous than some other option, the improvident election does not enable the taxpayers to revoke that election."[85]

This election may not be made by means of an amended return.[86]

§ 7.7   THE GENERAL 30 PERCENT LIMITATION

(a)   General Rules

Normally, an individual's charitable contributions made during a tax year, to one or more charitable organizations other than public charitable organizations, where the subject of the gift is money, are deductible to the extent that these contributions in the aggregate do

---

[84]*Woodbury* v. *Commissioner,* 900 F.2d 1457 (10th Cir. 1990).
[85]*Id.* at 1461. Also *Grynberg* v. *Commissioner,* 83 T.C. 255 (1984), where the court relied on a "doctrine of election," precluding the donor from revoking the election, because the donor had a free choice between the two alternatives and engaged in the overt act (by filing a tax return) of communicating that choice to the IRS.
[86]Rev. Rul. 77-217, 1977-1 C.B. 64.

not exceed 30 percent of the individual's contribution base for the tax year.[87] Separate rules apply where the property is long-term capital gain property and is contributed to charitable organizations other than public charitable organizations.[88]

This limitation is applicable to donees such as private foundations, veterans' organizations, fraternal organizations, and certain cemetery companies.[89]

Example 7.13

This example may be compared with Example 7.1. A had, for 1994, a contribution base of $100,000. During 1994, she made charitable contributions of money, in the amount of $45,000, to a private foundation. A was allowed a charitable contribution deduction for 1994 of $30,000 (30% of $100,000).

However, in some instances, the actual annual limitation on deductible gifts of this nature is less than the 30 percent limitation. This occurs when gifts of money and/or capital gain property to public charitable organizations are also made in the same contribution year. Thus, if the amount is lesser, the limitation will be an amount equal to the excess of 50 percent of the donor's contribution base for the year over the amount of deductible charitable contributions that are allowable under the 50 percent limitation.[90] This rule is discussed more fully below.[91]

As noted previously, these rules as applicable to "money" also apply to certain types of property. Thus, this general 30 percent limitation applies to gifts of money, ordinary income property, and short-term capital gain property.

(b) Carryover Rules

In general, the excess of

the amount of the charitable contribution or contributions of capital gain property made by an individual in a contribution year to one or more public charitable organizations,

[87] IRC § 170(b)(1)(B)(i).
[88] See § 11, *infra.*
[89] IRC § 170(c)(2)-(5).
[90] IRC § 170(b)(1)(B).
[91] See §§ 8 and 9, *infra.*

divided by

30 percent of his or her contribution base for the contribution year,

is treated as a charitable contribution paid by him or her to a public charitable organization, subject to the 30 percent limitation, in each of the five tax years immediately succeeding the contribution year in order of time.[92] As noted previously, for federal income tax purposes, an amount paid to a charitable organization in one year is, when the carryover rules are applied, treated as "paid" to a charitable organization in a subsequent year.

Example 7.14

This example is based on the facts of Example 7.13. A was allowed a charitable contribution deduction for 1994 of $30,000 (30% of $100,000) and a carryforward of $15,000 ($45,000 − $30,000).

---

§ 7.8 INTERPLAY OF THE 50 PERCENT/SPECIAL 30 PERCENT LIMITATIONS

In computing the charitable contribution deduction, contributions of money to public charitable organizations are taken into account before contributions of capital gain property to public charitable organizations.

This rule is illustrated by the following two examples:

Example 7.15

H and W (husband and wife) had a contribution base for 1993 of $50,000 and for 1994 of $40,000, and filed a joint return for both years. In 1993, H and W contributed $20,000 in money and $13,000 of capital gain property to PC, a public charitable organization. In

Continued

---

[92] IRC § 170(b)(1)(B), last sentence.

Example 7.15 Continued

1994, they contributed $5,000 in cash and $10,000 of capital gain property to PC. They were able to properly claim a charitable contribution deduction of $25,000 for 1993 (25% of $50,000) and the excess of $33,000 (contributed to PC) over $25,000 (50% of contribution base), or $8,000, constituted a charitable contribution carryover which was treated as a charitable contribution of capital gain property subject to the 30 percent limitation paid by them to a public charitable organization in each of the five succeeding tax years in order of time. Since 30 percent of the contribution base for H and W for 1994 ($12,000) exceeded the charitable contribution of capital gain property ($10,000) made by them in 1994 to a public charitable organization (computed without regard to the carryover rules), the portion of the 1993 carryover equal to the excess of $2,000 ($12,000 − $10,000) was treated as paid to a public charitable organization in 1994. The remaining $6,000 constituted an unused charitable contributions carryover in respect of capital gain property subject to the 30 percent limitation from 1993.[93]

Example 7.16

This example is based on the facts of Example 7.15, except that the $33,000 of charitable contributions in 1993 were all of capital gain property. Since the charitable contributions of H and W in 1993 exceeded 30 percent of their contribution base ($15,000) by $18,000 ($33,000 − $15,000), they were able to claim a charitable contribution deduction of $15,000 in 1993 and the excess of $33,000 over $15,000 ($18,000) constituted a charitable contribution carryover which was treated as a charitable contribution of capital gain property subject to the 30 percent limitation paid by them to a public charitable organization in each of the five succeeding tax years in order of time. Since they were allowed to treat only $2,000 of their 1994 contributions as paid in 1994, H and W had a remaining unused charitable contribution carryover of $16,000 in respect of capital gain property subject to the 30 percent limitation from 1993.[94]

---

[93] Reg. § 1.170A-10(c)(1), Example (1).
[94] Reg. § 1.170A-10(c)(1), Example (2).

§ 7.9   INTERPLAY OF THE 50 PERCENT/GENERAL 30 PERCENT LIMITATIONS

Where an individual donor makes, in the same year, gifts of money and/or capital gain property to one or more public charitable organizations and gifts of money in circumstances involving the general 30 percent limitation, the charitable contribution deduction is computed by first taking into consideration the gift or gifts to one or more public charitable organizations.[95] The contributions involving the 30 percent limitation are deductible, in whole or in part, only to the extent that (1) these gifts do not exceed the 30 percent limitation, or (2) the gift or gifts to one or more public charitable organizations do not, in the aggregate, exceed the amount allowable by the 50 percent limitation.

The actual deductible amount is the lesser of these two items. That is, the maximum amount deductible in any one year for gifts involving the 30 percent limitation in these circumstances is the lesser of the amount capped by the 30 percent limitation or the amount (if any) represented by the "gap" between the amount contributed to one or more public charitable organizations during the year and the maximum amount allowable under the 50 percent limitation for the year.

These rules concerning gifts of money are illustrated in the following two examples:

Example 7.17

B had, for 1994, a contribution base of $100,000. During 1994, B made charitable contributions of $70,000 in money, $40,000 of which was given to public charitable organizations and $30,000 of which was given to charitable organizations that are not public charitable organizations. B was allowed, for 1994, a charitable contribution deduction of $50,000 (50% of $100,000), which consisted of the $40,000 contributed to the public charities and $10,000 of the $30,000 contributed to the other organizations. Only $10,000 of the $30,000 contrib-

Continued

---

[95] IRC § 170(b)(1)(B).

Example 7.17 Continued

uted to the other charitable organizations was allowed as a deduction, since the contribution of $30,000 was allowed to the extent of the lesser of $30,000 (30% of $100,000) or $10,000 ([50% of $100,000] − $40,000, being the contributions allowed under the 50% limitation).[96]

Example 7.18

H and W (husband and wife) had a contribution base for 1994 of $50,000 and for 1995 of $40,000, and filed a joint return for both years. In 1994, H and W made a charitable contribution in money of $26,500 to PC, a public charitable organization, and $1,000 to PF, a charitable organization that is not a public charitable organization. In 1995, they made a charitable contribution in money of $19,000 to PC and $600 to PF. They were able to properly claim a charitable contribution deduction of $25,000 in 1994 (50 percent of $50,000). This deduction was of $25,000 of the gift to PC; none of the gift to PF was deductible in 1994.

The excess of $2,500 ($27,500 − $25,000) constituted a charitable contribution carryover which was subsequently treated by them as a charitable contribution paid by them to a public charitable organization ($1,500) and a non-public charitable organization ($1,000) in each of the five succeeding tax years in order of time. Their contribution of $19,000 to PC in 1995 was fully deductible in that year, because 50 percent of their contribution base was $20,000. Also, $1,000 of the $1,500 contributed to PC in 1994 was considered paid to PC in 1995 and was deductible in that year. Thus, H and W had a 1995 charitable contribution deduction of $20,000. Once again, none of the gift to PF was deductible in 1995. The remaining $500 contributed to PC in 1994 was treated as a carryover of gifts of money to public charitable organizations and the $1,000 carryover from 1994 and the $600 gift to PF in 1995 was treated as a carryover of gifts of money to charitable organizations that are not public charitable organizations.[97]

---

[96] Reg. § 1.170A-8(f), Example (1).
[97] Reg. § 1.170A-10(b)(1), Example (1).

§ 7.10   INTERPLAY OF THE SPECIAL 30 PERCENT/GENERAL 30 PERCENT LIMITATIONS

The federal income tax law favors gifts of capital gain property to public charitable organizations in relation to gifts of money to charitable organizations that are not public charitable organizations. Thus, a gift of money to, for example, a private foundation may not be fully deductible under the general 30 percent limitation because of a gift of capital gain property in the same year to a public charitable organization.

This rule is illustrated by the following example:

Example 7.19

X had a contribution base for 1994 of $100,000. During that year, X contributed an item of capital gain property, having a fair market value of $60,000, to PC, a public charitable organization, and contributed money in the amount of $5,000 to PF, a private foundation. The gift of money was not deductible in computing X's tax liability for 1994. This is because the fair market value of the property contributed was in excess of 50 percent of X's contribution base. (The actual charitable contribution deduction for this gift of property was limited to the amount equal to 30 percent of X's contribution base, or $30,000.) X thus has two carryovers to 1995. One was a carryover of $30,000 for the gift to PC (subject to the 30 percent limitation applicable to gifts of capital gain property) and the other was a carryover of the $5,000 (subject to the general 30 percent limitation).

---

§ 7.11   THE 20 PERCENT LIMITATION

(a)   General Rules

In general, contributions of capital gain property by individuals to charitable organizations that are not public charitable organizations are subject to a 20 percent limitation.[98] This limitation is a percentage of the donor's contribution base for the contribution year.

---

[98] IRC § 170(b)(1)(D)(i).

Example 7.20

A had, for 1994, a contribution base of $100,000. During 1994, she contributed an item of capital gain property to PF, a private foundation. The fair market value of the property was $25,000. A made no other charitable gifts in 1994. A was allowed a federal income tax charitable contribution deduction for 1994 of $20,000 (20% of $100,000).

However, in some instances, the actual annual limitation on deductible gifts of this nature is less than the 20 percent limitation. This occurs when gifts of capital gain property to public charitable organizations are also made in the same contribution year. Thus, the charitable deduction for this type of gift is confined to the lesser of

- the amount allowable under the 20 percent limitation, or
- an amount equal to the excess of 30 percent of the donor's contribution base for the year over the amount of charitable contributions of capital gain property to public charitable organizations that are allowable under the 30 percent limitation.[99]

This 20 percent limitation applies to contributions of property where the amount of the gift, for deduction purposes, was reduced under the deduction reduction rule that is discussed in Chapter 6.[100]

(b) Carryover Rules

In general, the excess of

The amount of the charitable contribution or contributions of capital gain property made by an individual in a contribution year to one or more charitable organizations that are not public charitable organizations,

divided by

20 percent of his or her contribution base for the contribution year,

[99] *Id.*
[100] *Id.*

is treated as a charitable contribution paid by him or her to a non-public charitable organization, subject to the 20 percent limitation, in each of the five tax years immediately succeeding the contribution year in order of time.[101]

Example 7.21

The facts of this Example are the same as in Example 7.20. A had a carryforward of $5,000 to be treated as a gift of capital gain property to charitable organizations that are not public charitable organizations for years subsequent to 1994.

---

§ 7.12   GIFTS "FOR THE USE OF" CHARITY

The federal income tax law provides for a charitable contribution deduction for gifts "to or for the use of" one or more qualified charitable donees.[102] Charitable contributions discussed in other sections of this chapter are gifts "to" a charitable organization. Contributions "for the use of" a charitable organization are discussed in Chapter 9 § 10.

Contributions for the use of a charitable organization are subject to the general 30 percent limitation.[103]

§ 7.13   BLENDING THE THREE PERCENTAGE LIMITATIONS

A donor, who is an individual, may make gifts of various types to charitable organizations of various tax classifications in a single year. These gifts may be partly of money and partly of property. The property may or may not be capital gain property. The charitable donees may be public charities, private foundations, veterans' organizations, or other charitable recipients.

---

[101] IRC § 170(b)(1)(D)(ii).
[102] IRC § 170(c).
[103] IRC § 170(b)(1)(B).

The law provides for application of the various percentages in situations where differing types of gifts are made and/or where differing categories of charitable organizations are recipients of the gifts.

Where an individual contributes cash to public and private charities in the same year, there is an interplay between the 50 percent limitation and the 30 percent limitation.[104] Where an individual contributes money and capital gain property to one or more public charities in the same year, there is an interplay between the 50 percent limitation and the special 30 percent limitation. Also, there can be an interplay between percentage limitations where capital gain property is contributed in the same year to both one or more public charities and one or more charitable organizations that are not public ones. In some instances, all of the percentage limitations are applicable.

No matter what the mix of gift subjects and gift recipients may be, the maximum amount that may be deducted by an individual in any one year, as the result of one or more charitable gifts, is an amount equal to 50 percent of the donor's contribution base. Contributions of money to public charitable organizations are considered before contributions of money to charitable organizations that are not public charitable organizations. Contributions of money are taken into account before contributions of capital gain property. Contributions of capital gain property to public charitable organizations are taken into account before contributions of such property to non-public charitable organizations.

Amounts of charitable gifts that exceed these various limitations can be, as discussed in the above sections of this chapter, carried forward and be potentially deductible in subsequent years. However, just as there can be an interplay of gifts and money in the same year, there can be an interplay of two or more years in conjunction with a single gift (because of one or more carryovers). A charitable contribution in a current year is considered, in computing allowable deductions for that year, before taking into account contribution deductions based on carryovers.[105]

---

[104]See § 8, *supra*.
[105]IRC § 170(d)(1); Reg. § 1.170A-8; Reg. § 1.170A-10.

§ 7.14   INDIVIDUALS' NET OPERATING LOSS CARRYOVERS AND CARRYBACKS

(a)   Carryovers

An individual having a net operating loss carryover[106] from a prior tax year which is available as a deduction in a contribution year must apply a special rule for net operating loss carryovers[107] in computing the excess charitable contributions for the contribution year. In determining the amount of excess charitable contributions that must be treated as paid in each of the five tax years succeeding the contribution year, the excess charitable contributions described above must be reduced by the amount by which the excess reduces taxable income (for purposes of determining the portion of a net operating loss which must be carried to tax years succeeding the contribution year under the general rule concerning net operating loss carryovers[108]) and increases the net operating loss which is carried to a succeeding tax year. In reducing taxable income under these rules, an individual who has made charitable contributions in the contribution year to public organizations and to other charitable organizations must first deduct contributions made to the public charitable organizations from his or her adjusted gross income, computed without regard to his or her net operating loss deduction before any of the contributions made to other charitable organizations may be deducted from adjusted gross income. Thus, if the excess of the contributions made in the contribution year to public charitable organizations over the amount deductible in the contribution year is utilized to reduce taxable income (under the general rules concerning net operating loss carryovers[109]) for the year, thereby serving to increase the amount of the net operating loss carryover to a succeeding year or years, no part of the excess charitable contributions made in the contribution year may be treated as paid in any of the five immediately succeeding tax years. If only a portion of the excess charitable contributions is so used, the excess charitable contributions need be reduced only to that extent.[110]

---

[106] IRC § 172.
[107] IRC § 170(d)(1)(B).
[108] IRC § 170(b)(2), second sentence.
[109] Id.
[110] Reg. § 1.170A-10(d)(1).

These rules may be illustrated by the following three examples:

Example 7.22

B, for 1993, had adjusted gross income (computed without regard to any net operating loss deduction) of $50,000. During 1993, B made charitable contributions of money in the amount of $30,000, all of which were to public charitable organizations. B had a net operating loss carryover from 1992 of $50,000. In the absence of the net operating loss deduction, B would have been allowed a deduction for charitable contributions of $25,000 (50% of $50,000). After the application of the net operating loss deduction, B was not allowed any deduction for charitable contributions, and there was (before applying the special rule for net operating loss carryovers) a tentative excess charitable contribution of $30,000. For purposes of determining the net operating loss which remained to be carried over to 1994, B computed his taxable income for 1993 under the general rule concerning net operating loss carryovers by deducting the $25,000 charitable contribution. After the $50,000 net operating loss carryover was applied against the $25,000 of taxable income for 1993 (computed in accordance with this general rule, assuming no deductions other than the charitable contribution deduction were applicable in making the computation), there remained a $25,000 net operating loss carryover to 1994. Since application of the net operating loss carryover of $50,000 from 1992 reduced the 1993 adjusted gross income (for purposes of determining 1993 tax liability) to zero, no part of the $25,000 of charitable contributions in 1993 was deductible, under the percentage limitation rules for individuals. However, in determining the amount of the excess charitable contributions which must have been treated as paid in tax years 1994, 1995, 1996, 1997, and 1998, the $30,000 must be reduced to $5,000 by the portion of the excess charitable contributions ($25,000) which was used to reduce taxable income for 1993 (as computed for purposes of the general rule concerning net operating loss carryovers) and which thereby served to increase the net operating loss carryover to 1994 from zero to $25,000.[111]

Example 7.23

The facts of this example are the same as those in Example 7.33, except that B's total charitable contributions of $30,000 in money made during 1993 consisted of $25,000 to public charitable organiza-
Continued

---

[111]Reg. § 1.170A-10(d)(1), Example (1).

Example 7.23 Continued

tions and $5,000 to other charitable organizations. There was a tentative excess charitable contribution of $25,000, rather than $30,000 as in Example 5.33. For purposes of determining the net operating loss which remained to be carried over to 1994, B computed his taxable income for 1993 under the general rule concerning net operating loss carryovers by deducting the $25,000 of charitable contributions to public charitable organizations. Since the excess charitable contribution of $25,000 was used to reduce taxable income for 1993 (as computed for purposes of this general rule) and thereby served to increase the net operating loss carryover to 1994 from zero to $25,000, no part of the excess charitable contributions made in the contribution year could have been treated as paid in any of the five immediately succeeding tax years. A carryover is not allowed with respect to the $5,000 of charitable contributions made in 1993 to the other charitable organizations.[112]

Example 7.24

This example is based on the facts in Example 7.34, except that B's total charitable contributions of $30,000 made during 1993 were of capital gain property subject to the 30 percent limitation. There was a tentative excess charitable contribution of $30,000. For purposes of determining the net operating loss which remained to be carried over to 1994, B computed his taxable income for 1993 under the general rule concerning net operating loss carryovers by deducting the $15,000 (30% of $30,000) contribution of capital gain property which would have been deductible in 1993 absent the net operating loss deduction. Since $15,000 of the excess charitable contribution of $30,000 was used to reduce taxable income for 1993 (as computed for purposes of this general rule) and thereby served to increase the net operating loss carryover to 1994 from zero to $15,000, only $15,000 ($30,000 − $15,000) of the excess was able to have been treated as paid in tax years 1994, 1995, 1996, 1997, and 1998.[113]

---

[112] Reg. § 1.170A-10(d)(1), Example (2).
[113] Reg. § 1.170A-10(d)(1), Example (3).

(b) Carrybacks

The amount of the excess charitable contribution for a contribution year may not be increased because a net operating loss carryback is available as a deduction in the contribution year.

Example 7.25

In 1993, D had an excess charitable contribution of $50,000 which was to be carried to the five succeeding tax years. In 1996, D had a net operating loss which was able to be carried back to 1993, the excess contribution of $50,000 for 1993 could not have been increased by reason of the fact that D's adjusted gross income for 1993 (on which the excess contribution was based) was subsequently decreased by the carryback of the net operating loss from 1996. In addition, in determining under the general rule concerning net operating loss carry-overs the amount of the net operating loss for any year subsequent to the contribution year which is a carryback or carryover to tax years succeeding the contribution year, the amount of contributions made to public charitable organizations is limited to the amount of the contributions which did not exceed 50 percent of the donor's contribution base, computed without regard to any of the net operating loss deduction modifications rules,[114] for the contribution year. Thus, D had a net operating loss in 1996 which was carried back to 1993 and in turn to 1994 and D had made charitable contributions in 1993 to public charitable organizations. In determining the maximum amount of the charitable contributions which were deductible in 1993 for purposes of determining the taxable income for 1993 which was deducted under the general rule from the 1996 loss in order to ascertain the amount of that loss which was carried back to 1994, the 50 percent limitation was based on D's adjusted gross income for 1993 computed without taking into account the net operating loss carryback from 1996 and without making any of the modifications.[115]

The amount of the charitable contribution from a preceding tax year which is treated as paid in a current tax year (the "deduction year") may not be reduced because a net operating loss carryback is available as a deduction in the deduction year. Additionally, in deter-mining[116] the amount of the net operating loss for any tax year subse-

---

[114]IRC § 172(d).
[115]Reg. § 1.170A-10(d)(2).
[116]IRC § 172(b)(2).

quent to the deduction year which is a carryback or carryover to tax years succeeding the deduction year, the amount of contributions made to public charitable organizations in the deduction year must be limited to the amount of these contributions, which were actually made in the deduction year and those which were treated as paid in that year.[117] Moreover, these contributions may not exceed the 50 percent limitation or, in the case of capital gain property, the 30 percent limitation, computed without regard to any of the net operating loss deduction modifications[118] for the deduction year.[119]

§ 7.15 SPECIAL RULES FOR SPOUSES

If a husband and wife

1. file a joint return for a contribution year,
2. compute an excess charitable contribution for that year, and
3. file separate returns for one or more of the five tax years immediately succeeding the contribution year,

any excess charitable contribution for the contribution year which is unused at the beginning of the first of these five tax years for which separate returns are filed must be allocated between the husband and wife. For purposes of this allocation, a computation must be made of the amount of any excess charitable contribution which each spouse would have computed if separate returns had been filed for the contribution year.

The portion of the total unused excess charitable contribution for the contribution year allocated to each spouse must be an amount which bears the same ratio to the unused excess charitable contribution as the spouse's excess contribution, based on the separate return computation, bears to the total excess contributions of both spouses, based on the separate return computation. To the extent that a portion of the amount allocated to either spouse is not treated as a charitable contribution to a public charitable organization in the tax year in which separate returns are filed, each spouse must treat his or her respective unused portion as the available charitable contribu-

---

[117]Reg. § 1.170A-10(d)(3).
[118]IRC § 172(d).
[119]Reg. § 1.170A-10(d)(3).

tion carryover to the next succeeding tax year in which the joint excess charitable contribution may be treated as paid. If a husband and wife file a joint return for one of the five tax years immediately succeeding the contribution year with respect to which a joint excess charitable contribution is computed and following the first tax year for which the husband and wife filed a separate return, the amounts allocated to each spouse for this first tax year, reduced by the portion of the amounts treated as paid to a public charitable organization in this first tax year and in any tax year intervening between this first tax year and the succeeding tax year in which the joint return is filed, must be aggregated for purposes of determining the amount of the available charitable contribution carryover to the succeeding tax year.[120]

These rules may be illustrated by the following example:

Example 7.26

H and W filed joint returns for 1993, 1994, and 1995, and in 1996 they filed separate returns. In each of these years, H and W itemized their deductions in computing taxable income. The following facts apply with respect to H and W for 1993:

		H	W	Joint return
Contribution base	. . . .	$50,000	$40,000	$90,000
Contributions of cash to public charitable organizations (no other contributions)	. . . .	37,000	28,000	65,000
Allowable charitable contribution deductions	. . . .	25,000	20,000	45,000
Excess contributions to be treated as paid in five succeeding tax years	. . . .	12,000	8,000	20,000

The joint excess charitable contribution of $20,000 had to be treated as having been paid to a public charitable organization in the five suc-

Continued

---

[120]Reg. § 1.170A-10(d)(4)(i).

Example 7.26 Continued

ceeding tax years. In 1994, the portion of the excess treated as paid by H and W was $3,000 and in 1995 the portion of the excess treated as paid was $7,000. Thus, the unused portion of the excess charitable contribution made in the contribution year was $10,000 ($20,000 − $3,000 [amount treated as paid in 1994] and $7,000 [amount treated as paid in 1995]). Since H and W filed separate returns in 1996, $6,000 of the $10,000 was allocable to H and the remaining $4,000 was allocable to W. This was determined as follows:

$$\frac{\$12,000 \text{ (excess charitable contributions made by } H \text{ (based on separate return computation) in 1993)}}{\$20,000 \text{ (total excess charitable contributions made by } H \text{ and } W \text{ (based on separate return compotation) in 1993}} \times \$10,000 = \$6,000$$

$$\frac{\$8,000 \text{ (excess charitable contributions made by } W \text{ (based on separate return computation) in 1993)}}{\$20,000 \text{ (total excess charitable contributions made by } H \text{ and } W \text{ (based on separate return computation) in 1993}} \times \$10,000 = \$4,000$$

In 1996, H had a contribution base of $70,000 and he contributed $14,000 in cash to a public charitable organization. In 1996, W had a contribution base of $50,000 and she contributed $10,000 in cash to a public charitable organization. Accordingly, H was able to properly claim a charitable contribution deduction of $20,000 in 1996 and W was able to properly claim a charitable contribution deduction of $14,000 in 1996. H's $20,000 deduction consisted of the $14,000 contribution in 1996 and the $6,000 carried over from 1993 and treated as a charitable contribution paid by him to a public charitable organization in 1996. W's $14,000 deduction consisted of the $10,000 contribution in 1996 and the $4,000 carried over from 1993 and treated as a charitable contribution paid by her to a public charitable organization in 1996.

The $6,000 contribution treated as paid in 1996 by H and the $4,000 contribution treated as paid in 1996 by W were computed as follows:

Continued

Example 7.26 Continued

		H	W
Available charitable contribution carryover	. . . .	$6,000	$4,000
50% of contribution base	. . . .	35,000	25,000
Contributions of cash made in 1996 to public charitable organizations (no other contributions)	. . . .	14,000	10,000
		$21,000	$15,000

Amount of excess contributions treated as paid in 1996:

The lesser of $6,000 (available carryover of H to 1996) or $21,000 (excess of 50% of contribution base ($35,000) over contributions actually made in 1996 to a public charitable organization ($14,000) $6,000

The lesser of $4,000 (available carryover of W to 1996) or $15,000 (excess of 50% of contribution base ($25,000) over contributions actually made in 1996 to a public charitable organization ($10,000) $4,000

For purposes of this example, it was assumed that H and W did not make any contributions of capital gain property during the years involved. Had they done so, however, there would have been similar adjustments based upon the 30 percent limitation.[121]

In the case of a husband and wife, where

- either or both of the spouses filed a separate income tax return for a contribution year,
- they computed an excess charitable contribution for the year under these rules, and
- they filed a joint income tax return for one or more of the tax years succeeding the contribution year,

their excess charitable contribution for the contribution year which

[121] *Id.*

was unused at the beginning of the first tax year for which a tax return was filed must be aggregated for purposes of determining the portion of the unused charitable contribution which must be treated (in determining the amount considered as paid in years succeeding a contribution year) as a charitable contribution paid to a public charitable organization. This rule also applies in the case of two single individuals who are subsequently married and file a joint return. A remarried individual who filed a joint return with a former spouse in a contribution year with respect to which an excess charitable contribution was computed, and who in any one of the five tax years succeeding the contribution year filed a joint return with his or her present spouse, must treat the unused portion of the excess charitable contribution allocated to him or her in the same manner as the unused portion of an excess charitable contribution computed in a contribution year in which he or she filed a separate return, for purposes of determining the amount considered as paid in years succeeding a contribution year to a public charitable organization in the succeeding year.[122]

In case of the death of one spouse, any unused portion of an excess charitable contribution allowable to that spouse is not treated as paid in the tax year in which the death occurs, or in any subsequent tax year, except on a separate return made for the deceased spouse by a fiduciary for the tax year which ends with the date of death, or on a joint return for the tax year in which the death occurs.[123]

The application of this rule may be illustrated as follows:

Example 7.27

The facts are the same as in Example 7.26, except that H died in 1995 and W filed a separate return for 1996. W filed a joint return for H and W for 1995. In Example 5.36, the unused excess charitable contribution as of January 1, 1996, was $10,000, of which $6,000 was allocable to H and $4,000 to W. No portion of the $6,000 allocable to H may be treated as paid by W or by any other person in 1996 or in any subsequent tax year.[124]

---

[122]Reg. § 1.170A-10(d)(4)(ii).
[123]Reg. § 1.170A-10(d)(4)(iii).
[124]*Id.*

§ 7.16 SPECIAL INFORMATION REQUIREMENTS

If, in a tax year, a deduction is claimed in respect of an excess charitable contribution which, in accordance with the rules for determining an amount considered as paid in years succeeding a contribution year, is treated (in whole or in part) as paid in the year, the donor must attach to his or her return a statement showing the following:.

- the contribution year (or years) in which the excess charitable contributions were made,
- the excess charitable contributions made in each contribution year, and the amount of the excess charitable contributions consisting of capital gain property,
- the portion of the excess, or of each excess, treated as paid in any tax year intervening between the contribution year and the tax year for which the return is filed, and the portion of the excess which consists of capital gain property,
- whether or not an election, under the rules allowing the 50 percent limitation with respect to contributions of capital gain property,[125] has been made which affects any of the excess contributions of capital gain property, and
- whatever other information the tax returns or the instructions accompanying them may reasonably require.[126]

§ 7.17 PERCENTAGE LIMITATION FOR CORPORATIONS

(a) General Rules

The deduction by a corporation subject to income taxation in a tax year for charitable contributions is limited to ten percent of its taxable income for the year, computed with certain adjustments.[127]

(b) Carryovers

Any charitable contributions made by a corporation in a tax year (a "contribution year") in excess of the amount deductible in the contri-

---

[125]See § 6, *supra.*
[126]Reg. § 1.170A-10(e).
[127]IRC § 170(b)(2); Reg. § 1.170A-11(a).

bution year under the ten-percent limitation are deductible in each of the five immediately succeeding tax years in order of time but only to the extent of the lesser of the following amounts:.

- the excess of the maximum amount deductible for the succeeding tax year under the ten-percent limitation, over the sum of the charitable contributions made in that year, plus the aggregate of the excess contributions which were made in tax years before the contribution year and which are deductible under these rules in the succeeding tax year,
- in the case of the first tax year succeeding the contribution year, the amount of the excess charitable contributions, or
- in the case of the second, third, fourth, and fifth tax years succeeding the contribution year, the portion of the excess charitable contributions not deductible under these rules for any tax year intervening between the contribution year and the succeeding tax year.[128]

These rules apply to excess charitable contributions by a corporation, whether or not the contributions are made to or for the use of[129] the recipient charitable organization and whether or not the donee is a public charitable organization. These rules may be illustrated by the following example:

Example 7.28

Corporation X, which reports its income on the calendar year basis, made a charitable contribution of $20,000 in 1993. X's taxable income (determined without regard to any deduction for charitable contributions) for 1993 was $100,000. Accordingly, the charitable contribution deduction for 1993 was $10,000 (10% of $100,000). The excess charitable contribution deduction not deductible in 1993 ($10,000) was a carryover to 1994.

X had taxable income (determined without regard to any deduction for charitable contributions) of $150,000 in 1994 and made a charitable contribution of $10,000 in 1994. For 1994, X properly deducted as a charitable contribution the amount of $15,000 (10% of $150,000).

Continued

---

[128]IRC § 170(d)(2)(A).
[129]See Chapter 9 § 10.

Example 7.28 Continued

This amount consisted of the $10,000 contribution made in 1994 and of $5,000 of the amount carried over from 1993. The remaining $5,000 carried over from 1993 and not allowable as a deduction for 1994 because of the 10 percent limitation was carried over to 1995.

X had taxable income (determined without regard to any deduction for charitable contributions) of $200,000 in 1995 and made a charitable contribution of $18,000 in 1995. For 1995, X was able to deduct the amount of $20,000 (10% of $200,000). This amount consisted of the $18,000 contribution made in 1995 and of $2,000 of the amount ($5,000) carried over from 1993 to 1995. The remaining $3,000 of the carryover from 1993 was available for purposes of computing the charitable contribution carryover from 1993 to 1996, 1997, and 1998.[130]

---

§ 7.18   CORPORATIONS' NET OPERATING LOSS CARRYOVERS AND CARRYBACKS

(a)   Carryovers

A corporation having a net operating loss carryover from any tax year must apply a special rule concerning these carryovers[131] before computing the excess charitable contributions carryover from any tax year. This special rule is as follows: In determining the amount of excess charitable contributions that may be deducted in tax years succeeding the contribution year, the excess of the charitable contributions made by a corporation in the contribution year over the amount deductible in that year must be reduced by the amount by which the excess (1) reduces taxable income for purposes of determining the net operating loss carryover under the net operating loss deduction rules[132] and (2) increases a net operating loss carryover to a succeeding tax year. Thus, if the excess of the contributions made in a tax year over the amount deductible in a tax year is utilized to reduce taxable income (under the rules for determining net operating

---

[130] Reg. § 1.170A-11(c)(1).
[131] IRC § 170(d)(2)(B).
[132] IRC § 172(b)(2), second sentence.

loss carryovers[133]) for the year, thereby serving to increase the amount of the net operating loss carryover to a succeeding tax year or years, a charitable contributions carryover is not available. If only a portion of the excess charitable contribution is so used, the charitable contributions carryover must be reduced only to that extent.

These rules may be illustrated by the following example:

Example 7.29

Corporation Y, which reports its income on the calendar year basis, made a charitable contribution of $20,000 during 1993. Y's taxable income for 1993 was $80,000 (computed without regard to any net operating loss deduction and without regard to any deduction for charitable contributions). Y had a net operating loss carryover from 1992 of $80,000. In the absence of the net operating loss deduction, Y would have been allowed a charitable contribution deduction for 1993 of $8,000 (10% of $80,000). After the application of the net operating loss deduction, Y was not allowed a deduction for charitable contributions, and there was a tentative charitable contribution carryover from 1993 of $20,000. For purposes of determining the net operating loss carryover to 1994, Y computed its taxable income for 1993 by deducting the $8,000 charitable contribution. Thus, after the $80,000 net operating loss carryover was applied against the $72,000 of taxable income for 1993, there remained an $8,000 net operating loss carryover to 1994. Since the application of the net operating loss carryover of $80,000 from 1992 reduced the taxable income of Y for 1993 to zero, no part of the $20,000 of charitable contributions in that year was deductible. However, in determining the amount of the allowable charitable contribution carryover from 1993 to 1994, 1995, 1996, 1997, and 1998, the $20,000 had to be reduced by the portion of it ($8,000) which was used to reduce taxable income for 1993 and which thereby served to increase the net operating loss carryover from 1992 to 1994 from zero to $8,000.[134]

(b) Carrybacks

The amount of the excess contribution for a contribution year is not increased because a net operating loss carryback is available as a deduction in the contribution year. In addition, in determining the

---

[133]IRC § 172(b)(2).
[134]Reg. § 1.170A-11(c)(2).

amount of the net operating loss for any year subsequent to the contribution year which is a carryback or carryover to tax years succeeding the contribution year, the amount of any charitable contributions must be limited to the amount of the contributions which did not exceed 10 percent of the donor's taxable income for the contribution year.[135]

The amount of the charitable contribution from a preceding tax year which is deductible in a current tax year (the "deduction year") cannot be reduced because a net operating loss carryback is available as a deduction in the deduction year. In addition, in determining the amount of the net operating loss for any tax year subsequent to the deduction year which is a carryback or a carryover to tax years succeeding the deduction year, the amount of contributions made in the deduction year must be limited to the amount of these contributions, actually made in that year,[136] which did not exceed 10 percent of the donor's taxable income for the deduction year.[137]

(c) Year Contribution Is Made

Contributions made by a corporation in a contribution year include contributions which are considered as paid during the contribution year.[138]

---

[135] Reg. § 1.170A-11(c)(3).
[136] IRC § 170(d)(2).
[137] Reg. § 1.170A-11(c)(4).
[138] Reg. § 1.170A-11(c)(5).

8

Estate and Gift Tax Considerations

by Michael E. Murphree

§ 8.1 INTRODUCTION

Federal estate and gift tax law came into existence in 1916, and has been a continuous part of the federal tax scheme ever since. Unlike federal income tax law, federal estate and gift taxes are an excise tax, on the transfer of property of individuals, either during their lives or upon their death.

The federal estate and gift taxes are frequently referred to as estate tax. This is a tax upon the value of estate property of individuals passing to others either during their lives, or upon their death. This is not the same as state law inheritance taxes, which tax the beneficiary or recipient of property from a decedent.

The federal estate and gift tax is a unified transfer tax comprising two elements; the first element is the "gift" tax; the second element is the "estate" tax. The tax is unified in that both gift and estate transfers are taxed as an integrated whole. They comprise a unified transfer tax system. (This has not always been the case during the history of the federal estate and gift tax.)

Another transfer tax is the tax on generation skipping transfers. The generation skipping transfer tax is not integrated with the gift and estate transfer tax system, but is a separate tax on transfers. However, it is complementary to, and works in conjunction with, the unified gift and estate tax system. It reaches transfers of wealth that are otherwise missed by the unified transfer tax. As its name implies, it purports to tax transferred wealth that skips a generation. A "generation" is specifically defined by the law.

Separate and apart from its function as a revenue device, the federal transfer taxes serve an important social function. These taxes tend to lessen the concentration of wealth, particularly family wealth, in the society.

Although the federal estate and gift tax applies to any transfer, the traditional focus of concern has been upon transfers within the family context. More precisely, the focus is upon generational transfers of family wealth to successive generations.

The income tax, as a progressive tax, has a greater bite as income levels rise. However, as a tax on income, it has little effect on previously accumulated wealth. It may lessen the ability of individuals to accumulate wealth, but it has no effect on previously accumulated wealth, typically family wealth, that is passed from generation to generation.

Unlike the federal income tax, the federal estate tax is, fundamentally, a tax on wealth. It is a tax on personal wealth whenever it is transferred gratuitously during an individual's life, or upon transfer by that individual's death.

The estate tax lessens concentrations of wealth through its progressive tax rate structure. For 1992, the graduated rates for federal estate and gift taxes start at 18% (for estates up to $10,000) and rise progressively to a steep 55% (for estates over $3,000,000). In 1993, the top rate drops to 50% (for estates over $2,500,000). Although the estate and gift taxes do not prevent passing of large estates, they take a sizable bite out of large estates, and so tend to lessen the concentration of family wealth.

Families with small concentrations of wealth are given a break. Through the availability of a credit known as the unified credit, estates of up to $600,000 can pass free of federal estate and gift tax.

Additionally, small amounts of wealth can be transferred annually to other individuals free of gift tax. Through what is known as the annual (gift tax) exclusion, as much as $10,000 per individual may be transferred each year free of the unified estate and gift tax during a person's lifetime.

Given the sizable tax bite associated with large estates, and the natural tendency and desire on the part of individuals to pass as much of their family wealth as possible to the next generation, there has been a great deal of attention paid to estate tax planning. Estate planning has developed as a means of minimizing or reducing the amount of estate transfer taxes incurred in passing on family wealth.

§ 8.2   FEDERAL GIFT TAX

Federal tax law imposes an excise tax on the value of an individual's lifetime transfers of property. However, not all transfers are subject to the tax. Only those transfers that are "gifts" fall within the ambit of the tax.

A gift, in common parlance, is understood to be a present or donation. Frequently one makes a gift as an act or expression of love, affection, friendship, or respect. The gift is generally understood to be gratuitous, and not for any consideration or remuneration. The term gift may have a different meaning for federal gift tax purposes.

(a)   Imposition of Gift Tax—General Elements

Under federal gift tax law, a tax is imposed "on the transfer of property by gift during [the] calender year by any individual."[1]

The federal gift tax applies generally to all individuals, whether they are residents or non-residents of the United States.[2] Special rules apply throughout the gift tax area to non-residents, and non-residents not citizens of the United States. Corporations and other artificial entities are not subject to the tax, only natural persons.

A United States citizen who resides in a U.S. possession is considered a citizen.[3] However, if such person acquired U.S. citizenship solely by being a citizen of the possession, or birth or residence in the possession, such person is considered a non-resident and not a citizen of the United States.[4]

(b)   Scope of Covered Transfers and Property

Generally all property of every kind is included within the scope of the tax. It applies to real or personal, tangible or intangible property.[5] It applies to property situated inside or outside the United States.[6] However, only transfers of property situated within the

---

[1] IRC § 2501.
[2] IRC § 2501(a)(1).
[3] IRC § 2501(b).
[4] IRC § 2501(c).
[5] IRC § 2511(a).
[6] *Id.*

United States are covered in the case of a non-resident not a resident of the United States.

Transfers of intangible property by a non-resident not a citizen of the United States are not included[7], unless the intangible property is stock in a domestic corporation or debt obligations of the United States, its political subdivisions, or its citizens.[8] But note a special exception in cases of lost U.S. citizenship.[9]

Also, the tax applies to all types of transfers, "whether the transfer is in trust or otherwise, whether the gift is direct or indirect."[10] Certain other transfers of property, or property interests, are specifically included in the federal gift tax law.

(c) Powers of Appointment

Generally, the exercise, release, or lapse of a general power of appointment is considered to be a transfer subject to the gift tax.[11] A "general power of appointment" over property is the power of an individual to appoint property to oneself, one's estate, creditors, or the creditor's of that estate.[12]

Certain powers are not considered to be general powers of appointment.[13] These powers are generally limited by an ascertainable standard, or in conjunction with some other person. Powers to "consume, invade, or appropriate property for the benefit of the possessor" limited by an ascertainable standard concerning health, education, support, or maintenance are not general powers.[14] Powers exercisable only in conjunction with the person creating the power are not considered general.[15]

Certain lapses are not treated as releases of general powers over property. Where property can be appointed annually that does not

[7]IRC § 2501(2).
[8]IRC § 2511(b).
[9]IRC § 2501(3).
[10]IRC § 2511(a).
[11]IRC § 2514. Special rules apply to powers created on or before October 21, 1942.
[12]IRC § 2514(c).
[13]IRC § 2514.
[14]IRC § 2514(c)(1).
[15]IRC § 2514(c)(3)(A).

exceed the greater of $5,000 or 5% of the value of the asset, the lapse of such power is not considered to be the release of a general power over the property. Such a qualifying lapse will not be subjected to imposition of a gift tax.

The term "gift" is not defined in the federal tax law. The Internal Revenue Service has stepped in to provide guidance by construing the term gift.[16] A gift is defined as any transfer whereby property, or property rights, are gratuitously conferred on another. The essential characteristics of a gift are:

- transfer of money, property, or property rights sufficient to vest legal or equitable title in the donee;
- relinquishment of dominion and control over the gift property by the donor;
- absence of full and adequate consideration for the transfer;
- no disclaimer or renunciation of the gift by the donee; and
- competence of the donor to make the gift

The criteria establishing a gift's essential characteristics do not take into account the objective or subjective gratuitousness in the transfer. Intention or motivation is not a governing factor. If any transfer is made for less than full and adequate consideration, it is deemed a gift if all the other criteria are present.

(d) Transfers Deemed Non-Gifts

Gifts are transfers for less than adequate consideration. Under the federal gift tax law, certain transfers are deemed to be for full and adequate consideration, and hence do not fall within the definition of a "gift." These transfers are all made pursuant to a written marital property settlement agreement that meets certain other conditions.[17] A divorce must occur within a three year period that begins one year before the date the agreement was entered into. Further, the transfers must be to the other spouse in settlement of marital or property rights, or to provide for child support during minority of children born to the marriage.

---

[16]Reg. § 25.2511-1(c).
[17]IRC § 2516.

(e)   Taxable Gifts

Gift and estate taxes are unified and aggregated to take account of all lifetime transfers and transfers taking effect at death. However, death is not the taxable event for purposes of gift tax. Taxable gifts are accounted for and taxed on an annual basis during the life of an individual.[18] A "taxable gift" is defined as "the total amount of gifts made during the calendar year" above the annual exclusion (if applicable), and less allowable gift tax deductions.[19]

(f)   Exclusions from Taxable Gift

Certain transfers are excluded from the definition of a taxable gift tax.

(i)   Tuition for Education

The federal gift tax law excludes from tax transfers of property (typically cash payments) made directly to a qualified educational organization for tuition, on behalf of some individual (typically a son or daughter).[20] The tax law encourages the private funding of education free of potential transfer tax.

(ii)   Medical Care Costs

The federal gift tax law excludes from tax transfers of property (again, typically cash payments) made directly to a medical care provider for medical care services on behalf of some individual (typically a family member).[21] Recognizing that health care is expensive and can be a significant financial burden, the federal tax law does not impose an additional financial burden on those who come to the aid of family members (or others) in the payment of costly medical services.

(iii)   Waiver of Pension Rights

The third exclusion from the definition of a taxable gift is for waivers of certain pension survivor benefits, or the rights thereto.[22]

[18] IRC § 2501(a)(1).
[19] IRC § 2503.
[20] IRC § 2503(e).
[21] Id.
[22] IRC § 2503(f).

(iv) Loans of Art Work

The fourth exclusion from the definition of a taxable gift involves a loan of any work of art that is archaeological, historic, or creative tangible personal property. The federal tax law excludes from tax loans of art work made to an exempt organization described in 501(c)(3) and used for its exempt purpose.[23]

(v) Transfers to Political Organizations

The fifth exclusion from the definition of a taxable gift is for transfers to certain defined political parties for the use of such organizations.[24]

(g) Annual Exclusion

As noted above, taxable gifts are all gifts made during a calendar year after taking into account the annual exclusion, less allowable deductions. The annual exclusion is a fixed dollar amount that is allowed as an exclusion from gift tax. Currently, the amount of the exclusion is $10,000.[25]

There are a number of restrictions on the availability or applicability of the annual exclusion.

First, the exclusion is available annually. It may not be carried over to another year if it is unused or under used.

Second, the exclusion is available for the first $10,000 of a gift to each recipient thereof, termed a donee. There is no limit on the number of donees that may be gifted property covered by the annual exclusion.

Third, only present interests are considered for purposes of the annual exclusion. Future interests in property,[26] including reversions and remainder interests,[27] are denied the exclusion.

Certain transfers made for the benefit of minors are not considered to be future interests under the annual exclusion. A transfer for the benefit of a minor qualifies for the annual exclusion where:

[23] IRC § 2503(g).
[24] IRC § 2501(a)(5).
[25] IRC § 2503.
[26] IRC § 2503(b).
[27] Reg. § 25.2503-3.

- the property, and income therefrom, may be used by or for the benefit of the minor before he or she reaches 21, and
- where any remaining property and income is distributed to the minor upon reaching 21, and if he or she dies before reaching 21, to his or her estate before 21, or as he or she appoints pursuant to a general power of appointment[28]

(h) Valuation of Gift Transfers

The federal gift transfer tax applies only to the value of the property transferred as of the date of transfer.[29] Where the gift is also a direct skip within the meaning of the generation skipping transfer tax, the value of such a gift is increased by the amount of the generation skipping transfer tax imposed.[30] The value of money gifts is the amount given. Gifts of property other than money are valued at their fair market value.[31]

In the case of transfers of property for less than full and adequate consideration, the value of the transferred gift is the fair market value of the property less the consideration received.[32] Suppose a parent had purchased real estate which has greatly appreciated in value. It was purchased years ago for $50,000. Today it has a fair market value of $250,000. The parent decides to give the realty to an only child, and transfers the property to his or her child for cost, $50,000. Since insufficient consideration was received, part of the transfer represents a taxable gift. The value of the taxable gift would be $200,000, the fair market value of the property ($250,000) less the amount of consideration received (($50,000).

(i) Basis of Gifted Property

The basis of gift property in the hands of the recipient is generally the transferor's basis plus the gift tax paid as a result of the transfer.[33] To account for the transferor's investment in property, the federal income tax law provides that the basis in gifted property to a trans-

---

[28] IRC § 2503(c); Reg. § 25.2503-4(a).
[29] IRC § 2512(a).
[30] IRC § 2515.
[31] Reg. § 25.2512-1.
[32] IRC § 2512(b); Reg 25.2512-1.
[33] IRC § 1015(d).

feree is the transferor's basis. This is known as a transferred or carryover basis. The basis of the property in the hands of the gift giver, the transferor, is transferred with the gift, and becomes the basis in the property in the hands of the recipient, the transferee, of the gift. As noted, the amount of the transferred basis in gifted property is increased by the amount of gift tax paid by the transferor as a result of the gift.

There is one important limitation on the carryover of the transferor's basis. The transferee's basis in gifted property is the same as the basis in the hands of the transferor, except that the basis cannot exceed the fair market value of the property at the time of the gift. What this means is that tax wealth can be transferred, but not tax losses. Should loss property (property in which the basis exceeds the fair market value of the asset) be transferred by gift, the transferee will not be able to recognize the transferor's loss on the property.

An example of the basis rule is a bargain sale of property, which is a sale for less than fair market value (insufficient consideration). It is also known as a part gift/part sale transaction, as intention of the transferor is to make a gift of a part of the property.

Taking the previous example, suppose the transferor wishes to sell his $250,000 investment property which he purchased years ago for $50,000, for less than its value. The intent is to make a gift of part of the appreciation.

If the transferor sold the property for $40,000, less than the basis in the property, no loss would be allowed to result on the sale. The amount of the taxable gift would be $210,000, the difference between the fair market value of the gift ($250,000), and the amount of consideration received ($40,000).

If the transferor sold the property for $60,000, there would be a gain of $10,000 on the transaction. The amount of the taxable gift would be $190,000, the difference between the fair market value of the gift ($250,000), and the amount of consideration received ($60,000).

On the $40,000 sale, the transferee's basis would be the gift tax plus the greater of the amount paid by the transferee ($40,000) or the transferor's basis ($50,000). In this case the transferee assumes the transferor's basis of $50,000.

On the $60,000 sale, the transferee's basis would be the gift tax plus the greater of the amount paid by the transferee ($60,000) or the transferor's basis ($50,000). In this case the transferee takes his or her own cost basis of $60,000.

(j) Gift Tax Deductions

The federal gift tax law provides two deductions from taxable gifts: the marital deduction and the charitable deduction.

(i) Marital Deduction

The federal gift tax law provides an unlimited gift tax deduction for transfers between spouses.[34] Spouses can make any number of transfers between themselves, in any amount, free of gift tax. However, the unlimited marital deduction is subject to a number of conditions and limitations.

Generally, life estates and other terminable interests may not qualify for the marital deduction. Terminable interests are interests in property that may be terminated. If a transfer is made to the other spouse of an interest that may terminate that other spouse's rights and interest in the property, such a transfer does not qualify for the marital deduction if:

- the transferor spouse retains or gifts to someone other than the other spouse an interest in the property, and such person may enjoy use or possession of the property upon a termination; or
- the transferor spouse retains a power of appointment over use or possession of the property upon a termination

Qualified terminable interest property (QTIP) will qualify for the marital deduction if certain conditions are met. The spouse must receive income for life, and no other person may have a power of appointment over the property except to appoint to the other spouse during the other spouse's life.[35] An election must be made to take advantage of the QTIP provisions.

A qualified charitable remainder trust will not be disqualified from a marital deduction if the other spouse is the only non-charitable beneficiary of the trust.[36]

The deduction is disallowed in its entirety if the other spouse is not a citizen of the United States. In its place is substituted the

---

[34] IRC § 2523.
[35] IRC § 2523(f).
[36] IRC § 2523(g).

annual exclusion with a limit of $100,000 rather than $10,000.[37]
Other special rules apply in this context.

(ii) Charitable Deduction

Like federal income tax law, the federal gift tax law also provides a
deduction for gifts to charities.[38]

Citizens and residents of the United States are allowed to deduct
all gift transfers to or for the use of

- the United States, any State (including the District of Columbia), and political subdivisions thereof for exclusively public
  purposes
- organizations organized and operated exclusively for religious,
  charitable, scientific, literary or educational purposes, to foster
  amateur sports competition (but not athletic facilities or equipment), and to encourage art and the prevention of cruelty to
  children or animals (no net earnings to private shareholders or
  individuals, and not a disqualified organization for attempted
  legislative influence, and no participation in political campaigns)
- fraternal societies for use exclusively for religious, charitable,
  scientific, literary or educational purposes, including encouragement of art and the prevention of cruelty to children or
  animals
- veterans' organizations organized in the United States or a possession (no net earnings to private shareholder or individual)

Non-residents not citizens of the United States are allowed to
deduct all gift transfers to or for the use of

- the United States, any State (including the District of Columbia), and political subdivisions thereof for exclusively public
  purposes
- domestic corporations organized and operated exclusively for
  religious, charitable, scientific, literary or educational purposes,
  and to encourage art and the prevention of cruelty to children

---

[37] IRC § 2523(i).
[38] IRC § 2522.

or animals (no net earnings to private shareholders or individuals, and not a disqualified organization for attempted legislative influence, and no participation in political campaigns)

- trust fund, community chest, or foundation organized and operated exclusively for religious, charitable, scientific, literary or educational purposes, and to encourage art and the prevention of cruelty to children or animals (no substantial part of activities for propaganda or to influence legislation, and no participation in political campaigns) and are used exclusively within the United States for such purposes
- fraternal societies for use exclusively for religious, charitable, scientific, literary or educational purposes, including encouragement of art and the prevention of cruelty to children or animals
- veterans' organizations organized in the United States or a possession (no net earnings to private shareholder or individual)

The charitable deduction is subject to disallowance in certain cases. Transfers to organizations described in Section 508(d) or 4948(c)(4) of the Internal Revenue Code do not enjoy the charitable deduction. Generally, a transfer of a remainder interest in property to a charity is not entitled to a charitable gift tax deduction where the transferor retains an interest, or transfers his or her retained interest, to a donee for a use other than the charitable uses described above under donations by citizens, residents, and nonresidents not citizens.[39]

A charitable deduction is allowed for remainder transfers (remainder interests) to charities by the following methods:

- a charitable remainder annuity trust
- a charitable remainder unitrust
- a pooled income fund for other interests
- a guaranteed annuity
- an annual fixed percentage distribution of fair market value of property

Citizens and residents are also allowed a deduction for the transfer of certain qualified real estate easements.[40]

[39] IRC § 2522(c).
[40] IRC § 2522(d).

(k) Liability for Gift Tax

Gift tax is computed on the value of taxable gift transfers. Liability to pay the tax imposed is upon the donor, the transferor of the gift property.[41]

(l) Split Gifts Between Spouses

The federal gift tax law allows spouses to agree to share, equally, in gifts made by the other spouse.[42] This permits use of the other spouse's annual exclusion as well as the unified credit. If the annual exclusion is split, a $20,000 gift tax free transfer can be made in lieu of the regular $10,000 exclusion per donee.

When both spouses consent[43] to a split gift, each becomes jointly and severally liable for the entire gift tax liability.[44]

Gift splitting is not permitted on transfers where one spouse gives the other spouse a general power of appointment over the property.[45]

(m) Disclaimers

Persons who hold interests in property, including powers with respect to property, may disclaim their interest without the disclaimer being treated as a taxable transfer to that person.[46] Such a disclaimer is termed a "qualified disclaimer," meaning an irrevocable and unqualified refusal to accept a property interest.[47] To be effective the disclaimer must meet certain other prescribed form and notice requirements.

Where property, or an interest therein, passes to another as a result of a qualified disclaimer, the person disclaiming is not treated as having made a taxable transfer.[48]

[41] IRC § 2502(c).
[42] IRC § 2513.
[43] Required by IRC § 2513(a)(2).
[44] IRC § 2513(d).
[45] IRC § 2513.
[46] IRC § 2518.
[47] IRC § 2518(b).
[48] Reg. § 25.2518-1(b).

§ 8.3   FEDERAL ESTATE TAX

The second part of the unified federal transfer tax system is the estate tax. This aspect of the system concerns transfers of property that take place upon the death of an individual.

(a)   Gross Estate

The first step in determining estate tax liability is the determination of the value of the decedent's "gross estate." The value of the gross estate is defined as including the date of death value of "all property, real or personal, tangible or intangible, wherever situated."[49] The value of the gross estate also includes "the value of all property to the extent of the interest therein of the decedent at the time of his death."[50]

The gross estate encompasses a broad spectrum of property. The gross estate includes within its reach the probate estate, contractual payments (such as insurance), and jointly titled property. In addition to the broad sweep of the gross estate given by its statutory definition, the federal estate tax law provides for other specific inclusions in the gross estate. Included within the gross estate are:

- dower or curtesy interests
- transfers within 3 years of death
- retained life estates
- transfers taking effect at death
- revocable transfers
- annuities
- joint interests
- powers of appointment
- life insurance
- transfers for insufficient consideration

There are basic policy reasons for inclusion of these property interests in the decedent's estate. Although the decedent has parted with the legal ownership of these property interests, where significant

[49] IRC § 2031.
[50] IRC § 2033.

beneficial interests are retained in the property, the decedent should be treated as the owner for purposes of imposing the estate transfer tax. Where the retained powers and control over property are such that the decedent has the ability to affect the beneficial use and enjoyment of property during life, or upon death, particularly with respect to transferring such interests, the decedent can in all fairness be treated as though he or she were the owner of such property. As a deemed owner, the decedent is taxed on such property as though it were a part of his or her transferable estate on death.

(i) Dower or Curtesy Interests

The full value of all property subject to dower, curtesy, or other similar marital estate interests of the surviving spouse in the decedent's estate, are specifically included in the gross estate.[51]

(ii) Transfers Within 3 Years of Death

At one time the federal estate tax law required that transfers in contemplation of death be included back in the estate of the decedent. The policy reason was obvious. A person, nearing death, with knowledge that they would soon die, could bypass the heavy estate tax bite through deathbed lifetime gifts of most or all of their property.[52]

To close this glaring loophole, transfers in contemplation of death were recaptured and added back to the taxable estate. However, this provision also generated a great deal of litigation over whether certain transfers were in contemplation of death.

To forestall deathbed type transfers, and to avoid litigation over whether certain transfers were in contemplation of death, a "bright line" rule was adopted. All transfers within three years of the decedent's death were added back to the estate.

Presently, except for certain kinds of transfers, the three year rule no longer applies.[53] The transfers made within three years of death and included back in the estate are:

---

[51] IRC § 2034.
[52] IRC § 2035.
[53] IRC § 2035(d).

- transfers with retained life interests
- transfers taking effect at death
- revocable transfers
- life insurance proceeds

Certain other gifts within three years of death are included back in the gross estate, but only for special purposes and calculations.[54]

(iii) Retained Life Estates

The gross estate includes property in which the decedent retained for life (or a period ascertainable by reference to the decedent's life) the right to, or the right to appoint, the possession, enjoyment, or the right to income from the property.[55]

(iv) Transfers Taking Effect at Death

The gross estate includes the value of all property in which the decedent has transferred an interest that can be enjoyed only by surviving the decedent, and the decedent has retained a reversionary interest that exceeds 5 percent of the value of the property.[56] A retained interest includes any interest to the decedent, his or her estate, or subject to a power of appointment in the decedent.[57]

Where the value of a retained reversion is 5 percent or less, such reversion may be included back in the estate.[58]

(v) Revocable Transfers

This provision recognizes that property ownership is more than mere legal title. Ownership, in its broader sense, includes a bundle of rights tied up in the property. Legal title is but one of the many rights bundled up in property. These other rights include beneficial rights, such as the power to control use and enjoyment of proper-

---

[54] IRC § 2035(d)(3).
[55] IRC § 2036.
[56] IRC § 2037(a).
[57] IRC § 2037(b).
[58] Reg. § 20.2037-1(c).

ty. One may sever legal title to property and yet retain so many other powers and rights that control of property (through its use and enjoyment) has been retained. In such cases, the person controlling the property is in effect the de facto owner of the property.

The gross estate includes the value of all property over which the decedent had a power to alter, amend, revoke, or terminate an interest in property. Any form of a revocable transfer is includable.[59]

(vi) Annuities

An annuity is a contractual arrangement whereby a stream of income is paid in exchange for a premium payment. An annuity (periodic income payments) is paid to a beneficiary for a stated period of time. The payments are usually of a specified amount (fixed dollar amount), payable at certain intervals (weekly, monthly, yearly), over a certain period of time (number of years or for life).

The gross estate includes the value of any annuity or other payment receivable by any beneficiary by reason of surviving the decedent under any form of contract or agreement (other than insurance) if any payment was payable to the decedent, or the decedent had a right to receive a payment, alone or with another, for life or a period not ascertainable without reference to the decedent's life.[60] The amount of payments includable in the gross estate are the amounts proportionate to the purchase price paid by the decedent.

(vii) Joint Interests

Except for spouses, the gross estate includes the value of all property held as joint tenants unless it can be shown that the interest held originally belonged to some other person. Spouses include only one-half of property owned as joint tenants or as tenants by the entireties. Jointly held property acquired by gift, bequest, devise, or inheritance includes only the decedent's fractional share of the property.[61]

---

[59] IRC § 2038.
[60] IRC § 2039.
[61] IRC § 2040.

(viii) Powers of Appointment

The gross estate includes the value of property over which the decedent had a general power of appointment at the time of death.[62]

Certain lapses are not treated as releases of general powers over property. Where property can be appointed annually and does not exceed the greater of $5,000 or 5 percent of the value of the asset, the lapse of such power is not considered to be the release of a general power over the property. Such a qualifying lapse will not be subjected to imposition of a gift tax.

(ix) Life Insurance

The gross estate includes the value of life insurance receivable by the executor on the life of the decedent, and insurance receivable by other beneficiaries where the decedent retained any incidents of ownership at the time of death, exercisable alone or in conjunction with another.[63] A reversionary interest of more than 5% of the value of the policy immediately before death is considered an incident of ownership.

Incidents of ownership include the power to change beneficiaries, revoke an assignment of the policy, pledge the policy for a loan, cancel, surrender, or transfer the policy.[64]

The amount or value of the insurance policy includable in the owner's estate is the policy's face amount, and not its cash surrender value.

(x) Transfers for Insufficient Consideration

The gross estate includes the following property transferred for less than full and adequate consideration:

- transfers within 3 years of death
- retained life estate
- transfers taking effect at death
- revocable transfers
- powers of appointment

[62] IRC § 2041.
[63] IRC § 2042.
[64] Reg. § 20.2042-1(c)(2).

(b) Taxable Estate

The taxable estate is defined in the federal estate tax law as the value of the gross estate less allowable deductions.[65]

The following items are deductions allowable from the gross estate to arrive at the taxable estate:

- funeral expenses
- administration expenses
- claims against the estate
- unpaid indebtedness included in gross estate
- losses and other casualties
- charitable deduction
- marital deduction

The two most significant deductions are the charitable and marital estate tax deductions.

(i) Charitable Estate Tax Deduction

A charitable estate tax deduction[66] is allowed for the value of all estate transfers of the decedent to or for the use of the following organizations:

- the United States, any State (including the District of Columbia), and political subdivisions thereof for exclusively public purposes
- organizations organized and operated exclusively for religious, charitable, scientific, literary or educational purposes, to foster amateur sports competition (but not athletic facilities or equipment), and to encourage art and the prevention of cruelty to children or animals (no net earnings to private shareholders or individuals, and not a disqualified organization for attempted legislative influence, and no participation in political campaigns)
- fraternal societies for use exclusively for religious, charitable, scientific, literary or educational purposes, including encour-

[65] IRC § 2051.
[66] IRC § 2055(a).

agement of art and the prevention of cruelty to children or animals (not a disqualified organization for attempted legislative influence, and no participation in political campaigns)

- veterans' organizations organized by Act of Congress, or its departments or local chapters or posts (no net earnings to private shareholder or individual)

The charitable deduction is disallowed in certain cases. Transfers to organizations described in Section 508(d) or 4948(c)(4) of the Internal Revenue Code do not enjoy the charitable deduction. Generally, a transfer of a split interest in property to a charity is not entitled to a charitable estate tax deduction where an interest in the same property is transferred to a person, or for a use, other than the charitable uses described above.[67]

A charitable deduction is allowed for such split interests in property where the interest (remainder interest) transferred is:

- a charitable remainder annuity trust
- a charitable remainder unitrust
- a pooled income fund for other interests
- a guaranteed annuity
- an annual fixed percentage distribution of fair market value of property

Contributions of split interests in copyrighted tangible works of art are not denied a charitable contribution where the art work is conveyed separately from the copyright in such work.[68] The split gifts of the art work and its copyright are treated as separate properties. The contribution must be made to a qualified organization where the use of the property is related to the organization's function. A qualified organization is a 501(c)(3) organization other than a private foundation.

(ii) Marital Estate Tax Deduction

An unlimited marital deduction is allowed to a decedent for the value of any property transferred to his or her surviving spouse.[69]

---

[67] IRC § 2055(e).
[68] IRC § 2055(e)(4).
[69] IRC § 2056(a).

However, transfers of terminable interests in property, interests that fail after a certain period of time, the occurrence of a contingency, or failure of some event,[70] generally do not qualify for the marital deduction.[71]

An interest which is conditional on the survival of the surviving spouse will not be considered a terminable interest where such a condition does not exceed six months.[72]

A terminable life estate to the surviving spouse is entitled to the marital deduction where the spouse is entitled to receive all the income from the interest (or a specific portion thereof) at least annually with power of appointment in the surviving spouse (or the spouse's estate) over all the property (or a specific portion thereof).[73]

Similarly, in the case of proceeds from a life insurance policy, or an annuity, if the proceeds are payable in installments (or held to pay interest thereon) and the installments are payable at least annually (beginning at least 13 months after the decedent's death), such payments qualify for the marital deduction.[74] The payments must be payable only to the surviving spouse. Further, the surviving spouse (or the estate) must have a power of appointment over the property.

The marital deduction is available, by election, for qualified terminable interest property ("QTIP").[75] Under a QTIP election, a qualified terminable income interest for the life of the surviving spouse is granted a marital deduction. The interest qualifies where the surviving spouse has a right to income from the property (or a specific portion thereof) for life, payable at least annually, or has a life usufruct interest in the property. Further, no person may have a power of appointment over the property during the life of the surviving spouse.

Interests passing to the surviving spouse through a qualified charitable remainder trust do qualify for the marital deduction.[76] A trust is qualified where it is a charitable remainder annuity trust or a charitable remainder unitrust. The only non-charitable beneficiary under such a trust must be the surviving spouse.

---

[70] Reg. § 20.2056(b)-1(b).
[71] IRC § 2056(b).
[72] IRC § 2056(3).
[73] IRC § 2056(5).
[74] IRC § 2056(b)(6).
[75] IRC § 2056(b)(7).
[76] IRC § 2056(b)(8).

Special rules apply to a surviving spouse who is not a United States citizen. Generally, transfers to such spouses are not entitled to the marital deduction.[77] However, a transfer through a qualified domestic trust is entitled to a marital deduction.[78]

(c) Time of Valuation of Gross Estate

The general rule is that the gross estate is valued as of the date of death of the decedent.[79] However, an alternate valuation date can be elected by the executor of the estate. The election generally allows the gross estate to be valued as of six months after death for undistributed property, and the date of transfer for distributions within six months of death.[80] However, the election is allowable only where it will result in a decrease in both the value of the gross estate, and the sum of the transfer tax imposed.[81]

Generally, the value of the estate is the fair market value of the property on the date of death.[82] Special valuation rules are provided for farm and other qualified real estate.[83]

Unlisted stocks and securities are valued by taking into consideration value of similar securities of other corporations in the same or similar line of work.[84]

(d) Basis of Transferred Property

One significant difference between lifetime transfers, and transfers that take place on death, involves the basis of the property transferred. For lifetime transfers, the basis of property in the hands of the transferor is carried over and becomes the basis in the hands of the tranferee.

In contrast, transfers on death receive special preferential treatment. The basis to the recipient is not a carryover basis, but the fair

[77] IRC § 2056(d)(1).
[78] IRC § 2056(d)(2), 2056A.
[79] IRC § 2031(a).
[80] IRC § 2032(a).
[81] IRC § 2032(c).
[82] IRC § 2031, Reg. § 20.2031-1(b).
[83] IRC § 2032A.
[84] IRC § 2031(b).

market value of the property as of the date of death (or the alternate valuation date).[85] The recipient of a decedent's estate enjoys a stepped-up basis in the transferred property. Any appreciation in the asset will escape income tax free as a result of the testamentary transfer.

§ 8.4 UNIFIED TAX

The unified federal transfer tax is a progressive tax. It taxes the value of transfered property in brackets ranging (in 1992) from a low of 18 percent to a high of 55 percent for estates over $3 million. As of the time Congress was considering the Revenue Act of 1992, which would have been applicable with respect to transfers occurring after 1992, the maximum federal estate and gift tax rates were scheduled to decline to 50 percent on taxable transfers over $2.5 million. While that Act would have deferred for five years (until after 1997) these estate and gift tax rate reductions, the measure was vetoed.

Below is the unified tax rate table for 1992:

| Amount of Estate | | Amount of Bracket Tax |
Over	Not Over	Percentage
0	10,000	18
10,000	20,000	20
20,000	40,000	22
40,000	60,000	24
60,000	80,000	26
80,000	100,000	28
100,000	150,000	30
150,000	250,000	32
250,000	500,000	34
500,000	750,000	37
750,000	1,000,000	39
1,000,000	1,250,000	41
1,250,000	1,500,000	43
1,500,000	2,000,000	45
2,000,000	2,500,000	49
2,500,000	3,000,000	53
3,000,000	———	55

[85]IRC § 1014.

Here is the unified tax rate table for 1993:

Amount of Estate		Amount of Bracket Tax Percentage
Over	Not Over	
0	10,000	18
10,000	20,000	20
20,000	40,000	22
40,000	60,000	24
60,000	80,000	26
80,000	100,000	28
100,000	150,000	30
150,000	250,000	32
250,000	500,000	34
500,000	750,000	37
750,000	1,000,000	39
1,000,000	1,250,000	41
1,250,000	1,500,000	43
1,500,000	2,000,000	45
2,000,000	2,500,000	49
2,500,000	———	50

(a)   Estate and Gift Tax Credits

(i)   Unified Credit

A credit is available to offset the taxes imposed under the unified estate and gift transfer tax. Known as the "unified credit," it is available to offset, dollar for dollar, taxes imposed on both lifetime gift transfers and transfers by reason of death.[86]

Unified Transfer Tax Credit

Year of Gift/Death	Unified Credit Amount	Exemption Equivalent
1992	$192,800	$600,000

[86] IRC §§ 2010, 2505.

Under the unified credit, tax free transfers of up to $600,000 in asset value can be made during an individual's life and/or upon that person's death.

(ii) Other Credits

Under the unified transfer tax system, other credits are available to offset or reduce tax liability:

- credit for state death taxes[87]
- credit for foreign death taxes[88]
- credit for prior transfer[89]
- credit for death taxes on remainders[90]

§ 8.5 GENERATION SKIPPING TRANSFER TAX

A new transfer tax was added to the federal tax system by the Tax Reform Act of 1976.[91] The reason for the new tax was to curb a perceived abuse involving the use of trust vehicles in estate planning.

As will be seen, trusts can be used effectively as a means for passing wealth on to successive generations at minimum tax cost to the decedent's estate. Indeed, one of the guiding principles of estate planning is the passing down of wealth to "lower" or successive generations at a minimum tax cost.

Since decedent's estates are taxed on the value of their property, and trusts are only taxed on the income they generate, trusts have become convenient vehicles, or depositories, for generational wealth. A decedent's wealth (denominated first generation) can be transferred to a trust. The transfer may or may not involve the imposition of a transfer tax. Typically, the trust retains the property (known as trust corpus or principal) and distributes income to the next generational level (denominated second generation), typically the sons and daughters of the decedent. Tax is paid on the trust income, but not

---

[87] IRC § 2011.
[88] IRC § 2014.
[89] IRC § 2013.
[90] IRC § 2015.
[91] IRC § 2601 et. seq.

the trust property. The trust property is not included in the estates of the decedent's children upon their death. Therefore, there is no estate tax at the second generational level. The trust, upon the death of the decedent's children, typically distributes its property to the grandchild of the decedent (denominated third generation) free of transfer tax. Through the use of a trust vehicle, a generation is skipped over along with that generations level estate transfer tax.

Example-Diagram:

1st Gen.	2nd Gen.	3rd Generation
Grantor ———————	Children ———————	Grand Children

Income———————Income for life
(no estate tax)
Limited Power of Appointment
–invade principal under an
ascertainable standard,
or
–discretion within 5 and 5 powers

Principal————(By-pass)————Principal (one level of
estate tax)

Wealth——————————————————Wealth

To curb generational skipping transfers of wealth through use of trusts, and preserve the integrity of uniform generation to generation transfer taxes, the generation skipping transfer tax was adopted.

Application of the Generation Skipping Transfer Tax

A transfer tax is imposed on every generation skipping transfer.[92] The tax rate is a flat amount equal to the maximum unified estate and gift tax rate.[93] For 1992 the flat generation skipping transfer (referred to as "GST") tax is 55 percent. The rate drops to 50 percent for 1993 and later years. The tax itself, although a transfer tax, is not unified with the estate and gift tax. It is a separate tax on transfers of

[92] IRC § 2601.
[93] IRC § 2602.

property. The source for payment of the tax is the property subject to the GST tax.[94]

(i)   Generational Assignment

The federal tax code provides rules for determining to which generation a transferor of a generation skipping transfer belongs.[95] Generally, generational levels are assigned based upon lineal descent. Adopted persons, and persons related by half-blood, are treated as lineal descendants. Married individuals are assigned to the same generational level as their spouse. Non-lineal descendants are assigned to generations based upon their age. An individual within 12½ years of a transferor is assigned to the same generation as the transferor. An individuals between 12½ and 37½ years of a transferor is assigned to the next younger and lower generational level. New generational levels are added for each additional 25 year difference.

(ii)   Taxable Generation Skipping Transfers

A generation skipping transfer is defined as any:

- taxable distribution[96]
- taxable termination[97]
- direct skip[98]

Certain transfers are excluded from the definition.

Taxable Distribution. A taxable distribution is any distribution from a trust to a skip person,[99] that is, a person two or more generations below the transferor of the interest.[100]

The amount of a taxable distribution is the value received on the transfer reduced by expenses of the transferee related to the tax.[101]

---

[94] IRC § 2603.
[95] IRC § 2651.
[96] IRC § 2611(a)(1).
[97] IRC § 2611(a)(2).
[98] IRC § 2611(a)(3).
[99] IRC § 2612(b).
[100] IRC § 2613.
[101] IRC § 2621.

Taxable Termination. A taxable termination is any termination of an interest in property held in trust and such interest is for the benefit of a skip person.[102] The amount of a taxable termination is the value received on the transfer reduced by expenses related to the property.[103]

Direct Skip. A direct skip is the transfer of an interest to a skip person.[104] The amount of the taxable gift is the value received.

(iii)   Valuation of Generation Skipping Transfer

The valuation of the transfer is as of the time of the transfer.[105] The estate tax alternate valuation period may apply to direct skips or taxable terminations at death.[106]

(iv)   Exemptions from Generation Skipping Transfer Tax

An exemption of $1,000,000 is allowed to every individual with respect to the value of property transferred.[107] As with the gift tax annual exclusion, spouses are permitted to split the generation skipping transfer tax exemption. This allows married couples to transfer up to $2,000,000 free of GST tax.

Another exemption is permitted for transfers to grandchildren.[108] If a parent of a grandchild, who is a lineal descendant of the transferor, is dead, the grandchild is treated as the child of the transferor. In such a case, the generation skipping gap is closed up so that no GST tax is applicable to the transaction.

All lifetime gifts entitled to the annual gift tax exclusion, or the education and medical exclusion, are exempt from the GST tax.[109]

---

[102]IRC § 2612(a).
[103]IRC § 2621.
[104]IRC § 2612(c).
[105]IRC § 2624.
[106]IRC § 2624.
[107]IRC § 2631.
[108]IRC § 2612(c).
[109]IRC § 2642(c)(3).

(v) *Estate Planning*

Estate planning is a term that applies to lifetime financial and tax planning for an individual (and his or her family), as well as planning for the transfer of accumulated lifetime wealth. Typically the estate planner focuses on the lifetime financial resources, needs and desires of an individual. At the same time, the estate planner looks at that person's needs and desire to provide for others during their life and after death. The estate planner attempts to meet these needs and desires by utilizing techniques and devices to reduce or eliminate tax consequences to the individual.

§ 8.6 ESTATE PLANNING PRINCIPLES

There are a number of principles that guide an estate planner in his or her work to reduce the federal transfer tax.

(a) Estate Reduction

The first principle is estate reduction. The federal transfer tax ultimately reaches only that property remaining in, or by tax law included back in, the decedent's gross estate. To avoid or minimize tax, one can reduce an estate so that by the time death (and taxes) arrives, little or nothing remains to be taxed.

There are a number of techniques available to accomplish this result. The $10,000 annual gift tax exclusion is one method for getting assets out of the estate. An individual can give up to $10,000 annually to any number of individuals. If that person is married, he or she can split their spouses annual exclusion and give away $20,000 per year.

The annual exclusion can be leveraged to convey away assets that will (or can be expected to) appreciate greatly over time. A $10,000 (or $20,000) tax-free gift of appreciating property today may over time shelter several times that amount.

Likewise, an individual can take advantage of the unified credit to make lifetime transfers of more than the annual exemption amount to remove large assets that will (or can be expected to) appreciate over time. Up to $600,000 in assets can be transferred away tax free, and with it any appreciation over the life of the donor.

(b) Estate Freezes

A complementary device for controlling appreciation in the estate is through what is known as an estate freeze. Instead of transferring the entire asset that is expected to appreciate over time, the amount of appreciation in the asset can be frozen at its current level, and the appreciation potential conveyed away at little or no tax cost.

One technique involves the recapitalization of stock in a corporation. The older members of the corporation could maintain their interests in the corporation through ownership of common stock. The value of the stock could be fixed. New preferred stock could then be issued. Such stock would have little current value, but could be expected to appreciate in value as the company grows. By such a stock recapitalization, the present value of the company could be frozen for the owners, while the future appreciation could be passed on to the younger generation in the form of preferred stock with little or no value (and hence little or no transfer tax cost).

New valuation rules have been adopted which limit the ability to of an estate planner to freeze the estate of a business owner.[110]

(c) Deferral

Another technique is deferral of estate tax. The time value of money principle suggests that the deferred or delayed enjoyment of one dollar a year from now is worth less than a dollar today. Therefore, the same amount of money today is worth more than the same amount of money in the future. The greater the deferral, the greater the present value of money.

Deferral of transfer taxes can be accomplished in a number of ways. The most significant method is by transfers to a spouse. The marital deduction is unlimited. Except for the exclusion of certain unqualified terminable interests, taxes can be deferred through transfers to a spouse qualifying for the marital deduction.

Another popular deferral device has been the trust. Assets placed in trust could provide for support of a spouse, with distribution upon death to the children. Similarly, a trust could provide for support of children, with a distribution upon death to grandchildren. In either event, taxation of the trust assets would be deferred until after they were distributed to the children or grandchildren. The generation

[110]IRC §§ 2701-2704.

skipping transfer tax must now be carefully considered with respect to these types of transactions.

(d) Generation Skipping Transfers

Like deferral, an estate planning goal has traditionally been to pass assets down to as many lower generations as possible with little or no tax. Bypass trusts were used for this purpose. A trust could be set up to provide for your children, and the remainder to the grandchildren. The next lower generation would be skipped over free of estate tax at that level.

Today, that device is limited to a degree by the generation skipping transfer tax. However, by utilizing the $1,000,000 exclusion, opportunities to skip generations tax free still exist.

(e) Credit Maximizing Trusts and Transactions

Another technique has been to use the available credits to shield assets from tax, and maximize tax savings. As an example, assume Husband and Wife have the following estate:

H	W
$800,000	$400,000

Either spouse could transfer assets to the other free of tax. However, the surviving spouse would end up with a $1,200,000 estate. The unified credit would shield only $600,000, half of the estate. The remaining $600,000 would be subject to tax. If either spouse transferred up to $600,000 of their assets out of their estate, and to someone other than their spouse, the transfer would be shielded by the unified credit and be a tax-free transfer.

If Husband transferred $600,000 in trust, shielded by the credit, and the remaining $200,000 to his wife, shielded by the marital deduction, there would be no estate tax payable by either spouse on their respective estates. Upon the death of the wife, her estate of $600,000 would be shielded from tax. This transaction maximizes the credit available to both spouses.

(f) Estate Balancing

In the above example, the joint estate of the married couple was $1,200,000, equalling the credit available to both spouses. Where the combined estate of a married couple exceeds $1,200,000 (the combined amount of the couple's unified credit), some of their assets will be subject to transfer tax.

Because of the progressive nature of the estate tax, larger estates are taxed more than small estates. If one or the other spouse ends up with a proportionately larger estate than the other, higher estate taxes will be due.

To take advantage of the tax savings of progressive rates, the estate planner will seek to balance the estates of spouses so that they are approximately equal. By avoiding large imbalances in estates of married couples, an estate tax savings can be enjoyed.

Now assume that the estate of Husband is $2,000,000 and the estate of Wife is $500,000. Assume further that one spouse dies and transfers all assets to the other spouse free of tax under the marital deduction. The value of the surviving spouse's estate is now $2,500,000. If the surviving spouse were to be taxed on their combined marital estate, a tax of $735,800 would be due.

	Surviving Spouse
Value of Gross Estate	$2,500,000
Less Unified Credit	600,000
Taxable Estate	1,900,000
Tax	735,800

By transferring all property from one spouse to the survivor free of tax under the marital deduction, the value and benefit of one spouse's $600,000 unified credit is lost. Additionally, the aggregate of both spouse's estates pushes their combined value into the upper levels of the progressive estate tax resulting in a higher level of tax.

If each spouse were to be taxed separately on the value of their estates, a combined estate tax of $606,550 would be due.

	H	W
Value of Gross Estate	$2,000,000	$500,000
Less Unified Credit	600,000	600,000
Taxable Estate	1,400,000	-0-
Tax	606,550	-0-

Combined Tax = $606,550

Each spouse would have the advantage of the $600,000 unified credit. Also, the separate estates would be taxed at lower marginal rates than if they were combined into one estate.

However, the two separate estates are unequal in value. One is rather large and is subjected to high marginal tax rates. The other estate is smaller than the available unified credit, resulting in a loss of $100,000 of available unified credit to Wife.

Now assume that Husband makes a qualifying marital deduction transfer to Wife of $750,000. The transfer is tax free and equalizes the estates of both spouses at $1,250,000. If each spouse were now separately taxed on the value of their estates, a combined estate tax of only $422,600 would be due.

	H	W
Value of Gross Estate	$1,250,000	$1,250,000
Less Unified Credit	600,000	600,000
Taxable Estate	650,000	650,000
Tax	211,300	211,300

Combined Tax = $422,600

A significant tax savings was realized by taking advantage of the progressive estate tax structure through estate balancing. The combined tax on the equalized estates was $422,600, resulting in a tax savings of $312,400, or nearly one-half, over the combined estate. A tax savings of $312,400, or almost one-third, was obtained over the unequal and separately taxed estates.

The estate taxes saved by the use of the various estate methods is shown on the accompanying chart.

Tax Savings of Estate Method

Estate	Combined over—	Separate over—	Equalized over—
Combined	———	129,250	312,400
Separate	———	———	183,950
Equalized	———	———	———

Nearly half the tax on the combined estate is saved through equalizing the estates. Almost one-third of the combined tax on each spouse's separate estate is saved by equalization.

These are the principle methods used in estate planning to reduce the federal transfer tax. Many other devices and techniques are available in order to accomplish a given estate planning goal.

§ 8.7 REMAINDER INTERESTS

(a) Will Settlements

Outright and planned gifts can be eligible for these charitable deductions. If a remainder interest gift is made using a split-interest trust, the trust must be a charitable remainder trust[111] or a pooled income fund.[112]

An estate tax charitable deduction is not available for the bequest to charity of a contingent remainder interest in a farm.[113] Under a will, a decedent bequeathed a farm to a child for life, with the remainder to a charitable organization. However, the will also provided that if another child survived the first child, the remainder interest in the farm will vest in the second child instead of the charity. Both individuals were forty-five years of age as of the death of the decedent. It was this remainder interest that the IRS found to be too contingent to merit a charitable deduction. The law is that, in the case of a charitable transfer subject to a condition, no deduction is available "unless the possibility that the charitable transfer will not become effective is so remote as to be negligible."[114] The IRS returned to its position that a charitable deduction is not allowable where the probability exceeds five percent that a noncharitable beneficiary will survive the exhaustion of a fund in which the charity has a remainder interest.[115] Under this rule, any probability in excess of five percent that such a contingency will occur and defeat the charity's interest is not considered so remote as to be negligible. Because

[111] See Chapter 11.
[112] See Chapter 12.
[113] Rev. Rul. 85-23, 1985-1 C.B. 327.
[114] Reg. § 20.2055-2(b).
[115] Rev. Rul. 70-452, 1970-2 C.B. 199; and Rev. Rul. 77-374, 1977-2 C.B. 329.

the two children were of equal age, the actuarial possibility that the second child will survive the first (and thus divest the charity of its remainder interest) was 50 percent. Obviously, 50 percent is greater than five percent, so the IRS held that "the possibility that the charitable remainder transfer in this case will not take effect in possession and enjoyment is not so remote as to be negligible."[116] Thus, the IRS concluded that the bequest did not give rise to an estate tax charitable contribution deduction even though it was otherwise in compliance with the requirements.

The IRS, in 1989, ruled that, in situations involving settlements of bona fide will contests, it will no longer challenge the deductibility of immediate payments to charitable organizations on the ground that they were made in lieu of a split interest that would not constitute an allowable estate tax charitable contribution deduction.[117] In so doing, the IRS revoked its prior contrary position[118] and modified a 1978 pronouncement.[119] This alteration of position was prompted by court opinions.[120]

Consider the situation where someone dies, leaving a charitable bequest in the form of a gift to a trust, with income payable to an individual and the remainder interest to a charitable organization. The trust fails to qualify as a charitable remainder trust or pooled income fund, so that there is no estate tax charitable deduction. There is a will contest, resulting in a settlement, pursuant to which the estate makes a single payment to the income beneficiary and a distribution to the charitable organization. The original position of the IRS in this regard was that no estate tax charitable deduction is available in these circumstances because the accelerated payment to the charity under the settlement was, in effect, a post mortem modification of a will that did not satisfy the statutory requirements.[121] However, the courts held that these requirements are not applicable on the ground that the settlements do not create split interests, in that the interests passing to the charitable and non-charitable benefi-

---

[116]Rev. Rul. 85-23, supra, n. 113, at 328.
[117]Rev. Rul. 89-31, 1989-1 C.B. 277.
[118]Rev. Rul. 77-491, 1977-2 C.B. 332.
[119]Rev. Rul. 78-152, 1978-1 C.B. 296.
[120]E.g., *Flanagan* v. *United States*, 810 F.2d 930 (10th Cir. 1987); and *Strock, Estate of* v. *United States*, 655 F. Supp. 1334 (W.D. Pa. 1987).
[121]IRC § 2055(e)(2)(A).

ciaries were not interests in the same property. Despite this change in position, the IRS warned that "settlements of will contests will continue to be scrutinized in order to assure that the settlement in question is not an attempt to circumvent . . . [the rule requiring split interests to be in certain forms] by instituting and settling a collusive contest."[122]

In one instance, the estate tax charitable deduction was denied because the recipient of a bequest did not qualify as a charitable entity. The executor of the estate secured from the organization an affidavit certifying that it is a charitable organization. However, he failed to review the IRS' Cumulative List of Charitable Organizations[123]; the organization had been deleted from the list prior to the transfer from the estate.[124]

(b)   Reformations

As discussed in Chapter 11, the law requires that certain provisions be in a charitable remainder trust if a charitable deduction is to be available. These requirements apply with respect to the income, estate, or gift tax charitable deduction. However, there is a procedure by which these trusts, both those created during lifetime and testamentary trusts, can be adjusted to bring them into compliance with the appropriate tax law requirements, for income tax,[125] estate tax,[126] and gift tax[127] consequences. Federal law permits a charitable deduction for a "qualified reformation" of a trust, which does not meet the requirements of a charitable remainder annuity trust or a charitable remainder unitrust, for purposes of qualifying for the estate tax charitable deduction.[128] The qualified reformation procedure requires that the interest be a "reformable interest" that can be changed (such as by amendment or construction) into a "qualified

---

[122]Rev. Rul. 89-31, *supra*, n. 117, at 278.
[123]IRS Publication No. 78.
[124]*Clopton, Estate of* v. *Commissioner*, 93 T.C. 275 (1989).
[125]IRC § 170(f)(7).
[126]IRC § 2055(e)(3).
[127]IRC § 2522(c)(4).
[128]IRC § 2055(e)(3)(A).

interest."[129] Also, for the reformation to be effective,

- any difference between the actuarial value (determined as of the date of the decedent's death) of the qualified interest and the actuarial (as so determined) of the reformable interest may not exceed five percent of the actuarial value (as so determined) of the reformable interest,[130]
- in the case of a charitable remainder interest, the nonremainder interest (before and after the qualified reformation) must terminate at the same time,[131]
- In the case of any other interest, the reformable interest and the qualified interest must be for the same period,[132] and
- The change must be effective as of the date of death of the decedent.[133]

A nonremainder interest (before reformation) for a term of years in excess of twenty years is treated as satisfying the second of these requirements if the interest (after reformation) is for a term of twenty years.[134]

In general, a reformable interest, for estate tax law purposes, is any interest for which a charitable deduction would be allowable at the time of the death of the decedent but for the requirement that the interest be in one of the specified forms.[135]

The term "reformable interest" does not include any interest unless, before the remainder vests in possession, all payments to noncharitable persons[136] are expressed either in specified dollar amounts or a fixed percentage of the property.[137] However, this rule does not apply to any interest if a judicial proceeding is commenced to change the interest into a qualified interest not later than the 90th day after the last date (including extensions) for filing the return (if an estate tax return is required to be filed), or the last date (including exten-

---

[129] IRC § 2055(e)(3)(B).
[130] IRC § 2055(e)(3)(B)(i).
[131] IRC § 2055(e)(3)(B)(ii)(I).
[132] IRC § 2055(e)(3)(B)(ii)(II).
[133] IRC § 2055(e)(3)(B)(iii).
[134] IRC § 2055(e)(3)(B), last sentence.
[135] IRC § 2055(e)(3)(C)(i).
[136] That is, entities that are the income interest beneficiaries.
[137] IRC § 2055(e)(3)(C)(ii).

sions) for filing the income tax return for the first tax year for which a return is required to be filed by the trust (if an estate tax return is not required to be filed).[138] Moreover, this rule does not apply in the case of any interest passing under a will executed before January 1, 1979, or under a trust created before that date.[139] There has been considerable litigation in this setting, particularly with respect to application of the estate tax rules.

In one case, a court held that the estate tax charitable contribution deduction was not available for a transfer to a charitable organization because the gift flowed through a nonqualifying charitable trust.[140] The decedent left a will that created a trust with three purposes: to support his three sisters, to maintain the graves of his family members, and to provide funds for religious education in certain parishes in a state. Two years after the estate tax return was filed, the estate secured from a state court the authority to establish a charitable foundation. The court later authorized the funding of the foundation with substantial assets from the estate. The estate claimed a charitable deduction for the funds transferred to the foundation; the IRS denied the claim. Five years later, two of the three sisters having died, the state court interpreted the will to establish three trusts: one for support of the surviving sister, one for grave maintenance, and one for the education of future clergy. The net assets of the trust for the surviving sister were to roll over to the foundation. A federal court ruled that the decedent's will provided for three trusts and that, therefore, a split-interest bequest inconsistent with the tax rules was not created. An appellate court disagreed, ruling that the estate's claim for a refund on the basis of a charitable deduction must fail because the estate did not satisfy any of the specifically prescribed methods of creating[141] or reforming a split interest trust. In part, the court was concerned about the amount that might have to be expended for medical care and other support for the surviving sister. Wrote the appellate court: "There is no justification for a judicial divination of an unstated congressional intent to make an exception for the charitable bequest in this case."[142]

---

[138] IRC § 2055(e)(3)(C)(iii).
[139] IRC § 2055(e)(3)(C)(iv).
[140] *Johnson, Estate of* v. *United States*, 941 F.2d 1318 (5th Cir. 1991).
[141] See Chapter 11.
[142] *Johnson, Estate of* v. *United States*, *supra*, n. 140, at 1321.

The estate in this case relied heavily on an earlier opinion from another court of appeals, in which an estate tax charitable deduction was allowed where a split-interest problem was resolved so that the entire estate could be accurately and permanently separated between charitable and noncharitable beneficiaries.[143] In that case, the government made the same argument as it did in the more recent case. However, the court distinguished the earlier case from the more recent case, on the ground that in the prior case "the amount payable to the noncharitable beneficiaries was limited, and could be firmly assessed and separated from the charitable bequest."[144] Moreover, in the earlier case, the split interest could have been reformed. For the outcome in the prior case to occur, held the court, the property in which the noncharitable beneficiary had an interest must be capable of being measured and severed from the solely charitable property in the estate. In the more recent case, the court continued, "there is no way to divide the entire estate between the charitable and noncharitable beneficiaries because their interests continue to conflict."[145]

In another case, a court held that a trust met the requirements for reformation, for federal estate tax charitable deduction purposes, including the requirement that the will containing the trust be executed prior to 1979, even though a codicil to the will was executed in 1982.[146] An individual executed her first will in 1971, creating a trust with a charitable remainder for the benefit of a college and an annuity payment to an individual. A 1972 codicil changed a non-trust portion of the will, a 1977 codicil again made some non-trust changes and increased the annuity payment; a 1982 codicil again increased the annuity amount. Each codicil stated that, in all other respects, the provisions of the will were confirmed. After this individual died, the personal representative of the estate caused the trust to be reformed, in that it originally did not meet the statutory requirements, so that the estate could benefit from the estate tax charitable deduction. The IRS subsequently determined that the trust did not meet certain of the reformation requirements, including the rule that the will be executed before 1979,[147] and denied the refund claim for

[143]*Oetting* v. *United States*, 712 F.2d 358 (8th Cir. 1983).
[144]*Johnson, Estate of* v. *United States*, *supra*, n. 140, at 1320.
[145]*Id.* at 1321.
[146]*Wells Fargo Bank* v. *United States*, 91-1 U.S.T.C. ¶ 60,067 (C.D. Cal. 1990).
[147]See the text accompanied by n. 139, *supra*.

estate taxes paid. The IRS contended that a codicil republishes a will as of the date the codicil was executed, so that the will must be deemed to have been executed in 1982—and thus not before 1979, so that the trust was not reformable. The representative of the estate contended that, under applicable state law, the doctrine of republication is not applied where it would defeat a testator's intent. The court accepted the representative's view and gave strict construction to the statutory language which states that the will must be executed before 1979.

In this same case, another requirement at issue was the rule that the value of a charitable interest must be presently ascertainable so that it is severable from the noncharitable interest.[148] The government argued that provisions in the will providing for payment of improvements to the income beneficiary's residence, his unusual and exceptional expenses, and his income taxes made the value of the charitable interest not ascertainable. However, the court ruled that the determination of "presently ascertainable" requires that the court look to certain facts as of the time of the testator's death. The court found that any expenses with respect to the residence could be satisfied out of the income interest. The fact that the trust could pay for the income interest beneficiary's unusual and exceptional expenses was neutralized by the facts of his age (87), independent sources of income, and insurance coverage. Having made these determinations as to the execution of the will and the standards for determining whether the will provides a "sufficiently definite standard" limiting the extent of possible invasion of the trust corpus for the benefit of the income interest beneficiary, the court refused to grant complete summary judgment against the IRS and deferred to another occasion the decision as to whether the possibility that the bequest to charity will be defeated is so remote as to be negligible.

In another case, a court held that a split-interest charitable trust that failed to qualify for the estate tax charitable deduction cannot be converted into a qualifying trust under the reformation rules because there was not a timely judicial proceeding.[149] The trust involved did not qualify as an eligible charitable remainder trust. It was subsequently amended pursuant to state law; the estate contended that this amendment constituted a change in the trust so that it was reformed into a qualified remainder trust, eligible for the estate tax

---

[148]See the text accompanied by n. 129, *supra*.
[149]*Hall, Estate of* v. *Commissioner*, 93 T.C. 745 (1990).

charitable deduction. The IRS, however, asserted that the reformation was not timely,[150] in that the proceeding that led to amendment of the trust took place nearly two years after the deadline. The estate argued that a filing with the state probate court commenced the requisite judicial proceeding (the filing was before the deadline). The filing was technically corrected on a point of law; this gave the estate the contention that, since the correction was made shortly before the case was submitted, the reformation was timely. But the court rejected that reasoning, observing that it contravened congressional intent, in that it would enable an estate to qualify simply by, after passage of the reformation rules deadline, obtaining a retroactive trust amendment.

It has been held that the federal government is not entitled to interest against an estate, where the entirety of the estate's assets passed to a charitable organization following reformation of a testamentary trust.[151] The decedent's will contained a defective split-interest trust. The estate tax return included a claim for a charitable deduction for the value of the remainder interest passing to charity, in anticipation of a successful reformation. Subsequently, the IRS assessed interest on the premise that no deduction was allowable at the time the estate tax return was filed until the reformation of the trust. The first court to review this matter read overall tax law as meaning that a tax is due as of the time a return must be filed and that interest begins to accumulate as of the return due date. In this case, wrote the court, the estate was not entitled to the charitable deduction at the time the return was due, so the interest obligation began to run. However, an appellate court disagreed, holding that an amendment to a will made pursuant to the reformation procedure is retroactive to the date of the testator's death. It concluded that the legislative history of the provision established that this retroactivity is applicable for all purposes. The court of appeals wrote that, in enacting this provision, "Congress took the unusual step of allowing a will to be amended after the testator's death for the purpose of eliminating estate taxes that diminished bequests to charity."[152] This court decided that "[e]xacting a price from charities in the form of interest on the eliminated tax is inconsistent with congressional intent to benefit charities."[153]

[150]See the text accompanied by n. 138, *supra*.
[151]*Oxford Orphanage, Inc. v. United States*, 775 F.2d 570 (4th Cir. 1985).
[152]*Id.* at 575.
[153]*Id.*

9

Special Gift Situations

§ 9.1 WORKS OF ART

(a) Gifts

Contributions of works of art may be made to charitable organizations. In general, the federal income tax charitable contribution deduction for a gift of a work of art is an amount equal to the fair market value of the property.[1] However, there are exceptions to this general rule.

1. The charitable deduction for any one year may be limited by one of the percentage limitations.[2]

2. The work of art that is contributed may be the creation of the donor, in which case the deduction is confined to the donor's basis in the property.[3]

3. The work of art may be put to an unrelated use by the charitable recipient, in which case the deduction is confined to the donor's basis in the property.[4]

4. The actual charitable deduction may be limited by application of the alternative minimum tax.[5]

---

[1] In general, see Chapter 6.
[2] See Chapter 7.
[3] IRC §§ 170(e)(1) and 1221. See § 12, *infra*.
[4] See Chapter 6 § 6.
[5] See Chapter 10.

Of these four elements, the third is the most likely to occur. A work of art is an item of tangible personal property. There is a special rule concerning gifts of tangible personal property, which may be reiterated in this context. The rule is this: Where a gift of tangible personal property is made, the amount of the charitable deduction that would otherwise be determined must be reduced by the amount of gain which would have been long-term capital gain if the property contributed had been sold by the donor at its fair market value, determined at the time of the contribution, where the use by the donee is unrelated to its tax-exempt purposes.[6]

The greatest controversy surrounding the charitable deduction of a work of art is likely to be the value of the item. Not infrequently, there is a dispute between the IRS and a donor as to the fair market value of a work of art. Usually, these disputes are settled; sometimes they are resolved by a court. The appropriate value for an item of property is a question of fact, not law; thus, the testimony of one or more expert witnesses can be significant. A trial court's valuation for an item of property will be set aside on appeal only if the finding of value is clearly erroneous.[7]

Examples of the court opinions concerning the valuation of works of art for charitable deduction purposes follow.

- A promoter designed a plan to dispose of excess inventories of "reprint books" (republication of books in the public domain). Having located public libraries interested in receiving the books, the promoter solicited individuals to invest in the plan. Persons executed documents evidencing the purchase of the books at a cost equal to one-third of the catalog list price, waited the capital gain holding period, then executed additional documents evidencing the gift of the books to the libraries. The charitable deduction was claimed to be an amount equal to the full publishers' list prices. The government argued that the transactions were shams, in that the donors neither really owned nor contributed the books, which remained in warehouses. Nonetheless, the court gave substantive effect to the documentation (including "bills of sale" and "warehouse receipts") and the role of the promoter as the investors' "agent,"

[6]IRC § 170(e)(1)(B)(i); Reg. § 1.170A-4(b)(2)(ii).
[7]E.g. *Anselmo* v. *Commissioner*, 757 F.2d 1208 (11th Cir. 1985).

holding that title to the books and risk of loss passed to them. Having given economic effect to the transaction, the court disemboweled the plan on the basis of valuation. In determining the fair market value of the books, the court said that the retail market must be used. Focusing on the immense number of books involved and the weak market for scholarly reprints, the court found the market price for them to have been substantially depressed. The court concluded that the fair market value of the books was 20 percent of the catalog retail list prices for the books, and allowed a charitable deduction for that amount. (As noted, the donors purchased the books for one-third of the list price.)[8]

- Individuals purchased a substantial number of unframed lithographs, held them for the long-term capital gain treatment period, then donated them to charitable organizations. The court valued the lithographs on the basis of the market in which the donors purchased them, not "on the prices paid in only a few sales."[9]

- An individual was denied an income tax charitable deduction in excess of the amount allowed by the IRS for artwork and copyrights contributed to a museum. The court essentially rejected the opinions of the expert witnesses on both sides of the case.[10]

- An individual purchased a substantial number of Indian artifacts and etchings, held them for the requisite capital gain holding period, and then donated most of them to a museum. The court found that the donated items were grossly overvalued and that there was a pattern of abuse designed to achieve excessive valuations of the items. The value asserted by the IRS was found to be the appropiate value.[11]

- Individuals contributed African art objects to a charitable organization. The court substantially reduced the value of the items, in relation to that claimed by the donors, finding that

[8]*Skripak* v. *Commissioner*, 84 T.C. 285 (1985).
[9]*Lio* v. *Commissioner*, 85 T.C. 56, 71 (1985), aff'd, 813 F.2d 837 (7th Cir. 1987). Also *Orth* v. *Commissioner*, 85 T.C. 56 (1985), aff'd, 813 F.2d 837 (7th Cir. 1987).
[10]*Harken* v. *Commissioner*, 50 T.C.M. 994 (1985).
[11]*Johnson* v. *Commissioner*, 85 T.C. 469 (1985).

most of the artwork was not "traditional" African art but "tourist" or "airport" art..[12]

- Individuals contributed art objects to a museum and claimed charitable contribution deductions based on appraisals. The IRS contested the claimed charitable deduction. The court upheld the donor's value in full.[13]

- An individual contributed a statue to a state. The donor claimed a value of $800,000. The IRS asserted that the value was $50,000. The court found the value to be $600,000, concluding that the donor's expert witness was more persuasive than the witness provided by the government.[14]

- A court found that charitable contribution deductions claimed for gifts of artwork to colleges were deliberately inflated and were tax-motivated transactions.[15]

- A court denied charitable deductions claimed for gifts of paintings and sculptures to museums because of valuation overstatements. The court based its valuations on expert testimony.[16]

- Two donors contributed lithographs to a charitable organization. They claimed each lithograph had a value of $300. The IRS contested this valuation. The court found that each lithograph had a value of $100.[17] On appeal, the court wrote: "This was an interesting taxsaving arrangement devised as an art transaction, but the art will have to be treasured for art's sake and not as a tax deduction."[18]

- Individuals made a gift of posters to a charitable organization. They asserted a value of $5 per poster; the court allowed a deduction on the basis of 73 cents per poster—the amount originally determined by the IRS.[19]

- Individuals contributed works of art to a charitable organization. The value selected by the court for nine of these items was about halfway between the donor's values and the government's values.[20]

[12]*Neely* v. *Commissioner*, 85 T.C. 934 (1985).
[13]*Biagiotti* v. *Commissioner*, 52 T.C.M. 588 (1986).
[14]*Koftinow* v. *Commissioner*, 52 T.C. 261 (1986).
[15]*Angell* v. *Commissioner*, 52 T.C.M. 939 (1986).
[16]*Frates* v. *Commissioner*, 53 T.C.M. 96 (1987).
[17]*Orth* v. *Commissioner*, *supra*, n. 9.
[18]*Id.*, 813 F.2d at 843.
[19]*Ferrell* v. *Commissioner*, 53 T.C.M. 209 (1987).
[20]*Winokur* v. *Commissioner*, 90 T.C. 733 (1988).

Gifts of art are likely to be subject to the appraisal requirements.[21]

There are penalties that apply to the overvaluation of property for tax purposes[22] and these penalties are frequently applied in the context of a gift of artwork.

(b) Loans

Rather than contribute a work of art to a charitable organization, a person may instead decide to loan the work of art to a charity. This type of transfer does not give rise to a federal income tax charitable contribution deduction. The transaction is nonetheless a gift. However, the transaction is disregarded as a transfer for gift tax purposes where

- the recipient organization is a charitable entity,[23]
- the use of the artwork by the charitable donee is related to the purpose or function constituting the basis for its tax exemption, and
- the artwork involved is an archaeological, historic, or creative item of tangible personal property.[24]

§ 9.2   GEMS

Contributions of gems may be made to a charitable organization. Essentially, the law concerning the deductibility of gifts of works of art is applicable in this context.[25] However, the specter of "tax shelters" hangs over these gifts, because of the various deduction promotions that have transpired in recent years. Once again, the principal issue in this setting is the value of the items transferred.

What follows are some examples of court opinions concerning the valuation of gems for charitable deduction purposes.

- A court considered a gift of gems to a museum, with the claimed charitable deduction based upon the value of $80,680. Finding essentially for the government, the court concluded

---

[21] See Chapter 23.
[22] See Chapter 11 § 5.
[23] That is, an organization described in IRC § 501(c)(3).
[24] IRC § 2503(g).
[25] See § 1, *supra*.

that the date-of-gift value of the gems was $16,800. The court, which delved deeply into the practices of the jewelry trade, rejected the view that the gems should be valued by reference to the prices charged by jewelry stores for individual items of jewelry and held that the value should be based on the price that would have been paid by a jewelry store to a wholesaler, with the sales of the gems individually rather than in bulk. Despite the emphasis in the opinion on valuation, the court was influenced by the tax results attempted by the donor in this case. The donor held the gems just long enough to satisfy the long-term capital gain holding period requirements, claimed a charitable deduction that was nearly five times the amount paid for the gift property, and purchased the gems after becoming motivated by tax shelter promotional material.[26]

- Two donors purchased gemstones over a three-year period and contributed them to a museum approximately one year after the last of the purchases. A court found that the fair market value of the gems was the cost of them to the donors.[27]

- A charitable deduction was claimed for gifts of gemstones and similar items to a museum; a court found the transfers to be tax-motivated and found the value of the items to be equal to the acquisition cost.[28]

- A donor contributed opals to a museum. A court confined the deduction amount to the donor's cost, having not found evidence that there was any increase in value in the jewels since the time of their purchase.[29]

- Two donors contributed an opal to a university. They claimed a value of $70,000. The IRS contested this valuation. The court concluded that the opal had a value of $50,000, largely because the jewel was part of a set, so that the separate gift diminished its value.[30]

Gifts of gems may be subject to the appraisal requirements.[31]

---

[26] *Anselmo* v. *Commissioner, supra,* n. 7.
[27] *Chiu* v. *Commissioner,* 84 T.C. 716 (1985).
[28] *Dubin* v. *Commissioner,* 52 T.C.M. 456 (1985).
[29] *Schachter* v. *Commissioner,* 51 T.C.M. 1428 (1986).
[30] *Rhoades* v. *Commissioner,* 55 T.C.M. 1159 (1988).
[31] See Chapter 23.

There are penalties that apply to the overvaluation of property for tax purposes[32] and these penalties are frequently applied in the context of gifts of gems.

§ 9.3 PROPERTY SUBJECT TO DEBT

Property may be the subject of charitable gifts.[33] When, however, the property is subject to a debt, unique tax consequences are likely to arise.

One of these consequences is that the transaction is likely to be a bargain sale.[34] This is because the transfer of property that was subject to a debt relieved the donor of that obligation, which is a form of consideration, so that the donor received something in return for the gift (relief from the debt).[35] This is a topic that has been the subject of some litigation.

The federal tax law is clear that "[t]he gain from the sale or other disposition of property shall be the excess of the amount realized therefrom over the adjusted basis . . ."[36] The general rule is that "[t]he adjusted basis for determining the gain or loss from the sale or other disposition of property, whenever acquired, shall be the basis" for federal tax law purposes, as "adjusted."[37] The phrase "other disposition of property" includes a gift of property. Thus, "[a] disposition of property includes a gift of the property or a transfer of the property in satisfaction of the liabilities to which it is subject."[38] However, the bargain sale rules entail a somewhat different definition of the term basis, which is that, if a deduction is allowed for a federal income tax charitable contribution deduction "by reason of a sale, then the adjusted basis for determining the gain from such sale shall be that portion of the adjusted basis which bears the same ratio to the adjusted basis as the amount realized bears to the fair market value of the property."[39] Thus, the general rule uses the term "sale or

---

[32] See Chapter 11 § 5.
[33] See, e.g., Chapter 6.
[34] In general, see § 5, *infra*.
[35] Reg. § 1.1011-2(a)(3). E.g., Rev. Rul. 81-163, 1981-1 C.B. 433.
[36] IRC § 1001(a).
[37] IRC § 1011(a). The rules concerning "adjusted" basis are the subject of IRC § 1016.
[38] Reg. § 1.1001-2(a)(4)(iii).
[39] IRC § 1011(b).

other disposition," while the bargain sale rule only uses the term "sale." This led to the contention that a "sale" occurs in this setting only where the transferor received a direct benefit from the transaction such as cash on mortgaging the property or a depreciation deduction with respect to the property prior to transferring it to the charity.[40] This argument leads to the collateral argument that the general rule for determining basis applies, rather than the bargain sale rule.

However, a U.S. Supreme Court opinion made it clear that taxation on relief from debt is not dependent upon any theory of economic benefit and applies to situations such as those not involving the taking of any depreciation deductions.[41] The court stated:

> This, however, does not erase the fact that the mortgagor received the loan proceeds taxfree and included them in his basis on the understanding that he had an obligation to repay the full amount. . . . When the obligation is cancelled, the mortgagor is relieved of his responsibility to repay the sum he originally received and thus realizes value to that extent within the meaning of . . . [the tax law defining "amount received"[42]]. From the mortgagor's point of view, when his obligation is assumed by a third party who purchases the encumbered property, it is as if the mortgagor first had been paid with cash borrowed by the third party from the mortgagee on a nonrecourse basis, and then had used the cash to satisfy his obligation to the mortgagee.[43]

The Supreme Court put the matter this way (as a contrast):

> When a taxpayer receives a loan, he incurs an obligation to repay that loan at some future date. Because of this obligation, the loan proceeds do not qualify as income to the taxpayer. When he fulfills the obligation, the repayment of the loan likewise has no effect on this tax liability.[44]

Another court subsequently completed this argument:

[40]This was the taxpayers' contention in *Ebben* v. *Commissioner*, 783 F.2d 906, 911-912 (9th Cir. 1986). There were grounds for this argument (*Crane* v. *Commissioner*, 331 U.S. 1 (1947)).

[41]*Commissioner* v. *Tufts*, 461 U.S. 300 (1983).

[42]IRC § 1001(b).

[43]*Commissioner* v. *Tufts*, *supra*, n. 41, at 312 (citation omitted).

[44]*Id.* at 307.

But when someone else relieves him of his obligation to pay the loan, it is as though the taxpayer had received cash and the transfer of the encumbered property to the charity is the equivalent of a sale without regard to any tax benefit theory.[45]

In the particular case, the taxpayers contributed mortgaged property to a college, which took the property subject to a debt. The court wrote that "it was as if the taxpayers had been paid with cash borrowed by . . . [the college] from the mortgagee on a nonrecourse basis, and then had used the cash to satisfy their obligation to the mortgagee."[46]

The IRS has consistently interpreted the term "sale" in the bargain sale context to include gifts of mortgaged property to a charity. Thus:

If property is transferred subject to an indebtedness, the amount of indebtedness must be treated as an amount realized for purposes of determining whether there is a sale or exchange . . ., even though the transferee does not agree to assume or pay the indebtedness.[47]

This approach has been upheld as a reasonable one by a court.[48]

This doctrine of law causes the transaction to be partially a "purchase" and partially a gift. The tax basis of the property must be allocated to both the purchase and gift portions of the transaction in determining the capital gain to be reported.[49]

Example 9.1

M contributed an item of capital gain property to PC, a public charitable organization. At the time of the gift, the property had a fair market value of $35,000. M's basis in the property was $15,000. The property was the subject of a $10,000 mortgage.

M's charitable contribution deduction for the year was $20,000 ($35,000 − $15,000). M also is treated as having received $10,000—a form of consideration (relief from the mortgage obligation).

Continued

---

[45]*Ebben* v. *Commissioner, supra,* n. 40, at 912. Also *Commissioner* v. *Peterman,* 118 F.2d 973 (9th Cir. 1941); and *Guest* v. *Commissioner,* 77 T.C. 9 (1981); *Freeland* v. *Commissioner,* 74 T.C. 970 (74 T.C. 970 (1980).
[46]*Ebben* v. *Commissioner, supra,* n. 40, at 912.
[47]Reg. § 1.1011-2(a)(3).
[48]*Ebben* v. *Commissioner, supra,* n. 40, at 913–915.
[49]IRC § 1011(b).

> ### Example 9.1 Continued
>
> Of the $15,000 basis in the property, $4,286 was allocated to the purchase element of the transaction (10/35 × $15,000) and $10,714 was allocated to the gift element of the transaction (25/35 × $15,000). Thus, M had a long-term capital gain of $5,714 as the result of this transaction.

For these purposes, it is immaterial whether the donee organization pays the debt or agrees to assume it. The relief from the obligation is regarded as an item of consideration in either event.[50]

This principle of law also applies in the planned giving context.[51]

Thus, the contribution to a charitable organization, by means of a pooled income fund, of an item of property that is subject to a debt causes the donor to be treated as though he or she received income in an amount equal to the amount of the debt.[52] The taxable gain is determined using the bargain sale rules, which entail allocation of the basis in the property to the purchase and gift elements (see above).

It appears that these same rules apply in the context of charitable giving by means of charitable remainder trusts.[53]

In the setting of charitable remainder trusts, the consequences of transferring property encumbered with debt can be more severe than is the case with pooled income funds. As discussed, a form of unrelated business income is unrelated debt-financed income.[54] A gift of mortgaged property to a charitable remainder trust can cause unrelated debt-financed income to be received by the trust.[55] When a charitable remainder trust receives unrelated business income in a year, it loses its tax exemption for the year.[56] If an individual transfers mortgaged property to a charitable remainder trust, where the individual is personally liable on the mortgage, the trust may become disqualified on the ground that the discharge of the obligation causes the donor to become the owner of the trust. The IRS has so held.[57]

---

[50] *Ebben* v. *Commissioner, supra,* n. 40.
[51] In general, see Part III.
[52] Reg. § 1.642(c)-5(a)(3).
[53] Rev. Rul. *supra,* n. 35; IRS Private Letter Ruling 8526015.
[54] See Chapter 4 § 4.
[55] IRC §§ 51(c)(2)(A) and (B).
[56] See Chapter 12 § 2.
[57] IRS Private Letter Ruling 9015049.

§ 9.4   GIFTS OF INVENTORY

There are special federal tax rules governing charitable contributions
of items of inventory. The term "inventory" is assigned to property
that is stock in trade of a business enterprise, held for sale to customers; the resulting income is ordinary income.[58]

In general, the amount of the charitable deduction for contributions of property is measured by using the fair market value of the
property.[59] However, where a donor makes a charitable contribution
of property out of its inventory, the gift deduction is generally confined to an amount which may not exceed the donor's cost basis in
the property.[60] That is, the amount that might otherwise be deductible must be reduced by the amount of ordinary income that would
have resulted had the items been sold.

Nevertheless, a special rule provides an augmented deduction under certain circumstances, pursuant to which the charitable deduction for contributions of inventory may be an amount equal to as
much as twice the cost basis in the property.[61] These gifts of inventory are known as "qualified contributions."[62]

(a)   Basic Rules

In the case of a gift of inventory, the charitable contribution generally must be reduced by an amount equal to one-half of the amount
of gain that would not have been long-term capital gain if the property had been sold by the donor at fair market value at the date of
the contribution.[63] If, after this reduction, the amount of the deduction would be more than twice the basis in the contributed property,
the amount of the deduction must be further reduced to an amount
equal to twice the cost basis in the property.[64]

This augmented deduction is available where the following circumstances are present:

[58]The term "inventory" is discussed in Chapter 2.
[59]IRC § 170(e). See Chapter 6.
[60]IRC § 170(e)(1)(A).
[61]IRC § 170(e)(3); Reg. § 1.170A-4A(a).
[62]IRC § 170(e)(3)(A).
[63]Reg. § 1.170A-4A(a).
[64]*Id.*

1. The gift is of property that is

    –   Stock in trade of the taxpayer or other property of a kind which would properly be included in the inventory of the taxpayer if on hand at the close of the tax year,[65]

    –   Property held by the taxpayer primarily for sale to customers in the ordinary course of the trade or business,[66]

    –   Property, used in a trade or business, of a character which is subject to the allowance for depreciation,[67] or

    –   Real property used in a trade or business;[68]

2. The donor is a corporation (other than a small business corporation[69]).

3. The donee is a charitable organization;[70]

4. The donee is not a private foundation;[71]

5. The use of the property by the donee is related to its tax-exempt purposes;

6. The property "is to be used by the donee solely for the care of the ill, the needy, or infants";

7. The property is not transferred by the donee in exchange for money, other property, or services;

8. The donor receives from the donee a written statement representing that its use and disposition of the property will be in accordance with these rules; and

9. The property is in compliance with all applicable requirements of the Federal Food, Drug, and Cosmetic Act.

A contribution of property, to be deductible pursuant to these

---

[65] IRC § 1221(1).
[66] *Id.*
[67] IRC § 1221(2).
[68] *Id.*
[69] This type of entity is technically known as an "S" corporation (IRC § 1371(b)).
[70] That is, is an organization described in IRC § 501(c)(3).
[71] See Chapter 4 § 3. However, the donee can be a private operating foundation.

rules, must be a "qualified contribution." A qualified contribution is one which satisfies the foregoing nine requirements.[72]

(b) Restrictions on Use

For a contribution to qualify under these rules, the contributed property must be subject to certain restrictions in use. If the transferred property is used or transferred by the donee organization (or by any subsequent transferee that furnished to the donee the requisite written statement[73]) in a manner inconsistent with the requirements of these rules, the donor's deduction is only the amount allowable with regard to gifts of inventory in general.[74] As noted, this general deduction is confined to the donor's cost basis.

However, if the donor is able to establish that, at the time of the contribution, the donor reasonably anticipated that the property would be used in a manner consistent with these requirements, then the donor's deduction would nonetheless be computed using these special rules.[75]

(i) Exempt Purpose Use

Under these rules, the use of the property must be related to the purpose or function constituting the ground for tax exemption as a charitable entity of the organization to which the contribution is made.[76]

The gift property may not be used in connection with any activity which gives rise to unrelated business income.[77]

(ii) Ultimate Beneficiaries

The gift properties must be used for the care of the ill, needy, or infants. The property itself must ultimately either be transferred to

---

[72] Reg. § 1.170A-4A(b)(1).
[73] See text accompanying n. 98, *infra*.
[74] Reg. § 1.170A-4A(b)(2).
[75] *Id.*
[76] Reg. § 1.170A-4A(b)(2)(i).
[77] *Id.* The unrelated business income rules are summarized at Chapter 4 § 4.

(or for the use of) the ill, needy, or infants for their care or be retained for their care. No other person may use the contributed property except as incidental to primary use in the care of the ill needy or infants. The donee organization may satisfy these requirements by transferring the property to a relative, custodian, parent, or guardian of the ill or needy individual or infant, or to any other individual if it makes a reasonable effort to ascertain that the property will ultimately be used primarily for the care of the ill or needy individual, or infant, and not for the primary benefit of any other person.[78]

The donee organization may transfer the gift properties to other qualified tax-exempt public charitable organizations, within or outside the United States. However, for these rules to be satisfied, the transferring organization must obtain a written statement from the transferee organization.[79] If the property is ultimately transferred to, or used for the benefit of, ill or needy persons, or infants, who are outside the United States, the organization which transfers the property outside the United States must be a corporation. For these purposes, if the donee organization charges for its transfer of contributed property (other than an allowable fee[80]), these rules are not met.[81]

The term "ill" person is defined for these purposes as follows:

> An ill person is a person who requires medical care . . . .[82] Examples of ill persons include a person suffering from physical injury, a person with a significant impairment of a bodily organ, a person with an existing handicap, whether from birth or later injury, a person suffering from malnutrition, a person with a disease, sickness, or infection which significantly impairs physical health, a person partially or totally incapable of self-care (including incapacity due to old age). A person suffering from mental illness is included [in this definition] if the person is hospitalized or institutionalized for the mental disorder, or, although the person is nonhospitalized or noninstitutionalized, if the person's mental illness constitutes a significant health impairment.[83]

---

[78] Reg. § 1.170A-4A(b)(2)(ii)(A).
[79] This written statement must conform to the requirements described in ns. 94–97, *infra*.
[80] See the text accompanied by ns. 89–90, 92, *infra*.
[81] Reg. § 1.170A-4A(b)(2)(ii)(A).
[82] This term is, in turn, defined in Reg. § 1.213-1(e).
[83] Reg. § 1.170A-4A(b)(2)(ii)(B).

The term "care of the ill" means "alleviation or cure of an existing illness and includes care of the physical, mental, or emotional needs of the ill."[84]

The term "needy" is defined for these purposes as follows:

A needy person is a person who lacks the necessities of life, involving physical, mental, or emotional well-being, as a result of poverty or temporary distress. Examples of needy persons include a person who is financially impoverished as a result of low income and lack of financial resources, a person who temporarily lacks food or shelter (and the means to provide for it), a person who is the victim of a natural disaster (such as fire or flood), a person who is the victim of a civil disaster (such as a civil disturbance), a person who is temporarily not self-sufficient as a result of a sudden and severe personal or family crisis (such as a person who is the victim of a crime of violence or who has been physically abused), a person who is a refugee or immigrant and who is experiencing language, cultural, or financial difficulties, a minor child who is not self-sufficient and who is not cared for by a parent or guardian, and a person who is not self-sufficient as a result of previous institutionalization (such as a former prisoner or a former patient in a mental institution).[85]

The phrase "care of the needy" is defined as follows:

Care of the needy means alleviation or satisfaction of an existing need. Since a person may be needy in some respects and not needy in other respects, care of the needy must relate to the particular need which causes the person to be needy. For example, a person whose temporary need arises from a natural disaster may need temporary shelter and food but not recreational facilities.[86]

These rules define an "infant" as "a minor child" (as determined under the laws of the jurisdiction in which the child resides).[87] The phrase "care of an infant" means "performance of parental functions and provision for the physical, mental, and emotional needs of the infant."[88]

[84]Reg. § 1.170A-4A(b)(2)(ii)(C).
[85]Reg. § 1.170A-4A(b)(2)(ii)(D).
[86]Reg. § 1.170A-4A(b)(2)(ii)(E).
[87]Reg. § 1.170A-4A(b)(2)(ii)(F).
[88]Reg. § 1.170A-4A(b)(2)(ii)(G).

(c) Restrictions on Transfer of Contributed Property

In general, a contribution will not satisfy these rules if the donee organization or any transferee of it requires or receives any money, property, or services for the transfer or use of the property contributed. For example, if an organization provides temporary shelter for a fee, and also provides free meals to ill or needy individuals, or infants, using food contributed under these rules, the determination of the deduction for the contribution of food is subject to these rules. However, the fee charged by the organization for the shelter may not be increased merely because meals are served to the ill or needy individuals or infants.[89]

However, a contribution may qualify under these rules if the donee organization charges a fee to another organization in connection with its transfer of the donated property, if (1) the fee is "small or nominal in relation to the value of the transferred property and is not determined by this value," and (2) the fee is "designed to reimburse the donee organization for its administrative, warehousing, or similar costs."[90]

An example of the application of these rules follows:

Example 9.2

A pharmaceutical company (not an S corporation) had a basis in certain products (inventory) of $1. The products are normally sold for a price of $10. The company donated the products to charity for qualified purposes shortly before the date of their expiration; because of the imminence of the expiration date, the products were valued at $5 at the time of the gift. The corporation claimed a charitable deduction of $10 per item. However, following an audit, the IRS said that the proper deduction was $2 per item. This conclusion was reached as follows.

First, the amount of the potential deduction had to be reduced by one-half of the amount of gain that would not have been long-term capital gain if the property had been sold by the donor at its fair market value on the date of the contribution. If the amount of the

Continued

---

[89] Reg. § 1.170A-4A(b)(3)(i).
[90] Reg. § 1.170A-4A(b)(3)(ii).

Example 9.2 Continued

charitable contribution that remains after this reduction exceeds twice the basis of the contributed property, the amount of the charitable contribution must be reduced a second time to an amount that is equal to twice the amount of the basis of the property.

Under these rules, if the company had sold the property at its fair market value on the date of its contribution, the company's amount of gain would have been $4 per item. This gain would have been ordinary income, rather than long-term capital gain. Thus, the company was required to reduce the fair market value of its contribution ($5 per item) by one-half of the gain ($4 per item ÷ $2 per item), leaving an amount of $3 per item. Since the amount of the charitable deduction that remained after the first reduction (that is, $3 per item) is in excess of twice the basis of the contributed property, a second reduction must occur in the amount of $1 per item, resulting in a charitable contribution deduction of $2 (twice the basis) per item.[91]

Here is an example of this rule as it concerns fees:

Example 9.3

X is a food bank, organized and operated as a tax-exempt charitable organization. X receives surplus food from donors out of their inventory and distributes the food to other charities, which in turn give the food to needy persons. X charges a small fee to cover administrative, warehousing, and similar costs. X permissibly charges this fee on the basis of the total number of pounds of food distributed to the transferee charities. However, X may not charge a fee on the basis of the value of the food distributed.[92]

---

[91] Rev. Rul. 85-8, 1985-1 C.B. 59. The IRS had some difficulties with this rule. A substantially similar ruling was published in 1983 (Rev. Rul. 83-29, 1983-1 C.B. 65) but the formula was incorrectly applied. The IRS tried to correct this mistake later in the year (Ann. 83-128, 1983-32 I.R.B. 30) but again misapplied the formula. The 1983 ruling as permanently published correctly applied the formula. Nonetheless, the IRS clarified it in the 1985 ruling by stating that "[n]o inference should be drawn [from this ruling] as to the fair market value of any products donated by any corporation shortly before the expiration date of the products" and that the "fair market value of the products donated will depend on the facts and circumstances surrounding those particular products at that particular time" (Rev. Rul. 85-8, *supra*, at 60).

[92] *Id.*

This special rule does not apply to a transfer of donated property directly from an organization to ill or needy individuals, or infants.[93]

(d) Requirements of a Written Statement

(i) Statement To Donor

Under these rules, the donee organization must furnish each donor with a written statement that

1. describes the contributed property, stating the date of its receipt;

2. represents that the property will be used in compliance with this body of law;[94]

3. represents that the donee organization is a charitable organization and is not a private foundation;[95] and

4. represents that adequate books and records will be maintained and made available to the IRS upon request.[96]

This written statement must be furnished within a "reasonable period" after the contribution. However, it must be furnished no later than the date (including extensions) by which the donor is required to file his federal corporate income tax return for the year of the contribution. The required books and records need not trace the receipt and disposition of specific items of donated property if they disclose compliance with the requirements by reference to "aggregate quantities" of donated property. The books and records are "adequate" if they reflect "total amounts received and distributed" (or used), and outline the procedure used for determining that the ulti-

---

[93] *Id.*

[94] It is expected by the IRS that this written statement specifically provides as follows: "The property will be used in compliance with section 170(c)(3) of the Internal Revenue Code and paragraphs (b)(2) and (3) of Regulation § 1.170A-4A."

[95] As noted, however (see n. 71, *supra*), the donee may be a private operating foundation).

[96] Reg. § 1.170A-4A(b)(4)(i).

mate recipient of the property is an ill or needy individual, or infant. However, these books and records need not reflect the names of the ultimate individual recipients or the property distributed to (or used by) each one.[97]

(ii) Statements To Transferring Organization

If an organization that received a contribution under these rules transfers the contributed property to another organization, the transferee organization must furnish to the transferring organization a written statement which contains the information referenced in the first, second, and fourth requirements for a statement to a donor (see above). This statement must also represent that the transferee organization is a charitable organization that is not a private foundation (or, if a foreign organization, that it would meet that test). This written statement must be furnished within a "reasonable period" after the transfer.[98]

(e) Requirement of Compliance with the Federal Food, Drug, and Cosmetic Act

In the case of contributed property that is subject to the Federal Food, Drug, and Cosmetic Act, the property must comply with that law at the date of contribution and for the immediately preceding 180 days. In the case of specific items of contributed property not in existence for the entire period of 180 days immediately preceding the date of contribution, this requirement is met if the contributed property complied with that law during the period of its existence and at the date of contribution and if, for the 180-day period prior to contribution, other property (if any) held by the donor at any time during that period (which property was fungible with the contributed property) was in compliance with that law during the period held by the donor.[99]

---

[97] Reg. § 1.170A-4A(b)(4)(i).
[98] Reg. § 1.170A-4A(b)(4)(ii).
[99] Reg. § 1.170A-4A(b)(5)(i).

Example 9.4

Z, a grocery store, contributed 12 crates of naval oranges to a public charity for distribution to the needy. The oranges were picked and placed in the grocery store's stock two weeks before the date of contribution. The contribution satisfied the requirements of these rules if Z complied with the Act for 180 days prior to the date of contribution with respect to all naval oranges in stock during that period.[100]

(f) Amount of Reduction

The amount of the charitable contribution under these rules must be reduced before application of the percentage limitation on the charitable deduction.[101] These rules mandate two reductions. The amount of the first reduction is equal to one-half of the amount of gain which would not have been long-term capital gain if the property had been sold by the donor at its fair market value on the date of its contribution, excluding, however, any amount involving certain recapture rules (see below). If the amount of the charitable contribution which remains after this reduction exceeds twice the basis of the contributed property, then the amount of the charitable contribution is reduced a second time to an amount which is equal to twice the amount of the basis of the property.[102]

The basis of contributed property that is inventory must be determined under the donor's method of accounting for inventory for purposes of federal income tax. The donor must use as the basis of the contributed item the inventoriable carrying cost assigned to any similar item not included in closing inventory.[103] For example, under

---

[100] Reg. § 1.170A-4A(b)(5)(ii).

[101] IRC § 170(e)(3)(B); Reg. § 1.170A-4A(c)(1). These rules are also applied without regard to the deduction reduction rules, which are the subject of Chapter 6 §§ 4, 5 and 6 (also see the text accompanied by ns. 60–62, *supra*). The percentage limitation applicable to corporations is discussed in Chapter 7 § 17.

[102] Reg. § 1.170A-4A(c)(1).

[103] Reg. § 1.170A-4A(c)(2).

the "last in-first out" (LIFO) dollar value method of accounting for inventory, the tax regulations provide that "where there has been an invasion of a prior year's layer, the donor may choose to treat the item contributed as having a basis of the unit's cost with reference to the layer(s) of prior year(s) cost or with reference to the current year cost."[104]

The donor of the property which is inventory contributed under these rules must make a corresponding adjustment to cost of goods sold, decreasing the cost of goods sold by the lesser of the fair market value of the contributed item or the amount of basis (determined under the rules described in the preceding paragraph.[105]

Example 9.5

During 1993, Y, a corporation on the calendar-year basis of reporting taxes, made a qualified contribution of women's coats.[106] The fair market value of the property at the date of contribution was $1,000 and the basis of the property was $200. The amount of the charitable contribution which would have been taken into account under the general charitable deduction rules is $1,000. The amount of gain which would not have been long-term capital gain if the property had been sold was $800 ($1,000 − $200). The amount of the contribution had to be reduced by one-half of the amount which would not have been capital if the property had been sold, or $400 ($\frac{1}{2}$ of $800).

After this reduction, the amount of the contribution which was taken into account was $600 ($1,000 − $400) A second reduction had to be made in the amount of the charitable contribution because this amount (as first reduced to $600) was more than an amount equal to twice the basis of the property, or $400. The amount of the further reduction is $200 [$600 − (2 × $200)], and the amount of the contribution as finally reduced was $400 [$1,000 − ($400 + $200)]. Y also had to reduce its cost of goods sold for the year of the contribution by $200.[107]

---

[104]*Id.*
[105]Reg. § 1.170A-4A(c)(3).
[106]The coats were stock in trade of Y (inventory)(IRC § 1221(1)). See the text accompanied by ns. 65–66, *supra*.
[107]Reg. § 1.170A-4A(c)(4), Example (1).

Example 9.6

The facts of this Example are based on Example 9.5, except that the basis of the property was $600. The amount of the first reduction was $200 (($1,000 − $600)/2). As reduced, the amount of the contribution which was taken into account was $800 ($1,000 − $200). There was no need for a second reduction because $800 is less than $1,200, which is twice the basis of the property. However, Y had to decrease its cost of goods sold for the year of contribution by $600.[108]

(g) Recapture Excluded

A deduction is not allowed under these rules for any amount which, if the property had been sold by the donor on the date of its contribution for an amount equal to its fair market value, would have been treated as ordinary income.[109] Thus, before making either of the two reductions (see above), the fair market value of the contributed property must be reduced by the amount of gain that would have been recognized (if the property had been sold) as ordinary income by reason of one of these recapture rules.[110]

§ 9.5 BARGAIN SALES

As discussed in Chapter 6, the charitable deduction for an item of capital gain property is often based on the fair market value of the property and the donor is not required to recognize gain on the capital gain element in the property. However, one of the exceptions to that rule involves the so-called "bargain sale."

(a) Definition of "Bargain Sale"

A bargain sale is a transfer of property which is in part a sale or exchange of the property and in part a charitable contribution of the property.[111] Basically, a bargain sale is a sale of an item of property to

---

[108]Reg. § 1.170A-4A(c)(4), Example (2).
[109]This property might be treated as ordinary income property pursuant to IRC §§ 617, 1245, 1250, 1251, or 1252.
[110]Reg. § 1.170A-4A(d).
[111]Reg. § 1.170A-4(c)(2)(ii).

a charitable organization at a price that is an amount that is less than the fair market value of the property, with the seller/donor regarding the amount equal to the fair market value of the property less the amount that is the sales price as a contribution to the charitable organization.

(b) Allocation of Basis

The charitable deduction arising from the making of a bargain sale may be an amount equal to the value of the gift portion of the property transferred. However, the charitable deduction may be less, inasmuch as the deduction reduction rules that are the subject of Chapter 6 potentially apply to the contribution element in a bargain sale. (The deduction reduction rule requires that, under certain circumstances, the amount that is equal to the fair market value of the property be reduced by the ordinary income or capital gain element in the property.)

There must be allocated to the contributed portion of the property that portion of the adjusted basis of the entire property that bears the same ratio to the total adjusted basis as the fair market value of the contributed portion of the property bears to the fair market value of the entire property. Further, for these purposes, there must be allocated to the contributed portion of the property the amount of gain that is not recognized on the bargain sale, but that would have been recognized if the contributed portion of the property had been sold by the donor at its fair market value at the time of its contribution to the charitable organization.[112]

The amount of long-term capital gain or ordinary income which would have been recognized if the contributed portion of the property had been sold by the donor at its fair market value at the time of its contribution is the amount which bears (a) the same ratio to the ordinary income (or long-term capital gain) which would have been recognized if the entire property had been sold by the donor at its fair market value at the time of its contribution (b) as the fair market value of the contributed portion of the property at that time bears to the fair market value of the entire property at that time.[113] The fair market value of the contributed portion of the property is the

---

[112]IRC § 1011(b); Reg. § 1.1011-2(a)(1).
[113]Reg. § 1.170A-4(c)(3).

amount determined by subtracting from the fair market value of the entire property the amount realized on the sale.[114]

The adjusted basis of the contributed portion of the property must be used by the donee in applying to the contributed portion of the property such rules of law as[115]

- determining the adjusted basis of debt-financed property;[116]
- determining the basis of property acquired by gift;[117]
- determining capital gains and losses in the calculation of the net investment income of private foundations;[118] and
- determining net short-term capital gain in calculating the tax on failure to distribute income imposed on private foundations.[119]

The fair market value of the contributed portion of the property at the time of the contribution may not be used by the donee as the basis of the contriblulted portion.[120]

The contribution element arising from a bargain sale is subject to the percentage limitations that are the subject of Chapter 7. The gain that is generated as the consequence of a bargain sale transaction must be recognized in the year of the sale.[121]

These rules as applied to a bargain sale may be illustrated by the following example:

Example 9.7

H has long-term capital gain property that has a fair market value of $20,000. H's basis in the property is $8,000. H sold the property to a hospital for $8,000. Consequently, H made a charitable contribution to the hospital of $12,000 ($20,000 − $8,000). The transaction was thus partially a contribution ($12,000) and partially a sale ($8,000).

Continued

---

[114]*Id.*
[115]Reg. § 1.170A-4(c)(4).
[116]IRC § 514(a)(1). See Chapter 4 § 4.
[117]IRC § 1015(a).
[118]IRC § 4940(c)(4).
[119]IRC § 4942(f)(2)(B).
[120]Reg. § 1.170A-4(c)(4), last sentence.
[121]Reg. § 1.1011-2(a)(2). Also Reg. § 1.1011-2(c), Example (2).

Example 9.7 Continued

H thus received a gain of $8,000. To determine the net gain, H had to reduce the gain by the amount of the basis allocable to it. The basis allocated to the sale portion of the transaction was $3,200 ($8,000/ $20,000 × $8,000). The basis allocated to the gift element of the transaction was $4,800 ($12,000/$20,000 × $8,000).

A bargain sale will also arise where the property transferred to a charitable organization is subject to a debt, even though the donor does not receive any payment for the transfer of the property.[122]

In one case, a court held that a charitable contribution of property, subject to a nonrecourse indebtedness, constituted a bargain sale that gives rise to taxable gain.[123] A dissent observed that the holding is erroneous because the donors were not relieved of any personal liability by the transfer of the land.

A court upheld a bargain sale transaction, where persons sold stock to a city for less than the fair market value of the securities. The city wanted the property represented by the stock for use as part of a sewage treatment program. The stock had a value of $7.9 million and was sold for $4 million.[124]

(c) Interplay with Deduction Reduction Rule

A court ruled that the federal tax regulations accompanying the appreciation reduction rules[125] were invalid to the extent that they required reduction of a donor's charitable deduction, arising by reason of a bargain sale, by the amount of the unrealized appreciation of the sale portion of the property.[126] Under the facts of the case, the donors sold appreciated long-term capital gain property to a charitable organization as a bargain sale. The regulations accompanying these rules[127] provided, in the case of a bargain sale to which the deduction reduction rule applies, that no deduction is allowable unless the gift exceeds the appreciation reduction amount for all of the

---

[122] See § 3, *supra.*
[123] *Ebben* v. *Commissioner, supra,* n. 40.
[124] *Waranch* v. *Commissioner,* 58 T.C.M. 584 (1989).
[125] IRC § 170(e)(1). See Chapter 6.
[126] *Bullard, Estate of* v. *Commissioner,* 87 T.C. 261 (1986).
[127] Reg. §§ 1.170A-4(c) and 1.1011-2.

property. Because this interpretation of the rules would have eliminated any charitable contribution deduction, the donors contended that the deduction reduction rule only causes a reduction in their charitable deduction of the inherent gain in the donated portion of the property. In agreeing with the donors, the court parsed the language of the deduction reduction rule, which speaks of the "property contributed," and concluded that Congress referenced, in connection with bargain sales, only the property donated and not the property sold as well. Therefore, the court pronounced the regulations "unreasonable" and thus invalid.[128] The regulations were subsequently revised to reflect this opinion.

(d) Interplay with the Carryover Rules

In a case, a donor made a bargain sale of capital gain property to a charitable organization. Earlier in the same year, the same donor made another gift of different capital gain property to another charitable recipient, resulting in a charitable deduction (prior to application of the percentage limitations[129]). This deduction exceeded the amount allowable for the donor for gifts of capital gain property for the year, thus forcing all of the deduction attributable to the bargain sale to be carried forward.

The tax regulations state that a charitable deduction arising from a bargain sale of property is an "allowable" deduction, even if part or all of the contribution must be carried forward, irrespective of whether the portion carried over is ever used as a deduction.[130] In this case, the donors challenged the regulation, claiming that the deduction resulting from the first gift must be deducted in its entirety before any part of the contribution for the second gift can be deducted. If that were true, it so worked out that the entire allowable deduction relating to capital gain property in the year of the gift and in the subsequent year would be charged against the first contribution, leaving nothing to be deductible attributable to the second contribution. But the court held that there is no basis in law for the "first-in first out" rule as the donors suggested.[131]

[128]*Bullard* v. *Commissioner, supra,* n. 123.
[129]See Chapter 7.
[130]Reg. § 1.1011-2(a)(2).
[131]*Hodgdon* v. *Commissioner,* 98 T.C. No. 424 (1992).

The court construed the term "allowable" in the context of the five-year carryover rule. That is, the deductibility of a gift may not be known until the expiration of six years—long after the expiration of the period of limitations for assessment of a deficiency in respect to the year of contribution. Wrote the court: "We think it unlikely that Congress intended the substantive rights of taxpayers and the Government to be imperiled by a rule providing that no deduction was 'allowable' for [these] purposes . . . unless it eventually turned out, long after the taxable year, that the contribution actually reduced the taxpayer's taxable income in any of the 5 succeeding taxable years."[132] The court continued: "We think that if the statute is read in the context of all relevant provisions, the word 'allowable' must be interpreted as referring to a contribution available for deduction even though the contribution does not ultimately result in a deduction by reason of future events entirely unrelated to the nature of the charitable contribution."[133] This interpretation of the law, concluded the court, "strongly supports" the regulation.[134]

§ 9.6   GIFTS FOR CONSERVATION PURPOSES

The federal tax law contains special rules for contributions to charity of real property for conservation purposes. These rules are an exception to the general rule that there is no charitable deduction for contributions of "partial interests" in property.[135] This exception involves a so-called "qualified conservation contribution."[136]

A qualified conservation contribution has three characteristics; it is a contribution

- of a "qualified real property interest,"[137]
- to a "qualified organization,"[138]
- exclusively for "conservation purposes."[139]

---

[132]*Id.* at 434.
[133]*Id.*
[134]*Id.*
[135]IRC § 170(f)(3)(A).
[136]IRC § 170(f)(3)(B)(iii). Reg. § 1.170A-14(a).
[137]IRC § 170(h)(1)(A).
[138]IRC § 170(h)(1)(B).
[139]IRC § 170(h)(1)(C).

(a) Qualified Real Property Interests

A qualified real property interest is any of the following interests in real property:

- the entire interest of the donor other than a "qualified mineral interest,"[140]
- a remainder interest,[141]
- a restriction (granted in perpetuity) on the use which may be made of the real property.[142]

A "qualified mineral interest" is the donor's interest in subsurface oil, gas, or other minerals, and the right to access to these minerals.[143]

A real property interest is not treated as an entire interest (other than a qualified mineral interest) if the property in which the donor's interest exists was divided prior to the contribution in order to enable the donor to retain control of more than a qualified mineral interest or to reduce the real property interest donated.[144] However, minor interests, such as rights-of-way, that will not interfere with the conservation purposes of the gift, may be transferred prior to the conservation contribution without adversely affecting the treatment of a property interest as a qualified real property interest.[145] An entire interest in real property may consist of an undivided interest in the property.[146]

A "perpetual conservation restriction" is a qualified real property interest. A perpetual conservation restriction is a "restriction granted in perpetuity on the use which may be made of real property— including an easement or other interest in real property that under state law has attributes similar to an easement (e.g., a restrictive covenant or equitable servitude).[147] This definition does not preclude

---

[140] IRC § 170(h)(2)(A).

[141] IRC § 170(h)(2)(B).

[142] IRC § 170(h)(2)(C).

[143] IRC § 170(h)(6), Reg. § 1.170A-l4(b)(1)(i).

[144] Reg. § 1.170A-14(b)(1)(ii). Also Reg. § 1.170A-7(a)(2)(i).

[145] Reg. § 1.170A-14(b)(1), last sentence.

[146] Reg. § 1.170A-14(b)(ii). However, as discussed *infra*, the conservation purpose which is the subject of the contribution must be protected in perpetuity.

[147] Reg. § 1.170A-14(b)(2). For these purposes, the terms "easement," "conservation restriction," and "perpetual conservation restriction" have the same meaning (*id.*).

the deductibility of a gift of affirmative rights to use a land or water area.[148] Any rights reserved by a donor in the contribution of a perpetual conservation restriction must conform to the law on this subject.

(b) Qualified Organizations

A qualified organization is an organization which is

* a unit of government,[149]
* a publicly supported charitable organization of the "donative" variety,[150]
* a publicly supported charitable organization of the "service provider" variety,[151]
* a supporting organization that is controlled by one or more of the foregoing three types of organizations.[152]

In addition, to be an eligible donee, an organization must have "a commitment to protect the conservation purposes of the donation, and have the resources to enforce the restrictions."[153] A qualified organization need not set aside funds to enforce the restrictions that are the subject of the contribution.[154]

A deduction is allowed for a contribution under these rules only if, in the instrument of conveyance, the donor prohibits the donee from

[148]*Id.* See the text accompanying ns. 161–162 *infra*.

[149]IRC § 170(h)(3)(A). A "governmental unit" is described in IRC § 170(b)(1)(A)(v). See Chapter 4 § 3, text accompanied by ns. 193–194.

[150]IRC § 170(h)(3)(A). This type of publicly supported organization is described in IRC §§ 170(b)(1)(A)(vi) and 509(a)(1). See Chapter 4 § 3, text accompanied by ns. 195–213.

[151]IRC § 170(h)(3)(B)(i). This type of publicly supported organization is described in IRC § 509(a)(2). See Chapter 4 § 3, text accompanied by ns. 216–232.

[152]IRC § 170(h)(3)(B)(ii). Reg. § 1.170A-14(c)(1). A supporting organization is an organization that is not a private foundation by reason of IRC § 509(a)(3). See Chapter 4 § 3, text accompanied by ns. 233–249.

[153]Reg. § 1.170A-14(c)(1). A conservation group organized or operated primarily or substantially for one of the "conservation purposes" (see the text accompanying ns. 137–178, *infra*) is considered to have the requisite commitment (*id.*).

[154]*Id.*

subsequently transferring the easement (or, in the case of a remainder interest or the reservation of a qualified mineral supporting organization is an organization that is not a private foundation by reason of interest, the property), whether or not for consideration, unless the donee, as a condition of the subsequent transfer, requires that the conservation purposes which the contribution was originally intended to advance be carried out. Moreover, subsequent transfers must be restricted to organizations qualifying, at the time of the subsequent transfer, as eligible donees.[155] Nonetheless, when a later "unexpected" change in the conditions surrounding the property that is the subject of a donation makes "impossible or impractical" the continued use of the property for conservation purposes, these requirements will be met if the property is sold or exchanged and any proceeds are used by the donee organization in a manner consistent with the conservation purposes of the original contribution.[156]

(c)   Conservation Purpose

The term "conservation purpose" means the

- preservation of land areas for outdoor recreation by, or the education of, the general public;[157]
- protection of a relatively natural habitat of fish, wildlife, or plants, or similar ecosystem;[158]
- preservation of open space (including farmland and forest land) where the preservation is
  - for the scenic enjoyment of the general public,
  - pursuant to a clearly delineated federal, state, or local governmental education policy, and will yield a significant public benefit;[159]
- preservation of an historically important land area or a "certified historic structure."[160]

[155] Reg. § 1.170A-14(c)(2).
[156] Id.
[157] IRC § 170(h)(4)(A)(i).
[158] IRC § 170(h)(4)(A)(ii).
[159] IRC § 170(h)(4)(A)(iii).
[160] IRC § 170(h)(4)(A)(iv); Reg. § 1.170A-14(d)(1).

In connection with the first of these definitions (recreation or education), conservation purposes include the preservation of a water area for the use of the public for boating or fishing, or a nature or hiking trail for the use of the public.[161] However, the recreation or education must be for the substantial and regular use of the general public.[162]

In connection with the second of these definitions (protection of an environmental system), the fact that the habitat or environment has been altered to some extent by human activity will not result in a denial of a charitable deduction under these rules if the fish, wildlife, or plants continue to exist there in a relatively natural state. For example, the preservation of a lake formed by a man-made dam or a salt pond formed by a man-made dike would meet the conservation purposes test if the lake or the pond were a natural feeding area for a wildlife community that included rare, endangered, or threatened native species.[163]

Also, in connection with the second of these definitions, the tax regulations add the requirement that the "relatively natural habitat" be "significant."[164] Significant habitats and ecosystems include: habitats for rare, endangered, or threatened species of animals, fish, or plants; natural areas that represent high quality examples of a terrestrial community or aquatic community, such as islands that are undeveloped or not intensely developed where the coastal ecosystem is relatively intact; and natural areas which are included in, or which contribute to, the ecological viability of a local, state, or national park, nature preserve, wildlife refuge, wilderness area, or other similar conservation area.[165]

As to the third of these definitions (preservation of open space), the preservation (1) must be pursuant to a clearly delineated federal, state, or local governmental conservation policy and will yield a significant public benefit, or (2) must be for the scenic enjoyment of the general public and will yield a significant public benefit.[166] A governmental policy in this regard must be more than a general

[161]Reg. § 1.170A-14(d)(2)(i).
[162]Reg. § 1.170A-14(d)(2)(ii).
[163]Reg. § 1.170A-14(d)(3)(i).
[164]Id.
[165]Reg. § 1.170A-14(d)(3)(ii).
[166]Reg. § 1.170A-14(d)(4)(i).

declaration of conservation goals by a single official or legislative body; the requirement will be met by contributions that further a specific, identified conservation project, that preserve a wild or scenic river, or that protect the scenic, ecological, or historic character of land that is contiguous to or an integral part of the surroundings of existing recreation or conservation sites.[167] A contribution made for the preservation of open space may be for the scenic enjoyment of the general public. Preservation of land may be for the scenic enjoyment of the general public if development of the property would impair the scenic character of the local rural or urban landscape or would interfere with a scenic panorama that can be enjoyed from a park, nature preserve, road, body of water, trail, or historic structure or land area, and the area or transportation way is open to or utilized by the public. The regulations contain criteria for evaluating the requisite "scenic enjoyment"[168] and, for both definitions, the necessary "significant public benefit."[169]

In connection with the fourth of these definitions (historic preservation), the donation of a qualified real property interest to preserve an historically important land area or a certified historic structure meets the requirements.[170] When restrictions to preserve a building or land area within a registered historic district permit future development on the site, a charitable contribution deduction is allowed under these rules only if the terms of the restrictions require that the development conform with appropriate local, state, or federal standards for construction or rehabilitation within the district.

An "historically important land area" includes

- an independently significant land area, including any related historic resources that meet the National Register Criteria for Evaluation,[171]
- any land area within a registered historic district, including any buildings on the land area that can reasonably be considered as contributing to the significance of the district,

---

[167]Reg. § 1.170A-14(d)(4)(iii).
[168]Reg. § 1.170A-14(d)(4)(ii)(A).
[169]Reg. § 1.170A-14(d)(4)(iv).
[170]Reg. § 1.170A-14(d)(5)(i).
[171]36 C.F.R. 60.4.

• any land area adjacent to a property listed individually in the National Register of Historic Places, in a case where the physical or environmental features of the land area contribute to the historic or cultural integrity of the property.[172]

A "certified historic structure" is a building, structure, or land area which is (1) listed in the National Register, or (2) located in a registered historic district[173] and is certified by the Secretary of the Interior to the Secretary of the Treasury as being of historic significance to the district.[174] The structure must satisfy this definition either as of the date of the transfer or on the due date (including extensions) for filing the transferor's tax return for the year in which the transfer is made.[175]

For a conservation contribution to be deductible, some visual public access to the donated property is required. In the case of an historically important land area, the entire property need not be visible to the public for a donation to qualify under these rules.[176] The regulations contain criteria for determining the required type and amount of public access.[177] The amount of access afforded the public by the contribution of an easement is determined with reference to the amount of access permitted by the terms of the easement which are established by the donor, rather than the amount of access actually provided by the donee charitable organization.[178]

(d) Exclusivity Requirement

To satisfy these rules, a contribution must be exclusively for conservation purposes. However, a conservation deduction will not be denied where incidental benefit inures to the donor merely as a result of conservation restrictions limiting the uses to which the donor's property may be put.[179] In general, a conservation deduction will not be allowed if the contribution would accomplish one of the enumer-

---

[172]Reg. § 1.170A-14(d)(5)(ii).
[173]This term is defined in IRC § 47(c)(3)(B).
[174]IRC § 170(h)(4)(B); Reg. § 1.170A-14(d)(5)(iii).
[175]IRC § 170(h)(4)(B), last sentence.
[176]Reg. § 1.170A-14(d)(5)(iv)(A).
[177]Reg. § 1.170A-14(d)(5)(iv)(B).
[178]Reg. § 1.170A-14(d)(5)(iv)(C).
[179]Reg. § 1.170A-14(e)(1).

ated conservation purposes but would permit destruction of other significant conservation interests.[180] Nonetheless, a use that is destructive of conservation interests will be permitted if the use is necessary for the protection of the conservation interests that are the subject of the contribution.[181]

A contribution cannot be treated as being "exclusively" for conservation purposes unless the conservation purpose is protected in perpetuity.[182] Thus, any interest in the property retained by the donor (and the donor's successors in interest) must be subject to legally enforceable restrictions that will prevent uses of the retained interest that are inconsistent with the conservation purposes of the donation.[183] A deduction is not permitted under these rules for a contribution of an interest in property which is subject to a mortgage unless the mortgagee subordinates its rights in the property to the right of the charitable organization to enforce the conservation purposes of the gift in perpetuity.[184] However, a conservation deduction will not be disallowed merely because the interest which passes to, or is vested in, the donee charitable organization may be defeated by the performance of some act or the happening of some event, if on the date of the gift it appears that the possibility that the act or event will occur is so remote as to be negligible.[185]

In general, in the case of a contribution of any interest where there is a retention of a "qualified mineral interest," this requirement of "exclusivity" is not regarded as met if at any time there may be extraction or removal of minerals by any surface mining method.[186] Also, the requirement that the conservation purposes be protected in perpetuity is not satisfied if any method of mining that is inconsistent with the particular conservation purposes of a contribution is permitted at any time.[187] A "qualified mineral interest" is the donor's interest in subsurface oil, gas, or other minerals and the right of access to the minerals.[188]

---

[180] Reg. § 1.170A-14(e)(2).
[181] Reg. § 1.170A-14(e)(3).
[182] IRC § 170(h)(5)(A); Reg. § 1.170A-14(a).
[183] Reg. § 1.170A-14(g)(1).
[184] Reg. § 1.170A-14(g)(2).
[185] Reg. § 1.170A-14(g)(3).
[186] IRC § 170(h)(5)(B)(i).
[187] Reg. § 1.170A-14(g)(4).
[188] Reg. § 1.170A-14(b)(1)(i).

(e) Valuation

The value of the charitable contribution in the case of a contribution of a donor's entire interest in property (other than a qualified mineral interest) is the fair market value of the surface rights in the property contributed.[189] The value for the deduction is computed without regard to the mineral rights.[190] In the case of a contribution of a remainder interest in real property, depreciation and depletion of the property must be taken into account in determining the value of the interest.[191] The value of a charitable contribution of a perpetual conservation restriction is the fair market value of the perpetual conservation restriction at the time of the contribution.[192] In the case of a contribution of a qualified real property interest for conservation purposes, the basis of the property retained by the donor must be adjusted by the elimination of that part of the total basis of the property that is properly allocable to the qualified real property interest granted.[193]

(f) Substantiation Requirement

If a donor makes a qualified conservation contribution and claims a charitable contribution deduction for it, the donor must maintain written records of

- the fair market value of the underlying property before and after the donation,
- the conservation purpose furthered by the donation.

This information may have to be part of the donor's income tax return.[194]

This requirement is in addition to the general charitable contribution substantiation requirements, discussed in Chapter 23.

---

[189] E.g., *The Stanley Works and Subsidiaries* v. *Commissioner*, 87 T.C. 389 (1986) (where it was held that the value of a conservation easement donated to charity is based on the highest and best use of the land).
[190] Reg. § 1.170A-14(h)(1).
[191] IRC § 197(f)(4); Reg. § 1.170A-14(h)(2).
[192] Reg. § 1.170A-14(h)(3).
[193] Reg. § 1.170A-14(h)(3)(iii).
[194] Reg. § 1.170A-14(i).

(g) Relationship to Rehabilitation Tax Credit

It has been held that a partnership must recapture a portion of a rehabilitation tax credit and reduce its basis in the underlying rehabilitated property upon its donation to a charitable organization of an historical facade easement, where the gift occurred in the same year it claimed the tax credit.[195] The partnership was formed to acquire, rehabilitate, and operate a building, which became designated as a "certified historic structure."[196] The partnership "substantially rehabilitated" the building, causing it to become a "qualified rehabilitation building."[197] The partnership incurred "qualified rehabilitation expenditures"[198] in the amount of $2.8 million in the course of restoring the building. Later in the same year, the partnership deeded a facade and conservation easement to a charitable organization formed to preserve and protect the architectural heritage of the state involved. The easement was granted in perpetuity, was intended to benefit the public, and constituted a "qualified conservation contribution."[199] Thus, the transaction qualified as a charitable contribution.[200] The fair market value of the easement was $422,000. The parties stipulated that the easement value was allocable as follows: $4,413 to the building "shell," $41,267 to the land, and $376,320 to the rehabilitated building. The partnership claimed a rehabilitation tax credit in the amount of $2.2 million—the amount expended during the year in rehabilitation of the building. The IRS concluded, and the court agreed, that the tax credit should be $1.8 million—the amount expended less the portion of the easement value allocated to the rehabilitated building ($376,320).

The law is that, if property for which an investment tax credit[201] has been taken in prior years is disposed of or otherwise ceases to qualify for the credit before the end of the useful life used in computing the credit, a portion of the tax credit must be recaptured.[202] The tax regulations provide that this requirement is triggered when a person disposes of a portion of the basis of a qualified rehabilitated

[195] *Rome I Ltd.* v. *Commissioner*, 96 T.C. 697 (1991).
[196] IRC § 48(g)(3)
[197] IRC § 48(g)(1)(A).
[198] IRC § 48(g)(2)(A)
[199] IRC § 170(h)(1).
[200] IRC § 170(f)(3)(B)(iii).
[201] IRC § 38.
[202] IRC § 47(a).

building that is attributable to qualified rehabilitated expenditures. In this case, the IRS took the position that the donation of the facade easement was a "disposition" of the property. The partnership contended that the federal tax law does not require the recapture of a portion of a rehabilitation tax credit upon the donation of a facade easement. It also argued that the charitable donation of a facade easement is not a "disposition" for these purposes because it was not a "gift" within the meaning of the regulations. However, the court concluded that the "plain meaning" of the term "disposition" is "to transfer or otherwise relinquish ownership of property."[203] The court added that "[w]e believe that requiring recapture of a portion of the rehabilitation tax credit upon the donation of a facade easement is in accordance with Congress' purpose in enacting" these rules.[204]

The matter troubling the court was the creation of a double deduction if this recapture was not required. Therefore, it ruled that the donation of the facade easements was a "gift." Consequently, since the easement qualified as property eligible for an investment tax credit, the court followed the requirement of the tax regulations that this disposition triggered the recapture provision. Thus, the court announced that "[t]he rehabilitation credit, like the investment tax credit, is subject to recapture in the event of the early disposition of the property attributed to the qualified rehabilitation expenditures."[205] Consequently, this rule was announced: "When a qualified real property interest is donated for conservation purposes, the basis of the donor's remaining property is adjusted by eliminating that part of the total basis of the property that is properly allocable to the donated qualified real property interest" and the donor must recapture a portion of the rehabilitation tax credit.[206]

The IRS published its stance in this regard in 1989.[207] However, the court wrote that it agreed with the IRS position, "not because we rely upon it for authority, but because we have independently arrived at the same conclusion."[208]

---

[203] *Rome I Ltd.* v. *Commissioner, supra*, n. 195.
[204] *Id.* at 704.
[205] *Id.* at 706.
[206] *Id.*
[207] Rev. Rul. 89-90, 1989-2 C.B. 3.
[208] *Rome I Ltd* v. *Commissioner*, supra, n. 195, at 707. Cf. IRS General Counsel Memorandum 39664 (where the IRS took the position that recapture of a rehabilitation tax credit under these circumstances was not required).

(h) Donative Intent

A court has ruled that a gift of a scenic easement was a transfer of value to the charitable recipient, despite a variety of restrictions imposed by the donors, but also that the motivation of the donors for making the gift must be subsequently explored.[209] The issues in the case related to a contribution to a conservancy organization of a scenic easement over approximately 170 acres of the donors' real property. The IRS, in challenging the tax deductions claimed for this gift, asserted that there was no true "gift" because the donors reserved numerous rights in the scenic easement property, and that they lacked the requisite donative intent and exclusive conservation purpose when they conveyed the scenic easement.

Because of the reservation of certain rights, the IRS contended that the donors retained dominion and control over the easement property and thus transferred nothing of value to the charitable organization. But the court ruled that some of these restrictions enabled the recipient charity to "adequately preserve the scenic quality of the easement property."[210] Thus, the court held that the donors transferred "value" to the conservancy organization through the scenic easement conveyance and concluded that the easement placed material restrictions on the donors' use of the property, as required by the law.[211]

The issue the court declined to resolve at the time was that of the donors' intent in making the contribution. The court observed that, in general, the tax law "permits charitable deductions for bona fide gifts irrespective of a taxpayer's motivations."[212] But, the court added, a donor "must not expect a substantial benefit as a *quid pro quo* for the transfer."[213] To this end, then, the court will be looking at the "external features"[214] of the transaction.

The IRS took the position that the donors did not transfer the scenic easement for an exclusive conservation easement purpose.

---

[209]*McLennan* v. *United States*, 91-1 U.S.T.C. ¶ 50,230 (Cl. Ct. 1991); 91-2 U.S.T.C. ¶ 50,447 (Ct. Cl. 1991).

[210]*Id.*, 91-1 U.S.T.C. ¶§50,230, at 87,925.

[211]Reg. § 1.170A-7(b)(1)(ii).

[212]*McLennan* v. *United States, supra*, n. 209, 91-1 U.S.T.C. ¶ 50,230, at 87,926.

[213]*Id.*

[214]*Id.*

This assertion was in addition to the one that the donors lacked the necessary "donative intent." The donors argued that they granted the scenic easement for the "purpose of protecting the area . . . from further development so as to preserve the beauty and environmental systems of that area."[215] The IRS, however, countered that the donors granted the easement with the "expectation of preserving property values and achieving desired zoning restrictions for the property."[216] The court wrote that it was unable at the time to determine whether the benefits which accrued to the donors (other than the tax savings generated by the charitable deduction) "were merely incidental to a greater public conservation benefit derived from the scenic easement conveyance" and that the facts require "further ventilation."[217] The court observed that the donors bear the burden "of proving at trial that . . . [they] transferred the easement to the [c]onservancy with the requisite donative intent and exclusive conservation purpose."[218]

§ 9.7 SCIENTIFIC RESEARCH PROPERTY

There are special federal tax rules governing charitable contributions of scientific research property.[219] To qualify under these rules, the property that is the subject of the gift must be

- tangible personal property, and
- stock in trade of a corporation or other property of a kind which would properly be included in the inventory of the cor-

---

[215]*Id.*

[216]*Id.*

[217]*Id.*

[218]*Id.* The matter of donative intent in the general charitable giving context is explored in Chapter 4 § 1.

In *Osborne* v. *Commissioner*, 87 T.C. 575 (1986), a charitable deduction was allowed for the installation and transfer of drainage facilities and easements to a city. The IRS challenged the deduction, alleging that the facilities enhanced the value of the donors' property. The court allowed the deduction only to the extent the transfer "gratuitously benefited" the city (at 583). The court allowed the deduction, using a value about twice that asserted by the government.

[219]IRC § 170(e)(4).

poration[220] if on hand at the close of the tax year, or property held by the corporation primarily for sale to customers in the ordinary course of its trade or business.[221]

This deduction is available only to corporations.[222] However, it is not available to a small business corporation,[223] a personal holding company,[224] or a service corporation.[225]

In addition to the foregoing, for this charitable deduction to be available, all of the following requirements must be satisfied.

* The contribution must be to an eligible institution of higher education,[226] or an eligible scientific research organization.[227]

[220]See the discussion of the term "inventory" in Chapter 2 and in § 4, *supra*.
[221]IRC § 170(e)(4)(B). This second criterion is the subject of IRC § 1221(1).
[222]*Id.*
[223]These are known as "S corporations" (IRC § 1371(b)).
[224]IRC § 542.
[225]IRC § 170(e)(4)(D). A "service corporation" is the subject of IRC § 414(m)(3).
[226]That is, an institution of higher education that normally maintains a regular faculty and curriculum and normally has a regularly enrolled body of pupils or students in attendance at the place where its educational activities are regularly carried on (IRC § 170(b)(1)(A)(ii)). See Chapter 4 § 3, text accompanied by ns. 172–176. This type of eligible institution is required by IRC § 170(e)(3)(4)(B)(i), by cross-reference to IRC § 41(e)(6)(A), which in turn cross-references to IRC § 3304(f), which imposes the following additional criteria: the institution (1) admits as regular students only individuals having a certificate of graduation from a high school or the recognized equivalent of this type of certificate, (2) is legally authorized within a state to provide a program of education beyond high school, (3) provides an educational program for which it awards a bachelor's degree or higher degree, or provides a program which is acceptable for full credit toward this type of degree, or offers a program of training to prepare students for gainful employment in a recognized occupation, and (4) is a public or other nonprofit institution.
[227]That is, to an organization that meets the following criteria: it is (1) not an eligible institution of higher education (see n. 226, *supra*), (2) exempt from federal income taxation under IRC § 501(a) because it is described in IRC § 501(c)(3) (see Chapter 4 § 2), (3) organized and operated primarily to conduct scientific research, and (4) not a private foundation (see Chapter 4 § 3) (IRC § 170(e)(3)(4)(B)(i), by cross-reference to IRC § 41(e)(6)(B)).

- The property must be constructed by the donor corporation.[228]
- The contribution must be made not later than two years after the date the construction of the property is substantially completed.[229]
- The original use of the property must be by the charitable recipient.[230]
- The property must be scientific equipment or apparatus substantially all of the use of which by the charitable recipient is for research or experimentation,[231] or for research training, in the United States in physical or biological sciences.[232]
- The property must not be transferred by the charitable recipient in exchange for money, other property, or services.[233]
- The corporation must receive from the charitable recipient a written statement representing that its use and disposition of the property will be in accordance with the fifth and sixth of these requirements.[234]

This deduction is computed in the same manner as it is pursuant to the special rule concerning gifts of inventory.[235]

§ 9.8   FUTURE INTERESTS IN TANGIBLE PERSONAL PROPERTY

A charitable contribution consisting of a transfer of a future interest in tangible personal property is treated as made only when all intervening interests in, and rights to the actual possession or enjoyment

[228]IRC § 170(e)(4)(B)(ii). Property is considered constructed by the donor corporation only if the cost of the parts used in the construction of the property (other than parts manufactured by the corporation or a related person) do not exceed 50 percent of the corporation's basis in the property (IRC § 170(e)(4)(C)).
[229]IRC § 170(e)(4)(B)(iii).
[230]IRC § 170(e)(4)(B)(iv).
[231]This phrase is referenced in IRC § 174.
[232]IRC § 170(e)(4)(B)(v).
[233]IRC § 170(e)(4)(B)(vi).
[234]*Id.*
[235]IRC § 170(e)(4)(A). See the text accompanied by ns. 100–107, *supra*.

of, the property (1) have expired, or (2) are held by persons other than the donor or those related to the donor.[236]

The term "future interest" includes

- reversions, remainders, and other interests or estates, whether vested or contingent, and whether or not supported by a particular interest or estate, which are limited to commence in use, possession, or enjoyment at some future date or time,[237] and
- situations in which a donor purports to give tangible personal property to a charitable organization but has an understanding, arrangement, agreement, or the like, whether written or oral, with the charitable organization which has the effect of reserving to, or retaining in, the donor a right to the use, possession, or enjoyment of the property.[238]

These rules do not apply with respect to a transfer of an undivided present interest in property. For example, a contribution of an undivided one-quarter interest in a painting with respect to which the charitable donee is entitled to possession during three months of each year is treated as made upon the receipt by the donee of a formally executed and acknowledged deed of gift. However, the period of initial possession by the donee may not be deferred in time for more than one year.[239]

Thus, these rules do not have application in respect of a transfer of a future interest in intangible personal property or of a transfer of a future interest in real property.[240] However, a fixture which is intended to be severed from real property is treated as tangible personal property.[241] For example, a contribution of a future interest in a chandelier attached to a building is considered a contribution that consists of a future interest in tangible personal property if the

---

[236] IRC § 170(a)(3); Reg. § 1.170A-5(a)(1). The rules of IRC § 267(b) (relating to losses, expenses, and interest with respect to transactions between related taxpayers) are used to measure the requisite relationships.
[237] Reg. § 25.2503-3(b).
[238] Reg. § 1.170A-5(a)(4).
[239] Reg. § 1.170A-5(a)(2).
[240] Reg. § 1.170A-5(a)(3).
[241] IRC § 170(a)(3), last sentence; Reg. § 1.170A-5(a)(3).

transferor intends that it be detached from the building at or prior to the time when the charitable organization's right to possession or enjoyment of the chandelier is to commence.[242]

In the case of a charitable contribution of a future interest, the other rules of the law of charitable giving are inapplicable to the contribution until the time the contribution is treated as made under these rules.[243]

These rules may be illustrated by the following example:

Example 9.8

On December 31, 1994, A, an individual who reports his income on the calendar year basis, conveyed by deed of gift, to a museum, title to a painting, but reserved to himself the right to use, possess, and enjoy the painting during his lifetime. There was no intention on the part of A to avoid the application of the partial interest gift rules[244] by the conveyance. At the time of the gift, the value of the painting was $200,000. Since the contribution consisted of a future interest in tangible personal property in which the donor retained an intervening interest, A did not make a deductible charitable contribution to the museum in 1994.[245]

Example 9.9

The facts are the same as in Example 9.8, except that on December 31, 1995, A relinquished all of his right to the use, possession, and enjoyment of the painting, and delivered the painting to the museum. The value of the painting had increased to $220,000. A is treated as having made a charitable contribution of $220,000 in 1995 for which a deduction is allowable (without regard to the partial interest gift rules).[246]

---

[242] Reg. § 1.170A-5(a)(3).
[243] Reg. § 1.170A-5(a)(5).
[244] IRC § 170(f)(3)(A). See § 9, *infra*.
[245] Reg. § 1.170A-5(b), Example (1).
[246] Reg. § 1.170A-5(b), Example (2).

Example 9.10

The facts are the same as in Example 9.8, except that A died without relinquishing his right to the use, possession, and enjoyment of the painting. Since A did not relinquish his right to the use, possession, and enjoyment of the property during his life, A is treated as not having made a charitable contribution of the painting for income tax purposes.[247]

Example 9.11

The facts are the same as in Example 9.8, except that A, on December 31, 1995, transferred his interest in the painting to his daughter, B. Since A and B are related, no contribution of the remainder interest in the painting is considered to have been made in 1995.[248]

Example 9.12

The facts are the same as in Example 9.11. On December 31, 1996, B conveyed to the museum the interest measured by A's life. B thus made a charitable contribution of the present interest in the painting conveyed to the museum. In addition, since all intervening interests in, and rights to the actual possession or enjoyment of, the property have expired, a charitable contribution of the remainder interest is treated as having been made by A in 1996, for which a charitable contribution deduction is allowable (without regard to the partial interest gift rules). The value of the remainder interest is determined by subtracting the value of B's interest measured by A's life expectancy in 1996, and B receives a charitable contribution deduction in 1996 for the life interest measured by A's life expectancy.[249]

---

[247] Reg. § 1.170A-5(b), Example (3).
[248] Reg. § 1.170A-5(b), Example (4).
[249] Reg. § 1.170A-5(b), Example (5).

Example 9.13

On December 31, 1994, C, an individual, transferred a valuable paint-ing to a qualified pooled income fund[250] which is maintained by a university. C retained for himself for life an income interest in the painting, the remainder interest in the painting being contributed to the university. Since the contribution consists of a future interest in tangible personal property in which the donor has retained an inter-vening interest, no charitable deduction is considered to have been made in 1994.[251]

Example 9.14

On January 15, 1994, D, an individual, transferred a painting (a long-term capital asset) to a pooled income fund, which is maintained by a university, and created an income interest in the painting for E, for her life. D and E are not related individuals. The remainder interest in the property was contributed by D to the university. The trustee of the pooled income fund put the painting to an unrelated use.[252] Accord-ingly, D was allowed a charitable deduction in 1994 for the present value of the remainder interest in the painting (after reducing the amount as required[253]). This reduction in the amount of the contribution is required since the use by the pooled income fund of the painting is a use which would have been an unrelated use if it had been made by the university.[254]

§ 9.9   CONTRIBUTIONS IN TRUST

(a)   General Rules

A charitable deduction is not allowed for the fair market value of a contribution of any interest in property which is less than the donor's

---

[250]See Chapter 13.
[251]Reg. § 1.170A-5(b), Example (6).
[252]See Chapter 4 § 4.
[253]*Id.*
[254]Reg. § 1.170A-5(b), Example (7).

entire interest in the property and which is transferred in trust unless the transfer meets certain requirements.[255] However, if a donor's entire interest in the property is transferred in trust and contributed to a charitable organization, a charitable deduction is allowed.[256] For example, if an item of property is transferred in trust with the requirement that the income of the trust be paid for a term of twenty years to a church and thereafter the remainder is to be paid to an educational institution, a deduction is allowed for the value of the property.[257]

These rules do not apply with respect to a contribution of a partial interest in property if the interest is the donor's entire interest in the property (an income interest or remainder interest). However, if the property in which a partial interest exists was divided in order to create the interest and thus avoid these rules, the deduction is not allowable.[258]

Example 9.15

X, an individual, desired to contribute to a charitable organization the reversionary interest in certain securities which she owns. X transferred the securities in trust with the requirement that the income of the trust be paid to her son for life and that the reversionary interest be paid to herself. Immediately after creating the trust, X contributed the reversionary interest to the charitable organization. X was not allowed a charitable contribution deduction for the gift of her entire interest, namely, the reversionary interest in the trust.[259]

A charitable contribution deduction is not allowed for the fair market value of a gift, to a charitable organization, of a remainder interest in property which is less than the donor's entire interest in the property and which the donor transfers in trust, unless the trust is

- a pooled income fund (see Chapter 12),
- a charitable remainder annuity trust (see Chapter 11 § 5), or

---

[255]IRC § 170(f)(2); Reg. § 1.170A-6(a)(1).
[256]IRC § 170(f)(2)(D).
[257]Reg. § 1.170A-6(a)(1).
[258]Reg. § 1.170A-6(a)(2).
[259]Id.

- a charitable remainder unitrust (see Chapter 11 § 6).[260]

A charitable contribution deduction is not allowed for the fair market value of a gift, to a charitable organization, of an income interest in property which is less than the donor's entire interest in the property and which the donor transfers in trust, unless the income interest is a guaranteed annuity interest or a unitrust interest, and the grantor is treated as the owner of the interest.[261]

(b) Guaranteed Annuity Interests

An income interest is a "guaranteed annuity interest" only if it is an irrevocable right pursuant to the governing instrument of the trust to receive a guaranteed annuity. A guaranteed annuity is an arrangement under which a determinable amount is paid periodically but not less than annually, for a specified term and/or for the life or lives of an individual or individuals, each of whom must be living at the date of transfer and can be ascertained at that date. For example, the annuity may be paid for the life of A plus a term of years. An amount is determinable if the exact amount which must be paid under the conditions specified in the governing instrument of the trust can be ascertained as of the date of transfer. For example, the amount to be paid may be a stated sum for a term, or for the life of an individual, at the expiration of which it may be changed by a specified amount but may not be redetermined by reference to a fluctuating index, such as the cost of living index. The amount to be paid may be expressed in terms of a fraction or percentage of the cost of living index on the date of transfer.[262]

An income interest is a guaranteed annuity interest only if it is a guaranteed annuity interest in every respect. For example, if the income interest is the right to receive from a trust each year a payment equal to the lesser of a sum certain or a fixed percentage of the net fair market value of the trust assets, determined annually, the interest is not a guaranteed annuity interest.[263]

Where a charitable interest is in the form of a guaranteed annuity interest, the governing instrument of the trust may provide that

[260] IRC § 170(f)(2)(A); Reg. § 1.170A-6(b)(1).
[261] IRC § 170(f)(2)(B); Reg. § 1.170A-6(c)(1).
[262] Reg. § 1.170A-6(c)(2)(i)(A).
[263] Reg. § 1.170A-6(c)(2)(i)(B).

income of the trust, which is in excess of the amount required to pay the guaranteed annuity interest, may be paid to or for the use of a charitable organization. Nevertheless, the amount of the charitable deduction is limited to the fair market value of the guaranteed annuity interest.[264]

If the present value on the date of transfer of all the income interests for a charitable purpose exceeds 60 percent of the aggregate fair market value of all amounts in the trust (after the payment of liabilities), the income interest will not be considered a guaranteed annuity interest unless the governing instrument of the trust prohibits both the acquisition and the retention of assets which would give rise to the private foundation tax on jeopardizing investments[265] if the trustee had acquired assets of that nature.[266]

An income interest consisting of an annuity transferred in trust is not a guaranteed annuity interest if any amount other than an amount in payment of a guaranteed annuity interest may be paid by the trust for a private purpose before the expiration of all the income interests for a charitable purpose, unless the amount for a private purpose is paid from a group of assets which, pursuant to the governing instrument of the trust, are devoted exclusively to private purposes and to which the split-interest trust rules[267] are inapplicable by reason of an exception to them.[268] This exception applies only if the obligation to pay the annuity for a charitable purpose begins as of the date of creation of the trust, and the obligation to pay the guaranteed annuity for a private purpose does not precede in point of time the obligation to pay the annuity for a charitable purpose, and only if the governing instrument of the trust does not provide for any preference or priority in respect of any payment of the guaranteed annuity for a private purpose as opposed to any payment for a charitable purpose. In this context, an amount is not paid for a private purpose if it is paid for an "adequate and full consideration" in money or money's worth.[269]

[264]Reg. § 1.170A-6(c)(2)(i)(C).
[265]IRC § 4944. See *The Law of Tax-Exempt Organizations*, Chapter 23.
[266]Reg. § 1.170A-6(c)(2)(i)(D).
[267]IRC § 4947(a)(2). See Chapter 3; also *The Law of Tax-Exempt Organizations*, Chapter 27 § 2.
[268]This exception is the subject of IRC § 4947(a)(2)(B).
[269]Reg. § 1.170A-6(c)(2)(i)(E).

Example 9.16

E transferred $75,000 in trust with the requirement that an annuity of $5,000 a year, payable annually at the end of each year, be paid to B, an individual, for five years and thereafter an annuity of $5,000 a year, payable annually at the end of each year, be paid to M, a charitable organization, for five years. The remainder is to be paid to C, an individual. A charitable deduction is not allowed under these rules with respect to the charitable annuity because it is not a "guaranteed annuity interest."[270]

(c) Unitrust Interests

An income interest is a "unitrust interest" only if it is an irrevocable right pursuant to the governing instrument of the trust to receive payment, not less often than annually, of a fixed percentage of the net fair market value of the trust assets, determined annually. In computing the net fair market value of the trust assets, all assets and liabilities must be taken into account without regard to whether particular items are taken into account in determining the income of the trust. The net fair market value of the trust assets may be determined on any one date during the year or by taking the average of valuations made on more than one date during the year, provided that the same valuation date or dates and valuation methods are used each year. Where the governing instrument of the trust does not specify the valuation date or dates, the trustee is to select the date or dates and indicate the selection on the first return which the trust is required to file with the IRS (Form 1041). Payments under a unitrust interest may be paid for a specified term or for the life or lives of an individual or individuals, each of whom must be living at the date of transfer and can be ascertained at that date. For example, a unitrust interest may be paid for the life of A plus a term of years.[271]

An income interest is a unitrust interest only if it is a unitrust interest in every respect. For example, if the income interest is the

---

[270] Id.
[271] Reg. § 1.170A-6(c)(2)(ii)(A).

right to receive from a trust each year a payment equal to the lesser of a sum certain or a fixed percentage of the net fair market value of the trust assets, determined annually, the interest is not a unitrust interest.[272]

Where a charitable interest is in the form of a unitrust interest, the governing instrument of the trust may provide that income of the trust in excess of the amount required to pay the unitrust interest is to be paid to or for the use of a charitable organization. Nevertheless, the amount of the deduction under these rules must be limited to the fair market value of the unitrust interest.[273]

An income interest in the form of a unitrust interest is not a unitrust interest if any amount other than an amount in payment of a unitrust interest may be paid by the trust for a private purpose before the expiration of all the income interests for a charitable purpose, unless the amount for a private purpose is paid from a group of assets which, pursuant to the governing instrument of the trust, are devoted exclusively to private purposes and to which the split-interest trust rules are inapplicable by reason of an exception to them.[274] This exception applies only if the obligation to pay the unitrust interest for a charitable purpose begins as of the date of creation of the trust, and the obligation to pay the unitrust interest for a private purpose does not precede in point of time the obligation to pay the unitrust interest for a charitable purpose, and only if the governing instrument of the trust does not provide for any preference or priority in respect of any payment of the unitrust interest for a private purpose as opposed to any payment for a charitable purpose. In this context, an amount is not paid for a private purpose if it is paid for an "adequate and full consideration" in money or money's worth.[275]

(d)   Valuations

The charitable contribution deduction allowed for a gift of a guaranteed annuity interest is limited to the fair market value of the interest on the date of the contribution.[276] The same is true with respect

---

[272] Reg. § 1.170A-6(c)(2)(ii)(B).
[273] Reg. § 1.170A-6(c)(2)(ii)(C).
[274] See ns. 268 and 269, *supra*.
[275] Reg. § 1.170A-6(c)(2)(ii)(D).
[276] Reg. § 1.170A-6(c)(3)(i).

to the gift of a unitrust interest.[277] The fair market value of a unitrust interest is determined by subtracting the present value of all interests in the transferred property, other than the unitrust interest, from the fair market value of the transferred property.[278] If, by reason of all the conditions and circumstances surrounding a transfer of an income interest in property in trust, it appears that the charitable organization may not receive the beneficial enjoyment of the interest, a charitable deduction is allowed under these rules only for the minimum amount it is evident the charity will receive.[279]

(e) Recapture Requirement

If the donor of an income interest in property, at any time before the termination of the interest, ceases to be treated as the owner of the interest (such as by reason of death of the donor), the donor must be considered as having received, on the date of cessation of the ownership, an amount of income equal to (1) the amount of any charitable deduction the donor was allowed for the contribution of the interest, reduced by (2) the discounted value of all amounts which were required to be, and actually were, paid with respect to the interest under the terms of the trust to the charitable organization before the time at which the donor ceases to be treated as the owner of the interest.

The discounted value of these amounts is computed by treating each amount as a contribution of a remainder interest after a term of years and valuing each amount as of the date of contribution of the income interest by the donor, consistent with the manner in which the fair market value of the income interest was determined. This rule is not to be construed to disallow a deduction to the trust for amounts paid by the trust to the charitable organization after the time at which the donor ceased to be treated as the owner of the trust.[280]

(f) Denial of Deduction for Certain Contributions

If a charitable contribution deduction is allowed for the fair market value of an income interest transferred in trust, neither the grantor

---

[277] Reg. § 1.170A-6(c)(3)(ii).
[278] *Id.*
[279] Reg. § 1.170A-6(c)(3)(iii).
[280] IRC § 170(f)(2)(B); Reg. § 1.170A-6(c)(4).

of the income interest, the trust, nor any other person may be allowed a charitable or any other type of deduction for the amount of any charitable contribution made by the trust with respect to, or in fulfillment of, the income interest.[281] However, this rule is not to be construed to

- disallow a deduction to the trust[282] for amounts paid by the trust after the grantor ceases to be treated as the owner of the income interest[283] and which are not taken into account in determining the amount of recapture,[284] or
- disallow a deduction to the grantor[285] for a charitable contribution made to the trust in excess of the contribution required to be made by the trust under the terms of the trust instrument with respect to, or in fulfillment of, the income interest.[286]

§ 9.10 USE OF PROPERTY

A person may contribute, to a charitable organization, the right to use an item of property. An example of this would be a contribution, by an owner of an office building, of the rent-free use of office space to a charitable organization for a period of time. Another example would be a gift by an owner of vacation property of the right to use the property for a period of time (such as two weeks). However, there is no federal income tax charitable deduction for this type of gift.[287]

The reason for the lack of a deduction for a gift of this nature is the fact that the contribution is of a partial interest in the property,[288] which is not one of the forms of partial interests the gift of which gives rise to a charitable deduction.[289] Also, since the donor of the right to use an item of property rarely takes the value of the use of

---

[281] IRC § 170(f)(2)(C); Reg. § 1.170A-6(d)(1).
[282] IRC § 642(c)(1).
[283] IRC § 671.
[284] See the text accompanying n. 280, *supra.*
[285] IRC § 671.
[286] Reg. § 1.170A-6(d)(2).
[287] Reg. § 1.170A-7(a)(1).
[288] IRC § 170(f)(3)(A).
[289] See Part IV.

the property into income as imputed rent, to allow a charitable deduction for the use of the property by a charitable organization would be to allow a double deduction under the circumstances.

The IRS has provided an example of the application of this rule. The example concerns a common situation, which is an auction sponsored by a charitable organization, where one of the items that is donated to the charity is the right to use a vacation home for one week, with the donor of the home being its owner. The value of the fair rental amount foregone by the property owner is not the basis for a federal income tax charitable contribution deduction.[290] (Moreover, use of the property by the successful bidder at the auction is considered "personal use" by the owner, for purposes of determining any business expense deduction allowable with respect to the property.[291])

§ 9.11   SERVICES

An individual may contribute, to a charitable organization, his or her services. This is, of course, the action of a volunteer. However, there is no federal income tax charitable deduction for the contribution of services.[292]

Since the donor of services rarely takes the value of the services into income as imputed income, to allow a charitable deduction for the contribution of the services to a charitable organization would be to allow a double deduction under the circumstances. Also, it is the view of the IRS that the difficulties associated with the valuation of services is alone a policy reason for not allowing this type of deduction (along with the associated revenue loss).

In one case, a lawyer performed legal services for charitable organizations over a three-year period, for which he was not compensated. For each of these years, he deducted amounts reflecting the value of his time expended in rendering the services. The court involved found the regulation that bars the deduction to be valid and held that the lawyer was not entitled to a charitable deduction for

---

[290] Rev. Rul. 89-51, 1989-1 C.B. 89.

[291] *Id.* See IRC § 280A(d)(2)(C).

[292] Reg. § 1.170A-1(g). The lack of a charitable deduction for the gift of services does not defeat a charitable deduction for unreimbursed expenditures made incident to the rendering of the services. See § 13, *infra.*

the gift of his time to charity.[293] The court rejected the argument that the lawyer was donating property, namely, the product of his services in the form of pleadings, resolutions, opinion letters, reports, deeds, and the like.[294]

In other instances, the IRS ruled that there is no tax deduction for the gift by a radio station to a charitable organization of broadcast time as part of the station's programming,[295] and that the contribution to a charitable organization by a newspaper of space in the newspaper is not deductible.[296] This rule of law should be contrasted with the rule that a contribution of a contract right to receive purchased services is deductible, because it is not a contribution of the donor's services.[297]

Under the facts of the case that gave rise to this rule, a radio station received lodging and transportation rights from hotels and airlines in exchange for the provision of advertising time. The radio station included the value of the lodging and transportation in its gross income, and the hotels and airlines included in their gross incomes the value of the advertising time. The radio station donated the lodging and transportation rights to a governmental agency.

The IRS concluded that the radio station was entitled to a charitable deduction for the fair market value of the donated rights. In so doing, the IRS made an analogy with an earlier ruling, in which it upheld the deductibility of a gift to a charitable organization of a right to receive dancing lessons that the donor purchased from a dancing school.[298] Again the gift was of property, namely, a purchased contract right to receive dancing lessons.

[293]*Grant* v. *Commissioner*, 84 T.C. 809 (1985), aff'd, 800 F.2d 260 (4th Cir. 1986). Also *Levine* v. *Commissioner*, 54 T.C.M. 209 (1987).
[294]Even if this regulation (see n. 292, *supra*) was held invalid, there nonetheless would not be any charitable deduction for an amount in excess of basis because of the rule denying a deduction for an amount in excess of basis for gifts of property created by the donor (IRC §§ 170(e)(1)(A) and 1221(3)).
[295]Rev. Rul. 67-236, 1967-2 C.B. 103.
[296]Rev. Rul. 57-462, 1957-2 C.B. 157.
[297]Rev. Rul. 84-1, 1984-1 C.B. 39.
[298]Rev. Rul. 68-113, 1968-1 C.B. 80.

§ 9.12 DONORS' CREATIONS

An individual may make a contribution to a charitable organization of an item of property which was created by the donor, such as a painting or a manuscript. The charitable deduction for this type of gift is not based on the fair market value of the property; instead, it is confined to the donor's cost basis in the property.

This tax result is occasioned by the rule that requires a reduction in the charitable contribution deduction, occasioned by a gift of property, by an amount equal to the amount of gain that would not have been long-term capital gain had the property been sold by the donor at its fair market value at the time of the contribution.[299] The federal tax law specifically excludes from the definition of "capital asset" a "copyright, a literary, musical, or artistic composition, a letter or memorandum, or similar property," held by

- a person "whose personal efforts created such property,"
- "[i]n the case of a letter, memorandum, or similar property, a taxpayer [person] for whom such property was prepared or produced," or
- "[a] taxpayer [person] in whose hands the basis of such property is determined, for purposes of determining gain from a sale or exchange, in whole or in part by reference to the basis of such property in the hands of" a person described in either of the foregoing two categories.[300]

Thus, as noted, the charitable deduction is confined to the amount equal to the cost to the donor of the creation of the item of property.

§ 9.13 UNREIMBURSED EXPENSES

In general, the expenses incurred by an individual in the course of assisting the work of charitable organizations are deductible; the expenses are treated as charitable contributions.[301] This type of deduction is in contrast with the lack of a charitable deduction for a gift of

---

[299] IRC § 170(e)(1)(A). See Chapter 6.
[300] IRC § 1221(3).
[301] Reg. § 1.170A-1(g).

the services themselves[302] or for payments made directly to individuals by others who are assisting the individuals in their charitable endeavors.[303]

The basic law in this regard is as follows:

> . . . "[U]nreimbursed expenditures made incident to the rendition of services to an organization contributions to which are deductible may constitute a deductible contribution. For example, the cost of a uniform without general utility which is required to be worn in performing donated services is deductible. Similarly, out-of-pocket transportation expenses necessarily incurred in performing donated services are deductible. Reasonable expenditures for meals and lodging necessarily incurred while away from home in the course of performing donated services also are deductible.[304]

The rationale for this rule is that these expenses are not incurred for the benefit of the individual involved but rather for the benefit of the charitable organization.[305]

The IRS has ruled that the following unreimbursed expenses, incurred by volunteers, are deductible as a charitable contribution:

- those incurred by a member of the Civil Air Patrol that are directly attributable to the performance of volunteer services (such as the expenses of acquiring and maintaining uniforms, and of maintenance and repair of a telescope)[306]
- those incurred by elected or appointed governmental officials that are directly connected with and solely attributable to the performance of their official duties[307]
- those incurred in rendering services at and for a church[308]
- those incurred while rendering services to the American Red

---

[302] See § 11, *supra.*

[303] See Chapter 11 § 2.

[304] Reg. § 1.170A-1(g). Also Rev. Rul. 55-4, 1955-1 C.B. 291.

[305] Rev. Rul. 56-508, 1956-2 C.B. 126, modified by Rev. Rul. 84-61, 1984-1 C.B. 39.

[306] Rev. Rul. 58-279, 1958-1 C.B. 145.

[307] Rev. Rul. 59-160, 1959-1 C.B. 59.

[308] Rev. Rul. 61-46, 1961-1 C.B. 51 (also holding that individuals attending church conventions, assemblies, or other meetings in accordance with their rights, privileges, or obligations as members of a church are not deductible); and Rev. Rul. 56-508, *supra,* n. 305.

Cross as a nurses' aide (such as local transportation costs and expenses of acquiring and maintaining uniforms)[309]

- those incurred by civil defense volunteers in the performance of their duties (such as traveling expenses and expenses of attending meetings)[310]

- those incurred by a lay member of a church in attending a church convention as a delegate[311]

- those incurred by a member of the American Legion who is appointed as a delegate to and attends an American Legion convention[312]

- those incurred while assisting underprivileged juveniles selected by a charitable organization (such as admission costs and expenses of meals)[313]

- those incurred by an individual while participating in a church-established program[314]

- those incurred by volunteer pilots in providing training services for organization that promotes, fosters, and engages in aviation education activities.[315]

By contrast, the IRS has ruled that unreimbursed expenses incurred by an individual as a participant in a "study mission" to Europe and Asia authorized by a charitable organization are not deductible as charitable contributions.[316]

The unreimbursed, out-of-pocket expenses, directly attributable to the performance of volunteer services for a charitable organization, incurred for the operation, maintenance, and repair of an automobile (or similar item, such as an airplane) are deductible as charitable

---

[309]*Id.*

[310]Rev. Rul. 56-509, 1956-2 C.B. 129.

[311]Rev. Rul. 58-240, 1958-1 C.B. 141.

[312]*Id.*

[313]Rev. Rul. 70-519, 1970-2 C.B. 62, modified by Rev. Rul. 84-61, *supra*, n. 305.

[314]Rev. Rul. 76-89, 1976-1 C.B. 89. Also Rev. Rul. 73-597, 1973-2 C.B. 69.

[315]IRS Private Letter Ruling 9243043.

[316]Rev. Rul. 71-135, 1971-1 C.B. 94, clarifying Rev. Rul. 58-240, *supra*, n. 311.

contributions.[317] Certain items, such as the proportionate share of general maintenance and general repairs, liability insurance, or depreciation in connection with the use of an automobile for charitable purposes are not deductible.[318] Since depreciation may not be taken into account in determining the deduction for charitable contributions, no adjustment to the basis of the automobile is required because of its use for charitable purposes.[319]

The standard mileage rate to use (rather than itemization of expenses) in calculating the charitable deduction for use of a passenger automobile is 12 cents per mile.[320]

Notwithstanding the foregoing, there is no charitable deduction for traveling expenses (including amounts expended for meals and lodging) while way from home, whether paid directly or by reimbursement, "unless there is no significant element of personal pleasure, recreation, or vacation in such travel."[321]

In amplification of this prohibition, the IRS issued this guidance:

> For example, a taxpayer who sails from one Caribbean Island to another and spends eight hours a day counting whales and other forms of marine life as part of a project sponsored by a charitable organization generally will not be permitted a charitable deduction. By way of further example, a taxpayer who works on an archaeological excavation sponsored by a charitable organization for several hours each morning, with the rest of the day free for recreation and sightseeing, will not be allowed a deduction even if the taxpayer works very hard during those few hours. In contrast, a member of a local chapter of a charitable organization who travels to New York City and spends an entire day attending the organization's regional meeting will not be subject to this provision even if he or she attends the theatre in the evening.[322]

The IRS added: "This provision applies whether the travel expenses are paid directly by the taxpayer or by some indirect means

[317]Rev. Rul. 58-279, *supra*, n. 306. Also *Orr* v. *United States*, 343 F.2d 553 (5th Cir. 1965); *Tranquilli* v. *Commissioner*, 39 T.C.M. 874 (1980); and *Clark* v. *Commissioner*, 29 T.C.M. 460 (1970).
[318]Rev. Proc. 82-61, 1982-2 C.B. 849 § 3.02, 1(a).
[319]*Id.*, § 3.02, 1(b).
[320]IRC § 170(i).
[321]IRC § 170(j).
[322]IRS Notice 87-23, 1987-1 C.B. 467, 469.

such as by contribution to the charitable organization that pays for the taxpayer's travel expenses."[323]

§ 9.14 SECTION 306 STOCK

The federal tax law recognizes a special type of stock known as "section 306 stock" (the term is derived from the section of the Internal Revenue Code that provides the tax rules for this type of security). Section 306 stock essentially is stock distributed to a shareholder in circumstances where the value of the stock distributed is not includible in the recipient's gross income.[324] The proceeds from the sale of section 306 stock are treated as ordinary income (rather than as capital gain).[325]

In one case, an individual acquired section 306 stock as a dividend on common stock, the receipt of which was not recognized as income.[326] He contributed the stock to a public charitable organization and claimed a contribution deduction for the full fair market value of the stock, while simultaneously not diminishing his control over the corporation. The IRS litigated the claimed deduction; the court involved held that this donor must reduce what would otherwise be the charitable contribution deduction (based upon the fair market value of the stock) by the amount of ordinary income that would have been realized upon a sale of the stock.[327]

In a similar case, two individuals made charitable contributions of section 306 stock to a school and a college, and claimed charitable contribution deductions based upon the fair market value of the stock. Once again, the IRS litigated the matter; in defense, the donors asserted an exception to the general rule concerning section 306 stock, which is that a disposition of section 306 stock will receive capital gains treatment "[i]f it is established to the satisfaction of the Secretary [IRS] that the distribution, and the disposition or redemption, was not in pursuance of a plan having as one of its principal purposes the avoidance of Federal income tax."[328]

---

[323]*Id.*
[324]IRC § 306(c)(1)(A).
[325]IRC § 306(a).
[326]IRC § 305(a).
[327]*Bialo* v. *Commissioner*, 88 T.C. 1132 (1987). The deduction reduction rule involved is discussed in Chapter 6.
[328]IRC § 306(b)(4)(A).

During the trial, it was shown that the stock was issued as part of a reorganization that took the form it did to enable the individuals to retain control of and participate in the future growth of the issuing company and to "freeze" the value of a portion of their equity in the corporation for estate tax planning purposes. The trial court concluded: "We are not persuaded that he [one of the taxpayers] was unaware that the consequences of such a [charitable] deduction would be avoidance of ordinary income tax on the bail-out of corporate earnings."[329] The court concluded that the individuals did not meet their burden to "clearly negate" the assertion that avoidance of federal income tax was not one of the principal purposes of the disposition of the section 306 stock.[330]

On appeal, the appellate court held that the burden of proof on the donors was "heavy"; it disagreed with the individuals' position. The appellate court concluded that "a finder of fact could reasonably infer that . . . [the principal individual] knew of the tax consequences at the time he made his donations."[331] This individual was characterized as a "successful and sophisticated businessman"; the court noted that he sought and received a ruling from the IRS that the stock, when originally issued, was section 306 stock.[332] His testimony at trial that he did not have the tax consequences of his charitable contributions in mind at the time he made them was held by the court of appeals to be self-serving and thus was disregarded. Although these charitable actions were found to be "generous, sincere, and praiseworthy,"[333] the appellate court found that these individuals failed to meet their burden of proof, thereby defeating their attempt to secure capital gain treatment for the stock should it have been sold and to secure a full fair market valuation for their gifts.

§ 9.15 PUBLIC POLICY CONSIDERATIONS

There is a doctrine in the law of tax-exempt organizations that states that a nonprofit organization cannot be tax-exempt as a charitable

[329] *Pescosolido v. Commissioner*, 91 T.C. 52 (1988).
[330] *Id.* at 60.
[331] *Pescosolido v. Commissioner*, 883 F.2d 187 (1st Cir. 1989).
[332] *Id.* at 190.
[333] *Id.*

entity[334] if it engages in one or more activities that are contrary to "public policy."[335] This rule is infrequently applied in the charitable giving setting.

However, in one case, an individual contributed certain Native American artifacts to a museum; a portion of the collection consisted of elements protected by the Eagle Protection Act and the Migratory Bird Treaty Act. The IRS contended that there should not be any charitable deduction for this portion of the gift, on the ground that the acquisition of them was contrary to public policy. However, a court held that the donors had a sufficient ownership interest in these elements to contribute them to the museum, even though the donors may have violated federal law when they purchased the items.[336]

[334]That is, an organization that is tax-exempt under IRC § 501(a) as an entity described in IRC § 501(c)(3).
[335]See *The Law of Tax-Exempt Organizations*, Chapter 5 §§ 4 and 5.
[336]*Sammons* v. *Commissioner*, 51 T.C. 1968 (1986).

10

Other Aspects of
Deductible Giving

The complexities of the law of charitable giving are manifold and
limited only by the intricacies of the tax law and the imaginations of
regulators and litigants. Some of these other aspects of deductible
charitable giving are treated in this chapter.

§ 10.1 VALUATION OF PROPERTY

As discussed in Chapter 6, charitable gifts may be made of property.
These gifts may be outright contributions of property to charity, or of
a partial interest in an item of property to charity. The gift may
entail a reduction of the otherwise deductible amount[1] or may impli-
cate one or more of the percentage limitations.[2] The income tax
rules, or the gift and estate tax rules,[3] may be involved. The property may be personal property or real property, tangible property or
intangible property.

Whatever the circumstances, the determination of a federal income tax charitable contribution deduction for a gift of property to
charity is likely to require valuation of the property. As discussed in
Chapter 23, the valuation of property can be an integral part of the
substantiation requirements.

In litigation, the court may be called upon to decide the value of
an item of gift property. This issue is one of fact, not law. In this
type of litigation, it is common for one or both sides to use one or

[1]See Chapter 6.
[2]See Chapter 7.
[3]See Chapter 8.

more expert witnesses in an attempt to convince the court of the merits of a particular value. The court may rely on the expertise of one or more of these witnesses or may disregard all of them and set a value on the basis of its own belief as to value. As with any witness, the credibility of the expert witness (and of the donor) in the eyes of a court is critical in formulating the outcome.[4] A finding by a trial court of a value for an item of property will be set aside on appeal only if the finding of the value is clearly erroneous.[5]

The value that is to be found in this context is the "fair market value" of the property. As a general rule, the fair market value of an item of property is the price at which the property would change hands between a willing buyer and a willing seller, neither being under any compulsion to buy or sell and both having reasonable knowledge of relevant facts.[6]

The IRS has amplified this rule, holding that "[t]he most probative evidence of fair market [value] is the prices at which similar quantities of . . . [the property] are sold in arms'-length transactions."[7] The IRS has also determined that the fair market value of gift property is determined by reference to the "most active and comparable market place at the time of the donor's contribution," in a ruling concerning the deductibility of bibles initially purchased at a "discount."[8]

The amount of a charitable contribution, determined for deduction purposes, is affected by a restriction placed by the donor on the use of the donated property.[9] In one instance, an agricultural college sought to acquire a parcel of land, consisting of one hundred acres, to use in connection with its operations in farming research and development of new farming techniques. The owner of the property contributed fifty acres to the college under a deed of gift that carried a restrictive covenant providing that the land may be used only for agricultural purposes. Use of the land for agricultural purposes would

---

[4]In one case, the court ruled that the donors of mining claims are not entitled to any charitable deduction because the claims lacked any value. In rejecting the donors' expert witness' testimony, the court noted that his values were "financial fantasies" (*Snyder v. Commissioner*, 86 T.C. 567, 585 (1986). Also *Parker v. Commissioner*, 86 T.C. 547 (1986)).

[5]*Anselmo v. Commissioner*, 757 F.2d 1208 (11th Cir. 1985).

[6]Reg. § 1.170A-1(c)(2).

[7]Rev. Rul. 80-69, 1980-1 C.B. 55.

[8]Rev. Rul. 80-233, 1980-2 C.B. 69.

[9]Rev. Rul. 85-99, 1985-2 C.B. 83.

not result in a special benefit to the donor. The "highest and best" use of the land was for a more valuable use.

The IRS said that the value of property contributed to a charitable organization is "the price that a reasonably knowledgeable willing buyer would pay a reasonably knowledgeable willing seller for the property subject to any restrictions imposed at the time of the contributions."[10] Added the IRS: "Property otherwise intrinsically more valuable [,] that is encumbered by some restriction or condition limiting its marketability or use, must be valued in light of such limitation."[11]

In recent years, the courts have had to decide a substantial number of charitable gift "tax shelter" cases, where property is sold to putative donors with the expectation that the donors would hold the property long enough for it to become long-term capital gain property and then donate the property to charity, at a point in time where the value of the property has appreciated in relation to the original purchase price. These tax shelter cases frequently involve gifts of gems[12] or works of art.[13] The courts have not looked favorably on these transactions.[14]

Some examples of court opinions that have addressed the question of the valuation of property follow.

- A case concerned contribution of a partial interest in property for conservation purposes.[15]
- A case concerned the valuation of land and improvements contributed to a college.[16]
- A case concerned the valuation of a mineral interest contributed to a governmental agency.[17]
- Two donors contributed wastewater treatment equipment to a university. The donors claimed a deduction of $201,000. The

---

[10]*Id.*

[11]*Id.*

[12]See Chapter 9 § 2.

[13]See Chapter 9 § 1.

[14]E.g., *Anselmo* v. *Commissioner, supra,* n. 5.

[15]*Hilborn* v. *Commissioner,* 85 T.C. 677 (1985).

[16]*Palmer, Estate of D.D.* v. *Commissioner,* 86 T.C. 66 (1985), rev'd and rem'd, 839 F.2d 420 (8th Cir. 1988).

[17]*Stark* v. *Commissioner,* 86 T.C. 243 (1985).

IRS asserted that the value of the property was $20,500. The court that heard the case settled, without explanation, on a deduction value of $75,000. On appeal, this decision was reversed and remanded. The appellate court wrote: "Unlike the original judgment of Solomon, the true rationale of which has been readily apparent to generations of disinterested observers . . . the judgment appealed from here has no discernable logic. We are not prepared to permit the . . . [court below], whenever it disagree with the valuations offered by both sides, simply to shut its eyes and pick at random any number that happens to lie somewhere between the Commissioner's valuation and the taxpayer's. Only by happenstance will such a blind choice avoid a valuation that is either unacceptably low or unacceptably high. The random walk approach, which leaves no trail for the appellate court to follow, may be a sensible way to pick stocks, but it is not an appropriate way to determine the value of a charitable donation."[18]

- A donor contributed 30 gravesites to a church. The donor claimed a deduction of $15,000. The IRS contested that valuation. The court concluded that the sites had a value of $4,000.[19]
- The fair market value of a donated scenic easement was determined, with the court basing the value on the basis of the property as a single parcel rather than on the basis of its potential for subdivision into 24 lots.[20] The court wrote that, in ascertaining the value of the land, "the appropriate question is what a hypothetical Malcolm Forbes would have paid for it as one tract, rather than what two dozen hypothetical yuppies would have paid for it" as 24 lots.[21]
- Two donors contributed gravesites to charitable organizations. They claimed a charitable deduction of $300 per site. The IRS contested that valuation. The court found the value to be $60 per site.[22]

[18]*Start* v. *Commissioner*, 1986 P.H. 61,000 (5th Cir. 1986).
[19]*Sandler* v. *Commissioner*, 52 T.C.M. 563 (1986).
[20]*Akers* v. *Commissioner*, 799 F.2d 243 (6th Cir. 1986), aff'g, 48 T.C.M. 1113 (1984).
[21]*Id.*, 799 F.2d at 245. The appellate court termed the difference between the two valuations as being "rather like the difference between the worth of a gravid or potentially gravid sow and the postpartum worth of sow-cum-shoats" (id.).

- A charitable deduction was allowed for the installation and transfer of drainage facilities and easements to a city. The IRS denied the deduction. The court found the value to be about twice that asserted by the IRS.[23]

- A court held that there was no deduction for a contribution, by the spouse of a deceased psychoanalyst, of the decedent's correspondence and manuscripts.[24]

- A donor contributed bandages to an international relief organization. The donor claimed a value of $45,600. The IRS contested the valuation. The court found the property to have a value of $4,211.[25]

- A number of individuals contributed an easement to a natural wildlife habitat. The value of the easement was litigated. The IRS asserted a pre-gift value of $475,000 and a post-gift value of $47,500. The court found that the property was valued at $1,165,000 prior to the contribution of the easement and $100,000 after the contribution.[26]

- A donor contributed a conservation easement to a historic preservation organization. The donor claimed a value of $350,000. The IRS asserted the value was $70,000. The court found the value to be $130,000.[27]

- A donor contributed a "facade servitude" to a charitable organization. The donor claimed a value of $350,000. The IRS contended the value was $86,000. The court found the value to be $168,700.[28]

- A donor contributed interests in a collection of antique stereoscopic negative glass plates and related items to a university. The donor claimed a deduction for the gift of $1,427,253. The IRS originally asserted that the property did not have any value: During the court proceedings, it tried to compromise at $450,000. The court allowed a deduction of $1,250,000.[29]

[22] *Broad* v. *Commissioner,* 52 T.C.M. 12 (1986).
[23] *Osborne* v. *Commissioner,* 87 T.C. 575 (1986).
[24] *Strasser* v. *Commissioner,* 52 T.C.M. 1130 (1986).
[25] *Tallal* v. *Commissioner,* 52 T.C.M. 1017 (1986).
[26] *Stotler* v. *Commissioner,* 53 T.C.M. 973 (1987).
[27] *Losch* v. *Commissioner,* 55 T.C.M. 909 (1988).
[28] *Nicoladis* v. *Commissioner,* 55 T.C.M. 624 (1988).
[29] *Mast* v. *Commissioner,* 56 T.C.M. 1522 (1989).

§ 10.2   GIFTS "FOR THE USE OF" CHARITY

The federal tax law provisions concerning charitable giving frequently make reference, in addition to gifts "to" a charitable organization, to gifts "for the use of" a charitable organization. The definition of a "charitable contribution" for federal income tax law purposes states that it is "a contribution to or for the use of" qualified charitable organizations.[30]

There is little law on the point. One court had the occasion to peruse the legislative history of the law that added this phrase to the Internal Revenue Code (in 1921) and concluded that the words mean "roughly the equivalent of" the words "in trust for."[31] In the previous year, the then Bureau of Internal Revenue had ruled that charitable deductions could not be taken for contributions to trusts, community chests, and other types of charitable foundations on the ground that these organizations were not organized and operated for charitable purposes, but merely served as a conduit for contributions to charitable organizations.[32] These organizations were common law trusts; legal title to the contributions remained vested in a trustee which invested the funds prior to disbursement to various charitable organizations.

The legislative history of this phrase indicates that Congress intended by this law change to make contributions in trust for the benefit of charitable organizations eligible for deduction as charitable gifts.[33] Over the intervening years, courts and the IRS have adhered to this interpretation of the words "for the use of."[34]

The matter found its way to the U.S. Supreme Court, in connection with the issue as to whether funds transferred by parents to their children while the children served as full-time, unpaid missionaries for a church are deductible as charitable contributions. Inasmuch as the gifts were not "to" the church, the argument advanced by the parents turned on whether the gifts were "for the use of" the

---

[30] IRC § 170(c), opening clause.

[31] *Rockefeller* v. *Commissioner*, 676 F.2d 35, 40 (2d Cir. 1982).

[32] O.D. 669, 3 C.B. 187 (1920).

[33] E.g., H. Rep. No. 350, 67th Cong., 1st Sess. 12 (1921).

[34] E.g., *Danz* v. *Commissioner*, 18 T.C. 454 (1952), aff'd on other grounds, 231 F.2d 673 (9th Cir. 1955), cert. den., 352 U.S. 828 (1956); *Bowman* v. *Commissioner*, 16 B.T.A. 1157 (1956); Rev. Rul. 53-194, 1953-2 C.B. 128; and Rev. Rul. 55-275, 1955-1 C.B. 295.

church. The Supreme Court, in reaffirming that the words mean "in trust for," concluded that the payments were not deductible as charitable contributions.[35]

The Court observed that, while this interpretation of the phrase "does not require that the qualified [charitable] organization take actual possession of the contribution, it nevertheless reflects that the beneficiary must have significant legal rights with respect to the disposition of donated funds."[36] The Court rejected the claim that a charitable deduction should be allowed merely where the charitable organization has "a reasonable opportunity to supervise the use of contributed funds."[37] The Court observed that the IRS "would face virtually insurmountable administrative difficulties in verifying that any particular expenditure benefited a qualified donee," were a looser interpretation of the phrase utilized.[38] The larger interpretation would, wrote the Court, "create an opportunity for tax evasion that others might be eager to exploit," although the Court was quick to note that "there is no suggestion whatsoever in this case that the transferred funds were used for an improper purpose."[39]

Under the facts, the Supreme Court found that the funds were not transferred "in trust for" the church. The money was transferred to the children's personal bank accounts on which they were the sole authorized signatories. No trust or "similar legal arrangement"[40] was created. The children lacked any legal obligation to use the money in accordance with guidelines of the church, nor did the church have any legal entitlement to the money or a cause of action against missionaries who used their parents' money for purposes not approved by the church.

Recall that a charitable contribution deduction is not allowed for a gift of services.[41] However, unreimbursed expenses made incident to the rendition of services to charitable organizations are deductible. At the outset, the position of the IRS was that expenses incurred for charitable purposes were gifts for the use of, and not to, charitable organizations. However, this position was reviewed in litigation and

---

[35]*Davis* v. *United States*, 110 S. Ct. 2014 (1990).
[36]*Id.* at 2021.
[37]*Id.* at 2022.
[38]*Id.*
[39]*Id.*
[40]*Id.*
[41]See Chapter 9 § 11.

the government lost the cases.[42] The IRS thereafter abandoned this position and ruled that unreimbursed expenses incurred by an individual in rendering gratuitous services to a charitable organization are gifts "to" the charity.[43]

A contribution of an income interest in property, whether or not the contributed interest is transferred in trust, for which a charitable deduction is allowed,[44] must be construed as made for the use of rather than to a charitable organization.[45] A contribution of a remainder interest in property, whether or not the contributed interest is transferred in trust, for which a charitable deduction is allowed,[46] must generally be considered as made to the charitable organization.[47] However, if a remainder interest is transferred in trust and, pursuant to the terms of the trust instrument, the interest contributed is, upon termination of the predecessor estate, to be held in trust for the benefit of the organization, the contribution must be considered as made for the use of the organizations.[48]

The following example illustrates these points:

Example 10.1

A transferred property to a charitable remainder annuity trust[49] includes the requirement to pay to B for life an annuity equal to five percent of the initial fair market value of the property transferred in trust. The trust instrument provides that after B's death the remainder interest in the trust is to be transferred to M, a church, or, in the event that M is not a charitable organization at the time when the amount is to be irrevocably transferred to it, to another qualifying charitable organization. The contribution by A of the remainder interest was made to M. However, if in the trust instrument A had directed that after B's death the remainder interest is to be held in trust for the benefit of M, the contribution would have to be considered as made for the use of M.[50]

---

[42]*Rockefeller* v. *Commissioner, supra,* n. 31.
[43]Rev. Rul. 84-61, 1984-1 C.B. 39.
[44]IRC § 170(f)(2)(B) or (3)(A).
[45]Reg. § 1.170A-8(a)(2).
[46]IRC § 170(f)(2)(A) or (3)(A).
[47]*Id.*
[48]*Id.*
[49]See Chapter 12.
[50]*Id.*

§ 10.3 CONDITIONAL GIFTS

A donor may make a contribution to a charitable organization but place conditions on the gift. Depending upon the type of condition, there may not be a charitable deduction for the transfer, at least not until the time the condition is satisfied. Conversely, a condition may not have any bearing on the deductibility of the charitable gift.

There are three types of conditions in this regard:

1. A condition (sometimes termed a "contingency") that is material, so that the transfer is not considered complete until the condition is satisfied,

2. A condition involving a possible occurrence, where the likelihood of the event occurring is so remote as to be negligible, in which case the condition is ignored for purposes of deductibility, and/or

3. A condition that is material but that is in furtherance of a charitable purpose, so that the condition is more in the nature of a "restriction."

(a) Material Conditions—Nondeductibility

As to the first two of the above categories, the standard is as follows: If, as of the date of a gift, a transfer for charitable purposes is dependent upon the performance of some act or the happening of a precedent event in order that it might become effective, no deduction is allowable unless the possibility that the charitable transfer will not become effective is so remote as to be negligible.[51] If the possibility is not negligible, if it occurs, and if the charitable transfer becomes effective, the charitable deduction arises at the time the condition is satisfied or eliminated.

As an illustration, a charitable organization wishes to construct a building to be used for its program purposes. It has developed a building fund that is sufficient to cover 90 percent of the construction costs for the building; the organization will seek the remaining funds from the general public. The organization represents to donors that, if the contributions are not sufficient to meet the balance of the costs of construction, the contributions will be returned to the do-

---

[51] Reg. § 1.170A-1(e).

nors. If the contributions received exceed the necessary amount, the organization will retain the excess funds for general program purposes. Thus, as of the date of the gifts, the transfers for charitable purposes are dependent upon the performance of an act or the happening of a precedent event in order to become effective. Furthermore, whether the contributions will be returned depends solely on whether the donors contribute an amount equal to the difference between the cost of the construction of the building and the amount already in the building fund. Under these circumstances, the possibility that the charitable transfer will not become effective is not so remote as to be negligible. Consequently, the gifts are not deductible as of the time of the transfer but will become deductible at the time the condition is satisfied or eliminated (that is, when the public gifts are transferred to the building fund, because the needed amount was raised, or are retained by the organization to be expended for general program purposes).[52]

In some instances, a condition may affect only a portion of the gift. For example, the Department of Parks, Recreation, and Tourism of a state obtained sponsors who agreed to pay any deficit that the department might incur in conducting an international steeplechase race to promote tourism. The department represented to the sponsors that any funds not used to meet the deficit would be returned to the sponsors on a pro rata basis. Thus, only the pro rata portion of any sponsorship advance that the department used for racing expenses was a payment to the state for exclusively public purposes. Therefore, only the portion of each advance actually used to meet the deficit is deductible by the sponsor as a charitable contribution. No portion of the advance is considered to be a payment of a contribution until such time as the net amount actually going to the state is definitely determined by a final accounting.[53]

A condition or battery of conditions may be so extensive that the matter goes to the question of the donor's intent. In one instance, a gift of land was burdened with so many conditions, including sale of the land, that a court found that the "donor," at best, had an intent to make a gift of future sales proceeds rather than an intent to make a present gift of the land.[54]

[52]Rev. Rul. 79-249, 1979-2 C.B. 104.
[53]Rev. Rul. 72-194, 1972-1 C.B. 94.
[54]Dayton v. Commissioner, 32 T.C.M. 782 (1973).

(b) Negligible Conditions

As noted, a condition that is so remote as to be negligible is ignored for gift deductibility purposes. This phrase has been defined as "a chance which persons generally would disregard as so highly improbable that it might be ignored with reasonable safety in undertaking a serious business transaction."[55] It has also been defined as "a chance which every dictate of reason would justify an intelligent person in disregarding as so highly improbable and remote as to be lacking in reason and substance."[56]

In one case, a court found conditions that were not so remote as to be negligible. One condition was found to have a "good chance" of occurring.[57] Another condition was characterized as "certainly foreseeable" and "quite likely."[58] Still another condition was labeled as having a "high probability," "probable." and "quite possible."[59] Thus, a charitable gift was not deductible at the time originally made. In another case, a charitable deduction was not allowable because there was a "realistic possibility" that the condition involved would occur.[60]

Finders of fact, such as courts or the IRS, rarely conclude, in this context, that a condition is so remote as to be negligible.

(c) Material Conditions—Deductibility

There is one type of material condition that will not defeat a charitable deduction and, indeed, must be satisfied if the deduction is to be allowed. This is a condition that the gift be used for one or more program purposes; as noted, this is frequently known as a "restricted" gift. Some examples of a restricted gift are the following:

- a gift to a charitable organization restricted to use for scholarships

---

[55] *United States* v. *Dean*, 224 F.2d 26, 29 (1st Cir. 1955).

[56] *Briggs* v. *Commissioner*, 72 T.C. 646, 657 (1979), aff'd without published opinion, 665 F.2d 1051 (9th Cir. 1981), citing *Woodworth, Estate of* v. *Commissioner*, 47 T.C. 193 (1966), and *United States* v. *Provident Trust Co.*, 291 U.S. 272 (1934).

[57] *Briggs* v. *Commissioner, supra*, n. 56, 72 T.C. at 657.

[58] *Id.*

[59] *Id.* at 658.

[60] *885 Investment Co.* v. *Commissioner*, 95 T.C. 156, 162 (1990).

- a gift to a university restricted to a fund underlying a chair in a particular department
- a gift to a museum restricted to its endowment fund, and
- a gift to a hospital restricted to its building fund

These types of conditions or restrictions will not cause a charitable contribution deduction to be disallowed.

§ 10.4   REALLOCATION OF DEDUCTIONS

Congress has provided the IRS with broad authority to undo a taxpayer's "creative" tax planning by readjusting the facts to more correctly state the taxpayer's tax position. This authority empowers the IRS to closely scrutinize transactions between mutually controlled parties. This process is known as "reallocation" of items of income, deductions, and credits; it is done where necessary to prevent the evasion of taxes or to ensure the clear reflection of each taxpayer's income.[61] It has been held that the IRS can use this authority to reallocate, in the charitable giving context, in order to adjust (reduce) a claimed charitable contribution deduction.

In one instance, two partners, who were an individual and a corporation wholly owned by him, caused their partnership to distribute to them a tract of land in the form of two tracts of approximately equal value but not equal size. The individual received a 76 percent interest in one tract and a 24 percent interest in the other. The individual held a 49 percent interest in the partnership. The land was donated to a city and the individual claimed a charitable contribution deduction based on a 76 percent interest in the real estate. (He also reported 24 percent of the gain from the sale of the other tract.) The IRS reallocated the amount of the charitable contribution deduction (and the capital gain) between the two partners on the basis of their respective percentage interests in the partnership. The IRS was successful in court in forcing this donor to confine his deduction to an amount equal to the 49 percent interest in the land.[62]

---

[61] IRC § 482.
[62] *Dolese v. Commissioner*, 82 T.C. 830 (1984), aff'd 811 F.2d 543 (10th Cir. 1987).

§ 10.5 PENALTIES

The federal tax law contains a variety of penalties for violation of
various aspects of the law of charitable giving. These penalties are
part of a broader range of so-called "accuracy-related" penalties.[63]

This accuracy-related penalty is an addition to tax of an amount
equal to 20 percent of a tax underpayment.[64] This body of law relates
to the portion of any underpayment which is attributable to one or
more specified acts, including the following:

- negligence[65]
- disregard of rules or regulations[66]
- any substantial underpayment of income tax[67]
- any substantial income tax valuation misstatement[68]
- any substantial estate or gift tax valuation understatement[69]

The term "negligence" is defined for this purpose as including
"any failure to make a reasonable attempt to comply with" the applicable law.[70] The term "disregard" includes "any careless, reckless, or
intentional disregard."[71]

A "substantial overstatement" occurs where the amount of the
understatement of tax for the year exceeds the greater of ten percent
of the tax that is required or $5,000.[72] These rules apply with respect
to "tax shelters"; that term is defined to include any "plan or ar-

---

[63] IRC § 6662. Prior law contained similar penalties in IRC §§ 6621(d) and
6653, and many court opinions that have invoked these penalties in the
charitable giving setting make reference to IRC § 6653 penalties. IRC
§ 6662 took effect with respect to returns due after 1989.
[64] IRC § 6662(a).
[65] IRC § 6662(b)(1).
[66] Id.
[67] IRC § 6662(b)(2).
[68] IRC § 6662(b)(3).
[69] IRC § 6662(b)(5).
[70] IRC § 6662(c).
[71] Id.
[72] IRC § 6662(d)(1)(A). The term "understatement" of tax is defined in IRC
§ 6662(d)(2).

rangement" if the "principal purpose" of it "is the avoidance or evasion of Federal income tax."[73]

An income tax substantial valuation misstatement generally occurs if the value of any property (or the adjusted basis of any property) claimed on a tax return is 200 percent or more of the amount determined to be the correct amount of the valuation (or adjusted basis).[74] For this penalty to be imposed, the substantial misstatement must exceed $5,000 ($10,000 for most corporations).[75]

This penalty may be increased in the event of a "gross valuation misstatement," which is an amount equal to 40 percent of the portion of the underpayment.[76] An income tax gross valuation misstatement generally occurs if the value of any property (or the adjusted basis of any property) claimed on a tax return is 400 percent or more of the amount determined to be the correct amount of the valuation (or adjusted basis).[77] For this penalty to be imposed, the gross misstatement must exceed $5,000 ($20,000 for most corporations).[78]

There is a "substantial estate or gift tax valuation understatement if the value of any property claimed on a tax return is 50 percent or less of the amount determined to be the correct amount of the valuation."[79] This penalty applies when the underpayment exceeds $5,000.[80] A gross valuation misstatement in this context takes place if the value of any property claimed on a tax return is 25 percent or less of the amount determined to be the correct amount of the valuation.[81]

Finally, there is a fraud penalty with respect to tax returns due after 1989.[82]

There have been several court opinions concerning the application of these penalties in the charitable giving setting under pre-1990 law.

---

[73]IRC § 6662(d)(2)(C)(ii)(III).
[74]IRC § 6662(e)(1)(A).
[75]IRC § 6662(e)(2).
[76]IRC § 6662(h)(1).
[77]IRC § 6662(h)(2)(A)(i).
[78]IRC § 6662(h)(2)(A)(iii).
[79]IRC § 6662(g)(1).
[80]IRC § 6662(g)(2).
[81]IRC § 6662(h)(2)(C).
[82]IRC § 6663.

These include

- application of an underpayment penalty where a lawyer intentionally disregarded the tax regulations in claiming a charitable contribution deduction for gifts of legal services[83]
- application of penalties where the claimed values were based on "financial fantasies"[84]
- application of penalty where gift property was valued at $45,600 and court found the value to be $4,211[85]
- application of penalties where the value of gift property was deliberately inflated and the transactions were tax-motivated[86]
- application of negligence penalty where parties participated in a circular flow of funds arrangement designed for tax avoidance[87]

§ 10.6   ALTERNATIVE MINIMUM TAX CONSIDERATIONS

The federal tax law includes an "alternative minimum tax."[88] This tax is termed an "alternative" tax because it may be paid instead of the "regular" income tax. It is called a "minimum" tax because it is designed to force a person of wealth to pay some federal tax, notwithstanding the sophistication of their tax planning.

Some persons are able to avoid taxation, in whole or in part, through the use of deductions, credits, exemptions, and the like. These items are generally known as "items of tax preference" or "tax preference items." A very general summary of the alternative minimum tax is that it is a tax, albeit computed with some adjustments, on many of a person's tax preference items.

For a period of about six years, the appreciation element inherent in a charitable contribution of appreciated property was considered an item of tax preference for purposes of the alternative minimum

---

[83]*Grant* v. *Commissioner*, 84 T.C. 809 (1985), aff'd, 800 F.2d 260 (4th Cir. 1986).
[84]*Snyder* v. *Commissioner, supra,* n. 4. Also *Parker* v. *Commissioner, supra,* n. 4.
[85]*Tallal* v. *Commissioner, supra,* n. 25.
[86]*Angell* v. *Commissioner*, 52 T.C.M. 939 (1986).
[87]*Allen* v. *Commissioner*, 91-1 U.S.T.C. ¶ 50,080 (9th Cir. 1991), aff'g 92 T.C. 1 (1989).
[88]IRC §§ 55–59.

tax.[89] This rule would have been permanently repealed had the Revenue Act of 1992 been enacted; instead, it was repealed.

The rule that, for purposes of computing alternative minimum taxable income, the deduction for charitable contributions of capital gain property (real, tangible personal, or intangible personal) is disallowed to the extent that the fair market value of the property exceeds its adjusted basis, was enacted in 1986. This rule of law was adopted as somewhat of a compromise in the face of an effort to subject this type of appreciation element to the regular capital gains tax.

However, the charitable community that is highly dependent upon contributions of appreciated property (such as institutions of higher education and museums) experienced a substantial decline in giving of property and began to work to change, if not eliminate, the rule. Congress, in 1990, created a partial exception, concerning contributions made in a tax year beginning in 1991, or made before July 1, 1992, in a tax year beginning in 1992, in the case of contributions of tangible personal property.[90]

The legislative history of this potential 1992 law change contains the following explanation of the change:

> The [Senate Finance] [C]ommittee believes that the temporary AMT [alternative minimum tax] exception for contributions of appreciated tangible personal property has induced additional charitable giving. Thus, by permanently extending this rule and expanding it to apply to all appreciated property gifts, taxpayers will be allowed the same charitable contribution deduction for both regular tax and alternative minimum tax purposes. This will provide an additional incentive for taxpayers to make contributions of appreciated property.[91]

As note, this proposed change in the law was not enacted. Nonetheless, an attempt in 1993 to repeal this alternative minimum tax rule, in relation to gifts of all categories or property, is quite likely.

---

[89] Former IRC § 57(a)(6).

[90] Former IRC § 57(a)(6)(B). In general, Wittenbach, "Window of Opportunity for Gifts of Tangible Personal Property," 69 *Taxes* 706 (1991).

[91] "Technical Explanation of the Finance Committee Amendment" ("Technical Explanation"), at 579-580. The Technical Explanation was not formally printed; it is, however, reproduced in the Congressional Record (138 *Cong. Rec.* (No. 112) S11246 (Aug. 3, 1992)).

Part IV

Planned Giving

11

Gifts by Means of Charitable Remainder Trusts

The federal tax law provides for a form of planned giving that utilizes a split-interest trust called a "charitable remainder trust."[1]

In general, a charitable remainder trust is a vehicle by which money or property is split into two types of interests: one or more "income interests" and one or more "remainder interests." The remainder interest is destined for one or more charitable organizations, while the income interest or interests are usually retained by or created for noncharitable beneficiaries. In the normal course of events, the gift of the remainder interest gives rise to a federal tax deduction. This chapter focuses on the income tax deduction; Chapter 8 discusses the use of charitable remainder trusts in the estate and gift tax context.

§ 11.1 DEFINITIONS

Generally, a charitable remainder trust provides for a specified distribution, at least annually, to one or more beneficiaries, at least one of which is not a charitable organization, for life or for a term of years, with an irrevocable remainder interest to be paid over to, or held for the benefit of, charity.[2] The contribution of the remainder interest must be deductible for federal income, gift, and/or estate tax purposes.[3]

[1]The concepts of planned giving and split-interest trusts are discussed in Chapter 3. That chapter also contains a general description of charitable remainder trusts.
[2]Reg. § 1.664-l(a)(l)(i).
[3]Reg. § 1.664-l(a)(l)(iii)(a).

369

Basically, there are two types of charitable remainder trusts: a "charitable remainder annuity trust" and a "charitable remainder unitrust."

A "charitable remainder annuity trust" is a trust

- from which a sum certain is to be paid, not less often than annually, to one or more persons (at least one of which is not a charitable organization[4] and, in the case of individuals, only to an individual who is living at the time of the creation of the trust),
- from which the sum certain is to be paid for a term of years (not in excess of 20 years) or for the life (or lives) of the individuals,
- where the sum certain is not less than five percent of the initial net fair market value of all property placed in the trust,
- from which no amount other than the income interest payments may be paid to or for the use of any person other than a charitable organization, and
- following the termination of the income interest payments, the remainder interest in the trust is to be transferred to, or for the use of, a charitable organization or is to be retained by the trust for a charitable use.[5]

A "charitable remainder unitrust" is a trust

- from which a fixed percentage of the net fair market value of its assets, valued annually, is to be paid, not less often than annually, to one or more persons (at least one of which is not a charitable organization and, in the case of individuals, only to an individual who is living at the time of the creation of the trust),
- from which the sum certain is to be paid for a term of years (not in excess of 20 years) or for the life (or lives) of the individual(s).

---

[4]For this purpose, the term "charitable donee" means an organization described in IRC § 170(c). These entail nearly all IRC § 501(c)(3) organizations and certain other eligible donees. See Chapter 4 § 2.
[5]IRC § 664(d)(1); Reg. §§ 1.664-1(a)(1)(a), 1.664-1(a)(1)(iii)(b).

- where the sum certain is not less than five percent of the net fair market value of its assets,
- from which no amount other than the income interest payments may be paid to or for the use of any person other than a charitable organization, and
- following the termination of the income interest payments, the remainder interest in the trust is to be transferred to, or for the use of, a charitable organization or is to be retained by the trust for a charitable use.[6]

There are, however, variations on the concept of the charitable remainder unitrust. The standard charitable remainder unitrust is the one that is in conformity with the foregoing criteria. Another is the charitable remainder unitrust that pays out all of the trust income, where that amount is less than the five percent payout amount, as long as the trust begins in subsequent years to pay out the full required payout amount.[7] Another type of charitable remainder unitrust is one that is as described in the preceding sentence but allows the income beneficiary or beneficiaries to receive "make up" payments for the years in which the amounts paid out were less than the five percent payout amount.[8]

A trust is a charitable remainder trust only if it is either a charitable remainder annuity trust in every respect or a charitable remainder unitrust in every respect.[9] For example, a trust which provides for the payment each year to a noncharitable beneficiary of the greater of a sum certain or a fixed percentage of the annual value of the trust assets is not a charitable remainder trust inasmuch as the trust is neither a charitable remainder annuity trust (for the reason that the payment for the year may be a fixed percentage of the annual value of the trust assets, which is not a "sum certain") nor a charitable remainder unitrust (for the reason that the payment for the year may be a sum certain, which is not a "fixed percentage" of the annual value of the trust assets).[10]

The IRS assessed the governing instrument of an otherwise quali-

---

[6]IRC § 664(d)(2); Reg. §§ 1.664-1(a)(1)(a), 1.6641(a)(1)(iii)(c).
[7]IRC § 664(d)(3).
[8]*Id.*
[9]Reg. § 1.664-1(a)(2).
[10]*Id.*

fying charitable remainder trust, which provided that the annual payment of the specified distribution (a five percent annuity or unitrust amount, as the case may be[11]) to the income beneficiaries will be as follows: A is to receive $25x, B is to receive $15x, and C is to receive the balance. Upon the death of any income beneficiary, the amount of income that the beneficiary would have been entitled to receive will be retained by the trust until the death of the last income beneficiary. Upon the death of the last income beneficiary, the assets of the trust are to be distributed to the charitable organization that is the remainder interest beneficiary under the trust.

The IRS held that this trust could not qualify as a charitable remainder trust.[12] The Service observed that, if C dies before either A or B, the total of the designated amounts payable annually would be less than the annuity amount that must be paid out annually, in the case of a charitable remainder annuity trust, or it is possible that the total of the designated amounts payable annually will be different from the unitrust amount that must be paid out annually, in the case of a charitable remainder unitrust. The IRS further noted that, even if C did not die before A or B, the designated amounts payable annually may exceed the unitrust amount in the case of a charitable remainder unitrust. For example, if in a particular tax year five percent of the net fair market value of the trust assets on the valuation date equals an amount that is less than $40x, the designated payments to A and B would exceed the unitrust amount for that tax year.

A trust is not a charitable remainder trust if the provisions of the trust include a provision which restricts the trustee from investing the trust assets in a manner which could result in the annual realization of a reasonable amount of income or gain from the sale or disposition of trust assets.[13] It has been held that this rule does not preclude a bank, in its capacity as a trustee of a charitable remainder trust, from investing the assets of the trust in common trust funds maintained by the bank.[14] Similarly, this rule does not prevent the charitable remainder beneficiary, as trustee of charitable remainder

---

[11]See §§ 5 and 6, *infra.*
[12]Rev. Rul. 76-280, 1976-2 C.B. 195.
[13]Reg. § 1.664-1(a)(3).
[14]Rev. Rul. 73-571, 1973-2 C.B. 213.

trusts, from investing the assets of the trusts in its general endowment fund.[15]

In contrast, the IRS ruled that a trust did not qualify as a charitable remainder trust where the grantor of the trust contributed to the trust a collection of antiques in addition to income-producing assets at the time of its creation. The governing instrument of the trust provided that the grantor's spouse, who was the sole income beneficiary of the trust for her life, would have use of the antique collection for her life. At her death, the antique collection and all of the remaining assets in the trust were to be distributed to a charitable organization. The Service held that the retention of the life estate in the antique collection for the grantor's spouse restricted the trustee from investing all of the trust assets in a manner that could result in the annual realization of a reasonable amount of income or gain from the sale or disposition of trust assets, so that the trust did not qualify as a charitable remainder trust.[16]

In order for a trust to be a charitable remainder trust, it must meet the definition of, and function exclusively as, a charitable remainder trust from the creation of the trust.[17] For this purpose, the trust will be deemed to be created at the earliest time that neither the grantor nor any other person is treated as the owner of the entire trust but in no event prior to the time property is first transferred to the trust.[18] Neither the grantor nor his or her spouse is treated as the owner of the trust merely because the grantor or his or her spouse is named as an income interest beneficiary.[19]

In this setting, the income interest beneficiary is often termed the "recipient."[20] The term "income interest" is used to embrace all of the interests other than the remainder interest, even though some or all

[15]Rev. Rul. 83-19, 1983-1 C.B. 115. The IRS ruled that a trustee could borrow from the assets of an insurance policy held by a charitable remainder trust without disqualifying the trust (IRS Private Letter Ruling 8745013).
[16]Rev. Rul. 73-610, 1973-2 C.B. 213.
[17]Reg. § 1.664-1(a)(4).
[18]Id.
[19]Id.
[20]Reg. § 1.664-1(a)(1)(iii)(d), which defines a "recipient" as "the beneficiary who receives the possession or beneficial enjoyment of the annuity amount or the unitrust amount."

of the income may have characteristics other than "income" for tax purposes.[21]

For federal estate tax purposes, a charitable remainder trust is deemed to be created on the date of death of the decedent (even though the trust is not funded until the end of a reasonable period of administration or settlement) if the obligation to pay the annuity or unitrust amount with respect to the property passing in trust at the death of the decedent begins as of the date of death of the decedent, notwithstanding the fact that the requirement to pay the amount is deferred.[22] If permitted by applicable local law or authorized by the provisions of the governing instrument of the trust,[23] the requirement to pay the annuity or unitrust amount may be deferred until the end of the tax year of the trust in which occurs the complete funding of the trust. Within a reasonable period after that time, the trust must pay the income beneficiary (in the case of an underpayment) or must receive from the income beneficiary (in the case of an overpayment) the difference between (1) any annuity or unitrust amounts actually paid, plus interest on these amounts computed at the appropriate rate of interest[24] computed annually, and (2) the annuity or unitrust amounts payable, plus interest on these amounts computed at the appropriate rate of interest[25] computed annually. The amounts payable must be retroactively determined by using the tax year, valuation method, and valuation dates which are ultimately adopted by the charitable remainder trust.[26] The governing instrument of a testamentary charitable remainder trust must provide rules conforming to these requirements.[27]

For purposes of retroactively determining the unitrust amount payable, plus interest, the governing instrument of a charitable remainder unitrust may, alternatively, provide that the unitrust amount with respect to property passing in trust at the death of the decedent (for the period which begins on the date of death of the decedent and ends on the earlier of the date of death of the last income

---

[21] See § 3, *infra.*

[22] Reg. § 1.664-1(a)(5)(i).

[23] The term "governing instrument" means the document by which the trust was created (Reg. § 1.664-l(a)(l)(iii)(e)).

[24] Reg. § 1.664-1(a)(5)(v).

[25] Reg. § 1.664-l(a)(5)(iv).

[26] Reg. § 1.664-1(a)(5)(i). A sample provision to reflect this requirement appears in Rev. Rul. 82-165, 1982-2 C.B. 117 § (1).

[27] Rev. Rul. 80-123, 1980-1 C.B. 205.

beneficiary or the end of the tax year of the trust in which occurs the complete funding of the trust) be computed by a formula contained in the tax regulations.[28] This alternative is available because, in many cases (for example, in the case of a residuary bequest to a charitable remainder unitrust), the unitrust payments the beneficiary would have received if the trust had been fully funded and functioning on the date of death, plus interest, are difficult to calculate.[29]

The application of the rules concerning the creation of a charitable remainder trust is illustrated by the following examples:

Example 11.1

On September 19, 1990, H transferred property to a trust over which he retained an inter vivos power of revocation. The trust was to pay W 5 percent of the value of the trust assets, valued annually, for her life, with the remainder to charity. The trust would have satisfied all of the requirements of the charitable remainder trust rules if it were irrevocable. However, the trust was not deemed created in 1990 because H was treated as the owner of the entire trust. On May 26, 1993, H predeceased W, at which time the trust became irrevocable. For purposes of the charitable trust rules, the trust was deemed created on May 26, 1993, because that was the earliest date on which H was not treated as the owner of the entire trust. The trust became a charitable remainder trust on May 26, 1993, because it met the definition of a charitable remainder trust from its creation.[30]

Example 11.2

The facts are the same as in Example 11.1, except that H retained the inter vivos power to revoke only one-half of the trust. For purposes of the charitable remainder trust rules, the trust was deemed created on September 19, 1990, because on that date the grantor was not treated as the owner of the entire trust. Consequently, a charitable deduction was not allowable either at the creation of the trust or at the death of H because the trust did not meet the definition of a charitable remainder trust from the date of its creation. This is so because from the date of its creation, the trust was subject to a partial power to revoke on that date.[31]

---

[28] Reg. § 1.664-1(a)(5)(ii).
[29] See Rev. Rul. 92-57, 1992-29 I.R.B. 4.
[30] Reg. § 1.664-1(a)(6), Example (1).
[31] Reg. § 1.664-1(a)(6), Example (2).

Example 11.3

The facts are the same as in Example 11.1, except that the residue of H's estate was to be paid to the trust and the trust was required to pay H's debts. The trust was not a charitable remainder trust at H's death because it did not function exclusively as a charitable remainder trust from the date of its creation which, in this case, was the date it became irrevocable.[32]

Example 11.4

In 1990, H transferred property to Trust A over which he retained an inter vivos power of revocation. Trust A, which is not a charitable remainder trust, was to provide income or corpus to W until the death of H. Upon H's death, the trust was required by its governing instrument to pay the debts and administrative expenses of H's estate, and then to terminate and distribute all of the remaining assets to Trust B which met the definition of a charitable remainder annuity trust.

Trust B was a charitable remainder trust from the date of its funding because it functioned as a charitable remainder trust from its creation. For purposes of the estate tax charitable deduction,[33] Trust B was deemed created at H's death if the obligation to pay the annuity amount began on the date of H's death. For purposes of the charitable remainder trust rules, Trust B became a charitable remainder trust as soon as it was partially or completely funded. Consequently, unless Trust B has unrelated business taxable income,[34] the income of the trust is exempt from federal tax and any distributions by the trust, even before it is completely funded, are governed by the charitable remainder trust rules. Any distributions made by Trust A, including distributions to a recipient in respect of annuity amounts are governed by general trust rules[35] rather than the charitable remainder trust rules.[36]

[32] Reg. § 1.664-1(a)(6), Example (3).
[33] IRC § 2055. See Chapter 8.
[34] See the text accompanying ns. 39–43, *infra*, and Chapter 4 § 4.
[35] IRC Subchapter J, Chapter 1, Subtitle A.
[36] Reg. § 1.664-1(a)(6), Example (4).

Example 11.5

In 1992, *H* died intestate, leaving the net residue of his estate (after payment by the estate of all debts and administrative expenses) to a trust which met the definition of a charitable remainder unitrust. For purposes of the estate tax charitable deduction, the trust was deemed created at *H*'s death if the requirement to pay the unitrust amount began on H's death and is a charitable remainder trust, even though the estate was obligated to pay debts and administrative expenses. For purposes of the charitable remainder trust rules, the trust became a charitable remainder trust as soon as it was partially or completely funded. Consequently, unless the trust has unrelated business income, the income of the trust is exempt from federal tax, and any distributions by the trust, even before it is completely funded, are governed by the charitable remainder trust rules. Any distributions made by *H*'s estate, including distributions to a recipient in respect of unitrust amounts, are governed by general trust rules rather than the charitable remainder trust rules.[37]

§ 11.2   TAXATION OF CHARITABLE REMAINDER TRUSTS

If a charitable remainder trust has any unrelated business taxable income for a tax year, the trust is subject to federal tax for that year.[38]

In applying this rule, activities of the trust deemed unrelated are those unrelated activities of the charitable organization that is the remainder interest beneficiary of the trust.[39]

This rule may be illustrated by the following example:

Example 11.6

In 1994, a charitable remainder trust, which has a calendar year as its tax year, has $1,000 of ordinary income including $100 of unrelated business taxable income, and no deductions other than those under general trust rules.[40] The trust is required to pay out $700 for 1994 to

Continued

[37]Reg. § 1.664-1(a)(6), Example (5).
[38]Reg. § 1.664-1(c).
[39]The unrelated business income rules are summarized in Chapter 4 § 4.
[40]That is, under IRC §§ 642(b) and 661(a).

Example 11.6 Continued

a noncharitable recipient. Because the trust had some unrelated business income in 1994, it was not tax-exempt for that year. Consequently, the trust was taxable on all of its income for that year as a complex trust. The trust was allowed a deduction for the $700.[41] The trust was also allowed a deduction of $100.[42] Consequently, the taxable income of the trust for 1994 was $200 ($1,000 − $700 − $100).[43]

---

§ 11.3 TAX TREATMENT OF ANNUAL DISTRIBUTIONS

Annuity and unitrust distributions are treated as having the following characteristics in the hands of the recipients (whether or not the trust is tax-exempt):

- First, the amounts are treated as ordinary income, to the extent of the sum of the trust's ordinary income for the tax year of the trust and its undistributed ordinary income for prior years. An ordinary loss for the current year must be used to reduce undistributed ordinary income for prior years and any excess must be carried forward indefinitely to reduce ordinary income for future years.[44]

- Second, the amounts are treated as capital gain, to the extent of the charitable remainder trust's undistributed capital gains.[45]
  - If, in any tax year of a charitable remainder trust, the trust has both undistributed short-term capital gain and undistributed long-term capital gain, then the short-term capital

---

[41] IRC § 661(a).

[42] IRC § 642(b).

[43] Reg. § 1.664-1(c).

[44] Reg. § 1.664-1(d)(1)(i)(a). For these purposes, the amount of current and prior years' income must be computed without regard to the deduction for net operating losses provided by IRC §§ 172 or 642(d) (*ibid*).

[45] Reg. § 1.664-1(d)(1)(i)(b). Undistributed capital gains of a charitable remainder trust are determined on a cumulative net basis without regard to the capital loss carrybacks and carryover rules (IRC § 1212) (*ibid*).

gain must be deemed distributed prior to any long-term capital gain.[46]

– If a charitable remainder trust has for any tax year capital losses in excess of capital gains, any excess of the net short-term capital loss over the net long-term capital gain for the year must be a short-term capital loss in the succeeding tax year, any excess of the net long-term capital loss over the net short-term capital gain for the year must be a long-term capital loss in the succeeding tax year.[47]

– If a charitable remainder trust has for any tax year capital gains in excess of capital losses, any excess of the net short-term capital gain over the net long-term capital loss for the year must be, to the extent not deemed distributed, a short-term capital gain in the succeeding tax year, and any excess of the net long-term capital gain over the net short-term capital loss for the year must be, to the extent not deemed distributed, a long-term capital gain in the succeeding tax year.[48]

• Third, the amounts are treated as other income to the extent of the sum of the trust's other income for the taxable year and its undistributed other income for prior years. A loss in this category for the current year must be used to reduce undistributed income in this category for prior years and any excess must be carried forward indefinitely to reduce this income for future years.[49]

• Finally, the amounts are treated as a distribution of trust corpus. For these purposes, the term "corpus" means the net fair market value of the trust's assets less the total undistributed income (but not loss) in each of the above categories.[50]

The application of these rules concerning capital gains and losses may be illustrated by the following example:

---

[46] Reg. § 1.664-1(d)(1)(i)(b)(1).
[47] Reg. § 1.664-1(d)(1)(i)(b)(2).
[48] Reg. § 1.664-1(d)(i)(b)(3).
[49] Reg. § 1.664-1(d)(1)(i)(c).
[50] Reg. § 1.664-1(d)(1)(i)(d).

Example 11.7

The X Trust is a charitable remainder trust created on January 1, 1993. It utilizes the calendar year as its tax year. During the years indicated, the trust had the following capital transactions:

1993:

Long-term capital loss $10
Short-term capital gain 5

1994:

Short-term capital gain $20
Short-term capital loss 5

1995:

Long-term capital gain $15

Distributions for 1993 and 1994 were not in excess of current and accumulated ordinary income for those years. In 1995, distributions exceeded current and accumulated ordinary income by $5.

The treatment of the 1993 and 1994 transactions is as follows:

1993:

Long-term capital loss recognized .... $(10)
Short-term capital loss recognized .... (5)
Net long-term capital loss carried
    forward to 1994 .... $(5)

1994:

Short-term capital gain recognized $20
Short-term capital loss recognized .... (5)
Long-term capital loss carried
    forward from 1993 .... $(5)
Net short-term capital gain carried
    forward to 1995 .... $ 10

1995:

Long-term capital gain recognized .... $ 15
Net short-term capital gain carried
    forward from 1994 10

In 1995, the trust had long-term capital gain of $15 and short-term capital gain of $10. If the trust had both short-term capital gain and

Continued

Example 11.7 Continued

long-term capital gain for the same tax year, the short-term capital gain would be deemed distributed prior to the long-term capital gain. Therefore, the distribution of $5 in 1995 was deemed to be short-term capital gain. The undistributed net short-term capital gain of $5 was a short-term capital gain carried forward to 1996. The undistributed net long-term capital gain of $15 was a long-term capital gain carried forward to 1996.[51]

The determination of the character of amounts distributed must be made as of the end of the tax year of the trust. There are various classes of items within the four preceding categories of income. Amounts treated as paid from one of the categories must be viewed as consisting of (a) the same proportion of each class of items included in such category as (b) the total of the current and accumulated income of each class of items bears to the total of the current and accumulated income for that category. A loss in one of these categories may not be used to reduce a gain in any other category.[52]

Items of deduction of a charitable remainder trust for a tax year of the trust, which are deductible in determining taxable income[53] and which are directly attributable to one or more classes of items within a category of income or to corpus, must be allocated to these classes of items or to corpus. All other allowable deductions for the tax year, not directly attributable to one or more classes of items within a category of income or to corpus,[54] must be allocated among the classes of items within the category (excluding classes of items with net losses) on the basis of the gross income of these classes for the tax year, reduced by the deductions allocated to them. However, in no event may the amount of expenses allocated to any class of items exceed the income of that class for the tax year. Items of deduction which are not allocable under these rules as previously stated may be allocated in any manner.[55] All unrelated income taxes[56] and all

---

[51] Reg. § 1.664-1(d)(1)(i)(b).

[52] Reg. § 1.664-1(d)(1)(ii).

[53] This phrase is inapplicable to the deductions permitted by IRC §§ 642(b), 642(c), 661, and 1202.

[54] *Id.*

[55] *Id.*

[56] See Chapter 4 § 4.

private foundation excise taxes[57] must be allocated to corpus. Any expense which is not deductible in determining taxable income and which is not allocable to any class of items must be allocated to corpus.[58]

If there are two or more income beneficiaries, each is treated as receiving his or her pro rata portion of the categories of income and corpus.[59] The application of this rule may be illustrated by the following example:

Example 11.8

X transferred $40,000 to a charitable remainder annuity trust which is to pay $3,000 per year to X and $2,000 per year to Y for a term of five years. During the first of its tax years, the trust had $3,000 of ordinary income, $500 of capital gain, and $500 of tax-exempt income after allocation of all expenses. X was treated as receiving ordinary income of $1,800 ($3,000/$5,000 × $3,000), capital gain of $300 ($3,000/$5,000 × $500), tax-exempt income of $300 ($3,000/$5,000 × $500), and corpus of $600 ($3,000/$5,000 × [$5,000 − $4,000]). Y was treated as receiving ordinary income of $1,200 ($2,000/$5,000), capital gain of $200 ($2,000/$5,000 × $500), tax-exempt income of $200 ($2,000/$5,000 × $500), and corpus of $400 ($2,000/$5,000 × [$5,000 − $4,000]).[60]

The annuity or unitrust amount is includible in the income beneficiary's (or beneficiaries') gross income for the tax year in which the amount is required to be distributed. This is the case even though the annuity or unitrust amount is not distributed until after the close of the tax year of the trust. If a recipient of an income interest has a tax year[61] that is different from the tax year of the trust, the amount the beneficiary is required to include in gross income must be included in the tax year in which or with which ends the tax year of the trust in which the amount is required to be distributed.[62]

---

[57] See *The Law of Tax-Exempt Organizations*, Chapters 20–24.
[58] Reg. § 1.664-1(d)(2). The deductions allowable to a trust under IRC §§ 642(b), 642(c), 661, and 1202 are not allowed in determining the amount or character of any class of items within a category of income or corpus (*id*).
[59] Reg. § 1.664-1(d)(3).
[60] *Id.*
[61] IRC §§ 441 or 442.
[62] Reg. § 1.664-(d)(4)(i).

However, any payments which are made or required to be distributed by a charitable remainder trust because of

- the rules applicable to testamentary transfers,[63]
- an amendment to the governing instrument of certain trusts pursuant to special effective dates rules,[64] or
- an incorrect valuation,[65]

must be included in the gross income of the income interest beneficiary in his or her tax year in which or with which ends the tax year of the trust in which the amount is paid, credited, or required to be distributed. A recipient is allowed a deduction from gross income for amounts repaid to a charitable remainder trust because of an overpayment during the reasonable period of administration or settlement or until the trust is fully funded, because of an amendment, or because of an incorrect valuation, to the extent these amounts were included in his or her gross income.[66]

If the tax year of the trust does not end with or within the last tax year of the income beneficiary because of the recipient's death, the extent to which the annuity or unitrust amount required to be distributed to him or her is included in the gross income of the recipient for his or her last tax year, or in the gross amount of his or her estate, is determined by making the computations for the tax year of the trust in which his or her last tax year ends. The gross income for the last tax year of an income beneficiary on the cash basis includes amounts actually distributed to the recipient before his or her death. Amounts required to be distributed which are distributed to his or her estate are included in the gross income of the estate as income in respect of a decedent.[67]

---

[63] See Chapter 8.

[64] Generally, the rules concerning charitable remainder trusts are effective with respect to transfers in trust made after July 31, 1969 (Reg. § 1.664-1(f)(1)). However, there are special rules concerning the amendment of nonqualifying trusts that are created subsequent to July 31, 1969, and prior to December 31, 1972 (Reg. § 1.664-1(f)(3)).

[65] See the text accompanied by ns. 80–81, 129, *infra*.

[66] Reg. § 1.664-1(d)(4)(ii). IRC § 1341 contains rules relating to the computation of tax where an individual restores substantial amounts held under a claim of right.

[67] Reg. § 1.664-1(d)(4)(iii). The tax rules concerning income in respect of a decedent are contained in IRC § 691.

The annuity or unitrust amount may be paid in money or in other property. In the case of a distribution made of property other than money, the amount paid, credited, or required to be distributed must be considered as an amount realized by the trust from the sale or other disposition of property. The basis of the property in the hands of the recipient is its fair market value at the time it was paid, credited, or required to be distributed.[68]

The application of these rules may be illustrated by the following example:

Example 11.9

On January 1, 1993, X created a charitable remainder annuity trust, the tax year of which is the calendar year. X receives an annuity of $5,000 annually. During 1993, the trust received $500 of ordinary income. On December 31, 1993, the trust distributed money in the amount of $500 and a capital asset of the trust having a fair market value of $4,500 and a basis of $2,200. The trust was deemed to have realized a capital gain of $2,300. X properly treated the distribution of $5,000 in 1993 as being $500 of ordinary income, capital gain of $2,300, and trust corpus of $2,200. The basis of the undistributed property is $4,500 in the hands of X.[69]

---

§ 11.4   TAX TREATMENT OF OTHER DISTRIBUTIONS

An amount distributed by a charitable remainder trust to a charitable organization (other than an annuity or unitrust amount) must be considered a distribution of corpus and of those categories of income specified above[70] in an order inverse to that prescribed in those rules. The character of the amount must be determined as of the end of the trust tax year in which the distribution is made after the character of the annuity or unitrust amount has been determined.[71]

In the case of this type of distribution, no gain or loss is realized by the trust by reason of a distribution in kind unless the distribution is in satisfaction of a right to receive a distribution of a specific dollar amount or in specific property other than that distributed.[72]

---

[68] Reg. § 1.664-1(d)(5).
[69] *Id.*
[70] See § 3. *supra.*
[71] Reg. § 1.664-1(e)(1).
[72] Reg. § 1.664-1(e)(2).

§ 11.5 CHARITABLE REMAINDER ANNUITY TRUSTS—SPECIFIC RULES

A charitable remainder annuity trust is a trust that complies with the foregoing rules[73] and the rules described in this section.[74]

(a) Required Payment of Annuity Amount

A qualifying charitable remainder annuity trust must pay a sum certain not less often than annually to an eligible person or persons[75] for each tax year of the appropriate period,[76] all as provided in the governing instrument of the trust.[77]

A "sum certain" is a stated dollar amount, which is the same either as to each income beneficiary or as to the total amount payable for each year of the period of the trust. The payment requirement is satisfied by, for example, the provision for an amount which is the same every year to A until his death and concurrently an amount which is the same every year to A until her death, with the amount to each recipient to terminate at his or her death. The provision for an amount to A and B for their joint lives and then to the survivor of them also satisfies this requirement. In the case of a distribution to a charitable organization at the death of an income beneficiary or the expiration of a term of years, the governing instrument of a charitable remainder annuity trust may provide for a

---

[73] See §§ 1–4, *supra.*

[74] Reg. § 1.664-2(a).

[75] See the text accompanied by ns. 88–90, 96, *infra.*

[76] See the text accompanied by ns. 100–102, *infra.*

[77] Reg. § 1.664-2(a)(1)(i). A trust is not deemed to have engaged in an act of self-dealing (IRC § 4941; see *The Law of Tax-Exempt Organizations*, Chapter 20), to have unrelated debt-financed income (IRC § 514; see Chapter 4 § 4), to have received an additional contribution (see the text accompanied by n. 112, *infra*), or to have failed to function exclusively as a charitable remainder trust (see the text accompanied by n. 5, *supra*) merely because payment of the annuity amount is made after the close of the tax year, as long as the payment is made within a reasonable time after the close of the tax year (*id*). For these purposes, a reasonable time does not ordinarily extend beyond the date by which the trustee is required to file the trust's income tax return (Form 1041-B) (including extensions) for the year (*id.*).

reduction of the stated amount payable after the distribution as long as

- the reduced amount payable is the same either as to each income beneficiary or as to the total amount payable for each year of the balance of the period, and
- the minimum annuity amount requirements[78] are met.[79]

The stated dollar amount may be expressed as a fraction or a percentage of the initial net fair market value of the property irrevocably passing in trust as finally determined for federal tax purposes. If the stated dollar amount is expressed in this manner and the market value is incorrectly determined by the fiduciary, this requirement is satisfied if the governing instrument of the trust provides that, in this event, the trust must pay to the recipient (in the case of an undervaluation) or be repaid by the recipient (in the case of an overvaluation) an amount equal to the difference between the amount which the trust should have paid the recipient if the correct value were used and the amount which the trust actually paid the recipient. The payment or payments must be made within a reasonable period after the final determination of the value. Any payment due to an income beneficiary by reason of an incorrect valuation is considered to be a payment required to be distributed at the time of the final determination for purposes of the year-of-inclusion rules.[80]

The application of the rule permitting the stated dollar amount to be expressed as a fraction or a percentage of the initial net fair market value of the property irrevocably passing in trust as finally determined for federal tax purposes may be illustrated as follows:

Example 11.10

The will of X provided for the transfer of one-half of his residuary estate to a charitable remainder annuity trust. The trust is required to pay to W for life an annuity equal to five percent of the initial net fair

Continued

---

[78] See the text accompanied by n. 86, *infra*.
[79] Reg. § 1.664-2(a)(1)(ii).
[80] Reg. § 1.664-2(a)(1)(iii). Those rules are the subject of the text accompanied by n. 66, *supra*. Rules relating to the subject of future contributions are the subject of the text accompanied by n. 112, *infra*. Rules relating to required adjustments for underpayments or overpayments of these amounts in respect of payments made during a reasonable period of administration are the subject of the text accompanied by ns. 22–28, *supra*.

Example 11.10 Continued

market value of the interest passing in trust as finally determined for federal tax purposes. The annuity is to be paid on December 31 of each year computed from the date of X's death. The will also provided that if this initial net fair market value is incorrectly determined, the trust must pay to W, in the case of an undervaluation, or be repaid by W, in the case of an overvaluation, an amount equal to the difference between the amount which the trust should have paid if the correct value were used and the amount which the trust actually paid. X died on March 1, 1993. The executor filed an estate tax return showing the value of the residuary estate as $250,000 before reduction for taxes and expenses of $50,000. The executor paid to W $4,192 ([$250,000 − $50,000] × ½ × 5 % × 306/365) on December 31, 1993. On January 1, 1994, the executor transferred one-half of the residue of the estate to the trust. The trust adopted the calendar year as its tax year. The value of the residuary estate is finally determined for federal tax purposes to be $240,000 ($290,000 − $50,000). Accordingly, the amount which the executor should have paid to W was $5,030 ([$290,000 − $50,000] × ½ × 5 % × 306/365). Consequently, an additional amount of $838 ($5,030—$4,192) had to be paid to W within a reasonable period after the final determination of value for federal tax purposes.[81]

The governing instrument of a charitable remainder annuity trust must provide that, in the case of a tax year which is for a period of less than twelve months (other than the tax year in which the end of the trust period occurs), the annuity amount must be the amount otherwise determined, prorated for the trust year. That is, the annuity amount must be multiplied by a fraction the numerator of which is the number of days in the tax year of the trust and the denominator of which is 365 (366 if February 29 is a day included in the numerator).[82] The trust will not qualify as a charitable remainder trust absent a provision that provides a formula for prorating the specified distribution in the tax year when the noncharitable interests terminate.[83]

The governing instrument of a charitable remainder annuity trust must also provide that, in the tax year in which the end of the trust period occurs, the annuity amount to be distributed must be the

---

[81] Reg. § 1.664-2(a)(1)(iii).
[82] Reg. § 1.664-2(a)(1)(iv)(a).
[83] Rev. Rul. 79-428, 1979-2 C.B. 253.

amount otherwise determined, prorated for the trust year. That is, the annuity amount must be beginning on the first day of that tax year and ending on the last day multiplied by a fraction, the numerator of which is the number of days in the of the period, and the denominator of which is 365 (366 if February 29 is a day included in the numerator).[84]

(b) Minimum Annuity Amount

The total amount payable as an annuity amount may not be less than five percent of the initial net fair market value of the property placed in a charitable remainder annuity trust as finally determined for federal tax purposes.[85]

However, a trust will not fail to meet the minimum annuity amount requirement by reason of the fact that it provides for a reduction of the stated amount payable upon the death of an income beneficiary or the expiration of a term of years, provided that

- a distribution is made to a charitable organization at the death of the recipient or the expiration of a term of years, and
- the total amounts payable each year after the distribution are not less than a stated dollar amount which bears the same ratio to five percent of the initial net fair market value of the trust assets as the net fair market value of the trust assets immediately after the distribution bears to the net fair market value of the trust assets immediately before the distribution.[86]

In the case where the grantor of an inter vivos trust underestimates in good faith the initial net fair market value of the property placed in trust as finally determined for federal tax purposes and specifies a fixed dollar amount for the annuity which is less than five percent of the initial net fair market value of the property placed in trust as initially determined for federal tax purposes, the trust is deemed to have met the five percent requirement if the grantor or his or her representative consents, by appropriate agreement with the IRS, to accept an amount equal to twenty times the annuity as

[84]Reg. § 1.664-2(a)(1)(iv)(b).
[85]Reg. § 1.664-2(a)(2)(i).
[86]Reg. § 1.664-2(a)(2)(ii).

the fair market value of the property placed in trust for purposes of determining the appropriate charitable contribution deduction.[87]

(c) Permissible Income Recipients

The annuity amount must be payable to or for the use of a named person[88] or persons, at least one of which is not a charitable organization. If the amount is to be paid to an individual or individuals, all of them must be living at the time of the creation of the trust. A named person or persons may include members of a named class provided that, in the case of a class which includes any individual, all of the individuals must be alive and ascertainable at the time of the creation of the trust, unless the period for which the annuity amount is to be paid to the class consists solely of a term of years. For example, in the case of a testamentary trust, the testator's will may provide that am amount shall be paid to his children living at his death.[89]

However, the IRS approved an arrangement where an otherwise qualifying charitable remainder annuity trust made distributions to a second trust where the only function of the second trust was to receive and administer the distributions for the benefit of the named individual lifetime beneficiary of the trust, who was incompetent.[90] The income beneficiary was regarded as receiving the distributions directly from the first trust.

A trust is not a charitable remainder annuity trust if any person has the power to alter the amount to be paid to any named person (other than a charitable organization), if the power would cause any person to be treated as the owner of the trust or any portion of it, or if the rules treating grantors and others as substantial owners[91] were applicable to the trust.[92] For example, the governing instrument of a

---

[87] Reg. § 1.664-2(a)(2)(iii).
[88] The term "person" is defined for federal income tax purposes in IRC § 7701.
[89] Reg. § 1.664-2(a)(3)(i).
[90] Rev. Rul. 76-270, 1976-2 C.B. 194.
[91] IRC subpart E, Part 1, subchapter J, chapter 1, subtitle A.
[92] Reg. § 1.664-2(a)(3)(ii). Cf. the text accompanying n. 97, *infra* (a rule permitting the retention by a grantor of a testamentary power to revoke or terminate the interest of an income beneficiary other than a charitable organization).

charitable remainder annuity trust may not grant the trustee the power to allocate the annuity among members of a class unless the power falls within one of the exceptions to the rules concerning the power to control beneficial enjoyment.[93] In contrast, this rule is not violated where the grantor has reserved the right to remove the trustee for any reason and substitute any other person (including the grantor) as trustee.[94]

In one instance, the IRS reviewed a trust that was intended to qualify as a charitable remainder annuity trust. The trust had an independent trustee. The governing instrument of the trust provides that the trustee is to pay the specified distribution to or among the named individuals, B, C, and D, in such amounts and proportions as the trustee, in its sole discretion, shall from time to time determine until the death of the survivor of B, C, or D. B is a child of A. C is unrelated to, but was a former employee of, A. D is unrelated to and was never employed by A. The IRS held that, since the trustee is independent, the payments may be allocated as described without precluding the trust from qualifying as a charitable remainder trust, inasmuch as the power to make the allocation would not cause any person to be treated as the owner of the trust or any portion of it.[95]

A pet animal is not a "person" for this purpose; thus, an otherwise qualifying charitable remainder annuity trust that provides care for a pet animal during its lifetime does not qualify as a charitable remainder annuity trust.[96]

(d) Other Payments

No amount other than the annuity amount may be paid to or for the use of any person other than a charitable organization. An amount is not paid to or for the use of any person other than a charitable organization if the amount is transferred for full and adequate consideration. The trust may not be subject to a power to invade, alter, amend, or revoke for the beneficial use of a person other than a charitable organization. However, the grantor may retain the power

[93] Reg. § 1.664-2(a)(3)(ii). The rules concerning the power to control beneficial enjoyment are the subject of IRC § 674(a). The exceptions to these rules are in IRC § 674(b).
[94] Rev. Rul. 77-285, 1977-2 C.B. 213.
[95] Rev. Rul. 77-73, 1977-1 C.B. 175.
[96] Rev. Rul. 78-105, 1978-1 C.B. 295.

exercisable only by will to revoke or terminate the interest of any recipient other than a charitable organization.[97]

Also, the grantor may reserve the power to designate a substitute charitable remainder beneficiary without disqualifying an otherwise qualifying charitable remainder annuity trust.[98]

The governing instrument of a charitable remainder annuity trust may provide that any amount other than the annuity amount shall be paid (or may be paid in the discretion of the trustee) to a charitable organization, provided that, in the case of distributions in kind, the adjusted basis of the property distributed is fairly representative of the adjusted basis of the property available for payment on the date of payment. For example, the governing instrument of a charitable remainder annuity trust may provide that a portion of the trust assets may be distributed currently, or upon the death of one or more of the income beneficiaries, to a charitable organization.[99]

(e) Period of Payment of Annuity Amount

The period for which an annuity amount is payable must begin with the first year of the charitable remainder annuity trust and continue either

- for the life or lives of a named individual or individuals, or
- for a term of years not to exceed twenty years.

Only an individual or a charitable organization may receive an amount for the life of an individual. If an individual receives an amount for life, it must be solely for his or her life. Payment of an annuity amount may terminate with the regular payment next preceding the termination of the annuity amount period. (The annuity amount period ceases upon the death of the income beneficiary(ies).) The fact that the income beneficiary may not receive the last payment cannot be taken into account for purposes of determining the present value of the remainder interest.[100]

In the case of an annuity amount payable for a term of years, the length of the term of years must be ascertainable with certainty at

[97] Reg. § 1.664-2(a)(4).
[98] Rev. Rul. 76-8, 1979-1 C.B. 179.
[99] Reg. § 1.664-2(a)(4).
[100] Reg. § 1.664-2(a)(5)(i).

the time of the creation of the trust, except that the term may be terminated by the death of the income beneficiary, or by the grantor's exercise by will of a retained power to revoke or terminate the interest of any recipient other than a charitable organization. In any event, the period may not extend beyond either the life (or lives) of a named individual (or individuals) or a term of years not to exceed twenty years. For example, the governing instrument of a charitable remainder annuity trust may not provide for the payment of an annuity amount to A for his life and then to B for a term of years because it is possible for the period to last longer than either the lives of recipients living (technically, "in being") at the creation of the trust or a term of years not to exceed twenty years. Conversely, the governing instrument of the trust may provide for the payment of an annuity amount to A for his life and then to B for his life or a term of years (not to exceed twenty years), whichever is shorter (but not longer), if both A and B are living at the creation of the trust because it is not possible for the period to last longer than the lives of recipients living at the creation of the trust.[101]

The five percent requirement must be met until the termination of all of the annuity payments. For example, the following provisions are satisfactory:

- an amount equal to at least five percent of the initial net fair market value of the property placed in trust to A and B for their joint lives and then to the survivor of them for his life;
- an amount equal to at least five percent of the initial net fair market value of the property placed in trust to A for life or for a term of years not longer than twenty years, whichever is longer (or shorter);
- an amount equal to at least five percent of the initial net fair market value of the property placed in trust to A for a term of years not longer than twenty years and then to B for life (as long as B was living at the date of creation of the trust);
- an amount to A for her life and concurrently an amount to B for her life (the amount to each recipient to terminate at her death) if the amount given to each individual is not less than five percent of the initial net fair market value of the property placed in trust; or

[101] *Id.*

- an amount to *A* for his life and concurrently an equal amount to *B* for his life, and at the death of the first to die, the trust to distribute one-half of the then value of its assets to a charitable organization, if the total of the amounts given to *A* and *B* is not less than five percent of the initial net fair market value of the property placed in trust.[102]

(f) Permissible Remainder Interest Beneficiaries

At the end of the annuity payment period, the entire corpus of the trust must be irrevocably transferred, in whole or in part, to or for the use of one or more charitable organizations or retained, in whole or in part, for charitable use.[103] The trustee may have the power, exercisable during the donor's life, to add and/or substitute additional charitable organizations as remainder interest beneficiaries.[104]

If all of the trust corpus is to be retained for charitable use, the tax year of the trust must terminate at the end of the annuity payment period and the trust must cease to be treated as a charitable remainder trust for all purposes. If all or any portion of the trust corpus is to be transferred to or for the use of a charitable organization or organizations, the trustee must have a reasonable time after the annuity payment period to complete the settlement of the trust. During this time, the trust will continue to be treated as a charitable remainder trust for all purposes. Upon the expiration of the period, the tax year of the trust must terminate and the trust must cease to be treated as a charitable remainder trust for all purposes. If the trust continues in existence, it will be subject to the charitable trust rules[105] unless the trust is tax-exempt,[106] in which case the trust shall be deemed to have been created at the time it ceases to be treated as a charitable remainder trust.[107]

Where interests in the corpus of a charitable remainder annuity trust are given to more than one charitable organization, the interests may be enjoyed by them either concurrently or successively.[108]

---

[102] Reg. § 1.664-2(a)(5)(ii).
[103] Reg. § 1.664-2(a)(6)(i).
[104] Rev. Rul. 76-371, 1976-2 C.B. 305.
[105] IRC § 4947(a)(1). See *The Law of Tax-Exempt Organizations*, Chapter 27 § 1.
[106] That is, tax-exempt by reason of IRC § 501(c)(3).
[107] Reg. § 1.664-2(a)(6)(ii).
[108] Reg. § 1.664-2(a)(6)(iii).

The governing instrument of a charitable remainder annuity trust must provide that (1) if an organization to or for the use of which the trust corpus is to be transferred or for the use of which the trust corpus is to be retained is not a charitable organization at the time any amount is to be irrevocably transferred to or for the use of the organization, then (2) the amount shall be transferred to or for the use of one or more alternative charitable organizations at that time or retained for charitable use. The alternative organization or organizations may be selected in any manner provided by the terms of the trust's governing instrument.[109]

In general the allowable charitable deduction for property transferred to a valid charitable remainder trust will be subject to the 20 percent contributions limitation when the organization designated to receive the remainder interest may be redesignated from a public charity to a nonpublic charity.[110] However, this will not be the outcome where the likelihood that the remainder interest will not go to a public charitable organization is so remote as to be negligible.[111]

(g) Additional Contributions

A trust is not a charitable remainder annuity trust unless its governing instrument provides that no additional contributions may be made to it after the initial contribution. For this purpose, all property passing to a charitable remainder annuity trust by reason of death of the grantor is considered one contribution.[112]

(h) Calculation of Remainder Interest

For purposes of the federal income, gift, and estate charitable contribution deductions, the fair market value of the remainder interest of a charitable remainder annuity trust is the net fair market value (as of the appropriate valuation date) of the property placed in the trust less the present value of the annuity. For these purposes, the term "appropriate valuation date" means the date on which the property is

---

[109] Reg. § 1.664-2(a)(6)(iv).
[110] Rev. Rul. 79-368, 1979-2 C.B. 109. See Chapter 7.
[111] Rev. Rul. 80-38, 1980-1 C.B. 56.
[112] Reg. § 1.664-2(b).

transferred to the trust by the donor, except that, for estate tax charitable deduction purposes, it means the date of death unless the alternative valuation date is elected,[113] in which event it means the alternative valuation date.[114]

(i) Charitable Deductions

Any claim for a charitable deduction on any return for the value of a remainder interest in a charitable remainder annuity trust must be supported by a full statement attached to the return showing the computation of the present value of the interest. The federal income tax charitable contribution deduction is limited to the fair market value of the remainder interest of a charitable remainder annuity trust regardless of whether a charitable organization also receives a portion of the annuity.[115]

§ 11.6 CHARITABLE REMAINDER UNITRUSTS— SPECIFIC RULES

A charitable remainder unitrust is a trust that complies with the foregoing rules[116] and the rules described in this section.[117]

(a) Required Payment of Unitrust Amount

A qualifying charitable remainder unitrust must pay, not less often than annually, a fixed percentage of the net fair market value of the trust assets, determined annually, to an eligible person or persons[118]

---

[113]IRC § 2032.
[114]Reg. § 1.664-2(c).
[115]Reg. § 1.664-2(d). For the rules relating to the reduction of the amount of a charitable contribution deduction with respect to a contribution of certain ordinary income property or capital gain property, see Chapters 6 and 7. For rules for postponing the time for deduction of a charitable contribution of a future interest in tangible personal property, see Chapter 9 § 8.
[116]See §§ 1–4, *supra.*
[117]Reg. § 1.664-3(a).
[118]See the text accompanied by ns. 139–140, 145, *infra.*

for each tax year of the appropriate period,[119] all as provided in the governing instrument of the trust.[120]

Instead of the foregoing unitrust amount, the governing instrument of the trust may provide that the trust shall pay for any year either of the following:

- the amount of trust income[121] for a tax year to the extent that the amount is not more than the general unitrust amount (the "income only" exception), or
- the total of
  - the amount of trust income for a tax year to the extent that the amount is not more than the general unitrust amount, and
  - an amount of trust income for a tax year which is in excess of the general unitrust amount for the year, to the extent that (by reason of the first of these two items) the aggregate of the amounts paid in prior years was less than the aggregate of the required amounts (the income only plus prior year(s) make-up exception).[122]

Thus, in this regard, there are three types of unitrusts: (1) the "standard" unitrust which is described in this section of the chapter; (2) the "income-only" unitrust; and (3) the income-only unitrust with the make-up feature.

[119] See the text accompanied by ns. 150–153, *infra*. A change in the annual valuation date of a charitable remainder unitrust does not result in disqualification of the trust (e.g., IRS Private Letter Ruling 8822035).

[120] Reg. § 1.664-3(a)(1)(i)(a). A trust is not deemed to have engaged in an act of self-dealing (IRC § 4941; see *The Law of Tax-Exempt Organizations*, Chapter 20), to have unrelated debtfinanced income (IRC § 514; see Chapter 4 § 4), to have received an additional contribution (see the text accompanied by ns. 164–166, *infra*), or to have failed to function exclusively as a charitable remainder trust (see the text accompanied by n. 6, *supra*) merely because payment of the unitrust amount is made after the close of the tax year, as long as the payment is made within a reasonable time after the close of the tax year (id). For these purposes, a reasonable time does not ordinarily extend beyond the date by which the trustee is required to file the trust's income tax return (Form 1041-B) (including extensions) for the year (*id.*).

[121] IRC § 643(b).

[122] Reg. § 1.664-3(a)(1)(i)(b).

On one occasion, the IRS ruled that a trust did not satisfy the requirements of the income-only exception. The governing instrument of the trust, which otherwise qualified as a charitable remainder unitrust, provided that the trustee was to pay income to the grantor for his lifetime, with income to be paid to his spouse, should she survive the grantor. The trust instrument also provided that, upon the death of the grantor's spouse, or upon the grantor's death if his spouse predeceased him, the trustee was to divide the then remaining trust assets into two equal parts. Each part is to be operated separately for the respective benefit of A and B, the children of the grantor and his spouse. The trustee is to pay to A the lesser of five percent of the net fair market value of one equal part of the total trust assets valued annually or the annual income of this equal part. Upon the death of A, the trustee must make the payments to B. Likewise, the trustee is to pay to B the lesser of five percent of the net fair market value of the other equal part of the total trust assets valued annually or the annual income of this equal part. Upon the death of B, the trustee must make the payments to A. Thereafter, the trust assets are destined for a charitable remainder beneficiary.

The IRS held that the income exception was not satisfied in this situation. The Service said that the provisions of the trust agreement directing the separate operation of these parts may cause the trustee, in some tax years, to not distribute the amount required to be paid from the entire trust in accordance with legal requirements. The IRS wrote: "For example, in some taxable years of the trust, it is possible that one part of the total trust assets will earn little or no income while the other part of the total trust assets will earn income exceeding five percent of the net fair market value of its assets. Thus, under the income exception form of payment and in accordance with the provisions of the trust instrument that directs the separate operation of the two equal parts, the total payments in some taxable years, which consist of the trust income of one part limited by the amount of income earned plus the trust income of the other part limited by the amount that is not more than the designated fixed percentage of the net fair market value of that part's assets, could be less than the total of all trust income earned by the entire trust assets and required to be distributed by the trustee" under these rules.[123] These

[123]Rev. Rul. 76-310, 1976-2 C.B. 197.

provisions precluded the trust from qualifying as a charitable remainder unitrust.

The "fixed percentage" may be expressed either as a fraction or as a percentage and must be payable each year for the specified period.[124] A percentage is "fixed" if the percentage is the same either as to each income beneficiary or as to the total percentage payable each year of the period. For example, provision for a fixed percentage which is the same every year to A until his death and concurrently a fixed percentage which is the same every year to B until her death, the fixed percentage to each recipient to terminate at his or her death, would satisfy this requirement. Similarly, provision for a fixed percentage to A and B for their joint lives and then to the survivor would satisfy this rule. In the case of a distribution to a charitable organization at the death of an income beneficiary or the expiration of a term of years, the governing instrument may provide for a reduction of the fixed percentage payable after the distribution, provided that

- the reduced fixed percentage is the same either as to each recipient or as to the total amount payable for each year of the balance of the period, and
- the appropriate minimum unitrust amount requirements[125] are met.[126]

In one instance, the IRS reviewed the governing instrument of a trust which provided that the trustee will pay A, the unitrust amount beneficiary, seven percent of the net fair market value of the trust assets, valued annually, until the death of the donor. Upon the donor's death, the trustee is to pay A nine percent of the net fair market value of the trust assets until death. This arrangement was held to not constitute a "fixed" percentage and the trust did not qualify as a charitable remainder unitrust for that reason.[127] A similar situation, that also failed, was this: The trustee is to pay A seven percent of the property's value until A's death and nine percent thereafter to B until B's death.[128]

[124]The requisite period is the subject of the text accompanied by ns. 150–153, *infra.*
[125]See the text accompanied by n. 138, *infra.*
[126]Reg. § 1.664-3(a)(1)(ii).
[127]Rev. Rul. 80-104, 1980-1 C.B. 135.
[128]*Id.*

The governing instrument of a charitable remainder unitrust must provide that in the case where the net fair market value of the trust assets is incorrectly determined by the fiduciary, the trust must pay to the income beneficiary (in the case of an undervaluation) or be repaid by the income beneficiary (in the case of an overvaluation) an amount equal to the difference between the amount the trust should have paid the income beneficiary if the correct value were used and the amount which the trust initially paid the income beneficiary. These payments or repayments must be made within a reasonable period after the final determination of the value. Any payment due to an income beneficiary by reason of an incorrect valuation must be considered to be a payment required to be distributed at the time of the final determination for purposes of the year-of-inclusion rules.[129]

In computing the net fair market value of the trust assets, there must be taken into account all assets and liabilities without regard to whether particular items are taken into account in determining the income of the trust. The net fair market value of the trust assets may be determined on any one date during the tax year of the trust, or by taking the average of valuations made on more than one date during the tax year of the trust, as long as the same valuation date or dates and valuation methods are used each year. If the governing instrument of the trust does not specify the valuation date or dates, the trustee must select the date or dates and indicate his or her selection on the first tax return (Form 1041-B) which the trust is required to file. The unitrust amount which must be paid each year must be based on the valuation for that year.[130]

The governing instrument of the trust must provide that, in the case of a tax year of the trust which is for a period of less than twelve months, other than the tax year in which occurs the end of the trust's income payment period,

- the unitrust amount must be the amount otherwise determined under the general rules[131] multiplied by a fraction, the numerator of which is the number of days in the tax year of the trust and the denominator of which is 365 (366 if February 29 is a day included in the numerator),

---

[129] Reg. § 1.664-3(a)(1)(iii). The year-of-inclusion rules are the subject of the text accompanied by n. 66, *supra.*

[130] Reg. § 1.664-3(a)(1)(iv).

[131] See the text accompanied by ns. 118–120, *supra.*

- the unitrust amount must be the amount otherwise determined under the income-only exception[132] (if applicable), and
- if no valuation date occurs before the end of the tax year of the trust, the trust assets must be valued as of the last day of the tax year of the trust.[133]

The governing instrument of the trust must provide that, in the case of the tax year in which occurs the end of the trust's income payment period,

- the unitrust amount which must be distributed will be the amount otherwise determined under the general unitrust amount rules prorated for the trust year. That is, the unitrust amount must be multiplied by a fraction, the numerator of which is the number of days in the period beginning on the first day of this last tax year and ending on the last day of the period and the denominator of which is 365 (366 if February 29 is a day included in the numerator),
- the unitrust amount must be the amount otherwise determined under the income-only exception (if applicable), and
- if no valuation date occurs before the end of the period, the trust assets shall be valued as of the last day of the period.[134]

The trust will not qualify as a charitable remainder trust absent a provision that provides a formula for prorating the specified distribution in the tax year when the noncharitable interests terminate.[135]

There is a special rule that allows termination of payment of the unitrust amount with the regular payment next preceding the termination of the income payment period.[136]

---

[132] See the text accompanied by n. 122, *supra.*

[133] Reg. § 1.664-3(a)(1)(v)(a). A sample provision to reflect this requirement appears in Rev. Rul. 82-165, *supra,* n. 26, § (2).

[134] Reg. § 1.664-3(a)(1)(v)(b)(1). The IRS has set forth an acceptable method for determining the net fair market value of the assets of a charitable remainder unitrust from which payments are made to the income beneficiary prior to the annual valuation date (Rev. Rul. 76-467, 1976-2 C.B. 198).

[135] Rev. Rul. 79-428, *supra,* n. 83.

[136] Reg. § 1.664-3(a)(1)(v)(b)(2). This special rule is the subject of the text accompanied by ns. 150–153, *infra.*

(b)   Minimum Unitrust Amount

The fixed percentage (see above) with respect to all income beneficiaries taken together may not be less than five percent.[137]

However, a trust will not fail to meet the minimum unitrust amount by reason of the fact that it provides for a reduction of the fixed percentage payable upon the death of an income beneficiary or the expiration of a term of years, provided that

- a distribution is made to a charitable organization at the death of the income beneficiary or the expiration of the term of years, and
- the total of the percentage after the distribution is not less than five percent.[138]

(c)   Permissible Income Beneficiaries

The unitrust amount must be payable to or for the use of a named person or persons, at least one of which is not a charitable organization. If the unitrust amount is to be paid to an individual or individuals; all of these individuals must be living at the time of creation of the trust. A named person or persons may include members of a named class, except in the case of a class which includes any individual, all of the individuals must be alive and ascertainable at the time of the creation of the trust unless the period for which the unitrust amount is to be paid to the class consists solely of a term of years. For example, in the case of a testamentary trust, the testator's will may provide that the required amount is to be paid to his children living at his death.[139]

However, the IRS approved an arrangement where an otherwise qualifying charitable remainder unitrust made distributions to a second trust where the only function of the second trust was to receive and administer the distributions for the benefit of the named individual lifetime beneficiary of the trust, who was incompetent.[140] The income beneficiary was regarded as receiving the distributions directly from the first trust.

[137]Reg. § 1.664-3(a)(2)(i).
[138]Reg. § 1.664-3(a)(2)(ii).
[139]Reg. § 1.664-3(a)(3)(i).
[140]Rev. Rul. 76-270, 1976-2 C.B. 194.

A trust is not a charitable remainder unitrust if any person has the power to alter the amount to be paid to any named person, other than a charitable organization, if that power would cause any person to be treated as the owner of the trust or any portion of it. For example, in general, the governing instrument of the trust may not grant the trustee the power to allocate the fixed percentage among members of a class.[141] (However, the grantor may retain a testamentary power to revoke or terminate the interest of an income beneficiary other than a charitable organization.)[142] In contrast, this rule is not violated where the grantor has reserved the right to remove the trustee for any reason and substitute any other person (including the grantor) as trustee.[143]

In one instance, the IRS reviewed a trust that was intended to qualify as a charitable remainder annuity trust. The trust had an independent trustee. The governing instrument of the trust provides that the trustee is to pay the specified distribution to or among the named individuals, B, C, and D, in such amounts and proportions as the trustee, in its sole discretion, shall from time to time determine until the death of the survivor of B, C, or D. B is a child of A. C is unrelated to, but was a former employee of, A. D is unrelated to and was never employed by A. The IRS held that, since the trustee is independent, the payments may be allocated as described without precluding the trust from qualifying as a charitable remainder trust, inasmuch as the power to make the allocation would not cause any person to be treated as the owner of the trust or any portion of it.[144]

A pet animal is not a "person" for this purpose; thus, an otherwise qualifying charitable remainder unitrust that provides care for a pet animal during its lifetime does not qualify as a charitable remainder unitrust.[145]

---

[141] Reg. § 1.664-3(a)(3)(ii). In one instance, the IRS ruled that a trust would be disqualified as a charitable remainder unitrust if the trust document was amended to change the order in which the life income beneficiaries receive payment (IRS Private Letter Ruling 9143030).

[142] See the text accompanied by n. 147, *infra.*

[143] Rev. Rul. 77-285 *supra* n. 94.

[144] Rev. Rul. 77-73, *supra,* n. 95.

[145] Rev. Rul. 78-105, *supra,* n. 96.

(d) Other Payments

No amount other than the unitrust amount may be paid to or for the use of any person other than a charitable organization. An amount is not paid to or for the use of any person other than a charitable organization if the amount is transferred for full and complete consideration. The trust may not be subject to a power to invade, alter, amend, or revoke for the beneficial use of a person other than a charitable organization.[146] However, the grantor may retain the power exercisable only by will to revoke or terminate the interest of any income beneficiary other than a charitable organization.[147]

Also, the grantor may reserve the power to designate a substitute charitable remainder beneficiary without disqualifying an otherwise qualifying charitable remainder unitrust.[148]

The governing instrument of the trust may provide that any amount other than the unitrust amount may be paid (or may be paid in the discretion of the trustee) to a charitable organization provided that, in the case of a distribution in kind, the adjusted basis of the property distributed is fairly representative of the adjusted basis of the property available for payment on the date of payment. For example, the governing instrument of the trust may provide that a portion of the trust assets may be distributed currently, or upon the death of one or more income beneficiaries, to a charitable organization.[149]

(e) Period of Payment Unitrust Amount

The period for which a unitrust amount is payable begins with the first year of the charitable remainder trust and continues either for the life (or lives) of a named individual (or individuals) or for a term of years not to exceed twenty years. Only an individual or a charitable organization may receive an amount for the life of an individual.[150] If an individual receives an amount for life, it must be solely

---

[146] Reg. § 1.664-3(a)(4).
[147] E.g., Rev. Rul. 74-149, 1974-1 C.B. 157.
[148] Rev. Rul. 76-8, *supra*, n. 98.
[149] Reg. § 1.664-3(a)(4).
[150] Thus, a corporation can be an income interest beneficiary of a charitable remainder unitrust where the unitrust amount payment period is a qualified term of years (IRS Private Letter Ruling 9205031).

for his or her life. Payment of a unitrust amount may terminate with the regular payment next preceding the termination of the period. (Again, the income payment period terminates at the death of the income beneficiary(ies)). The fact that the income beneficiary may not receive this last payment may not be taken into account for purposes of determining the present value of the remainder interest.

In the case of an amount payable for a term of years, the length of the term of years must be ascertainable with certainty at the time of the creation of the trust, except that the term may be terminated by the death of the income beneficiary or by the grantor's exercise by will of a retained power to revoke or terminate the interest of any income beneficiary other than a charitable organization. In any event, the period may not extend beyond either the life or lives of a named individual or individuals or a term of years not to exceed twenty years. For example, the governing instrument of a charitable remainder unitrust may not provide for the payment of a unitrust amount to A for his life and then to B for a term of years because it is possible for the period to last longer than either the lives of recipients living at the creation of the trust or a term of years not to exceed twenty years. By contrast, the governing instrument of the trust may provide for the payment of a unitrust amount to A for her life and then to B for her life or a term of years (not to exceed twenty years), whichever is shorter (but not longer), if both A and B are living at the creation of the trust because it is not possible for the period to last longer than the lives of income beneficiaries living at the creation of the trust[151]

The five percent requirement[152] must be met until the termination of all of the income payments. For example, the following provisions would satisfy this requirement:

- a fixed percentage of at least five percent to A and B for their joint lives and then to the survivor for his or her life,
- a fixed percentage of at least five percent to A for life or for a term of years not longer than twenty years, whichever is longer (or shorter),
- a fixed percentage of at least five percent to A for a term of years not longer than twenty years and then to B for life (assuming B was living at the creation of the trust),

[151] Reg. § 1.664-3(a)(5)(i).
[152] See the text accompanied by ns. 137–138, *supra*.

- a fixed percentage to *A* for his life and concurrently a fixed percentage to *B* for her life (the percentage to each recipient to terminate at his or her death) if the percentage given to each individual is not less than five percent,
- a fixed percentage to *A* for his life and concurrently an equal percentage to *B* for her life, and at the death of the first to die, the trust to distribute one-half of the then value of its assets to a charitable organization if the total of the percentages is not less than five percent for the entire period.[153]

The IRS also approved the following unitrust provision. Each year, quarterly distributions at an annual rate of six percent of the net fair market value of the trust assets, determined annually, are to be made to *B* for a term of 20 years. If *B* dies before the expiration of the twenty-year term, the payments will be made to *C* for the balance of the term remaining. If *C* also dies before the expiration of the twenty-year period, then distributions for the balance of the period remaining are to be made to *C*'s heirs at law excluding the donor and his spouse. At the end of the twenty-year term, the balance remaining in the trust is to be distributed to the remainder interest beneficiary.[154]

(f) Permissible Remainder Beneficiaries

At the end of the income payment period (see above), the entire corpus of the trust must be irrevocably transferred, in whole or in part, to or for the use of one or more charitable organizations or retained, in whole or in part, for charitable use.[155] The trustee may have the power, exercisable during the donor's life, to add and/or substitute additional charitable organizations as remainder interest beneficiaries.[156]

If all of the trust corpus is to be retained for charitable use, the tax year of the trust must terminate at the end of the income payment period and the trust will cease to be treated as a charitable

---

[153]Reg. § 1.664-3(a)(5)(ii).
[154]Rev. Rul. 74-39, 1974-1 C.B. 156.
[155]Reg. § 1.664-3(a)(6)(i).
[156]Rev. Rul. 76-371, *supra*, n. 104. A charitable remainder unitrust does not fail to qualify because the grantor retains the power to change the charitable remainder beneficiary (IRS Private Letter Ruling 9204036).

remainder trust for all purposes. If all or any portion of the trust corpus is to be transferred to or for the use of a charitable organization or organizations, the trustee must have a reasonable time after the income payment period to complete the settlement of the trust. During that time, the trust must continue to be treated as a charitable remainder trust for all purposes. Upon the expiration of the period, the tax year of the trust must terminate and the trust must cease to be treated as a charitable remainder trust for all purposes. If the trust continues in existence, it will be considered a charitable trust[157] unless the trust becomes a tax-exempt organization.[158] For purposes of determining whether the trust is tax-exempt as a charitable organization,[159] the trust is deemed to have been created at the time it ceased to be treated as a charitable remainder trust.[160]

Where interests in the corpus of a charitable remainder unitrust are given to more than one charitable organization, the interests may be enjoyed by them either concurrently or successively.[161]

The governing instrument of a charitable remainder trust must provide that (1) if an organization to or for the use of which the trust corpus is to be transferred or for the use of which the trust corpus is to be retained is not a charitable organization at the time any amount is to be irrevocably transferred to or for the use of the organization, then (2) the amount will be transferred to or for the use of or retained for the use of one or more alternative organizations which are charitable entities at that time. This alternative organization (or these alternative organizations) may be selected in any manner provided by the terms of the governing instrument of the trust.[162]

In general, the allowable charitable deduction for property transferred to a valid charitable remainder trust will be subject to the 20 percent contributions limitation when the organization designated to receive the remainder interest may be redesignated from a public charity to a nonpublic charity.[163] However, this will not be the out-

---

[157]IRC § 4947(a)(1).

[158]That is, becomes tax-exempt under IRC § 501(a), presumably by reason of qualification under IRC § 501(c)(3).

[159]That is, an IRC § 501(c)(3) organization. See Chapter 4 § 2.

[160]Reg. § 1.664-3(a)(6)(ii).

[161]Reg. § 1.664-3(a)(6)(iii).

[162]Reg. § 1.664-3(a)(6)(iv).

[163]Rev. Rul. 79-368, *supra*, n. 110. See Chapter 7.

come where the likelihood that the remainder interest will not go to a public charitable organization is so remote as to be negligible.[164]

(g) Additional Contributions

A trust is not a charitable remainder unitrust unless its governing instrument either prohibits additional contributions to the trust after the initial contribution or provides that for the tax year of the trust in which the additional contribution is made:

- where no valuation date occurs after the time of the contribution and during the tax year in which the contribution is made, the additional property must be valued as of the time of contribution, and
- the unitrust amount must be computed by multiplying the fixed percentage by the sum of (1) the net fair market value of the trust assets (excluding the value of the additional property and any earned income from and any appreciation on the property after its contribution) and (2) that proportion of the value of the additional property (that was excluded), with the number of days in the period which begins with the date of contribution and ends with the earlier of the last day of the tax year or the last day of the income payment period bears to the number of days in the period which begins with the first day of the tax year and ends with the earlier of the last day of the tax year or the last day of the income payment period.

For these purposes, all property passing to a charitable remainder unitrust by reason of death of the grantor must be considered one contribution.[165]

The application of these rules is illustrated by the following examples:

Example 11.11

On March 1, 1993, X made an additional contribution of property to a charitable remainder unitrust. The tax year of the trust is the calendar

Continued

---

[164] Rev. Rul. 80-38, *supra*, n. 111.
[165] Reg. § 1.664-3(b).

Example 11.11 Continued

year, and the regular valuation date is January 1 of each year. For purposes of computing the required payout with respect to the additional contribution for the year of contribution, the additional contribution is valued on March 2, 1993 (the date of contribution). The property had a value on that date of $5,000. Income from this property in the amount of $250 was received on December 31, 1993. The required payout with respect to the additional contribution for the year of contribution was $208 (5% × $5,000 × 305/365). The income earned after the date of contribution and after the regular valuation date did not enter into the computation.[166]

Example 11.12

On July 1, 1993, X made an additional contribution of $10,000 to a charitable remainder unitrust. The tax year of the trust is the calendar year and the regular valuation date is December 31 of each year. The fixed percentage is five percent. Between July 1, 1993, the additional property appreciated in value to $12,500 and earned $500 of income. Because the regular valuation date for the year of contribution occurred after the date of the additional contribution, the additional contribution including income earned by it is valued on the regular valuation date. Thus, the required payout with respect to the additional contribution is $325.87 (5% × [$12,500 + $500] × 183/365).[167]

(h) Charitable Deductions

The federal income tax charitable contribution deduction is limited to the fair market value of the remainder interest of a charitable remainder unitrust regardless of whether a charitable organization also receives a portion of the unitrust amount.[168]

---

[166] *Id*, Example (1).

[167] Reg. § 1.664-3(b), Example (2). Also Rev. Rul. 74-481, 1974-2 C.B. 190.

[168] Reg. § 1.664-3(d). For the rules relating to the reduction of the amount of a charitable contribution deduction with respect to a contribution of certain ordinary income property or capital gain property, see Chapters 6 and 7. For rules for postponing the time for deduction of a charitable contribution of a future interest in tangible personal property, see Chapter 9 § 8.

§ 11.7 CALCULATION OF CHARITABLE DEDUCTION

In the case of a charitable contribution by means of a charitable remainder annuity trust or a charitable remainder unitrust, the charitable deduction is equal to the value of the remainder interest. The value of the remainder interest is equal to the fair market value of the property less the value of the income interest.

The value of an annuity, any interest for life or a term of years, or any remainder or reversionary interest is determined by using an interest rate (rounded to the nearest two-tenths of one percent) equal to 120 percent of the federal midterm rate, used to determine the issue price (value) of certain debt instruments,[169] in effect for the month in which the valuation date falls.[170] The IRS occasionally determines, by private letter ruling, the present value of a charitable remainder interest created by a charitable remainder trust or supplies the factor needed to make the computation.[171]

This valuation is made by means tables prepared by the IRS[172] using the most recent mortality experience available.[173] These tables must be revised at least once every ten years to take into account the most recent mortality experience available as of the time of the revision.[174]

If an income, estate, or gift tax charitable contribution is allowable for any part of the property transferred, the individual involved may elect to use the federal midterm rate for either of the two months preceding the month in which the valuation date falls in determining the value.[175] Otherwise, the rate that is used is the rate in effect in the month of the gift. In the case of transfers of more than one interest in the same property with respect to which a person may use the same rate, the person must use the same rate with respect to each interest.[176]

As directed, the IRS has published valuation tables. These tables reflect the use of interest rates or adjusted payout rates ranging from

---

[169] IRC § 1274(d)(1).
[170] IRC § 7520(a)(2). A chart of these rates appears as Appendix G.
[171] E.g., IRS Private Letter Ruling 8601033.
[172] IRC § 7520(a)(1).
[173] IRC § 7520(c)(3).
[174] *Id.*
[175] IRC § 7520(a).
[176] *Id.*

2.2 percent to 26 percent. These tables are in the following publications:

- Actuarial Values—Alpha Volume (IRS Publication 1457), which provides remainder, income, and annuity factors for one life, two lives, and terms certain. These factors are used for purposes of income, gift, and estate tax calculations.
- Actuarial Values—Beta Volume (IRS Publication 1458), which provides unitrust remainder factors for one life, two lives, and terms certain. These factors are also used for income, gift, and estate tax purposes.
- Actuarial Values—Gamma Volume (IRS Publication 1459), which provides depreciation adjustment factors. These factors are used only for income tax purposes.

§ 11.8   MANDATORY PROVISIONS

As references throughout the foregoing portions of this chapter indicate, there are a variety of provisions that must appear in a charitable remainder trust instrument, as a condition of qualification of the trust under the applicable federal tax rules.

Many of these mandatory provisions are required by the tax regulations. Others are required by various IRS pronouncements.[177] Following the issuance of these requirements, the IRS published prototypes of charitable remainder trusts.[178] Thereafter, the IRS announced that it ordinarily would not issue rulings as to the qualification of charitable remainder trusts.[179]

[177]Rev. Rul. 72-395, 1972-2 C.B. 340; Rev. Rul. 80-123, *supra*, n. 27; Rev. Rul. 82-128, 1982-2 C.B. 71; Rev. Rul. *supra*, n. 26; and Rev. Rul. 88-81, 1988-2 C.B. 127.
[178]Rev. Proc. 89-20, 1989-1 C.B. 841; Rev. Proc. 89-21, 1989-1 C.B. 842; Rev. Proc. 90-30, 1990-1 C.B. 534; Rev. Proc. 90-31, 1990-1 C.B. 539; and Rev. Proc. 90-32, 1990-1 C.B. 546 (see Appendix E).
[179]Rev. Proc. 91-3, 1991-1 C.B. 364 § 4.01 subpar. 34. Prior to that time, the IRS issued rulings as to the qualification of charitable remainder trusts (e.g., IRS Private Letter Ruling 7842062).

§ 11.9 APPLICATION OF PRIVATE FOUNDATION RULES

In addition, since charitable remainder trusts are split-interest trusts,[180] they are subject to at least some of the prohibitions that are imposed on private foundations, most particularly the rules concerning self-dealing[181] and so-called taxable expenditures.[182] While reference to the other private foundation rules may not be necessary,[183] it is common practice to include references in the trust instrument to the other private foundation restrictions—namely, the requirement of income distribution,[184] and the prohibitions on excess business holdings[185] and jeopardizing investments.[186]

The interplay of the private foundation rules in the charitable remainder trust context was illustrated in a private letter ruling issued by the IRS concerning a gift of a joint venture interest to a charitable remainder unitrust.[187] The donor owned an interest in and to a joint venture, which was created by an agreement dated January 15, 1969. The donor acquired all of the interest by July 13, 1977. The sole asset of the joint venture was an apartment complex, which was subject to a nonrecourse mortgage indebtedness. The mortgage indebtedness was placed on the real property in 1970. As a nonrecourse debt, none of the venturers had any personal liability with respect to the indebtedness. Furthermore, under the terms of the agreement, all other debts, obligations, or liabilities of the venture were to be borne severally, according to the percentage ownership interest. Thus, no venturer was personally liable for the venture debt or any of the debts of obligations of any of the other venturers. Each venturer was liable for any future cash calls in the event the venture needs additional capital and the venture does not borrow the money from commercial sources.

---

[180]IRC § 4947(a)(2); Reg. § 53.4947-1(c)(1)(ii). See *The Law of Tax-Exempt Organizations*, Chapter 27 § 2.
[181]IRC § 4941. See *The Law of Tax-Exempt Organizations*, Chapter 20.
[182]IRC § 4945. See *The Law of Tax-Exempt Organizations*, Chapter 24.
[183]Reg. §§ 1.508-2(b)(1)(vi); 1.664-1(b).
[184]IRC § 4942. See *The Law of Tax-Exempt Organizations*, Chapter 21.
[185]IRC § 4943. See *The Law of Tax-Exempt Organizations*, Chapter 22.
[186]IRC § 4944. See *The Law of Tax-Exempt Organizations*, Chapter 23.
[187]IRS Private Letter Ruling 8536061.

The joint venture agreement required that any transferor of venture interests remains primarily and directly liable for the performance of any obligations of a transferee. The proposed gift agreement stated that the donor "agrees to indemnify and hold harmless the trust from and against all expenses, losses, and payments, or obligations which might arise as a result of its ownership of the venture interest."

The owner of the joint venture interest wanted to contribute the interest to charity by means of a charitable remainder unitrust. The trustee would not be restricted from investing the trust assets in a manner which could result in the annual realization of a reasonable amount of income or gain. The grantor remained primarily liable for any obligation arising under the venture agreement for which the trust might otherwise be liable. The trust did not assume any portion of the venture debt, since it was nonrecourse and without personal liability.

The IRS reasoned that, inasmuch as the venture debt was placed on the venture property in 1970 and because the joint venture was not a disqualified person[188] with respect to the donor, the transfer of the venture interest by the grantor to the trust would not constitute a sale or exchange of property for purposes of the self-dealing rules and thus that the gift of the venture interest would not constitute an act of self-dealing between the trust and the grantor.[189]

---

[188]IRC § 4946. See *The Law of Tax-Exempt Organizations*, Chapter 19.
[189]For further reading about charitable remainder trusts, see Appendix H.

12

Gifts by Means of Pooled Income Funds

The federal tax law provides for a form of planned giving that utilizes a split-interest trust called a "pooled income fund."[1]

Basically, a pooled income fund is a vehicle by which money or property is split into two types of interests: one or more "income interests" and one or more "remainder interests." The remainder interest is destined for one or more charitable organizations, while the income interest or interests are usually retained by or created for noncharitable beneficiaries.[2] In the normal course of events, the gift of the remainder interest gives rise to a federal tax deduction.[3] This chapter focuses on the income tax deduction; Chapter 8 discusses the use of pooled income funds in the estate and gift tax context.

§ 12.1 DEFINITIONS

The rules concerning qualified pooled income funds employ a variety of definitions. These definitions include the following:

- The term "income" has the same meaning as it does under general income tax rules.[4]

---

[1] The concepts of planned giving and split-interest trusts are discussed in Chapter 3. That chapter also contains a general description of pooled income funds.
[2] IRC § 642(c)(5).
[3] IRC § 170(f)(2)(A). See Chapter 9 § 9.
[4] Reg. § 1.642(c)-5(a)(5)(i). The term "income" is generally defined in IRC § 643(b).

- The term "donor" includes a decedent who makes a testamentary transfer of property to a pooled income fund.[5]
- The term "governing instrument" means either the governing plan under which the pooled income fund is established and administered or the instrument of transfer, as the context requires.[6]
- The term "public charity" means certain charitable organizations that are not private foundations because they are institutions such as churches, universities, colleges, and hospitals, or are certain publicly supported charities.[7] To be a public charity for these purposes, an organization need only be described in one of the applicable provisions of the federal tax law,[8] even though it has been classified as another type of public charity.[9] Nonetheless, not all charitable organizations that are generically termed "public charities" or "publicly supported charities" qualify as "public charities" under these rules.
- The term "fair market value," when used with respect to property, means its value in excess of the indebtedness or charges against the property.[10]
- The term "determination date" means each day within the tax year of a pooled income fund on which a valuation is made of the property in the fund. The property in the fund must be valued on the first day of the tax year of the fund and on at least three other days within the tax year. The period between

---

[5] Reg. § 1.642(c)-5(a)(5)(ii).
[6] Reg. § 1.642(c)-5(a)(5)(iii).
[7] Reg. § 1.642(c)-5(a)(5)(iv).
[8] IRC § 170(b)(1)(A)(i)-(vi).
[9] Reg. § 1.642(c)-5(a)(5)(iv). For example, a charitable organization may not be a private foundation by reason of the fact that it is classified as a publicly supported charity under IRC § 509(a)(2), and yet also satisfy the public support test of IRC § 509(a)(1). Because of this, the organization is one that is described in IRC § 170(b)(1)(A)(vi) and thus qualifies as a "public charity" under these rules. By contrast, if the organization satisfied only the IRC § 509(a)(2) public support test, and not the IRC § 509(a)(1) public support test, it would not be a "public charity" under this definition (unless it otherwise qualified) because IRC § 509(a)(2) is referenced in IRC § 170(b)(1)(A)(viii), which is outside the scope of the tax law provisions defining public charities in this context. In general, see Chapter 4 § 3.
[10] Reg. § 1.642(c)-5(a)(5)(v).

any two consecutive determination dates within a tax year may not be greater than three calendar months. In the case of a tax year of less than twelve months, the property in the fund must be valued on the first day of that tax year and on such other days within the year as occur at successive intervals of no greater than three calendar months. Where a valuation date falls on a Saturday, Sunday, or legal holiday,[11] the valuation may be made on either the next preceding day which is not a Saturday, Sunday, or a legal holiday or the next succeeding day which is not a Saturday, Sunday, or a legal holiday, as long as the next such preceding day or next such succeeding day is consistently used where the valuation date falls on a Saturday, Sunday, or legal holiday.[12]

§ 12.2   QUALIFYING POOLED INCOME FUNDS

To qualify under these rules, a pooled income fund must satisfy the following requirements.

(a)   Remainder Interests

Each donor to a pooled income fund must transfer property (which includes money) to the fund and contribute an irrevocable remainder interest in the property to or for the use of a qualified public charity,[13] retaining for himself or herself, or creating for another beneficiary or beneficiaries, a life income interest in the transferred property.[14] A contingent remainder interest is not treated as an irrevocable remainder interest.[15]

(b)   Life Income Interests

Each donor to a pooled income fund must retain for himself or herself for life an income interest in the property transferred to the fund, or create an income interest in the property for the life of one or more beneficiaries, each of whom must be living at the time of

[11] The term "legal holiday" is defined in IRC § 7503.
[12] Reg. § 1.642(c)-5(a)(5)(vi).
[13] See the text accompanied by n. 7, *supra*.
[14] IRC § 642(c)(5)(A); Reg. § 1.642(c)-5(b)(1).
[15] Reg. § 1.642(c)-5(b)(1).

the transfer of the property to the fund by the donor.[16] The term "one or more beneficiaries" includes those members of a named class who are alive and can be ascertained at the time of the transfer of the property to the fund. In the event more than one beneficiary of the income interest is designated, the beneficiaries may enjoy their shares of income from the fund concurrently, consecutively, or both concurrently and consecutively.[17]

These income interest beneficiaries must be individuals. An income interest beneficiary of a pooled income fund cannot be a pet animal, even where the measuring period of the income interest is the lifetime of the animal.[18]

However, it is not required that a donor to a pooled income fund be an individual. The law allows a donor, by means of a pooled income fund gift, to create an income interest in gift property for the life of one or more beneficiaries.[19] Thus, a donor to a pooled income fund may be a person other than an individual, such as a corporation.[20] However, where the donor is not an individual, it cannot (lacking a "natural" life) retain an income interest in its favor, nor can it retain a power exercisable only by will to revoke or terminate the income interest of a designated beneficiary.

The measuring period of an income interest for an income beneficiary of a pooled income fund must be the life of the beneficiary. That is, an individual beneficiary of an income interest may not receive an income interest where the duration of the enjoyment of the income interest is measured by the lifetime of another individual.[21] This is the case even where the other individual is also a beneficiary of an income interest established by the same gift.[22] A provision in the governing instrument of a pooled income fund authorizing the creation of such an interest would prevent the fund from qualifying as a pooled income fund.[23]

---

[16] IRC § 642(c)(5)(A).
[17] Reg. § 1.642(c)-5(b)(2).
[18] Rev. Rul. 78-105, 1978-1 C.B. 295 (so held in the case of a charitable remainder trust (see Chapter 11); presumably, the holding is the same for pooled income funds).
[19] See the text accompanied by n. 14, *supra*.
[20] Rev. Rul. 85-69, 1985-1 C.B. 183.
[21] Rev. Rul. 79-81, 1979-1 C.B. 220.
[22] *Id.*
[23] *Id.*

The donor may retain the power exercisable only by will to revoke or terminate the income interest of any designated beneficiary other than the public charity. The governing instrument must specify at the time of the transfer the particular beneficiary or beneficiaries to whom the income is payable and the share of income distributable to each person so specified.[24]

The public charity to or for the use of which the remainder interest is contributed may be designated as one of the beneficiaries of an income interest. The donor need not retain or create a life interest in all of the income from the property transferred to the fund, provided that any income not payable under the terms of the governing instrument to an income beneficiary is contributed to, and within the tax year in which it is received is paid to, the same public charity to or for the use of which the remainder interest is contributed. However, a charitable contribution deduction is not allowed to the donor for the value of the income interest of the public charity or for the amount of any such income paid to the organization.[25]

(c)   Commingling Requirement

The property transferred to a pooled income fund by each donor must be commingled with, and invested or reinvested with, other property transferred to the fund by other donors in satisfaction of the above requirements.[26] The governing instrument of the pooled income fund must contain a provision reflecting this requirement.[27]

The public charity to or for the use of which the remainder interest is contributed may maintain more than one pooled income fund, provided that each fund is maintained by the organization and is not a device to permit a group of donors to create a fund which may be subject to their manipulation.[28]

The fund must not include property transferred under arrangements other than those specified in these rules.[29] For example, if a contribution to a pooled income fund is made subject to a provision that the income interest of the designated beneficiary is to be mea-

---

[24]*Id.*
[25]*Id.*
[26]IRC § 642(c)(5)(B).
[27]Reg. § 1.642(c)-5(b)(3).
[28]*Id.*
[29]IRC § 642(c)(5)(D).

sured by the life of another individual, that contribution would be a transfer in violation of this requirement.[30]

However, a fund will not be disqualified as a pooled income fund under these rules because any portion of its properties is invested or reinvested jointly with other properties, not a part of the pooled income fund, which are held by, or for the use of, the public charity which maintains the fund. An example of this practice, which is frequently used to "seed" a fund, is transfer to a fund of securities in the general endowment fund of the public charity to or for the use of which the remainder interest is contributed. Where this type of joint investment or reinvestment of properties occurs, records must be maintained which sufficiently identify the portion of the total fund which is owned by the pooled income fund and the income earned by, and attributable to, that portion. Such a joint investment or reinvestment of properties is not treated as an association or partnership for federal tax purposes.[31]

A bank which serves as trustee of more than one pooled income fund may maintain a common trust fund[32] for the collective investment and reinvestment of moneys of such funds.[33]

(d) Prohibition Against Exempt Securities

The property transferred to a pooled income fund by a donor must not include any securities the income from which is exempt from federal income tax, and the fund must not invest in this type of security.[34] The governing instrument of the fund must contain specific prohibitions against accepting or investing in these securities.[35]

(e) Maintenance Requirement

A qualifying pooled income fund must be maintained by the same public charity to or for the use of which the irrevocable remainder

---

[30] Rev. Rul. 79-81, *supra*, n. 21.
[31] *Id.*
[32] These common trust funds are defined in IRC § 584.
[33] Reg. § 1.642(c)-5(b)(3).
[34] IRC § 642(c)(5)(C). This prohibition is chiefly aimed at tax-exempt municipal bonds, the income from which is exempt from federal income taxation by IRC § 103.
[35] Reg. § 1.642(c)-5(b)(4).

interest is contributed.[36] This requirement of maintenance is satisfied where the public charity exercises control directly or indirectly over the fund. For example, this requirement of control is ordinarily met when the public charity has the power to remove the trustee or trustees of the fund and designate a new trustee or trustees.[37]

A national organization that carries out its purposes through local organizations, chapters, or auxiliary bodies with which it has an identity of aims and purposes may maintain a pooled income fund (otherwise satisfying the requirements of these rules) in which one or more local organizations, chapters, or auxiliary bodies that are public charities have been named as recipients of the remainder interests. For example, a national church body may maintain a pooled income fund where donors have transferred property to the fund and contributed an irrevocable remainder interest in it to or for the use of various local churches or educational institutions of the body. The fact that the local organizations or chapters are separately incorporated is immaterial.[38]

A national organization may wish to maintain a pooled income fund for the benefit of local or other charitable organizations but not meet the foregoing criteria. In this circumstance, a donor could recommend (but not direct) that an amount equal to the remainder interest amount associated with the gift be paid by the remainder interest beneficiary over to the other charitable organization, following the death of the income beneficiary or beneficiaries.

(f) Prohibitions on Identity of Trustees

A pooled income fund may not have, and its governing instrument must prohibit the fund from having, as a trustee a donor to the fund or a beneficiary (other than the public charity to or for the use of which the remainder interest is contributed) of an income interest in any property transferred to the fund.[39]

Thus, if a donor or beneficiary (other than the public charity) directly or indirectly has general responsibilities with respect to the fund which are ordinarily exercised by a trustee, the fund does not qualify under these rules. The fact that a donor of property to the

[36] IRC § 642(c)(5)(E).
[37] Reg. § 1.642(c)-5(b)(5).
[38] *Id.* See § 11, *infra.*
[39] IRC § 642(c)(5)(E); Reg. § 1.642(c)-5(b)(6).

fund, or a beneficiary of the fund, is a trustee, officer, director, or other official of the public charity to or for the use of which the remainder interest is contributed ordinarily will not prevent the fund from meeting these requirements.[40]

(g) Income of Beneficiaries

Each beneficiary of a pooled income fund entitled to income of any tax year of the fund must receive the income in an amount determined by the rate of return earned by the fund for that tax year with respect to his or her income interest, compounded as provided below.[41] The governing instrument of the fund must direct the trustee to distribute income currently or within the first sixty-five days following the close of the tax year in which the income is earned. Any such payment made after the close of the tax year must be treated as paid on the last day of the tax year. A statement must be attached to the return of the pooled income fund indicating the date and amount of these payments after the close of the tax year. The beneficiary must include in his or her gross income all amounts properly paid, credited, or required to be distributed to the beneficiary during the tax year or years of the fund ending within or with his or her tax year. The governing instrument of the fund must provide that the income interest of any designated beneficiary must either terminate with the last regular payment which was made before the death of the beneficiary or be prorated to the date of his or her death.[42]

(h) Termination of Life Income Interest

Upon the termination of the income interest retained or created by any donor, the trustee of a pooled income fund must sever from the fund an amount equal to the value of the remainder interest in the property upon which the income interest is based. The value of the remainder interest for this purpose may be either

- its value as of the determination date next succeeding the termination of the income interest, or

---

[40] Reg. § 1.642(c)-5(b)(6).
[41] IRC § 642(c)(5)(F). See § 3, *infra*.
[42] Reg. § 1.642(c)-5(b)(7).

- its value as of the date on which the last regular payment was made before the death of the beneficiary if the income interest is terminated on the payment date.

In one instance, a charitable organization established a fund to attract contributions. The governing instrument of the fund provided that the income interest of each income beneficiary would terminate with the income payment immediately preceding the beneficiary's death. The valuation dates selected were January 1, April 1, July 1, and October 1. The payment dates were March 15, June 15, September 15, and December 15. A beneficiary of an income interest died on May 15. The property to be severed from the fund was valued as of July 1, since that was the valuation date immediately following the date of death (May 15). The determination date that next succeeded the termination on March 15 of the income interest was April 1. The last regular payment prior to the death of the beneficiary was made on March 15. The IRS held that the fund did not qualify as a pooled income fund because the property was neither valued as of the determination date next succeeding the termination of the income interest nor valued as of the date on which the last regular payment was made before the death of the beneficiary.[43]

The amount so severed from the fund must either be paid to, or retained for the use of, the designated public charity, as provided in the governing instrument.[44]

§ 12.3   ALLOCATION OF INCOME TO BENEFICIARY

Every income interest retained or created in property transferred to a pooled income fund must be assigned a proportionate share of the annual income earned by the fund, such share or unit of participation being based on the fair market value of the property on the date of transfer.[45]

(a)   Units of Participation

On each transfer of property by a donor to a pooled income fund, one or more units of participation in the fund must be assigned to

---

[43] Rev. Rul. 76-196, 1976-1 C.B. 178.
[44] Reg. § 1.642(c)-5(b)(8).
[45] Reg. § 1.642(c)-5(c)(1).

the beneficiary or beneficiaries of the income interest retained or created in the property, the number of units of participation being equal to the number obtained by dividing the fair market value of the property by the fair market value of a unit in the fund at the time of the transfer.[46] This is known as the "unit plan."

Under the unit plan, the fair market value of a unit in a pooled income fund at the time of the transfer must be determined by dividing the fair market value of all property in the fund at that time by the number of units then in the fund. The initial fair market value of a unit in a pooled income fund is the fair market value of the property transferred to the fund divided by the number of units assigned to the income interest in that property. The value of each unit of participation will fluctuate with each new transfer of property to the fund in relation to the appreciation or depreciation in the fair market value of the property in the fund, but all units in the fund will always have equal value.[47]

Under the unit plan, the share of income allocated to each unit of participation must be determined by dividing the income of the fund for the tax year by the outstanding number of units in the fund at the end of the year, except that, consistent with the rate of return requirements,[48] income must be allocated to units outstanding during only part of the year by taking into consideration the period of time the units are outstanding. For this purpose, the actual income of the part of the tax year, or a prorated portion of the annual income, may be used, after making such adjustments as are reasonably necessary to reflect fluctuations during the year to the fair market value of the property in the fund.[49]

The governing instrument of a pooled income fund may provide any other reasonable method not described under the unit plan rules for assigning units of participation in the fund and allocating income to the units which reaches a result reasonably consistent with the unit plan rules.[50]

If a transfer of property to the fund by a donor occurs on other than a determination date, the number of units of participation assigned to the income interest in the property may be determined by

[46] Reg. § 1.642(c)-5(c)(2)(i)(a).
[47] Reg. § 1.642(c)-5(c)(2)(i)(b).
[48] See the text accompanied by ns. 41–42, *supra*.
[49] Reg. § 1.642(c)-5(c)(2)(i)(c).
[50] Reg. § 1.642(c)-5(c)(2)(ii).

using the fair market value of the property in the fund on the determination date immediately preceding the date of transfer (determined without regard to the property so transferred), subject, however, to appropriate adjustments on the next succeeding determination date. These adjustments may be made by any reasonable method, including the use of a method whereby the fair market value of the property in the fund at the time of the transfer is deemed to be the average of the fair market values of the property in the fund on the determination dates immediately preceding and succeeding the date of transfer. For purposes of determining this average, any property transferred to the fund between the preceding and succeeding dates, or on the succeeding date, must be excluded.[51]

The application of this rule may be illustrated by the following example:

Example 12.1

The determination dates of a pooled income fund are the first day of each calendar month. On April 1, 1993, the fair market value of the property in the fund was $100,000, at which time 1,000 units of participation are outstanding with a value of $100 each. On April 15, 1993, B transferred property with a fair market value of $50,000 to the fund, retaining for himself for life an income interest in the property. No other property is transferred to the fund after April 1, 1993. On May 1, 1993, the fair market value of the property in the fund, including the property transferred by B, was $160,000. The average of the fair market values of the property in the fund (excluding the property transferred by B) on April 1 and May 1, 1993, was $105,000 ($100,000 + [$160,000 − $50,000] ÷ 2). Accordingly, the fair market value of a unit of participation in the fund on April 15, 1993, at the time of B's transfer may be deemed to be $105 ($105,000/1,000 units), and B was assigned 476.19 units of participation in the fund ($50,000/$105) [52]

(b) Partial Allocation of Income to Charity

Notwithstanding the above rules concerning units of participation, the governing instrument of a pooled income fund may provide that a unit of participation is entitled to share in the income of a fund in

---

[51] Reg. § 1.642(c)-5(c)(2)(iii).
[52] *Id.*

a lesser amount than would otherwise be determined under those rules, provided that the income otherwise allocable to the unit under the rules is paid within the tax year in which it is received to the public charity to or for the use of which the remainder interest is contributed under the governing instrument of the fund.[53]

Application of the foregoing may be illustrated by the following examples:

Example 12.2

On July 1, 1993, A and B transferred separate properties with a fair market value of $20,000 and $10,000, respectively, to a newly created pooled income fund that is maintained by Y University and that uses as its tax year the fiscal year ending June 30. A and B each retain for themselves for life an income interest in the property, the remainder interest being contributed to Y University. The pooled income fund assigned an initial value of $100 to each unit of participation in the fund, and under the governing instruments, A received 200 units and B received 100 units, in the fund. On October 1, 1993, which is a determination date, C transferred property to the fund with a fair market value of $12,000, retaining in herself for life an income interest in the property and contributing the remainder interest to Y University. The fair market value of the property in the fund at the time of C's transfer was $36,000. The fair market value of A's and B's units at the time of the transfer was $120 each ($36,000/300). By reason of her transfer of property, C was assigned 100 units of participation in the fund ($12,000/$120).[54]

Example 12.3

The pooled income fund in Example 12.2 earned $2,000 for its tax year ending June 30, 1994. There were no further contributions of property to the fund in that year. $300 was earned in the first quarter ending September 30, 1993. Therefore, the fund earned $1 per unit for the first quarter ($300 ÷ 300 units outstanding) and $5.75 per unit for the remainder of the tax year ([$2,600 − $300] ÷ 400 units outstanding). The fund distributed its income for the year based on its actual earnings per quarter. The income had to have been distributed as follows:

Continued

---

[53]Reg. § 1.642(c)-5(c)(3).
[54]Reg. § 1.642(c)-5(c)(4), Example (1).

Example 12.3 Continued

Beneficiary		Share of Income
A	$1,350	([200 × $1] + [200 × $5.75])
B	675	([100 × $1] + [100 × $5.75])
C	575	(100 × $5.75).[55]

Example 12.4

On July 1, 1993, A and B transferred separate properties with a fair market value of $10,000 and $20,000, respectively, to a newly created pooled income fund that is maintained by X Hospital and that uses as its tax year the fiscal year ending June 30. A and B each retained in themselves an income interest for life in the property, the remainder interest being contributed to X Hospital. The governing instrument provides that each unit of participation in the fund shall have a value of not more than its initial fair market value; the instrument also provides that the income allocable to appreciation in the fair market value of each unit (to the extent in excess of its initial fair market value) at the end of each quarter of the fiscal year is to be distributed currently to X Hospital. On October 1, 1993, which was a determination date, C contributed to the fund property with a fair market value of $60,000 and retained in herself an income interest for life in the property, the remainder interest being contributed to X Hospital. The initial fair market value of the units assigned to A, B, and C was $100. A, B, and C's units of participation are as follows:

Beneficiary		Units of Participation
A	100	($10,000 ÷ $100)
B	200	($20,000 ÷ $100)
C	600	($60,000 ÷ $100)

The fair market value of the property in the fund at the time of C's contribution was $40,000. The fair market value of the property in the fund was $100,000 on December 31, 1993. The income of the fund for the second quarter ending December 31, 1993, was $2,000. The income was shared by the income beneficiaries and X Hospital as follows:

Continued

---

[55] Reg. § 1.642(c)-5(c)(4), Example (2).

Example 12.4 Continued

Beneficiary	Allocation of Income
A, B, and C	90% ($90,000 ÷ $100,000)
X Hospital	10% ($10,000 ÷ $100,000)

For the quarter ending December 31, 1993, each unit of participation was allocated $2 (90% × $2,000 ÷ 900) of the income earned for that quarter. A, B, C, and X Hospital shared in the income as follows:

Beneficiary	Share of Income	
A	$ 200	(100 × $2)
B	400	(200 × $2)
C	1,200	(600 × $2)
X University	200	(10% × $2,000)[56]

---

§ 12.4   TAX STATUS OF FUND AND BENEFICIARIES

A qualified pooled income fund is not treated as an association for tax purposes,[57] nor does such a fund have to be a trust under local law.[58] Generally, a pooled income fund and its beneficiaries are subject to federal income taxation.[59]

§ 12.5   RECOGNITION OF GAIN OR LOSS ON TRANSFERS

No gain or loss is recognized to a donor on the transfer of property to a pooled income fund.[60] In this instance, the basis of the fund and its holding period with respect to property transferred to the fund by a donor is determined pursuant to the general rules concerning the

---

[56] Reg. § 1.642(c)-5(c)(4), Example (3).
[57] Reg. § 1.642(c)-5(a)(2). The definition of an "association" for tax purposes is the subject of IRC § 7701(a)(3).
[58] Reg. § 1.642(c)-5(a)(2).
[59] *Ibid.* This taxation is under IRC, Part 1, Subchapter J, Chapter 1, although the provisions of Subpart E (relating to grantors and others treated as substantial owners) does not apply to pooled income funds (*id*).
[60] Reg. § 1.642(c)-(5)(a)(3).

basis of property acquired by gift and transferred in trust.[61] If, however, a donor transfers property to a pooled income fund and, in addition to creating or retaining a life income interest in the fund, receives property from the fund, or transfers property to the fund which is subject to an indebtedness, this rule does not apply to the gain realized by reason of the receipt of the property or the amount of the indebtedness (whether or not assumed by the pooled income fund), which is required to be treated as an amount realized on the transfer.[62]

§ 12.6   CHARITABLE CONTRIBUTION DEDUCTION

A charitable contribution deduction is allowed for a transfer of property to a pooled income fund.[63]

In the case of a charitable contribution by means of a pooled income fund, the charitable deduction is equal to the value of the remainder interest. The value of the remainder interest is equal to the fair market value of the property less the value of the income interest.

The value of any interest for life or any remainder interest is determined by using an interest rate (rounded to the nearest two-tenths of one percent) equal to 120 percent of the federal midterm rate, used to determine the issue price (value) of certain debt instruments,[64] in effect for the month in which the valuation date falls.[65]

This valuation is made using tables prepared by the IRS[66] using the most recent mortality experience available.[67] These tables must be revised at least once every ten years to take into account the most recent mortality experience available as of the time of the revision.[68]

If an income, estate, or gift tax charitable contribution is allowable for any part of the property transferred, the individual involved may elect to use the federal midterm rate for either of the two months preceding the month in which the valuation date falls in determining

---

[61] *Ibid.* These rules are the subject of IRC §§ 1015(b) and 1223(2).
[62] *Id.* See Chapter 9 § 5 for a discussion of the bargain sale rules.
[63] IRC § 170(f)(2)(A); Reg. § 1.642(c)-5(a)(4).
[64] IRC § 1274(d)(1).
[65] IRC § 7520(a)(2). A chart of these rates appears as Appendix G.
[66] IRC § 7520(a)(1).
[67] IRC § 7520(c)(3).
[68] *Ibid.*

the value.[69] Otherwise, the rate that is used is the rate in effect in the month of the gift. In the case of transfers of more than one interest in the same property with respect to which a person may use the same rate, the person must use the same rate with respect to each interest.[70]

As directed, the IRS has published valuation tables. These tables reflect the use of interest rates ranging from 2.2 percent to 26 percent. The tables used for determining the value of pooled income fund remainder interests are in *Actuarial Values—Alpha Volume* (IRS Publication 1457), which provides remainder and income factors for one life and two lives. These factors are used for purposes of income, gift, and estate tax calculations.

§ 12.7 MANDATORY PROVISIONS

As references throughout the foregoing portions of this chapter indicate, there are a variety of provisions that must appear in a pooled income fund instrument, as a condition of qualification of the fund under the applicable federal tax rules.

Many of these mandatory provisions are required by the tax regulations. The IRS published sample provisions for inclusion in a pooled income fund declaration of trust and instrument of transfer.[71] Subsequently, the IRS published sample forms of a declaration of trust and instruments of transfer that meet the requirements for a qualified pooled income fund.[72]

Concurrently with the publication of this prototype of a qualifying pooled income fund, the IRS announced that it would no longer issue rulings as to whether a transfer to a pooled income fund qualifies for a charitable deduction or whether a pooled income fund is a qualified one.[73]

---

[69] IRC § 7520(a).
[70] *Id.*
[71] Rev. Rul. 82-38, 1982-1 C.B. 96; Rev. Rul. 85-57, 1985-1 C.B. 182.
[72] Rev. Proc. 88-53, 1988-2 C.B. 712. See Appendix F.
[73] Rev. Proc. 88-54, 1988-2 C.B. 715, amplifying Rev. Proc. 88-3, 1988-1 C.B. 579. This announcement applied to all ruling requests received in the National Office of the IRS after November 28, 1988. Also Rev. Proc. 91-3, 1991-1 C.B. 364, 372 § 4.01, subpar. 33. Prior to that time, the IRS issued rulings as to the qualification of pooled income funds (e.g., IRS Private Letter Ruling 8601041).

Thereafter, the IRS published additional pooled income fund language, concerning the establishment of depreciation reserve funds.[74]

§ 12.8   PRIVATE FOUNDATION RULES

Since pooled income funds are split-interest trusts,[75] they are subject to at least some of the prohibitions that are imposed on private foundations, most particularly the rules concerning self-dealing[76] and so-called taxable expenditures.[77] While reference to the other private foundation rules may not be necessary,[78] it is common practice to include references in the pooled income fund declaration of trust to the other private foundation restrictions—namely, the requirement of income distribution,[79] and the prohibitions on excess business holdings[80] and jeopardizing investments.[81]

§ 12.9   PASSTHROUGH OF DEPRECIATION

In private letter rulings, the IRS recognized that the tax deduction for depreciation can flow through a pooled income fund to the income beneficiaries of the fund in determining their federal income tax liability.[82] However, the benefits arising from this circumstance were initially curbed when the IRS required application of the tax-exempt entity rules in certain of these circumstances, which had the effect of reducing the allowable depreciation deduction.[83] These circumstances arise where the property that is the (or a) medium of investment of the pooled income fund is located on the premises of the charitable organization that maintains the fund or is otherwise available to those who are served by the charitable organization. This

---

[74] Rev. Rul. 90-103, 1990-2 C.B. 159.
[75] IRC § 4947(a)(2); Reg. § 53.4947-1(c)(1)(ii). See *The Law of Tax-Exempt Organizations*, Chapter 27 § 2.
[76] IRC § 4941. See *The Law of Tax-Exempt Organizations*, Chapter 20.
[77] IRC § 4945. See *The Law of Tax-Exempt Organizations*, Chapter 24.
[78] Reg. § 1.642(c)-5(a)(6).
[79] IRC § 4942. See *The Law of Tax-Exempt Organizations*, Chapter 21.
[80] IRC § 4943. See *The Law of Tax-Exempt Organizations*, Chapter 22.
[81] IRC § 4944. See *The Law of Tax-Exempt Organizations*, Chapter 23.
[82] E.g., IRS Private Letter Ruling 8616020.
[83] The tax-exempt entity leasing rules are the subject of *The Law of Tax-Exempt Organizations*, Chapter 47.

430 GIFTS BY MEANS OF POOLED INCOME FUNDS   Ch. 12

is because of the provision of the tax-exempt entity rules that includes within the definition of a "lease" the grant of the "right to use" property, thereby causing the grant of a right to use property to be a so-called "disqualified lease."[84]

Thereafter, however, the IRS ruled that a pooled income fund, to qualify under these rules, must have adequate language concerning a depreciation reserve fund.[85] Specifically, the IRS held that

- if a trustee of a trust that otherwise qualifies as a pooled income fund is not required by the governing instrument of the trust or state law to establish a depreciation reserve fund with respect to any depreciable property held by the trust, the trust does not meet the requirements for a pooled income fund under these rules, and
- if a trustee of a trust that otherwise qualifies as a pooled income fund is required by the governing instrument of the trust to establish a depreciation reserve fund with respect to any depreciable property held by the trust, but the depreciation to be added to the reserve is not required to be determined in accordance with general accepted accounting principles ("GAAP"), the trust does not meet the requirements for a pooled income fund under these rules.

The IRS explained the rationale for these requirements as follows:

. . . [T]he purpose of establishing a depreciation reserve for a pooled income fund is the preservation of the value of the property which will pass to the charitable remainderman. This can be accomplished only by a method that systematically allocates the cost of a capital asset to the years in which the asset is expected to produce income. . . . It is . . . appropriate for a pooled income fund to use a GAAP standard in calculating depreciation, since a GAAP method ensures that the cost of the asset will be allocated systematically over its useful life.

§ 12.10 COMPARISON WITH CHARITABLE REMAINDER TRUSTS

The vehicle used most commonly in planned giving transactions is the charitable remainder trust—the subject of Chapter 11. There are

---

[84] Reg. § 1.168(j)-1T, Q-5, A-5.
[85] Rev. Rul. 90-103, *supra*, n. 74, amplifying Rev. Rul. 82-38, *supra*, n. 71.

some important distinctions between charitable remainder trusts and pooled income funds that warrant highlighting.

First, the remainder interest beneficiary of a charitable remainder trust can be any type of charitable organization.[86] The remainder interest beneficiary of a charitable remainder trust can be any type of public charity or a private foundation.[87] By contrast, the remainder interest beneficiary of a pooled income fund must be a public charity—and can only be particular types of public charities.[88]

Second, the income interest created by a charitable remainder trust must be either an annuity amount or a unitrust amount, both subject to a minimum payout amount.[89] However, the income interest created by a pooled income fund is the pro rata share of the earnings of the fund, whatever they may be.[90]

Third, the income interest term of a charitable remainder trust can be measured by one or more lifetimes or a term of years not to exceed twenty years.[91] By contrast, the income interest term created by a pooled income fund must be for the life of the income beneficiary.[92]

Fourth, a pooled income fund cannot receive or invest in tax-exempt securities.[93] There is no comparable limitation in the case of a charitable remainder trust.

Fifth, a pooled income fund must be maintained by the charitable organization that is the holder of the remainder interests contributed.[94] There is no comparable limitation in the case of a charitable remainder trust.

[86] The term "charitable" is used in this context to mean an organization that is tax-exempt under IRC § 501(a) by reason of being described in IRC § 501(c)(3). See Chapter 4 § 2.
[87] See Chapter 4 § 3.
[88] See the text accompanied by ns. 7–9, *supra*.
[89] See Chapter 12 §§ 5 and 6.
[90] See the text accompanied by ns. 16–25, *supra*.
[91] See Chapter 12 §§ 5 and 6.
[92] See the text accompanied by ns. 21–23, *supra*.
[93] See the text accompanied by ns. 34–35, *supra*.
[94] See the text accompanied by ns. 36–38, *supra*.

§ 12.11   MULTI-ORGANIZATION POOLED INCOME FUNDS

The conventional pooled income fund is established and maintained by one charitable organization. The organization uses the fund as a fund-raising vehicle, and the gifts flow to the fund and thereafter the remainder interest portion in the gifts is transferred to that charitable organization.

However, in some situations, a pooled income fund is established in circumstances where more than one charitable organization is the ultimate beneficiary of the remainder interest in property transferred to the fund. There has been some confusion and controversy over the extent to which there can be multiple charitable beneficiaries of a pooled income fund. The IRS has been studying this matter and, late in 1992, issued two revenue rulings on the point.

(a)   National Organizations With Affiliates

It is common for a national charitable organization to have local charitable organizations (such as state chapters) that are affiliated with it. The local organizations are generally under the supervision and control of the national organization; these entities have an identity of aims and purposes.

One of the issues presented to the IRS was whether a national organization such as this can establish a pooled income fund that it will maintain for itself and for those of the local organizations that expressly consent to participate in the fund.[95] The declaration of trust and instruments of transfer (collectively, the "governing instrument") meet all of the other requirements of the law, so that the fund would qualify as a pooled income fund if the maintenance requirement is satisfied.[96] Under the terms of the governing instrument of this fund, a donor can designate that the remainder interest in the gift be transferred either to the national charitable organization or to one of

---

[95] It is assumed for purposes of this analysis that the national organization and each of the participating local organizations is the type of organization that is qualified to maintain a pooled income fund (that is, an organization described in at least one of the provisions of IRC § 170(b)(1)(A)(i)-(vi)). (See § 1, *supra*, text accompanied by ns. 7–9).

[96] That is, the qualification of the fund turned on compliance with IRC § 642(c)(5)(E) (see § 2, *supra*, text accompanied by ns. 36–38).

the participating local charitable organizations. The governing instrument also provides that a designated local organization may not sever its interest in the fund prior to the death of the named income beneficiary. The governing instrument further provides that, if the designated local organization is no longer affiliated with the national organization when the remainder interest would be transferred, the remainder interest will be transferred to the national organization or to another affiliated local organization selected by the national organization.

The tax law requirements for a pooled income fund include the rule that the fund must be maintained "by the organization to which the remainder interest is contributed" and of which no donor or income interest beneficiary is a trustee.[97] This requirement of maintenance is satisfied where the public charity exercises control, directly or indirectly, over the fund.[98] These requirements also provide that a national organization that carries out its purposes through local organizations (such as chapters) with which it has an identity of aims and purposes may maintain a pooled income fund in which one or more local organizations that are public charities have been named as recipients of the remainder interests.[99] For example, a national church body may maintain a pooled income fund where donors have transferred property to the fund and contributed an irrevocable remainder interest in it to, or for the use of, various local churches or educational institutions of the body. All the facts and circumstances are to be examined to determine whether a national organization and its local organizations meet this standard; the fact that the local organizations are incorporated is immaterial for this purpose.[100] The IRS concluded that this maintenance requirement ensures "that the charitable organization [that maintains a pooled income fund] would look out for its own best interests by not manipulating the investments and by preserving the value of the remainder."[101]

Reviewing these facts, the IRS ruled that the various provisions in the governing instruments of the pooled income fund ensure that there will always be an identity of aims and interests between the national organization and any local organization that actually receives

---

[97] IRC § 642(c)(5)(E).
[98] Reg. § 1.642(c)-5(b)(5).
[99] *Id*. See § 2, *supra*, text accompanied by n. 38.
[100] *Id*.
[101] Rev. Rul. 92-107, 1992-51 I.R.B. 4.

a remainder interest in the fund. The IRS concluded that the maintenance requirement would be achieved in these circumstances because of the "close relationship" between the national organization and its local organizations.[102] Thus, this pooled income fund was held to qualify under the federal tax law requirements.

(b) Pooled Income Funds of Community Trusts

The IRS also reviewed the situation where a pooled income fund is maintained by a community trust[103] and either

1. The donor permits the community trust to determine the charitable organizations that will benefit from the remainder interest, or

2. The donor may designate the specific charitable organization for whose benefit the community trust will use the remainder interest.

In this connection, the IRS reviewed two situations.[104]

In the first of these situations, a community trust proposed to establish a pooled income fund that it will maintain. Under the terms of the governing instrument, the donor contributes a remainder interest in property to the community trust and it will determine how, and by whom, the remainder interest will be used for charitable purposes.

In the second of these situations, a community trust proposed to establish a pooled income fund that it will maintain. Under the terms of the governing instrument, the donor contributes a remainder interest in property to the community trust but the donor may designate the specific charitable organization for whose benefit the

---

[102] *Id.*

[103] A "community trust" (or "community foundation") is a publicly supported charity that is described in Reg. § 1.170A-(e)(10)) (see *The Law of Tax-Exempt Organizations*, Chapter 17 § 2, text accompanied by ns. 95–104).

[104] Again, there are two underlying assumptions: (1) each of the potential beneficiary organizations qualifies as a public charity eligible to maintain a pooled income fund (see n. 95, *supra*), and (2) the pooled income fund would otherwise qualify under the tax law requirements, so that the only issue is with respect to the maintenance requirement (see n. 96, *supra*).

community trust will use the remainder interest. As required by law, the governing body of the community trust has the power to modify any restriction on the distribution of designated funds if in the sole judgment of the governing body the restriction becomes unnecessary, incapable of fulfillment, or inconsistent with the charitable needs of the community or area served.[105]

In the first of these situations, the IRS ruled that the fund meets the federal tax law requirements of a pooled income fund. There, the community trust has the discretion to determine how the remainder interest is to be used for charitable purposes. Although the community trust cannot itself use the property contributed to the pooled income fund, the trust is accorded the "broadest latitude" in choosing the charitable organizations that will benefit from the remainder interest.[106] Thus, for purposes of the pooled income fund requirements, the IRS held that a donor in this circumstance would be making a gift of the remainder interest to the community trust.[107]

In the second of these circumstances, the community trust wanted to maintain a pooled income fund through which donors would transfer remainder interests to the trust. However, each donor would be able to designate the charitable organization for whose benefit the community trust must use the remainder interest. Except for certain unusual circumstances,[108] the community trust has no discretion as to which organization will benefit from the remainder interest. Thus, the IRS ruled that a donor in this circumstance would be treated as having made a contribution of the remainder interest, not to the community trust, but rather to the charitable organization designated by the donor.[109] Thus, because the charitable organization designated by the donor does not maintain the pooled income fund, the IRS ruled that the fund, if established, would fail to meet the tax law requirements and, therefore, would fail to qualify as a pooled income fund.[110]

[105]Reg. § 1.170A-(e)(11)(v)(B)(i).
[106]Rev. Rul. 92-108, 1992-51 I.R.B. 5.
[107]Id. Situation 1.
[108]Reg. § 1.170A-(e)(11)(v)(B)(i).
[109]Rev. Rul. 92-108, supra, n. 106, Situation 2.
[110]Id. This revenue ruling is effective for all pooled income funds with respect to contributions made after December 31, 1992 (id.).
As this book went to publication, the IRS revoked Rev. Rul. 92-108, supra, n. 106 (Rev. Rul. 93-8, 1993 I.R.B.), deciding to subject the matter to "further study" (Notice 93-9, 1993 I.R.B.).

(c) Other Circumstances

There may be other circumstances where a multi-organization pooled income fund (or something approximating it) may be established. For example, there may be a national organization with chapters (or local organizations bearing other designations) where all of the facts in the first of these two revenue rulings exist but for the fact that the chapters, while loosely affiliated, are not under the general supervision and control of the national organization. Or, there may be a national organization where the local organizations are members of it, so that there is no general supervision and control and perhaps not the requisite "affiliation." The question arises—which is not answered by either of these 1992 rulings—whether the national organization can maintain a qualified pooled income fund for itself and either of these categories of local organizations.

Presumably, the rule as developed by the first of these revenue rulings would lead to the conclusion that a pooled income fund established for the benefit of the local organizations would not qualify. This is because of an absence of the requisite affiliation.

However, the rule as developed by the second of these revenue rulings, in the first situation, would seem to cause the pooled income fund to qualify. Nonetheless, where the fund meets the second of these situations, it would not qualify. Therefore, a national organization in these circumstances would be best advised to allow a donor to recommend the local organization to which the remainder interest in the gift will be transferred, rather than allow the donor to designate the local organization beneficiary.[111]

---

[111] For further reading about pooled income funds, see Appendix H.

13

Charitable Gift Annuities

A form of planned gift vehicle is the "charitable gift annuity,"[1] created by means of an agreement between a donor and a charitable organization, rather than by means of a split-interest trust.[2] The income interest is reflected in an annuity obligation of the donee charitable organization. Once the requirement to pay the annuity has expired, the remaining property becomes that of the charitable organization involved. A federal income tax deduction is generally available for the value of the remainder interest that was created by the contract.

§ 13.1 CONTRACT AS VEHICLE FORM

Unlike the charitable remainder trust, the pooled income fund, and the charitable lead trust,[3] the charitable gift annuity is not based upon use of a split-interest trust. Rather, the annuity is reflected in an agreement between the donor and charitable donee, where the donor agrees to make a gift of money and/or property and the donee agrees, in return, to provide the donor (and/or someone else) with an annuity. (Recall that an annuity is a fixed amount, paid annually.)

The charitable gift annuity is nonetheless a planned giving method that is based upon the concept of split interests—an income interest and a remainder interest (though not, as noted, established through a trust).

In fact, the donor, in the process of creating a charitable gift annuity, is engaging in two transactions, albeit with one payment:

---

[1]The concept of planned giving is discussed in Chapter 3. That chapter also contains a general description of charitable gift annuities.
[2]The concept of the split-interest trust is discussed in Chapter 3.
[3]See Chapters 11, 12 and 15, respectively.

the purchase of an annuity and the making of a charitable gift. It is the latter that gives rise to the charitable deduction. One sum (money and/or property) is transferred; the amount in excess of that necessary to purchase the annuity is the charitable gift portion of the transaction. There is generally a federal income tax charitable contribution deduction for the value of the remainder interest created in this manner.[4]

§ 13.2   DETERMINING THE CHARITABLE DEDUCTION

As with the annuity paid out of a charitable remainder annuity trust,[5] the annuity resulting from the creation of a charitable gift annuity arrangement is a fixed amount paid at regular intervals. The amount paid is dependent upon the age of the beneficiary, determined at the time the contribution is made.

As noted, the amount that generates the charitable deduction is basically the amount equal to the fair market value of the money and/or property transferred, reduced by the value of the income interest. The annuity is usually calculated using a rate of return set by the Committee on Gift Annuities.

The value of any interest for life or any remainder interest is determined by using an interest rate (rounded to the nearest two-tenths of one percent) equal to 120 percent of the federal midterm rate, used to determine the issue price (value) of certain debt instruments,[6] in effect for the month in which the valuation date falls.[7]

This valuation is made using tables prepared by the IRS[8] that chart the most recent mortality experience available.[9] These tables must be revised at least once every ten years to take into account the most recent mortality experience available as of the time of the revision.[10]

If an income, estate, or gift tax charitable contribution is allowable for any part of the property transferred, the individual involved may elect to use the federal midterm rate for either of the two months

---

[4]Reg. § 1.170A-1(d)(1).
[5]See Chapter 11 § 5.
[6]IRC § 1274(d)(1).
[7]IRC § 7520(a)(2). A chart of these rates appears as Appendix G.
[8]IRC § 7520(a)(1).
[9]IRC § 7520(c)(3).
[10]*Id.*

preceding the month in which the valuation date falls in determining the value.[11] Otherwise, the rate that is used is the rate in effect in the month of the gift. In the case of transfers of more than one interest in the same property with respect to which a person may use the same rate, the person must use the same rate with respect to each interest.[12]

As directed, the IRS has published valuation tables. These tables reflect the use of interest rates ranging from 2.2 percent to 26 percent. The tables used for determining the value of charitable gift annuity remainder interests are in *Actuarial Values—Alpha Volume*.[13]

§ 13.3   TAX TREATMENT TO DONOR

A portion of the annuity paid is tax-free, being a return of capital. This amount is a function of the donor's life expectancy, obtained by calculating the "expected return multiple."[14] The tax-free portion of the annuity payment is determined by ascertaining the "exclusion ratio," which is an amount equal to the investment on the contract divided by the expected return.

The balance of the annuity payment is ordinary income, which is taxable.[15] All of the annuity becomes taxable once the capital element is returned.

Where appreciated securities are given, there will be—in addition to the foregoing consequences—capital gain on the appreciation that is attributable to the value of the annuity. It is because of this feature of this type of transaction that the charitable gift annuity transfer constitutes a "bargain sale."[16] Thus, the basis in the gift property must be allocated between the gift portion and the sale (annuity) portion of the transfer.

The manner in which capital gain is recognized in this setting is dependent upon the language in the annuity agreement. If the donor is the annuitant, the capital gain can be recognized ratably over the individual's life expectancy. More specifically, the capital gain can be

[11] IRC § 7520(a).
[12] *Id.*
[13] IRS Publication 1457.
[14] Reg. § 1.1011-2(c).
[15] IRC § 72; Reg. § 1.1011-2(c).
[16] See Chapter 9 § 5.

recognized ratably in this context where

- the annuity is
  - nonassignable, or
  - assignable but only to the charitable organization involved, and
- one of the following is the case
  - the transferor is the only annuitant, or
  - the transferor and a designated survivor annuitant or annuitants are the only annuitants.[17]

In other circumstances, the gain must be recognized in the year of the charitable gift annuity transaction.

§ 13.4   DEFERRED PAYMENT GIFT ANNUITIES

Frequently, the annuity payment period begins with the creation of the annuity payment obligation. However, with the charitable gift annuity planned giving transaction, the initiation of the payment period can be postponed to a future date. The term usually used in this connection is "deferred" (rather than "postponed"), so that this type of arrangement is called the "deferred payment" charitable gift annuity.

The timing of receipt of the annuity can be deferred to lower-income years (such as retirement years), to reduce income taxation of the annuity, with the gift element of the transaction deductible in higher-income years.

§ 13.5   ESTATE AND GIFT TAX CONSEQUENCES

Where a donor names another individual as the annuitant, the donor is making a gift to that other individual. The amount of this gift is the value of the annuity.[18] Where the spouse of the donor is the only annuitant, the gift is sheltered from the federal gift tax by the gift tax marital deduction.[19]

Where another individual is the annuitant under a charitable gift annuity arrangement, and where the donor dies within three years of

[17] Reg. §§ 1.1011-2(a)(4)(ii) and 1.1011-2(c), Example (8).
[18] IRC § 2503(a).
[19] IRC § 2523(a), (b)(1).

the date of the transaction, any gift tax paid because of the gift must be included in the donor's estate.[20]

§ 13.6 UNRELATED BUSINESS INCOME IMPLICATIONS

An otherwise tax-exempt charitable organization[21] will lose or be denied tax exemption if a substantial part of its activities consists of the provision of "commercial-type insurance."[22] Otherwise, the activity of providing commercial-type insurance is treated as the conduct of an unrelated trade or business[23] and taxed under the rules pertaining to taxable insurance companies.[24]

The term "commercial-type insurance" generally means any insurance of a type provided by commercial insurance companies.[25]

For this purpose, the issuance of annuity contracts is considered the provision of insurance.[26] However, these rules do not apply to a charitable gift annuity, which is defined for this purpose as an annuity where

- a portion of the amount paid in connection with the issuance of the annuity is allowable as a charitable deduction for federal income or estate tax purposes, and
- the annuity is described in the special rule for annuities in the law concerning unrelated debt-financed income[27] (determined as if any amount paid in money in connection with the issuance of the annuity were property).[28]

§ 13.7 UNRELATED DEBT-FINANCED INCOME IMPLICATIONS

A form of income that can be taxable to charitable and other types of tax-exempt organizations is "unrelated debt-financed income." Basi-

---

[20] IRC § 2035(c).
[21] That is, an organization described in IRC § 501(c)(3).
[22] IRC § 501(m).
[23] See Chapter 4 § 4.
[24] IRC Subchapter L.
[25] See *The Law of Tax-Exempt Organizations*, Chapter 28 § 7.
[26] IRC § 501(m)(4).
[27] See the text accompanied by n. 33, *infra*.
[28] IRC § 501(m)(3)(E), (5).

cally, this is a form of unrelated income, which is investment income that is traceable in one way or another to borrowed funds.[29]

In computing a tax-exempt organization's unrelated business taxable income, there must be included with respect to each debt-financed property which is unrelated to the organization's exempt function—as an item of gross income derived from an unrelated trade or business—an amount of income from the property, subject to tax in the proportion in which the property is financed by the debt.[30] The term "debt-financed property" means (with certain exceptions) all property held to produce income and with respect to which there is an "acquisition indebtedness" at any time during the tax year (or during the preceding 12 months, if the property was disposed of during the year).[31]

Acquisition indebtedness, with respect to debt-financed property, means the unpaid amount of (1) the indebtedness incurred by the tax-exempt organization in acquiring or improving the property, (2) the indebtedness incurred before any acquisition or improvement of the property if the indebtedness would not have been incurred but for the acquisition or improvement, and (3) the indebtedness incurred after the acquisition or improvement of the property if the indebtedness would not have been incurred but for the acquisition or improvement and the incurrence of the indebtedness was reasonably foreseeable at the time of the acquisition or improvement.[32]

There are several exceptions to the scope of the definition of "acquisition indebtedness." One of these exceptions is that the term does not include an obligation to pay an annuity which is

- the sole consideration issued in exchange for property if, at the time of the exchange, the value of the annuity is less than 90 percent of the value of the property received in the exchange,
- payable over the life of one individual who is living at the time the annuity is issued, or over the lives of two individuals living at that time, and
- payable under a contract which does not guarantee a minimum amount of payments or specify a maximum amount of payments

[29] IRC § 514. See *The Law of Tax-Exempt Organizations*, Chapter 20.
[30] IRC §§ 514(a)(1), 512(b)(4).
[31] IRC § 514(b)(1).
[32] IRC § 514(c)(1).

and does not provide for any adjustment of the amount of the annuity payments by reference to the income received from the transferred property or any other property.[33]

§ 13.8 CONTRAST WITH OTHER PLANNED GIFT METHODS

Because the arrangement creating a charitable gift annuity is by contract between donor and donee, all of the assets of the charitable organization are subject to the liability for ongoing payment of the annuities. (By contrast, with most planned giving techniques, the resources for payment of income are confined to those in a split-interest trust.) That is why a few states impose a requirement that charities establish a reserve for the payment of gift annuities, and why many charitable organizations are reluctant to embark upon a gift annuity program. However, charitable organizations that are reluctant to commit to the ongoing payment of annuities can eliminate the risk by reinsuring them.

With the charitable gift annuity, the gift portion of the transaction is made immediately available to the recipient charitable organization for its use.[34]

[33]IRC § 514(c)(5).
[34]For further reading about charitable gift annuities, see Appendix H.

14

Other Gifts of Remainder Interests

An earlier chapter[1] considered how the federal income tax law under-lying planned giving is based on the concept of partial interests. The charitable contribution deduction (if there is one) is for the gift of a remainder interest or an income interest.

§ 14.1 OVERVIEW

The law is quite specific as to the circumstances where a charitable contribution deduction arises, particularly where the gift is made using a trust. Basically, there is no federal income tax charitable contribution deduction unless the gift meets one of a variety of stringent tests.[2] Related to this point is the rule of law that a charita-ble contribution consisting of a transfer of a future interest in tangi-ble personal property is treated as made only when all intervening interests in, and rights to the actual possession or enjoyment of, the property have expired or are held by persons other than the donor or those related to the donor.[3]

Otherwise, there are few situations where a federal income tax charitable contribution deduction is available for a gift of a partial interest. (The rules in this regard are essentially the same in the gift and estate tax setting.[4] One exception is the special set of rules concerning certain gifts of works of art, as distinct from the copy-

---

[1]See Chapter 3.
[2]IRC § 170(f)(3)(A). See Chapter 9 § 9.
[3]IRC § 170(a)(3). See Chapter 9 § 8.
[4]See Chapter 8.

rights of then, which can lead to an estate and gift tax charitable deduction.[5])

Indeed, there are only three of these situations. They are the following:

- so-called "qualified conservation contributions;"[6]
- contributions of remainder interests in a personal residence or farm;[7]
- contributions of an undivided portion of the donor's entire interest in the property.[8]

§ 14.2   CONTRIBUTIONS OF REMAINDER INTERESTS IN PERSONAL RESIDENCE OR FARM

There may be a federal income tax charitable contribution deduction arising from a gift of a remainder interest in a personal residence or farm, even though the gift is not made in trust and is irrevocable.[9]

The deduction is based on the value of the remainder interest.[10] In determining this value, depreciation (computed on the straight-line method) and depletion of the property may be taken into account.[11]

(a)   Personal Residence

A "personal residence" is defined for this purpose as a property that is used by its owner as a personal residence; it does not have to be the owner's principal residence.[12] For example, a vacation home would likely qualify under this definition.[13] Indeed, there is no restriction on the form which a personal residence may take. All that is

---

[5]IRC §§ 2055(e)(4) and 2522(c)(3). See Chapter 9 § 1.
[6]IRC § 170(f)(3)(B)(iii). See Chapter 9 § 6.
[7]IRC § 170(f)(3)(B)(i). See § 2, *infra*.
[8]IRC § 170(f)(3)(B)(ii). See § 3, *infra*.
[9]IRC § 170(f)(3)(B)(i); Reg. § 1.170A-7(b)(3), (4).
[10]*Id.*
[11]IRC § 170(f)(4); Reg. § 1.170A-12(b)(2).
[12]Reg. § 1.170A-7(b)(3).
[13]*Id.*

required for a facility to qualify as a personal residence is that it contain facilities for cooking, sleeping, and sanitation.[14]

The term "personal residence" also includes stock owned by a donor as a tenant-stockholder in a cooperative housing corporation[15] if the dwelling which the donor is entitled to occupy as a stockholder is used by the donor as his or her personal residence.[16]

In general, a "personal residence" does not include household furnishings that are not fixtures.[17] Thus, there is no charitable deduction for a contribution of a remainder interest in household furnishings contained in a decedent's personal residence at the time of death.[18]

In this context, the charitable remainder interest must be in the residence itself and not simply in the proceeds to be derived from the sale of the residence at a future date.[19] The IRS so held in the setting of a contribution of a remainder interest in a decedent's personal residence bequeathed to charity, under a will which provided that the property is to be sold upon the life tenant's death and the entire proceeds of the sale are to be paid to a charitable organization.[20] However, a charitable deduction will be allowed for the value of a remainder interest in a personal residence where the residence is to be sold and the proceeds distributed to a charitable organization, as long as local law permits the charity to elect distribution of the residence itself.[21] The charitable deduction will be allowed, because a gift of a remainder interest in a personal residence is given to charity and to an individual as tenants in common, for the value of the interest received by the charity.[22] The deduction

---

[14]Rev. Rul. 74-241, 1974-1 C.B. 68. The IRS held that a yacht which "contains all of the amenities found in a house" qualifies as a "personal residence" (IRS Private Letter Ruling 8015017).

[15]IRC § 216(b)(1), (2).

[16]Reg. § 1.170A-7(b)(3).

[17]E.g., Reg. § 1.1034-1(c)(3).

[18]Rev. Rul. 76-165, 1976-1 C.B. 279.

[19]Rev. Rul. 76-543, 1976-2 C.B. 287, amp. by Rev. Rul. 77-169, 1977-1 C.B. 286.

[20]Rev. Rul. 77-169, *supra*, n. 19.

[21]Rev. Rul. 83-158, 1983-2 C.B. 159, distinguishing Rev. Rul. 77-169, *supra*, n. 19; and Rev. Rul. 76-543, *supra*, n. 19. Also *Blackford, Estate of* v. *Commissioner*, 77 T.C. 1246 (1981).

[22]Rev. Rul. 87-37, 1987-1 C.B. 295.

will also be allowed, notwithstanding the fact that the applicable law (known as "mortmain art") requires the charitable recipient to dispose of the property within ten years of the date of acquisition.[23] In the last of these situations, the IRS noted that the "circumstance does not lend itself to abuse" because the charitable organization is receiving the . . . [property] in its original form and can sell the property for itself in the way that is most advantageous and most likely to realize the full value of the property."[24]

As noted, this type of remainder interest gift cannot be made by means of a trust. (The nontrust contribution to a charitable organization of a remainder interest in a personal residence, with retention of an estate in the property for life or for a term of years is not considered a transfer in trust.[25])

One court had the opportunity to review this matter in some detail (albeit in the context of the federal estate tax charitable deduction) and construed the provision as meaning that the remainder interest, to result in a charitable deduction, cannot pass through a trust.[26] An individual created a trust in his will by which a life estate was created in two personal residences for the benefit of his sister, with the remainder interest destined for charitable organizations. The court traced the legislative history of the general rule requiring gifts of this nature to be in a qualifying trust and the rule creating an exception for nontrust gifts of remainder interests in personal residences. It found that the trust did not conform to the requirements of a charitable remainder trust (in part because of authority granted to the trustee), the rules as to which were created "to eliminate possible abuses in the administration of trusts which might operate to deprive the charity of the future remainder interest" for which there has been a charitable deduction.[27] The court added that "[t]his concern is no less present with respect to personal residences which first pass through a trust not approved" by the general rules.[28] The court wrote that "[u]nlike an outright gift of a remainder interest in a residence where the charity is guaranteed the eventual deed upon

---

[23] Rev. Rul. 84-97, 1984-2 C.B. 196.

[24] *Id.* at 197.

[25] Reg. § 1.170A-7(b)(3).

[26] *Ellis First National Bank of Bradenton v. United States*, 550 F.2d 9 (Ct. Cl. 1977).

[27] *Id.* at 16.

[28] *Id.*

the termination of the life estate, a remainder interest which passes through a trust and is subject to the trustee's exercise of discretionary powers, is not certain to be realized by the charity."[29] The court found that the "potential for abuse is dramatically evident" in the trust involved in the case[30] and upheld the tax regulations making it clear that these gifts, to qualify for charitable deductions, cannot be in trust.

The IRS ruled that a charitable deduction is not allowable for a gift of a remainder interest in a decedent's personal residence passing to charity upon the death of the decedent's child for whom the residence was held in a testamentary trust, valid under local law, that was neither a charitable remainder annuity trust, charitable remainder unitrust, or pooled income fund.[31]

Also, as noted, this type of gift must be irrevocable. Thus, the IRS ruled that a charitable deduction was not allowable for the gift of a remainder interest in a personal residence to a charitable organization where the donors placed a condition on the gift requiring the donee to sell its remainder interest and receive cash in lieu of it if the donors decided to sell the residence before they die.[32] Indeed, a contingency of any type is likely to eliminate the deduction, such as a provision that the property in the remainder interest will pass to another individual instead of a charitable organization under certain circumstances.[33]

The charitable organization must be given the right to possession, dominion, and control of the property.[34] The deduction is not defeated simply because the charitable organization that is the donee fails to actually take possession of the property.[35]

(b)   Farm

A "farm" is defined for this purpose as any land used by the donor or a tenant of the donor for the production of crops, fruits, or other

[29] *Id.*
[30] *Id.*
[31] Rev. Rul. 76-357, 1976-2 C.B. 285. Also *Cassidy, Estate of* v. *Commissioner*, 49 T.C.M. 580 (1985).
[32] Rev. Rul. 77-305, 1977-2 C.B. 72.
[33] Rev. Rul. 85-23, 1985-1 C.B. 327.
[34] Reg. § 1.170A-7(b)(1)(i).
[35] *Winokur* v. *Commissioner*, 90 T.C. 733 (1988).

agricultural products or for the sustenance of livestock.[36] A farm includes the improvements on it.[37] The term "livestock" is defined to include cattle, hogs, horses, mules, donkeys, sheep, goats, captive fur-bearing animals, chickens, turkeys, pigeons, and other poultry.[38] The words "any land" does not mean the entire farm acreage owned and used by the donor or his or her tenant for the production of crops or the sustenance of livestock; it can include any portion of farm acreage so used.[39] It can be property that is subject to a conservation easement.[40]

As noted, this type of gift, to be deductible, cannot be made in trust.[41] A contribution not in trust to a charitable organization of a remainder interest in a farm, with retention of an estate in the farm for life or for a term of years, would give rise to a charitable deduction for the value of the remainder interest not transferred in trust.

The various points of law concerning the charitable contribution deduction for gifts of remainder interests in personal residences[42] should also apply in the setting of gifts of remainder interests in farms.

§ 14.3 UNDIVIDED PORTIONS OF ENTIRE INTERESTS IN PROPERTY

There is a federal income tax charitable contribution deduction for a gift of an undivided portion of the donor's entire interest in an item of property.[43] This type of deduction is available only where the gift is not in trust.[44]

An undivided portion of a donor's entire interest in property must

---

[36]Reg. § 1.170A-7(b)(4).
[37]Id.
[38]Id.
[39]Rev. Rul. 78-303, 1978-2 C.B. 122.
[40]IRS Private Letter Ruling 8202137.
[41]Of course, if the trust qualifies (such as a qualified charitable remainder trust (see Chapter 11)), a deduction for the remainder interest would be available. If the trust does not qualify, once again there would not be a charitable deduction (e.g., IRS Private Letter Ruling 8110016).
[42]See § 2, supra.
[43]IRC § 170(f)(3)(B)(ii); Reg. § 1.170A-7(b)(1)(i).
[44]Reg. § 1.170A-7(b)(1)(i).

- consist of a fraction or percentage of each and every substantial interest or right owned by the donor in the property, and
- extend over the entire term of the donor's interest in the property and in other property into which the property may be converted.[45]

Example 14.1

In 1988, B was given a life estate in an office building for the life of A. B had no other interest in the office building. B was allowed an income tax charitable deduction for his contribution in 1993 to charity of a one-half interest in the life estate in a transfer which was not made in trust. The contribution by B was a contribution of an undivided portion of the donor's entire interest in property.[46]

Example 14.2

In 1989, C was given the remainder interest in a trust created under the will of her father. C had no other interest in the trust. C was allowed an income tax charitable contribution deduction for her contribution in 1993 to charity of a 20 percent interest in the remainder interest in a transfer which was not made in trust. This contribution by C was considered a contribution of an undivided portion of her entire interest in the property.[47]

Also, an income tax charitable contribution is allowed:

- if a person owns 100 acres of land and makes a contribution of 50 acres to a charitable organization,[48] or
- for a contribution of property to a charitable organization where the organization is given the right, as a tenant in common with the donor, to possession, dominion, and control of the property for a portion of each year appropriate to its interest in the property.[49]

[45] *Id.*
[46] *Id.*
[47] *Id.*
[48] *Id.*
[49] *Id.*

However, a charitable contribution in perpetuity of an interest in property not in trust, where the donor transfers some specific rights and retains other substantial rights, is not considered a contribution of an undivided portion of the donor's interest in property under this rule.[50] Thus, for example, a charitable deduction is not allowable for the value of an immediate and perpetual gift not in trust of an interest in original historic motion picture films to a charitable organization where the donor retains the exclusive right to make reproductions of the films and to exploit the reproductions commercially.[51] Likewise, a charitable deduction was not allowed for the contribution of an overriding royalty interest or a net profits interest to a charitable organization by the owner of a working interest under an oil and gas lease, because the owner carved out and contributed only a portion of the interest.[52]

This body of law allows for creative tax and charitable planning, as indicated in the following examples.

- An individual transferred an undivided two-fifths interest in land to a charitable organization and retained an undivided three-fifths interest in the property. At the time of this transfer, this individual intended to make a gift to the same charitable organization of the retained interest. However, the individual leased the retained interest to the charitable organization at a fair rental value, with an option in the donee to purchase the retained interest. The lease provided that if, during its term, the individual made further gifts to the charitable organization of all or part of the three-fifths interest, the rent payable under the lease would be proportionately reduced. The IRS ruled that there was a charitable contribution deduction for the fair market value of the undivided two-fifths interest in the property contributed to the organization and that contributions of all or a part of the retained three-fifths interest in the property to the charitable organization would also give rise to a charitable deduction.[53]

- An individual owned approximately 30 acres of improved real property. This individual planned to retain all rights to approxi-

[50] *Id.*
[51] *Id.*
[52] Rev. Rul. 88-37, 1988-1 C.B. 97.
[53] Rev. Rul. 58-261, 1958-1 C.B. 143.

mately two acres of the property. The individual planned to make a series of contributions to a charitable organization of undivided interests as tenant in common in the balance of the acreage. Under each deed conveying an undivided interest, the charitable organization will have the right to possession, dominion, and control of the approximately 28 acres for a portion of each year appropriate to the interest conveyed. To enable the charitable organization to use the entire 30 acres for the entirety of the first year in which the individual conveyed the 28 acres, the individual planned to grant to the charitable organization a one-year lease of the retained undivided interest in the 28 acres and the two acres not subject to any undivided interest in the charity. The lease required the charity to pay all expenses for upkeep, maintenance, and repair, and any taxes and assessments levied upon the 30 acres. The charitable organization was also required to bear the expense of any improvements it made on the 30 acres, without regard as to whether the improvements are made to the two acres or the 28 acres. The IRS ruled that the fair market value of the undivided interests conveyed to the charitable organization will be deductible as charitable contributions in the years made (and that the amounts equal to any expenses paid or incurred, or any improvements made, by the charitable organization with respect to the 30 acres during the one-year lease term will be items of gross income to this individual).[54]

• An individual had an extensive collection of paintings and sculptures that were kept in the individual's home. A museum (a public charity[55]) wanted to acquire the entire collection at one time but could not because of a lack of exhibit space and money. So the parties agreed that the museum would acquire the collection by means of a series of bargain sales.[56] Under the terms of the agreement, the museum paid a total of $8x for the

[54]IRS Private Letter Ruling 8204220.
[55]This distinction is noted because, if the museum were a private foundation, the ensuing charitable deductions would have to be confined to allocable portions of the donor's basis in the property (see Chapter 6, text accompanied by n. 30). Also, no reduction in the deduction was required because the donated property was used by the charitable donee for purposes related to its tax exemption (see Chapter 6 § 6).
[56]Bargain sales are the subject of Chapter 9 § 5.

collection, an amount that was substantially less than the fair market value of the collection. The initial payment was $2x. The remaining $6x was payable in equal installments of $1x over the six successive years following the year in which the initial payment was made. After making a payment, the museum acquired an undivided ownership interest in each and every item contained in the collection. The amount of undivided interest acquired by the museum was computed as follows: the percentage of ownership interest, less the total amount paid by the museum, divided by $8x. Because of the space difficulties, the collection was displayed at this individual's personal residence. During those years, the museum and the general public had access to the collection for at least the portion of the year as was determined by multiplying 365 days by the museum's undivided ownership interest. The museum had the right to have the days of access spread evenly throughout the year, by calendar quarter. The museum also had the right, prior to acquisition of full ownership of the collection, to removal of it to its facilities for the number of access days then available to the museum. When the museum acquired full ownership of the collection, it had the right to the sole possession and custody of it. The IRS ruled that, to the extent each transfer to the museum of a percentage of an undivided ownership interest was made for an amount less than the fair market value of the interest, the difference between the fair market value of the interest and that amount was deductible as a charitable gift.[57]

---

[57] IRS Private Letter Ruling 8333019. A similar transaction, without the bargain sale feature, is reflected in IRS Private Letter Ruling 8535019.

15

Gifts by Means of
Charitable Lead Trusts

The federal tax law provides for a form of planned giving that utilizes a split-interest trust that is termed a "charitable lead trust."[1]

In general, a charitable lead trust is a vehicle by which money or property is split into two interests: One or more "income interests" and one or more "remainder interests." The income interest is to be paid over to one or more charitable organizations, while the remainder interest is destined for one or more noncharitable beneficiaries. (This type of planned giving is so named because the income interest created for charitable objectives precedes—or "leads"—the remainder interest.)

The forms of planned giving discussed in the foregoing three chapters have this common element: The donor transfers to a charitable organization the remainder interest in the money or property involved, with one or more noncharitable beneficiaries retaining the income interest. However, the reverse may occur—and that is the essence of the "charitable lead trust."

§ 15.1 GENERAL RULES

A charitable lead trust is a vehicle by which property transferred to it is apportioned into an income interest and a remainder interest. Like the charitable remainder trust and the pooled income fund,[2] it

---

[1] The concepts of planned giving and split-interest trusts are discussed in Chapter 3. That chapter also contains a general description of charitable lead trusts.

[2] See Chapters 11 and 12, respectively.

is a split-interest trust. Pursuant to a charitable lead trust, an income interest in property is contributed to a charitable organization, either for a term of years or for the life of one individual or the lives of more than one individual. The remainder interest in the property is reserved to return, at the expiration of the income interest (the "lead period"), to the donor or some other noncharitable beneficiary or beneficiaries; often the property passes from one generation (the donor's) to another.

The charitable lead trust can be used to accelerate a series of charitable contributions, that would otherwise be made annually, into one year, with a corresponding single-year deduction for the "bunched" amount of charitable gifts.

In some sets of circumstances, a charitable deduction is available for the transfer of an income interest in property to a charitable organization. There are stringent limitations, however, on the deductible amount of charitable contributions of these income interests.

A charitable lead trust can be funded by a donor or donors during lifetime, as well as by means of transfers from an estate.

The charitable lead trust is frequently used to transfer property from one member of a family to another, usually from one generation to the next. For example, a father may establish a charitable lead trust, providing income from the trust to a charitable organization for a term of years, with the trust corpus to thereafter pass to his daughter. This type of transfer may be subject to a gift tax, but the actual tax cost of the gift is substantially reduced because of the reduction in the amount transferred to the ultimate beneficiary by the value of the income interest contributed to a charitable organization. If a charitable lead trust is used to shift property to a generation other than the immediate next one, the transfer may be subject to the generation-skipping transfer tax.[3]

§ 15.2   THE INCOME INTEREST

The income interest created for a charitable organization by means of a charitable lead trust is defined in one of two ways. The income interest may be stated as a guaranteed annuity or as an annual payment equal to a fixed percentage of the fair market value of the trust property, valued annually.[4] These interests have the same

[3]IRC § 2642.
[4]IRC § 170(f)(2)(B); Reg. § 1.170A-6(c)(4).

names as in the charitable remainder trust context; the first of these interests is an "annuity interest" and the other is "unitrust interest."[5] Thus, there can be a charitable lead annuity trust or a charitable lead unitrust. The annuity interest or unitrust interest must be received at least annually.[6]

As with a charitable remainder trust, the charitable lead trust annuity interest or unitrust must qualify as one or the other in all respects.[7]

The IRS held (in the gift tax context) that annuity interests that will continue for a term of years or for a period of lives in existence (technically, "in being") plus a term of years can qualify as annuity interests.[8] In the case, an individual, A, created a trust and funded it with $250,000. The trust instrument provided that the trustee of the trust must distribute at the end of each tax year an annuity of $20,000 to qualified charitable organizations. The trust is to terminate on the earlier of a period of 30 years after the funding of the trust or 21 years after the death of the last survivor of A's children living on the date when the trust was created, in favor of A's surviving children. When A created the trust, she had three children of the age of 53, 60, and 63. The IRS concluded that each of the payment periods is an allowable payment period and that the lesser value of the two can be computed.

The trust must provide for a specified distribution (as noted, at least annually) to one or more income beneficiaries for the life or lives of one or more individuals or for a term of years.[9] These individuals must be alive and ascertainable as of the funding of the trust.[10]

§ 15.3　INCOME TAX CHARITABLE DEDUCTION

A transfer of money or property to a charitable lead trust may or may not result in a current "front end" income tax charitable contribution deduction for the donor.

If certain conditions are met, a charitable deduction will be availa-

[5]See Chapter 11 §§ 5 and 6.
[6]Reg. § 1.170A-6(c)(2)(i)(A), (ii)(A).
[7]Reg. § 1.170A-6(c)(2)(i)(B), (ii)(B).
[8]Rev. Rul. 85-49, 1985-1 C.B. 330.
[9]Reg. § 1.170A-6(c)(2)(1)(A), (ii)(A).
[10]*Id.*

ble for the value of an income interest created by means of a charitable lead trust. These conditions are principally twofold. First, as noted, the income interest must be in the form of an annuity interest or a unitrust interest.[11] Where this is done, the charitable contribution deduction is available for federal income, gift, and estate tax purposes, when other requirements are satisfied.[12] Second, for purposes of the income tax charitable deduction, the donor must be treated as the owner of the income interest, pursuant to the so-called "grantor trust" rules.[13] (This is a federal tax law requirement, with the donor being the "grantor.") This latter requirement means that the income as received by the charitable lead trust is taxed to the donor/grantor. As discussed below, this fact makes an income tax deduction for a charitable gift in this context of limited likelihood and use.

A charitable lead trust may be established in such a fashion that there is no income tax charitable contribution deduction for the income interest involved. Under this approach, the trust is written so that the grantor trust rules are inapplicable; this is accomplished by causing the donor to not be considered the owner of the income interest. The tax consequence of such a charitable lead trust is that the donor forgoes a charitable contribution deduction at the front end, but he or she concurrently avoids taxation on the income of the trust for each of the years that the trust is in existence. In this situation, while there is no charitable deduction, there is nonetheless a "deduction" in the sense that the income generated by the property involved is outside the stream of taxable income flowing to the donor.

From an income tax standpoint, the facts and circumstances of each case must be evaluated to ascertain whether a charitable lead trust is appropriate for an individual (or family) and, if so, whether or not the charitable contribution deduction should be utilized. A person with a year of abnormally high income may find considerable advantage in a charitable lead trust that yields a charitable deduction, since that deduction will be of greatest economic advantage in relation to the higher income taxation, and the trust income subsequently attributable to the donor will be taxable in a relatively lower amount. Conversely, the charitable lead trust without the deduction

---

[11] See § 2, *supra*.
[12] IRC §§ 170(f)(2)(B), 2055(e)(2)(B), and 2522(c)(2)(B).
[13] IRC § 170(f)(2)(B), Reg. § 1.170A-6(c)(1).

is sometimes utilized in support of a charitable organization by an individual where outright contributions by him or her to the organization cannot be fully deductible because of the percentage limitations on annual charitable contribution deductions.

§ 15.4 VALUING THE CHARITABLE DEDUCTION

The value of any interest for life or any remainder interest is determined by using an interest rate (rounded to the nearest two-tenths of one percent) equal to 120 percent of the federal midterm rate, used to determine the issue price (value) of certain debt instruments,[14] in effect for the month in which the valuation date falls.[15]

This valuation is made using tables prepared by the IRS[16] charting the most recent mortality experience available.[17] These tables must be revised at least once every ten years to take into account the most recent mortality experience available as of the time of the revision.[18]

If an income, estate, or gift tax charitable contribution deduction is allowable for any part of the property transferred, the individual involved may elect to use the federal midterm rate for either of the two months preceding the month in which the valuation date falls in determining the value.[19] Otherwise, the rate that is used is the rate in effect in the month of the gift. In the case of transfers of more than one interest in the same property with respect to which a person may use the same rate, the person must use the same rate with respect to each interest.[20]

As directed, the IRS has published valuation tables. These tables reflect the use of interest rates ranging from 2.2 percent to 26 percent. The tables used for determining the value of charitable lead annuity trust income interests are in *Actuarial Values—Alpha Volume*[21] and of charitable lead unitrust income interests are in *Actuarial Values—Beta Volume*.[22]

---

[14] IRC § 1274(d)(1).
[15] IRC § 7520(a)(2). A chart of these rates appears as Appendix G.
[16] IRC § 7520(a)(1).
[17] IRC § 7520(c)(3).
[18] *Ibid.*
[19] IRC § 7520(a).
[20] *Ibid.*
[21] IRS Publication 1457.
[22] IRS Publication 1458.

§ 15.5 TAX TREATMENT OF THE CHARITABLE LEAD TRUST

A qualified charitable remainder trust is an entity that generally is exempt from federal income taxation.[23] However, a charitable lead trust is not exempt from income taxation. Consequently, the tax treatment accorded a charitable lead trust is dependent upon whether or not the "grantor trust" rules are applicable.

If the grantor trust rules are applicable, so that the donor is treated as the owner of the trust, the income of the trust will be taxable to the donor and not to the trust.[24] This means that the trust will not have any income tax liability.

If the grantor trust rules are inapplicable, so that the donor is not treated as the owner of the trust, the income of the trust will be taxable to the trust. In this situation, the charitable lead trust is allowed an unlimited charitable deduction for the payments from it, pursuant to the trust agreement, to the charitable organization that is the income beneficiary.[25]

A charitable lead trust is not entitled to an income tax deduction for payments to charitable organizations in excess of the income interest payable under the terms of the trust agreement.[26] Under the facts of a particular case, four individuals established a trust and transferred $15 million to it. The trust qualified as a charitable lead trust, with provision for specified annuity payments (totalling $975,000 annually) to charities. The lead period is 45 years. The trust agreement enables the trustees to pay charitable annuities in excess of the $975,000 amount and in advance of the 45-year term if the payments are in commutation of future annuity payments. However, while the trustees did in fact make excess payments to charitable organizations, they did not commute any future annuity payments as a result. The trust claimed income tax deductions for these excess payments.[27] The IRS and the court denied the deduction.

The law essentially allows a trust to deduct charitable contribu-

---

[23] Chapter 11 § 2.

[24] IRC § 671.

[25] IRC § 642(c)(1).

[26] *Crown Income Charitable Fund, Rebecca K. v. Commissioner*, 98 T.C. No. 25 (1992).

[27] IRC § 642(c)(1).

tions to the full extent of gross income as long as the transfers are made pursuant to the terms of the governing instrument. Under the trust agreement, if payments in excess of the annual annuity would adversely affect the maximum charitable deduction allowable, the trustees are not supposed to make them but instead accumulate the income and add it to principal. The parties quarreled over whether the trust document, in referring to the "maximum charitable deduction," was referencing the income tax charitable deduction or the gift tax charitable deduction. The court decided it was the latter.

The court found that commutation is necessary before it can be said that the amounts in dispute were paid pursuant to the trust agreement. The court construed the term "commutation" to mean a computation in the formal sense contemporaneously with payments to charity in excess of the annual annuity amount. It held that a "definite formula" for a valid commutation must exist.

Thus, the court held that, since the amounts in question were not transferred in commutation of future annuity payments, the amounts were not transferred pursuant to the terms of the trust and thus that the claimed deduction was not available. (The court sidestepped the question of whether the ability of the trustees to accelerate the payment of a charitable lead annuity is consistent with the federal gift tax requirement[28] that the charitable (income) interest be in the form of guaranteed annuity.)

The court also denied a deduction under the rules by which a trust is allowed a deduction for the payment of income or principal,[29] on the ground that the regulations under that section expressly require that any amounts paid by trusts for charitable purposes can only be deductible under the general rules providing a deduction for payments for a charitable purpose.[30] The court had previously so held,[31] and it refused to reverse its prior position.

The court, however, rejected the government's contention that the trust was liable for additions to tax for substantial understatements.[32] It held that the trust disclosed sufficient information on its tax returns to allow the IRS to identify the issues involved.

---

[28] IRC § 2522(c)(2)(B).
[29] IRC § 661(a)(2).
[30] IRC § 642(c).
[31] *O'Conner, Estate of* v. *Commissioner,* 69 T.C. 165 (1977).
[32] IRC § 6661. See Chapter 10 § 5.

§ 15.6   TESTAMENTARY USE OF LEAD TRUSTS

Like the other forms of planned giving, a charitable lead trust can be used to benefit a charitable organization out of the assets of a decedent's estate. That is, the income interest thereby created for a charitable organization can be transferred as a charitable bequest by means of such a trust. The remainder interest would be reserved for one or more noncharitable beneficiaries, such as the decedent's heirs.

In this situation, a charitable deduction is available to the estate. Again, the deduction is for the present value of the income interest being transferred to a charitable organization.

When a federal estate tax charitable deduction becomes available, there is no need for anyone to recognize the income of the charitable lead trust. That is, there is no application of the equivalent of the grantor trust rules (whereby an individual is considered the owner of the trust) in this context.

§ 15.7   PERCENTAGE LIMITATION RULES

There are percentage limitations, under the federal tax law, applicable to charitable contributions by individuals that can limit the extent of deductibility for charitable gifts in any one year.[33] One set of these limitations applies where the contribution is "for the use of" a charitable organization, rather than "to" a charitable organization.[34]

A contribution made by means of a charitable lead trust is considered a contribution "for the use of" the charitable organization that is entitled to the income interest.[35] Thus, in general, a 30 percent limitation is applicable on these gifts for income tax purposes.[36] Where the charitable donee is not a public charitable organization[37] and the subject of the gift is capital gain property, the 20 percent limitation is applicable.[38] Nonetheless, amounts in excess of these limitations may be carried forward to subsequent years.[39]

---

[33] See Chapter 7.
[34] See Chapter 10 § 2.
[35] Reg. § 1.170A-8(a)(2).
[36] IRC § 170(b)(1)(B).
[37] See Chapter 4 § 3.
[38] IRC § 170(b)(1)(D).
[39] IRC §§ 170(b)(1)(B) and 170(b)(1)(D)(ii).

§ 15.8 PRIVATE FOUNDATION RULES

As is the case with many types of trusts used in the planned giving context, a charitable lead trust—being a split-interest trust[40]—is treated as a private foundation for certain purposes.[41]

In general, the private foundation rules that pertain to a charitable lead trust are those concerning self-dealing,[42] excess business holdings,[43] jeopardizing investments,[44] and taxable expenditures.[45] However, a charitable lead trust is exempt from the excess business holdings and jeopardizing investments rules where all of the amounts in the trust for which a charitable contribution deduction was allowed (namely, the income interest), and none of the remainder interest, have an aggregate value of no more than 60 percent of the total fair market value of all amounts in the trust.[46]

The IRS applied these rules (in the gift tax setting), in considering a trust where trust income in excess of the guaranteed annuity payable to charity is to be added to trust corpus for distribution to noncharitable remainder beneficiaries upon expiration of the guaranteed annuity period, although all of the excess income along with any other property held by the trust may be applied, if necessary, to pay the guaranteed annuity during the term of the annuity and is not available for any private purpose during the term. Because, in the case considered, the value of the income interest did not exceed 60 percent of trust corpus and because the income interest of the trust was devoted solely to charitable purposes, the value of the annuity was held to be deductible even though the trust instrument lacked references to the excess business holdings and jeopardizing investments rules. However, if the trust provided that all income earned by the trust in any year in excess of the amount needed for the annuity payment is to be paid currently to the individuals named as remainder interest beneficiaries, the value of the annuity interest would not be deductible because (1) the income interest in the trust

---

[40] IRC § 4947(a)(2); Reg. § 53.4947-1(c)(1)(ii). See *The Law of Tax-Exempt Organizations*, Chapter 27 § 2.
[41] The definition of a "private foundation" is summarized in Chapter 4 § 3.
[42] IRC § 4941. See *The Law of Tax-Exempt Organizations*, Chapter 20.
[43] IRC § 4943. See *The Law of Tax-Exempt Organizations*, Chapter 22.
[44] IRC § 4944. See *The Law of Tax-Exempt Organizations*, Chapter 23.
[45] IRC § 4945. See *The Law of Tax-Exempt Organizations*, Chapter 24.
[46] IRC § 4947(b)(3).

would not be devoted solely to charitable purposes and (2) the trust instrument does not contain references to the excess business holdings and jeopardizing investments rules, even though the value of the charitable interest is less than 60 percent of the trust corpus.[47]

§ 15.9   CHARITABLE INCOME TRUSTS

Broadly comparable to the charitable lead trust is the so-called "charitable income trust." In the case of this type of trust, the charitable organization that is the income interest beneficiary is—literally— only entitled to the income of the trust. (In the case of the usual charitable lead trust, the income beneficiary is to be paid an annuity amount or a unitrust amount, and those amounts must be satisfied out of principal if the trust's income is insufficient to fund the payout(s).) There is no income, gift, or estate tax deduction available for this type of gift. This is because the trust is not one of the two required forms.[48]

The charitable income trust has been used in the context of gifts made during the donor's lifetime to

- deflect the income of the trust from the income of the donor, and/or
- transfer property to a member of the donor's family with a minimum of tax exposure.

§ 15.10   COMPARISON WITH REMAINDER TRUSTS

An annuity interest or a unitrust interest in property may be created by means of a charitable remainder trust. These interests are subject to minimum amounts that must be payable to the income beneficiaries.[49] However, an income interest created by a charitable lead trust is not governed by any minimum or maximum payout requirement.[50]

Also, an income interest in property created by means of a charitable remainder trust may be measured by a term of years. The income interest term established by a charitable remainder trust

[47] Rev. Rul. 88-82, 1988-2 C.B. 336.
[48] See § 2, *supra*.
[49] See Chapter 11 §§ 5 and 6.
[50] IRC § 170(f)(2)(B).

cannot be longer than twenty years.[51] By contrast, there is no restriction in federal law on the length of the term during which the income interest is payable to a charitable organization out of a charitable lead trust.[52,53]

---

[51] See Chapter 11 § 1, text accompanied by ns. 5 and 6.
[52] IRC § 170(f)(2)(B).
[53] For further reading about charitable lead trusts, see Appendix H.

16

Gifts of Life Insurance

Life insurance can be the subject of a charitable gift. It can be considered part of the panoply of planned gifts, although a split-interest trust is not usually involved.

A gift of life insurance is a particularly good way for the younger donor to make a major gift to a charitable organization.

§ 16.1 INTRODUCTION

A person may make a gift of life insurance to a charitable organization. Where a federal income tax charitable contribution deduction is desired, the donor must make the charity the owner and beneficiary of the insurance policy.

An individual can contribute a fully paid-up life insurance policy or a single premium policy to a charitable organization and deduct, for income tax purposes, its replacement value.[1] Or, an individual can acquire a life insurance policy, contribute it to a charitable organization, pay the premiums, and create a charitable contribution deduction for each premium payment made.

For an income tax deduction for a gift of life insurance to be available, the insurance contract must be enforceable. (A contribution by means of a contract that is void or likely to be voidable is a gift of something without value.) To be enforceable, there must be a form of "insurable interest" between the insured and the beneficiary.[2]

---

[1]Reg. § 25.2512-6(a), Example (3). Also *United States* v. *Ryerson*, 312 U.S. 260 (1941).
[2]See § 4, *infra*.

467

§ 16.2   THE CONCEPTS OF LIFE INSURANCE[3]

(a)   The Basics

Life insurance is represented by a contract—known as an insurance policy—that involves at least three parties:

- an insured person,
- the owner of the insurance policy (usually the purchaser of the policy), and
- the insurer (the insurance company that is the provider of the policy).

Another party to this arrangement is the beneficiary of the insurance proceeds. The owner of the insurance policy may be the beneficiary, or the beneficiary may be another person. Also, two or more persons may be the beneficiary of an insurance policy.

If the insured qualifies and if the requisite consideration for the insurance contract—the premium—is paid by the policy owner, the insurance company promises to pay a cash benefit (death benefit) in the event the insured dies while the policy is in force. Depending on the type of life insurance, a portion of the premium may go into a cash account (and accumulate as cash value). The cash value is available to the policy owner at any time during the insured's lifetime, by canceling ("cashing in") the insurance policy.

The insured and the owner of the policy may be the same person, or they may be different persons. For example, one may purchase a policy on his or her own life. Alternatively, a spouse may purchase an insurance policy on the other spouse's life. Where one spouse purchases a policy on the other spouse's life, the purchasing spouse is the policy owner and the other spouse is the insured.

The distinction between the insured and the policy owner is also important for the reason of taxes. At one's death, all of one's property is tabulated for the purpose of determining if one's estate must pay estate taxes. Property includes the death benefits from life insurance unless the decedent was merely the insured but not the policy owner. If the decedent was not the policy owner and if he or she had

---

[3]This section of the chapter is based in part on an analysis of life insurance and charitable giving prepared by Robert E. Tucker and published as Special Analysis No. 86-2, *The Nonprofit Counsel* (1986).

no rights (for example, to use the cash value or to name the beneficiary), the death benefit paid at death will not be included in the
estate for estate tax purposes.

(b) Types of Life Insurance

Broadly speaking, there are two categories of life insurance—term
insurance and permanent insurance. Each has many different types.
For example, term insurance can be classified as level term, decreasing term, and increasing term. Permanent insurance can be catego-
rized as whole life, variable life, adjustable life, and universal life.

Term insurance is analogous to renting a house. One agrees to pay
a regular payment in exchange for the protection afforded by the
house. Each year, the landlord raises the rent as expenses increase.
No matter how long an individual rents, he or she receives nothing
back in the event of a move. With term insurance, in exchange for a
"rent payment" (premium), the insurance company provides protection (the death benefit). Each year (typically), the rent payment
(premium) is increased. If one "leaves" (cancels the insurance policy),
he or she receives nothing back, no matter how long the premium
payments were made.

Permanent insurance is analogous to purchasing a house. The same
protection as a rented house is provided, but the monthly payments
are (usually) higher. However, the monthly payments are fixed and
do not increase. In addition, each month the house is owned, the
value may increase (at least over the long term). This value is called
"equity," which can be used during lifetime by either borrowing,
using the property as collateral, or selling the house and receiving
the net equity in a lump sum.

In a permanent insurance contract one pays the mortgage payments (premiums) in exchange for both protection (death benefit)
and equity (cash value). If one dies while insured, the death benefit
is paid. If an individual wants to use the cash value while alive, he
or she may do so by borrowing or by cancelling the policy and taking
the cash value. Some policies also allow for withdrawals without
borrowing or surrendering. Premium payments are generally fixed
during lifetime.

To summarize, term insurance is initially less expensive, offers
death protection, and does not build up any cash value during one's
lifetime. Permanent insurance is more expensive in the early years,
provides the same death benefit, and also builds cash value during
lifetime.

A new generation type of permanent insurance is "universal life." To understand this form of insurance, one can visualize a bucket with two spigots, one on each side.

One deposits premium dollars into the bucket, and each month the insurance company turns on one of the spigots and drains off the dollars necessary to pay all of the following: one month's cost of death protection, expense charges, and administrative charges. The spigot is then turned off, and the dollars remaining in the bucket are invested and earn interest. These excess dollars and the interest earned make up the policy's cash value.

As one continues to deposit more premium dollars and as more interest is earned, the cash value becomes larger. At any time, one may cease depositing premium dollars as long as there are enough dollars in the bucket to pay for the cost of insurance, and the expense and administrative charges. Conversely, if one wants the cash value to build faster, he or she may pay more premium dollars.

The cash value can be taken out of the policy during lifetime in three ways. First, some of the money can be borrowed at a rate of interest; if the money is borrowed, it reduces the death benefit by the same amount. However, the money may be paid back at any time. Second, one can withdraw some of the money without incurring a loan. This method also reduces the death benefit, but it cannot be paid back without satisfying certain requirements. Third, one can surrender the policy (terminate the insurance) and take all of the cash value. The money available in all three methods may, however, be reduced by a surrender charge, illustrated by the second spigot. In the first ten to fifteen years, the insurance company imposes this charge on a sliding scale and it reduces to zero by the tenth to fifteenth policy year.

Universal life offers additional flexibility in that it allows one to select either of two death benefit options. One chooses to have a level death benefit or an increasing death benefit.

Two other types of insurance contracts have evolved. One is called "survivorship whole life." It is unique in that it simultaneously insures two or more lives. The second type is group-term life insurance provided by an employer to an employee. An employee may be provided up to $50,000 of this type of insurance without having to recognize taxable income.[4] The cost of any coverage over that amount must be recognized as income.

---

[4] IRC § 79(a).

(c) Valuation

There are three ways in which a life insurance policy can be valued:

- The replacement value, which is the amount which the issuer of the insurance would charge to issue an identical policy to a person of the same age as the insured. This value is usually used in the gift and estate context.[5]
- The cash surrender value, which is the amount the insurance company is willing to pay in the event the policy is surrendered. This value has been applied in the income tax context.[6]
- The potential net death benefit amount, which is the amount which the beneficiary would receive if the insured died immediately, which would be the difference between the face amount and any loan outstanding.

Since the potential net death benefit value is relevant only where special circumstances suggest that because of ill health the insured's death is imminent, the values usually used are the replacement value and the cash value (or an intermediate amount).

§ 16.3 CHARITABLE GIVING AND INSURANCE

Essentially, there are three situations where a contribution of life insurance can give rise to a charitable deduction.

In the first situation, an individual may have an existing life insurance policy that is fully paid up, or is a single premium policy, and is not needed for the protection of his or her family. A gift of the policy to a charitable organization would, in general, occasion a charitable deduction in an amount equal to the replacement value of the policy, as noted.[7] An exception to this rule is derived from the fact that a disposition of the insurance policy would not be a transaction generating long-term capital gain, so that the charitable deduction cannot be greater than the basis of the donor in the policy.[8] It has been held that, when valuing a paid-up life insurance policy that was contributed to a charitable organization, where the policy was subject

[5]Reg. §§ 25.2512-6(a), Example (3), 20.2031-8, Example (2).
[6]For example, see the text accompanied by n. 9, *infra*.
[7]See n. 2, *supra*.
[8]See Chapter 6 § 4, particularly the text accompanied by n. 17.

to a substantial loan, the proper valuation is the cash surrender value of the policy on the date it was surrendered.[9] In so holding, the court was influenced by the fact that no party had any interest in maintaining the life insurance policy as an investment.

Second, an individual may own an insurance policy where premium payments are still being made. The charitable deduction for a gift of a policy in this circumstance is an amount equal to the "interpolated terminal reserve value" of the policy at the date of the sale, plus the proportionate part of any premium paid by the donor prior to the date of the gift which is applicable to a period subsequent to the date of the gift.[10] As in the prior situation, the deduction in any event cannot exceed an amount equal to the donor's basis in the property. Where all other requisite conditions are met, a charitable deduction is available for the remaining premium payments.

In the third of these situations, the insurance policy that is donated is a new one. Thus, there is no charitable deduction for the gift of the policy but, as in the previous circumstance, there is a charitable deduction for the premium payments as made.

If the donor of a life insurance policy retains any "incidents of ownership" (see below) in the policy during lifetime, he or she is not permitted to deduct, for federal income tax purposes, the cost of the premiums as a charitable gift.[11] For example, the IRS ruled that the irrevocable assignment of the cash surrender value of a life insurance policy to a college, with the donor retaining the right to designate the beneficiary and to assign the balance of the policy, whether the policy is paid up and the college is given possession or the policy is not fully paid up and the donor retains possession, constitutes a charitable contribution of a partial interest for which a deduction is not allowable.[12] Incidents of ownership, in this context, means the right of the insured, or of his or her estate, to the economic benefits of the policy and includes the following:

- the power to change the beneficiary,
- the power to surrender the policy,

---

[9]*Tuttle* v. *United States*, 436 F.2d 69 (2d Cir. 1970).
[10]Reg. § 25.2512-6(a); Rev. Rul. 59-195, 1959-1 C.B. 18.
[11]This is because the gift would be of a nondeductible partial interest (see Chapter 9 § 9).
[12]Rev. Rul. 76-143, 1976-1 C.B. 63.

- the power to cancel the policy,
- the power to assign the policy,
- the power to revoke an assignment,
- the power to pledge the policy for a loan,
- the power to obtain from the insurer a loan against the surrender value of the policy,[13] and
- a reversionary interest in the policy or its proceeds, whether arising by the express terms of the policy or other instrument or by operation of law, but only if the value of the reversionary interest immediately before the death of the decedent exceeded five percent of the value of the policy.[14]

If the individual has not changed his or her mind on the subject prior to death, the charitable organization will receive the death benefit. This death benefit will be included in the estate for estate tax calculations but the estate will receive an estate tax charitable deduction for gifts to charitable organizations. Therefore, the death benefit will not create any estate tax burden.

Thus, it is not enough, for an income tax charitable deduction, to simply cause a charitable organization to be named as the (or a) beneficiary of a life insurance policy. Full ownership rights in the policy must be conveyed for a charitable deduction to be allowed.

If one gives an amount equal to a premium payment to a charitable organization and authorizes the charity to purchase an insurance policy on the donor's life, the value of the gift is greatly multiplied. The charitable organization is able to use the annual gifts to purchase an insurance policy having a face value that is greater than the annual amounts combined. Since, in this instance, the charitable organization is the policy owner and the beneficiary, and the donor is merely the insured, the annual gift is a deductible charitable contribution.

From the charitable organization's point of view, two transactions occur each year. First, premium dollars plus investment earnings are added to the cash value. Second, the cost of insurance, expense charges, and administrative charges are deducted from the cash value. The net cash value is available to the charitable organization if there is a current need for cash. Borrowing or withdrawing cash

---

[13]The foregoing seven examples are listed in Reg. § 20.2042-1(c)(2).
[14]Reg. § 20.2042-1(c)(3).

value will, however, reduce the death benefit and require additional future premium payments in order to keep the policy in force.

This concept can also be effectively utilized when a donor wishes to make a single, large contribution. If the amount given is used to purchase life insurance, a much greater gift is likely to result.

The foregoing discussion focused on the direct use of life insurance in the context of charitable giving. One or more donors make a substantial gift to charity (via the insurance death benefit) with relatively small incremental gifts. The charity is benefitted in that it can use the policy cash values while the donor is alive, although the major portion of the gift is received at the death of the donor.

However, there are instances of the "indirect" use of life insurance in the charitable giving setting.

An individual may have a valuable parcel of property that produces very little income and is not important to his or her financial welfare; at the same time, sale of the property might generate a significant capital gains tax liability. An illustration of this would be a tract of raw land that originally cost very little but has substantially grown in value. Another example would be highly appreciated securities that pay little or no dividends. If the individual were to sell the property, capital gains tax would have to be paid on the gain (the difference between the original cost and the current fair market value of the property).

But if this individual made an outright gift of the property to a public charity, the donor's federal income tax charitable deduction would be based on the fair market value of the property.[15] The capital gains tax would be avoided. In general, regarding this gift, the individual could deduct an amount up to thirty percent of his or her adjusted gross income,[16] with any excess carried forward up to five immediately succeeding years.[17] The tax savings may offset the gift cost; the donor's estate is reduced by the amount of the contribution, so that the estate tax burden is reduced.

One major deterrent to a gift of this nature is that the property itself is contributed to charity and is not passed on to the donor's heirs. However, life insurance can solve this problem and make it possible for the donor to make a current gift of the property to charity. The individual in this situation can make tax-free gifts (up to

[15] See Chapter 6 § 2.
[16] See Chapter 7 § 5.
[17] *Id.*

$10,000 per year per donee[18]) of part or all of the tax savings. Adult heirs (assuming they have an insurable interest) can purchase life insurance on the donor's life in an amount equal to or greater than the value of the property given to charity. The cost of the insurance is paid by the tax-free gifts they received from the donor.

Two purposes are served by this approach. First, the heirs receive the same (or approximately the same) economic benefit (by means of life insurance) that they would have received if the gift had not been made. Second, neither the property given nor the life insurance purchased on the life of the donor by the heirs will be included in the estate of the donor.

The same result can be achieved by the creation by the donor of an irrevocable life insurance trust. The donor makes tax-free gifts of the tax savings to an irrevocable trust for the benefit of his or her heirs. The trust purchases life insurance on the donor with the money received from the donor. At the donor's death, the insurance is paid to the trust free of income or estate taxes, and it replaces the property given to charity by the donor. (The insurance may be includible in the decedent's estate if the death occurs within three years of the transaction.)

However, the donor may need income from the property during lifetime. This can be accomplished by the creation of a charitable remainder trust.[19] Instead of making an outright gift of property to the charity, the donor transfers the property to a charitable remainder trust. During the donor's lifetime, the donor retains the right to a certain amount of annual income but at the donor's death the amount remaining in the trust is paid to the charitable organization or organizations that are the remainder interest beneficiaries. The annual amount payable to the donor must either be a fixed amount of money[20] or a fixed percentage of the trust assets.[21] Payments can be made to the donor for his or her lifetime or for a term of years. If appropriate, the trust can provide for payments for the donor's lifetime and the lifetime of the donor's spouse.

The donor in this circumstance receives a current income tax deduction for the present value of the future gift of trust assets to the charity. A small annual income payment to the donor (and

[18] IRC § 2503(b).
[19] See Chapter 11.
[20] Id. § 5.
[21] Id. § 6.

spouse) during lifetime will result in a larger gift to charity, inasmuch as the trust assets will not be as depleted. As a result, the current income tax charitable deduction will be higher. If larger income payments are desired, the current tax deduction will be lower.

In order to preserve the assets passing to the donor's heirs, the donor can create an irrevocable life insurance trust, make tax-free gifts of the donor's tax savings to the trust, and allow the trust to insure the donor's life. This use of the survivorship whole life policy is ideal in the event the charitable remainder trust pays an income to both the donor and his or her spouse.

An individual, perhaps, cannot afford to contribute a major asset to charity at the time, yet wants to provide for income to his or her spouse for life and would like to make a major gift to charity. Life insurance can assist an individual in this situation.

First, the individual establishes a charitable remainder unitrust.[22] This trust provides for payment of a fixed percentage of income for the life of the individual and his or her spouse. Second, the trust purchases insurance on the donor's life. The trust pays for the insurance from annual gifts of premium, which the donor makes to the trust. During the donor's lifetime, there is little if any payment to the donor and spouse, since the trust asset is the life insurance policy on the donor. At the donor's death, the trust receives the death proceeds and pays income to the surviving spouse for his or her lifetime. At the death of the spouse, the trust distributes the remaining assets to the charity or charities that are the remainder interest beneficiaries.

This arrangement benefits the donor in two ways. The spouse receives a guaranteed income and, because a remainder interest is paid to charity, the donor is allowed to deduct a portion of the annual gift of premium payments to the charitable remainder unitrust. In effect, it is a way to purchase life insurance on a partially tax-deductible basis. During lifetime, the donor may be allowed to change the charitable remainder beneficiaries and may revoke the spouse's income interest by a provision to that effect in the donor's will.

Mention was made above of the rule concerning employer-provided group term life insurance.[23] The point was made that such coverage in excess of $50,000 of insurance gives rise to gross income

---

[22]*Id.*
[23]See the text accompanied by n. 4, *supra.*

for the employee recipient. However, there is an exception to that rule, pertaining to situations where a charitable organization is named as the beneficiary of the insurance that is in excess of the $50,000 threshold.[24]

§ 16.4 THE REQUIREMENT OF INSURABLE INTEREST

A contract of insurance—that is, an insurance policy—is valid (enforceable), only where there is an insurable interest between the insured and the beneficiary. Basically, one person has an insurable interest in another person where the person that is the beneficiary of the insurance is better off economically with the insured alive rather than dead. Thus, the concept of insurable interest is that the beneficiary would suffer an economic loss if the insured were to die. (Without putting too fine a point on the subject, the insurable interest doctrine emanated from the common law, to prevent an individual from purchasing insurance on the life of another and then seeing to it that the other person's life was terminated soon thereafter. The law evolved the idea of insurable interest to prevent "gambling" on individuals' lives.) The most common example of a relationship involving insurable interest is the marital relationship; likewise, "key" individuals are often insured by their companies.

The IRS, in a private letter ruling, held that a charitable contribution deduction is not available, for federal income tax purposes, for the payment by a donor of premiums for a life insurance policy donated to a charitable organization, where the charity is the sole beneficiary of the policy proceeds.[25] The donor was characterized by the IRS as conceding that the charitable organization involved lacked an insurable interest in the donor's life.

The IRS view in this private letter ruling was based upon two doctrines of law. One of these is that the transfer of the policy to the charitable organization was not a transfer of all of the donor's rights associated with it. The IRS characterized the donation as a gift of a partial interest in the policy, not in trust, so that a deduction was not available.[26] The interest retained was portrayed as the ability of the donor, through a will, to name the heirs who would benefit, if the proceeds of the policy were returned to the estate. That is, the IRS

[24]IRC § 79(b)(2)(B); Reg. § 1.79-2(c)(3).
[25]IRS Private Letter Ruling 9110016.
[26]See Chapter 9 § 9.

relied on the fact that the personal representative of the estate may successfully maintain an action to recover the benefits of the policy and distribute them to others.

The second doctrine of law in this regard is that a deduction for this type of charitable gift will not be disallowed merely because the interest which passes to, or is vested in, the charity may be defeated by the performance of some act or the happening of some event, if on the date of the gift it appears that the possibility that the act or event will occur is negligible.[27] The potential of the exercise of the rights to be retained by the insurance company and by the personal representative of the estate was found to be not remote. Also, the IRS pointed out that the donor could discontinue payments of the premiums on the insurance, causing the policy to lapse unless the charitable organization paid them.

The facts underlying this ruling involved an individual who had previously made gifts to the charitable organization. This individual intended to apply for a life insurance policy and name the charity as the sole beneficiary of the policy proceeds. Upon receipt of the policy from the insurance company, the individual intended to irrevocably assign the policy to the charity, and to continue payment of the insurance policy premiums.

The state (New York) insurance law involved prohibited anyone, without an insurable interest in an insured, from obtaining an insurance policy on the life of another person unless the benefits are to be paid to someone with an insurable interest. As noted, it was conceded that the charitable organization did not have an insurable interest in the donor's life. The intent of the donor to procure the policy and transfer it to the charity, rather than have the charity obtain it directly, was seen as a circumvention of the state law prohibition.

If the transaction was a violation of state law, then, upon the death of the donor, the insurance company may not have to pay the proceeds of the policy to the charity or, if it did, the representative of the estate may be able to bring a lawsuit to recover the proceeds from the organization and distribute them to other beneficiaries of the estate.

The facts of this ruling involved, as noted, a concession that the charitable organization lacked the requisite insurable interest in the donor. At first thought, it may appear that a charitable organization

[27] See Chapter 10 § 3.

in these circumstances would be more financially advantaged with an insured dead than alive—that the charity would be in a preferential position with the insurance proceeds in hand. However, in many instances, this is not the case, and a charitable organization will have an insurable interest in the life of a donor of a life insurance policy. For example, the donor may be a valuable volunteer and/or a major donor in other and ongoing respects. There should not always be an assumption that a charitable organization that is the owner (by gift) and beneficiary of a life insurance policy is always better off with that donor deceased.

Some states' statutory law has been amended to invest an insurable interest in charitable organizations that are the owners and beneficiaries of donated insurance policies. Indeed, the state involved in this ruling subsequently amended its law, on a retroactive basis, to provide for an insurable interest in charitable organizations with respect to donors of life insurance policies. Thereafter, the IRS revoked its ruling, noting that the individual was not proceeding with the gift.[28]

A state court in 1992 held that an ex-spouse has an insurable interest in the life of the other ex-spouse, even though the beneficiary ex-spouse also has a substantial interest in the insured's death.[29] This opinion is of particular applicability in connection with the continuing uncertainty as to whether a charitable organization can have an insurable interest in the life of a contributor of a life insurance policy. In this case, the ex-wife wished to purchase insurance on the life of her ex-husband, who was paying alimony to her, to continue a stream of income to her in the event of his demise. However, the former husband refused to cooperate, fearing that his former wife would soon see to his passing. He indicated that he did not want to be "worth more dead than alive" to his former wife. She sued to force him to consent to the purchase of the insurance.

The court found that the ex-wife had an insurable interest in the life of the ex-husband, based on the state's statutory law. The court also decided that, divorce notwithstanding, a former wife who is entitled to alimony has an insurable interest in her former husband's life. The court recognized that the "primary purpose of the prohibition [on life insurance absent insurable interest] is to prevent wagering on the life of another, . . . although, as other authorities

[28] IRS Private Letter Ruling 9147040.
[29] *Hopkins* v. *Hopkins*, _____ A.2d _____ (Ct. App. Md. 1992).

recognize, . . . the prevention of murder is another rationale."[30] It quoted another court as writing that the rule as to insurable interest stems from the need "to avoid extending to the beneficiary the temptation to hasten by improper means the time when he [or she] will receive the benefits of the policy."[31] (The court noted the "rancorous history" between the parties, which was cited by the ex-husband as the basis for his position.[32]) However, the court also found that this ex-wife had, as beneficiary of the policy, an interest in the ex-husband's death. Instead of finding that that interest obviates any insurable interest, the court recognized a "conflict of interest." That is, the ex-wife was held to have both an interest in the insured's continued life (the insurable interest) and an interest in his death. The court wryly observed, quoting from another court opinion, that "this conflict might be a fruitful source of crime."[33] This conflict of interest was held to be resolvable by the consent of the would-be insured. The putative insured was said to be able to "evaluate the risk to his own interest" in deciding whether or not to become an insured.[34] Thus, the case turned on a state statute requiring consent by an insured to the insurance coverage even where the potential beneficiary has an insurable interest in the life of the insured. In the case, the court said that the former husband "emphatically does not consent" to this insurance and that he cannot be compelled to consent[35]; the ex-wife thus was unable to obtain the insurance coverage.

This opinion has a substantial bearing on the matter of insurable interest in the setting of charitable giving. In the instance, as noted, of an individual who is a valued volunteer and a major annual contributor to a charitable organization, it would seem that the organization has an insurable interest in this individual's life, at least in connection with the gift of a life insurance policy by him or her. Certainly, the charity has an economic interest in the ongoing life of the individual. Being the beneficiary of an insurance policy is not likely to cause someone representing the charity to succumb to the "temptation to hasten by improper means the time when . . . [the charity] will receive the benefits of the policy."

[30] *Id.* at _____.
[31] *Id.* at _____.
[32] *Id.* at _____.
[33] *Id.* at _____.
[34] *Id.* at _____.
[35] *Id.* at _____.

There is nearly always an interest for a charitable organization in the death of an individual, particularly when that individual is the insured on a life insurance policy of which the charity is the owner and beneficiary. But one of the important aspects of this opinion is that the court did not find that the interest in the beneficiary's death undercut or eliminated the insurable interest—it found that the interest in death *conflicted* with the insurable interest. Thus, this case is authority for the thought that a charity's interest in receiving the proceeds of an insurance policy is not automatically a basis for a finding that there is no insurable interest. As noted, the court found that this conflict of interest can be cured through consent. Obviously, a contributor of an insurance policy to a charity has consented to being an insured where the charity is the beneficiary. Thus, it would seem that, if an ex-spouse can have an insurable interest in the life of the other ex-spouse, where the beneficiary ex-spouse also has an economic interest in the demise of the other ex-spouse (that is, where the potential decedent ex-spouse is "worth more dead than alive"), a charitable organization that is an owner/beneficiary of an insurance policy by gift would have an insurable interest as well. This opinion offers a new approach to thinking about the relationship between charitable giving and insurable interests.

§ 16.5   UNRELATED DEBT-FINANCED INCOME CONSIDERATIONS

It has been held that the investment income resulting from life insurance gift programs can be unrelated business income.[36]

This court held that loans against the accumulated cash value of life insurance policies constitutes "indebtedness," so that the income derived from the reinvestment of the proceeds in marketable securities is treated as income from debt-financed property.[37] The court decided, on the basis of court opinions finding that insurance policy loans have generally been regarded as a form of indebtedness and that this type of borrowing has been held sufficient to support a federal income tax interest deduction, that the withdrawals are a form of indebtedness for purposes of the debt-financed income rules.

The court placed great emphasis on the legislative history of the

---

[36] *Mose and Garrison Siskin Memorial Foundation, Inc.* v. *United States*, 790 F.2d 480 (6th Cir. 1986).
[37] IRC § 514.

1964 revision of the federal tax law, which disallows a deduction for certain insurance loans.[38] However, the court wrote, since Congress thus intended to preserve the interest deduction for payments on other types of insurance loans, Congress implicitly considers loans against the accumulated cash value of life insurance policies as "indebtedness." The court noted that federal tax law[39] allows a deduction for all interest paid or accrued on indebtedness. Consequently, the court reasoned that if a life insurance loan involves an indebtedness in one tax context, it must be an indebtedness in all tax contexts, including the rules for taxation of unrelated debt-financed income.

Universal life insurance offers (or appears to offer) a solution to this problem. As noted above, cash value may be withdrawn from universal life policies without creating a policy loan. Thus, a charitable organization could withdraw cash value, re-invest it, and avoid the problem of having the property considered "debt-financed" property which generates unrelated business income.

[38] IRC § 264.
[39] IRC § 163(a).

17

Establishing and Maintaining a Planned Giving Program

§ 17.1 INTRODUCTION

Charitable organizations are underutilizing planned giving. Part of the reason for this phenomenon, which is rather remarkable considering the extent of gifts that can be developed by means of the planned giving techniques, lies in the mystery that surrounds planned giving. For all too many individuals and organizations, it is perceived as far too complex.

Another reason for this underuse of planned giving can be found in the name that this type of giving used to have: deferred giving. Since planned giving seems so intricate and is believed not to generate badly needed current dollars, the implementation of a planned giving program is usually deferred, literally, to another day, a day that, all too often, never seems to come.

Still another reason for this less than full utilization of planned giving is found in the belief that planned giving is only for the larger charitable organizations, those that have been in existence for some time and that have an existing constituency (such as churches and universities). Finally, the lack of planned giving programs can be traced to the belief that the initial process of establishing a planned giving program is too expensive.

None of these reasons (excuses, really) for delaying a planned giving program are valid. Nearly every charitable organization, no matter how small or how new, should have some semblance of a planned giving program.

The very term "planned giving" usually causes some uncertainty.

The two words obviously do not mean that all other gifts are un-planned. A far better term would be "integrated giving," in that the concept of planned giving means a gift that is of sufficient magnitude that the making of it is integrated with the donor's personal financial plan or estate plan. A planned gift, then, is not a gift made on an impulse; it is planned in the sense that the consequences of the gift (other than those to the charitable donee) as they relate, for example, to the donor's family or business, are taken into account before the gift is made and in determining the type of gift it will be.

Probably the simplest of planned gifts is a bequest in a will.[1] The larger the gift or the more complicated the terms (such as the inclusion of one or more trusts), the greater the extent of the planning—but a planned gift it is. Writing a will means formulating a plan; so does the writing of a trust.

Usually an outright gift of money or property is not regarded as a planned gift, although sometimes an outright contribution of property can be, such a gift of a business or a partnership interest. A mere gift of an insurance policy may not be a planned gift, but the process of deliberately selecting a particular policy for donation to a charity and the giving of it can easily entail some serious planning.[2]

Most planned gifts are those that are based on the fundamental principle that property consists of two interests: an income interest and a remainder interest.[3] Planned gifts usually involve the donation to charity of either an income interest or a remainder interest. A gift of an income interest is made by means of a charitable lead trust.[4] Most remainder interest gifts are made using a charitable remainder trust,[5] a pooled income fund,[6] or a charitable gift annuity.[7]

The fund-raiser's delight in working in the planned giving area is that he or she can do more than ask for gifts and collect them. He or she can simultaneously render valuable services to the donor. The donor may end up with more income as the result of the gift. The donor's earnings may become taxed at capital gains rates rather than

[1]See Chapter 8.
[2]See Chapter 16.
[3]See Chapter 3.
[4]See Chapter 15.
[5]See Chapter 11.
[6]See Chapter 12.
[7]See Chapter 13.

ordinary income rates, or perhaps not taxed at all. The donor has been enabled to dispose of property without paying capital gains taxes or of property he or she really did not need. The donor may become able to pass property to other family members without incurring estate taxes. Planned giving can be the foundation for retirement plans, tuition payments, and memorial gifts. The list goes on and on.

So, if planned giving is so beneficial to both donor and donee, why is every charitable organization not using it? The principal reasons were given at the outset. However, another reason may be that the organization simply does not quite know how to begin. Here, then, are the ten steps—from a legal viewpoint—to implementation of a planned giving program.

§ 17.2 STEPS OF IMPLEMENTATION

The ten steps for implementing a planned giving program (each of which are discussed next) are the following:

1.   The board of directors or trustees passed a "planned giving program launch resolution."
2.   A brief presentation is made at a board meeting.
3.   Prototype documents are developed.
4.   Registration is made at a board meeting.
5.   Marketing literature is prepared or purchased.
6.   A cadre of volunteers is started.
7.   Prospective donors are identified.
8.   Prospective donors are contacted.
9.   Planned gifts are obtained.
10. The staff and volunteers begin the never-ending task of learning the techniques and procedures of planned giving.

(a) Step 1

First and foremost, the members of the organization's board of directors or board of trustees must be involved. At this point, "being involved" does not mean as donors; that part comes later. It means being involved in the launching of the program.

The best way to start this process is by causing the board to pass a planned giving program launch resolution. This is a resolution that states that there is to be such a program, who on the staff and among the officers is principally responsible for it, and—most importantly—what planned giving methods are going to be used. On this last point, the resolution should expressly identify the vehicles: wills, charitable remainder trusts, insurance, pooled income fund, or whatever.

(b)   Step 2

Most of the board members will not have heard of these vehicles (other than wills) and that opens the way to step two. At a board meeting, some time should be set aside for a brief presentation on the basics of planned giving. The presentation should be made by an outsider: a lawyer, professional development counsel, or bank trust officer, for example. The board members should be given some written material to peruse afterward.

(c)   Step 3

Once the board has received its initial training and has adopted the launch resolution, step three is to develop some prototype instruments. These are documents, with the organization's name already in the appropriate places, that can be shown to interested parties. These documents may include will clauses, charitable remainder trusts (both annuity trust and unitrust, and one life and two lives), stock powers, pooled income fund transfer agreements, and/or charitable gift annuity contracts.

Donors will rarely be interested in these prototype documents. Some of the board members may be. Certainly those who are going to be asking for planned gifts should have some basic familiarity with them. However, the greatest use of these instruments will be to provide them to the potential donor's counsel, be it lawyer, accountant, financial planner, insurance agent, securities broker, or advisor. These persons, too, may be unfamiliar with planned giving and will find actual documents very helpful.

(d)   Step 4

Government regulation of planned giving programs is unavoidable, so step four is to adhere to the requirements of law. Asking for the planned gift is still asking for a gift, so it is important to register in each of the states that have charitable solicitation acts if the charity has not already done so.[8] If charitable gift annuities are to be used, state insurance law requirements must be complied with. Some states' securities laws will apply in this context, particularly with respect to pooled income fund gifts.

(e) Step 5

Step five is the beginning of the marketing phase. This step may involve a myriad of alternatives, but the first must be the acquisition of some easy-to-understand brochures on the concept and methods of planned giving that will be distributed to prospective donors. It is far preferable to have separate brochures on each of the techniques rather than to have one large (and likely unread) booklet. The organization can either write and print these brochures itself or purchase them commercially.

The board of directors have now been provided copies of the literature. Now starts the process of getting some (preferably all) of the directors or trustees to commit to some form of planned gift. It is not easy causing others to give when the organization's own leadership has not (or worse, will not).

(f) Step 6

In step six, the organization should start the process of building a network or cadre of volunteers who will be planned giving advocates to the outside world. This group should be comprised, in part, of members of the board of directors. Other possibilities include persons from the organization's prior leadership, active members, community leaders, and volunteer professionals (such as lawyers and accountants). These individuals will assist in procuring planned gifts, by making such gifts themselves, by asking others, and/or by influencing others who will do the asking.

This cadre of volunteers will need some training before they are sent out looking for gifts. Special sessions with someone knowledgeable about planned giving is essential, as is the provision of written materials. The intent is not to make these persons planned giving experts overnight or even to expect them to procure the gift. Their job is to become sufficiently familiar with planned giving so they

[8]See *The Law of Fund-Raising*, principally, Chapters 3 and 4.

know the basics about each method and something about how to correlate those basics with the facts and circumstances of each prospect's situation. The actual "ask" will probably be by a staff person or a professional planned giving consultant.

(g) Step 7

Step seven is to identify prospective donors. Of course, this step is, in actuality, an ongoing process. If the organization has a membership, that obviously is the base of individuals with which to begin. The giving history of donors (frequency and amount of gifts) should be reviewed to determine planned giving prospects. Others who are interested in the organization's programs are prospects as well. Even new organizations have those who are supporters and thus who are potential planned givers.

(h) Step 8

Once the prospective donors are identified, they must be contacted; this is step eight. It is, in essence, the marketing phase, and how it is done will vary from group to group. One tried-and-true approach is to send a letter to the prospective contributors explaining the planned giving program and inviting them to request additional information; those who respond are sent the appropriate brochures. Another approach is to concentrate on one vehicle, such as the pooled income fund or insurance, and market just that method by sending the brochure with the introductory letter. Some organizations like to lead with a wills program.

There are many other marketing techniques. Some organizations have had success with financial planning seminars, where planned giving is stressed. Others hold seminars, not for donors but for those in the community who advise donors (again, lawyers, financial planners, accountants, and the like). If the organization has a magazine or newsletter, it should regularly publish items on planned giving in these publications. If the organization has an annual meeting, a presentation on planned giving should be on the agenda. One favorite is the annual membership meeting, where a planned giving booth is among the other displays in the exhibit hall.

The marketing aspects of planned giving must be ongoing ones. Some organizations can use all of these techniques. For launching a planned giving program, a combination of a special mailing, a seminar, and coverage in the organization's regular publications can be powerful.

(i) Step 9

Step nine—obviously a crucial one—is the process of actually obtaining the gift ("closing the deal") once a bona fide prospect has signaled some interest. On this point, it is hard to generalize. For organizations with an emerging planned giving program, the best way to proceed is to have a staff person or a volunteer meet with the prospective contributor and work out a general plan, then have a subsequent session with a planned giving professional who can advise the parties as to the specific giving method that is best for all concerned. Thereafter, a lawyer or other individual can prepare the specific instrument.[9]

A recent gift unfolded in this way, resulting in the organization's first charitable remainder trust. An individual had been contacted about the planned giving program. Having coincidentally received a large amount of money as the result of a sale of property, he was looking for some tax relief. He had an interest in the organization, so he and a staff person met and worked out these general guidelines: he needed a charitable deduction of X amount and an annual income of Y amount. The parties subsequently met with a lawyer, the numbers were run on a computer, the deduction and income amounts for each planned giving method were reviewed, and a specific arrangement (using a charitable remainder trust) was developed.

(j) Step 10

One thing is clear: The organization's staff and volunteers will only learn by doing. As the gifts come in and the various processes that led to the gift are experienced, the parties involved will gain greater confidence and thus will need to rely on the outside professional less. Nonetheless, it is advisable to have a planned giving professional on call at the outset, and thereafter use him or her as circumstances warrant. This is step ten, which may have occurred much earlier in the process: the selection of legal counsel who can work

---

[9]As noted in Chapters 11 and 12, the IRS has published prototypes of many forms of charitable remainder trusts and pooled income funds. See Appendices E and F.

with the organization in the launching and ongoing administration of the program.

As noted at the outset, one of the excuses frequently given for postponing the inauguration of a planned giving program (or ignoring the idea of such a program altogether) is that it is not suitable for a new organization. There is no question that a university with decades of graduations has a much more solid donor base than a community service group incorporated last week. But that university's relative advantage is not an authentic reason for doing nothing. Every organization has a support base or it would not exist. It may be that, on day one, there is only one planned gift prospect, yet that is no reason to not ask that one prospect. The largest planned giving program in the country started with one gift.

§ 17.3   OBTAINING CURRENT INCOME

Another excuse for not implementing a planned giving program is that the organization must channel all of its fund-raising energies into the generation of current dollars. Of all the excuses for not beginning, this is the most plausible. Nonetheless, it is still an excuse, not a reason.

There are two aspects of planned giving that are misunderstood when it comes to the need for current support. One is that there are some forms of planned giving that produce current dollars. Planned giving is not simply waiting thirty years for someone to die. Three planned giving methods that yield current dollars are

- the charitable lead trust, where the donor gives immediate income, rather than the deferred remainder interest,[10]
- the charitable remainder trust, where the donor (in addition to giving the remainder interest) gives a portion of the income interest to the charity,[11]
- gifts of life insurance, where the policy can be surrendered if necessary for its cash value or the charity can borrow money using the cash value as collateral.[12]

[10]See Chapter 15.
[11]See Chapter 11.
[12]See Chapter 16.

The other misunderstanding is that planned gifts generate usable support much more quickly than is generally realized. Individuals can die sooner than expected (or, to state the matter more diplomatically, not everyone reaches their life expectancy). The odds being what they are, the larger the stable of planned gifts, the greater the likelihood of a speedy return.

Also, the planned gift is ideal for the organization that is amassing a general endowment, scholarship, memorial, research, building, or similar fund. While everyone likes current gift dollars, once a base of investment assets (principal) is established, the investment income can nicely complement the gift support, and the organization has the security of knowing that the assets remain in place.

The more it is understood that planned giving means service to the donors and large gifts, the more appreciated it will be. Some money will have to be expended at the outset, but it will be minimal in relation to the gifts received. It is simply a matter of getting started—of taking the "deferral" out of this form of giving. Once the program is launched, the mystery will fall away and planned giving will become the most enjoyable and remunerative part of the fundraising and development program.

Part V

Cross-Border Charitable Giving

18

International Giving by Individuals During Lifetime

by Carole S. George

The charitable impulse is not confined to any national borders. Individuals, business corporations, private foundations, and other charitable and noncharitable organizations in the United States are increasingly finding the means by which to transfer materials and funds to troubled areas of the world. Although not always as simple as domestic giving, international charitable giving is not only feasible, but may be the way of the future as collectively individuals and organizations strive to meet large global social, cultural, and environmental needs.

§ 18.1 INTRODUCTION

Some would say that the nations of the world are uniting. Others insist that a process of Balkanization is underway. Few would deny that the frontiers of the world are being redefined.

Attendant to geopolitical changes are internal national restructurings, which are weakening sovereignties that have traditionally financed all social needs. Nearly everyone has been impressed by the deep and critical needs in all sectors of life within, for example, the Central and Eastern European countries. Yet the rise of charitable organizations and the necessity for them is truly an international phenomenon.

This chapter describes the legal requirements underlying the United States income tax charitable deduction for gifts to foreign charities made by American individuals. In general, contributions by individuals during lifetime to overseas organizations do not result in an income tax charitable deduction, due to historic policies that restrict deductibility to those charitable activities that essentially relieve expenditures of United States public funds. Nonetheless, these gifts, in certain situations, will be deductible if the requisite control over their disbursement to foreign charitable organizations and activities is strictly controlled and managed by domestic incorporated charitable bodies.

An increase in the mobility of managers of multinational companies and a tendency toward retirement in foreign countries have led to greater foreign property ownership. These facts, coupled with the increase in trans-border philanthropic activity by residents and businesses in industrialized countries, have greatly expanded the likelihood that transborder charitable mechanisms will be an important part of planning estates.

The extent to which gifts by bequest to foreign charitable organizations will be deductible under the American estate and gift tax schemes is discussed in Chapter 19. These tax provisions do not prohibit the use of funds overseas. Gifts to foreign corporations serving charitable purposes and donations to governmental entities that act as trustees in directing the funds to charitable purposes may be deductible.

Chapter 20 describes the methods by which an American company can obtain tax benefits through the practice of overseas corporate giving. Particular attention is focused on the utility of a corporate foundation. In this sense, the chapter also discusses the rules and regulations governing overseas activities of American private foundations, inasmuch as corporate grant-making foundations are generally technically classified as private foundations.[1]

§ 18.2 BACKGROUND

Prior to passage of the Revenue Act of 1938, United States individual taxpayers were allowed to make deductible contributions to charitable organizations regardless of where the organizations had been created or were located. Corporations did not enjoy this freedom: The Revenue Act of 1935,[2] which first allowed a deduction for corporate charitable contributions, limited that deduction to contributions

---

[1]A summary of the definition of the term "private foundation" is in Chapter 4 § 3.
[2]Section 102(c).

to organizations established in the United States that used the contributions within the United States.

The rule treating individual contributions was modified by the Revenue Act of 1938. That Act[3] provided that contributions by individuals were deductible only if the recipient was a domestic organization. The House Ways and Means committee report in this regard[4] declared that the rationale for allowing these deductions was that any loss of tax revenue was seen to be offset by relief of an obligation that otherwise would require public funds. Obviously gifts to foreign institutions did not produce any of these benefits.

According to this committee report:

> Under the 1936 Act the deduction of charitable contributions by corporations is limited to contributions made to domestic institutions . . . . The bill provides that the deduction allowed to taxpayers other than corporations be also restricted to contributions made to domestic institutions. The exemption from taxation of money or property devoted to charitable and other purposes is based upon the theory that the Government is compensated for the loss of revenue by its relief from financial burden which would otherwise have to be met by appropriations from public funds, and by the benefits resulting from the promotion of the general welfare. The United States derives no such benefit from gifts to foreign institutions, and the proposed limitation is consistent with the above theory. If the recipient, however, is a domestic organization the fact that some portion of its funds is used in other countries for charitable and other purposes (such as missionary and educational purposes) will not affect the deductibility of the gift.[5]

The Revenue Act of 1939[6] changed the requirement that a qualifying organization be "domestic" to the requirement that it have been "created or organized in the United States or in any possession thereof. . . ." In virtually identical form, this requirement was re-enacted[7] as part of the Internal Revenue Code of 1954 and carried over to today's Internal Revenue Code of 1986.

Since 1939, the IRS has consistently held that donations by individuals to or for the use of domestic charitable organizations are deductible even though they are entirely used abroad, subject to the

---

[3] Section 23(o).
[4] H.R. Rep. No. 1860, 75th Cong., 3rd Sess. 19-20 (1938).
[5] *Id.*
[6] Section 224.
[7] IRC § 170(c)(2)(A).

"conduit" and "earmarking" restrictions discussed below. This long-standing position was stated in a general counsel memorandum in 1958. In 1972, the position was expressly incorporated into the tax regulations,[8] which provide as follows:

> A charitable contribution by an individual to or for the use of an organization described in section 170(c) [that is, a charitable organization] may be deductible even though all, or some portion, of the funds of the organization may be used in foreign countries for charitable or educational purposes.

On the other hand, gifts given directly to foreign charities are not deductible as charitable contributions because of the requirement that the recipient organization be a domestic entity, that is, a corporation, trust or community chest, fund or foundation that is established in the United States.[9]

The classification of domestic versus foreign organizations is not necessarily transparent. For example, one court denied a charitable deduction for a direct gift from an American taxpayer to the First Church of Christ, Scientist, in Berne, Switzerland, a Swiss corporation. The organization's claim to United States provenance was grounded on the fact that it was an affiliate of The First Church of Christ, Scientist, in Boston, Massachusetts, a Massachusetts corporation. The court reviewed the organizational documents of the Swiss organization, and discovered the provision:

> The Mother Church of Christ, Scientist, shall assume no general official control of other churches, and it shall be controlled by none other.

> Each Church of Christ, Scientist, shall have its own form of government. No conference of churches shall be held, unless it be when our churches, located in the same State, convene to confer on a statute of said State, or to confer harmoniously on individual unity and action of the churches in said State.

The court determined that this statement negated the contention that the Mother Church and the Berne branch were inseparable. The Swiss organization was thus held to be legally independent of the American church. Therefore, the individual's contribution to the

---

[8]Reg. § 1.170A-8(a)(1).
[9]IRC § 170(c)(2)(A).

First Church of Christ, Scientist, Berne (Switzerland), was held to be not deductible.[10]

However, in another situation, the same court decided in favor of the American donor. In this instance, a school had been created in France under French corporation laws and had operated there for many years before incorporating in Delaware. The IRS maintained that the United States corporation had no activities and was merely a shell created to attract tax-deductible American contributions. The Tax Court found that the organization was created in the United States by virtue of the Delaware incorporation. Further, the court observed that the organization did not distribute any of its funds to a foreign organization operating a school in France. Rather, the organization itself was found to be operating the Paris school and applied contributions received toward operation of that school. This was sufficient to characterize the entity as a domestic charity for United States law purposes, notwithstanding the school's foreign origin. The operational nexus with the United States organization, even though essentially technical, was sufficient to distinguish the domestic organization from a mere shell (discussed below).[11]

The second of these two opinions is difficult to reconcile with the "earmarking" and "conduit" restrictions discussed below. Application of the teachings of this case to any factual situation would have to be made with caution.[12]

§ 18.3   THE "EARMARKING" AND "CONDUIT" RESTRICTIONS

As discussed above, an American taxpayer who is an individual is not permitted to claim an income tax charitable deduction for a gift that flows directly to a foreign charitable organization, based upon fundamental policies underlying the charitable deduction framework. Nonetheless, an American individual taxpayer may be permitted to make a contribution to an incorporated American charity that devotes some or all of its funds to overseas activities. The ability to claim the deduction depends upon the degree of control exerted by the Ameri-

---

[10] *Welti* v. *Commissioner*, 1 T.C. 905 (1943).

[11] *Bilingual Montessori School of Paris, Inc.*, v. *Commissioner*, 75 T.C. 480 (1980).

[12] Further analysis of this body of law is in *The Law of Tax-Exempt Organizations*, Chapter 44 § 5.

can charitable organization and the lack of control imposed by the donor in directing that the gift be applied to foreign charitable activities.

Following a basic American tax law principle, deductibility of a contribution does not necessarily depend upon its payment to a qualifying organization. If the gift is "earmarked" for a further destination, it is appropriate to look beyond the immediate recipient, although a qualifying organization, to determine whether the payment is a charitable contribution that will bring an income tax deduction to the donor.

In one instance, a court considered the question whether amounts paid to a foster home for the care of a named individual were furnished for the use and benefit of the home and hence qualified as deductible charitable contributions. The earmarking in this instance transformed the gift to the foster home into a gift to a particular individual. In the eyes of the court, the "contributions" were not to be used in any manner as deemed appropriate by the home, but were for the use of a single individual in whom the "donor" felt a keen fatherly and personal interest. The charitable contribution deduction was denied in this circumstance.[13]

The IRS, in applying this principle to transfers of contributions from United States sources to foreign organizations, concluded:

> 'A given result at the end of a straight path is not made a different result because reached by following a devious path.' . . . Moreover, it seems clear that the requirements of . . . [the federal income tax law] would be nullified if contributions inevitably committed to a foreign organization were held to be deductible solely because, in the course of transmittal to a foreign organization, they came to rest momentarily in a qualifying domestic organization. In such case the domestic organization is only nominally the donee; the real donee is the ultimate foreign recipient.[14]

IRS ruling policy permits a United States charitable organization to fund a foreign charitable organization and/or individual when

- the domestic organization's purpose can be furthered by granting funds to one or more foreign entities,

[13] *Thomason v. Commissioner*, 2 T.C. 441 (1943).
[14] Rev. Rul. 63-252, 1963-2 C.B. 101. In reaching this conclusion, the IRS relied on *Minnesota Tea Co. v. Helvering*, 302 U.S. 609, 613 (1938); and *Griffiths v. Helvering*, 308 U.S. 355, 358 (1939).

- the domestic organization has reviewed and approved of the foreign entity's purposes, and
- the grants are paid from general funds rather than from special funds solicited on behalf of the foreign organization.[15]

Difficulty arises, from the IRS's point of view, when a domestic charity is empowered in such a way that it is no more than an agent of or trustee for a particular foreign organization, has purposes so narrow that its funds can go only to a particular foreign organization, or solicits funds on behalf of a particular foreign organization.

The IRS has analyzed five situations:

1. A foreign organization that caused a domestic organization to be formed in order to conduct a fundraising campaign in the United States, pay administrative expenses from the collected funds, and remit any balance to the foreign organization.

2. Certain persons in the United States, desirous of furthering the work of a foreign organization, who formed a domestic charitable organization to receive contributions and send them periodically to the foreign organization.

3. A foreign organization and a domestic organization that had previously received a ruling that contributions to it would be deductible as charitable gifts entered into an agreement under which the domestic organization was to conduct a fund-raising campaign on behalf of the foreign organization, representing to prospective contributors that the raised funds would go to the foreign organization.

4. A domestic organization that conducts a variety of charitable activities in a foreign country, sometimes grants funds to foreign charitable organization to further the domestic organization's purposes. These grants are made for purposes that the domestic organization has reviewed and approved, and the grants are made from the organization's general funds rather than from a special fund raised on behalf of the foreign organization.

5. A domestic organization that does work in a foreign country and forms a subsidiary in that country to facilitate its opera-

---

[15]Rev. Rul. 63-252, *supra*, n. 14.

tion. The subsidiary was formed for purposes of administrative convenience, and the domestic organization controls all facets of its operations. The domestic organization will solicit funds for the specific purpose of carrying out its charitable activities in the foreign country, as it had before forming the foreign subsidiary, but will now transmit such funds directly to the foreign subsidiary.[16]

A common theme in the first three of these cases is that the organizations are charitable organizations nominally created in the United States. They are organized or operated solely to solicit funds on behalf of pre-existing foreign entities. The domestic entities are effectively agents or conduit organizations for the foreign beneficiaries. As such, contributions to them are not deductible under United States law as charitable gifts. Examples four and five describe organizations that solicit funds without any express understanding that they will be forwarded to foreign entities. They are independent organizations with their own charitable programs. These organizations exercise "discretion and control" over the funds solicited from United States sources. Consequently, gifts to them are deductible. The view of the IRS is that the real donees in the first, second, and third of these situations are the foreign organizations and, thus, contributions ostensibly to the domestic organization are not deductible under United states law. In contrast, the IRS has concluded that contributions to the domestic organizations in the fourth and fifth situations are deductible as charitable gifts because the domestic organizations in these situations actually received and essentially controlled the use of the funds.

The seminal IRS ruling on the point ends with the following language that draws on the principles enunciated in the case law:

> It is recognized that special earmarking of the use or destination of funds paid to a qualifying charitable organization may deprive the donor of a deduction . . . [citations omitted.] These cases indicate that an inquiry as to the deductibility of a contribution need not stop once it is determined that an amount has been paid to a qualifying organization; if the amount is earmarked then it is appropriate to look beyond the fact that the immediate recipient is a qualifying organization to determine whether the payment constitutes a deductible contribution.

[16]*Id.*

Similarly, if an organization is required for other reasons,
specific provision in its charter, to turn contributions, or an,
contributions it receives, over to another organization, then in deπ.
mining whether such contributions are deductible, it is appropriate to
determine whether the ultimate recipient of the contribution is a qualifying organization. . . . Moreover, it seems clear that the requirements of . . . [the federal tax law] would be nullified if contributions
inevitably committed to go to a foreign organization were held to be
deductible solely because, in the course of transmittal to the foreign
organization, they came to rest momentarily in a qualifying domestic
organization. In such cases, the domestic organization is only nominally the donee; the real donee is the ultimate foreign recipient.[17]

Thus, the problem of earmarking that arises when the American
donee organization acts as a conduit for the American donor is resolved when the American organization exercises meaningful "control
and discretion" as to the ultimate use of the contributions.

An important test in this regard is who solicited whom: Did the
individual taxpayer seek out the recipient organization's cooperation
to facilitate application of the funds to a designated project, or did
the American donee organization seek the donor's support of a project identified by the organization? Where the recipient charitable
organization designated the overseas use of the funds, the donor's
contribution produces an allowable deduction. The donor may specify
among overseas uses presented as options by the charitable organization. Where, however, the donor identifies a desired overseas use,
and employs the charitable organization as a funding agent or conduit, the gift is not allowed as a charitable deduction to the donor.

§ 18.4 CONTROL OVER FOREIGN TRANSFEREES

The matter of what constitutes adequate control of the donated funds
has been clarified by the IRS.[18] This ruling discussed a situation
where a domestic charitable organization solicited contributions in
the United States for a specific project of a foreign counterpart
organization. The charity's charter provided that in furtherance of its
educational, scientific, and charitable purposes it had the power to
receive and to allocate contributions—within the discretion of the
board of directors—to any organization organized and operated ex-

---

[17]Id. at 104.
[18]Rev. Rul. 66-79, 1966-1 C.B. 48.

clusively for charitable or educational purposes within the meaning of the United States tax law. The board of directors had exercised effective review of the project before approving any funding. The board monitored the foreign distributing organization's on-going adherence to the domestic charity's goals. Notwithstanding that the donations were technically "earmarked," the domestic organization demonstrated that it had exercised full control over the donated funds and had retained substantial responsibility as to their use. These standards entail more than merely being able to decide whether or not to contribute and being able to require the foreign recipient to furnish a periodic accounting. In stating its decision, the IRS referred to an earlier ruling which held that, where gifts to a charitable organization were not earmarked by the donor for a particular individual, the deduction would be allowable where it was established that a gift was intended by the donor for the use of the organization and not actually as a gift to a specific individual for whose benefit the gift would be used by the donee organization.[19] The test, said the IRS, is whether the organization retains full control of the donated funds to ensure they will be used to carry out its own charitable purposes.

The conclusion in another IRS pronouncement was that because the trustees of the subject organization were unable to state that all the funds would be used in the United States, this inability led to the result that they did not have sufficient control and discretion over the use of any contributions that they made to foreign distributees.[20] The problem in this case was that the domestic organization did not seem to have any formal operating system by which it could control the selection of projects to be funded—not any means of effective supervision over the use of the funds for a project, not the ability to withhold or control the funds once committed. In this regard, the IRS concluded that it appeared that the domestic organization was intending to remit the monies to the foreign distributee before even considering possible projects and then discussing with the foreign organization the possible uses of its funds. Thus, the operating procedures and inability of the domestic organization to supervise the use of funds by the foreign organization did not evidence that degree of control and discretion required under the law.[21]

[19] Rev. Rul. 62-113, 1962-2 C.B. 10.
[20] IRS General Counsel Memorandum 37444.
[21] Reg. § 1.170A-8(a)(1).

The IRS has presented another analysis of the control and accountability requirement.[22] This ruling discussed a domestic charity formed to address the problem of plant and wildlife ecology in a foreign country through programs that include grants to foreign private organizations. The domestic charity maintains control and responsibility over the use of any funds granted to a foreign organization by first making an investigation of the purpose to which the funds will be directed, by then entering into a written agreement with the recipient organization, and ultimately by making site visits to see that the agreement is being followed. Any foreign organization that receives financial assistance from the charitable organization must be organized and operated in a manner analogous to a United States tax-exempt charitable organization and be completely independent of foreign governments. The charitable organization exercises accountability for the funds dispensed to these programs. Accordingly, it was held that contributions to the organization are deductible as charitable gifts.

In yet another illustration of this form of control and accountability, the IRS considered a domestic association that was organized for the relief of poor, distressed, and displaced persons of certain countries. This domestic association was incapable of listing in advance the names of the ultimate recipients of the monies it would turn over to a foreign organization. Even though the foreign organization promised to use the funds for humanitarian purposes such as furnishing food, clothing, shelter, medical supplies and services for distressed persons, and even though both the foreign organization and its distributees were required to account for the use of the funds, there was too little discretion and control by the domestic organization to meet these standards.[23]

Conversely, a tax-exempt charitable organization does not jeopardize its exemption by making controlled distributions assuredly in furtherance of its own exempt purposes to organizations that are not themselves tax-exempt as charitable entities. "We do not believe this [tax-exempt] status of the distributees is a requirement for the distributor's qualifications" as a charitable organization, the lawyers for the IRS have observed.[24] They added: "It can be readily understood that such status for the foreign distributee is a safeguard for insuring

[22] Rev. Rul. 75-65, 1975-1 C.B. 79.
[23] IRS General Counsel Memorandum 35319.
[24] *Id.*

that charitable funds will be expended solely in furtherance of charitable purposes."

In reaching its conclusion in this particular case, the IRS emphasized that the domestic organization did not know how the funds would be used. This IRS pronouncement further stated that it may not be necessary for a domestic charitable organization to know in advance the precise nature of ultimate distributees to ensure that its qualification as a charitable entity is not jeopardized, if it can establish that its methods of operation include the following types of procedures:

- The domestic charitable organization apprises its agents at the outset of the limitations imposed on it by the terms of United States law in this regard with respect to eligible recipients of its funds and makes clear to its agents that they are subject to the same limitations in distributing its funds;

- The domestic charitable organization reviews proposed projects in detail and approves those reasonably calculated to accomplish one or more of its qualified charitable objectives before turning over any funds to its agents for expenditure for these purposes;

- The domestic charitable organization turns over funds to its agents only as needed for specific projects. This form of expenditure control encourages compliance with the dictates of the domestic organization;

- The domestic charitable organization or an independent agent selected by it for the purpose, makes periodic audits of programs and requires periodic financial statements by its agents. This continuing check provides assurance that the charitable funds in question are not being misspent.

Adoption of these guidelines, as subsequently cited with approval by the IRS,[25] can assist in strengthening the case for the deductibility of contributions as charitable gifts.

§ 18.5 SUMMARY

Although the requirements of the United States tax law with respect to tax exemption as a charitable organization[26] and deductibility of

[25] IRS General Counsel Memorandum 37444.
[26] IRC § 501(c)(3).

charitable gifts[27] are parallel in many respects, they are not identical. In some situations, contributions to or for the use of a foreign organization are not deductible for income tax purposes because the domestic organization requirement[28] is not met.

As respects the case of a domestic organization that serves as a conduit for a foreign charitable organization, contributions to the domestic organization are no more deductible as charitable gifts than if they had been made directly to the foreign organization.

In most other situations, these two provisions operate in parallel fashion. If a domestic organization transmits its funds to a foreign private organization but retains the required control and discretion over the funds—as detailed in examples four and five of the IRS ruling discussed earlier[29]—contributions to it will be deductible as charitable gifts. Conversely, a domestic organization otherwise qualified as a charitable entity forfeits its qualification for tax-exempt and charitable donee status if it regularly transmits its funds to any organization that is not described in the United States rules for charitable organizations,[30] because it then cannot demonstrate that it is operated exclusively for charitable purposes. Further, if the domestic organization fails to exercise discretion and control over the use of funds transmitted to a foreign organization to assure their use exclusively for purposes that qualify as charitable under United States law, those contributions to it will not be deductible.

§ 18.6 TREATY PROVISIONS

The foregoing analysis has concentrated on the general principles of United States law as articulated in the statutes and by the IRS. However, there also are treaty provisions that are relevant to deductibility of cross-border donations.

The only income tax treaty currently in force that references the subject is the Income Tax Treaty Between Canada and The United States, brought into force August 16, 1984. The IRS is currently working with Canada to develop rules for implementing this agreement.

Article XXI of this treaty permits United States persons a deduction for contributions to Canadian charitable organizations and Cana-

[27] IRC § 170(c)(2).
[28] IRC § 170(c)(2)(A).
[29] Rev. Rul. 63-252, *supra*, n. 14.
[30] IRC § 501(c)(3).

dian persons a deduction for contributions to United States charitable organizations. Because of the requirement that the recipient charitable organization be tax-exempt in both countries, or that it would be tax-exempt if it applied for recognition of exemption in both countries, the provision has never been implemented.

The relevant portion of this treaty[31] was essentially carried over from a 1942 convention. It is more generous to colleges and universities. Deductions for contributions, other than to a Canadian college or university at which the United States citizen or resident or a family member of such person is enrolled, are limited to the Canadian source income of the United States citizen or resident. Therefore, a United States citizen with no Canadian income would be unable to benefit from this provision. In addition, the percentage limitations of the United States tax law[32] apply after the limitations established by the treaty.

This portion of that treaty states as follows:

> For the purposes of United States taxation, contributions by a citizen or resident of the United States to an organization which is resident in Canada, which is generally exempt from Canadian tax and which could qualify in the United States to receive deductible contributions if it were resident in the United States shall be treated as charitable contributions; however, such contributions (other than such contributions to a college or university at which the citizen or resident or a member of his family is or was enrolled) shall not be deductible in any taxable year to the extent that they exceed an amount determined by applying the percentage limitations of the laws of the United States in respect to the deductibility of charitable contributions to the income of such citizen or resident arising in Canada. The preceding sentence shall not be interpreted to allow in any taxable year deductions for charitable contributions in excess of the amount allowed under the percentage limitations of the laws of the United States in respect to the deductibility of charitable contributions.

The United States Senate Committee on Foreign Relations Report of May 21, 1984, on the Tax Convention and Proposed Protocols with Canada, stated:

> The Committee recognizes that the special relationship between the United States and Canada may arguably warrant the treaty's expanded

---

[31] Article XXI ¶ 5.
[32] See Chapter 7.

allowance of deductions for contributions to charities of the other country. . . . However, the Committee remains deeply concerned about the granting of deductions to U.S. persons by treaty where the [United States Internal Revenue] Code does not otherwise grant the deductions. . . . The Committee does not believe that treaties are a proper forum for providing deductions not otherwise permitted under domestic law. . . . The Committee wishes to stress that the inclusion of special charitable and convention expense deduction rules in the proposed treaty should not be taken as precedent for future treaty negotiations.

19

International Giving by Individuals Through Estates

by Carole S. George

§ 19.1 INTRODUCTION AND OVERVIEW

The treatment of gifts and bequests under United States estate and gift tax provisions[1] does not limit the use of funds overseas.

The federal estate tax deduction[2] and the federal gift tax deduction[3] permit bequests and gifts by United States residents to foreign organizations for charitable purposes. For estate and gift tax purposes, an individual is considered to be a resident of the United States if that individual maintains his or her domicile in the United States at the time of death or at the time of the gift, whichever is applicable.[4]

The federal estate tax charitable deduction provision is similar to the federal income tax charitable deduction provision[5] in allowing deductions for gifts to United States governmental entities but not to foreign governmental units. Unlike the income tax rule, however, the federal estate tax rule permits deductions for bequests to charitable trusts without requiring that the trusts be domestic organizations.

In the case of a nonresident who is not a United States citizen, gifts will be subject to the gift tax if they are not made to a domestic

---

[1] In general, see Chapter 8.
[2] IRC § 2055(a)(2).
[3] IRC § 2522(a)(2).
[4] Reg. §§ 20.0-1(b)(1); 25.2502-1(b).
[5] IRC § 170(c).

511

charitable corporation.[6] A gift made to any charitable trust, community chest, fund or foundation, by a nonresident who is not a citizen, must be used exclusively within the United States.[7]

§ 19.2   ESTATE TAX PROVISIONS

Federal tax law allows an unlimited charitable deduction from the gross estate of a United States citizen or resident decedent for transfers to qualifying donees for public, charitable, educational, religious, and other similar purposes.[8] The estate tax provisions do not restrict qualifying donees to domestic charitable organizations. Under certain circumstances, transfers to foreign governments for charitable purposes may be allowed.

(a)   Transfer to a Foreign Corporation Serving Charitable Ends

An estate tax deduction is allowed for transfers to or for the use of "any corporation" organized and operated exclusively for religious, charitable, scientific, literary, or educational purposes, including the encouragement of art, or to foster national or international amateur sports competition . . . . and the prevention of cruelty to children or animals.[9]

It is significant to note that this provision of law refers to transfers "to or for the use of any corporation," and does not limit the contemplated transfers to American corporations. The accompanying regulations echo this provision in referring to "any corporation or association."[10]

To qualify as a suitable donee corporation, the foreign organization must meet certain standards. For example, the foreign organization must satisfy the prohibitions against private inurement[11] and political activities.[12] The lobbying restriction applicable to domestic tax-

---

[6]IRC § 2106(a)(2).
[7]IRC § 2522(b)(2) and (3).
[8]IRC § 2055(a).
[9]IRC § 2055(a)(2).
[10]Reg. § 20.2055-1(a)(2).
[11]See *The Law of Tax-Exempt Organizations*, Chapter 13.
[12]*Ibid*, Chapter 15.

exempt charitable organizations[13] extends to foreign associations as well.[14]

This body of law does not define with precision when an organization will be considered "organized and operated exclusively for religious, charitable, scientific, literary or educational purposes." However, the statutory language of the estate tax deduction provision is parallel to that of the income tax deduction provision.[15]

Generally, the term "charitable" is construed in its common law sense and includes, among other concepts:

- relief of the poor and distressed or of the underprivileged,
- advancement of religion, and
- advancement of education or science.

The concept of what constitutes a foreign charitable corporation was discussed in a court opinion.[17] A charitable deduction had been claimed for a proportional residuary bequest to a governmentally owned Canadian hospital as a nonprofit organization operated exclusively for the purpose of providing care for the sick and for medical educational facilities. The gift was determined to qualify for an estate tax charitable deduction under the provision which allows a deduction for bequests to charitable corporations.[18] In this case, involving a private hospital that had been turned over to a city, the hospital was found not to be a political subdivision in the sense that it was either a political unit or an integral governmental instrumentality exercising sovereign powers. Rather, the court determined that the hospital was a nonintegral governmental instrumentality, a clear counterpart of a private charitable corporation organized and operated exclusively for charitable purposes.

(b) Transfer to a Foreign Government Serving Public Purposes

An estate tax charitable deduction is allowed for transfers to or for the use of the United States, any political subdivision thereof, or the

[13]*Id.* Chapter 14.
[14]IRC § 2055(a)(2).
[15]See Chapter 1.
[16]Reg. § 1.501(c)(3)-1(d)(2).
[17]*Old Colony Trust Company* v. *United States.* 433 F.2d 684 (1st Cir. 1971).

District of Columbia, for exclusively public purposes.[19] Although a transfer to a United States governmental subdivision for its general or public purposes would qualify for the deduction, the same gift to a foreign government would not.

In the facts of one court case, an individual died, having bequeathed his entire estate to the Hammer School District of Vrads Parish in Denmark, "[t]o be used by said school district in any manner it may wish for the betterment of the schools or aid to the students of said district." In determining whether a United States estate tax deduction for the gift was allowable, the court referred to the statutory language.[20] The court specifically chose to determine whether the Danish school district was a political subdivision of a foreign government, not whether it was a corporation. Although the Danish school district was a corporation operated exclusively for educational purposes, the law[21] limits deductible bequests to political subdivisions to those that are subdivisions of the American government. Thus the court held that this bequest was not deductible for estate tax purposes.[22]

(c) Transfer to a Trustee

An estate tax charitable deduction is allowed for "contributions or gifts to a trustee or trustees . . . to be used by such trustee or trustees . . . exclusively for religious, charitable, scientific, literary or educational purposes, or for the prevention of cruelty to children or animals."[23]

The question of whether a bequest to a foreign governmental body to be used exclusively for charitable purposes could be deductible as a bequest to a foreign charitable trust has arisen. A growing body of federal case law holds that a bequest to a foreign governmental entity can be instilled with a charitable purpose. In such case, it would be deductible under the rule concerning bequests to a trustee for charitable purposes.[24]

[18] IRS § 2055(a)(2).
[19] IRC § 2055(a)(1).
[20] IRC § 2055(a).
[21] IRC § 2055(a)(1).
[22] *Edwards* v. *Phillips*, 373 F.2d 618 (10th Cir. 1067), *cert. den.*, 389 U.S. 834 (1967).
[23] IRC § 2055(a)(3).
[24] See the text accompanied by n. 23, *supra*.

The two courts that have considered this matter subsequent to this court opinion have expressly rejected the court's rationale and have adopted instead another approach to statutory construction.[25] Both cases involved bequests to foreign governmental units. Both courts applied this rule, allowing a deduction for a bequest to a trustee for exclusively charitable purposes. The precedent was therefore set that a transfer to a foreign government, subdivision or instrumentality may qualify for the estate tax charitable deduction, provided it is restricted exclusively for charitable purposes and the government subdivision acts in a fiduciary capacity.

In another case,[26] the question was whether a clause in the will of an individual constituted a charitable trust and thus qualified as an allowable deduction in the computation of New York state taxes. A controversial paragraph in the decedent's will provided in part as follows:

> I hereby give, devise and bequeath the entire collection of gold and platinum coins left me by my late beloved husband, to the State of Israel, upon condition that the same be kept and exhibited in the State of Israel, in an appropriate museum, that the same be marked and identified to the viewing public as 'The Collection of Dr. Aron A. Kaplun' and that the State of Israel will undertake to keep said collection in perpetuity, never to be sold or otherwise disposed of . . . .

Obviously, the State of Israel is not a domestic governmental body as defined under the law,[27] nor is it a corporation organized and operating exclusively for charitable purposes as described in the law.[28] Thus, the claimed deduction had to stand under the rule concerning gifts to a trustee for a charitable purpose.[29] Whereas the bequest in the earlier case[30] had been given outright to a Danish city school district, the coin collection in this case had been donated to a governmental subdivision to be maintained in trust for the decedent. In drawing a line between what Congress may have intended in limiting an estate tax deduction for gifts that were made directly to foreign governments and those that were given "in trust" to foreign govern-

---

[25] *Schoellkopf* v. *United States*, 124 F.2d 982 (2d Cir. 1942).
[26] *Kaplun* v. *United States*, 436 F.2d 799 (2d Cir. 1970).
[27] IRC § 2055(a)(1).
[28] IRC § 2055(a)(2).
[29] IRC § 2055(a)(3).
[30] *Edwards* v. *Phillips*, *supra*, n. 22.

ments for charitable purposes, the court in this case relied on the reasoning in another court opinion.[31]

In that case, a devise (bequest) had been made to "the mayor and magistratsraete of Fureth, Bayern, Germany to be used and expended for the benefit of said City of Fuerth." A majority of the court refused to apply the reasoning of the prior court opinion, and although the court disallowed the deduction because the bequest was left to a foreign city outright and not in trust, it noted in its ruling that "contributions and gifts to foreign cities for exclusively charitable purposes are deductible," notwithstanding the political nature of the trustee.[32]

The majority and dissent in this case emphasized that Congress logically could have differentiated between public purposes that could be advanced only under the general estate tax deduction rule[33] and the charitable purposes contemplated under the rule concerning bequests to a charitable trustee.[34] The court wrote:

> It seems to us that the word 'public' embodies a broader concept, and envisions gifts to domestic government bodies for purposes other than the ordinary philanthropic purposes most people associate with 'charity.' Consequently, it is our opinion that the use of the word 'public' shows a Congressional intention to bring within the statutory exemption gifts which could be used for such standard governmental functions as the payment of salaries to policemen and firemen. We think there is a clear indication that Congress considered that many contributions which would benefit domestic municipalities are not charitable, because the exemption permits different and broader uses of a bequest than those which are exclusively for charitable purposes.[35]

In another case, an estate was able to take a residuary bequest as a charitable deduction where the devise was made to a foreign political unit in trust for building a home for the aged.[36]

---

[31]*Continental Illinois National Bank and Trust Company of Chicago* v. *United States*, 403 F.2d 721 (Ct.Cl. 1968), cert. den., 394 U.S. 973 (1969).
[32]*Id*, 403 F.2d at 727.
[33]IRC § 2055(a)(1).
[34]IRC § 2055(a)(3).
[35]*Continental Illinois National Bank and Trust Company of Chicago* v. *United States*, *supra*, n. 31, 403 F.2d at 724.
[36]*National Savings and Trust Company* v. *United States*, 436 F.2d 458 (Ct. Cl. 1971).

After these court decisions, the IRS announced that a deduction is allowable under the estate tax rules[37] with respect to a transfer of property to a foreign government or political subdivision thereof for exclusively charitable purposes.[38] The IRS noted the earlier court decision.[39] However, the IRS looked to the more recent decisions,[40] which concluded that where the use of property is limited to exclusively charitable purposes,[41] a gift by bequest to a foreign government body or political subdivision will qualify for a charitable deduction.

The essence of this IRS announcement was the basis of a subsequent court opinion.[42] The issue was the reformation of a provision in a will. The decedent, according to the court, had intended the municipality of Kerasitsa, Greece, rather than his children, to be the ultimate heir of a hospital built there from proceeds of the sale of his United States real estate. The court generally restated the IRS position: "[The IRS] makes no argument that if we find the remainder interest vested in some entity other than decedent's heirs that the bequest is still outside the bounds of . . . [the federal estate tax charitable deduction]. Petitioner asserts that the decedent intended for the hospital to pass to the village government upon its completion and that this intent establishes the charitable nature of the bequest."[43]

A further demonstration of the utility of the IRS position appears in an IRS private letter ruling.[44] An attempt had been made by a court to reform a bequest to meet the estate tax law requirements.[45] The IRS determined, however, that in order for the taxpayer to be able to reform a nonqualifying charitable remainder trust, the beneficiary designated in the will had to be an organization or purpose described or defined in the law of charity.[46] The State of Israel had

[37] IRC § 2055.
[38] Rev. Rul. 74-523, 1974-2 C.B. 304.
[39] *Edwards* v. *Phillips, supra,* n. 22.
[40] *Old Colony Trust company* v. *United States, supra,* n. 17; *Kaplun* v. *United States, supra,* n. 26; and *National Savings and Trust Company* v. *United States, supra,* n. 36.
[41] IRC §§ 2055(a)(2) and 2055(a)(3).
[42] *Orphanos, Estate of* v. *Commissioner,* 67 T.C. 780 (1977).
[43] *Id* at 782.
[44] IRS Private Letter Ruling 7938001.
[45] IRC §§ 2055(a) and 2055(e).
[46] IRC § 2055(a).

been named as the beneficiary. The IRS announced: "If the beneficiary designated in the will had been a . . . [charitable] organization or purpose, the trust established under the decedent's will, as conformed by a probate court order, would have constituted a charitable remainder annuity trust . . ."[47]

In another instance, an executor of an estate attempted to salvage a bequest of residuary property given in trust to a foreign government. The foreign country acknowledged that the bequest would be used for an agricultural high school in that country. The issue was whether the actual charitable use to which the funds were applied would qualify the gift for the deduction when in fact the will had not specifically so directed. The IRS concluded that "the fact [the foreign country] has agreed to use its gift for charitable purposes does not convert an otherwise general gift into a charitable gift."[48]

(d)   Special Rule for Testamentary Charitable Remainder Trusts

A charitable organization to or for the use of which the remainder interest passes must meet the requirements of the estate tax deduction[49] as well as the remainder trust rules.[50] Therefore the charitable entity to which the remainder interest in a charitable remainder annuity trust passes may not be a foreign corporation.[51]

§ 19.3   GIFT TAX PROVISIONS

The federal tax law allows an unlimited gift tax charitable deduction for gifts to qualifying donees.[52] This deduction is not subject to the percentage limitations applicable to the income tax charitable deduction.[53]

Although a donor may be willing to forego an income tax charitable deduction in order to benefit a foreign charitable organization,

---

[47]The charitable remainder annuity trust rules are the subject of Chapter 11.
[48]IRS Technical Advice Memorandum 8748001.
[49]IRC § 2055(a).
[50]IRC §§ 642(c)(5)(A), 664(d)(1)(C), or 664(d)(2)(C), whichever applies.
[51]Reg. § 20.2055-2(e)(2)(v).
[52]IRC § 2522(a).
[53]See Chapter 7.

care should be taken to ensure that the donor does not inadvertently make a taxable gift. The rules governing the gift tax charitable deduction are similar to those applicable to the estate tax charitable deduction: A gift tax deduction is not limited to gifts to or for the use of domestic charitable corporations.

§ 19.4   CHARITABLE GIVING OF NONRESIDENT WHO IS NOT A CITIZEN

(a)   Estate Tax Provisions

When the decedent is a nonresident who is not a citizen of the United States, the federal tax law allows a charitable deduction from the United States gross estate for transfers to qualifying donees "to or for the use of the United States, any political subdivision thereof, or the District of Columbia" for exclusively public purposes: "charitable, educational, religious and other similar purposes."[54] The deduction is limited to transfers to domestic charitable corporations and transfers to trustees for use in the United States.[55]

Transfers to a foreign government for exclusively charitable purposes do not qualify for the federal estate tax deduction. Transfers to foreign organizations including foreign governments exclusively for charitable purposes may be deductible[56] as a transfer to a trustee, provided the funds are restricted to use within the United States.

An individual, a citizen and resident of Ontario, Canada, provided as follows in his will: "If and when the Michigan College of Mining and Technology, Houghton, Michigan, U.S.A., establishes in Canada to the satisfaction of my Trustees, a charitable foundation corporation or a charitable trust so that monies may be received by it in Canada from my estate and others and the said money spent in Canada without income tax or succession duty levies of any kind, then on that happening, and only then, my Trustees are to pay the remaining twenty-five percent of the net annual income to the said charitable foundation corporation or charitable trust when established . . . ." The bequest was to be used to pay tuition and related expenses of Canadian students at the Michigan college. The court held that the be-

[54] IRC § 2106(a)(2).
[55] IRC § 2106(a)(2)(A).
[56] IRC § 2106(a)(2)(iii).

quest was "to a trustee or trustees . . . to be used within the United States," since the funds were to be expended in the United States.[57] Hence the decedent's estate was held to be entitled to the claimed deduction for a charitable contribution.[58]

(b)   Gift Tax Provisions

A gift of real property or tangible personal property situated in the United States made by a nonresident not a citizen is subject to the federal gift tax.[59] The gift tax charitable deduction provisions that apply to nonresidents who are not citizens parallel the estate tax provisions.

A gift tax charitable deduction is allowed for gifts to domestic organizations for charitable purposes and gifts to trustees for charitable purposes within the United States.[60]

(c)   Treaty Provisions

In 1980, language to be used as model treaty provisions was prepared by the Department of the Treasury. This language is recommended as reasonable practice. Since that time, several United States bilateral tax treaties governing estate and gift tax have provided treatment for charitable gifts. The estate tax convention with Canada is likely to be changed, in the near future, to include these provisions. The pending estate and gift tax treaty with Germany, now in the discussion stage, also is likely to incorporate the spirit of the model provisions.

At the present, there are only three United States bilateral tax treaties in force that contain references to the deductibility of charitable gifts in bequests. These are the treaties with Denmark, France, and Sweden.

The United States–Denmark Estate and Gift Tax Treaty, which entered into force on November 7, 1984, contains the following paragraph:

---

[57] *McAllister, Estate of* v. *Commissioner,* 54 T.C. 1407 (1970).
[58] IRC § 2106(a)(2)(A)(iii).
[59] IRC § 2522(b).
[60] *Id.*

The transfer or deemed transfer of property to or for the use of a Contracting State or a political subdivision or local authority thereof, or to a corporation or organization of a Contracting State operated exclusively for religious, charitable, scientific, literary, or educational purposes, if such transfer is exempt from tax or taxed at a reduced rate in that State, shall be treated by the other Contracting State as if such transfer or deemed transfer were made to a similar corporation or organization of that other state.[61]

The United States–France Estate and Gift Tax Treaty, in force since October 1, 1980, provides as follows:

(1) A transfer to a legal entity created or organized in a Contracting State shall be exempt from tax, or fully deductible from the gross value subject to tax, in the other Contracting State with respect to its taxes referred to in Article 2, provided the transfer would be eligible for such exemption or deduction if the legal entity had been created or organized in that other Contracting State.

(2) The provisions of paragraph (1) shall apply only if the legal entity:

(a) Has a tax-exempt status in the first Contracting State by reason of which transfers to such legal entity are exempt or fully deductible;

(b) Is organized and operated exclusively for religious, charitable, scientific, literary, or educational purposes; and

(c) Receives a substantial part of its support from contributions from the public or governmental funds.

(3) This Article shall not apply to transfers to a Contracting State or a political or administrative subdivision thereof unless specifically limited to a purpose described in paragraph (2)(b).[62]

The United States–Sweden Estate and Gift Tax Treaty, which entered into force on September 5, 1984, contains a paragraph that provides as follows:

The transfer or deemed transfer of property to or for the use of a corporation or organization of one Contracting State organized and operated exclusively for religious, charitable, scientific, or educational

[61] Article 9 of the Treaty.
[62] Article 10 of the Treaty.

purposes shall be exempt from tax by the other Contracting State if and to the extent that the transfer:

a) is exempt from tax in the first-mentioned Contracting State; and

b) would be exempt from tax in the other Contracting State if it were made to a similar corporation or organization of that other State.[63]

The provision in the treaty with Sweden directly follows the model treaty language. The speculation is that as other estate and gift tax treaties with the United States are updated, provisions governing the deductibility of charitable gifts will be included.

[63] Article 8 § 7 of the Treaty.

20

International Giving by Corporations

by Carole S. George

A dynamic aspect of the new global market environment is the extension of corporate philanthropy practiced by American companies that are doing business abroad. The tax law of the United States imposes certain limitations on overseas charitable giving, depending upon the character of the donor and of the donee. These constraints are by no means barriers to transborder corporate giving. A United States corporation planning to conduct philanthropic activities in a foreign country has several methods available for transferring contributions abroad.

§ 20.1 CORPORATE CONTRIBUTIONS TO AMERICAN CHARITY FOR OVERSEAS USE

A United States corporation may deduct, as charitable contributions,[1] up to ten percent of its pre-tax net profits,[2] for gifts made to United States charitable corporations[3] even though the gift may ultimately be used overseas. Certain adjustments to pretax net profits are required for purposes of this computation.[4] A corporate charitable contribution may be used for overseas purposes if it is made to an organization that is incorporated under American laws and qualified as a charitable entity. In contrast, a gift to an unincorporated trust, chest, fund,

---

[1]IRC § 170(a)(1).
[2]IRC § 170(b)(2).
[3]That is, corporations that are charitable by reason of IRC § 170(c)(2).
[4]IRC § 170(b)(2)(A)-(D).

or foundation is deductible only if it is to be used within the United States or its possessions.[5] A corporate contribution that is made directly to a tax-exempt organization established under the laws of any foreign country, even if the recipient has charitable status under United States law, does not attract a charitable deduction.

Because organizations such as the American National Red Cross, The United Way, and The Salvation Army were established and incorporated in the United States, they are frequently used by corporations for facilitating foreign giving objectives. Overseas giving achieved through the mechanism of support of United States organizations with charitable status raises no legal or procedural questions not already contemplated in a domestic giving program.

Another category of international agencies that is useful for this purpose are the so-called "private voluntary organizations," which receive their principal support from the U.S. Agency for International Development. Agencies such as CARE, Save the Children Fund, American Friends Service Committee, Overseas Education Fund, and the Population Council are private voluntary organizations. Typically, these agencies address large problems in developing countries, such as disaster relief and food aid. Since they are qualified as tax-exempt charitable organizations under United States law, they are able to receive charitable donations to be applied to their foreign charitable activities.

§ 20.2 GIFTS OF MONEY FROM A FOREIGN AFFILIATE OF A U.S. PARENT TO AN OVERSEAS CHARITABLE AGENCY

An American corporation can make contributions to foreign charitable (and/or governmental) organizations directly through one or more of its foreign subsidiaries. The ability of the company to obtain a tax deduction for the gift depends on the tax laws of the country involved, as well as the company's position with respect to computation of the United States foreign tax credit.[6]

In general, corporations may elect to claim a credit against United States tax liability for certain foreign taxes which they incur. This foreign tax credit is limited to the amount of United States tax

[5]Rev. Rul. 69-80, 1969-1 C.B. 65.
[6]IRC § 27.

otherwise payable on foreign source taxable income. Thus, the foreign tax credit is not available against United States tax on United States source taxable income. A shift in the source of net income from foreign operations to those in the United States may increase net United States tax for some corporations by reducing the foreign tax credit limitation and thus the amount of the foreign tax credit which may be claimed.

For purposes of the foreign tax credit limitation, foreign source taxable income generally is computed by (1) determining the items of gross income that are from foreign sources and then (2) subtracting from those items the corporation's deductions that are allocated or apportioned to foreign source gross income. A shift in the allocation or apportionment of expenses from United States source to foreign source gross income decreases foreign source taxable income and thus may increase United States tax by reducing the foreign tax credit limitation.

In general, the primary statutory rule for allocating and apportioning deductions between foreign and domestic income is that there shall be deducted from foreign and domestic source gross income, respectively, the expenses, losses, and other deductions properly apportioned or allocated to them and a ratable part of any expenses, losses, or other deductions which cannot definitively be allocated to some item or class of gross income.[7] In addition, for a corporation that is a member of an affiliated group of corporations, expenses that are not directly allocated or apportioned to any specific income-producing activity generally must be allocated and apportioned under the so-called "one taxpayer" rule, that is, as if all of the members of the affiliated group were a single corporation.[8]

Charitable contribution deductions generally are treated as not definitely related to any gross income or income-producing activity and, therefore, are apportioned ratably and subject to the one taxpayer rule.[9]

The Department of the Treasury proposed regulations in March of 1991 that would have altered the general rule requiring ratable apportionment of charitable contributions in cases where the use of the contribution is restricted either to purely domestic or purely foreign

[7]IRC §§ 861(b), 862(b), and 863(b).
[8]IRC § 864(e)(6).
[9]Reg. § 1.861-8(e)(9)(iv); IRS Notice 89-91, 1989-2 C.B. 408.

uses.[10] Under the proposal, a charitable contribution deduction generally would be allocated solely to United States source gross income if the corporation both designates the contributions for use solely in the United States and reasonably believes that the contribution would be so used. Conversely, a charitable contribution deduction would be allocated solely to foreign source gross income if the corporation knows or has reason to know that the contribution would be used solely outside the United States or that the contribution necessarily may be used only outside the United States.

A hearing was held by the IRS on this proposal on August 1, 1991. The charitable community testified in opposition to the proposal and asked the IRS to adjust the proposed rule regarding the allocation of charitable contributions, so as not to discourage charitable giving for international philanthropy.[11] Considerable pressure built in opposition to the proposal throughout the balance of 1991, stimulated largely by charitable organizations that were fearful that their corporate support for international charitable programs would significantly decline.

The U.S. Senate responded by proposing to revise this body of law by means of an amendment contained in the Revenue Act of 1992.[12] However, this provision was not included in the final version of this legislation (which was vetoed), although the provision may be contained in a subsequent tax measure.

In a technical explanation of the legislation accompanying its version of the 1992 Act, the Senate Finance Committee wrote the following:

> The committee understands that [,] to the extent a taxpayer's charitable contribution deductions are apportioned to foreign source income, a reduction in the taxpayer's allowable foreign tax credit may occur. The committee is concerned that the limitation on the foreign tax credit resulting from the present-law apportionment of such deductions might discourage certain taxpayers with multinational business operations from making donations to charities. The committee also is concerned that the approach for allocating and apportioning charitable deductions set forth in the 1991 proposed Treasury regulations would have the effect of creating an inappropriate distinction between contri-

[10]Prop. Reg. § 1.861-8(e)(12), INTL-116-90, 1991-1 C.B. 949.
[11]A detailed analysis of this proposed regulation and the reasons for opposition to it appears in VIII *The Nonprofit Counsel* (No. 9) 1 (1991).
[12]H.R. 11, 102d Cong., 2d Sess. (1992).

butions put to foreign charitable uses, on the one hand, and domestic charitable uses, on the other. In order to provide an incentive for multinational companies to make charitable donations, and to avoid creating a disparity between charities on the basis of the location of their beneficiaries, the committee believes it is appropriate to mandate that a specified portion of all charitable contribution deductions be allocated solely to U.S. source gross income.[13]

Under this proposal, for purposes of computing the source of taxable income for the foreign tax credit limitation, corporations would be permitted to allocate 40 percent of their charitable contribution deductions to gross income from United States sources. The remaining 60 percent of charitable contribution deductions would have to be apportioned ratably between United States gross income and foreign source gross income. As under present law, all corporations included in an affiliated group would be treated as a single corporation for purposes of the ratable apportionment of the residual 60 percent of charitable contribution deductions.

§ 20.3   DONATION OF GOODS OR SERVICES TO BENEFIT A FOREIGN CHARITY

A company may choose to support charitable endeavors by making expenditures from its marketing or advertising budgets. In this situation, funds benefiting charitable organizations overseas may be able to flow through the business expense budget category and be deductible as a business expense under United States tax law.[14] United States law, however, disallows a business expense deduction of any amount that meets the definition of a charitable contribution but cannot be deducted under that section because of the percentage limitations, dollar limitations, or time of payment requirements.[15] These expenditures are sponsorship of broadcasts or concerts of performing arts groups, museum exhibits, public service advertising in support of a charitable cause, purchase of tickets to fund-raising events, and other activities that directly or indirectly promote sales

---

[13]Technical Explanation of the Finance Committee Amendment" ("Technical Explanation"), at 583. The Technical Correction was not formally printed; it is, however, reproduced in the Congressional Record (138 *Cong. Rec.* (No. 112) S11246 (Aug. 3, 1992)).

[14]IRC § 162(a).

[15]*Id.*

of a company's products or services through association with cultural or other charitable activities. To qualify for deduction as business expenses, the corporation must be prepared to justify how the expenditures in fact serve to promote the corporation's business interests.

In-kind gifts of company products are also deductible. Examples include pharmaceutical products that are sent to an overseas hospital or computer equipment that is given to a school. The amount of the deduction for such gifts is governed by the general rules applicable to gifts for use outside the United States (discussed in this chapter). There are special rules relating to gifts of inventory by virtue of which the deduction may be as great as twice the cost basis inherent in the donated property.[16] In general, the rules concerning gifts of tangible personal property allow a donor to deduct only the acquisition cost of the property, rather than current fair market value, if the property is of a type the donor normally sells in its business.[17]

Another method of supporting a charity is to make in-kind gifts of the use of a corporation's facilities or personnel. This type of charitable giving includes occupancy of surplus office space, use of corporate printing or computer facilities, and loan of corporate staff services. As expenses of these facilities and personnel would have been incurred regardless of the donation, the expenses associated with this type of giving are deductible under United States law as business expenses. (There is no United States charitable deduction for gifts of the use of property[18] or for gifts of services.[19])

§ 20.4 GRANTS OF MONEY FROM AN AMERICAN CORPORATION-RELATED FOUNDATION TO A FOREIGN CHARITY

Several large American corporations are currently considering the idea of establishing overseas foundations. However, the present practice is that an American company with an established philanthropic program makes its outbound grants through its United States corporate foundation. A corporate foundation is almost always a "private

[16] IRC § 170(c)(3). See Chapter 9 § 4.
[17] See Chapter 6 § 4.
[18] See Chapter 9 § 10.
[19] See Chapter 9 § 11.

foundation" under United States law.[20] And nothing in the United States tax statutes or regulations prohibits overseas grant-making by private foundations.

(a) Taxable Expenditures

Of paramount concern to a private foundation is avoidance of making a "taxable expenditure" while engaging in grant-making. United States law categorizes certain types of expenditures as taxable ones if made by private foundations and contains significant penalties for engaging in these practices.[21]

The term "taxable expenditure" means any amount paid or incurred by a private foundation

- as a grant to an organization unless
    - the organization is a public charity or an exempt operating foundation,[22] or
    - the private foundation exercises "expenditure responsibility" with respect to the grant,[23] or
- for any purpose other than a charitable purpose.[24]

The penalty for making a "taxable expenditure" begins at ten percent of the expenditure against the foundation and two and one-half percent (maximum $5,000) against any foundation manager (such as a trustee or officer) who agreed to the expenditure.[25] If the expenditure is not timely "corrected,"[26] the penalty increases to 100 percent against the foundation and 50 percent (maximum $10,000) against the foundation manager.[27]

To avoid exposure to taxable expenditure liability, a private foundation must make two preliminary determinations with regard to an overseas grant:

[20] See Chapter 4 § 3.
[21] IRC § 4945. The rules concerning "taxable expenditures" are the subject of *The Law of Tax-Exempt Organizations*, Chapter 24.
[22] See Chapter 4 § 3.
[23] IRC § 4945(h).
[24] IRC § 4945(d).
[25] IRC § 4945(a).
[26] IRC § 4945(i)(1).
[27] IRC § 4945(b).

- whether the grant is for a charitable purpose, and
- whether the private foundation must exercise expenditure responsibility with respect to the grantee organization because it is not a public charity.

(b) Charitable Purpose

The United States regulatory scheme surrounding transborder grant-making parallels the rules concerning domestic grant-making. The most basic concept in this regard is that of "charitable purpose." A grant to a charitable organization will not alone satisfy the requirement. Yet a grant that is specifically designated for a charitable purpose but made to an organization that is not charitable can qualify.

To qualify as an eligible grantee, an organization must be organized and operated exclusively for religious, charitable, scientific, literary or educational purposes; to foster amateur sports competition; or for the prevention of cruelty to children or animals.[28] The emphasis is not on the structure of the organization; it is on the charitable purposes served.

Terms such as charitable, educational, and scientific purposes are specifically defined in the United States tax law.[29]

(c) Expenditure Responsibility

The United States tax law requires "expenditure responsibility" of private foundations to ensure that their grants are spent solely for the purpose for which they are made and that full and complete reports on how the funds are spent are submitted to the grantor by the grantee. This body of law requires private foundations to exercise "expenditure responsibility" with respect to grants to certain organizations.[30]

As noted, foundation grants to public charities need not be the subject of expenditure responsibility. But if the prospective grantee is a charitable organization other than a public charity, expenditure responsibility must always be exercised.

---

[28] IRC § 170(c)(2)(B).
[29] See Chapter 4 § 2.
[30] IRC § 4945(h): Reg. § 53.4945-5(h).

In making the determination that the prospective grantee organization is publicly supported, a private foundation must obtain documentation of the sources of the prospective grantee's financing. The prospective grantee must also inquire whether the proposed grant would reduce the general public and/or government support below the required level of public support to be a publicly supported charity, thus changing (or "tipping") the grantee from a public charity to a private charity.

If the grantee is a public charity and will remain so even with the proposed grant, the answer to the question as to whether the private foundation will have to exercise expenditure responsibility depends upon the nature of the organization under several categories established in United States tax law.

Determination of whether expenditure responsibility is required for grants to overseas donees takes the following five forms:

1. When the grant is made to a governmental unit, expenditure responsibility is generally not required.[31]

2. Where the IRS has determined that an organization is publicly supported, expenditure responsibility is generally not required.[32]

3. Whether or not the organization has been classified by the IRS as publicly supported or substantiated by its legal counsel as the equivalent of a publicly supported organization, expenditure responsibility is generally not required if two conditions are met. These are:

   – the organization, according to the reasonable judgment of the foundation manager, establishes that it is the equivalent of a publicly supported organization, and

   – supporting data is in the form of an affidavit or legal opinion provided by the donee organization's legal counsel.[33]

4. If the organization is a tax-exempt charitable organization by virtue of an IRS determination but is not publicly supported, or if legal counsel has submitted an opinion that the organization is an equivalent of a taxexempt charitable organization

[31] Reg. § 53.4945-5(a)(4)(iii).
[32] IRC § 4945(d)(4)(A).
[33] Reg. § 53.4945-5(a)(5).

but does not qualify as the equivalent of a publicly supported organization, expenditure responsibility must be exercised.

5. Otherwise, expenditure responsibility is mandatory. A further safeguard is required: Grant funds must be segregated into a separate accountable fund.

If the determination is made that expenditure responsibility must be exercised, the foundation must conduct a pre-grant inquiry of the potential grantee. This requirement entails "a limited inquiry . . . complete enough to give a reasonable man assurance that the grantee will use the grant for the proper purposes."[34]

The following data is usually sufficient to satisfy the pregrant inquiry:

- basic institutional character (such as educational institution and research institution),
- names and titles of its officers and managers,
- the tax status of the proposed grantee in its country of origin,
- any previous grant history with the private foundation,
- a summary of information reflecting the proposed grantee's accountability, and
- the private foundation's analysis of the suitability of the proposed grantee for the requested funds.

When a foundation is satisfied that the grantee will use the grant for its stated purposes, the actual grant must be accompanied by an agreement to be signed by an officer of the grantee organization, specifically covering limitations on the grant and providing the grantee's assurance of its intended compliance with all conditions.

(d) Overseas Grantee Categories

For both the "charitable purpose" determination and the analysis as to whether "expenditure responsibility" is necessary, the character of the grantee organization is important. Fundamentally, four categories of grantee organizations may be recipients of grants from United States private foundations. These are:

[34] Reg. § 53.4945-5(b)(2).

- foreign governmental units that do not have the status of tax-exempt charitable entities under United States law,
- foreign organizations that have obtained recognition as tax-exempt charitable organizations under United States law,
- foreign organizations that are recognized as "equivalent to" American tax-exempt charitable organizations, and
- foreign organizations that are within none of the above categories.

Governmental units are entities such as agencies and "instrumentalities" of foreign governments and other international agencies.[35] The terms "foreign government" and "agency of a foreign government" are used throughout the United States tax law in their generally accepted sense, including a state or local ministry or department, or a bureau or office of a ministry or department. An "instrumentality" of a government unit is slightly more complex. Taken in its generally accepted meaning, an instrumentality would be an entity furthering the purposes financed by a government unit, such as schools or universities.

To document the classification of an organization as an instrumentality of a government, a foundation manager is advised to obtain the following information:

- a copy of the document by which the organization was created (termed "articles of organization"), describing its purposes;
- a copy of documentation stating that the organization is exempt from taxation. In some cases, this documentation will consist of a certificate from an appropriate ministry. Where the organization is exempt from taxation because it belongs to a general class of organizations, a written statement from the taxation authorities acknowledging tax exemption is recommended. In systems where this is unobtainable, a legal opinion describing the nexus between this particular grantee organization and the classification of tax-exempt organizations will be satisfactory;
- further documentation provided by the organization's legal counsel in affidavit form that will detail the source of the organization's operating funds.[36]

[35] Reg. § 53.4945-5(a)(4)(iii).
[36] Reg. § 53.4945-5(a)(5).

The term "public international organizations"[37] is used to describe international organizations that are composed of governments as members and are designated as international organizations by executive order.[38] Examples of these organizations are the United Nations, the International Chamber of Commerce, the World Bank, and the World Health Organization. Should a private foundation seek to make a grant to an organization composed of governments but not so designated, it is advised to follow the procedure for establishing that the organization is an instrumentality of a government, as summarized above.

An American private foundation should not automatically assume that a governmental unit's use of a proposed grant will be for a "charitable purpose." This must be established by documents supporting the grant application.

Grants to governmental units are generally made for the purpose of carrying out educational, charitable, or social programs. The fact that the grant is made to a governmental unit supervising the pursuit of these activities is not necessarily conclusive, and care should be taken to ascertain that the particular grant supports the stated charitable purpose.

United States law provides that expenditure responsibility is not required if the grant is made to "a foreign government, or any agency or instrumentality thereof, or an international organization designated as such by [e]xecutive [o]rder . . ., even if it is not" a tax-exempt charitable organization.[39] Nonetheless, this body of law also states that "any grant to an organization referred to in this subparagraph must be made exclusively for charitable purposes . . . ."[40]

(e)   Grants to Charitable Organizations and "Equivalents"

The determination letter issued by the IRS, recognizing an organization to be a tax-exempt charitable entity, establishes that the Service has found the organization to be in pursuit of charitable purposes. This letter reflects the findings of the IRS that:

---

[37] Reg. § 53.4945-5(a)(4)(iii).
[38] 22 U.S.C. § 288.
[39] Reg. § 53.4945-5(a)(4)(iii).
[40] Id.

- the organization is organized and operated exclusively for religious, charitable, scientific, testing for public safety, literary or educational purposes; to foster national or international amateur sports competition; or for the prevention of cruelty to children or animals,
- no part of the net earnings of the organization inures to the benefit of any private shareholder or individual,
- no substantial part of the organization's activities is the carrying on of propaganda programs or otherwise attempting to influence legislation, and
- no part of the organization's activities is participating in or intervening in any political campaign on behalf of or in opposition to any candidate for public office.

The United States law permits foreign organizations to qualify for recognition of tax exemption. The tax exemption provision[41] merely refers to "an organization described in" appropriate categories as being tax-exempt, and another provision of law[42] refers specifically to restrictions on foreign organizations that can obtain tax exemption as charitable organizations. United States law defines "private foundation" as "a domestic or *foreign* organization" that is a charitable entity.[43]

According to the IRS, approximately five hundred foreign organizations, predominantly in the fields of education, agriculture, and health, have sought determination of exempt organization status.

As with domestic charitable organizations, a private foundation may in large part rely upon the tax exemption determination of the overseas exempt organization to support the determination that a grant to that organization is for a charitable purpose. This strong presumption is permissible because the recipient organization is itself answerable to the IRS (as is any charitable organization) on the question as to whether the funds are used for a charitable purpose.

Typically, however, a foreign organization will not have obtained recognition of tax exemption as a charitable entity from the IRS. Thus, an American private foundation that is a prospective grantor must establish that the potential donee organization is organized and

---

[41] IRC § 501(a).
[42] IRC § 4948.
[43] IRC § 509(a) (emphasis added).

operated in a manner consistent with a tax-exempt charitable organization, thus constituting the equivalent of a tax-exempt charitable organization.

Charitable organization "equivalents" are foreign organizations that have not obtained determination letters from the IRS but that are organized and operated in a manner so that they can quite easily be determined to be equivalent to public charities under United States law. A private foundation is well advised, in these circumstances, to develop its own form modeled after the IRS' application for recognition of tax-exempt status (Form 1023), because the foundation itself is assuming the burden of determining with convincing documentary evidence that the prospective grantee meets the essential requirements for public charity status. This includes evidence of the prospective grantee's nonprofit status and charitable purposes, copies of organizational documents, relevant statutory decrees, evidence (if any) of local tax standing, description of the intended uses of the grant, identification of the organization's directors and officers, and certification by an officer as to the correctness of the information (and compliance with the standards listed above). This documentation must be retained by the grant-maker to defend the grant in the case of an audit by the IRS.

According to United States law, if a grant is made to an organization which does not have a ruling or determination letter that it is a public charity, the grant will be considered as made to a public charitable organization if the grantor foundation has made a "good faith determination" that the grantee organization is a public charity.[44] The determination is based on an affidavit of the grantee organization or an opinion of either the grantee's counsel or the grantor's counsel that the grantee is a public charitable organization, setting forth sufficient facts concerning the operations and support of the grantee for the IRS to determine that the grantee would be likely to qualify as a public organization.

If an organization has been determined to be organized for charitable purposes and to be a public charity under United States law, there will be the strong presumption that grants to it are made for charitable purposes. Thus, a private foundation is allowed to rely on the IRS letter of determination in satisfying this portion of its inquiry. The presumption also follows where the foundation has made its good faith determination that the organization is organized and

[44]Reg. § 53.4945-5(a)(5).

operated for purposes which render it equivalent to a public charitable organization.

United States law requires expenditure responsibility concerning grants made to charitable organizations and their equivalents unless these organizations can be classified as public charities.[45] Several categories of public charitable organizations are embraced by this section, including various educational organizations, hospitals and medical research organizations, churches and associations of churches, organizations that receive sufficiently wide financial support from a governmental unit or from the "public," and organizations that support one of the above types of organizations and meet certain other criteria.[46]

(f) IRS Simplified Procedures

In 1992, the IRS developed a simplified procedure enabling private foundations in the United States to make grants to foreign charitable organizations, relying solely on an appropriate affidavit.[47] Essentially, this simplification is accomplished by eliminating the need for a lawyer's opinion as to the tax status of the foreign grantee.[48]

This procedure is not available where the grant is a transfer of assets pursuant to a liquidation, merger, redemption, recapitalization, or other similar adjustment, organization, or reorganization.

The procedure is engrafted onto the above-described regulations which set forth ways in which a U.S. private foundation can make a grant to a foreign charitable organization without contravening the qualifying distribution rules or the taxable expenditures limitations.[49] These circumstances relate to foreign charitable organizations that do not have an IRS determination letter recognizing them as charitable organizations and are equivalent to U.S. public charitable organizations or private operating foundations (which is usually the case).

Absent these rulings, the management of a private foundation must make a "reasonable judgment" that the prospective grantee is a charitable organization and a "good faith determination" that the potential recipient is a public charity or operating foundation.[50]

---

[45] IRC § 4945 (d)(4).
[46] See Chapter 4 § 3.
[47] Rev. Proc. 92-94, 1992-46 I.R.B. 34.
[48] See the text accompanied by n. 35, *supra.*
[49] See the text accompanied by ns. 27–39, *supra.*
[50] See the text accompanied by ns. 34–35, *supra.*

Under this procedure, both this reasonable judgment and good faith determination may be made on the basis of a "currently qualified" affidavit prepared by the grantee for the prospective grantor or for another grantor or prospective grantor. This procedure requires that the affidavit be written in English and state the substantive information that is required. An affidavit is considered current when it reflects the grantee's latest complete accounting year or (in the case of public charitable organizations whose public charity status is not dependent on public support) if the affidavit is updated at the request of the prospective grantor to reflect the grantee's current data.

(g) Grants to Organizations That Are Not Governmental Units, Not Charitable Organizations, and Not Equivalents to Charitable Organizations

When a private foundation decides to make a grant to an organization that is neither a governmental unit, a tax-exempt charitable organization, nor a charitable organization "equivalent," the grant must be highly nondiscretionary and clearly identified with a specific charitable purpose. In this situation, the grant supports a purpose, determined to qualify as a charitable purpose. The structure of the organization carrying out this purpose is therefore overlooked.

Where public charity status equivalency cannot be established, the private foundation may nonetheless make the grant, but the grant must be clearly identified for a precise charitable purpose. The tax laws of the United States do not provide a procedure for making this type of determination as to a specific charitable purpose. Those foundations that have experience in this area have followed a practice of securing from the prospective grantee a project description demonstrating how the grant is to be used for a charitable purpose and/or securing the written commitment that the grantee will use the grant only for its stated purposes.

Whenever a grant is made to a tax-exempt charitable organization or to an organization that is a charitable organization equivalent and is a public charity, the presumption that the grant will be used for charitable purposes is so strong that a foundation is well advised to seek public charity status equivalency for grants to foreign nongovernmental organizations, whenever possible. An additional advantage of establishing this equivalency is that operating or general support grants may be made to these organizations.

Expenditure responsibility must be exercised when a grant is made to this category of donee organization. Further, the grantee organization must agree to segregate the grant funds in a separate account designated for financing a charitable purpose.[51]

[51] In general, Hill, "Charitable Contributions and the Foreign Tax Credit," 3 *J. Tax. Exempt Orgs.* 22 (Summer 1991).

Part VI

Administration of Charitable Giving

21

Receipt, Record-Keeping, and Reporting Requirements

There is a battery of rules to which a donor to a charitable organization and the charitable organization that is the donee must adhere as a condition of allowance of the otherwise allowable federal income tax charitable contribution deduction. That is, where there is noncompliance with these rules, the donor will not be entitled to the charitable deduction, notwithstanding the fact that all other applicable rules have been followed. These rules—some of which are termed "substantiation" requirements—embrace receipt, record-keeping, and reporting requirements.

An individual who itemizes deductions must separately state (on Schedule A of the federal income tax return, Form 1040) the aggregate amount of charitable contributions of money and the aggregate amount of charitable gifts of property.

§ 21.1 RECEIPT AND RECORD-KEEPING REQUIREMENTS

(a) Existing Law

In the case of contributions of money to charity, a donor—individual or corporate—must keep some record of the gift. This record must be maintained irrespective of the size of the gift. Preferably, the record will be a cancelled check or a receipt from the charitable donee.[1] Otherwise, the record must be "written" and "reliable."[2] The record must show the name of the charitable donee, the date of the contribution, and the amount of the contribution.[3]

A letter or other communication from the charitable donee acknowledging receipt of the contribution, and showing the date and amount of the contribution, constitutes a "receipt."[4] A donor has the burden of establishing "reliability" of a written record other than a check or receipt. The reliability of this type of written record is determined on the basis of all of the facts and circumstances of a particular case. Factors indicating that this other written evidence is "reliable" include

- the contemporaneous nature of the writing that evidences the contribution,
- the regularity of the donor's record-keeping procedures, and
- in the case of a contribution of a "small amount" (and that term is not defined), any other written evidence from the recipient charitable organization evidencing the making of a gift that would not otherwise constitute a "receipt."[5]

As to the second of these factors, "a contemporaneous diary entry stating the amount and date of the donation and the name of the donee charitable organization made by a taxpayer who regularly makes such diary entries would generally be considered reliable."[6] As to the third of these factors, the evidence would include "an emblem, button, or other token traditionally associated with a charitable organization and regularly given by the organization to persons making cash donations."[7]

Concerning contributions of property (other than money) to a charitable organization, a corporate or individual donor must obtain a receipt from the recipient charitable organization and a reliable written record of specified information with respect to the donated prop-

---

[1]Reg. § 1.170A-13(a)(1)(i), (ii).
[2]Reg. § 1.170A-13(a)(1)(iii).
[3]*Id.*
[4]Reg. § 1.170A-13(a)(1)(ii).
[5]Reg. § 1.170A-13(a)(2)(i).
[6]Reg. § 1.170A-13(a)(2)(i)(B).
[7]Reg. § 1.170A-13(a)(2)(i)(C).

erty.[8] Where the property has a value of more than $5,000, the appraisal rules[9] apply rather than these receipt rules.

This receipt must include the name of the donee, the date and location of the contribution, and a "description of the property in detail reasonably sufficient under the circumstances."[10] When these regulations were initially promulgated (in proposed form), they required that the charitable organization donee provide a statement as to the value of the property. In response to complaints about that requirement, the regulations were revised to state that "[a]lthough the fair market value of the property is one of the circumstances to be taken into account in determining the amount of detail to be included on the receipt, such value need not be stated on the receipt."[11] For these purposes, a letter or other written communication from the donee acknowledging receipt of the contribution, showing the date of the contribution, and containing the required description of the property contributed constitutes a "receipt."[12]

However, a receipt is not required in instances where the gift is made in circumstances "where it is impractical to obtain a receipt (e.g., by depoisting property at a charity's unattended drop site)."[13] In these instances, however, the donor must "maintain reliable written records" with respect to each item of donated property.[14]

The donor of appreciated property to charity must also maintain a "reliable written record" of specified information with respect to each item of property.[15] This information must include the following:[16]

- the name and address of the charitable donee,
- the date and location of the contribution,
- a description of the property "in detail reasonable under the cirdumstances (including the value of the property),"[17]

[8] Reg. § 1.170A-13(b)(1).
[9] See § 2, *infra*.
[10] Reg. § 1.170A-13(b)(1)(i)–(iii).
[11] Reg. § 1.170A-13(b)(1)(iii).
[12] Reg. § 1.170A-13(b)(1).
[13] *Id*.
[14] *Id*.
[15] Reg. § 1.170A-13(b)(2)(i).
[16] Reg. § 1.170A-13(b)(2)(ii).
[17] Reg. § 1.170A-13(b)(2)(ii)(C).

- in the case of securities, the name of the issuing company, the type of security, and whether or not it is regularly traded on a stock exchange or in an over-the-counter market,
- the fair market value of the property at the time of the gift, the method utilized in determining the value, and a copy of the signed report of any appraiser,
- the cost or other basis of the property, if it is "ordinary income property" or other type of property where the deduction must be reduced by all or a portion of the gain, the reduction in the amount of the charitable contribution, and the manner in which the reduction was determined,[18]
- where the gift is of a "remainder interest" or an "income interest,"[19] the total amount claimed as a deduction for the year due to the gift and the amount claimed as a deduction in any prior year or years for gifts of other interests in the property, the name and address of each organization to which any such contribution was made, the place where any such property which is tangible property is located or kept, and the name of any person, other than the organizaton to which the property giving rise to the deduction was contributed, having actual possession of the property, and
- the terms of any agreement or understanding entered into by or on behalf of the donor "which relates to the use, sale, or other disposition of the property contributed,"[20] such as
  - any restriction, temporary or permanent, on the charity's right to use or dispose of the property,
  - a retention or conveyance of the right to the income from the donated property or to possession of the property, including the right to vote donated securities, to acquire the property by purchase or otherwise, or to designate the person having the income, possession, or right to acquire, or
  - an earmarking of the property for a particular use.[21]

Additional rules apply with respect to gifts of property (other than

[18]See Chapters 6 and 9 § 4.
[19]See Chapters 11–15.
[20]Reg. § 1.170A-13(b)(2)(ii)(G).
[21]*Id.*

money) for which the donor claims a federal income tax charitable contribution deduction in excess of $500.[22] (Again, these rules do not apply in cases where the appraisal rules apply.) In this situation, the donor is required to maintain additional records, regarding

- the manner of acquisition of the property, as, for example, by purchase, gift, bequest, inheritance, or exchange, and the approximate date of acquisition of the property by the donor or, if the property was created, produced, or manufactured by or for the donor, the approximate date the property was substantially completed,[23] and

- the cost or other basis of the property, other than publicly traded securities, held by the donor for a period less than the long-term capital gains holding period immediately preceding the date on which the contribution was made and, when the information is available, of property, other than publicly traded securities, held for the long-term capital gains holding period preceding the date on which the contribution was made.[24]

This information generally is to be provided as part of the donor's income tax return.[25] However, if the donor has "reasonable cause" for not being able to provide the information, the donor must attach an explanatory statement to the return.[26] If the donor can demonstrate this reasonable cause, the donor will not be disallowed a charitable contribution deduction for failure to comply with the rules pertaining to gifts of property having a value in excess of $500.[27]

(b) Proposed Law

The foregoing rules would have been altered somewhat, had the Revenue Act of 1992 been enacted rather than vetoed. That legislation would have introduced statutory law providing that a federal income tax charitable contribution deduction is not allowed for a gift of $750 or more unless the donor has written substantiation from the

---

[22] Reg. § 1.170A-13(b)(3).
[23] Reg. § 1.170A-13(b)(3)(i)(A).
[24] Reg. § 1.170A-13(b)(3)(i)(B).
[25] Reg. § 1.170A-13(b)(3)(ii).
[26] Id.
[27] Id.

charitable donee of the contribution.[28] This substantiation would have to include a good faith estimate of the value of any good or service that has been provided to the donor in exchange for making the gift to the donee.[29] If the charitable donee did not provide any goods or services to the donor in consideration of the contribution, the written substantiation would have to include a statement to that effect.

For purposes of computing the $750 threshold, separate payments would generally be treated as separate contributions and thus would not be aggregated in determining the threshold. In cases of contributions paid by withholding from wages, the deduction from each paycheck would have to be treated as separate payments.

This law would place responsibility upon donors who claim an itemized deduction for a contribution of $750 or more to request (and maintain in their records) substantiation from the charity of their contribution (and any good or service received in exchange).[30] Where a donor makes a non-money gift to a charitable organization, the donor would be required to obtain from the donee a receipt that describes the donated property (and indicates whether any good or service was given to the donor in exchange). (However, this rule would not require the charitable organization to value the property that it receives from the donor.) Donors could no longer rely on a cancelled check as substantiation for a contribution in excess of $750.

The written acknowledgment would have to provide information sufficient to substantiate the amount of the deductible contribution. However, this acknowledgment would not have to take any particular form. Thus, for example, acknowledgments could be made by letter, postcard, or computer-generated forms. Further, a charitable donee could prepare a separate acknowledgment for each contribution, or could provide donors with periodic (for example, annual) acknowledgments that set forth the required information for each contribution of $100 or more made by the donor during the period.

Congress expressed its "expectation" that a charitable organization that knowingly provides a false written substantiation to a donor will

---

[28] Proposed IRC § 170(f)(8).

[29] See Chapter 22.

[30] Earlier versions of this requirement would have caused donee charitable organizations to file information returns with the IRS reflecting contributions made to them. For example, such a proposal was part of the President's budget proposal for fiscal year 1993 (see IX *The Nonprofit Counsel* (No.3) 2–3 (1992)).

be subject to the penalties imposed for aiding and abetting an understatement of tax liability.[31]

However, this form of substantiation would not be required if the charitable donee filed a return with the IRS reporting information sufficient to substantiate the amount of the deductible contribution.

This substantiation would have to be obtained by the donor prior to the filing of his or her tax return for the tax year in which the contribution was made (or, if earlier, the due date, including extensions, for the return).

This body of law would have become effective for contributions made on or after January 1, 1993. Presumably, it would have completely superseded the body of law presently in effect.[32] It is believed, however, that this proposed body of law would not supplant the appraisal requirements.[33] This proposal is likely to appear in subsequent tax legislation.

§ 21.2 APPRAISAL REQUIREMENTS

Additional requirements are applicable relating to the substantiation of deductions claimed by an individual, a closely held corporation, a personal service corporation, a partnership, or a small business ("S") corporation for charitable contributions of certain property.[34] Property to which these rules apply is termed "charitable deduction property." If the contributed property is a partial interest in an item of property, the appraisal must be of the partial interest.[35] These substantiation requirements must be complied with if the charitable deduction is to be allowed.[36]

These requirements apply to contributions of property (other than money and publicly traded securities) if the aggregate claimed or reported value of the property (and all similar items of property for which deductions for charitable contributions are claimed or reported

---

[31] "Technical Explanation of the Finance Committee Amendment" ("Technical Explanation"), at 588, n. 12. The Technical Correction was not formally printed; it is, however, reproduced in the Congressional Record (138 *Cong. Rec.* (No. 112) S11246 (Aug. 3, 1992)). IRC § 6701. See Chapter 10 § 5.

[32] See the text accompanied by ns. 1–27, *supra*.

[33] See § 2, *infra*.

[34] Reg. § 1.170A-13(c).

[35] Reg. § 1.170A-13(c)(1)(ii).

[36] Reg. § 1.170A-13(c)(2).

by the same donor for the same tax year whether or not donated to the same charitable donee) is in excess of $5,000.[37]

The phrase "similar items of property" means "property of the same generic category or type," including stamp collections, coin collections, lithographs, paintings, photographs, books, nonpublicly traded stock, other non-publicly traded securities, land, buildings, clothing, jewelry, furniture, electronic equipment, household appliances, toys, everyday kitchenware, china, crystal, or silver.[38] For example, if a donor claimed for a year deductions of $2,000 for books given to College A, $2,500 for books given to College B, and $900 for books given to College C, the $5,000 threshold would be exceeded. Therefore, this donor would have to obtain a qualified appraisal for the books and attach to the appropriate income tax return three appraisal summaries for the books donated to the three colleges.

For this type of gift, the donor must obtain a "qualified appraisal" and attach an "appraisal summary" to the return on which the deduction is claimed.[39] However, in the case of nonpublicly traded stock, the claimed value of which does not exceed $10,000 but is greater than $5,000, the donor does not have to obtain a qualified appraisal but must attach a partially completed appraisal summary form to the tax or information return on which the deduction is claimed.[40]

A "qualified appraisal" is an appraisal document that

- relates to an appraisal that is made not earlier than 60 days prior to the date of contribution of the appraisal property,
- is prepared, signed, and dated by a "qualified appraiser" (or appraisers),
- contains the requisite information, and
- does not involve a prohibited type of appraisal fee.[41]

Certain information must be included in a qualified appraisal:

- a description of the property in sufficient detail for a person

---

[37] Reg. § 1.170A-13(c)(1)(i).
[38] Reg. § 1.170A-13(c)(7)(iii).
[39] Reg. § 1.170A-13(c)(2)(i)(A), (B).
[40] Reg. § 1.170A-13(c)(2)(ii).
[41] Reg. § 1.170A-13(c)(3)(i).

who is not generally familar with the type of property to ascertain that the property that was appraised is the property being
contributed,

- the physical condition of the property (in the case of tangible
  property),
- the date of contribution of the property,
- the terms of any agreement between the parties relating to any
  subsequent disposition of the property, including restrictions on
  the charity's use of the gift property,
- the name, address, and tax identification number of the appraiser,
- the qualifications of the qualified appraiser (or appraisers),
- a statement that the appraisal was prepared for income tax
  purposes,
- the date or dates on which the property was appraised,
- the appraised fair market value of the property on the date of
  contribution,
- the method of valuation used to determine the fair market
  value of the property, and
- the specific basis for the valuation.[42]

The qualified appraisal must be received by the donor before the
due date (including extensions) of the return on which the deduction
for the contributed property is first claimed or, in the case of a
deduction first claimed on an amended return, the date on which the
return is filed.[43]

A separate qualified appraisal is required for each item of property
that is not included in a group of similar items of property.[44] One
qualified appraisal is required for a group of similar items of property
contributed in the same tax year, as long as the appraisal includes all
of the required information for each item.[45] However, the appraiser
may select any items the aggregate value of which is appraised at
$100 or less, for which a group description (rather than a specific
description of each items) is adequate.[46]

[42] Reg. § 1.170A-13(c)(3)(ii).
[43] Reg. § 1.170A-13(c)(3)(iv)(B).
[44] Reg. § 1.170A-13(c)(3)(iv)(A).
[45] Id.
[46] Id.

The appraisal must be retained by the donor "for so long as it may be relevant in the administration of any internal revenue law."[47]

The "appraisal summary" must be made on a form prescribed by the IRS (Form 8283, Section B[48]), signed and dated by the charitable donee and qualified appraiser (or appraisers), and attached to the donor's return on which a deduction with respect to the appraised property is first claimed or reported.[49] The signature by the donee does not represent concurrence in the appraised value of the contributed property.

The following information must be included in the appraisal summary:

- the name and taxpayer identification number of the donor (for example, the social security number of an individual),
- a description of the property in requisite detail,
- a brief summary of the condition of the property at the time of the gift (in the case of tangible property),
- the manner and date of acquisition of the property by the donor,
- the cost basis of the property,
- the name, address, and taxpayer identification number of the charitable donee,
- the date the donee received the property,
- a statement explaining whether or not the charitable contribution was made by means of a bargain sale[50] and amount of any consideration received from the donee for the contribution,
- the name, address, and taxpayer identification number of the qualified appraiser (or appraisers),
- the appraised fair market value of the property on the date of contribution, and
- a declaration by the appraiser.[51]

The rules pertaining to separate appraisals, summarized above,

---

[47] Reg. § 1.170A-13(c)(3)(iv)(C).
[48] A copy of this form appears as Appendix C.
[49] Reg. § 1.170A-13(c)(4).
[50] See Chapter 9 § 5.
[51] Reg. § 1.170A-13(c)(4)(ii).

also apply with respect to appraisal summaries.[52] However, a donor who contributed similar items of property to more than one charitable donee must attach a separate appraisal summary for each donee.[53]

Every donor who presents an appraisal summary to a charitable organization for signature must furnish a copy of the appraisal summary to the charitable donee.[54] If the donor is a partnership or small business corporation, the donor must provide a copy of the appraisal summary to every partner or shareholder who receives an allocation of a deduction for a charitable contribution of property described in the appraisal summary.[55] The partner or shareholder must attach the appraisal summary to the partner's or shareholder's return.[56] If a donor (or partner or shareholder of a donor) fails to attach the appraisal summary to the return, a charitable deduction will not be disallowed if the donor (or partner or shareholder) submits an appraisal summary within 90 days of being requested to do so by the IRS, so long as the failure to attach the appraisal summary was a good faith omission and certain other requirements are met (including timely completion of the appraisal).[57]

The appraisal summary form (Form 8283, Section A) must be filed by contributors where the total value of all noncash contributions exceeds $500 and is less than $5,000. This portion of the form must also be used to report contributions of publicly traded securities, even where the value of them is in excess of $5,000.

Special rules apply for the substantiation of charitable deductions for gifts of non-publicly traded securities (such as Israeli bonds). When a five-part test is satisfied, charitable deductions are permitted for securities that are not publicly exchanged and for which there are no published quotations.

The term "qualified appraiser" means an individual who includes on the appraisal summary a declaration that

- he or she holds himself or herself out to the public as an appraiser or performs appraisals on a regular basis,

[52] Reg. § 1.170A-13(c)(4)(iv)(A).
[53] Reg. § 1.170A-13(c)(4)(iv)(B).
[54] Reg. § 1.170A-13(c)(4)(iv)(E).
[55] Reg. § 1.170A-13(c)(4)(iv)(F).
[56] Reg. § 1.170A-13(c)(4)(iv)(G).
[57] Reg. § 1.170A-13(c)(4)(iv)(H).

- because of the appraiser's qualifications as described in the appraisal, he or she is qualified to make appraisals of the type of property being valued,
- the appraiser is not one of the persons excluded by these rules from being a qualified appraiser, and
- the appraiser understands that an intentionally false or fraudulent overstatement of the value of the property described in the qualified appraisal or appraisal summary may subject the appraiser to a civil penalty for aiding and abetting an understatement of tax liability,[58] and consequently the appraiser may have appraisals disregarded.[59]

Notwithstanding these requirements, an individual is not a qualified appraiser if the donor had knowledge of facts which would cause a reasonable person to expect the appraiser to falsely overstate the value of the donated property.[60] Also, the donor, donee, or certain other related persons cannot be a "qualified appraiser" of the property involved in the gift transaction.[61]

More than one appraiser may appraise the donated property, as long as each appraiser complies with these requirements, including signing the qualified appraisal and appraisal summary.[62] If more than one appraiser appraises the property, the donor does not have to use each appraiser's appraisal for purposes of substantiating the charitable deduction.[63]

Generally, no part of the fee arrangement for a qualified appraisal can be based on a percentage of the appraised value of the property.[64] If a fee arrangement is based, in whole or in part, on the amount of the appraised value of the property (if any) that is allowed as a charitable deduction, after IRS examination or otherwise, it is treated as a fee based on a percentage of the appraised value of the

---

[58]IRC § 6701.
[59]Reg. § 1.170A-13(c)(5)(i).
[60]Reg. § 1.170A-13(c)(5)(ii).
[61]Reg. § 1.170A-13(c)(5)(iv). In formulating these rules, the IRS rejected the thought of including in the criteria for "qualified appraisers" certain professional standards or the establishment of a registry of qualified appraisers.
[62]Reg. § 1.170A-13(c)(5)(iii).
[63]Id.
[64]Reg. § 1.170A-13(c)(6)(i).

property.[65] (This rule does not apply in certain circumstance to appraisal fees paid to a generally recognized association that regulates appraisers.[66])

In any situation involving a gift of property, the charitable organization that is the recipient of the gift must value the property for its own record-keeping and reporting purposes. However, the charitable donee is not required (and, in some instances, may not be able[67]) to share that valuation with the donor.

Many of these requirements apply to the donor. Therefore, technically, compliance with them is the responsibility of the donor and not the charitable donee. However, as a matter of donor relations (if only because the charitable deduction usually depends upon adherence to the rules), the charitable organization will want to be certain that its donors are made aware of the rules and probably assist them in assembling the necessary records and in otherwise complying with the requirements.

A separate set of rules applies appraisal requirements to regular corporations (corporations other than those referenced above, termed "C" corporations). These rules, in general, require these corporations to obtain a qualified independent appraisal to validly claim a charitable contribution deduction for gifts of most non-money property having a value in excess of $5,000.[68]

These rules, when proposed, would have applied in instances when a regular corporation makes a charitable contribution of property that constitutes part of its inventory. Gifts of this nature are often the subject of a special deduction provision.[69] In response to complaints of burdens of overregulation by the corporate giving community, the IRS subsequently announced[70] a rule exempting certain corporations from the need to obtain appraisals for gifts of inventory.[71] These corporations, instead, are required to include summary

[65]Id.
[66]Reg. § 1.170A-13(c)(6)(ii).
[67]See the text accompanied by n. 61, *supra*.
[68]Reg. § 1.170A-13(c)(2)(ii).
[69]IRC § 170(e)(3). See Chapter 9 § 4.
[70]IR-88-137.
[71]The problem facing the charitable community in this regard was the fear that the more burdensome the regulatory process required in conjunction with gifts of inventory, the greater the likelihood that corporations would not make this type of gift. Also, the price set by these corporations for the

information in their annual tax return, such as a description of the inventory contributed and the valuation method used (such as retail pricing). This information is embodied in a "partially completed appraisal summary."

§ 21.3   REPORTING REQUIREMENTS

Federal law requires the filing of an information return by certain charitable donees that make certain dispositions of contributed property (so-called "charitable deduction property").[72]

A charitable donee that sells, exchanges, consumes, or otherwise disposes of gift property within two years after the date of the donor's contribution of the property must file an information return (Form 8282[73]) with the IRS. A copy of the donee information return must be provided to the donor and retained by the donee.

This information return must contain the following:

- the name, address, and taxpayer identification number of the donor and the donee,
- a sufficient description of the property,
- the date of the contribution,
- the amount received on the disposition, and

items they manufacture is based on their assessment of what the market will accept. In part, the price is determined by the cost of developing and marketing the items; the price is also partially a function of what the consuming public is willing to pay—the classic law definition of the fair market value of an item of property (see Chapter 10 § 1). An independent appraiser cannot provide any better determination of value than the contributing corporation. Further, an appraisal of inventory gifts is usually a pointless act. At best, the deduction will be an amount no greater than twice the corporation's cost basis in the property, so the fair market value of the property is likely to be irrelevant.

Section 62-81 of the Technical and Miscellaneous Revenue Act of 1988 authorized the Department of the Treasury to promulgate regulations allowing regular corporations to provide, in the case of charitable gifts of inventory, less detailed substantiation than that required for other corporations. However, the Treasury Department had already agreed to the above-described compromise by the time this legislation was finalized.

[72] IRC § 6050L.
[73] A copy of this form appears as Appendix D.

- the date of the disposition.

This reporting obligation is not required with respect to an item of charitable deduction property disposed of by sale if the appraisal summary signed by the donee with respect to the item contains, at the time of the donee's signature, a statement signed by the donor that the appraised value of the item does not exceed $500. For these purposes, items that form a set (for example, a collection of books written by the same author, components of a stereo system, or a group of place settings of a pattern of silverware) are considered one item. Also, all nonpublicly traded stock is considered one item, as are all nonpublicly traded securities other than nonpublicly traded stock.

This exception is designed to embrace the situation where a donor contributes items of property to a charity that altogether are worth more than $5,000 (thereby triggering the appraisal and appraisal summary requirements) and where the charity (within the two-year period) sells one of these items which, at the time the charity signed the appraisal summary, had a value of no more than $500. For example, if an individual donated the entire contents of a house to a charity, an appraisal summary may be done with respect to all of the items as a group; the charity may thereafter sell some of the items individually. To the extent that each item had a value that is less than $500, the charity would not have to file the information return with respect to the sale(s).

One of the vague aspects of this rule is the underlying assumption of application of the aggregation rule. For example, to build on the previous illustration, the contents of the house consisted of furniture valued at $5,000, jewelry valued at $5,000, clothing valued at $5,000, and art work valued at $5,000. While the safe approach may be to secure an appraisal for all of the $20,000 in property, an appraisal (and an appraisal summary) may not be required in the first instance because the properties are not "similar." If that is the case, the property is not "charitable deduction property" to begin with.

This reporting obligation also does not apply to a situation where the charitable donee consumes or distributes, without consideration, the property in the course of performing an exempt function.

This donee information return must be filed within 125 days of the disposition of the charitable deduction property.

A successor donee may be required to file this information return if it disposes of charitable deduction property within two years after the date of the donor's contribution to the original donee. A "successor donee" is any donee of charitable contribution property other than the original donee.[74]

[74]Ann. 88-120, 1988-38 I.R.B. 27.

22

Disclosure Requirements

There is a substantial and growing body of federal law that imposes on charitable and certain other tax-exempt organizations the obligation to make certain disclosures to donors in the context of giving to these organizations.

This area of the law differentiates between charitable and noncharitable tax-exempt organizations.

§ 22.1 DISCLOSURE BY CHARITABLE ORGANIZATIONS

(a) Existing Law

A tax-exempt charitable organization[1] is not required, by statute, to state explicitly, in its solicitations for support from members or the general public, whether an amount paid to it is deductible as a charitable contribution or whether all or part of the payment constitutes consideration for goods or services furnished by the organization to the payor.

However, it has long been the view of the IRS that, if any payment or portion of a payment to a charitable organization is not deductible as a charitable gift, the recipient charitable organization should so notify the payor.[2] That is, it is the position of the IRS that it is the responsibility of charitable organizations to inform their patrons of the distinction between deductible and nondeductible payments. The latter includes true dues, payments for admissions or

---

[1]That is, an organization that is tax-exempt pursuant to IRC § 501(a) by reason of description in IRC § 170(c)(2). See Chapter 4 § 2.
[2]Rev. Rul. 67-246, 1967-2 C.B. 104. See Chapter 23.

merchandise, and other material benefits and privileges received in return for the payment. The IRS expected charities, before solicitation, to determine the nondeductible portion of a payment and to clearly state the separate payments on a ticket or other evidence of payment furnished to a contributor.[3] Also, the federal individual income tax return (Form 1040, Schedule A) and the accompanying instructions inform individuals that, if they made a contribution and received a benefit in return, the value of that benefit must be subtracted in calculating any charitable contribution deduction.

This matter of adequate disclosure of the extent of deductibility of *quid pro quo* contributions has been a festering and growing problem from the standpoint of the IRS. Despite an explicit ruling posture on the subject since 1967,[4] many charitable organizations, either willfully or in ignorance of the IRS' position, did not adhere to the Service's requirements in this regard. In this sense, these rules were, on occasion, honored in their breach. The problem became so severe that in 1988 the Commissioner of Internal Revenue, in an unusual development, sent a written message to the nation's charities, saying: "I . . . ask your help in more accurately informing taxpayers as to the deductibility of payments by patrons of your fund-raising events."[5] The message announced a "Special Emphasis Program," by which the IRS sought to "ascertain the extent to which taxpayers are furnished accurate and sufficient information concerning the deductibility of their contributions."[6]

The Commissioner's message focused on fund-raising events, where part or all of a payment to a charitable organization is attributable to the purchase of admission or some other privilege. In this context, the law (at least as interpreted by the IRS) presumes that the total amount paid is equivalent to the benefits received in return. Of course, this presumption can be rebutted in appropriate instances, where there is a true gift element in the payment.

In general, this matter has three manifestations. One is the fund-raising event, where something of value is provided to the patron, such as dinner or entertainment. The charitable organization is expected by the IRS to determine the fair market value of the event and to notify the patron that only the amount of the payment that is

[3]See Chapter 4 § 1.
[4]See the text accompanied by n. 2, *supra*.
[5]IRS Publication 1391 (1988).
[6]*Id.* This Special Emphasis Program is discussed in Chapter 23.

in excess of that value is deductible as a charitable gift. For example, a fund-raising event may center around a dinner; the ticket is $75 and the dinner is worth $50; the IRS expected the charity to tell the patron that only $25 of the $75 is deductible as a charitable gift. (The portion that is reflective of a purchase, rather than a gift, may be deductible as an ordinary and necessary business expense.[7])

In determining fair value, a charitable organization must look to comparable circumstances. The cost to the charity is not relevant. Thus, a charity may have the dinner provided to it without cost (such as a donation from a caterer), yet the dinner still has a value to the recipient.

Another manifestation of this problem occurs when a donor donates and receives something of value in return, such as a package of greeting cards.[8] The IRS position in this connection is the same as receipt of a benefit or a privilege: The IRS expects the donor to claim as a charitable deduction only the amount in excess of value received and the Service expects the charity to provide the donor with that value.[9]

The third aspect of this is the payment to a charitable organization that is not deductible at all. Obvious examples of this include payments of tuition to schools and payment for healthcare services to hospitals. Other of these payments are dues, subscriptions, purchases made at auctions, and purchases of raffle and sweepstakes tickets.

The IRS conceded, in a 1988 private letter ruling, that there are no sanctions for violation of its disclosure rules.[10] However, there was discussion of application of the aiding and abetting (and other) penalties,[11] and of potential litigation in this area. There also was discus-

---

[7]IRC § 162(a).

[8]E.g., *Veterans of Foreign Wars, Department of Michigan v. Commissioner*, 89 T.C. 7 (1987); *Veterans of Foreign Wars of the United States, Department of Missouri, Inc. v. United States*, 85-2 U.S.T.C. § 9605 (W.D. Mo. 1984).

[9]There is a statutory exception to this rule. Where an individual makes a payment to or for the benefit of a college or university, which would be deductible as a charitable contribution but for the fact that the individual receives the right to purchase seating at an athletic event in the institution's athletic stadium, 80 percent of the payment may be treated as a charitable contribution (IRC § 170(m)).

[10]IRS Private Letter Ruling 8832003.

[11]See Chapter 10 § 5.

sion of the use of the unrelated income rules in this setting,[12] as well as of theories by which an organization's tax exemption could be revoked for failure to comport with these rules.

In 1988 the IRS also began reviewing tax returns filed by individuals, looking for situations where a charitable contribution deduction was being claimed, when in fact only a portion or perhaps none of the payment was deductible as a gift.

Congress adopted legislation in 1988 requiring disclosure of nondeductibility in the case of contributions to tax-exempt organizations that are not charitable ones.[13] The report of the Committee on the Budget of the House of Representatives accompanying this legislation contained a discussion of the problem from the standpoint of Congress, with the observation that the committee "is concerned that some charitable organizations may not make sufficient disclosure, in soliciting donations, membership dues, payments for admission or merchandise, or other support, of the extent (if any) to which the payors may be entitled to charitable deductions for such payments."[14]

This discussion focused on so-called "memberships" in a charitable entity, such as a museum or library, where the "members" receive benefits of some monetary value (such as free admission to events where others are charged, merchandise discounts, and free subscriptions). The Committee cautioned that some or all of these membership payments are not deductible as charitable contributions. The Committee's discussion also referenced payments to a charity that are not deductible at all as charitable gifts, such as sales of raffle tickets and the auctioning of property or services. However, the analysis stated that, concerning the amount paid as a winning bid at a charity's auction, the portion of the amount that is in excess of the fair market value of the item or service received may be deductible as a charitable gift. The discussion noted that some charities wrongfully imply that all such payments are fully deductible, while "many other charities carefully and correctly advise their supporters of the long-standing tax rules governing the deductibility of payments made to a charitable organization in return for, or with the expectation of, a financial or economic benefit to the payor."[15]

---

[12] See Chapter 4 § 4. The use of the unrelated income rules in the context of fund-raising regulation is the subject of Hopkins, *The Law of Fund-Raising* (John Wiley & Sons, Inc. New York, New York: 1991), Chapter 6 § 4.

[13] See § 2, *infra*.

[14] H.R. Rep. No. 100-391, 100th Cong., 1st Sess. 1607 (1988).

[15] *Id.* at 1607–1608.

The Committee wrote that it "anticipates" that the IRS "will monitor the extent to which taxpayers are being furnished accurate and sufficient information by charitable organizations as to the nondeductibility of payments to such organizations where benefits or privileges are received in return, so that such taxpayers can correctly compute their Federal income tax liability."[16] Moreover, the Committee expected the charitable community to do its part, noting its anticipation that groups representing the community will "further educate their members as to the applicable tax rules and provide guidance as to how charities can provide appropriate information to their supporters in this regard."[17]

The seriousness of the intensity of the IRS on this subject was revealed when, at the final meeting of the IRS Exempt Organization Advisory Group, on January 10, 1989, then-Commissioner of Internal Revenue Lawrence B. Gibbs opened the session with the charge that charities and their fund-raisers are engaged in "questionable" and "egregious" fund-raising practices, notably suggestions that certain payments are deductible charitable gifts when in fact they are not. Then-Assistant Commissioner for Employee Plans and Exempt Organizations Robert I. Brauer made clear that the IRS feels that these abuses are not isolated but are "widespread practices that involve quite legitimate charities." Mr. Gibbs stated that charities must "clean up their act in this regard" or face stiff regulation from the IRS.[18]

In 1990, the IRS issued guidelines to enable charitable organizations to properly advise their patrons as to the deductibility, if any, of payments made to them where the patrons are receiving something in return for their payments.[19] These guidelines were issued as part of a program at the IRS to require charitable organizations to disclose to donors and other payors the extent to which the payments are deductible, where a benefit or service is provided by the payor. These guidelines are also being used by reviewing IRS agents.

One of the many problems facing charitable organizations because of the disclosure requirement is what to do about small items or other benefits that are of token value in relation to the amount contributed. These guidelines contain rules whereby a benefit can be regarded as inconsequential or insubstantial, so that the full amount

[16]*Id.* at 1608.
[17]*Id.*
[18]VI *The Nonprofit Counsel* (No. 2) 7 (1989).
[19]Rev. Proc. 90-12, 1990-1 C.B. 471.

of a payment to a charity becomes deductible as a charitable gift.

Under these guidelines, benefits received in connection with a payment to a charitable organization will be considered to have insubstantial fair market value (so that the payment is fully deductible as a gift), for purposes of advising donors, whenever the following two requirements are met:

- the payment occurs in the context of a fund-raising campaign in which the charity informs patrons as to how much of their payment is a deductible contribution, and
- either of the following is the case:
  - the fair market value of all of the benefits received in connection with the payment is not more than the lesser of two percent of the payment or $50, or
  - the payment is $25 (adjusted for inflation[20]) or more and the only benefits received in connection with the payment are token items bearing the organization's name or logo.

For these purposes, "token items" include items such as bookmarks, calendars, key chains, mugs, posters, and T-shirts. Also, the costs of all of the benefits received by a donor must, in the aggregate, be within the statutory limits established for "low cost articles," which generally describe an article with a cost not in excess of $5 (indexed for inflation[21]) that is distributed incidental to a charitable solicitation.[22]

With respect to the first of these two requirements, where a charitable organization is providing only insubstantial benefits in return for a payment, disclosure of the fair market value of the benefits is not required. However, fund-raising materials should include a statement to this effect:

> Under Internal Revenue Service guidelines' the estimated value of [the benefits received] is not substantial; therefore, the full amount of your payment is a deductible contribution.

[20]The IRS has calculated that this amount for years beginning in 1991 is $28.58 and that the amount for years beginning in 1992 is $30.09 Rev. Proc. 92-58, 1992-29 I.R.B. 10.
[21]The IRS has calculated that this amount for years beginning in 1991 is $5.71 and that the amount for years beginning in 1992 is $6.01 (Rev. Rul. 92-58, *supra*, n. 20).
[22]IRC § 513(h)(2).

In a situation where it is impractical to state in every solicitation how much of a payment is deductible, the charitable organization can, under these guidelines, seek a ruling from the IRS concerning an alternative procedure. This circumstance can arise, for example, in connection with the offering of a number of premiums in an on-air fund-raising announcement by an educational organization.

Resolving what was a difficult problem for many organizations, these guidelines state that newsletters or program guides (other than commercial quality publications) are treated as not having measurable value or cost if their primary purpose is to inform members about the activities of an organization and if they are not available to non-members by paid subscription or through newsstand sales.

Example 22.1

In 1990, X, a broadcast organization, provided to donors who gave $30 a listener's guide for one year and a coffee mug bearing the organization's logo. The guide was of commercial quality. The cost of production and distribution of the guide was $4 per year per patron and its fair market value was $6. The cost of the mug was $3 and its fair market value was $5. The aggregate cost of these two items ($7) exceeded the 1990 limit for the definition of low-cost articles ($5.45). Consequently, this organization was expected to inform its patrons that, of the $30 payment, $19 is deductible (since the payor received items having a total value of $11).

The charitable community was unable to achieve a level of compliance with the general IRS disclosure guidelines that was of satisfaction to the IRS and Congress. The proposed legislation that is discussed next was the consequence.

(b) Proposed Law

Congress, in 1992, passed legislation (which was vetoed) that would have imposed certain disclosure requirements on charitable organizations that receive so-called "*quid pro quo* contributions."[23] A *quid pro quo* contribution would be defined as a payment to a charitable organization that was made partly as a contribution and partly in consideration for goods or services furnished to the donor.

---

[23]Revenue Act of 1992, H.R. 11, 102d Cong., 2d Sess. (1992) § 7203.

Charitable organizations that receive *quid pro quo* contributions would be required, in connection with the solicitation or receipt of the contribution, to

- inform the donor that the amount of the contribution that is deductible for federal income tax purposes is limited to the excess of the amount of any money, and the value of any property other than money, contributed by the donor over the value of the goods or services provided by the organization, and

- provide the donor with a good faith estimate of the value of goods and services furnished to the donor by the organization.

It was intended that this disclosure be made in connection with the solicitation or receipt of the contribution, such that the disclosure is reasonably likely to come to the attention of the donor. For example, a disclosure of the required information in small print set forth within a larger document might not meet this requirement.

With one exception, this disclosure requirement would apply to all *quid pro quo* contributions regardless of the dollar amount of the contribution involved (that is, even in situations with donations less than $100[24]). The disclosure would have to be made by the charitable organization in connection with either the solicitation or receipt of the contribution. Thus, for example, if a charitable organization received a $75.00 contribution, in exchange for which the donor received a dinner with a value of $40.00, the charity would have to inform the donor that only $35.00 is deductible as a charitable contribution. The exception would be that this rule would not apply where only *de minimis*, token goods or services are given to a donor.[25] Also, this rule would not apply with respect to transactions that do not have a donative element, such as sales of goods by a museum gift shop that are not in part donations.

The legislative history of this proposal contains the following explanation of the need for these rules:

> Difficult problems of tax administration arise with respect to fundraising techniques in which an organization that is eligible to receive

[24]See Chapter 21, text accompanied by ns. 28–33.

[25]In determining what is "*de minimis*" and "token," preexisting IRS ruling policy was followed. This policy is discussed in the text accompanied by ns. 19–22, *supra*.

deductible contributions provides goods or services in consideration for payments from donors. Organizations that engage in such fundraising practices often do not inform their donors that all or a portion of the amount paid by the donor may not be deductible as a charitable contribution. Consequently, the [Senate Finance] [C]ommittee believes . . . it appropriate that, in all cases where a charity receives a *quid pro quo* contribution (i.e., a payment made partly as a contribution and partly in consideration for goods or services furnished to the payor by the donee organization) the charity should inform the donor that the [federal income tax charitable contribution] deduction . . . is limited to the amount by which the payment exceeds the value of goods or services furnished, and provide a good faith estimate of the value of such goods or services.

Penalties could be imposed upon charitable organizations that fail to make the required disclosure, unless the failure was due to reasonable cause. The penalty would be $10.00 per contribution, capped at $5,000 per particular fund-raising event or mailing. The penalties would apply if an organization either (1) fails to make any disclosure in connection with a *quid pro quo* contribution, or (2) makes a disclosure that is incomplete or inadequate, such as an estimate not determined in good faith of the value of goods or services furnished to the donor.

§ 22.2   DISCLOSURE BY NON-CHARITABLE ORGANIZATIONS

Certain contributions disclosure rules were legislated by Congress late in 1987.[26] These rules are not applicable to charitable organizations.[27]

These disclosure rules are applicable to all types of taxexempt organizations (other than charitable ones), and are targeted princi-

---

[26] IRC § 6113. This section of the Internal Revenue Code, a consequence of hearings before the House Subcommittee on Oversight in 1987, is part of the deficit reduction legislation that was signed into law on Dec. 22, 1987 (Pub. L. No. 100-203, 100th Cong., 1st Sess. (1987)). The measure was initially introduced separately, as the "Tax-Exempt Organizations' Lobbying and Political Activities Accountability Act of 1987" (H.R. 2942, 100th Cong., 1st Sess. (1987)). The IRS published rules to accompany this law in 1988 (IRS Notice 88-120, 1988-2 C.B. 459).

[27] See n. 1, *supra*.

pally at social welfare organizations.[28] They are designed to prevent these noncharitable organizations from engaging in gift-solicitation activities under circumstances in which donors will assume, or be led to assume, that the contributions are tax-deductible, when in fact they are not. However, these rules do not apply to an organization that has annual gross receipts that are normally no more than $100,000.[29] Also, where all of the parties being solicited are tax-exempt organizations, the solicitation does not have to include the disclosure statement (inasmuch as these grantors have no need for a charitable deduction).[30]

Technically, this law applies in general to any organization to which contributions are not deductible as charitable gifts and which

- is tax-exempt,[31]
- is a political organization,[32]

---

[28]That is, organizations that are exempt under IRC § 501(a) by reason of being described in IRC § 501(c)(4). See *The Law of Tax-Exempt Organizations*, Chapter 28.

[29]IRC § 6113(b)(2)(A). In determining this threshold, the same principles that obtain in ascertaining the annual information return (Form 990) $25,000 filing threshold apply (Rev. Proc. 82-23, 1982-1 C.B. 687). (This $25,000 filing threshold is discussed in *The Law of Tax-Exempt Organizations*, Chapter 37, text accompanied by ns. 234–244). In general, these rules utilize a three-year average. The organization must include the required disclosure statement on all solicitations made more than 30 days after reaching $300,000 in gross receipts for the three-year period of the calculation (IRS Notice 88-120, *supra*, n. 25).

A local, regional, or state chapter of an organization with gross receipts under $100,000 must include the disclosure statement in its solicitations if at least 25 percent of the money solicited will go to the national, or other, unit of the organization that has annual gross receipts over $100,000, because the solicitation is considered as being in part on behalf of that unit. Also, if a trade association or labor union with over $100,000 in annual gross receipts solicits funds that will pass through to a political action committee with less than $100,000 in annual gross receipts, the solicitation must include the required disclosure statement. (These three types of tax-exempt organizations are the subject of *The Law of Tax-Exempt Organizations*, Chapters 29, 31, and 33, respectively.)

[30]IRS Notice 88-120, *supra*, n. 25.

[31]That is, is described in IRC § 501(a) and IRC § 501(c) (other than, as noted, in *supra*, n. 26, IRC § 501(c)(3)).

[32]That is, is described in IRC § 527.

- was either type of organization at any time during the five-year period ending on the date of the solicitation, or
- is a successor to one of these organizations at any time during this five-year period.[33]

The IRS is accorded the authority to treat any group of two or more organizations as one organization for these purposes where "necessary or appropriate" to prevent the avoidance of these rules through the use of multiple organizations.[34]

Under these rules, each "fund-raising solicitation" by or on behalf of a tax-exempt non-charitable organization must contain an express statement, in a "conspicuous and easily recognizable format," that gifts to it are not deductible as charitable contributions for federal income tax purposes.[35] (The IRS has promulgated rules as to this statement; these rules are summarized below.) A fund-raising solicitation is any solicitation of gifts made in written or printed form, by television, radio, or telephone (although there is an exclusion for letters or calls not part of a coordinated fund-raising campaign soliciting more than 10 persons during a calendar year).[36] Despite the clear reference in the statute to "contributions and gifts," the IRS interprets this rule to mandate the disclosure when any tax-exempt organization (other than a charitable one) seeks funds, such as dues from members.

Failure to satisfy this disclosure requirement can result in imposition of penalties.[37] The penalty is $1,000 per day (maximum of $10,000 per year), albeit with a reasonable cause exception. However, in an instance of "intentional disregard" of these rules, the penalty for the day on which the offense occurred is the greater of $1,000 or 50 percent of the aggregate cost of the solicitations that took place on that day, and the $10,000 limitation is inapplicable. For these purposes, the days involved are those on which the solicitation

---

[33]IRC § 6113(b)(1). For this purpose, a fraternal organization (one described in IRC § 170(c)(4) and discussed in Chapter 4 § 2) is treated as a charitable organization only with respect to solicitations for contributions that are to be used exclusively for purpose referred to in IRC § 170(c)(4) (IRC § 6113(b)(3)).

[34]IRC § 6113(b)(2)(B).

[35]IRC § 6113(a).

[36]IRC § 6113(c).

[37]IRC § 6710.

was telecast, broadcast, mailed, otherwise distributed, or telephoned.

The IRS promulgated rules in amplification of this law, particularly the requirement of a disclosure statement.[38] These rules, which include guidance in the form of "safe-harbor" provisions, address the format of the disclosure statement in instances of use of print media, telephone, television, and radio. They provide examples of acceptable disclosure language and methods (which, when followed, amount to the safe-harbor guidelines), and of included and excluded solicitations. They also contain guidelines for establishing the $100,000 threshold.[39]

The safe-harbor guideline for print media (including solicitations by mail and in newspapers) is fourfold:

- the solicitation should include language such as the following: "Contributions or gifts to [name of organization] are not deductible as charitable contributions for federal income tax purposes,"
- the statement should be in at least the same type size as the primary message stated in the body of the letter, leaflet, or advertisement,
- the statement should be included on the message side of any card or tear-off section that the contributor returns with the contribution, and
- the statement should be either the first sentence in a paragraph or itself constitute a paragraph.

The safe-harbor guidelines for telephone solicitations are the following:

- the solicitation includes language such as the following: "Contributions or gifts to [name of organization] are not deductible as charitable contributions for federal income tax purposes,"
- the statement must be made in close proximity to the request for contributions, during the same telephone call, by the same solicitor, and
- any written confirmation or billing sent to a person pledging to contribute during the telephone solicitation must be in compliance with the requirements for print media solicitations.

[38] IRS Notice 88-120, *supra*, n. 25.
[39] See the text accompanied by n. 28, *supra*.

To conform to the guideline, solicitation by television must include a solicitation statement that complies with the first of the print medium requirements. Also, if the statement is spoken, it must be in close proximity to the request for contributions. If the statement appears on the television screen, it must be in large, easily readable type appearing on the screen for at least five seconds.

In the case of a solicitation by radio, the statement must, to meet the safe-harbor test, comply with the first of the print medium requirements. Also, the statement must be made in close proximity to the request for contributions during the same radio solicitation announcement.

Where the soliciting organization is a membership entity, classified as a trade or business association or other form of business league,[40] or a labor or agricultural organization,[41] the following statement is in conformance with the safe-harbor guideline: "Contributions or gifts to [name of organization] are not tax deductible as charitable contributions. However, they may be deductible as ordinary and necessary business expenses."

If an organization makes a solicitation to which these rules apply and the solicitation does not comply with the applicable safe-harbor guidelines, the IRS will evaluate all of the facts and circumstances to determine whether the solicitation meets the disclosure rule. A "good faith effort" to comply with these requirements is an important factor in the evaluation of the facts and circumstances. Nonetheless, disclosure statements made in "fine print" do not comply with the statutory requirement.

This disclosure requirement applies to solicitations for voluntary contributions as well as solicitations for attendance at testimonials and like fund-raising events. The disclosure must be made in the case of solicitations for contributions to political action committees.

Exempt from this disclosure rule are: the billing of those who advertise in an organization's publications; billing by social clubs for food and beverages; billing of attendees of a conference; billing for insurance premiums of an insurance program operated or sponsored by an organization; billing of members of a community association for

---

[40]That is, an organization described in IRC § 501(c)(6) and tax-exempt under IRC § 501(a).

[41]That is, an organization described in IRC § 501(c)(5) and tax-exempt under IRC § 501(a).

mandatory payments for police and fire (and similar) protection; and billing for payments to a voluntary employees' beneficiary association[42] as well as similar payments to a trust for pension and/or health benefits.

General material discussing the benefits of membership in a tax-exempt organization, such as a trade association or labor union, does not have to include the required disclosure statement. However, the statement is required where the material both requests payment and specifies the amount requested as membership dues. If a person responds to the general material discussing the benefits of membership, the follow-up material requesting the payment of a specific amount in membership dues (such as a union check-off card or a trade association billing statement for a new member) must include the disclosure statement. General material discussing a political candidacy and requesting persons to vote for the candidate or "support" the candidate need not include the disclosure statement, unless the material specifically requests either a financial contribution or a contribution of volunteer services in support of the candidate.

[42]That is, an organization that is tax-exempt under IRC § 501(a) by reason of description in IRC § 501(c)(9). In general, see *The Law of Tax-Exempt Organizations*, Chapter 32 § 4.

23

Special Events and Corporate Sponsorships

As has been discussed throughout this section, a payment to a charitable organization is not always deductible as a charitable gift for federal income tax purposes.[1] Payments that can fall into these categories of questionable transfers are:

- a payment where the donor is provided some tangible item of property in exchange for the contribution, so that only a portion of the transaction is a charitable gift,
- a payment where the donor is provided some benefit, service, or privilege in exchange for the contribution, so that only a portion of the transaction is a charitable gift, and
- a payment where the donor is provided with an item of property, or a benefit, service, or privilege to the extent that none of the payment constitutes a charitable gift.

The IRS has launched a "Special Emphasis Program" to disseminate information about the law on these points and to provide audit guidance to its agents in the field. Two types of fund-raising practices have dominated the development of the law in this area: special events and donor recognition programs. This body of law addresses the question of whether the payments to a charitable organization are, in whole or in part, tax deductible as gifts, as well as the question of whether the charitable organization that is the recipient of these payments must pay the unrelated business income tax on them.

[1]See, e.g., Chapter 4 § 1.

§ 23.1　IRS AUDIT GUIDELINES

The IRS is aggressively using its inherent authority, in conjunction with its task of administering the federal tax laws, to regulate the field of fund-raising for charitable purposes. In part, this is the result of mandates from Congress to the IRS to increase its review and regulation of the processes of charitable giving.[2] Thus, the IRS is expanding its efforts to audit the fund-raising programs of charitable organizations. One of the tools it is employing in this regard is documentation issued in early 1990 to IRS agents in the field, including an extensive "checksheet."

(a)　Some Regulatory History

Prior to a discussion of this checksheet, some background is appropriate. Today's regulation of charitable giving by the federal government can best be appreciated in the light of its history.

For years, it has seemed that wide-ranging regulation of charitable giving by the IRS was inevitable. The new activism by the IRS in this regard is directly affecting the administration of giving programs by charitable organizations, as well as placing increased responsibilities and requirements on donors.

The broad regulation of charitable giving that is part of contemporary law did not materialize as most observers expected. No great scandal involving fraudulent "charitable" giving was uncovered by the media or IRS audit that led the IRS to act. Nor was there development of new regulations on the subject by the Department of the Treasury or enactment of a far-reaching statute by Congress.

Rather, regulation of charitable giving through the tax system arrived because the IRS decided to act with respect to a longstanding problem—some would characterize it as an "abuse." The problem/abuse is the casting of a payment to a charitable organization as a deductible gift when in fact the transaction does not involve a gift at all or is only partially a gift. Legislation enacted in 1992 characterizes these latter types of transactions as "*quid pro quo* gifts."[3]

The IRS position that a payment to a charitable organization is not a gift where the donor receives something of approximately equal value in return is not new. This position was made quite explicit on a

[2]See the discussion in Chapter 22, text accompanied by ns. 14–17.
[3]See Chapter 22, text accompanied by ns. 23–24.

number of occasions, including a pronouncement in 1967.[4] At that time and since, it has been the view of the IRS that charitable organizations have an obligation to notify their patrons when payments to them are not gifts, or are only partially gifts, particularly in the context of a special fund-raising event.[5]

There were, over the years, a few instances of deliberate and blatant wrongdoing in this area by "donors" and patrons. There were individuals who wrote a check, for example, to a school for something acquired at the school's annual auction and who could not resist the temptation to treat the payment as a charitable gift on their federal income tax returns. The same may be said of raffles, sweepstakes, book sales, sports tournaments, dinner and theater events, dues payments, and the like. However, most of the abuses of this nature were inadvertent, based on ignorance or misunderstanding of the legal requirements.

Matters changed somewhat when charitable organizations began explicitly or implicitly telling donors and patrons that their payments to the organizations were deductible as gifts, when in fact they were only partially deductible or not deductible at all. This practice became so overt and pervasive that the IRS decided that the time had come to enhance government review of these areas of fund-raising and giving.[6] The extent of regulation in this area was multiplied by reason of the increase in the extent of donor recognition efforts, particularly in the setting of corporate sponsorships.[7]

(b) Special Emphasis Program

The IRS launched its contemporary attack on these forms of fund-raising misperformance by inaugurating the so-called "Special Emphasis Program." This program evolved in two parts: an educational phase and an audit phase.

Phase I of this Special Emphasis Program took place throughout 1989. During this period, the IRS engaged in educational efforts to explain the rules to charitable organizations, who were expected to apply them when soliciting contributions and other payments. This aspect of the Program consisted of speeches by representatives of the

[4]Rev. Rul. 67-246, 1967-2 C.B. 104.
[5]See Chapter 22 § 1.
[6]*Id.*, text accompanied by n. 5.
[7]See § 3, *infra.*

IRS, workshops with charitable organizations, and the encouragement of educational efforts by national "umbrella" charitable organizations. (Some aspects of this educational phase are continuing.)

At this time, the IRS began reviewing annual information returns (Form 990) for 1988 filed by charitable organizations. Special emphasis was placed on the returns of organizations that are engaged in gift solicitation. Charitable organizations that were not in compliance with the disclosure requirements received letters from the IRS requesting immediate compliance with these rules. Some organizations (such as the Public Broadcasting Service[8]), working with the IRS, developed formal guidelines for their members. There was also talk of more audits of charitable organizations and donors by the IRS, review of lists of contributors by the IRS, and the imposition of various tax penalties.

The regulation by the IRS of charitable giving and other fundraising programs became much more serious when the second phase of the Special Emphasis Program was inaugurated, in early 1990. This aspect of the IRS's involvement and scrutiny is evidenced by the rather extraordinary checksheet sent by the National Office of the IRS to its agents in the field, to enable them to review the fundraising practices of charitable organizations.

(c) The Checksheet

The checksheet, bearing the title "Exempt Organizations Charitable Solicitations Compliance Improvement Program Study Checksheet" (Form 9215), reflected the beginning of the second phase of the IRS' Special Emphasis Program concerning solicitation practices of charitable organizations.[9]

This checksheet requires an auditing IRS agent to review, in conjunction with examinations of annual information returns (principally Form 990), the gift solicitation practices of charitable organizations, including the solicitation of gifts where the donor is provided a benefit, the use of special events, the conduct of bingo and other games of chance, travel tours, thrift stores, and the receipt of non-money contributions. A special section of the checksheet inquires about the use of professional fund-raisers. Overall, the checksheet consists of 82 questions, plus financial information.

[8]See n. 35, *infra.*
[9]This checksheet appears as Appendix B in *The Law of Fund-Raising.*

One question asks the IRS agent to determine whether the charitable organization is meeting the so-called "commensurate test." This is a standard, established by the IRS in 1964,[10] that looks to determine whether a charitable organization is carrying on charitable works that are commensurate in scope with its financial resources. The scope of the commensurate test in the context of charitable fund-raising is currently unclear,[11] but presumably the agent is supposed to ascertain whether the charitable organization is engaging in sufficient charitable activity in relation to its available resources, including gifts received through fund-raising campaigns, in relation to the time and expense of fund-raising.[12]

The checksheet focuses on the nature of benefits, goals, or services provided to donors. These items include retail merchandise, new and donated merchandise received at an auction, tickets for a game of chance, tuition at an educational institution, travel, tickets to an athletic or other event, discounts, free subscriptions, and preferential seating at a college or university athletic event.[13] The checksheet asks whether the charitable organization made any reference to the deductibility of a payment in its solicitation or professional literature or in any thank-you letter, receipt ticket, or other written receipt to donors.

As to contributions of property, the IRS wants a list of all non-money gifts, the fair market value of which is in excess of $500, during the year of examination. The checksheet inquires about the individual who valued the gift property, whether a proper receipt was provided, whether there is an agreement between the donor and the donee as to disposition of the property, and whether the requisite forms were properly completed and filed.[14]

---

[10] Rev. Rul. 64-182, 1964-1 C.B. (Part 1) 186.

[11] The issue is presently pending in the U.S. Tax Court, having been litigated in 1992, in *United Cancer Council, Inc.* v. *Commissioner* (U.S. Tax Ct. Docket No. 2008-91X).

[12] The commensurate test, as applied in the charitable fund-raising context, is the subject of *The Law of Fund-Raising*, Chapter 6 § 12 (1992 Supp., at 144).

[13] As to this latter item, see Chapter 22, text accompanied by n. 9.

[14] Other aspects of this checksheet, that inquire into fund-raising practices, is the subject of *The Law of Fund-Raising*, Chapter 6 § 1, pp. 368–370.

(d) Audit Guidance

In directions disseminated to its examining agents in 1990, and re-vised and re-disseminated in 1992,[15] concerning the Phase II exami-nations, the National Office of the IRS cautioned them that "the examinations must be thorough." The examiner is entreated to "pur-sue the examination to the point where he/she can conclude that all areas and data concerning fund-raising activities have been consid-ered."[16]

This guidance stated that the second phase of the Program focuses on "all aspects of fund-raising and charitable solicitations."[17] Some of the practices the IRS agents are looking for are the following:

- misleading statements in solicitations literature that imply de-ductibility of contributions, "where none probably exists,"
- contracts with professional "for-profit" fund-raisers, who use "questionable fund-raising methods" to solicit funds from the public,
- situations where other expenses, such as administrative and fund-raising costs, constitute an "unusually high portion" of the solicited funds and property, and
- fund-raising activities that result in consequences such as tax-able income or additional filing requirements.

These directions continued: "The scope and depth of the examina-tion should be sufficient to fully disclose the nature of abusive situa-tions involving fundraising activities that mislead donors to claim the incorrect charitable contribution deductions; misrepresent the use of the solicited funds; engage in questionable fund-raising practices, etc."[18] There was such an insistence on thoroughness because the results of these examinations[19] "are to be used in a report that will be submitted to Congress."[20]

---

[15]The directions that were sent in 1990 are the subject of *The Law of Fund-Raising*, Chapter 6 § 1, pp. 370-371. This guidance is contained in Manual Supplement (7(10)G-59).

[16]*Id.* § 11.02.

[17]*Id.* § 11.09.

[18]*Id.* § 11.03.

[19]These examinations collectively are referred to by the IRS as the "Charita-ble Solicitations Compliance Improvement Study."

[20]*Id.* § 11.02. Although this report has yet to be submitted, Congress al-ready acted (see Chapter 22 § 1, text accompanied by ns. 23–24).

Thus, what started out in 1967 as concern with overdeductibility in the context of gifts and other payments to charitable organizations has evolved into a nationwide examination by the IRS of all "questionable fund-raising practices and techniques."

§ 23.2 SPECIAL EVENTS

Special events (or benefit events) are social occasions that use ticket sales and underwriting to generate revenue. These events are typically the most expensive and least profitable method of charitable fund-raising. Nonetheless, they have a great value in public relations visibility, both for the charitable organization involved and its volunteers.[21]

Examples of these special events include:

- annual balls
- auctions
- bake sales
- car washes
- dinners
- fairs and festivals
- games of chance (such as bingo, raffles, and sweepstakes)
- luncheons
- sports tournaments (particularly golf and tennis)
- theater outings

There is some confusion in the law as to exactly what constitutes a "special event" in the charitable fund-raising context. For instance, one court defined a "fund-raising event" as "a single occurrence that may occur on limited occasions during a given year and its purpose is to further the exempt activities of the organization."[22] These events were contrasted with activities that "are continuous or continual activities which are certainly more pervasive a part of the organization than a sporadic event and [that are] . . . an end in themselves."[23] However, there is a wide variety of fund-raising methods, other than

[21] See Greenfield, *Fund-Raising: Evaluating and Managing the Fund Development Process* (New York: John Wiley & Sons, Inc. 1991), at 74–79.
[22] *U.S. CB Radio Association, No. 1, Inc. v. Commissioner*, 42 T.C.M. 1441, 1444 (1981).
[23] *Id.*

special events, that are "continuous" and "pervasive." Rarely, moreover, is the purpose of a special event to "further the exempt activities of the organization"; they are events that usually have no
relationship to a charitable organization's exempt purposes and activities, and are engaged in largely to generate some funds and favorable
publicity which in turn helps the organization advance its tax-exempt
activities. Finally, a fund-raising activity is rarely an end in itself, yet
many charitable organizations and institutions have major, ongoing
fund-raising and development programs that are permanent fixtures
in the totality of the organizations' functions.

Special events figure prominently in a charitable organization's
annual reporting to the IRS. In determining whether an annual information return (Form 990) is required, only net receipts (not gross
receipts) from special events are used in determining the $25,000
filing threshold. (Organizations, other than private foundations, with
gross receipts that are normally not in excess of $25,000, need not
file annual information returns.[24]) Part VII-A of the annual information return requires a tax-exempt organization to identify each
income-producing activity; a separate line is provided for special
fund-raising events.[25]

As discussed, it has been the view of the IRS for years that
charitable organizations that conduct special events have the obligation to notify the participants in these events of the amount (if any)
expended for their participation in the event that is deductible as a
charitable gift.[26] Also, as discussed, legislation that took effect in 1993
requires charitable organizations to make a good faith estimate of the
value of benefits, services, and/or privileges provided to a donor as
the consequence of a gift and to notify the donor that only an
amount in excess of that value is deductible.[27]

§ 23.3   DONOR RECOGNITION PROGRAMS

(a)   Proposed Donor Recognition Guidelines

The IRS caused a substantial stir in 1991 by determining that a
payment received by a college bowl association from a for-profit

---

[24]IRC § 6033(a)(2)(A)(ii).
[25]For more detail on the federal reporting requirements for charitable organizations in the fund-raising setting, see *The Law of Fund-Raising*, Chapter
6 § 6.
[26]See Chapter 22 § 1, text accompanied by ns. 1–22.
[27]See Chapter 22 § 1, text accompanied by ns. 23–24.

corporation sponsoring a bowl football game was taxable as unrelated business income, because the payment was for a package of "valuable" services rather than a "gift." This IRS pronouncement was a technical advice memorandum, passing on the federal tax consequences of so-called "corporate sponsorships," where the sponsoring business has the corporate name included in the name of the event.[28] (One of the most visible of these situations is the Mobil Oil Corporation sponsorship of the Cotton Bowl, now known as the Mobil Cotton Bowl.) The associations involved contended that the payment were gifts, but the IRS held that the companies received a substantial *quid pro quo* for the payments. This determination raised the question, once again, of whether a payment is a "gift" when the "donor" is provided something in return.

Charitable organizations throughout the United States became concerned about this IRS initiative. This was properly so, since it had implications far beyond college and university bowl games. The IRS bowl game technical advice memorandum raised the deeper question of when the extent of donor recognition renders a payment not a "gift."

The IRS promptly recognized this problem. Thus, it soon thereafter promulgated some proposed guidelines for its auditing agents to use when conducting examinations of tax-exempt organizations.[29]

(b) Proposed Guidelines—General Provisions

These guidelines, as the IRS put it, "set forth specific indicators to be considered in making a determination as to whether an organization is engaged in an unrelated trade or business activity."

These guidelines state that the provision of substantial valuable marketing and other services by a tax-exempt organization in return for its support in the form of funding may constitute unrelated business income. By contrast, this is not the case where there is no expectation that the organization will provide a substantial return benefit.

Before tax-exempt charitable organizations panic, it must be said that the IRS agrees that the mere recognition of a corporate contributor as a benefactor normally is incidental to the contribution and not of sufficient value to the contributor to constitute unrelated trade

---

[28] IRS Technical Advice Memorandum 9147007.
[29] IRS Ann. 92-15, 1992-6 I.R.B. 51.

or business. That is, "mere recognition" does not transform the gift into taxable advertising income.

For example, mere recognition occurs where a university names a professorship, where a scholarship or building is named after a benefactor, where an underwriting of a public radio or television program or museum exhibition is acknowledged, or where a contributor to a fund-raising event or a performing arts organization in an accompanying program is listed.

The IRS recognized that "[a]ssociating the name of the sponsor with the name of the exempt organization's event will not, in itself, trigger" the imposition of the unrelated income tax. Rather, says the IRS, "all the facts and circumstances of the relationship between the sponsor and [the] exempt organization must be considered." The IRS stated: "A determination of whether a substantial return benefit is present should include an analysis of: the value of the services provided in exchange for the payment; the terms under which payments and services are rendered; the amount of control that the sponsor exercises over the event; and whether the extent of the organization's exposure of the donor's name constitutes significant promotion."

(c) Exemptions

The IRS said that it will not apply these guidelines to organizations that are "of a purely local nature," that receive "relatively insignificant" gross revenue from corporate sponsors, and generally operate with significant amounts of volunteer labor. These organizations include youth athletic organizations such as little league baseball and soccer teams, and local theaters and youth orchestras.

(d) The Examination Guidelines

As indicated in the ruling concerning bowl association payments, the IRS is concerned wherever there is a written contract memorializing the relationship. Thus, the examination guidelines state that "the examiner should thoroughly review the corporate sponsorship contracts/arrangements (either written or oral) to determine whether the agreement requires the exempt organization to perform any services, including advertising, for the corporate sponsor in return for revenue." The guidelines advise the examining agent to "[r]equest any information that will assist you in thoroughly understanding the corporate sponsorship contracts/arrangements."

Examining agents were told to "[r]eview copies of minutes of the organization's board of directors or trustees meetings or any correspondence or other written statements between the exempt organization, corporate sponsor, or other party relating to the corporate sponsorship contract/arrangement." These agents are being urged to review films, videotapes, or photographs of the event over the years to determine the extent to which the corporate sponsor's name is mentioned or depicted.

If a tax-exempt charitable organization has corporate sponsorships/arrangements, the IRS examiner is supposed to "review the agreements to determine whether the organization is performing substantial services or providing other benefits in return for the payments received." The factors to be considered by the IRS as tending to indicate an unrelated trade or business include:

- whether the corporate sponsorship contract/arrangement requires
  - the corporate sponsor's name or logo to be included in the official event title (the bowl game situation),
  - the corporate sponsor's name or logo to be prominently placed throughout the stadium, arena, or other site where the event is held,
  - the corporate sponsor's name or logo to be printed on materials related to the event,
  - the corporate sponsor's name or logo to be placed on participant uniforms or other support personnel uniforms,
  - the corporate sponsor to refer to its sponsorship in advertisements over the course of the contract,
  - that participants be available to the corporate sponsor for personal appearances and endorsements, or
  - the tax-exempt organization to arrange for special seating, accommodations, transportation, and hospitality facilities at the event for corporate sponsor clients or executives;
- whether the corporate sponsorship contract/arrangement requires media coverage of the event;
- Whether the corporate sponsorship contract/arrangement provides for promotional arrangements that do more than merely acknowledge the sponsor. The agents are to consider
  - specification of size, color, and content of sponsorship acknowledgment,

- listing of corporate sponsor products or services in the acknowledgement;
- whether the payment is contingent upon the tax-exempt organization securing television, radio, or other marketing contracts to provide the sponsor's name logo widespread exposure. Also, the extent, if any, that the payment is based on the television ratings of the event is to be considered;
- whether the contract/arrangement includes extensions or renewals which are contingent upon continued public exposure;
- whether the arrangement can be terminated for failure to provide certain benefits;
- whether the segment of the public expected to see the identifying sponsorship information can reasonably be expected to purchase the sponsor's goods or services.

Concerning sporting events, the IRS examiners have been alerted to the possibility that the entity under audit might raise as a defense the fact that a portion of the sponsorship amount is paid to the participating tax-exempt organizations providing teams. In these situations, said the IRS, the examiner should obtain information from the participating institutions regarding terms and conditions, if any, governing the funds and the ultimate use made of the income. In this regard, the IRS notes, media reports have indicated that funds may be used for travel and other expenses related to attending the event rather than for the regular activities of the participating organization.

The IRS said that examiners should be alert to additional services provided to the corporate sponsor through the same or ancillary contracts. These services would include such items as tickets, travel, and lodging for VIPs, their family members, or the individuals that are guests of the corporate sponsor. Frequently, perquisites such as chauffeur-driven limousines, hospitality suites, and "lavish" receptions are also included, the IRS cautioned.

These proposed guidelines stated that, in determining whether amounts derived by tax-exempt organizations from corporate sponsors are subject to tax on unrelated business income, the examiner should first determine whether all of the technical requirements, under the federal tax law, are met. The examiner is advised to examine whether any of the modifications or exceptions to this body of law (such as for rent or royalties) are applicable.

The IRS has noted that it is not determinative, for purposes of unrelated business income tax, whether corporate sponsorship payments, where substantial services are required, are treated as contributions or business expenses by the sponsor.

The IRS has advised its agents that, if there is unrelated business income, they should analyze the overhead, administrative, and other expenses claimed by the tax-exempt organization and review the basis for allocation of the expenditures.

Finally, the IRS has advised its examiners that they should document the extent to which the sponsorship income is "accurately and consistently" reported on the organization's annual information return (Form 990) and unrelated business income tax return (Form 990-T).

In an unusual departure from procedure, the IRS sought public comment on the proposed examination guidelines. This was done, said the IRS, due to the "important and sensitive" issues these proposed guidelines raise.

(e) IRS Hearing and Questions

The IRS held a hearing, on July 21–23, 1992, on the proposed examination guidelines regarding the treatment of corporate sponsorship income received by tax-exempt organizations conducting public events.[30]

The Service was concerned that some tax-exempt organizations conducting "public events" may receive income from corporate sponsors that is income from the sale of advertising, rather than a gift. Advertising income is, of course, unrelated business income. This activity is distinguishable from situations where tax-exempt, charitable organizations are merely recognizing the generosity of corporate donors.

The proposed guidelines contained a framework for an analysis of the payments received by exempt organizations from corporate sponsorship arrangements and set forth specific indicators to be considered in making a determination as to whether an organization is engaged in an unrelated trade or business activity.

The IRS believed that this matter raises "important and sensitive" issues under present law with respect to charitable organizations. Thus, it invited public comment on the proposed examination guide-

---

[30]This hearing was announced in IRS Ann. 92-88, 1992-26 I.R.B. 34.

lines. After consideration of the comments received, the IRS concluded that a public hearing was warranted to further discuss the proposed examination guidelines before they are finalized.

In order to assist the IRS in its consideration of the proposed guidelines, the Service requested that oral comments at the hearing include a discussion of some or all of the following issues:

- Should the audit tolerance provision of the guidelines be replaced with a "safe harbor," which excludes from the examination guidelines
  - those exempt organizations below a specified size, and/or
  - any sponsorship payments which do not exceed a certain dollar amount?
- Should the "facts and circumstances" approach set forth in the proposed guidelines be replaced with a more mechanical test? If so, what should that test be?
- Should the guidelines list specific factors that are considered as tending only to show mere donor recognition? If so, what are those specific factors? What kinds of benefits are so insubstantial that they are merely "incidental" to the arrangement?
- What are important examples of mere recognition or acknowledgement of corporate contributors?
- What factors indicate that advertising is involved?
- When do identifying references to a corporate sponsor's products, services, or slogans constitute advertising? Is the frequency of these identifying references relevant?
- Should unrelated business income tax liability only arise where sponsorship income is used for advertising services? How should advertising services be defined? Are promotional and marketing services included?
- How should expenses that are not directly related to advertising be treated? Is the allocation rule governing exploitation of exempt activities the appropriate rule to use in sponsorship income cases? If the exploitation method does not apply, what is a reasonable method for allocating items of overhead expenses?
- How should certain expenses, such as payments to third-party exempt organizations, be treated?
- Should the guidelines provide that, under a reasonable alloca-

tion method, an exempt organization may use a fragmentation approach to demonstrate that the sponsorship income is partly a contribution or royalty?

In addition, the IRS has invited oral comments on any other issue relevant to the question of the treatment of corporate sponsorship income.

As 1992 closed, the IRS was writing the final version of these guidelines.

(f) Proposed Legislation

As the IRS was endeavoring to finalize its donor recognition guidelines, Congress attempted to intervene.[31] It wrote specific rules on this subject, as part of the Revenue Act of 1992;[32] the measure was subsequently vetoed.

Under this proposal, the term "unrelated trade or business" does not include the activity of soliciting and receiving "qualified sponsorship payments" with respect to any qualified public event.[33]

"Qualified sponsorship payments" would be defined as any payment by a person engaged in a trade or business with respect to which there is no arrangement or expectation that the person will receive any substantial return benefit other than the use of the name or logo of the person's trade or business in connection with a qualified public event.[34] For these purposes, use of a name or logo of a person's trade or business in connection with a public event would not include advertising or promotion of the person's particular products or

---

[31] It is possible that the IRS timed its announcement of its position on corporate sponsorship payments so that Congress, if it chose, could legislate on the subject in 1992. Technically, the IRS was correct on the position that it took, because the package of services offered in the college and university bowl context clearly went beyond mere recognition of a "gift" and constituted advertising. The policy considerations of this position are another matter. A parallel circumstance was the IRS position on "contributions" to college and university athletic scholarship funds—again, technically the correct position—which, as a policy matter, was altered by Congress (see Chapter 22 § 1, n. 9).

[32] H.R. 11, 102d Cong., 2d Sess. (1992) § 7303(a).

[33] Proposed IRC § 513(i)(1).

[34] Proposed IRC § 513(i)(2).

services. For example, advertising or promotion of a sponsor's products or services not within the safe harbor that would be provided by this law includes a call to action to purchase the sponsor's products, superlative description or qualitative claim about the company (or its products or services), direct comparison with other companies, price or value information, inducements to buy, or endorsements.[35]

The term "qualified public event" would mean any public event conducted by an eligible tax-exempt organization if

- substantially all of the activities of the organization in conducting the event are not subject to the unrelated business income tax (for example, the activities are substantially related to the exempt purposes of the organization, the activities are not regularly carried on, or the volunteer labor or some other exception in the unrelated income rules applies[36]), and
- the net proceeds from the event are used for a charitable purpose.[37]

The tax-exempt organizations that would be eligible to utilize this exception are the following:

- charitable, educational, religious, scientific, and like organizations,[38]
- social welfare organizations,[39]

---

[35]The legislative history of this measure states that corporate sponsorship announcements or representations that meet the Public Broadcasting System National Program Funding Standards and Practices (in *PBS National Program Funding Standards and Practices* (Feb. 1990)) generally would be considered permissible identification of a sponsor by use of its name or logo (or that of a division or subsidiary) and not advertising or promotion of the sponsor's particular services or products for purposes of the safeharbor rule.

[36]See Chapter 4 § 4.

[37]Proposed IRC § 513(i)(3). The "charitable purpose" is that described in IRC § 170(c)(2)(B), namely, a religious, charitable, scientific, literary, or educational purpose, as well as the fostering of national or international amateur sports competition, and the prevention of cruelty to children and animals.

[38]That is, those described in IRC § 501(c)(3).

[39]That is, those described in IRC § 501(c)(4).

- labor, agricultural, or horticultural organizations,[40]
- trade, business, and professional associations, and other types of business leagues,[41] and
- state colleges and universities.[42]

The legislative history of these proposed rules contains the following explanation for the development of them:

> The [Senate Finance] [C]ommittee believes that the UBIT [unrelated business income tax] should not apply to the receipt of sponsorship payments (in return for which the sponsor is identified) by tax-exempt organizations in connection with their conduct of public events, provided that substantially all activities in conducting the event are not subject to the UBIT and the net proceeds from the event are used for a charitable, educational, or other [similar] purpose. . . . In such a case, acknowledging support of a sponsor generally is incidental to the tax-exempt organization receiving such support. However, this safe harbor rule should not apply to payments in exchange for which the tax-exempt organization provides advertising or promotion of the payor's specific products or services.[43]

The legislative history of these rules also states that examples of public events that would be governed by this exception include intercollegiate athletic events, concerts, museum exhibitions, state and agricultural fairs, fine arts festivals, and golf tournaments (assuming that the other requirements are satisfied). Identifying a sponsor of a qualified public event (or incorporating the sponsor's name into the official name of the event) would fall into the safe-harbor exception, even if the amount of the sponsorship payment owed by the sponsor is contingent upon a factor such as attendance or broadcast ratings.[44]

---

[40]That is, those described in IRC § 501(c)(5).

[41]That is, those described in IRC § 501(c)(6).

[42]That is, those entities described in IRC § 511(d)(2)(B).

[43]"Technical Explanation of the Finance Committee Amendment" ("Technical Explanation"), at 591. The Technical Explanation was not formally printed; it is, however, reproduced in the Congressional Record (138 *Cong. Rec.* (No. 112) S11246 (Aug. 3, 1992)).

[44]*Id.* at 592. The legislative history also states that enactment of this proposed body of law would not create any inference as to the tax treatment, under prior law, of sponsorship (or other) payments not governed by the rule, or sponsorship payments received in connection with events held prior to its effective date (*id.*).

24

State Fund-Raising Regulation

The solicitation of charitable contributions in the United States involves practices that are recognized as being forms of free speech protected by federal and state constitutional law. Thus, there are limitations on the extent to which fund-raising for charitable, educational, scientific, religious, and like organizations can be regulated by government. Nevertheless, nonprofit organizations in the United States face considerable regulatory requirements at the federal and state levels when they solicit contributions for charitable purposes. The purpose of this chapter is to summarize this body of law.[1]

The process of raising funds for charitable purposes is heavily regulated by the states. At this time, all but five states have some form of statutory structure by which the fund-raising process is regulated.[2] Of these states, 33 have formal charitable solicitation acts.

§ 24.1 STATE REGULATION IN GENERAL

The various state charitable solicitation acts generally contain certain features. These are:

- a process by which a charitable organization registers or otherwise secures a permit to raise funds for charitable purposes in the state;

---

[1]This body of law is summarized in greater detail in *The Law of Fund-Raising.*

[2]The states that have no statutory or other regulatory law in this regard are Alaska, Delaware, Idaho, Montana, and Wyoming.

- requirements for reporting information (usually annually) about an organization's fund-raising program;
- a series of organizations or activities that are exempt from some or all of the statutory requirements;
- a process by which a professional fund-raiser, professional solicitor, and/or commercial co-venturer registers with, and reports to, the state;
- record-keeping requirements. applicable to charitable organizations, professional fund-raisers, professional solicitors, and/or commercial co-venturers;
- rules concerning the contents of contracts between a charitable organization and a professional fund-raiser, professional solicitor, and/or a commercial co-venturer;
- a series of so-called "prohibited acts";
- provision for reciprocal agreements among the states as to coordinated regulation in this field;
- a summary of the powers of the govermnental official having regulatory authority (usually the attorney general or secretary of state);
- a statement of the various sanctions that can be imposed for failure to comply with this law (such as injunctions, fines, and imprisonment).

These elements of the law are generally applicable to the fund-raising charitable organization. Yet there are several provisions of law that are directed at the fund-raising professional or the professional solicitor, and/or that go beyond traditional fund-raising regulation.

§ 24.2 HISTORICAL PERSPECTIVE

Until the mid-1950s, the matter of fund-raising practices was not addressed by state law. At that time, there was not much attention to those practices from an ethical perspective. Some counties had adopted some fund-raising regulation ordinances but there was not any state or federal law on the subject.

This began to change in the mid-1950s, as part of the disclosure and consumer protection movements. North Carolina was the first state to enact a fund-raising regulation law. However, others soon followed, generating a series of laws that came to be known as "charitable solicitation acts." New York was the second state to enact one of these acts, and this law became the prototype for the many that were to follow.

The New York law and its progeny involved a statutory scheme based on registration and reporting. Charitable organizations were required to register in advance of solicitation and to annually report; bond requirements came later. Subsequently, forms of regulation involving professional fund-raisers and professional solicitors were developed. Exceptions evolved, disclosure requirements expanded, and a variety of "prohibited acts" (see below) developed.

Today's typical charitable solicitation statute is far more extensive than its forebears of decades ago.

When charitable solicitation acts began to develop (as noted, beginning in the mid-1950s), the principal features were registration and annual reporting requirements. These laws were basically licensing statutes. They gave the states essential information about the fund-raising to be conducted, so that they would have a basis for investigation and review should there be suspicion of some abuse.

Time passed. Some states decided to go beyond the concept of licensing and began to affirmatively regulate charitable solicitations. This was done in part because of citizens' complaints; another part was political grandstanding. The regulation worked its way into the realm of attempting to prevent the "less qualified" (including out-of-the-mainstream) charities from soliciting in the states.

Structurally, the typical charitable solicitation statute originally did not have much to do with actual regulation of the efforts of either the fund-raising institution or the fund-raising professional. Rather, the emphasis was on information gathering and disclosure of it to desiring donors. As noted, its requirements were based on the submission of written information (registration statements, reports, and the like) by charitable organizations and their fund-raising advisers, bond requirements, and enforcement authority granted to the attorneys general, secretaries of state, or other governmental officials charged with administering and enforcing the law.

Later, however, law requirements began to creep in that sounded more like ethical precepts. These requirements were more than just mechanics—they went beyond registration requirements, filing due dates, and accounting principles. They went beyond telling the charity and the professional fund-raisers when to do something, and entered the realm of telling them how they must conduct the solicitation and what they cannot do in that regard.

From the regulators' viewpoint, the high point of this form of regulation came when the states could ban charitable organizations with "high" fund-raising costs. (As noted below, this form of regulation ultimately was found to be unconstitutional.) This application of constitutional law rights to charitable solicitation acts left the state regulators without their principal weapon. In frustration, they turned to other forms of law, these based on the principle of "disclosure" (see below).

In this aftermath, more state fund-raising law developed. The registration and annual reports became more extensive. The states tried, with limited success, to force charities and solicitors into various forms of point-of-solicitation disclosure of various pieces of information. Some states dictated the contents of the scripts of telephone solicitors. This disclosure approach failed to satisfy the regulatory impulse. More frustration ensued.

The regulators turned to even more ways to have a role in the charitable fund-raising process. They started to micro-manage charitable fund-raising. They began to substitute their judgment for that of donors, charities, and professional fund-raisers. Thus, they engendered laws that beefed up the record-keeping requirements, spelled out the contents of contracts between charities and fund-raising consultants and solicitors, stepped into commercial co-ventures, and even injected themselves into matters such as the sale of tickets for charitable events and solicitations by fire and police personnel.

The regulatory appetite still remained unsatisfied. Having accomplished the imposition of just about all of the "law" they could think of, they turned to principles of "ethics." Now, for example, in one state, charities that solicit charitable gifts and their professional fund-raisers and solicitors are "fiduciaries." This is a role historically confined to trustees of charitable trusts and more recently to directors of charitable corporations.

§ 24.3 THE POLICE POWER

Prior to a fuller analysis of state law regulation in this field, it is necessary to briefly reference the underlying legal basis for this body of law: the so-called "police power."

Each state (and local unit of government) inherently possesses the "police power." This power enables a state or other political subdivision of government to regulate—within the bounds of constitutional law principles (see below)—the conduct of its citizens and others, so as to protect the safety, health, and welfare of its people.

Generally, it is clear that a state can enact and enforce, in the exercise of its police power, a charitable solicitation act that requires a charity planning on fund-raising in the jurisdiction to first register with (or secure a license or permit from) the appropriate regulatory authorities and subsequently to render periodic reports about the results of the solicitation. There is nothing inherently unlawful about this type of law. It may also require professional fund-raisers and professional solicitors to register and report, or empower the regulatory authorities to investigate the activities of charitable organizations in the presence of reasonable cause to do so, and impose injunctive remedies, fines, and imprisonment for violation of the statute. It appears clear that a state can regulate charitable fund-raising notwithstanding the fact that the solicitation utilizes the federal postal system, uses television and radio broadcasts, or otherwise occurs in interstate commerce.

The rationale is that charitable solicitations may be reasonably regulated to protect the public from deceit, fraud, or the unscrupulous obtaining of money under a pretense that the money is being collected and expended for a charitable purpose.

However, despite the inherent police power lodged in the states (and local jurisdictions) to regulate the charitable solicitation process, and the general scope of the power, principles of law operate to confine its reach. Most of these principles are based on constitutional law precepts, such as freedom of speech, procedural and substantive due process, and equal protection of the laws, as well as the standards usually imposed by statutory law, which bars the exercise of the police power in a manner that is arbitrary.

§ 24.4 SOME DEFINITIONS

State law regulation of fund-raising of this nature pertains to fund-raising for "charitable" purposes. However, the use of the term "charitable" in this setting refers to a range of activities and organizations that are much broader than those embraced by the term as used in the federal tax context. That is, while the term includes organizations that are charitable, educational, scientific, and religious, as those terms are used for federal purposes, it also includes (absent specific exemption) organizations that are civic, social welfare, recreational, and fraternal. Indeed, the general definition is so encompassing as to cause some of these statutes to expressly exclude fund-raising by political action committees, labor organizations, and trade organizations.

Some of this regulation is applicable to a "professional fund-raiser" (or similar term). The majority of the states define a professional fund-raiser as one who, for a fixed fee under a written agreement, plans, conducts, advises, or acts as a consultant, whether directly or indirectly, in connection with soliciting contributions for, or on behalf of, a charitable organization. This definition usually excludes those who actually solicit contributions. Other terms used throughout the states include "professional fund-raising counsel," "professional fund-raiser consultant," and "independent fund-raiser."

Much of this regulation is applicable to those who are "professional solicitors." Most of the states that use this term define this type of person as one who, for compensation, solicits contributions for or on behalf of a charitable organization, whether directly or through others, or a person involved in the fund-raising process who does not qualify as a professional fund-raiser. A minority of states define the term as a person who is employed or retained for compensation by a professional fund-raiser to solicit contributions for charitable purposes.

There is considerable confusion in the law as to the appropriate line of demarcation between these two terms. Because the extent of regulation can be far more intense for a professional solicitor, it is often very important for an individual or company to be classified as a professional fund-raiser rather than a professional solicitor.

Some states impose disclosure requirements with respect to the process known as "commercial co-venturing." This process occurs when a business announces to the general public that a portion (a specific amount or a specific percentage) of the purchase price of a product or service will, during a stated period, be paid to a charitable organization. This activity results in a payment by the business to a charitable organization, the amount of which is dependent on consumer response to the promotion by, and positive publicity for, the business sponsor.

§ 24.5   REGISTRATION REQUIREMENTS

A cornerstone of each state's charitable solicitation law is the requirement that a charitable organization (as defined in that law and not exempt from the obligation (see below)) that intends to solicit—by any means—contributions from persons in that state must first apply for and acquire permission to undertake the solicitation. This permission is usually characterized as a "registration"; some states denominate it as a "license" or a "permit." If successful, the result is authorization to conduct the solicitation. These permits are usually valid for one year.

These state laws apply to fund-raising within the borders of each state involved. Thus, a charitable or like organization soliciting in more than one state must register under (and otherwise comply with) not only the law of the state in which it is located but also the law of each of the states in which it will be fund-raising. Moreover, many counties, townships, cities, and similar jurisdictions throughout the United States have ordinances that attempt to regulate charitable fund-raising within their borders.

As noted below, most states' charitable solicitation acts require a soliciting charity (unless exempt) to annually file information with the appropriate governmental agency. This is done either by an annual updating of the registration or the like, or by the filing of a separate annual report.

In many states, professional fund-raisers and professional solicitors are required to register with the state.

§ 24.6 REPORTING REQUIREMENTS

Nearly all of the state charitable solicitation acts mandate annual reporting to the state by registered charitable organizations, professional fund-raisers, and professional solicitors. This form of reporting can be extensive and may entail the provision of information concerning gifts received, funds expended for program and fund-raising, payments to service providers, and a battery of other information.

These reports are made on forms provided by the states. These forms, and the rules and instructions that accompany them, vary considerably in content. Underlying definitions and accounting principles can differ. There is no uniformity with respect to due dates for these reports.

In many states, professional fund-raisers and professional solicitors are required to file annual reports with the state.

§ 24.7 EXEMPTIONS FROM REGULATION

Many of the states exempt one or more categories of charitable organization from the ambit of their charitable solicitation statutes.

The basic rationale for these exemptions is that the exempted organizations are not part of the objective—the protection of its citizens from fund-raising fraud and other abuse—the state is endeavoring to achieve through this type of regulation. (Other rationales are the constitutional law limitations involved in the case of churches and the ability of one or more categories of organization to persuade the legislature to exempt them.)

The most common exemption in this context is for churches and their closely related entities. These entities include conventions of churches and associations of churches. Some states broadly exempt religious organizations. These exemptions are rooted in constitutional law principles, barring government from regulating religious practices and beliefs. Some states have run into successful constitutional law challenges when they have attempted to narrowly define the concept of "religion" for this purpose.

Some states exempt at least certain types of educational institutions from the entirety of their charitable solicitation acts. Usually, this exemption applies where the educational institution is accredited. The more common practice is to exempt educational institutions from only the registration or licensing, and reporting, requirements.

Some states, either as an alternative or in addition to the foregoing approach, exempt from the registration and reporting requirements educational institutions that confine their solicitations to their "constituency." That is, this type of exemption extends to the solicitation of contributions by an educational institution to its student body, alumni, faculty, and trustees, and their families. A few states exempt solicitations by educational institutions of their constituency from the entirety of their charitable solicitation laws.

Many educational institutions undertake some or all of their fund-raising by means of related "foundations." Some states expressly provide exemption, in tandem with whatever exemption their laws extend to educational institutions, to these supporting foundations. A few states exempt, from the registration requirements, alumni associations.

The rationale for exempting educational institutions from coverage under these laws is the general rationale articulated above. These institutions do not solicit the general public, there have not been any instances of abuses by these institutions of the fund-raising process, these institutions already adequately report to state agencies, and the inclusion of these institutions under the charitable solicitation statute would impose an unnecessary burden on the regulatory process.

Some states exempt hospitals (and, in some instances, their related foundations) and other categories of healthcare entities. Again, the exemption can be from the entirety of the statute or from its registration and reporting requirements. Other exemptions for organizations embrace veterans' organizations, police and firefighters' organizations, fraternal organizations, and, in a few states, organizations identified by name. Exemptions are also often available for membership organizations, "small" solicitations (ranging from $1,000 to $10,000), and solicitations for specified individuals.

Some of these exemptions are available as a matter of law. Others must be applied for, sometimes on an annual basis. Some exemptions are not available or are lost if the organization utilizes the services of a professional fund-raiser or professional solicitor.

§ 24.8   FUND-RAISING COST LIMITATIONS

Once, the chief weapon for state regulators in this regard was laws that prohibited charitable organizations with "high" fund-raising costs from soliciting in the states. Allegedly "high" fund-raising expenses were defined in terms of percentages of gifts received. These laws proliferated, with percentage limitations extended to the compensation of professional fund-raising consultants and professional solicitors. The issue found its way to the U.S. Supreme Court, where all of these percentage limitations were struck down as violating the charities' free speech rights. This application of the First and Fourteenth Amendments to the U.S. Constitution stands as the single most important bar to more stringent government regulation of the process of soliciting charitable contributions.

As noted, the states possess the "police power" to regulate the process of soliciting contributions for charitable purposes. However, the states cannot exercise this power in a manner that unduly intrudes on the rights of free speech of the soliciting charitable organizations and their fund-raising consultants and solicitors.

First, the Supreme Court held that a state cannot use the level of a charitable organization's fund-raising costs as a basis for determining whether a charity may lawfully solicit funds in a jurisdiction.[3] Four years later, the Court held that the free speech principles apply, even though the state offers a charitable organization an op-

---

[3] *Village of Schaumberg* v. *Citizens for a Better Environment*, 444 U.S. 620 (1980).

portunity to show that its fund-raising costs are "reasonable," despite the presumption that costs in excess of a specific ceiling are "excessive."[4] Another four years later, the Court held that these free speech principles applied when the limitation was not on a charity's fund-raising costs but on the amount or extent of fees paid by a charitable organization to professional fund-raisers or professional solicitors.[5] Subsequent litigation suggests that the courts are consistently reinforcing the legal principles so articulately promulgated by the Supreme Court during the 1980s.

§ 24.9   PROHIBITED ACTS

Most of the state's charitable solicitation acts contain a list of one or more acts in which a charitable organization (and perhaps a professional fund-raiser and/or professional solicitor) may not lawfully engage. These acts may be some or all of the following:

- A person may not, for the purpose of soliciting contributions, use the name of another person (except that of an officer, director, or trustee of the charitable organization by or for which contributions are solicited) without the consent of the other person. This prohibition usually extends to the use of an individual's name on stationery or in an advertisement or brochure, or as one who has contributed to, sponsored, or endorsed the organization.

- A person may not, for the purpose of soliciting contributions, use a name, symbol, or statement so closely related or similar to that used by another charitable organization or governmental agency that it would tend to confuse or mislead the public.

- A person may not use or exploit the fact of registration with the state so as to lead the public to believe that the registration in any manner constitutes an endorsement or approval by the state.

- A person may not represent to or mislead anyone, by any manner, means, practice, or device, to believe that the organization on behalf of which the solicitation is being conducted is

[4]*Secretary of State of Maryland* v. *Joseph H. Munson Co., Inc.*, 467 U.S. 947 (1984).

[5]*Riley* v. *National Federation of the Blind of North Carolina, Inc.*, 108 S. Ct. 2667 (1988).

a charitable organization or that the proceeds of the solicitation will be used for charitable purposes, when that is not the case.

- A person may not represent that the solicitation for charitable gifts is for or on behalf of a charitable organization or otherwise induce contributions from the public without proper authorization from the charitable organization.

In one state, it is a prohibited act to represent that a charitable organization will receive a fixed or estimated percentage of the gross revenue from a solicitation in an amount greater than that identified to the donor. In another state, it is a prohibited act for an individual to solicit charitable contributions if the individual has been convicted of a crime involving the obtaining of money or property by false pretenses, unless the public is informed of the conviction in advance of the solicitation.

In still another state, the following are prohibited acts for a charitable organization (or, in some instances, a person acting on its behalf):

- misrepresenting the purpose of a solicitation;
- misrepresenting the purpose or nature of a charitable organization;
- engaging in a financial transaction that is not related to the accomplishment of the charitable organization's exempt purpose;
- jeopardizing or interfering with the ability of a charitable organization to accomplish its charitable purpose;
- expending an "unreasonable amount of money" for fund-raising or for management.

Some states make violation of a separate law concerning "unfair or deceptive acts and practices" a violation of the charitable solicitation act as well.

§ 24.10 CONTRACTUAL REQUIREMENTS

Many of the state charitable solicitation acts require that the relationship between a charitable organization and a professional fund-raiser, and/or between a charitable organization and a professional solicitor, be evidenced in a written agreeraent. This agreement is required to be filed with the state soon after the contract is executed. These types of requirernents are clearly "law" and are not particularly unusual.

However, a few states have enacted requirements—some of them rather patronizing—that dictate to the charitable organization the contents of the contract. For example, under one state's law, a contract between a charitable organization and a fund-raising counsel must contain sufficient information "as will enable the department to identify the services the fund-raising counsel is to provide and the manner of his compensation." Another provision of the same law mandates that the agreement "clearly state the respective obligations of the parties."

The law in another state requires a contract between a charitable organization and a fund-raising counsel to contain provisions addressing the services to be provided, the number of persons to be involved in providing the services, the time period over which the services are to be provided, and the method and formula for compensation for the services.

Under another state's law, whenever a charitable organization contracts with a professional fund-raiser or other type of fund-raising consultant, the charitable organization has the right to cancel the contract, without cost or penalty, for a period of 15 days. Again, this type of law seems predicated on the assumption that charitable organizations are somehow not quite capable of developing their own contracts and tend to do so impetuously.

It can be argued that these laws are forms of overreaching, in terms of scope and detail, on the part of government, and that charitable organizations ought to be mature enough to formulate their own contracts.

§ 24.11 DISCLOSURE REQUIREMENTS

Many of the states that were forced to abandon or forgo the use of the percentage mechanism as a basis for preventing fund-raising for charity (see above) utilize the percentage approach in a disclosure setting. Several states, for example, require charitable organizations to make an annual reporting, either to update a registration or as part of a separate report, to the authorities as to their fund-raising activities in the prior year, including a statement of their fund-raising expenses. Some states require a disclosure of a charity's fund-raising costs, stated as a percentage, to donors at the time of the solicitation—although this requirement is of dubious constitutionality. In a few states, solicitation literature used by a charitable organization must include a statement that, upon request, financial and other information about the soliciting charity may be obtained directly from the state.

Some states require a statement as to any percentage compensation in the contract between the charitable organization and the professional fund-raiser and/or the professional solicitor. A few states require the compensation of a paid solicitor to be stated in the contract as a percentage of gross revenue; another state has a similar provision with respect to a professional fund-raiser. One state wants a charitable organization's fund-raising cost percentage to be stated in its registration statement.

An example of this type of law is a statute that imposed on the individual who raises funds for a charitable organization the responsibility to "deal with" the contributions in an "appropriate fiduciary manner." Thus, an individual in these circumstances owes a fiduciary duty to the public. These persons are subject to a surcharge for any funds wasted or not accounted for. A presumption exists in this law that funds not adequately documented and disclosed by records were not properly spent.

By direction of this law, all solicitations must "fully and accurately" identify the purposes of the charitable organization to prospective donors. Use of funds, to an extent of more than 50 percent, for "public education" must be disclosed under this law. Every contract with a professional fund-raiser must be approved by the charitable organization's governing board. Some of the provisions of this law probably are unconstitutional, such as the requirement that professional fund-raisers or solicitors must disclose to those being solicited the percentage of their compensation in relation to gifts received.

Another example is some of the provisions of another state's law, which makes an "unlawful practice" the failure of a person soliciting funds to "truthfully" recite, upon request, the percentage of funds raised to be paid to the solicitor. This state, like many other states, is using the concept of "prohibited acts" (see above) to impose a sort of "code of ethics" on all who seek to raise funds for charity.

Under one state's law, any person who solicits contributions for a charitable purpose and who receives compensation for the service must inform each person being solicited, in writing, that the solicitation is a "paid solicitation." In another state, where a solicitation is made by "direct personal contact," certain information must be "predominantly" disclosed in writing at the point of solicitation. In another state, the solicitation material and the "general promotional plan" for a solicitation may not be false, misleading, or deceptive, and must afford a "full and fair" disclosure.

Appendices

Appendix A

Sources of the Law

The law as described in this book is derived from many sources. For those not familiar with these matters and wishing to understand just what "the law" regarding charitable organizations and advocacy activities is, the following explanation should be of assistance.

FEDERAL LAW

At the federal (national) level in the United States, there are three branches of government as provided for in the U.S. Constitution. Article I of the Constitution established the U.S. Congress as a bicameral legislature, consisting of the House of Representatives and the Senate. Article II of the Constitution established the Presidency. Article III of the Constitution established the federal court system.

Congress

The legal structure underlying the federal law for nonprofit organizations in the United States has been created by Congress. Most of this law is manifested in the tax law and thus appears in the Internal Revenue Code (which is officially codified in Title 26 of the United States Code and referenced throughout the book as the "IRC" (see Chapter 1, n. 1)). Other laws written by Congress that can affect nonprofit organizations include the postal, employee benefits, antitrust, labor, and securities laws.

Tax laws for the United States must originate in the House of Representatives (U.S. Constitution, Article I § 7). Consequently, most of the nation's tax laws are initially written by the members and staff of the House Committee on Ways and Means. Frequently, these laws are generated by work done at the subcommittee level, usually the Subcommittee on Oversight or the Subcommittee on Select Revenue Measures.

Committee work in this area within the Senate is undertaken by the Committee on Finance. The Joint Committee on Taxation, consisting of members from both the House of Representatives and the Senate, also provides assistance in this regard. Nearly all of this legislation is finalized by a House–Senate conference committee, consisting of senior members of the House Ways and Means Committee and the Senate Finance Committee.

A considerable amount of the federal tax law for nonprofit organizations is found in the "legislative history" of these statutory laws. Most of this history is in congressional committee reports. Reports from committees in the House of Representatives are cited as "H. Rep." (see, e.g., Chapter 1 n. 26); reports from committees in the Senate are cited as S. Rep. (see, e.g., Chapter 1, n. 56); conference committee reports are cited as "H. Rep." (see, e.g., Chapter 1, n. 72). Transcripts of the debate on legislation, formal statements, and other items are printed in the Congressional Record ("*Cong. Rec.*") (see, e.g., Chapter 1, n. 16). The Congressional Record is published every day one of the houses of Congress is in session and is cited as "_____ *Cong. Rec.* _____ (daily ed., [date of issue]" (see, e.g., Chapter 20, n. 13). The first number is the annual volume number; the second number is the page in the daily edition on which the item begins. Periodically, the daily editions of the Congressional Record are republished as a hard-bound book and are cited as "_____ *Cong. Rec.* _____ ([year])" (see, e.g., Chapter 1, n. 16). As before, the first number is the annual volume number and the second is the beginning page number. The bound version of the Congressional Record then becomes the publication that contains the permanent citation for the item.

A Congress sits for two years, each of which is termed a "session." Each Congress is sequentially numbered. For example, the 102d Congress met during the calendar years 1991–1992. A legislative development that took place in 1991 is referenced as occurring during the 102d Congress 1st Session ("102d Cong., 1st Sess. (1991)").

A bill introduced in the House of Representatives or Senate during a particular Congress is given a sequential number in each house. For example, the 1,000th bill introduced in the House of Representative in 1991 is cited as "H.R. 1000, 102d Cong., 1st Sess.

(1991)" (see, e.g., Chapter 22, n. 23); the 500th bill introduced in the Senate in 1991 is cited as "S. 500, 102d Cong., 1st Sess. (1991)."

Executive Branch

A function of the Executive Branch in the United States is to administer and enforce the laws enacted by Congress. This "executive" function is performed by departments and agencies, and "independent" regulatory commissions (such as the Federal Trade Commission or the Securities and Exchange Commission). One of these functions is the promulgation of regulations, which are published by the U. S. government in the "Code of Federal Regulations" ("CFR"). When adopted, regulations are printed in the *Federal Register* (*"Fed. Reg."*). The federal tax laws are administered and enforced by the Department of the Treasury and the federal election laws are administered and enforced by the Federal Election Commission. Other laws in this field include those administered and enforced by the Office of Management and Budget ("OMB") and the Office of Personnel Management ("OPM").

One of the ways in which the Department of the Treasury executes these functions is by the promulgation of regulations ("Reg."), which are designed to interpret and amplify the related statute (see, e.g., Chapter 1, n. 36). These regulations (like other rules made by other departments, agencies, and commissions) have the force of law, unless they are overly broad in relation to the accompanying statute or are unconstitutional, in which case they can be rendered void by a court.

Within the Department of the Treasury is the Internal Revenue Service ("IRS"). The IRS is, among its many roles, a tax-collecting agency. The IRS, while headquartered in Washington, D.C. (its "National Office"), has regional and field offices throughout the country. Offices around the nation with specific jurisdiction over tax-exempt organizations are known as "key district" offices.

The IRS's jurisdiction over tax-exempt organizations is within the ambit of the Assistant Commissioner, Employee Plans and Exempt Organizations (EP/EO). Within that office is the Exempt Organizations Division. Within the Chief Counsel's office is an Employee Benefits and Exempt Organizations division.

The IRS (from its National Office) prepares and disseminates guidelines interpreting tax statutes and tax regulations. These guide-

lines have the force of law, unless they are overbroad in relation to
the statute and/or Treasury regulation involved, or are unconstitutional. IRS determinations on a point of law are termed "revenue
rulings" ("Rev. Rul."); those that are rules of procedure are termed
"revenue procedures" ("Rev. Proc.").

Revenue rulings (which may be based on one or more court opinions) and revenue procedures are sequentially numbered every calendar year, with that number preceded by a two-digit number
reflecting the year of issue. For example, the fiftieth revenue ruling
issued in 1991 is cited as "Rev. Rul. 91-50." Likewise, the twenty-
fifth revenue procedure issued in 1991 is cited as "Rev. Proc. 91-25."

These IRS determinations are published each week in the Internal
Revenue Bulletin ("I.R.B."). In the foregoing examples, when the
determinations are first published, the revenue ruling is cited as
"Rev. Rul. 91-50, 1991-__ I.R.B. __," with the number after the
hyphen being the number of the particular issue of the weekly Bulletin and the last number being the page number within that issue on
which the item begins. Likewise, the revenue procedure is cited as
"Rev. Proc. 91-25, 1991-__ I.R.B. __." Every six months, the
Internal Revenue Bulletins are republished as hard-bound books,
with the resulting publication termed the Cumulative Bulletin
("C.B."). The Cumulative Bulletin designation then becomes the permanent citation for the determination. Thus, the permanent citations
for these two IRS determinations are "Rev. Rul. 91-50, 1991-1 C. B.
__" (see, e. g., Chapter 3, n. 14) and "Rev. Proc. 91-25, 1991-1 C. B.
__" (see, e.g., Chapter 9, n. 318), with the first number being the
year of issue, the second number (after the hyphen) indicating
whether the determination is published in the first six months of the
year ("1" (as is the case in the example)) or the second six months of
the year ("2"), and the last number being the page number within
that semiannual bound volume at which the determination begins.

The IRS considers itself bound by its revenue rulings and revenue
procedures. These determinations are the "law," particularly in the
sense that the IRS regards them as precedential, although they are
not binding on the courts.

By contrast to these forms of "public" law, the IRS (again, from its
National Office) also issues "private" or nonprecedential determinations. These documents principally are private letter rulings, technical advice memoranda, and general counsel memoranda. These
determinations may not be cited as legal authority (IRC § 6110(j)(3)).
Nonetheless, these pronouncements can be valuable in understand-

ing IRS thinking on a point of law and, in practice (the statutory prohibition notwithstanding), these documents are cited as IRS positions on issues, such as in court opinions, articles, and books.

The IRS issues private letter rulings in response to written questions (termed "ruling requests") submitted to the IRS by individuals and organizations. An IRS district office may refer a case to the IRS National Office for advice (termed "technical advice"); the resulting advice is provided to the IRS district office in the form of a technical advice memorandum. In the course of preparing a revenue ruling, private letter ruling, or technical advice memorandum, the IRS National Office may seek legal advice from its Office of Chief Counsel; the resulting advice is provided in the form of a general counsel memorandum. These documents are eventually made public, albeit in redacted form.

Private letter rulings and technical advice memoranda are identified by seven-digit numbers, as in "IRS Private Letter Ruling 9126007" (see, e. g., Chapter 4, n. 55). (A reference to a technical advice memorandum appears in Chapter 4, n. 95.) The first two numbers are for the year involved (here, 1991), the second two numbers reflect the week of the calendar year involved (here, the twenty-sixth week of 1991), and the remaining three numbers identify the document as issued sequentially during the particular week (here, this private letter ruling was the seventh one issued during the week involved). General counsel memoranda are numbered sequentially since they have been written (e.g., General Counsel Memorandum 39457 is the thirty-nine thousand, four hundred, fifty-seventh general counsel memorandum ever written by the IRS's Office of Chief Counsel. (A reference to a general counsel memorandum appears in Chapter 4, n. 64.)

The Judiciary

The federal court system has three levels: trial courts (including those that initially hear cases where a formal trial is not involved), courts of appeal ("appellate" courts), and the U.S. Supreme Court. The trial courts include the various federal district courts (at least one in each state, the District of Columbia, and the U.S. territories), the U.S. Tax Court, and the U.S. Claims Court. There are thirteen federal appellate courts (the U.S. Courts of Appeal for the First through the Eleventh Circuits, the U.S. Court of Appeals for the

District of Columbia, and the U.S. Court of Appeals for the Federal Circuit).

Cases involving tax-exempt organization issues at the federal level can originate in any federal district court, the U.S. Tax Court, and the U.S. Claims Court (beginning in 1993, this Court is now termed the U.S. Court of Federal Claims). Under a special declaratory judgment procedure available only to charitable organizations (IRC § 7428), cases can originate only with the U.S. District Court for the District of Columbia, the U.S. Tax Court, and the U.S. Claims Court. Cases involving tax-exempt organizations are considered by the U.S. courts of appeal and the U.S. Supreme Court.

Most opinions emanating from a U.S. district court are published by the West Publishing Company in the "Federal Supplement" series ("Fed. Supp."). Thus, a citation to one of these opinions appears as "__ F. Supp. __," followed by an identification of the court and the year of the opinion. The first number is the annual volume number; the second number is the page in the book on which the opinion begins (see, e.g., Chapter 1, n. 27). Some district court opinions appear sooner in Commerce Clearinghouse or Prentice Hall publications (see, e.g., Chapter 1, n. 95); occasionally, these publications will contain opinions that are never published in the Federal Supplement.

Most opinions emanating from a U.S. court of appeals are published by the West Publishing Company in the "Federal Reporter Second" series ("Fed. 2d"). Thus, a citation to one of these opinions appears as "__ F. 2d. __," followed by an identification of the court and the year of the opinion. The first number is the annual volume number; the second number is the page in the book on which the opinion begins (see, e.g., Chapter 1, n. 25). Appellate court opinions appear sooner in Commerce Clearinghouse or Prentice Hall publications (see, e.g., Chapter 4, n. 88); occasionally, these publications will contain opinions that are never published in Federal Second. Opinions from the U.S. Claims Court are also published in Federal Second.

Opinions from the U.S. Tax Court are published by the U.S. government and are usually cited as "__ T.C. __," followed by the year of the opinion (see, e.g., Chapter 4, n. 11). Some Tax Court opinions that are of lesser precedential value are published as "memorandum decisions" and are cited as "__ T.C.M. __" followed by the year of the opinion (see, e.g., Chapter 4, n. 173). As always, the first number of these citations is the annual volume number; the second number is the page in the book on which the opinion begins.

U.S. district court and Tax Court opinions may be appealed to the appropriate U.S. court of appeals. For example, cases in the states of Maryland, North Carolina, South Carolina, Virginia, and West Virginia, and the District of Columbia, are appealable (from either court) to the U.S. Court of Appeals for the Fourth Circuit. Cases from any federal appellate or district court, the U.S. Tax Court, and the U.S. Claims Court may be appealed to the U.S. Supreme Court.

The U.S. Supreme Court usually has discretion as to whether to accept a case. This decision is manifested as a "writ of certiorari." When the Supreme Court agrees to hear a case, it grants the writ ("cert. gr."); otherwise, it denies the writ ("cert. den.") (see, e. g., Chapter 4, n. 11).

In this book, citations to Supreme Court opinions are to the "United States Reports" series, published by the U.S. government, when available ("__ U.S. __," followed by the year of the opinion) (see, e.g., Chapter 1, n. 18). When the United States Reports series citation is not available, the "Supreme Court Reporter" series, published by the West Publishing Company, reference is used ("__ S. Ct. __," followed by the year of the opinion) (see, e.g., Chapter 4, n. 15). As always, the first number of these citations is the annual volume number; the second number is the page in the book on which the opinion begins. There is a third way to cite Supreme Court cases, which is by means of the "United States Supreme Court Reports—Lawyers' Edition" series, published by The Lawyers Co-Operative Publishing Company and the Bancroft-Whitney Company, but that form of citation is not used in this book. Supreme Court opinions appear earlier in the Commerce Clearinghouse or Prentice Hall publications.

STATE LAW

The Legislative Branches

Statutory laws in the various states are created by their legislatures. There are a few references to state statutory laws in this book (see, e.g., Chapter 1, n. 22).

The Executive Branches

The rules and regulations published at the state level emanate from state departments, agencies, and the like. For nonprofit organizations, these departments are usually the office of the state's attorney general and the state's department of state. There are no references to state rules and regulations in this book (although most, if not all, of the states have such forms of law relating to the advocacy activities of nonprofit organizations).

The Judiciary

Each of the states has a judiciary system, usually a three-tiered one modeled after the federal system. Cases involving nonprofit organizations are heard in all of these courts. There are some references to state court opinions in this book (although most, if not all, of the states have court opinions relating to the advocacy activities of nonprofit organizations).

State court opinions are published by the governments of each state and the principal ones by the West Publishing Company. The latter sets of opinions (referenced in this book) are published in "Reporters" relating to court developments in various regions throughout the country. For example, the "Atlantic Reporter" contains court opinions issued by the principal courts in the states of Connecticut, Delaware, Maine, Maryland, New Hampshire, New Jersey, Pennsylvania, Rhode Island, and Vermont, and the District of Columbia, while the "Pacific Reporter" contains court opinions issued by the principal courts of Arizona, California, Colorado, Idaho, Kansas, Montana, Nevada, New Mexico, Oklahoma, Oregon, Utah, Washington, and Wyoming.

PUBLICATIONS

Articles, of course, are not forms of "the law." However, they can be cited, particularly by courts, in the development of the law. Also, as research tools, they contain useful summaries of the applicable law. In addition to the many law school "law review" publications, the following (which is not an exclusive list) periodicals contain material that is of help in following developments concerning charitable organizations, advocacy and the law.:

The Chronicle of Philanthropy
Daily Tax Report (Bureau of National Affairs, Inc.)
Exempt Organization Tax Review (Tax Analysts)
Foundation News (Council on Foundations)

The Journal of Taxation (Warren, Gorham & Lamont)
The Journal of Taxation of Exempt Organizations (Faulkner & Gray)
The Nonprofit Counsel (John Wiley & Sons, Inc.)
The Philanthropy Monthly (Non-Profit Reports, Inc.)
Tax Law Review (Rosenfeld Launer Publications)
The Tax Lawyer (American Bar Association)
Tax Notes (Tax Analysts)
Taxes (Commerce Clearinghouse, Inc.)

Appendix B

Internal Revenue Code Sections

Following are the various provisions of the Internal Revenue Code of 1986 which comprise the statutory framework for the federal tax law of charitable giving:

Section 27—foreign tax credit

Sections 55-59—alternative minimum tax rules

Section 162—income tax deduction for business expenses

Section 170—income tax deduction for charitable contributions, including percentage limitations, deduction reduction rules, and partial interest gift rules

Section 306—definition of so-called "section 306 stock"

Section 482—reallocation of deductions rules

Section 501—general requirements for income tax exemption

Section 501(m)—rules concerning commercial-type insurance, including exception for charitable gift annuities

Section 509—definition of public charity and private foundation status

Section 511—imposition of tax on unrelated business income

Section 512—definition of unrelated business taxable income

Section 513—definition of unrelated trade or business

Section 514—unrelated debt-financed income rules

Section 542(b)(2)—charitable contribution deduction in computing undistributed personal holding company income

Section 556(b)(2)—charitable contribution deduction in computing undistributed foreign personal holding company income

Section 642(c)—charitable contribution deduction for certain estates or trusts; rules concerning pooled income funds

Section 664—rules concerning charitable remainder trusts

Section 681—limitations on estate or trust charitable contribution deduction

Sections 861-864—determination of sources of income

Section 1011(b)—allocation of capital gain rules, applicable in bargain sale context

Section 2055— estate tax deduction for charitable contributions

Section 2106(a)(2)(A)—estate tax deduction for charitable contributions for estates of nonresidents not citizens

Section 2522—gift tax deduction for charitable contributions

Sections 2601 et seq.—Generation-skipping transfer tax rules

Section 4941—private foundation self-dealing rules

Section 4942—private foundation mandatory distribution rules

Section 4943—private foundation excess business holdings rules

Section 4944—private foundation jeopardizing investments rules

Section 4945—private foundation taxable expenditures rules

Section 4946—private foundation rules defining disqualified persons

Section 4947—application of private foundation rules to certain non-exempt trusts

Section 4948—private foundation rules as applied to foreign organizations

Section 6033—annual return filing obligations for most charitable and other tax-exempt organizations

Section 6113—rules concerning disclosure of non-deductibility of gifts by non-charitable organizations

Section 6701—penalty for aiding and abetting an understatement of tax liability

Section 6710—penalty for noncompliance with disclosure rules for non-charitable organizations

Section 7520—federal midterm monthly interest rate rules, used in computation of partial interests

Appendix C

Form **8283**

(Rev. November 1992)

Department of the Treasury
Internal Revenue Service

Noncash Charitable Contributions

▶ Attach to your tax return if the total deduction claimed
for all property contributed exceeds $500.

▶ See separate instructions.

OMB No. 1545-0908
Expires 11-30-95

Attachment
Sequence No. 55

Name(s) shown on your income tax return

Identifying number

Note: *Figure the amount of your contribution deduction before completing this form. See your tax return instructions.*

Section A—Include in this section **only** items (or groups of similar items) for which you claimed a deduction of $5,000 or less per item or group, and certain publicly traded securities (see instructions).

Part I Information on Donated Property—If you need more space, attach a statement.

1	(a) Name and address of the donee organization	(b) Description of donated property
A		
B		
C		
D		
E		

Note: *If the amount you claimed as a deduction for an item is $500 or less, you do not have to complete columns (d), (e), and (f).*

	(c) Date of the contribution	(d) Date acquired by donor (mo., yr.)	(e) How acquired by donor	(f) Donor's cost or adjusted basis	(g) Fair market value	(h) Method used to determine the fair market value
A						
B						
C						
D						
E						

Part II Other Information—If you gave less than an entire interest in property listed in Part I, complete lines 2a–2e. If restrictions were attached to a contribution listed in Part I, complete lines 3a–3c.

2 If less than the entire interest in the property is contributed during the year, complete the following:

  a Enter letter from Part I that identifies the property _____. If Part II applies to more than one property, attach a separate statement.

  b Total amount claimed as a deduction for the property listed in Part I: **(1)** For this tax year _____
    (2) For any prior tax years _____

  c Name and address of each organization to which any such contribution was made in a prior year (complete only if different than the donee organization above).

    Name of charitable organization (donee)

    Address (number, street, and room or suite no.)

    City or town, state, and ZIP code

  d For tangible property, enter the place where the property is located or kept _____
  e Name of any person, other than the donee organization, having actual possession of the property _____

3 If conditions were attached to any contribution listed in Part I, answer the following questions and attach the required statement (see instructions):

		Yes	No
a	Is there a restriction, either temporary or permanent, on the donee's right to use or dispose of the donated property?		
b	Did you give to anyone (other than the donee organization or another organization participating with the donee organization in cooperative fundraising) the right to the income from the donated property or to the possession of the property, including the right to vote donated securities, to acquire the property by purchase or otherwise, or to designate the person having such income, possession, or right to acquire?		
c	Is there a restriction limiting the donated property for a particular use?		

For Paperwork Reduction Act Notice, see separate instructions.   Cat. No. 62299J   Form **8283** (Rev 11-92)

Form 8283 (Rev. 11-92)   Page 2

Name(s) shown on your income tax return	Identifying number

Section B—Appraisal Summary—Include in this section only items (or groups of similar items) for which you claimed a deduction of more than $5,000 per item or group. Report contributions of certain publicly traded securities only in Section A.

If you donated art, you may have to attach the complete appraisal. See the **Note** in Part I below.

Part I   Information on Donated Property—To be completed by the taxpayer and/or appraiser.

4   Check type of property:

☐ Art* (contribution of $20,000 or more)   ☐ Real Estate   ☐ Gems/Jewelry   ☐ Stamp Collections
☐ Art* (contribution of less than $20,000) ☐ Coin Collections ☐ Books   ☐ Other

*Art includes paintings, sculptures, watercolors, prints, drawings, ceramics, antique furniture, decorative arts, textiles, carpets, silver, rare manuscripts, historical memorabilia, and other similar objects.

Note: *If your total art contribution deduction was $20,000 or more, you must attach a complete copy of the signed appraisal. See instructions.*

5	(a) Description of donated property (if you need more space, attach a separate statement)	(b) If tangible property was donated, give a brief summary of the overall physical condition at the time of the gift	(c) Appraised fair market value
A			
B			
C			
D			

	(d) Date acquired by donor (mo., yr.)	(e) How acquired by donor	(f) Donor's cost or adjusted basis	(g) For bargain sales, enter amount received	(h) Amount claimed as a deduction	(i) Average trading price of securities
A						
B						
C						
D						

Part II   Taxpayer (Donor) Statement—List each item included in Part I above that is separately identified in the appraisal as having a value of $500 or less. See instructions.

I declare that the following item(s) included in Part I above has to the best of my knowledge and belief an appraised value of not more than $500 (per item). Enter identifying letter from Part I and describe the specific item: _____

Signature of taxpayer (donor) ▶   Date ▶

Part III   Certification of Appraiser

I declare that I am not the donor, the donee, a party to the transaction in which the donor acquired the property, employed by, married to, or related to any of the foregoing persons, or an appraiser regularly used by any of the foregoing persons and who does not perform a majority of appraisals during the taxable year for other persons.

Also, I declare that I hold myself out to the public as an appraiser or perform appraisals on a regular basis; and that because of my qualifications as described in the appraisal, I am qualified to make appraisals of the type of property being valued. I certify that the appraisal fees were not based upon a percentage of the appraised property value. Furthermore, I understand that a false or fraudulent overstatement of the property value as described in the qualified appraisal or this appraisal summary may subject me to the civil penalty under section 6701(a) (aiding and abetting the understatement of tax liability). I affirm that I have not been barred from presenting evidence or testimony by the Director of Practice.

Sign Here

Signature ▶	Title ▶	Date of appraisal ▶

Business address (including room or suite no.)	Identifying number

City or town, state, and ZIP code

Part IV   Donee Acknowledgment—To be completed by the charitable organization.

This charitable organization acknowledges that it is a qualified organization under section 170(c) and that it received the donated property as described in Section B, Part I, above on _____
(Date)

Furthermore, this organization affirms that in the event it sells, exchanges, or otherwise disposes of the property (or any portion thereof) within 2 years after the date of receipt, it will file an information return (**Form 8282**, Donee Information Return) with the IRS and furnish the donor a copy of that return. This acknowledgment does not represent concurrence in the claimed fair market value.

Name of charitable organization (donee)	Employer identification number
Address (number, street, and room or suite no.)	City or town, state, and ZIP code
Authorized signature	Title	Date

Appendix D

Form **8282**
(Rev. Nov. 1992)
Department of the Treasury
Internal Revenue Service

Donee Information Return

(Sale, Exchange, or Other Disposition of Donated Property)

▶ See instructions on back.

OMB No. 1545-0908
Expires 11-30-95

Give Copy to Donor

Please Print or Type	Name of charitable organization (donee)	Employer identification number
	Address (number, street, and room or suite no.)	
	City or town, state, and ZIP code	

Note: *If you are the original donee, **DO NOT** complete Part II or column (c) of Part III.*

Part I   Information on ORIGINAL DONOR and DONEE You Gave the Property to

1a Name(s) of the original donor of the property	1b Identifying number

Note: *Complete lines 2a–2d only if you gave this property to another charitable organization (successor donee).*

2a Name of charitable organization	2b Employer identification number

2c Address (number, street, and room or suite no.)

2d City or town, state, and ZIP code

Part II   Information on PREVIOUS DONEES—Complete this part only if you were not the first donee to receive the property. If you were the second donee, leave lines 4a–4d blank. If you were a third or later donee, complete lines 3a–4d. On lines 4a–4d, give information on the preceding donee (the one who gave you the property).

3a Name of original donee	3b Employer identification number

3c Address (number, street, and room or suite no.)

3d City or town, state, and ZIP code

4a Name of preceding donee	4b Employer identification number

4c Address (number, street, and room or suite no.)

4d City or town, state, and ZIP code

Part III   Information on DONATED PROPERTY

(a) Description of donated property sold, exchanged, or otherwise disposed of (if you need more space, attach a separate statement)	(b) Date you received the item(s)	(c) Date the first donee received the item(s) (if you weren't the first)	(d) Date item(s) sold, exchanged, or otherwise disposed of	(e) Amount received upon disposition

For Paperwork Reduction Act Notice, see instructions on back.   Cat. No. 62307Y   Form **8282** (Rev. ··· 92)

General Instructions

(Section references are to the Internal Revenue Code.)

Paperwork Reduction Act Notice

We ask for the information on this form to carry out the Internal Revenue laws of the United States. You are required to give us the information. We need it to ensure that you are complying with these laws and to allow us to figure and collect the right amount of tax.

The time needed to complete this form will vary depending on individual circumstances. The estimated average time is:

Recordkeeping	3 hr., 7 min.
Learning about the law or the form.	30 min.
Preparing and sending the form to the IRS	34 min.

If you have comments concerning the accuracy of these time estimates or suggestions for making this form more simple, we would be happy to hear from you. You can write to both the **Internal Revenue Service**, Washington, DC 20224, Attention: IRS Reports Clearance Officer, T:FP; and the **Office of Management and Budget**, Paperwork Reduction Project (1545-0908), Washington, DC 20503. **DO NOT** send this form to either of these offices. Instead, see **Where To File** on this page.

Purpose of Form

Donee organizations use Form 8282 to report information to the IRS about dispositions of certain charitable deduction property made within 2 years after the donor contributed the property.

Definitions

Note: *For purposes of Form 8282 and these instructions, the term "donee" includes all donees, unless specific reference is made to "original" or "successor" donees.*

Original Donee.—The first donee to or for which the donor gave the property. The original donee is required to sign an appraisal summary presented by the donor for charitable deduction property.

Appraisal Summary.—Section B of Form 8283, Noncash Charitable Contributions.

Successor Donee.—Any donee of property other than the original donee.

Charitable Deduction Property.—Property (other than money or certain publicly traded securities) for which the original donee signed, or was presented with for signature, an appraisal summary on Form 8283.

Generally, only items or groups of similar items for which the donor claimed a deduction of more than $5,000 are included on an appraisal summary. There is an exception if a donor gives similar items to more than one donee organization and the total deducted for these similar items exceeds $5,000. For example, if a donor deducts $2,000 for books given to a donee organization and $4,000 for books to another donee organization, the donor must present a separate appraisal summary to each organization. For more information, see the Instructions for Form 8283.

Who Must File

Form 8282 must be filed by original and successor donee organizations who sell, exchange, consume, or otherwise dispose of (with or without consideration) charitable deduction property within 2 years after the date the original donee received the property.

Exceptions.—There are two situations where Form 8282 does not have to be filed.

1. Items valued at $500 or less.—You do not have to file Form 8282 if, at the time the original donee signed the appraisal summary, the donor had signed a statement on Form 8283 that the appraised value of the specific item was not more than $500. If Form 8283 contains more than one similar item, this exception applies only to those items that are clearly identified as having a value of $500 or less. However, for purposes of the donor's determination of whether the appraised value of the item exceeds $500, all shares of nonpublicly traded stock, or items that form a set, are considered one item. For example, a collection of books written by the same author, components of a stereo system, or six place settings of a pattern of silverware are considered one item.

2. Items consumed or distributed for charitable purpose.—You do not have to file Form 8282 if an item is consumed or distributed without consideration. The consumption or distribution must be in furtherance of your purpose or function as a tax-exempt organization. For example, no reporting is required for medical supplies consumed or distributed by a tax-exempt relief organization in aiding disaster victims.

When To File

If you dispose of charitable deduction property within 2 years of the date the original donee received it and you do not meet exception 1 or 2 above, you must file Form 8282 within 125 days after the date of disposition.

Exception.—If you did not file because you had no reason to believe the substantiation requirements applied to the donor, but you later become aware that they did apply, file Form 8282 within 60 days after the date you become aware you are liable. For example, this exception

would apply where an appraisal summary is furnished to a successor donee after the date that donee disposes of the charitable deduction property.

Missing Information

If Form 8282 is filed by the due date, you must enter your organization's name, address, and EIN and complete at least Part III, column (a). You do not have to complete the remaining items if the information is not available. For example, you may not have the information necessary to complete all entries if the donor's appraisal summary is not available to you.

Where To File

Send Form 8282 to the Internal Revenue Service Center, Cincinnati, OH 45944.

Penalty

You may be subject to a penalty if you fail to file this form by the due date, fail to include all of the information required to be shown on this form, or fail to include correct information on this form (see **Missing Information** above). The penalty is generally $50. For more details, see section 6721.

Other Requirements

Information You Must Give a Successor Donee.—If the property is transferred to another charitable organization within the 2-year period discussed earlier, you must give your successor donee the following information:

1. The name, address, and EIN of your organization,

2. A copy of the appraisal summary (the Form 8283) that you received from the donor or a preceding donee), and

3. A copy of this Form 8282, within 15 days after you file it.

You must furnish items 1 and 2 within 15 days after the latest of:

• The date you transferred the property,

• The date the original donee signed the appraisal summary, or

• If you are also a successor donee, the date you received a copy of the appraisal summary from the preceding donee.

Note: *The successor donee organization to whom you transferred this property is required to give you their organization's name, address, and EIN within 15 days after the later of:*

• *The date you transferred the property, or*

• *The date they received a copy of the appraisal summary.*

Information You Must Give the Donor.—You must give a copy of your Form 8282 to the donor of the property.

Appraisal Summary.—You must keep a copy of the appraisal summary in your records.

Appendix E

Charitable Remainder Trusts Prototype Instruments

In 1989, the IRS issued a sample form of declaration of trust that meets the requirements of a charitable remainder unitrust (Rev. Proc. 89-20, 1989-1 C.B. 841) and of a charitable remainder annuity trust (Rev. Proc. 89-21, 1989-1 C.B. 842). The full text of these documents is as follows:

Rev. Proc. 89-20

SECTION 1. PURPOSE

This revenue procedure makes available a sample form of declaration of trust that meets the requirements for a charitable remainder unitrust as described in section 664(d)(2) of the Internal Revenue Code.

SECTION 2. BACKGROUND

The Internal Revenue Service receives and responds to requests for rulings dealing with the qualification of trusts as charitable remainder trusts and the availability of deductions for contributions made to such trusts. In many of these requests, the trust instruments and charitable objectives are very similar. Consequently, in order to provide a service to taxpayers and to save the time and expense involved in requesting and processing a ruling on a proposed charitable remainder unitrust, taxpayers who make transfers to a trust that substantially follows the sample trust instrument contained herein can be assured that the Service will recognize the trust as meeting all of the requirements of a charitable remainder unitrust, provided the trust operates in a manner consistent with the terms of the trust instrument and provided it is a valid trust under applicable local law.

SECTION 3.   SCOPE AND OBJECTIVE

The sample declaration of trust made available by section 4 of this revenue procedure meets all of the applicable requirements under section 664(d)(2) of the Code for an inter vivos charitable remainder unitrust providing for unitrust payments during one life, followed by distribution of the trust assets to the charitable remainder beneficiary, if the trust document also creates a valid trust under local law. If the trust instrument makes reference to this revenue procedure and adopts a document substantially similar to the sample, the Service will recognize the trust as satisfying all of the applicable requirements of section 664(d)(2) of the Code and the corresponding regulations. Moreover, for transfers to a qualifying charitable remainder unitrust, the remainder interest will be deductible under sections 170(f)(2)(A) and 2522(c)(2)(A) for income and gift tax purposes, respectively. Therefore, it will not be necessary for a taxpayer to request a ruling as to the qualification of a substantially similar trust, and the Service generally will not issue such a ruling. * * * The Service, however, will continue to issue rulings to taxpayers who create trusts that are not substantially similar to the sample trusts.

SECTION 4.   SAMPLE CHARITABLE REMAINDER UNITRUST

On this _____ day of _____, 19_____, I, _____, (hereinafter referred to as "the Donor") desiring to establish a charitable remainder unitrust, within the meaning of Rev. Proc. 89-20 and section 664(d)(2) of the Internal Revenue Code (hereinafter referred to as "the Code") hereby create the _____ Charitable Remainder Unitrust and designate _____ as the initial Trustee.

1.   Funding of Trust. The Donor transfers to the Trustee the property described in Schedule A, and the Trustee accepts such property and agrees to hold, manage and distribute such property of the Trust under the terms set forth in this Trust instrument.

2.   Payment of Unitrust Amount. The Trustee shall pay to [a

living individual] (hereinafter referred to as "the Recipient") in each taxable year of the Trust during the Recipient's life a unitrust amount equal to [at least five] percent of the net fair market value of the assets of the Trust valued as of the first day of each taxable year of the Trust (the "valuation date"). The unitrust amount shall be paid in equal quarterly amounts from income and, to the extent that income is not sufficient, from principal. Any income of the Trust for a taxable year in excess of the unitrust amount shall be added to principal. If the net fair market value of the Trust assets is incorrectly determined, then within a reasonable period after the value is finally determined for Federal tax purposes, the Trustee shall pay to the Recipient (in the case of an undervaluation) or receive from the Recipient (in the case of an overvaluation) an amount equal to the difference between the unitrust amount properly payable and the unitrust amount actually paid.

3.   Proration of the Unitrust Amount. In determining the unitrust amount, the Trustee shall prorate the same on a daily basis for a short taxable year and for the taxable year of the Recipient's death.

4.   Distribution to Charity. Upon the death of the Recipient, the Trustee shall distribute all of the then principal and income of the Trust (other than any amount due Recipient or Recipient's estate, under paragraphs 2 and 3, above) to _____ (hereinafter referred to as the Charitable Organization). If the Charitable Organization is not an organization described in sections 170(c), 2055(a), and 2522(a) of the Code at the time when any principal or income of the Trust is to be distributed to it, then the Trustee shall distribute such principal or income to such one or more organizations described in sections 170(c), 2055(a), and 2522(a) as the Trustee shall select in its sole discretion.

5.   Additional Contributions. If any additional contributions are made to the Trust after the initial contribution, the unitrust amount for the year in which the additional contribution is made shall be [the same percentage as in paragraph 1] percent of the sum of (a) the net fair market value of the Trust assets as of the first day of the taxable year (excluding the assets so added and any income from, or appreciation on, such assets) and (b) that proportion of the value of the assets so added that was excluded under (a) that the number of days in the period that begins with the date of contribution and ends with the earlier of the last day of the taxable year or the Recipient's death bears to the number of days in the period that begins on the first day of such taxable year and ends with the earlier of the last day

in such taxable year or the Recipient's death. In the case where there is no valuation date after the time of contribution, the assets so added shall be valued at the time of contribution.

6. Prohibited Transactions. The income of the Trust for each taxable year shall be distributed at such time and in such manner as not to subject the Trust to tax under section 4942 of the Code. Except for the payment of the unitrust amount to the Recipient, the Trustee shall not engage in any act of self-dealing, as defined in section 4941(d), and shall not make any taxable expenditures, as defined in section 4945(d). The Trustee shall not make any investments that jeopardize the charitable purpose of the Trust, within the meaning of section 4944, or retain any excess business holdings, within the meaning of section 4943.

7. Successor Trustee. The Donor reserves the right to dismiss the Trustee and to appoint a successor Trustee.

8. Taxable Year. The taxable year of the Trust shall be the calendar year.

9. Governing Law. The operation of the Trust shall be governed by the laws of the State of _____. However, the Trustee is prohibited from exercising any power or discretion granted under said laws that would be inconsistent with the qualification of the Trust under section 664(d)(2) of the Code and the corresponding regulations.

10. Limited power of Amendment. The Trust is irrevocable. However, the Trustee shall have the power, acting alone, to amend the Trust in any manner required for the sole purpose of ensuring that the Trust qualifies and continues to qualify as a charitable remainder unitrust within the meaning of section 664(d)(2) of the Code.

11. Investment of Trust Assets. Nothing in this Trust instrument shall be construed to restrict the Trustee from investing the Trust assets in a manner that could result in the annual realization of a reasonable amount of income or gain from the sale or disposition of Trust assets.

IN WITNESS WHEREOF _____ and _____ [TRUSTEE] by its duly authorized officer have signed this agreement the day and year first above written.

[DONOR]

[TRUSTEE]

By

[Acknowledgements, Witnesses, etc.]

SECTION 5 APPLICATION

The Service will recognize a trust as meeting all of the requirements of a qualified charitable remainder unitrust under section 664(d)(2) of the Code if the trust instrument makes reference to this document and is substantially similar to the the sample provided in section 4, provided the trust operates in a manner consistent with the terms of the trust instrument and provided it is a valid trust under applicable local law. A trust that contains substantive provisions in addition to those provided by section 4 (other than provisions necessary to establish a valid trust under applicable local law) or that omits any of these provisions will not necessarily be disqualified, but neither will it be assured of qualification under the provisions of this revenue procedure.

SECTION 6.   EFFECTIVE DATE

This revenue procedure is effective for ruling requests received in the National Office after February 27, 1989, the date of publication of this revenue procedure in the Internal Revenue Bulletin.

Rev. Proc. 89-21

SECTION 1.   PURPOSE

This revenue procedure makes available a sample form of declaration of trust that meets the requirements for a charitable remainder annuity trust as described in section 664(d)(1) of the Internal Revenue Code.

SECTION 2.   BACKGROUND

The Internal Revenue Service receives and responds to requests for rulings dealing with the qualification of trusts as charitable remainder trusts and the availability of deductions for contributions made to such trusts. In many of these requests, the trust instruments and charitable objectives are very similar. Consequently, in order to provide a service to taxpayers and to save the time and expense involved in requesting and processing a ruling on a proposed charitable remainder annuity trust, taxpayers who make transfers to a trust that substantially follows the sample trust instrument contained herein can be assured that the Service will recognize the trust as meeting all of the requirements of a charitable remainder annuity trust, provided the trust operates in a manner consistent with the terms of the trust instrument and provided it is a valid trust under applicable local law.

SECTION 3.   SCOPE AND OBJECTIVE

The sample declaration of trust made available by section 4 of this revenue procedure meets all of the applicable requirements under section 664(d)(1) of the Code for an inter vivos charitable remainder annuity trust providing for annuity payments during one life, followed by distribution of the trust assets to the charitable remainder beneficiary, if the trust document also creates a valid trust under local law. If the trust instrument makes reference to this revenue procedure and adopts a document substantially similar to the sample, the Service will recognize the trust as satisfying all of the applicable requirements of section 664(d)(1) of the Code and the corresponding regulations. Moreover, for transfers to a qualifying charitable remainder annuity trust, the remainder interest will be deductible under sections 170(f)(2)(A) and 2522(c)(2)(A) for income and gift tax purposes, respectively. Therefore, it will not be necessary for a taxpayer to request a ruling as to the qualification of a substantially similar trust, and the Service generally will not issue such a ruling. * * * The Service, however, will continue to issue rulings to taxpayers who create trusts that are not substantially similar.

SECTION 4.   SAMPLE CHARITABLE REMAINDER ANNUITY TRUST

On this _____ day of _____, 19 _____, I, _____ (hereinafter referred to as "the Donor") desiring to establish a charitable remainder annuity trust, within the meaning of Rev. Proc. 89-21 and section 664(d)(1) of the Internal Revenue Code (hereinafter referred to as "the Code") hereby create the _____ Charitable Remainder Annuity Trust ("the Trust") and designate _____ as the initial Trustee.

1.   Funding of Trust. The Donor transfers to the Trustee the property described in Schedule A, and the Trustee accepts such property and agrees to hold, manage and distribute such property of the Trust under the terms set forth in this Trust instrument.

2.   Payment of Annuity Amount. The Trustee shall pay to [a living individual] (hereinafter referred to as "the Recipient") in each taxable year of the Trust during the Recipient's life an annuity

amount equal to [at least five] percent of the net fair market value of the assets of the Trust as of this date. The annuity amount shall be paid in equal quarterly amounts from income and, to the extent income is not sufficient, from principal. Any income of the Trust for a taxable year in excess of the annuity amount shall be added to principal. If the net fair market value of the Trust assets is incorrectly determined, then within a reasonable period after the value is finally determined for Federal tax purposes, the Trustee shall pay to the Recipient (in the case of an undervaluation) or receive from the Recipient (in the case of an overvaluation) an amount equal to the difference between the annuity amount(s) properly payable and the annuity amount(s) actually paid.

3.   Proration of the Annuity Amount. In determining the annuity amount, the Trustee shall prorate the same on a daily basis for a short taxable year and for the taxable year of the Recipient's death.

4.   Distribution to Charity. Upon the death of the Recipient, the Trustee shall distribute all of the then principal and income of the Trust (other than any amount due Recipient or Recipient's estate under paragraphs 2 and 3, above) to (hereinafter referred to as the Charitable Organization). If the Charitable Organization is not an organization described in sections 170(c), 2055(a), and 2522(a) of the Code at the time when any principal or income of the Trust is to be distributed to it, then the Trustee shall distribute such principal or income to such one or more organizations described in sections 170(c), 2055(a), and 2522(a) as the Trustee shall select in its sole discretion.

5.   Additional Contributions. No additional contributions shall be made to the Trust after the initial contribution.

6.   Prohibited Transactions. The income of the Trust for each taxable year shall be distributed at such time and in such manner as not to subject the Trust to tax under section 4942 of the Code. Except for the payment of the annuity amount to the Recipient, the Trustee shall not engage in any act of self-dealing, as defined in section 4941(d), and shall not make any taxable expenditures, as defined in section 4945(d). The Trustee shall not make any investments that jeopardize the charitable purpose of the Trust, within the meaning of section 4944, or retain any excess business holdings, within the meaning of section 4943.

7.   Successor Trustee. The Donor reserves the right to dismiss the Trustee and to appoint a successor Trustee.

8.   Taxable Year. The taxable year of the Trust shall be the calendar year.

9. Governing Law. The operation of the Trust shall be governed by the laws of the State of _____. However, the Trustee is prohibited from exercising any power or discretion granted under said laws that would be inconsistent with the qualification of the Trust under section 664(d)(1) of the Code and the corresponding regulations.

10. Limited Power of Amendment. The Trust is irrevocable. However, the Trustee shall have the power, acting alone, to amend the Trust in any manner required for the sole purpose of ensuring that the Trust qualifies and continues to qualify as a charitable remainder annuity trust within the meaning of section 664(d)(1) of the Code.

11. Investment of Trust Assets. Nothing in this Trust instrument shall be construed to restrict the Trustee from investing the Trust assets in a manner that could result in the annual realization of a reasonable amount of income or gain from the sale or disposition of Trust assets.

IN WITNESS WHEREOF _____ and _____ [TRUSTEE] by its duly authorized officer have signed this agreement the day and year first above written.

[DONOR]

[TRUSTEE]

By

[Acknowledgements, Witnesses, etc.]

SECTION 5.   APPLICATION

The Service will recognize a trust as meeting all of the requirements of a qualified charitable remainder unitrust under section 664(d)(2) of the Code if the trust instrument makes reference to this document and is substantially similar to the sample provided in section 4, provided the trust operates in a manner consistent with the terms of the trust instrument and provided it is a valid trust under applicable local law. A trust that contains substantive provisions in addition to those provided by section 4 (other than provisions necessary to establish a valid trust under applicable local law) or that omits any of these provisions will not necessarily be disqualified, but neither will it be assured of qualification under the provisions of this revenue procedure.

SECTION 6.   EFFECTIVE DATE

This revenue procedure is effective for ruling requests received in the National Office after February 27, 1989, the date of publication of this revenue procedure in the Internal Revenue Bulletin.

In 1990, the IRS issued five sample forms of trust that qualify as charitable remainder unitrusts (Rev. Proc. 90-30, 1990-1 C.B. 534). The full text of this document is as follows:

Rev. Proc. 90-30

SECTION 1.   PURPOSE

This revenue procedure makes available five sample forms of trust that meet the requirements for a charitable remainder unitrust as described in section 664(d)(2) of the Internal Revenue Code.

SECTION 2.   BACKGROUND

The Internal Revenue Service receives and responds to requests for rulings dealing with the qualification of trusts as charitable remainder trusts and the availability of deductions for contributions made to such trusts. In many of these requests, the trust instruments and charitable objectives are very similar. Consequently, in order to provide a service to taxpayers and to save the time and expense involved in requesting and processing a ruling on a proposed charitable remainder unitrust, this revenue procedure allows taxpayers who make transfers to a trust that substantially follows one of the sample forms of trust contained herein to be assured that the Service will recognize the trust as meeting all of the requirements of a charitable remainder unitrust, provided that the trust operates in a manner consistent with the terms of the instrument creating the trust and provided it is a valid trust under applicable local law.

SECTION 3.   SCOPE AND OBJECTIVE

Section 4 of Rev. Proc. 89-20, 1989-1 C.B. 841, provides a sample form of trust for an inter vivos charitable remainder unitrust providing for unitrust payments during one life that meets all of the applicable requirements of section 664(d)(2) of the Code. This revenue procedure amplifies Rev. Proc. 89-20 by providing the following additional sample forms of trust.

Section 4—Sample Inter Vivos Charitable Remainder Unitrust: Two Lives, Consecutive Interests;

Section 5—Sample Inter Vivos Charitable Remainder Unitrust: Two Lives, Concurrent and Consecutive Interests;

Section 6—Sample Testamentary Charitable Remainder Unitrust: One Life;

Section 7—Sample Testamentary Charitable Remainder Unitrust: Two Lives, Consecutive Interests; and

Section 8—Sample Testamentary Charitable Remainder Unitrust: Two Lives, Concurrent and Consecutive Interests.

In all cases, the termination of the life interests must be followed by distribution of the trust assets to the charitable remainder beneficiary, and the trust must be a valid trust under applicable local law. If the trust provisions are substantially similar to those in one of the samples provided in sections 4 through 8 of this revenue procedure or in section 4 of Rev. Proc. 89-20, the Service will recognize the trust as satisfying all of the applicable requirements of section 664(d)(2) of the Code and the corresponding regulations. A document will be considered to be substantially similar to one of the samples even though, for example, the wording is varied to comport with local law and practice as necessary to create trusts, define legal relationships, pass property by bequest, provide for the appointment of alternative and successor trustees, or designate alternative charitable remaindermen. Moreover, for transfers to a qualifying charitable remainder unitrust, the remainder interest will be deductible under sections 170(f)(2)(A), 2055(e)(2)(A), and 2522(c)(2)(A) for income, estate, and gift tax purposes, respectively, if the charitable remainder beneficiary otherwise meets all of the requirements of those provisions. Therefore, it will not be necessary for a taxpayer to request a ruling on the qualification of a substantially similar trust. A trust that contains substantive provisions in addition to those provided by sections 4 through 8 of this revenue procedure or by section 4 of Rev. Proc. 89-20 (other than provisions necessary to establish a valid trust under applicable local law) or that omits any of these provisions will not necessarily be disqualified but neither will it be assured of qualification under the provisions of this revenue procedure.

SECTION 4.   SAMPLE INTER VIVOS CHARITABLE REMAINDER UNITRUST: TWO LIVES, CONSECUTIVE INTERESTS

On this _____ day of _____, 19 _____, I, _____ (hereinafter referred to as "the Donor"), desiring to establish a charitable remainder unitrust, within the meaning of section 4 of Rev. Proc. 90-30 and section 664(d)(2) of the Internal Revenue Code (hereinafter referred to as "the Code") hereby create the _____ Charitable Remainder Unitrust and designate _____ as the initial Trustee. [Alternate or successor trustees may also be designated if desired.]

    1. Funding of Trust. The Donor transfers to the Trustee the property described in Schedule A, and the Trustee accepts such property and agrees to hold, manage, and distribute such property of the Trust under the terms set forth in this Trust instrument.

    2. Payment of Unitrust Amount. In each taxable year of the Trust, the Trustee shall pay to [a living individual] during his or her lifetime, and after his or her death to [a living individual] (hereinafter referred to as "the Recipients"), for such time as he or she survives, a unitrust amount equal to [at least 5] percent of the net fair market value of the assets of the Trust valued as of the first day of each taxable year of the Trust (the "valuation date"). The unitrust amount shall be paid in equal quarterly amounts from income and, to the extent that income is not sufficient, from principal. Any income of the Trust for a taxable year in excess of the unitrust amount shall be added to principal. If for any year the net fair market value of the Trust assets is incorrectly determined, then within a reasonable period after the value is finally determined for federal tax purposes, the Trustee shall pay to the Recipients (in the case of an undervaluation) or receive from the Recipients (in the case of an overvaluation) an amount equal to the difference between the unitrust amount properly payable and the unitrust amount actually paid.

    3. Payment of Federal Estate Taxes and State Death Taxes. The lifetime unitrust interest of the second Recipient will take effect upon the death of the first Recipient only if the second Recipient furnishes the funds for payment of any federal estate taxes or state death taxes for which the Trustee may be liable upon the death of the first Recipient. [This provision is mandatory only if all or a portion of the trust may be subject to such taxes on the death of the first recipient.]

    4. Proration of the Unitrust Amount. In determining the unitrust amount, the Trustee shall prorate the same on a daily basis for a short taxable year and for the taxable year ending with the survivor Recipient's death.

    5. Distribution to Charity. Upon the death of the survivor Recipient, the Trustee shall distribute all of the then principal and income of the Trust (other than any amount due either of the Recipients or

their estates under the provisions above) to _____ (hereinafter referred to as "the Charitable Organization"). If the Charitable Organization is not an organization described in sections 170(c), 2055(a), and 2522(a) of the Code at the time when any principal or income of the Trust is to be distributed to it, then the Trustee shall distribute such principal or income to such one or more organizations described in sections 170(c), 2055(a), and 2522(a) as the Trustee shall select in its sole discretion.

6.   Additional Contributions. If any additional contributions are made to the Trust after the initial contribution, the unitrust amount for the year in which the additional contribution is made shall be [the same percentage as in paragraph 2] percent of the sum of (a) the net fair market value of the Trust assets as of the valuation date (excluding the assets so added and any income from, or appreciation on, such assets) and (b) that proportion of the fair market value of the assets so added that was excluded under (a) that the number of days in the period that begins with the date of contribution and ends with the earlier of the last day of the taxable year or the date of death of the survivor Recipient bears to the number of days in the period that begins on the first day of such taxable year and ends with the earlier of the last day in such taxable year or the date of death of the survivor Recipient. In the case where there is no valuation date after the time of contribution, the assets so added shall be valued as of the time of contribution.

7.   Prohibited Transactions. The Trustee shall make distributions at such time and in such manner as not to subject the Trust to tax under section 4942 of the Code. Except for the payment of the unitrust amount to the Recipients, the Trustee shall not engage in any act of self-dealing, as defined in section 4941(d), and shall not make any taxable expenditures, as defined in section 4945(d). The Trustee shall not make any investments that jeopardize the charitable purpose of the Trust, within the meaning of section 4944 and the regulations thereunder, or retain any excess business holdings, within the meaning of section 4943(c).

8.   Taxable Year. The taxable year of the Trust shall be the calendar year.

9.   Governing Law. The operation of the Trust shall be governed by the laws of the State of _____. The Trustee, however, is prohibited from exercising any power or discretion granted under said laws that would be inconsistent with the qualification of the Trust under section 664(d)(2) of the Code and the corresponding regulations.

10.   Limited Power of Amendment. The Trust is irrevocable. The Trustee, however, shall have the power, acting alone, to amend the Trust in any manner required for the sole purpose of ensuring that the Trust qualifies and continues to qualify as a charitable remainder unitrust within the meaning of section 664(d)(2) of the Code.

11.   Investment of Trust Assets. Nothing in this Trust instrument shall be construed to restrict the Trustee from investing the Trust assets in a manner that could result in the annual realization of a reasonable amount of income or gain from the sale or disposition of Trust assets.

SECTION 5.   SAMPLE INTER VIVOS CHARITABLE REMAINDER UNITRUST: TWO LIVES, CONCURRENT AND CONSECUTIVE INTEREST

On this _____ day of _____, 19 _____, I, _____ (hereinafter referred to as "the Donor"), desiring to establish a charitable remainder unitrust, within the meaning of section 5 of Rev. Proc. 90-30 and section 664(d)(2) of the Internal Revenue Code (hereinafter referred to as "the Code") hereby create the _____ Charitable Remainder Unitrust and designate _____ as the initial Trustee. [Alternate or successor trustees may also be designated if desired.]

1.   Funding of Trust. The Donor transfers to the Trustee the property described in Schedule A, and the Trustee accepts such property and agrees to hold, manage, and distribute such property of the Trust under the terms set forth in this Trust instrument.

2.   Payment of Unitrust Amount. In each taxable year of the Trust, the Trustee shall pay to [a living individual] and [a living individual] (hereinafter referred to as "the Recipients"), in equal shares during their lifetimes, a unitrust amount equal to [at least 5] percent of the net fair market value of the assets of the Trust valued as of the first day of each taxable year of the Trust (the "valuation date"). Upon the death of the first of the Recipients to die, the survivor Recipient shall be entitled to receive the entire unitrust amount. The unitrust amount shall be paid in equal quarterly amounts from income and, to the extent that income is not sufficient, from principal. Any income of the Trust for a taxable year in excess of the unitrust amount shall be added to principal. If for any year the net fair market value of the Trust assets is incorrectly determined, then within a reasonable period after the value is finally

determined for federal tax purposes, the Trustee shall pay to the Recipients (in the case of an undervaluation) or receive from the Recipients (in the case of an overvaluation) an amount equal to the difference between the unitrust amount properly payable and the unitrust amount actually paid.

3.   Payment of Federal Estate Taxes and State Death Taxes. The lifetime unitrust interest of the survivor Recipient will continue in effect upon the death of the first Recipient to die only if the survivor Recipient furnishes the funds for payment of any federal estate taxes or state death taxes for which the Trustee may be liable upon the death of the first Recipient to die. [This provision is mandatory only if all or a portion of the trust may be subject to such taxes on the death of the first recipient to die.]

4.   Proration of the Unitrust Amount. In determining the unitrust amount, the Trustee shall prorate the same on a daily basis for a short taxable year and for the taxable year ending with the survivor Recipient's death.

5.   Distribution to Charity. Upon the death of the survivor Recipient, the Trustee shall distribute all of the then principal and income of the Trust (other than any amount due either of the Recipients or their estates under the provisions above) to _____ (hereinafter referred to as "the Charitable Organization"). If the Charitable Organization is not an organization described in sections 170(c), 2055(a), and 2522(a) of the Code at the time when any principal or income of the Trust is to be distributed to it, then the Trustee shall distribute such principal or income to such one or more organizations described in sections 170(c), 2055(a), and 2522(a) as the Trustee shall select in its sole discretion.

6.   Additional Contributions. If any additional contributions are made to the Trust after the initial contribution, the unitrust amount for the year in which the additional contribution is made shall be [the same percentage as in paragraph 2] percent of the sum of (a) the net fair market value of the Trust assets as of the valuation date (excluding the assets so added and any income from, or appreciation on, such assets) and (b) that proportion of the fair market value of the assets so added that was excluded under (a) that the number of days in the period that begins with the date of contribution and ends with the earlier of the last day of the taxable year or the date of death of the survivor Recipient bears to the number of days in the period that begins on the first day of such taxable year and ends with the earlier of the last day in such taxable year or the date of death of

the survivor Recipient. In the case where there is no valuation date after the time of contribution, the assets so added shall be valued as of the time of contribution.

7.   Prohibited Transactions. The Trustee shall make distributions at such time and in such manner as not to subject the Trust to tax under section 4942 of the Code. Except for the payment of the unitrust amount to the Recipients, the Trustee shall not engage in any act of self-dealing, as defined in section 4941(d), and shall not make any taxable expenditures, as defined in section 4945(d). The Trustee shall not make any investments that jeopardize the charitable purpose of the Trust, within the meaning of section 4944 and the regulations thereunder, or retain any excess business holdings, within the meaning of section 4943(c).

8.   Taxable Year. The taxable year of the Trust shall be the calendar year.

9.   Governing Law. The operation of the Trust shall be governed by the laws of the State of _____. The Trustee, however, is prohibited from exercising any power or discretion granted under said laws that would be inconsistent with the qualification of the Trust under section 664(d)(2) of the Code and the corresponding regulations.

10.   Limited Power of Amendment. The Trust is irrevocable. The Trustee, however, shall have the power, acting alone, to amend the Trust in any manner required for the sole purpose of ensuring that the Trust qualifies and continues to qualify as a charitable remainder unitrust within the meaning of section 664(d)(2) of the Code.

11.   Investment of Trust Assets. Nothing in this Trust instrument shall be construed to restrict the Trustee from investing the Trust assets in a manner that could result in the annual realization of a reasonable amount of income or gain from the sale or disposition of Trust assets.

SECTION 6.   SAMPLE TESTAMENTARY CHARITABLE REMAINDER UNITRUST: ONE LIFE

All the rest, residue, and remainder of my property and estate, real and personal, of whatever nature and wherever situated, [Alternatively, if not a residuary bequest, describe or identify the bequest] I give, devise, and bequeath to my Trustee in trust. It being my intention to establish a charitable remainder unitrust within the meaning of section 6 of Rev. Proc. 90-30 and section 664(d)(2) of the

Internal Revenue Code (hereinafter referred to as "the Code"), such Trust shall be known as the _____ Charitable Remainder Unitrust and I hereby designate _____ as the initial Trustee. [Alternate or successor trustees may also be designated if desired.]

1.   Payment of Unitrust Amount. In each taxable year of the Trust, the Trustee shall pay to [a living individual] (hereinafter referred to as "the Recipient") during the Recipient's life a unitrust amount equal to [at least 5] percent of the net fair market value of the assets of the Trust valued as of the first day of each taxable year of the Trust (the "valuation date"). The unitrust amount shall be paid in equal quarterly amounts from income and, to the extent that income is not sufficient, from principal. Any income of the Trust for a taxable year in excess of the unitrust amount shall be added to principal. If for any year the net fair market value of the Trust assets is incorrectly determined, then within a reasonable period after the value is finally determined for federal tax purposes, the Trustee shall pay to the Recipient (in the case of an undervaluation) or receive from the Recipient (in the case of an overvaluation) an amount equal to the difference between the unitrust amount properly payable and the unitrust amount actually paid.

2.   Deferral Provision. The obligation to pay the unitrust amount shall commence with the date of my death, but payment of the unitrust amount may be deferred from such date until the end of the taxable year of the Trust in which occurs the complete funding of the Trust. Within a reasonable time after the end of the taxable year in which the complete funding of the Trust occurs, the Trustee must pay to the Recipient (in the case of an underpayment) or receive from the Recipient (in the case of an overpayment) the difference between: (1) any unitrust amounts actually paid, plus interest, compounded annually, computed for any period at the rate of interest that the federal income tax regulations under section 664 of the Code prescribe for the Trust for such computation for such period; and (2) the unitrust amounts payable, plus interest, compounded annually, computed for any period at the rate of interest that the federal income tax regulations under section 664 prescribe for the Trust for such computation for such period.

3.   Proration of the Unitrust Amount. In determining the unitrust amount, the Trustee shall prorate the same on a daily basis for a short taxable year and for the taxable year ending with the Recipient's death.

4.   Distribution to Charity. Upon the death of the Recipient, the

Trustee shall distribute all of the then principal and income of the Trust (other than any amount due the Recipient or the Recipient's estate under the provisions above) to _____ (hereinafter referred to as "the Charitable Organization"). If the Charitable Organization is not an organization described in sections 170(c) and 2055(a) of the Code at the time when any principal or income of the Trust is to be distributed to it, then the Trustee shall distribute such principal or income to such one or more organizations described in sections 170(c) and 2055(a) as the Trustee shall select in its sole discretion.

5.   Additional Contributions. No additional contributions shall be made to the Trust after the initial contribution. The initial contribution, however, shall consist of all property passing to the Trust by reason of my death.

6.   Prohibited Transactions. The Trustee shall make distributions at such time and in such manner as not to subject the Trust to tax under section 4942 of the Code. Except for the payment of the unitrust amount to the Recipient, the Trustee shall not engage in any act of self-dealing, as defined in section 4941(d), and shall not make any taxable expenditures, as defined in section 4945(d). The Trustee shall not make any investments that jeopardize the charitable purpose of the Trust, within the meaning of section 4944 and the regulations thereunder, or retain any excess business holdings, within the meaning of section 4943(c).

7.   Taxable Year. The taxable year of the Trust shall be the calendar year.

8.   Governing Law. The operation of the Trust shall be governed by the laws of the State of _____. The Trustee, however, is prohibited from exercising any power or discretion granted under said laws that would be inconsistent with the qualification of the Trust under section 664(d)(2) of the Code and the corresponding regulations.

9.   Limited Power of Amendment. The Trustee shall have the power, acting alone, to amend the Trust in any manner required for the sole purpose of ensuring that the Trust qualifies and continues to qualify as a charitable remainder unitrust within the meaning of section 664(d)(2) of the Code.

10.   Investment of Trust Assets. Nothing herein shall be construed to restrict the Trustee from investing the Trust assets in a manner that could result in the annual realization of a reasonable amount of income or gain from the sale or disposition of Trust assets.

SECTION 7.   SAMPLE TESTAMENTARY CHARITABLE
REMAINDER UNITRUST: TWO LIVES, CONSECUTIVE
INTERESTS

All the rest, residue, and remainder of my property and estate, real
and personal, of whatever nature and wherever situated, [Alterna-
tively, if not a residuary bequest, describe or identify the bequest] I
give, devise, and bequeath to my Trustee in trust. It being my
intention to establish a charitable remainder unitrust within the
meaning of section 7 of Rev. Proc. 90-30 and section 664(d)(2) of the
Internal Revenue Code (hereinafter referred to as "the Code"), such
Trust shall be known as the _____ Charitable Remainder Unitrust and I hereby designate _____ as the initial Trustee. [Alter-
nate or successor trustees may also be designated if desired.]

    1.   Payment of Unitrust Amount. In each taxable year of the
Trust, the Trustee shall pay to [a living individual] during his or her
lifetime, and after his or her death to [a living individual] (hereinafter referred to as "the Recipients"), for such time as he or she
survives, a unitrust amount equal to [at least 5] percent of the net
fair market value of the assets of the Trust valued as of the first day
of each taxable year of the Trust (the "valuation date"). The unitrust
amount shall be paid in equal quarterly amounts from income and,
to the extent that income is not sufficient, from principal. Any income of the Trust for a taxable year in excess of the unitrust amount
shall be added to principal. If for any year the net fair market value
of the Trust assets is incorrectly determined, then within a reasonable period after the value is finally determined for federal tax purposes, the Trustee shall pay to the Recipients (in the case of an
undervaluation) or receive from the Recipients (in the case of an
overvaluation) an amount equal to the difference between the unitrust amount properly payable and the unitrust amount actually paid.

    2.   Deferral Provision. The obligation to pay the unitrust amount
shall commence with the date of my death, but payment of the
unitrust amount may be deferred from such date until the end of the
taxable year of the Trust in which occurs the complete funding of the
Trust. Within a reasonable time after the end of the taxable year in
which the complete funding of the Trust occurs, the Trustee must
pay to the Recipients (in the case of an underpayment) or receive
from the Recipients (in the case of an overpayment) the difference
between: (1) any unitrust amounts actually paid, plus interest, compounded annually, computed for any period at the rate of interest

that the federal income tax regulations under section 664 of the Code prescribe for the Trust for such computation for such period, and (2) the unitrust amounts payable, plus interest, compounded annually, computed for any period at the rate of interest that the federal income tax regulations under section 664 prescribe for the Trust for such computation for such period.

3.   Proration of the Unitrust Amount. In determining the unitrust amount, the Trustee shall prorate the same on a daily basis for a short taxable year and for the taxable year ending with the survivor Recipient's death.

4.   Distribution to Charity. Upon the death of the survivor Recipient, the Trustee shall distribute all of the then principal and income of the Trust (other than any amount due either of the Recipients of their estates under the provisions above) to _____ (hereinafter referred to as "the Charitable Organization"). If the Charitable Organization is not an organization described in sections 170(c) and 2055(a) of the Code at the time when any principal or income of the Trust is to be distributed to it, then the Trustee shall distribute such principal or income to such one or more organizations described in sections 170(c) and 2055(a) as the Trustee shall select in its sole discretion.

5.   Additional Contributions. No additional contributions shall be made to the Trust after the initial contribution. The initial contribution, however, shall consist of all property passing to the Trust by reason of my death.

6.   Prohibited Transactions. The Trustee shall make distributions at such time and in such manner as not to subject the Trust to tax under section 4942 of the Code. Except for the payment of the unitrust amount to the Recipient, the Trustee shall not engage in any act of self-dealing, as defined in section 4945(d), and shall not make any taxable expenditures, as defined in section 4945(d). The Trustee shall not make any investments that jeopardize the charitable purpose of the Trust, within the meaning of section 4944 and the regulations thereunder, or retain any excess business holdings, within the meaning of section 4943(c).

7.   Taxable Year. The taxable year of the Trust shall be the calendar year.

8.   Governing Law. The operation of the Trust shall be governed by the laws of the State of _____. The Trustee, however, is prohibited from exercising any power or discretion granted under said laws that would be inconsistent with the qualification of the

Trust under section 664(d)(2) of the Code and the corresponding regulations.

9.   Limited Power of Amendment. The Trustee shall have the power, acting alone, to amend the Trust in any manner required for the sole purpose of ensuring that the Trust qualifies and continues to qualify as a charitable remainder unitrust within the meaning of section 664(d)(2) of the Code.

10.   Investment of Trust Assets. Nothing herein shall be construed to restrict the Trustee from investing the Trust assets in a manner that could result in the annual realization of a reasonable amount of income or gain from the sale or disposition of Trust assets.

SECTION 8.   SAMPLE TESTAMENTARY CHARITABLE REMAINDER UNITRUST: TWO LIVES, CONCURRENT AND CONSECUTIVE INTERESTS

All the rest, residue, and remainder of my property and estate, real or personal, of whatever nature and wherever situated, [Alternatively, if not a residuary bequest, describe or identify the bequest] I give, devise, and bequeath to my Trustee in trust. It being my intention to establish a charitable remainder unitrust within the meaning of section 8 of Rev. Proc. 90-30 and section 664(d)(2) of the Internal Revenue Code (hereinafter referred to as "the Code"), such Trust shall be known as the _____ Charitable Remainder Unitrust and I hereby designate _____ as the initial Trustee. [Alternate or successor trustees may also be designated if desired.]

1.   Payment of Unitrust Amount. In each taxable year of the Trust, the Trustee shall pay to [a living individual] and [a living individual] (hereinafter referred to as "the Recipients"), in equal shares during their lifetimes, a unitrust amount equal to [at least 5] percent of the net fair market value of the assets of the Trust valued as of the first day of each taxable year of the Trust (the "valuation date"). Upon the death of the first of the Recipients to die, the survivor Recipient shall be entitled to receive the entire unitrust amount. The unitrust amount shall be paid in equal quarterly amounts from income and, to the extent that income is not sufficient, from principal. Any income of the Trust for a taxable year in excess of the unitrust amount shall be added to principal. If for any year the net fair market value of the Trust assets is incorrectly determined, then within a reasonable period after the value is finally determined for federal tax purposes, the Trustee shall pay to the

Recipients (in the case of an undervaluation) or receive from the Recipients (in the case of an overvaluation) an amount equal to the difference between the unitrust amount properly payable and the unitrust amount actually paid.

2.   Deferral Provision. The obligation to pay the unitrust amount shall commence with the date of my death, but payment of the unitrust amount may be deferred from such date until the end of the taxable year of the Trust in which occurs the complete funding of the Trust. Within a reasonable time after the end of the taxable year in which the complete funding of the Trust occurs, the Trustee must pay to the Recipients (in the case of an underpayment) or receive from the Recipients (in the case of an overpayment) the difference between: (1) any unitrust amounts actually paid, plus interest, compounded annually, computed for any period at the rate of interest that the federal income tax regulations under section 664 of the Code prescribe for the Trust for such computation for such period; and (2) the unitrust amounts payable, plus interest, compounded annually, computed for any period at the rate of interest that the federal income tax regulations under section 664 prescribe for the Trust for such computation for such period.

3.   Proration of the Unitrust Amount. In determining the unitrust amount, the Trustee shall prorate the same on a daily basis for a short taxable year and for the taxable year ending with the survivor Recipient's death.

4.   Distribution to Charity. Upon the death of the survivor Recipient, the Trustee shall distribute all of the then principal and income of the Trust (other than any amount due either of the Recipients or their estates under the provisions above) to _____ (hereinafter referred to as "the Charitable Organization"). If the Charitable Organization is not an organization described in sections 170(c) and 2055(a) of the Code at the time when any principal or income of the Trust is to be distributed to it, then the Trustee shall distribute such principal or income to such one or more organizations described in sections 170(c) and 2055(a) as the Trustee shall select in its sole discretion.

5.   Additional Contributions. No additional contributions shall be made to the Trust after the initial contribution. The initial contribution, however, shall consist of all property passing to the Trust by reason of my death.

6.   Prohibited Transactions. The Trustee shall make distributions at such time and in such manner as not to subject the Trust to tax

under section 4942 of the Code. Except for the payment of the unitrust amount to the Recipient, the Trustee shall not engage in any act of self-dealing, as defined in section 4941(d), and shall not make any taxable expenditures, as defined in section 4945(d). The Trustee shall not make any investments that jeopardize the charitable purpose of the Trust, within the meaning of section 4944 and the regulations thereunder, or retain any excess business holdings, within the meaning of section 4943(c).

7.   Taxable Year. The taxable year of the Trust shall be the calendar year.

8.   Governing Law. The operation of the Trust shall be governed by the laws of the State of _____. The Trustee, however, is prohibited from exercising any power or discretion granted under said laws that would be inconsistent with the qualification of the Trust under section 664(d)(2) of the Code and the corresponding regulations.

9.   Limited Power of Amendment. The Trustee shall have the power, acting alone, to amend the Trust in any manner required for the sole purpose of ensuring that the Trust qualifies and continues to qualify as a charitable remainder unitrust within the meaning of section 664(d)(2) of the Code.

10.   Investment of Trust Assets. Nothing herein shall be construed to restrict the Trustee from investing the Trust assets in a manner that could result in the annual realization of a reasonable amount of income or gain from the sale or disposition of Trust assets.

SECTION 9.   EFFECT ON OTHER REVENUE PROCEDURES

Rev. Proc. 89-20 is amplified.

SECTION 10.   EFFECTIVE DATE

This revenue procedure is effective on and after June 18, 1990, the date of publication of this revenue procedure in the Internal Revenue Bulletin.

In 1990, the IRS issued six sample forms of trust that qualify as charitable remainder unitrusts (Rev. Proc. 90-31, 1990-1 C.B. 539). The full text of this document is as follows:

Rev. Proc. 90-31

SECTION 1.   PURPOSE

This revenue procedure makes available six sample forms of trust that meet the requirements for a charitable remainder unitrust as described in section 664(d)(2) and (3) of the Internal Revenue Code.

SECTION 2.   BACKGROUND

The Internal Revenue Service receives and responds to requests for rulings dealing with the qualification of trusts as charitable remainder trusts and the availability of deductions for contributions made to such trusts. In many of these requests, the trust instruments and charitable objectives are very similar. Consequently, in order to provide a service to taxpayers and to save the time and expense involved in requesting and processing a ruling on a proposed charitable remainder unitrust, this revenue procedure allows taxpayers who make transfers to a trust that substantially follows one of the sample forms of trust contained herein to be assured that the Service will recognize the trust as meeting all of the requirements of a charitable remainder unitrust, provided that the trust operates in a manner consistent with the terms of the instrument creating the trust and provided it is a valid trust under applicable local law.

SECTION 3.   SCOPE AND OBJECTIVE

The sample forms of trust meet all of the applicable requirements of sections 664(d)(2) and (3) of the Code and include:

Section 4—Sample Inter Vivos Charitable Remainder Unitrust: One Life;

Section 5—Sample Inter Vivos Charitable Remainder Unitrust: Two Lives, Consecutive Interests;

Section 6—Sample Inter Vivos Charitable Remainder Unitrust: Two Lives, Concurrent and Consecutive Interests;

Section 7—Sample Testamentary Charitable Remainder Unitrust: One Life;

Section 8—Sample Testamentary Charitable Remainder Unitrust: Two Lives, Consecutive Interests; and

Section 9—Sample Testamentary Charitable Remainder Unitrust: Two Lives, Concurrent and Consecutive Interests.

In all cases, the termination of the life interests must be followed by a distribution of the trust assets to the charitable remainder beneficiary, and the trust must be a valid trust under applicable local law.

If the trust provisions are substantially similar to those in one of the samples provided in sections 4 through 9, the Service will recognize the trust as satisfying all of the applicable requirements of section 664(d)(2) and (3) of the Code and the corresponding regulations. A document will be considered to be substantially similar to one of the samples even though, for example, the wording is varied to comport with local law and practice as necessary to create trusts, define legal relationships, pass property by bequest, provide for the appointment of alternative and successor trustees, or designate alternative charitable remaindermen. Moreover, for transfers to a qualifying charitable remainder unitrust, the remainder interest will be deductible under sections 170(f)(2)(A), 2055(e)(2)(A), and 2522(c)(2)(A) for income, estate, and gift tax purposes, respectively, if the charitable remainder beneficiary otherwise meets all of the requirements of those provisions. Therefore, it will not be necessary for a taxpayer to request a ruling on the qualification of a substantially similar trust. A trust that contains substantive provisions in addition to those provided by sections 4 through 9 (other than provisions necessary to establish a valid trust under applicable local law) or that omits any of these provisions will not necessarily be disqualified, but it will not be assured of qualification under the provisions of this revenue procedure.

SECTION 4.   SAMPLE INTER VIVOS CHARITABLE REMAINDER UNITRUST: ONE LIFE

On this _____ day of _____, 19 _____, I, _____ (hereinafter referred to as "the Donor"), desiring to establish a charitable remainder unitrust within the meaning of section 4 of Rev. Proc. 90-31 and section 664(d)(2) and (3) of the Internal Revenue Code (hereinafter referred to as "the Code") hereby create the _____ *haritable Remainder Unitrust and designate _____ as the initial Trustee. [Alternate or successor trustees may also be designated if desired.]

1.   Funding of Trust. The Donor transfers to the Trustee the property described in Schedule A, and the Trustee accepts such property and agrees to hold, manage, and distribute such property of the Trust under the terms set forth in this Trust instrument.

2.   Payment of Unitrust Amount. In each taxable year of the

Trust, the Trustee shall pay to [a living individual] (hereinafter referred to as "the Recipient") during the Recipient's life a unitrust amount equal to the lesser of: (a) the Trust income for the taxable year, as defined in section 643(b) of the Code and the regulations thereunder, and (b) [at least 5] percent of the net fair market value of the assets of the Trust valued as of the first day of each taxable year of the Trust (the "valuation date"). The unitrust amount for any year shall also include any amount of Trust income for such year that is in excess of the amount required to be distributed under (b) (above) to the extent that the aggregate of the amounts paid in prior years was less than the aggregate of the amounts computed as [same percentage as in (b) above] percent of the net fair market value of the Trust assets on the valuation dates.

The unitrust amount shall be paid in quarterly installments. Any income of the Trust for a taxable year in excess of the unitrust amount shall be added to principal. If for any year the net fair market value of the Trust assets is incorrectly determined, then within a reasonable period after the value is finally determined for federal tax purposes, the Trustee shall pay to the Recipient (in the case of an undervaluation) or receive from the Recipient (in the case of an overvaluation) an amount equal to the difference between the unitrust amount properly payable and the unitrust amount actually paid.

3.   Proration of the Unitrust Amount. In determining the unitrust amount, the Trustee shall prorate the same on a daily basis for a short taxable year and for the taxable year ending with the Recipient's death.

4.   Distribution to Charity. Upon the death of the Recipient, the Trustee shall distribute all of the then principal and income of the Trust (other than any amount due the Recipient or the Recipient's estate under the provisions above) to _____ (hereinafter referred to as "the Charitable Organization"). If the Charitable Organization is not an organization described in sections 170(c), 2055(a), and 2522(a) of the Code at the time when any principal or income of the Trust is to be distributed to it, then the Trustee shall distribute such principal or income to such one or more organizations described in sections 170(c), 2055(a), and 2522(a) as the Trustee shall select in its sole discretion.

5.   Additional Contributions. If any additional contributions are made to the Trust after the initial contribution, the unitrust amount for the year in which the additional contribution is made shall be

equal to the lesser of (a) the Trust income for the taxable year, as defined in section 643(b) of the Code and the regulations thereunder, and (b) [the same percentage as in paragraph 2] percent of the sum of (1) the net fair market value of the Trust assets as of the valuation date (excluding the assets so added and any income from, or appreciation on, such assets) and (2) that proportion of the fair market value of the assets so added that was excluded under (1) that the number of days in the period that begins with the date of contribution and ends with the earlier of the last day of the taxable year or the day of the Recipient's death bears to the number of days in the period that begins on the first day of such taxable year and ends with the earlier of the last day in such taxable year or the day of the Recipient's death. In the case where there is no valuation date after the time of contribution, the assets so added shall be valued as of the time of contribution. The unitrust amount for any such year shall also include any amount of Trust income for such year that is in excess of the amount required to be distributed under (b) above to the extent that the aggregate of the amounts paid in prior years was less than the aggregate of the amounts computed as [same percentage as in (b) above] percent of the net fair market value of the Trust assets on the valuation dates.

6.   Prohibited Transactions. The Trustee shall make distributions at such time and in such manner as not to subject the Trust to tax under section 4942 of the Code. Except for the payment of the unitrust amount to the Recipient, the Trustee shall not engage in any act of self-dealing, as defined in section 4941(d), and shall not make any taxable expenditures, as defined in section 4945(d). The Trustee shall not make any investments that jeopardize the charitable purpose of the Trust, within the meaning of section 4944 and the regulations thereunder, or retain any excess business holdings, within the meaning of section 4943(c).

7.   Taxable Year. The taxable year of the Trust shall be the calendar year.

8.   Governing Law. The operation of the Trust shall be governed by the laws of the State of _____. The Trustee, however, is prohibited from exercising any power or discretion granted under said laws that would be inconsistent with the qualification of the Trust under section 664(d)(2) and (3) of the Code and the corresponding regulations.

9.   Limited Power of Amendment. The Trust is irrevocable. The Trustee, however, shall have the power, acting alone, to amend the

Trust in any manner required for the sole purpose of ensuring that the Trust qualifies and continues to qualify as a charitable remainder unitrust within the meaning of section 664(d)(2) and (3) of the Code.

10.   Investment of Trust Assets. Nothing in this Trust instrument shall be construed to restrict the Trustee from investing the Trust assets in a manner that could result in the annual realization of a reasonable amount of income or gain from the sale or disposition of Trust assets.

SECTION 5.   SAMPLE INTER VIVOS CHARITABLE REMAINDER UNITRUST: TWO LIVES, CONSECUTIVE INTERESTS

On this _____ day of _____, 19 _____, I, _____ (hereinafter referred to as "the Donor"), desiring to establish a charitable remainder unitrust within the meaning of section 5 of Rev. Proc. 90-31 and section 664(d)(2) and (3) of the Internal Revenue Code (hereinafter referred to as "the Code") hereby create the _____ Charitable Remainder Unitrust and designate _____ as the initial Trustee. [Alternate or successor trustees may also be designated if desired.]

1.   Funding of Trust. The Donor transfers to the Trustee the property described in Schedule A, and the Trustee accepts such property and agrees to hold, manage, and distribute such property of the Trust under the terms set forth in this Trust instrument.

2.   Payment of Unitrust Amount. In each taxable year of the Trust, the Trustee shall pay to [a living individual] (hereinafter referred to as "the Recipients"), for such time as he or she survives, a unitrust amount equal to the lesser of: (a) the Trust income for the taxable year, as defined in section 643(b) of the Code and the regulations thereunder, and (b) [at least 5] percent of the net fair market value of the assets of the Trust valued as of the first day of each taxable year of the Trust (the "valuation date"). The unitrust amount for any year shall also include any amount of Trust income for such year that is in excess of the amount required to be distributed under (b) (above) to the extent that the aggregate of the amounts paid in prior years was less than the aggregate of the amounts computed as [same percentage as in (b) above] percent of the net fair market value of the Trust assets on the valuation dates.

The unitrust amount shall be paid in quarterly installments. Any income of the Trust for a taxable year in excess of the unitrust amount shall be added to principal. If for any year the net fair market value of the Trust assets is incorrectly determined, then within a reasonable period after the value is finally determined for federal tax purposes, the Trustee shall pay to the Recipients (in the case of an undervaluation) or receive from the Recipients (in the case of an overvaluation) an amount equal to the difference between the unitrust amount properly payable and the unitrust amount actually paid.

3.   Payment of Federal Estate Taxes and State Death Taxes. The lifetime unitrust interest of the second Recipient will take effect upon the death of the first Recipient only if the second Recipient furnishes the funds for payment of any federal estate taxes or state death taxes for which the Trustee may be liable upon the death of the first Recipient. [This provision is mandatory only if all or a portion of the trust may be subject to such taxes on the death of the first recipient.]

4.   Proration of the Unitrust Amount. In determining the unitrust amount, the Trustee shall prorate the same on a daily basis for a short taxable year and for the taxable year ending with the survivor Recipient's death.

5.   Distribution to Charity. Upon the death of the survivor Recipient, the Trustee shall distribute all of the then principal and income of the Trust (other than any amount due either of the Recipients or their estates under the provisions above) to _____ (hereinafter referred to as "the Charitable Organization"). If the Charitable Organization is not an organization described in sections 170(c), 2055(a), and 2522(a) of the Code at the time when any principal or income of the Trust is to be distributed to it, then the Trustee shall distribute such principal or income to such one or more organizations described in sections 170(c), 2055(a), and 2522(a) as the Trustee shall select in its sole discretion.

6.   Additional Contributions. If any additional contributions are made to the Trust after the initial contribution, the unitrust amount for the year in which the additional contribution is made shall be equal to the lesser of (a) the Trust income for the taxable year, as defined in section 643(b) of the Code and the regulations thereunder, and (b) [the same percentage as in paragraph 2] percent of the sum of (1) the net fair market value of the Trust assets as of the valuation date (excluding the assets so added and any income from, or appreciation on, such assets) and (2) that proportion of the fair market value of the assets so added that was excluded under (1) that the number of days in the period that begins with the date of contribution and

ends with the earlier of the last day of the taxable year or the date of death of the survivor Recipient bears to the number of days in the period that begins on the first day of such taxable year and ends with the earlier of the last day in such taxable year or the date of death of the survivor Recipient. In the case where there is no valuation date after the time of contribution, the assets so added shall be valued as of the time of contribution. The unitrust amount for any such year shall also include any amount of Trust income for such year that is in excess of the amount required to be distributed under (b) above to the extent that the aggregate of the amounts paid in prior years was less than the aggregate of the amounts computed as [same percentage as in (b) above] percent of the net fair market value of the Trust assets on the valuation dates.

7. Prohibited Transactions. The Trustee shall make distributions at such time and in such manner as not to subject the Trust to tax under section 4942 of the Code. Except for the payment of the unitrust amount to the Recipients, the Trustee shall not engage in any act of self-dealing, as defined in section 4941(d), and shall not make any taxable expenditures, as defined in section 4945(d). The Trustee shall not make any investments that jeopardize the charitable purpose of the Trust, within the meaning of section 4944 and the regulations thereunder, or retain any excess business holdings, within the meaning of section 4943(c).

8. Taxable Year. The taxable year of the Trust shall be the calendar year.

9. Governing Law. The operation of the Trust shall be governed by the laws of the State of _____. The Trustee, however, is prohibited from exercising any power or discretion granted under said laws that would be inconsistent with the qualification of the Trust under section 664(d)(2) and (3) of the Code and the corresponding regulations.

10. Limited Power of Amendment. The Trust is irrevocable. The Trustee, however, shall have the power, acting alone, to amend the Trust in any manner required for the sole purpose of ensuring that the Trust qualifies and continues to qualify as a charitable remainder unitrust within the meaning of section 664(d)(2) and (3) of the Code.

11. Investment of Trust Assets. Nothing in this Trust instrument shall be construed to restrict the Trustee from investing the Trust assets in a manner that could result in the annual realization of a reasonable amount of income or gain from the sale or disposition of Trust assets.

SECTION 6.   SAMPLE INTER VIVOS CHARITABLE
REMAINDER UNITRUST: TWO LIVES, CONCURRENT
AND CONSECUTIVE INTERESTS

On this ＿＿＿＿ day of ＿＿＿＿, 19 ＿＿＿＿, I, ＿＿＿＿
(hereinafter referred to as "the Donor"), desiring to establish a charitable remainder unitrust, within the meaning of section 6 of Rev.
Proc. 90-31 and section 664(d)(2) and (3) of the Internal Revenue
Code (hereinafter referred to as "the Code") hereby create the
＿＿＿＿ Charitable Remainder Unitrust and designate ＿＿＿＿ as
the initial Trustee. [Alternate or successor trustees may also be designated if desired.]

  1.   Funding of Trust. The Donor transfers to the Trustee the
property described in Schedule A, and the Trustee accepts such
property and agrees to hold, manage, and distribute such property of
the Trust under the terns set forth in this Trust instrument.

  2.   Payment of Unitrust Amount. In each taxable year of the
Trust, the Trustee shall pay to [a living individual] and [a living
individual] (hereinafter referred to as "the Recipients") in equal
shares during their lifetimes, a unitrust amount equal to the lesser
of: (a) the Trust income for the taxable year, as defined in section
643(b) of the Code and the regulations thereunder, and (b) [at least
5] percent of the net fair market value of the assets of the Trust
valued as of the first day of each taxable year of the Trust (the
"valuation date"). The unitrust amount for any year shall also include
any amount of Trust income for such year that is in excess of the
amount required to be distributed under (b) (above) to the extent
that the aggregate of the amounts paid in prior years was less than
the aggregate of the amounts computed as [same percentage as in (b)
above] percent of the net fair market value of the Trust assets on the
valuation dates.

  Upon the death of the first of the Recipients to die, the survivor
Recipient shall be entitled to receive the entire unitrust amount.
The unitrust amount shall be paid in quarterly installments. Any
income of the Trust for a taxable year in excess of the unitrust
amount shall be added to principal. If for any year the net fair
market value of the Trust assets is incorrectly determined, then
within a reasonable period after the value is finally determined for
federal tax purposes, the Trustee shall pay to the Recipients (in the
case of an undervaluation) or receive from the Recipients (in the case
of an overvaluation) an amount equal to the difference between the

unitrust amount properly payable and the unitrust amount actually paid.

3.   Payment of Federal Estate Taxes and State Death Taxes. The lifetime unitrust interest of the survivor Recipient will continue in effect upon the death of the first Recipient to die only if the survivor Recipient furnishes the funds for payment of any federal estate taxes or state death taxes for which the Trustee may be liable upon the death of the first Recipient to die. [This provision is mandatory only if all or a portion of the trust may be subject to such taxes on the death of the first recipient to die.]

4.   Proration of the Unitrust Amount. In determining the unitrust amount, the Trustee shall prorate the same on a daily basis for a short taxable year and for the taxable year ending with the survivor's death.

5.   Distribution to Charity. Upon the death of the survivor Recipient, the Trustee shall distribute all of the then principal and income of the Trust (other than any amount due either of the Recipients or their estates under the provisions above) to _____ (hereinafter referred to as "the Charitable Organization"). If the Charitable Organization is not an organization described in sections 170(c), 2055(a), and 2522(a) of the Code at the time when any principal or income of the Trust is to be distributed to it, then the Trustee shall distribute such principal or income to such one or more organizations described in sections 170(c), 2055(a), and 2522(a) as the Trustee shall select in its sole discretion.

6.   Additional Contributions. If any additional contributions are made to the Trust after the initial contribution, the unitrust amount for the year in which the additional contribution is made shall be equal to the lesser of (a) the Trust income for the taxable year, as defined in section 643(b) of the Code and the regulations thereunder, and (b) [the same percentage as in paragraph 2] percent of the sum of (1) the net fair market value of the Trust assets as of the valuation date (excluding the assets so added and any income from, or appreciation on, such assets) and (2) that proportion of the fair market value of the assets so added that was excluded under (1) that the number of days in the period that begins with the date of contribution and ends with the earlier of the last day of the taxable year or the date of death of the survivor Recipient bears to the number of days in the period that begins on the first day of such taxable year and ends with the earlier of the last day in such taxable year or the date of death of the survivor Recipient. In the case where there is no valuation date

after the time of contribution, the assets so added shall be valued as of the time of contribution. The unitrust amount for any such year shall also include any amount of Trust income for such year that is in excess of the amount required to be distributed under (b) above to the extent that the aggregate of the amounts paid in prior years was less than the aggregate of the amounts computed as [same percentage as in (b) above] percent of the net fair market value of the Trust assets on the valuation dates.

7.   Prohibited Transactions. The Trustee shall make distributions at such time and in such manner as not to subject the Trust to tax under section 4942 of the Code. Except for the payment of the unitrust amount to the Recipients, the Trustee shall not engage in any act of self-dealing, as defined in section 4941(d), and shall not make any taxable expenditures, as defined in section 4945(d). The Trustee shall not make any investments that jeopardize the charitable purpose of the Trust, within the meaning of section 4944 and the regulations thereunder, or retain any excess business holdings, within the meaning of section 4943(c).

8.   Taxable Year. The taxable year of the Trust shall be the calendar year.

9.   Governing Law. The operation of the Trust shall be governed by the laws of the State of _____. The Trustee, however, is prohibited from exercising any power or discretion granted under said laws that would be inconsistent with the qualification of the Trust under section 664(d)(2) and (3) of the Code and the corresponding regulations.

10.   Limited Power of Amendment. The Trust is irrevocable. The Trustee, however, shall have the power, acting alone, to amend the Trust in any manner required for the sole purpose of ensuring that the Trust qualifies and continues to qualify as a charitable remainder unitrust within the meaning of section 664(d)(2) and (3) of the Code.

11.   Investment of Trust Assets. Nothing in this Trust instrument shall be construed to restrict the Trustee from investing the Trust assets in a manner that could result in the annual realization of a reasonable amount of income or gain from the sale or disposition of Trust assets.

SECTION 7.   SAMPLE TESTAMENTARY CHARITABLE REMAINDER UNITRUST: ONE LIFE

All the rest, residue, and remainder of my property and estate, real and personal, of whatever nature and wherever situated. [Alternatively, if not a residuary bequest, describe or identify the bequest.] I give, devise, and bequeath to my Trustee in trust. It being my intention to establish a charitable remainder unitrust within the meaning of section 7 of Rev. Proc. 90-31 and section 664(d)(2) and (3) of the Internal Revenue Code (hereinafter referred to as "the Code"), such Trust shall be known as the _____ Charitable Remainder Unitrust and I hereby designate _____ as the initial Trustee. [Alternate or successor trustees may also be designated if desired.]

1. Payment of Unitrust Amount. In each taxable year of the Trust, the Trustee shall pay to [a living individual] (hereinafter referred to as "the Recipient") during the Recipient's life a unitrust amount equal to the lesser of: (a) the Trust income for the taxable year, as defined in section 643(b) of the Code and the regulations thereunder, and (b) [at least 5] percent of the net fair market value of the assets of the Trust valued as of the first day of each taxable year of the Trust (the "valuation date"). The unitrust amount for any year shall also include any amount of Trust income for such year that is in excess of the amount required to be distributed under (b) (above) to the extent that the aggregate of the amounts paid in prior years was less than the aggregate of the amounts computed as [same percentage as in (b) above] percent of the net fair market value of the Trust assets on the valuation dates.

. The unitrust amount shall be paid in quarterly installments. Any income of the Trust for a taxable year in excess of the unitrust amount shall be added to principal. If for any year the net fair market value of the Trust assets is incorrectly determined, then within a reasonable period after the value is finally determined for federal tax purposes, the Trustee shall pay to the Recipient (in the case of an undervaluation) or receive from the Recipient (in the case of an overvaluation) an amount equal to the difference between the unitrust amount properly payable and the unitrust amount actually paid.

2. Deferral Provision. The obligation to pay the unitrust amount shall commence with the date of my death, but payment of the unitrust amount may be deferred from such date until the end of the taxable year of the Trust in which occurs the complete funding of the Trust. Within a reasonable time after the end of the taxable year in which the complete funding of the Trust occurs, the Trustee must pay to the Recipient (in the case of an underpayment) or receive from the Recipient (in the case of an overpayment) the difference between: (1) any unitrust amounts actually paid, plus interest compounded annually, computed for any period at the rate of interest

that the federal income tax regulations under section 664 of the Code prescribe for the Trust for such computation for such period; and (2) the unitrust amounts payable, plus interest compounded annually, computed for any period at the rate of interest that the federal income tax regulations under section 664 prescribe for the Trust for such computation for such period.

3. Proration of the Unitrust Amount. In determining the unitrust amount, the Trustee shall prorate the same on a daily basis for a short taxable year and for the taxable year ending with the Recipient's death.

4. Distribution to Charity. Upon the death of the Recipient, the Trustee shall distribute all of the then principal and income of the Trust (other than any amount due the Recipient or the Recipient's estate under the provisions above) to _____ (hereinafter referred to as "the Charitable Organization"). If the Charitable Organization is not an organization described in sections 170(c) and 2055(a) of the Code at the time when any principal or income of the Trust is to be distributed to it, then the Trustee shall distribute such principal or income to such one or more organizations described in sections 170(c) and 2055 (a) as the Trustee shall select in its sole discretion.

5. Additional Contributions. No additional contributions shall be made to the Trust after the initial contribution. The initial contribution, however, shall be deemed to consist of all property passing to the Trust by reason of my death.

6. Prohibited Transactions. The Trustee shall make distributions at such time and in such manner as not to subject the Trust to tax under section 4942 of the Code. Except for the payment of the unitrust amount to the Recipient, the Trustee shall not engage in any act of self-dealing, as defined in section 4941(d), and shall not make any taxable expenditures, as defined in section 4945(d). The Trustee shall not make any investments that jeopardize the charitable purpose of the Trust, within the meaning of section 4944 and the regulations thereunder, or retain any excess business holdings, within the meaning of section 4943(c).

7. Taxable Year. The taxable year of the Trust shall be the calendar year.

8. Governing Law. The operation of the Trust shall be governed by the laws of the State of _____. The Trustee, however, is prohibited from exercising any power or discretion granted under said laws that would be inconsistent with the qualification of the Trust under section 664(d)(2) and (3) of the Code and the corresponding regulations.

9. Limited Power of Amendment. The Trustee shall have the power, acting alone, to amend the Trust in any manner required for the sole purpose of ensuring that the Trust qualifies and continues to qualify as a charitable remainder unitrust within the meaning of section 664(d)(2) and (3) of the Code.

10. Investment of Trust Assets. Nothing herein shall be construed to restrict the Trustee from investing the Trust assets in a manner that could result in the annual realization of a reasonable amount of income or gain from the sale or disposition of Trust assets.

SECTION 8.   SAMPLE TESTAMENTARY CHARITABLE REMAINDER UNITRUST: TWO LIVES, CONSECUTIVE INTERESTS

All the rest, residue, and remainder of my property and estate, real and personal, of whatever nature and wherever situated. [Alternatively, if not a residuary bequest, describe or identify the bequest.] I give, devise, and bequeath to my Trustee in trust. It being my intention to establish a charitable remainder unitrust within the meaning of section 8 of Rev. Proc. 90-31 and section 664(d)(2) and (3) of the Internal Revenue Code (hereinafter referred to as "the Code"), such Trust shall be known as the _____ Charitable Remainder Unitrust and I hereby designate _____ as the initial Trustee. [Alternate or successor trustees may also be designated if desired.]

1. Payment of Unitrust Amount. In each taxable year of the Trust, the Trustee shall pay to [a living individual] during his or her lifetime, and after his or her death, to [a living individual] (hereinafter referred to as "the Recipients"), for such time as he or she survives, a unitrust amount equal to the lesser of: (a) the Trust income for the taxable year, as defined in section 643(b) of the Code and the regulations thereunder, and (b) [at least 5] percent of the net fair market value of the assets of the Trust valued as of the first day of each taxable year of the Trust (the "valuation date"). The unitrust amount for any year shall also include any amount of Trust income for such year that is in excess of the amount required to be distributed under (b) (above) to the extent that the aggregate of the amounts paid in prior years was less than the aggregate of the amounts computed as [same percentage as in (b) above] percent of the net fair market value of the Trust assets on the valuation dates.

The unitrust amount shall be paid in quarterly installments. Any income of the Trust for a taxable year in excess of the unitrust amount shall be added to principal. If for any year the net fair market value of the Trust assets is incorrectly determined, then within a reasonable period after the value is finally determined for federal tax purposes, the Trustee shall pay to the Recipients (in the case of an undervaluation) or receive from the Recipients (in the case of an overvaluation) an amount equal to the difference between the unitrust amount properly payable and the unitrust amount actually paid.

2.   Deferral Provision. The obligation to pay the unitrust amount shall commence with the date of my death, but payment of the unitrust amount may be deferred from such date until the end of the taxable year of the Trust in which occurs the complete funding of the Trust. Within a reasonable time after the end of the taxable year in which the complete funding of the Trust occurs, the Trustee must pay to the Recipients (in the case of an underpayment) or receive from the Recipients (in the case of an overpayment) the difference between: (1) any unitrust amounts actually paid, plus interest compounded annually, computed for any period at the rate of interest that the federal income tax regulations under section 664 of Code prescribe for the trust for such computation for such period; and (2) the unitrust amounts payable, plus interest compounded annually, computed for any period at the rate of interest that the federal income tax regulations under section 664 of Code prescribe for the Trust for such computation for such period.

3.   Proration of the Unitrust Amount. In determining the unitrust amount, the Trustee shall prorate the same on a daily basis for a short taxable year and for the taxable year ending with the survivor Recipient's death.

4.   Distribution to Charity. Upon the death of the survivor Recipient, the Trustee shall distribute all of the then principal and income of the Trust (other than any amount due either of the Recipients or their estates under the provisions above) to _____ (hereinafter referred to as "the Charitable Organization"). If the Charitable Organization is not an organization described in sections 170(c) and 2055(a) of the Code at the time when any principal or income of the Trust is to be distributed to it, then the Trustee shall distribute such principal or income to such one or more organizations described in sections 170(c) and 2055(a) as the Trustee shall select in its sole discretion.

5.   Additional Contributions. No additional contributions shall be made to the Trust after the initial contribution. The initial contribution, however, shall be deemed to consist of all property passing to the Trust by reason of my death.

6. Prohibited Transactions. The Trustee shall make distributions at such time and in such manner as not to subject the Trust to tax under section 4942 of the Code. Except for the payment of the unitrust amount to the Recipients, the Trustee shall not engage in any act of self-dealing, as defined in section 4941(d), and shall not make any taxable expenditures, as defined in section 4945(d). The Trustee shall not make any investments that jeopardize the charitable purpose of the Trust, within the meaning of section 4944 and the regulations thereunder, or retain any excess business holdings, within the meaning of section 4943(c).

7. Taxable Year. The taxable year of the Trust shall be the calendar year.

8. Governing Law. The operation of the Trust shall be governed by the laws of the State of _____. The Trustee, however, is prohibited from exercising any power or discretion granted under said laws that would be inconsistent with the qualification of the Trust under section 664(d)(2) and (3) of the Code and the corresponding regulations.

9. Limited Power of Amendment. The Trustee shall have the power, acting alone, to amend the Trust in any manner required for the sole purpose of ensuring that the Trust qualifies and continues to qualify as a charitable remainder unitrust within the meaning of section 664(d)(2) and (3) of the Code.

10. Investment of Trust Assets. Nothing herein shall be construed to restrict the Trustee from investing the Trust assets in a manner that could result in the annual realization of a reasonable amount of income or gain from the sale or disposition of Trust assets.

SECTION 9. SAMPLE TESTAMENTARY CHARITABLE REMAINDER UNITRUST: TWO LIVES, CONCURRENT AND CONSECUTIVE INTERESTS

All the rest, residue, and remainder of my property and estate, real and personal, of whatever nature and wherever situated, [Alternatively, if not a residuary bequest, describe or identify the bequest.] I give, devise, and bequeath to my Trustee in trust. It being my intention to establish a charitable remainder unitrust within the meaning of section 9 of Rev. Proc. 90-31 and section 664(d)(2) and (3) of the Internal Revenue Code (hereinafter referred to as "the Code"), such Trust shall be known as the _____ Charitable Remainder Unitrust and I hereby designate _____ as the initial Trustee. [Alternate or successor trustees may also be designated if desired.]

1.   Payment of Unitrust Amount. In each taxable year of the Trust, the Trustee shall pay to [a living individual] and [a living individual] (hereinafter referred to as "the Recipients"), in equal shares during their lifetimes, a unitrust amount equal to the lesser of: (a) the Trust income for the taxable year, as defined in section 643(b) of the Code and the regulations thereunder, and (b) [at least 5] percent of the net fair market value of the assets of the Trust valued as of the first day of each taxable year of the Trust (the "valuation date"). The unitrust amount for any year shall also include any amount of Trust income for such year that is in excess of the amount required to be distributed under (b) (above) to the extent that the aggregate of the amounts paid in prior years was less than the aggregate of the amounts computed as [same percentage as in (b) above] percent of the net fair market value of the trust assets on the valuation dates.

Upon the death of the first of the Recipients to die, the survivor Recipient shall be entitled to receive the entire unitrust amount. The unitrust amount shall be paid in quarterly installments. Any income of the Trust for a taxable year in excess of the unitrust amount and which is not paid pursuant to the second preceding sentence shall be added to principal. If for any year the net fair market value of the Trust assets is incorrectly determined, then within a reasonable period after the value is finally determined for federal tax purposes, the Trustee shall pay to the Recipients (in the case of an undervaluation) or receive from the Recipients (in the case of an overvaluation) an amount equal to the difference between the unitrust amount properly payable and the unitrust amount actually paid.

2.   Deferral Provision. The obligation to pay the unitrust amount shall commence with the date of my death, but payment of the unitrust amount may be deferred from such date until the end of the taxable year of the Trust in which occurs the complete funding of the Trust. Within a reasonable time after the end of the taxable year in which the complete funding of the Trust occurs, the Trustee must pay to the Recipients (in the case of an underpayment) or receive from the Recipients (in the case of an overpayment) the difference between: (1) any unitrust amounts actually paid, plus interest compounded annually, computed for any period at the rate of interest that the federal income tax regulations under section 664 of the Code prescribe for the Trust for such computation for such period; and (2) the unitrust amounts payable, plus interest compounded annually,

computed for any period at the rate of interest that the federal income tax regulations under section 664 of the Code prescribe for the Trust for such computation for such period.

3. Proration of the Unitrust Amount. In determining the unitrust amount, the Trustee shall prorate the same on a daily basis for a short taxable year and for the taxable year ending with the survivor Recipient's death.

4. Distribution to Charity. Upon the death of the survivor Recipient, the Trustee shall distribute all of the then principal and income of the Trust (other than any amount due either of the Recipients or their estates under the provisions above) to _____ (hereinafter referred to as "the Charitable Organization"). If the Charitable Organization is not an organization described in sections 170(c) and 2055(a) of the Code at the time when any principal or income of the Trust is to be distributed to it, then the Trustee shall distribute such principal or income to such one or more organizations described in sections 170(c) and 2055(a) as the Trustee shall select in its sole discretion.

5. Additional Contributions. No additional contributions shall be made to the Trust after the initial contribution. The initial contribution, however, shall be deemed to consist of all property passing to the Trust by reason of my death.

6. Prohibited Transactions. The Trustee shall make distributions at such time and in such manner as not to subject the Trust to tax under section 4942 of the Code. Except for the payment of the unitrust amount to the Recipients, the Trustee shall not engage in any act of self-dealing, as defined in section 4941(d), and shall not make any taxable expenditures, as defined in section 4945(d). The Trustee shall not make any investments that jeopardize the charitable purpose of the Trust, within the meaning of section 4944 and the regulations thereunder, or retain any excess business holdings, within the meaning of section 4943(c).

7. Taxable Year. The taxable year of the Trust shall be the calendar year.

8. Governing Law. The operation of the Trust shall be governed by the laws of the State of _____. The Trustee, however, is prohibited from exercising any power or discretion granted under said laws that would be inconsistent with the qualification of the Trust under section 664(d)(2) and (3) of the Code and the corresponding regulations.

9. Limited Power of Amendment. The Trustee shall have the

power, acting alone, to amend the Trust in any manner required for the sole purpose of ensuring that the Trust qualifies and continues to qualify as a charitable remainder unitrust within the meaning of section 664(d)(2) and (3) of the Code.

10. Investment of Trust Assets. Nothing herein shall be construed to restrict the Trustee from investing the Trust assets in a manner that could result in the annual realization of a reasonable amount of income or gain from the sale or disposition of Trust assets.

SECTION 10. EFFECTIVE DATE

This revenue procedure is effective on and after June 18, 1990, the date of publication of this revenue procedure in the Internal Revenue Bulletin.

In 1990, the IRS issued five sample forms of trust that qualify as charitable remainder annuity trusts (Rev. Proc. 90-32, 1990-1 C.B. 546). The full text of this document is as follows:

Rev. Proc. 90-32

SECTION 1. PURPOSE

This revenue procedure makes available five sample forms of trust that meet the requirements for a charitable remainder annuity trust as described in section 664(d)(1) of the Internal Revenue Code.

SECTION 2. BACKGROUND

The Internal Revenue Service receives and responds to requests for rulings dealing with the qualification of trusts as charitable remainder trusts and the availability of deductions for contributions made to such trusts. In many of these requests, the trust instruments and charitable objectives are very similar. Consequently, in order to provide a service to taxpayers and to save the time and expense involved in requesting and processing a ruling on a proposed charitable remainder annuity trust, this revenue procedure allows taxpayers who make transfers to a trust that substantially follows one of the sample forms of trust contained herein to be assured that the Service will recognize the trust as meeting all of the requirements of a charitable remainder annuity trust, provided that the trust operates in a manner consistent with the terms of the instrument creating the trust and provided it is a valid trust under applicable local law.

SECTION 3.   SCOPE AND OBJECTIVE

Section 4 of Rev. Proc. 89-21, 1989-1 C.B. 842, provides a sample form of trust for an inter vivos charitable remainder annuity trust providing for annuity payments during one life that meets all of the applicable requirements of section 664(d)(1) of the Code. This revenue procedure amplifies Rev. Proc. 89-21 by providing the following additional sample forms of trust.

Section 4—Sample Inter Vivos Charitable Remainder Annuity Trust: Two Lives, Consecutive Interests;

Section 5—Sample Inter Vivos Charitable Remainder Annuity Trust: Two Lives, Concurrent and Consecutive Interests;

Section 6—Sample Testamentary Charitable Remainder Annuity Trust: One Life;

Section 7—Sample Testamentary Charitable Remainder Annuity Trust: Two Lives, Consecutive Interests; and

Section 8—Sample Testamentary Charitable Remainder Annuity Trust: Two Lives, Concurrent and Consecutive Interests.

In all cases, the termination of the life interests must be followed by a distribution of the trust assets to the charitable remainder beneficiary, and the trust must be a valid trust under applicable local law.

If the trust provisions are substantially similar to those in one of the samples provided in sections 4 through 8 of this revenue procedure or in section 4 of Rev. Proc. 89-21, the Service will recognize the trust as satisfying all of the applicable requirements of section 664(d)(1) of the Code and the corresponding regulations. A document will be considered to be substantially similar to one of the samples even though, for example, the wording is varied to comport with local law and practice as necessary to create trusts, define legal relationships, pass property by bequest, provide for the appointment of alternative and successor trustees, or designate alternative charitable remaindermen. Moreover, for transfers to a qualifying charitable remainder annuity trust, the remainder interest will be deductible under sections 170(f)(2)(A), 2055(e)(2)(A), and 2522(c)(2)(A) for income, estate, and gift tax purposes, respectively, if the charitable remainder beneficiary otherwise meets all of the requirements of those provisions. Therefore, it will not be necessary for a taxpayer to request a ruling on the qualification of a substantially similar trust. A trust that contains substantive provisions in addition to those provided by sections 4 through 8 of this revenue procedure or by section 4 of Rev. Proc. 89-21 (other than provisions necessary to establish a valid trust under applicable local law) or that omits any of these provisions will not necessarily be disqualified, but it will not be assured of qualification under the provisions of this revenue procedure.

SECTION 4.   SAMPLE INTER VIVOS CHARITABLE REMAINDER ANNUITY TRUST: TWO LIVES, CONSECUTIVE INTERESTS

On this _____ day of _____, 19 _____, I, _____ (hereinafter referred to as "the Donor"), desiring to establish a charitable remainder annuity trust, within the meaning of section 4 of Rev. Proc. 90-32 and section 664(d)(1) of the Internal Revenue Code (hereinafter referred to as "the Code") hereby create the _____ Charitable Remainder Annuity Trust and designate _____ as the initial Trustee. [Alternate or successor trustees may also be designated if desired.]

1.   Funding of Trust. The Donor transfers to the Trustee the property described in Schedule A, and the Trustee accepts such property and agrees to hold, manage, and distribute such property of the Trust under the terms set forth in this Trust instrument.

2.   Payment of Annuity Amount. In each taxable year of the Trust, the Trustee shall pay to [a living individual] during his or her lifetime and, after his or her death, to [a living individual] (hereinafter referred to as "the Recipients"), for such time as he or she survives, an annuity amount equal to [at least 5] percent of the net fair market value of the assets of the Trust as of the date of this Trust. The annuity amount shall be paid in equal quarterly amounts from income and, to the extent that income is not sufficient, from principal. Any income of the Trust for a taxable year in excess of the annuity amount shall be added to principal. If the net fair market value of the Trust assets is incorrectly determined, then within a reasonable period after the value is finally determined for federal tax purposes, the Trustee shall pay to the Recipients (in the case of an undervaluation) or receive from the Recipients (in the case of an overvaluation) an amount equal to the difference between the annuity amount(s) properly payable and the annuity amount(s) actually paid.

3.   Payment of Federal Estate Taxes and State Death Taxes. The lifetime annuity interest of the second Recipient will take effect upon the death of the first Recipient only if the second Recipient furnishes the funds for payment of any federal estate taxes or state death taxes

for which the Trustee may be liable upon the death of the first Recipient. [This provision is mandatory only if all or a portion of the trust may be subject to such taxes on the death of the first recipient.]

4.   Proration of the Annuity Amount. In determining the annuity amount, the Trustee shall prorate the same on a daily basis for a short taxable year and for the taxable year ending with the survivor Recipient's death.

5.   Distribution to Charity. Upon the death of the survivor Recipient, the Trustee shall distribute all of the then principal and income of the Trust (other than any amount due either of the Recipients or their estates under the provisions above) to _____ (hereinafter referred to as "the Charitable Organization"). If the Charitable Organization is not an organization described in sections 170(c), 2055(a), and 2522(a) of the Code at the time when any principal or income of the Trust is to be distributed to it, then the Trustee shall distribute such principal or income to such one or more organizations described in sections 170(c), 2055(a), and 2522(a) as the Trustee shall select in its sole discretion.

6.   Additional Contributions. No additional contributions shall be made to the Trust after the initial contribution.

7.   Prohibited Transactions. The Trustee shall make distributions at such time and in such manner as not to subject the Trust to tax under section 4942 of the Code. Except for the payment of the annuity amount to the Recipients, the Trustee shall not engage in any act of self-dealing, as defined in section 4941(d), and shall not make any taxable expenditures, as defined in section 4945(d). The Trustee shall not make any investments that jeopardize the charitable purpose of the Trust, within the meaning of section 4944 and the regulations thereunder, or retain any excess business holdings, within the meaning of section 4943(c).

8.   Taxable Year. The taxable year of the Trust shall be the calendar year.

9.   Governing Law. The operation of the Trust shall be governed by the laws of the State of _____. The Trustee, however, is prohibited from exercising any power or discretion granted under said laws that would be inconsistent with the qualification of the Trust under section 664(d)(1) of the Code and the corresponding regulations.

10.   Limited Power of Amendment. The Trust is irrevocable. The Trustee, however, shall have the power, acting alone, to amend the

Trust in any manner required for the sole purpose of ensuring that the Trust qualifies and continues to qualify as a charitable remainder annuity trust within the meaning of section 664(d)(1) of the Code.

11.   Investment of Trust Assets. Nothing in this Trust instrument shall be construed to restrict the Trustee from investing the Trust assets in a manner that could result in the annual realization of a reasonable amount of income or gain from the sale or disposition of Trust assets.

SECTION 5.   SAMPLE INTER VIVOS CHARITABLE REMAINDER ANNUITY TRUST: TWO LIVES, CONCURRENT AND CONSECUTIVE INTERESTS

On this _____ day of _____, 19 _____, I, _____ (hereinafter referred to as "the Donor"), desiring to establish a charitable remainder annuity trust, within the meaning of section 5 of Rev. Proc. 90-32 and section 664(d)(1) of the Internal Revenue Code (hereinafter referred to as "the Code") hereby create the _____ Charitable Remainder Annuity Trust and designate _____ as the initial Trustee. [Alternate or successor trustees may also be designated if desired.]

1.   Funding of Trust. The Donor transfers to the Trustee the property described in Schedule A, and the Trustee accepts such property and agrees to hold, manage, and distribute such property of the Trust under the terms set forth in this Trust instrument.

2.   Payment of Annuity Amount. In each taxable year of the Trust, the Trustee shall pay to [a living individual] and [a living individual] (hereinafter referred to as "the Recipients"), in equal shares during their lifetimes, an annuity amount equal to [at least 5] percent of the net fair market value of the assets of the Trust as of the date of this Trust. Upon the death of the first of the Recipients to die, the survivor Recipient shall be entitled to receive the entire annuity amount. The annuity amount shall be paid in equal quarterly amounts from income and, to the extent that income is not sufficient, from principal. Any income of the Trust for a taxable year in excess of the annuity amount shall be added to principal. If the net fair market value of the Trust assets is incorrectly determined, then within a reasonable period after the value is finally determined for federal tax purposes, the Trustee shall pay to the Recipients (in the case of an undervaluation) or receive from the Recipients (in the case of an overvaluation) an amount equal to the difference between the

annuity amount(s) properly payable and the annuity amount(s) actually paid.

3.   Payment of Federal Estate Taxes and State Death Taxes. The lifetime annuity interest of the survivor Recipient will continue in effect upon the death of the first Recipient to die only if the survivor Recipient furnishes the funds for payment of any federal estate taxes or state death taxes for which the Trustee may be liable upon the death of the first Recipient to die. [This provision is mandatory only if all or a portion of the trust may be subject to such taxes on the death of the first recipient to die.]

4.   Proration of the Annuity Amount. In determining the annuity amount, the Trustee shall prorate the same on a daily basis for a short taxable year and for the taxable year ending with the survivor Recipient's death.

5.   Distribution to Charity. Upon the death of the survivor Recipient, the Trustee shall distribute all of the then principal and income of the Trust (other than any amount due either of the Recipients or their estates under the provisions above) to _____ (hereinafter referred to as "the Charitable Organization"). If the Charitable Organization is not an organization described in sections 170(c), 2055(a), and 2522(a) of the Code at the time when any principal or income of the Trust is to be distributed to it, then the Trustee shall distribute such principal or income to such one or more organizations described in sections 170(c), 2055(a), and 2522(a) as the Trustee shall select in its sole discretion.

6.   Additional Contributions. No additional contributions shall be made to the Trust after the initial contribution.

7.   Prohibited Transactions. The Trustee shall make distributions at such time and in such manner as not to subject the Trust to tax under section 4942 of the Code. Except for the payment of the annuity amount to the Recipients, the Trustee shall not engage in any act of self-dealing, as defined in section 4941(d), and shall not make any taxable expenditures, as defined in section 4945(d). The Trustee shall not make any investments that jeopardize the charitable purpose of the Trust, within the meaning of section 4944 and the regulations thereunder, or retain any excess business holdings, within the meaning of section 4943(c).

8.   Taxable Year. The taxable year of the Trust shall be the calendar year.

9.   Governing Law. The operation of the Trust shall be governed by the laws of the State of _____. The Trustee, however, is

prohibited from exercising any power or discretion granted under said laws that would be inconsistent with the qualification of the Trust under section 664(d)(1) of the Code and the corresponding regulations.

10.   Limited Power of Amendment. The Trust is irrevocable. The Trustee, however, shall have the power, acting alone, to amend the Trust in any manner required for the sole purpose of ensuring that the Trust qualifies and continues to qualify as a charitable remainder annuity trust within the meaning of section 664(d)(1) of the Code.

11.   Investment of Trust Assets. Nothing in this Trust instrument shall be construed to restrict the Trustee from investing the Trust assets in a manner that could result in the annual realization of a reasonable amount of income or gain from the sale or disposition of Trust assets.

SECTION 6.   SAMPLE TESTAMENTARY CHARITABLE REMAINDER ANNUITY TRUST: ONE LIFE

All the rest, residue and remainder of my property and estate, real and personal, of whatever nature and wherever situated, [Alternatively, if not a residuary bequest, describe or identify the bequest.] I give, devise and bequeath to my Trustee in trust. It being my intention to establish a charitable remainder annuity trust within the meaning of section 7 of Rev. Proc. 90-32 and section 664(d)(1) of the Internal Revenue Code (hereinafter referred to as "the Code"), such Trust shall be known as the _____ Charitable Remainder Annuity Trust and I hereby designate _____ as the initial Trustee. [Alternate or successor trustees may also be designated if desired.]

1.   Payment of Annuity Amount. In each taxable year of the Trust, the Trustee shall pay to [a living individual] during his or her lifetime, (hereinafter referred to as "the Recipient") during the Recipient's life an annuity amount equal to [at least 5] percent of the initial net fair market value of the assets passing in trust as finally determined for federal tax purposes, provided, however, that the payout percentage (as adjusted to reflect the timing and frequency of the annuity payments) shall not exceed the percentage that would result in a 5 percent probability that the Trust corpus will be exhausted before the death of the Recipient determined as of the date of my death (or the alternate valuation date, if applicable). [Note: The preceding sentence is one means of avoiding disallowance of the charitable deduction with respect to a charitable remainder annuity

trust for which there is a greater than 5 percent probability that the trust corpus will be exhausted before the death of the annuitant. See Rev. Rul. 77-374, 1977-2 C.B. 329.] The annuity amount shall be paid in equal quarterly amounts from income and, to the extent that income is not sufficient, from principal. Any income of the Trust for a taxable year in excess of the annuity amount shall be added to principal. If the net fair market value of the Trust assets is incorrectly determined, then within a reasonable period after the value is finally determined for federal tax purposes, the Trustee shall pay to the Recipient (in the case of an undervaluation) or receive from the Recipient (in the case of an overvaluation) an amount equal to the difference between the annuity amount(s) properly payable and the annuity amount(s) actually paid.

2.   Deferral Provision. The obligation to pay the annuity amount shall commence with the date of my death, but payment of the annuity amount may be deferred from such date until the end of the taxable year of the Trust in which occurs the complete funding of the Trust. Within a reasonable time after the end of the taxable year in which the complete funding of the Trust occurs, the Trustee must pay to the Recipient (in the case of an underpayment) or receive from the Recipient (in the case of an overpayment) the difference between: (1) any annuity amounts actually paid, plus interest, compounded annually, computed for any period at the rate of interest that the federal income tax regulations under section 664 of the Code prescribe for the Trust for such computation for such period; and (2) the annuity amounts payable, plus interest, compounded annually, computed for any period at the rate of interest that the federal income tax regulations under section 664 prescribe for the Trust for such computation for such period.

3.   Proration of the Annuity Amount. In determining the annuity amount, the Trustee shall prorate the same on a daily basis for a short taxable year and for the taxable year ending with the Recipient's death.

4.   Distribution to Charity. Upon the death of the Recipient, the Trustee shall distribute all of the then principal and income of the Trust (other than any amount due the Recipient or the Recipient's estate under the provisions above) to _____ (hereinafter referred to as "the Charitable Organization"). If the Charitable Organization is not an organization described in sections 170(c) and 2055(a) of the Code at the time when any principal or income of the Trust is to be distributed to it, then the Trustee shall distribute such principal or

income to such one or more organizations described in sections 170(c) and 2055(a) as the Trustee shall select in its sole discretion.

5.   Additional Contributions. No additional contributions shall be made to the Trust after the initial contribution. The initial contribution, however, shall be deemed to consist of all property passing to the Trust by reason of my death.

6.   Prohibited Transactions. The Trustee shall make distributions at such time and in such manner as not to subject the Trust to tax under section 4942 of the Code. Except for the payment of the annuity amount to the Recipient, the Trustee shall not engage in any act of self-dealing, as defined in section 4941(d), and shall not make any taxable expenditures, as defined in section 4945(d). The Trustee shall not make any investments that jeopardize the charitable purpose of the Trust, within the meaning of section 4944 and the regulations thereunder, or retain any excess business holdings, within the meaning of section 4943(c).

7.   Taxable Year. The taxable year of the Trust shall be the calendar year.

8.   Governing Law. The operation of the Trust shall be governed by the laws of the State of _____. The Trustee, however, is prohibited from exercising any power or discretion granted under said laws that would be inconsistent with the qualification of the Trust under section 664(d)(1) of the Code and the corresponding regulations.

9.   Limited Power of Amendment. The Trustee shall have the power, acting alone, to amend the Trust in any manner required for the sole purpose of ensuring that the Trust qualifies and continues to qualify as a charitable remainder annuity trust within the meaning of section 664(d)(1) of the Code.

10.   Investment of Trust Assets. Nothing herein shall be construed to restrict the Trustee from investing the Trust assets in a manner that could result in the annual realization of a reasonable amount of income or gain from the sale or disposition of Trust assets.

SECTION 7.   SAMPLE TESTAMENTARY CHARITABLE REMAINDER ANNUITY TRUST: TWO LIVES, CONSECUTIVE INTERESTS

All the rest, residue and remainder of my property and estate, real and personal, of whatever nature and wherever situated, [Alternatively, if not a residuary bequest, describe or identify the bequest.] I give, devise and bequeath to my Trustee in trust. It being my intention to establish a charitable remainder annuity trust within the meaning of section 7 of Rev. Proc. 90-32 and section 664(d)(1) of the Internal Revenue Code (hereinafter referred to as "the Code"), such Trust shall be known as the _____ Charitable Remainder Annuity Trust and I hereby designate _____ as the initial Trustee. [Alternate or successor trustees may also be designated if desired.]

1.   Payment of Annuity Amount. In each taxable year of the Trust, the Trustee shall pay to [a living individual] during his or her lifetime, and after his or her death, to [a living individual] (hereinafter referred to as "the Recipients"), for such time as he or she survives, an annuity amount equal to [at least 5] percent of the initial net fair market value of the assets passing in trust as finally determined for federal tax purposes, provided, however, that the payout percentage (as adjusted to reflect the timing and frequency of the annuity payments) shall not exceed the percentage that would result in a 5 percent probability that the Trust corpus will be exhausted before the death of the survivor Recipient determined as of the date of my death (or the alternate valuation date, if applicable). [Note: The preceding sentence is one means of avoiding disallowance of the charitable deduction with respect to a charitable remainder annuity trust for which there is a greater than 5 percent probability that the trust corpus will be exhausted before the death of the annuitant. See Rev. Rul. 77-374, 1977-2 C.B. 329.] The annuity amount shall be paid in equal quarterly amounts from income and, to the extent that income is not sufficient, from principal. Any income of the Trust for a taxable year in excess of the annuity amount shall be added to principal. If the net fair market value of the Trust assets is incorrectly determined, then within a reasonable period after the value is finally determined for federal tax purposes, the Trustee shall pay to the Recipients (in the case of an undervaluation) or receive from the Recipients (in the case of an overvaluation) an amount equal to the difference between the annuity amount(s) properly payable and the annuity amount(s) actually paid.

2.   Deferral Provision. The obligation to pay the annuity amount shall commence with the date of my death, but payment of the annuity amount may be deferred from such date until the end of the taxable year of the Trust in which occurs the complete funding of the Trust. Within a reasonable time after the end of the taxable year in which the complete funding of the Trust occurs, the Trustee must pay to the Recipients (in the case of an underpayment) or receive from the

Recipients (in the case of an overpayment) the difference between: (1) any annuity amounts actually paid, plus interest, compounded annually, computed for any period at the rate of interest that the federal income tax regulations under section 664 of the Code prescribe for the Trust for such computation for such period; and (2) the annuity amounts payable, plus interest, compounded annually, computed for any period at the rate of interest that the federal income tax regulations under section 664 prescribe for the Trust for such computation for such period.

3. Proration of the Annuity Amount. In determining the annuity amount, the Trustee shall prorate the same on a daily basis for a short taxable year and for the taxable year ending with the survivor Recipient's death.

4. Distribution to Charity. Upon the death of the survivor Recipient, the Trustee shall distribute all of the then principal and income of the Trust (other than any amount due either of the Recipients or their estates, under the provisions above) to _____ (hereinafter referred to as "the Charitable Organization"). If the Charitable Organization is not an organization described in sections 170(c) and 2055(a) of the Code at the time when any principal or income of the Trust is to be distributed to it, then the Trustee shall distribute such principal or income to such one or more organizations described in sections 170(c) and 2055(a) as the Trustee shall select in its sole discretion.

5. Additional Contributions. No additional contributions shall be made to the Trust after the initial contribution. The initial contribution, however, shall be deemed to consist of all property passing to the Trust by reason of my death.

6. Prohibited Transactions. The Trustee shall make distributions at such time and in such manner as not to subject the Trust to tax under section 4942 of the Code. Except for the payment of the annuity amount to the Recipients, the Trustee shall not engage in any act of self-dealing, as defined in section 4941(d), and shall not make any taxable expenditures, as defined in section 4945(d). The Trustee shall not make any investments that jeopardize the charitable purpose of the Trust, within the meaning of section 4944 and the regulations thereunder, or retain any excess business holdings, within the meaning of section 4943(c).

7. Taxable Year. The taxable year of the Trust shall be the calendar year.

8. Governing Law. The operation of the Trust shall be governed

by the laws of the State of _____. The Trustee, however, is prohibited from exercising any power or discretion granted under said laws that would be inconsistent with the qualification of the Trust under section 664(d)(1) of the Code and the corresponding regulations.

9.   Limited Power of Amendment. The Trustee shall have the power, acting alone, to amend the Trust in any manner required for the sole purpose of ensuring that the Trust qualifies and continues to qualify as a charitable remainder annuity trust within the meaning of section 664(d)(1) of the Code.

10.   Investment of Trust Assets. Nothing herein shall be construed to restrict the Trustee from investing the Trust assets in a manner that could result in the annual realization of a reasonable amount of income or gain from the sale or disposition of Trust assets.

SECTION 8.   SAMPLE TESTAMENTARY CHARITABLE REMAINDER ANNUITY TRUST: TWO LIVES, CONCURRENT AND CONSECUTIVE INTERESTS

All the rest, residue and remainder of my property and estate, real and personal, of whatever nature and wherever situated, [Alternatively, if not a residuary bequest, describe or identify the bequest.] I give, devise and bequeath to my Trustee in trust. It being my intention to establish a charitable remainder annuity trust within the meaning of section 8 of Rev. Proc. 90-32 and section 664(d)(1) of the Internal Revenue Code (hereinafter referred to as "the Code"), such Trust shall be known as the _____ Charitable Remainder Annuity Trust and I hereby designate _____ as the initial Trustee. [Alternate or successor trustees may also be designated if desired.]

1.   Payment of Annuity Amount. In each taxable year of the Trust, the Trustee shall pay to [a living individual] and [a living individual] (hereinafter referred to as "the Recipients"), in equal shares during their lifetimes, an annuity amount equal to [at least 5] percent of the initial net fair market value of the assets passing in trust as finally determined for federal tax purposes, provided, however, that the payout percentage (as adjusted to reflect the timing and frequency of the annuity payments) shall not exceed the percentage that would result in a 5 percent probability that the Trust corpus will be exhausted before the death of the survivor Recipient determined as of the date of my death (or the alternate valuation date, if applicable). [Note: The preceding sentence is one means of avoiding

disallowance of the charitable deduction with respect to a charitable remainder annuity trust for which there is a greater than 5 percent probability that the trust corpus will be exhausted before the death of the annuitant. See Rev. Rul. 77-374, 1977-2 C.B. 329.] Upon the death of the first of the Recipients to die, the survivor Recipient shall be entitled to receive the entire annuity amount. The annuity amount shall be paid in equal quarterly amounts from income and, to the extent that income is not sufficient, from principal. Any income of the Trust for a taxable year in excess of the annuity amount shall be added to principal. If the net fair market value of the Trust assets is incorrectly determined, then within a reasonable period after the value is finally determined for federal tax purposes, the Trustee shall pay to the Recipients (in the case of an undervaluation) or receive from the Recipients (in the case of an overvaluation) an amount equal to the difference between the annuity amount(s) properly payable and the annuity amount(s) actually paid.

2.   Deferral Provision. The obligation to pay the annuity amount shall commence with the date of my death, but payment of the annuity amount may be deferred from such date until the end of the taxable year of the Trust in which occurs the complete funding of the Trust. Within a reasonable time after the end of the taxable year in which the complete funding of the Trust occurs, the Trustee must pay to the Recipients (in the case of an underpayment) or receive from the Recipients (in the case of an overpayment) the difference between: (1) any annuity amounts actually paid, plus interest, compounded annually, computed for any period at the rate of interest that the federal income tax regulations under section 664 of the Code prescribe for the Trust for such computation for such period; and (2) the annuity amounts payable, plus interest, compounded annually, computed for any period at the rate of interest that the federal income tax regulations under section 664 prescribe for the Trust for such computation for such period.

3.   Proration of the Annuity Amount. In determining the annuity amount, the Trustee shall prorate the same on a daily basis for a short taxable year and for the taxable year ending with the survivor Recipient's death.

4.   Distribution to Charity. Upon the death of the survivor Recipient, the Trustee shall distribute all of the then principal and income of the Trust (other than any amount due either of the Recipients or their estates under the provisions above) to _____ (hereinafter referred to as "the Charitable Organization"). If the Charitable Orga-

nization is not an organization described in sections 170(c) and 2055(a) of the Code at the time when any principal or income of the Trust is to be distributed to it, then the Trustee shall distribute such principal or income to such one or more organizations described in sections 170(c) and 2055(a) as the Trustee shall select in its sole discretion.

5.   Additional Contributions. No additional contributions shall be made to the Trust after the initial contribution. The initial contribution, however, shall be deemed to consist of all property passing to the Trust by reason of my death.

6.   Prohibited Transactions. The Trustee shall make distributions at such time and in such manner as not to subject the Trust to tax under section 4942 of the Code. Except for the payment of the annuity amount to the Recipients, the Trustee shall not engage in any act of self-dealing, as defined in section 4941(d), and shall not make any taxable expenditures, as defined in section 4945(d). The Trustee shall not make any investments that jeopardize the charitable purpose of the Trust, within the meaning of section 4944 and the regulations thereunder, or retain any excess business holdings, within the meaning of section 4943(c).

7.   Taxable Year. The taxable year of the Trust shall be the calendar year.

8.   Governing Law. The operation of the Trust shall be governed by the laws of the State of _____. The Trustee, however, is prohibited from exercising any power or discretion granted under said laws that would be inconsistent with the qualification of the Trust under section 664(d)(1) of the Code and the corresponding regulations.

9.   Limited Power of Amendment. The Trustee shall have the power, acting alone, to amend the Trust in any manner required for the sole purpose of ensuring that the Trust qualifies and continues to qualify as a charitable remainder annuity trust within the meaning of section 664(d)(1) of the Code.

10.   Investment of Trust Assets. Nothing herein shall be construed to restrict the Trustee from investing the Trust assets in a manner that could result in the annual realization of a reasonable amount of income or gain from the sale or disposition of Trust assets.

SECTION 9.   EFFECT ON OTHER REVENUE PROCEDURES

Rev. Proc. 89-21 is amplified.

SECTION 10.   EFFECTIVE DATE

This revenue procedure is effective on and after June 18, 1990, the date of publication of this revenue procedure in the Internal Revenue Bulletin.

Appendix F

Pooled Income Funds Prototype Instruments

In 1988, the IRS issued a sample form of declaration of trust and instruments of transfer that meet the requirements of a pooled income fund (Rev. Proc. 88-53, 1988-2 C.B. 712). The full text of this document is as follows:

Rev. Proc. 88-53

SECTION 1. PURPOSE

This revenue procedure makes available a sample form of declaration of trust and instruments of transfer that meet the requirements for a pooled income fund as described in section 642(c)(5) of the Internal Revenue Code.

SECTION 2. BACKGROUND

The Internal Revenue Service receives and responds to many requests for rulings dealing with the qualification of trusts as pooled income funds and the availability of deductions for contributions made to such trusts. In many of these requests, the trust instruments and charitable objectives are very similar. Consequently, in order to provide a service to taxpayers and to save the time and expense involved in requesting and processing a ruling on a proposed pooled income fund, taxpayers who make transfers to a trust that substantially follows the model trust instrument contained herein can be assured that the Service will recognize the trust as meeting all of the requirements of a qualified pooled income fund, provided the trust operates in a manner consistent with the terms of the trust instrument and provided it is a valid trust under applicable local law.

SECTION 3.   SCOPE AND OBJECTIVE

The sample declaration of trust and instruments of transfer made available by this revenue procedure meet all of the applicable requirements for a pooled income fund under section 642(c)(5) of the Code, if the trust document also creates a valid trust under local law. If the public charity responsible for the creation and maintenance of a pooled income fund makes reference in the trust instrument of the fund to this revenue procedure, and adopts substantially similar documents, the Service will recognize the trust documents as satisfying all of the applicable requirements of section 642(c)(5) of the Code and the corresponding regulations. Moreover, for transfers to a qualifying pooled income fund, the remainder interest will be deductible under sections 170(f)(2)(A), 2055(e)(2)(A), and 2522(c)(2)(A) of the Code for income, estate, and gift tax purposes, respectively. Therefore, it will not be necessary for a taxpayer to request a ruling as to the qualification of a substantially similar trust, and the Service generally will not issue such a ruling. See Rev. Proc. 88-54, page 16, this Bulletin.

SECTION 4.   SAMPLE DECLARATION OF TRUST

On this _____ day of _____, 19_____, the Board of Trustees of the _____ Public Charity (hereinafter referred to as "Public Charity") desiring to establish a pooled income fund within the meaning of Rev. Proc. 88-53 and section 642(c)(5) of the Internal Revenue Code (hereinafter referred to as "the Code"), hereby creates the _____ Public Charity Pooled Income Fund (hereinafter referred to as "the Fund") and designates _____ as the initial trustee to hold, manage, and distribute such property hereinafter transferred to and accepted by it as part of the Fund under the following terms and conditions.

1.   Gift of Remainder Interest. Each donor transferring property to the Fund shall contribute an irrevocable remainder interest in such property to Public Charity.

2.   Retention of Life Income Interest. Each donor transferring property to the Fund shall retain for himself or herself an income

interest in the property transferred, or create an income interest in such property for the life of one or more named beneficiaries, provided that each income beneficiary must be a living person at the time of the transfer of property to the Fund by the donor. If more than one beneficiary of the income interest is named, such beneficiaries may enjoy their shares concurrently and/or consecutively. Public Charity may also be designated as one of the beneficiaries of the income interest. The donor need not retain or create a life interest in all of the income from the property transferred to the Fund and any income not payable to an income beneficiary shall be contributed to, and within the taxable year of the Fund in which it is received paid to, Public Charity.

3. Commingling of Property. The property transferred to the Fund by each donor shall be commingled with, and invested or reinvested with, other property transferred to the Fund by other donors satisfying the requirements of this instrument and of section 642(c)(5) of the Code or corresponding provision of any subsequent federal tax law. The Fund shall not include property transferred under arrangements other than those specified in this instrument and satisfying the said provisions of the Code.

All or any portion of the assets of the Fund may, however, be invested or reinvested jointly with other properties not a part of the Fund that are held by, or for the use of, Public Charity. When joint investment or reinvestment occurs, detailed accounting records shall be maintained by the Trustee specifically identifying the portion of the jointly invested property owned by the Fund and the income earned by, and attributable to, such portion.

4. Prohibition Against Exempt Securities. The property transferred to the Fund by any donor shall not include any securities whose income is exempt from taxation under subtitle A of the Code or the corresponding provisions of any subsequent federal tax law. The Trustee of the Fund shall not accept or invest in such securities as part of the assets of the Fund.

5. Maintenance by Public Charity. Public Charity shall always maintain the Fund or exercise control, directly or indirectly, over the Fund. Public Charity shall always have the power to remove any Trustee or Trustees and to designate a new Trustee or Trustees.

6. Prohibition Against Donor or Beneficiary Serving as Trustee. The Fund shall not have as a Trustee a donor to the Fund or a beneficiary (other than Public Charity) of an income interest in any property transferred to the Fund. No donor or beneficiary (other

than Public Charity) shall have, directly or indirectly, general responsibilities with respect to the Fund that are ordinarily exercised by a Trustee.

7.   Income of Beneficiary to be Based on Rate of Return of Fund. The taxable year of the Fund shall be the calendar year. The Trustee shall pay income to each beneficiary entitled thereto in any taxable year of the Fund in the amount determined by the rate of return earned by the Fund for the year with respect to the beneficiary's income interest. Payments must be made at least once in the year in which the income is earned. Until the Trustee determines that payments shall be made more or less frequently or at other times, the Trustee shall make income payments to the beneficiary or beneficiaries entitled to them in four quarterly payments on or about March 31, June 30, September 30, and December 31 of each year. An adjusting payment, if necessary, will be made during the taxable year or within the first 65 days following its close to bring the total payment to the actual income to which the beneficiary or beneficiaries are entitled for that year.

On each transfer of property by a donor to the Fund, there shall be assigned to the beneficiary or beneficiaries of the income interest retained or created in the property the number of units of participation equal to the number obtained by dividing the fair market value of the property transferred by the fair market value of a unit in the Fund immediately before the transfer. The fair market value of a unit in the Fund immediately before the transfer shall be determined by dividing the fair market value of all property in the Fund at that time by the number of units then in the Fund. The initial fair market value of a unit in the Fund shall be the fair market value of the property transferred to the Fund divided by the number of units assigned to the beneficiaries of the income interest in that property. All units in the Fund shall always have equal value.

If a transfer of property to the Fund by a donor occurs on other than a determination date, the number of units of participation assigned to the beneficiary or beneficiaries of the income interest in the property shall be determined by using the average fair market value of the property in the Fund immediately before the transfer, which shall be deemed to be the average of the fair market values of the property in the Fund on the determination dates immediately preceding and succeeding the date of transfer. For the purpose of determining the average fair market value, the property transferred by the donor and any other property transferred to the Fund between the preceding and succeeding dates, or on such succeeding date, shall be excluded. The fair market value of a unit in the Fund immediately before the transfer shall be determined by dividing the average fair market value of the property in the Fund at that time by the number of units then in the Fund. Units of participation assigned with respect to property transferred on other than a determination date shall be deemed to be assigned as of the date of the transfer.

A determination date means each day within a taxable year of the Fund on which a valuation is made of the property in the Fund. The property of the Fund shall be valued on January 1, April 1, July 1, and October 1 of each year; provided, however, that where such date falls on a Saturday, Sunday or legal holiday (as defined in section 7503 of the Code and the regulations thereunder), the valuation shall be made on the next succeeding day which is not a Saturday, Sunday or legal holiday.

The amount of income allocated to each unit of participation in the Fund shall be determined by dividing the income of the Fund for the taxable year by the outstanding number of units in the Fund at the end of the year, except that income shall be allocated to units outstanding during only part of the year by taking into consideration the period of time the units are outstanding during the year.

For purposes of this instrument, the term "income" has the same meaning as it does under section 643(b) of the Code or corresponding provision of any subsequent federal tax law and the regulations thereunder.

The income interest of any beneficiary of the Fund shall terminate with the last regular payment of income that was made before the death of the beneficiary. The Trustee of the Fund shall not be required to prorate any income payment to the date of the beneficiary's death.

8.   Termination of Life Income Interest. Upon the termination of the income interest of the designated beneficiary (or, in the case of successive income interests, the survivor of the designated beneficiaries) entitled to receive income pursuant to the terms of a transfer to the Fund, the Trustee shall sever from the Fund an amount equal to the value of the remainder interest in the property upon which the income interest is based. The value of the remainder interest for severance purposes shall be its value as of the date on which the last regular payment was made before the death of the beneficiary. The amount so severed from the Fund shall be paid to Public Charity. If at the time of severance of the remainder interest Public Charity has

ceased to exist or is not a public charity (an organization described in clauses (i) through (vi) of section 170(b)(1)(A) of the Code), the amount severed shall be paid to an organization selected by the Trustee that is a public charity.

9.   Prohibited Activities. The income of the Fund for each taxable year shall be distributed at such time and in such manner as not to subject the Fund to tax under section 4942 of the Code. Except for making the required payments to the life income beneficiaries, the Trustee shall not engage in any act of self-dealing as defined in section 4941(d) and shall not make any taxable expenditures as defined in section 4945(d). The Trustee shall not make any investments that jeopardize the charitable purpose of the Fund within the meaning of section 4944 or retain any excess business holdings within the meaning of section 4943.

10.   Depreciable or Depletable Assets. The Trustee shall not accept or invest in any depreciable or depletable assets.

11.   Incorporation by Reference. The provisions of this document may be, and are intended to be, incorporated by reference in any will, trust, or other instrument by means of which property is transferred to the Fund. Any property transferred to the Fund whereby an income interest is retained or created for the life of one or more named beneficiaries, where this document is not incorporated by reference, shall become a part of the Fund and shall be held and managed under the terms and conditions of this document, unless the instrument of transfer is inconsistent with such terms and conditions, in which case the Trustee shall not accept the property.

12.   Governing Law. The operation of the Fund shall be governed by the laws of the State of _____. However, the Trustee is prohibited from exercising any power or discretion granted under said laws that would be inconsistent with the qualification of the Fund under section 642(c)(5) of the Code and the corresponding regulations.

13.   Power of Amendment. The Fund is irrevocable. However, Public Charity shall have the power, acting alone, to amend this document and the associated instruments of transfer in any manner required for the sole purpose of ensuring that the Fund qualifies and continues to qualify as a pooled income fund within the meaning of section 642(c)(5).

IN WITNESS WHEREOF _____ [PUBLIC CHARITY] and _____, [TRUSTEE] by their duly authorized officers have signed this agreement the day and year first above written.

[PUBLIC CHARITY]
By
[TRUSTEE]
By

[Acknowledgements, Witnesses, etc.]

SECTION 5.   SAMPLE INSTRUMENT OF TRANSFER: ONE LIFE

On this _____ day of _____, 19_____, I hereby transfer to the _____ Public Charity Pooled Income Fund, under the terms and conditions set forth in its Declaration of Trust, the following property:

The income interest attributable to the property transferred shall be paid as follows:

A. To me during my lifetime.

B. To _____ during his or her life. However, I reserve the right to revoke, solely by will, this income interest.

Upon the termination of the income interest, the Trustee of the Fund will sever from the Fund an amount equal to the value of the remainder interest in the transferred property and transfer it to Public Charity:

A. For its general uses and purposes.

B. For the following charitable purpose(s): _____ However, if it is not possible for Public Charity in its sole discretion to use the severed amount for the specified purpose(s), then it may be used for the general purposes of Public Charity. This instrument and the transfer of property made pursuant thereto shall be effective after acceptance by both the Donor and the Trustee.

IN WITNESS WHEREOF _____ and _____ [TRUSTEE] by its duly authorized officer have signed this agreement the day and year first above written.
[DONOR]
[TRUSTEE]
By

(Acknowledgements, Witnesses, etc.)

SECTION 6.   SAMPLE INSTRUMENT OF TRANSFER: TWO LIVES, CONSECUTIVE INTERESTS

On this _____ day of _____, 19_____, I hereby transfer

to the _____ Public Charity Pooled Income Fund, under the terms and conditions set forth in its Declaration of Trust, the following property:

The income interest attributable to the property transferred shall be paid as follows:

A. To me during my lifetime, and after my death to _____ during his or her lifetime. However, I reserve the right to revoke, solely by will, his or her income interest.

B. To _____ during his or her lifetime, and after his or her death to _____ during his or her lifetime. However, I reserve the right to revoke, solely by will, the income interest of either or both beneficiaries.

Upon the termination of the income interest, the Trustee of the Fund will sever from the Fund an amount equal to the value of the remainder interest in the transferred property and transfer it to Public Charity:

A. For its general uses and purposes.

B. For the following charitable purpose(s): _____ However, if it is not possible for Public Charity in its sole discretion to use the severed amount for the specified purpose(s), then it may be used for the general purposes of Public Charity. This instrument and the transfer of property made pursuant thereto shall be effective after acceptance by both the Donor and the Trustee.

IN WITNESS WHEREOF _____ and _____, [TRUSTEE] by its duly authorized officer have signed this agreement the day and year first above written.
[DONOR]
[TRUSTEE]
By

(Acknowledgements, Witnesses, etc.)

SECTION 7. SAMPLE INSTRUMENT OF TRANSFER: TWO LIVES, CONCURRENT AND CONSECUTIVE INTERESTS

On this _____ day of _____, 19_____, I hereby transfer to the _____ Public Charity Pooled Income Fund, under the terms and conditions set forth in its Declaration of Trust, the following property:

The income interest attributable to the property transferred shall be paid as follows:

A. _____% to me during my lifetime, and _____% to _____ during his or her lifetime. After the death of the first income beneficiary to die, the survivor shall be entitled to the entire income. However, I reserve the right to revoke, solely by will, _____'s income interest.

B. _____% to _____ during his or her lifetime and _____% to _____ during his or her lifetime. Upon the death of the first income beneficiary to die, the survivor shall be entitled to receive the entire income. However, I reserve the right to revoke, solely by will, the income interest of either or both beneficiaries.

Upon the termination of the income interest, the Trustee of the Fund will sever from the Fund an amount equal to the value of the remainder interest in the transferred property and transfer it to Public Charity:

A. For its general uses and purposes.

B. For the following charitable purpose(s): _____ However, if it is not possible for Public Charity in its sole discretion to use the severed amount for the specified purpose(s), then it may be used for the general purposes of Public Charity.

This instrument and the transfer of property made pursuant thereto shall be effective after acceptance by both the Donor and the Trustee.

IN WITNESS WHEREOF _____ and _____, [TRUSTEE] by its duly authorized officer have signed this agreement the day and year first above written.

[DONOR]

[TRUSTEE]

By

(Acknowledgements, Witnesses, etc.)

SECTION 8.   APPLICATION

The Service will recognize a trust as meeting all of the requirements of a qualified pooled income fund under section 642(c)(5) of the Code if the public charity responsible for the creation and maintenance of the trust makes reference in the trust instrument of the fund to this revenue procedure and adopts substantially similar documents, provided the trust operates in a manner consistent with the terms of the trust instrument, and provided it is a valid trust under applicable local law. A trust that contains substantive provisions in addition to those provided by this revenue procedure (other than provisions necessary to establish a valid trust under applicable local law) or that omits any of those provisions will not necessarily be disqualified, but neither will it qualify under the provisions of this revenue procedure.

SECTION 9.   EFFECTIVE DATE

This revenue procedure is effective for ruling requests received in the National Office after November 28, 1988, the date of publication of this revenue procedure in the Internal Revenue Bulletin.

In 1988, the IRS issued a sample declaration of trust and instruments of transfer that meet the requirements of a pooled income fund (Rev. Proc. 88-54, 1988-2 C.B. 715). The full text of this document is as follows:

Rev. Proc. 88-54

SECTION 1.   BACKGROUND

Rev. Proc. 88-53, page 13, this Bulletin, makes available a sample declaration of trust and instruments of transfer that meet the applicable requirements under section 642(c)(5) of the Internal Revenue Code for a pooled income fund.

Rev. Proc. 88-3, 1988-1 I.R.B. 29, sets forth areas of the Internal Revenue Code under the jurisdiction of the Associate Chief Counsel (Technical and International) in which the Internal Revenue Service will not issue advance rulings or determination letters. Section 4 of Rev. Proc. 88-3 lists areas in which rulings or determination letters will not ordinarily be issued.

SECTION 2.   PROCEDURE

Rev. Proc. 88-3 is amplified by adding to section 4 the following:

Section 170—Charitable, Etc., Contributions and Gifts. Whether a transfer to a pooled income fund described in section 642(c)(5) of the Code qualifies for a charitable deduction under section 170(f)(2)(A).

Section 642—Pooled Income Funds. Whether a pooled income fund satisfies the requirements described in section 642(c)(5) of the Code.

Section 2055—Transfers for Public, Charitable and Religious Uses. Whether a transfer to a pooled income fund described in section 642(c)(5) of the Code qualifies for a charitable deduction under section 2055(e)(2)(A).

Section 2522—Charitable and Similar Gifts. Whether a transfer to a pooled income fund described in section 642(c)(5) of the Code qualifies for a charitable deduction under section 2522(c)(2)(A).

SECTION 3.   EFFECTIVE DATE

This revenue procedure will apply to all ruling requests received in the National Office after November 28, 1988, the date of publication of this revenue procedure.

SECTION 4.   EFFECT ON OTHER REVENUE PROCEDURES

Rev. Proc. 88-3 is amplified.

Appendix G

Monthly Federal Interest Rates Used in Valuing Partial Interests (IRC § 7520)

Month	Rate (%)	Rev. Rul.
July 1989	10.6	89-86
Aug. 1989	10.0	89-92
Sep. 1989	9.8	89-105
Oct. 1989	10.2	89-111
Nov. 1989	10.0	89-117
Dec. 1989	9.8	89-127
Jan. 1990	9.6	90-1
Feb. 1990	9.8	90-12
Mar. 1990	10.2	90-22
April 1990	10.6	90-28
May 1990	10.6	90-41
June 1990	11.0	90-48
July 1990	10.6	90-52
Aug. 1990	10.4	90-66
Sep. 1990	10.2	90-75
Oct. 1990	10.6	90-81
Nov. 1990	10.6	90-92
Dec. 1990	10.2	90-99
Jan. 1991	9.8	91-1
Feb. 1991	9.6	91-9

Month	Rate (%)	Rev. Rul.
Mar. 1991	9.6	91-15
April 1991	9.6	91-23
May 1991	9.6	91-29
June 1991	9.6	91-35
July 1991	9.6	91-39
Aug. 1991	9.8	91-41
Sep. 1991	9.6	91-48
Oct. 1991	9.0	91-53
Nov. 1991	8.6	91-57
Dec. 1991	8.6	91-62
Jan. 1992	8.2	92-1
Feb. 1992	7.6	92-8
Mar. 1992	8.0	92-13
April 1992	8.4	92-23
May 1992	8.6	92-33
June 1992	8.4	92-39
July 1992	8.2	92-50
Aug. 1992	7.8	92-59
Sep. 1992	7.2	92-67
Oct. 1992	7.0	92-87
Nov. 1992	6.8	92-90
Dec. 1992	7.4	92-104
Jan. 1993	7.6	93-1
Feb. 1993		93-

Appendix H

Planned Giving
Selected Bibliography

The professional literature in the field of planned giving is extensive; thus, these materials are collected here, rather than in footnotes throughout the text.

Chapter 3 The Concept of Planned Giving

Weithorn, "Trusts With Charitable Interests," 4 *Real Prop. Prob. & Trust* J. 624 (1969).

Clark, "Charitable Remainder Regulations Provide Guidelines for Operation of New Rules," 33 *J. Tax.* 214 (1970).

Fleming, "Charitable Trusts Under the Tax Reform Act," 48 *Taxes* 757 (1970).

Fremont-Smith, "Charitable Scene in Relation to the Tax Reform Act of 1969," 5 *Real Prop. Prob. & Trust J.* 393 (1970).

Myers, "Charitable Contributions," 4 *Ind. Legal Forum* (No. 1) 217 (1970).

Livsey, "Charitable Deductions: Planning Under the New Restrictions," 57 *A.B.A. J.* 274 (1971).

Olsen and Gleit, "Prop. Regs. Clarify Many Aspects of New Complex Charitable Contribution Deduction Rules," 35 *J. Tax.* 66 (Aug. 1971).

Peter, Jr., "Analytic Comparison of the Three Split-Interest Charitable Trusts Vehicles," 35 *J. Tax.* 240 (1971).

Turley, Jr., "Charitable Deductions, Remainders to Charity, and the Tax Reform Act" 8 *Houston L. Rev.* 411 (1971).

Haberman, "Trusts and the Tax Reform Act," 54 *Marq. L. Rev.* 117 (Spring 1971).

Jackson, "Gifts of Remainder Interests to Charity," 47 *Cal. S. B. J.* 22 (1972).

Riband, "Gifts in Trust of Income and Remainder Interests to Charity," 30 *N.Y.U. Inst. Fed. Tax.* 87 (1972).

Thomsen, "Split Interest Gifts to Charity," 7 *Real Prop. Prob. & Trust J.* 552 (1972).

Clark, "Inter-vivos and Testamentary Charitable Trusts Under the Tax Reform Act of 1969 and Regulations," 31 *N.Y.U. Inst. Fed. Tax.* 1127 (1973).

Hardingham, "Trusts Including Charitable and Noncharitable Purposes—Special Statutory Provisions," 47 *Austin L. J.* 68 (Feb. 1973).

Moore, "Split-Interest Charitable Trusts," 7 *Inst. Est. Plan.* 73 (1973).

Stevens, "Certainty and Charity—Recent Developments in the Law of Trusts," 52 *Can. B. Rev.* 372 (1974).

Tomeo, "Charitable Deferred Giving," 48 *Conn. B. J.* 48 (1974).

Wicker, "Charitable Trusts," 11 *Gonzaga L. Rev.* 1 (1975).

Horvitz, "Planning an Effective Gift Giving Program," 10 *Inst. Estate Plan.* 17.1 (1976).

Kannry, "Giving AFTER The 76 Tax Reform," X *Phil. Mon.* (No. 1) 19 (1977).

_____, "Planning Considerations for Charitable Contributions," 13 *Real Prop. Probs. & Trust J.* 581 (Fall 1978).

Brown, "All About Planned Giving," 117 *Trusts & Estates* 744 (1978).

Kennedy, "Ascertainable Standards, Discretionary Powers, and Charitable Remainders," 56 *Taxes* 78 (1978).

Lafferty, "Deferred Giving Developments," 117 *Trusts & Estates* 753 (1978).

_____, "Economic and Tax Ramifications of Charitable Giving Through Split-Interest Trusts," 52 *Temp. L. Q.* 1040 (1979).

_____, "Deferred Giving to Charity," XXXIII *Adv. Underwriter* (No. 3) 7 (Mar. 1979).

Peter, "Analytic Comparison of the Three Split-Interest Charitable Trust Vehicles," 35 *J. Tax.* 240 (1979).

Allinger, "Glossary of Terms Used in Planned Giving," 11 *Fund Raising Man.* (No. 6) 18 (1980).

Ruby, "Three Trust Documents," 4 *ALI-ABA Course Materials J.* 37 (April 1980).

DioGuardi, "Tax Economics of Charitable Giving," 120 *Trusts & Estates* (No. 2) 19 (1981).

Temple, "Using Deferred Charitable Gifts to Achieve Maximum Transmission of Family Wealth Tax Free," 30 *Tax. for Law.* 216 (1983).

Smith, "Deferred Giving: Letting the Donor Have His Cake While You Eat It Too," *Found. News*, 22 (Jan./Feb. 1984).

Carmichael, "Deferred Gifts for Youth: Weigh All Options," 16 *Fund Raising Man.* (No. 12) 56 (1986).

Greenberg and Hellige, "Overall Look at Planned Giving Options " 16 *Fund Raising Man.* (No. 12) 74 (1986).

Hobson, "Deferred Giving: Accent on Planning," 16 *Fund Raising Man.* (No. 12) 58 (1986).

Rosenbloom, Osherow, and Anderson, "Taking Advantage of the Opportunities Presented by IRS' 10% Valuation Tables," 64 *J. Tax.* 26 (1986).

Graham, "What Fund Raisers Should Know About Planned Giving," 16 *Fund Raising Man.* (No. 12) 28 (1986).

Geary, "The 'Now' Value of Deferred Gifts," 17 *Fund Raising Man.* (No. 12) 62 (1987).

Graham, "Is Planned Giving Dead?," 17 *Fund Raising Man.* (No. 12) 48 (1987).

Recer, "How Planned Charitable Gifts Benefit Heirs," 17 *Fund Raising Management* (No. 12) 38 (1987).

Sharpe, Jr., "Planned Giving—Key to Prosperity, Professionalism," 17 *Fund Raising Man.* (No. 12) 69 (1987).

Giese and Murray, "Planned Giving in A Capital Campaign," 18 *Fund Raising Man.* (No. 13) 43 (1988).

Boyle, "Evaluating Split-Interest Valuation," 24 *Ga. L. Rev.* 1 (1989).

Moerschbaecher, "Planned Caring: Planned Giving of Tomorrow?," 20 *Fund Raising Man.* (No. 1) 28 (1989).

Sharpe, "Planned Gifts Come of Age," 20 *Fund Raising Man.* (No. 2) 78 (1989).

Freeman and Klein, "The Economics of Charitable Gift Planning," 131 *Trusts & Estates* 22 (Aug. 1992).

Chapter 8   Estate and Gift Tax Considerations

Lauritzen, "Charitable Bequests and Powers of Invasion," 13 *Tax Coun. Q.* 395 (1969).

_____, "Restrictions on Charitable Testamentary Gifts," 5 *Real Prop. Prob. & Trusts J.* 290 (1970).

Lauritzen, "Charitable Bequests and Powers of Invasion," 14 *Tax Coun. Q.* 1 (1970).

Lewis, "Testamentary Charitable Remainder Trusts Under the Tax Reform Act of 1969," 48 *Taxes* 464 (1970).

Moore, "Estate Planning Under the Tax Reform Act of 1969: The Uses of Charity," 56 *Va. L. Rev.* 565 (1970).

Myers and Quiggle, "Charitable Contributions and Bequests by Individuals: The Impact of the Tax Reform Act," 39 *Ford. L. Rev.* 185 (1970).

Fratcher, "Bequests for Charitable Purposes," 56 *Ia. L. Rev.* 773 (1971).

Lemann, "Charitable Split-Interest Trusts in Estate Planning," 18 *La. B. J.* 259 (1971).

Morrison and Marcus, "Estate Planning Considerations for Charitable Trusts and Charitable Remainder Trusts Under the Tax Reform Act of 1969," 75 *Dick. L. Rev.* 185 (1971).

Galant, "Planning Opportunity: The Gifting of Closely Held Stock to Charitable Organizations," 51 *Taxes* 645 (1973).

Snyder, "Role of Charitable Contributions in Estate Planning: How to Eat Part of Your Cake and Keep Almost All of It," 9 *Wake Forest L. Rev.* 343 (1973).

Teitell, "Philanthropy and Estate Planning," 9 *Law Notes* 71 (Spring 1973).

Aulino, "Estate Distributions to Charitable Remainder Trusts," 114 *Trusts & Estates* 458 (1975).

Burke, "Charitable Giving and Estate Planning," 28 *Tax Law.* 289 (1975).

Echter, "Equitable Treatment for the Artist's Estate," 114 *Trusts & Estates* 394 (1975).

—————, "Donations Mortis Causa," 22 *Loyola L. Rev.* 768 (1976).

Browder, "Giving or Leaving—What Is a Will?," 75 *Mich. L. Rev.* 845 (April/May 1977).

Caffrey, "Charitable Bequests: Delegating Discretion to Choose the Objects of the Testator's Beneficence," 44 *Tenn. L. Rev.* 307 (1977).

Engel, "Pre and Post Mortem Planning for Charitable Giving," 116 *Trusts & Estates* 392 (1977).

Snyder, "The Tax Reform Act of 1976—Its Impact on the Role of Charitable Contributions in Estate Planning," 4 *N. Ky. L. Rev.* 283 (1977).

Cowley and Jones, "Estate and Gift Tax Unification: The Concepts and Selected Giving Problems,'" 36 *N.Y.U. Inst. Fed. Tax.* 273 (1978).

Mangum, "'Charitable Transfers and Estate Planning," 38 *N.Y.U. Inst. Fed. Tax.* 40-1 (1980).

Sugarman and Thomson, "Use of Charitable Giving in Estate Planning Under the 1981 Tax Act," 3 *Found. News* 66 (Nov./Dec. 1981).

Kirchick and Beckwith, "The Internal Revenue Service Changes the Odds On Death and Taxes," 62 *Taxes* 699 (1984).

Schmolka, "Income Taxation of Charitable Remainder Trusts and Decedents' Estates: Sixty-six Years of Astigmatism," 40 *Tax L. Rev.* 5 (1984).

Taylor, "The Charitable Remainder Trust: A Unique Estate Planning Technique," 69 *Taxes* 106 (1991).

Chapter 11   Gifts by Means of Charitable Remainder Trusts

Clark, "Charitable Remainder Regulations Provide Guidelines for Operation of New Rules," 33 *J. Tax.* 214 (1970).

Lewis, "Testamentary Charitable Remainder Trusts Under the Tax Reform Act of 1969," 48 *Taxes* 464 (1970).

Sanders, "How to Draft Charitable Remainder Trusts in View of New Proposed Regs," 33 *J. Tax.* 258 (1970).

_____, "Accumulation Trusts and Charitable Remainder Trusts: A Panel," 23 So. *Cal. Tax Inst.* 501 (1971).

_____, "Charitable Remainder Trusts Under the Tax Reform Act," 6 *Real Prop. Prob. & Trust J.* 384 (1971).

Gillon, "In a Strait Jacket on the Bed of Procrustes—Charitable Remainder Trusts Under the Tax Reform Act of 1969," 32 *Ala. Law.* 243 (1971).

Sacher, "Proposed Regs on Charitable Remainder Trusts Point Up Value of Unitrusts," 35 *J. Tax.* 380 (1971).

Sanders, "Charitable Remainder Trusts Under the Tax Reform Act of 1969," 12 *B.C. Ind. & Com. L. Rev.* 409 (1971).

Swados, "Charitable Remainder Trusts—Drafting and Valuation Guidelines," 29 *N.Y.U. Inst. Fed. Tax.* 2023 (1971).

Ashby, "Charitable Remainder Trusts: The New Look," 111 *Trusts & Estates* 530 (1972).

Garibaldi, "Some Final Problems for the Charitable Taxpayer: Gift Annuities; Pooled Income Funds; Split Interest Trusts; Valuation of Charitable Gifts," 30 *N.Y.U. Inst. Fed. Tax.* 117 (1972).

Olsen and Ledwith, "Final Regulations Point the Way to Effectively Use Charitable Remainder Trusts," 37 *J. Tax.* 368 (1972).

Teitell, "Charitable Remainder Unitrusts Under the Tax Reform Act," 111 *Trusts & Estates* 858 (1972).

―――――, "Charitable Remainder Trusts, Pooled Income Funds and the 1976 Tax Reform Act," 46 *U.M.B.C. L. Rev.* 357 (1973).

Moore, "Split-Interest Charitable Trusts," 7 *Inst. Estate Plan.* 73 (1973).

Olsen and Ledwith, "Final Regulations Liberalize Income Option Unitrust Treatment," 38 *J. Tax.* 142 (1973).

Olsen and Ledwith, "Charitable Remainder Trusts: How to Comply With the Final Regulations," 38 *J. Tax.* 2 (1973).

Seymour, "Charitable Remainder Trusts," 45 *N.Y.S. B. J.* 301 (1973).

Sneed, "Charitable Remainder Trusts," 25 *So. Cal. Tax Inst.* 87 (1973).

Willis "The Unitrust: An Income and Estate Planning Tool" 112 *Trusts & Estates* 821 (1973).

Wren, "Charitable Remainder Trusts: Some Considerations to Draftsmanship," 8 *U. Richmond L. Rev.* 25 (1973).

Crockett, "Charitable Remainder Trusts—New Trust Vehicles for Tax Planning," 19 St. *Louis U. L. J.* 161 (1974).

Ibach and Lehrfeld, "Dysfunctions in Deferred Giving: Working Out Problems of Unqualified Charitable Remainder Trusts," 113 *Trusts & Estates* 372 (1974).

Seymour, "Charitable Remainder Trusts," 37 *Tex. B. J.* 827 (1974).

―――――, "Charitable Remainder Trusts: Reforming and Drafting Split-Interest Trusts Under the New Law," 52 *Chi-Kent L. Rev.* 83 (1975).

―――――, "Model Charitable Remainder Unitrust," 10 *Real Prop. & Trusts* 535 (1975).

Cannon, "Charitable Remainder Trusts: A Study of Current Problems," 1975 *Brigham Young U. L. Rev.* 49 (1975).

Petroff, "How to Choose the Right Charitable Remainder Trust," 114 *Trusts & Estates* 871 (1975).

Teitell, "How to Work With Charitable Remainder Annuity Trusts," 114 *Trusts & Estates* 863 (1975).

Whaley, "Charitable Remainder Trusts and Pooled Income Funds: Internal Revenue Service Ruling Policy," 3 *J. Coll. & U. L,* 15 (1975).

Wicher, "Charitable Trusts," 11 *Gonzaga L. Rev.* 1 (1975).

Flannery, "Variation of the Charitable Remainder Trust," 1977 *N.Z. L. J.* 368 (1977).

_____, "Charitable Remainder Trusts, Pooled Income Funds and the 1976 Tax Reform Act," 46 *U.M.K.C. L. Rev.* 357 (1978).

Ashby, "Charitable Remainder Unitrusts as a Refuge for Low Basis Property," 117 *Trusts & Estates* 312 (1978).

Kennedy, "Ascertainable Standards, Discretionary Powers, and Charitable Remainders," 56 *Taxes* 78 (Feb. 1978).

Moore, "Income Taxation of Charitable Trusts," 37 *N.Y.U. Inst. Fed. Tax.* 41.1 (1979).

Peckham and Milstein, "Charitable Remainder Trusts: Tax Planning and Drafting Considerations," 14 *New England L. Rev.* 442 (1979).

Thiewes, "Charitable Remainder Trusts," 35 *Mo. B. J.* 107 (1979).

Tidd, "Charitable Remainder Trusts: Funding and Investment Considerations," 57 *Taxes* 577 (1979).

Fowler, "Charitable Remainder Trusts and Pooled Income Funds—Using Computer Simulation to Rank the Benefits," 11 *Tax Advisor* 68 (1980).

Lichter, "Highlights of Modern Charitable Remainder Trusts," 119 *Trusts & Estates* 46 (1980).

Teitell, "Technical Remainder Trust Ruling Reduces Deduction," 119 *Trusts & Estates* 61 (1980).

Recer, "Using the Charitable Remainder Trust in Real Estate," XII *NSFRE J.* (No. 2) 34 (1987).

Mering, "Combination of Charitable Remainder and Insurance Trusts can Increase Wealth," 17 *Est. Plan.* 356 (1990).

Whitney, "Unique Funding for Charitable Remainder Trusts," *J. Amer. Soc. CLU & ChFC* 36 (1990).

Hakala, "Turning Appreciation Into Income—Without Triggering Tax Using a Charitable Remainder Trust," 1 *J. Tax. Exempt Orgs.* 15 (Winter 1990).

Fischer and Jones, "Charitable Remainder Trusts: Planning and Designing Issues," 131 *Trusts & Estates* 45 (Jan. 1992).

McDonald, "Charitable Remainder Trusts: Realities and Proper Planning," 131 *Trusts & Estates* 45 (July 1992).

Lochray and Hunt, "Using Real Estate Options in Charitable Remainder Trusts," 131 *Trusts & Estates* 49 (Dec. 1992).

Chapter 12   Gifts by Means of Pooled Income Funds

Boggs, "Pooled Income Funds May Now Be the Best Method of Charitable Giving," 35 *J. Tax.* 162 (1971).

Teitell, "Pooled Income Funds Under the Tax Reform Act," 110 *Trusts & Estates* 625 (1971).

Garibaldi, "Some Final Problems for the Charitable Taxpayer: Gift Annuities; Pooled Income Funds; Split Interest Trusts; Valuation of Charitable Gifts," 30 *N.Y.U. Inst. Fed. Tax.* 117 (1972).

_____, "Charitable Remainder Trusts, Pooled Income Funds and the 1976 Tax Reform Act," 46 *U.M.K.C. L. Rev.* 357 (1973).

_____, "Pooled Income Funds Under the Internal Revenue Code—Are They Subject to Securities and Exchange Commission Regulation?," 20 *Wayne L. Rev.* 1287 (1974).

Steward, "Pooled Income Funds: The New Spearhead of Deferred Giving," 114 *Trusts & Estates* 306 (1975).

Whaley, "Charitable Remainder Trusts and Pooled Income Funds: Internal Revenue Service Ruling Policy," 3 *J. Coll. & Univ. L.* 15 (Fall 1975).

Fowler, "Charitable Remainder Trusts and Pooled Income Funds— Using Computer Simulation to Rank the Benefits," 11 *Tax Advisor* 68 (1980).

Veres, "Using Pooled Income Funds to Pass ITC and Depreciation Through to Life-Income Donors," 61 *J. Tax.* 28 (July 1984).

Lochray, "Pooled Income Funds and the Depreciable Property Requirements," 3 *J. Tax. Exempt Orgs.* 31 (Fall 1991).

Chapter 13   Charitable Gift Annuities

Garibaldi, "Some Final Problems for the Charitable Taxpayer: Gift Annuities; Pooled Income Funds; Split Interest Trusts; Valuation of Charitable Gifts," 30 *N.Y.U. Inst. Fed. Tax.* 117 (1972).

Teitell, "Federal Tax Implications of Charitable Gift Annuities," 19 *N.Y. L. F.* 269 (1973).

_____, "Federal Tax Implications of Charitable Gift Annuities," 113 *Trusts & Estates* 642 (1974).

_____, "Federal Tax Implications of Charitable Gift Annuities," 3 *J. Coll. & Univ. L.* 26 (Fall 1975).

Eyre, "Annuity Agreement—'Simplicity Itself'," 1977 *B.T.R.* 379 (1977).

Mudry, "Higher Rates for Charitable Annuities—How Charitable Annuities Work," XVI *Phil. Mon.* (No. 8) 30 (1983).

Baglia, "Dramatic Changes in New Planned Giving Tables—New IRS Tables for Charitable Gift Annuities," XVII *Phil. Mon.* (No. 11) 5 (1984).

Canter III, "Charitable Gift Annuity: An Attractive Alternative," 16 *Fund Raising Man.* (No. 10) 104 (1986).

Berry, "Federal Tax and State Regulation of Charitable Gift Annuities," 3 *J. Tax. Exempt Orgs.* 15 (Summer 1991).

Chapter 15   Gifts by Means of Charitable Lead Trusts

Ashby, "Uses of Charitable Income Interests in Estate Planning," 115 *Trusts & Estates* 12 (1976).

Callahan, "Charitable 'Lead' Trusts—the Forgotten Member of the Trilogy," 11 *Inst. Estate & Plan.* 5.1 (1977).

Muchin, Lubelchek, and Grass, "Charitable Lead Trusts Can Provide Substantial Estate Planning Benefits," 49 *J. Tax.* 2 (1978).

O'Brien and Raabe, Jr., "High Interest Rates Increase Attractiveness of Charitable Lead Annuity Trusts and Unitrusts," 9 *Est. Plan.* 130 (1982).

Chapter 16   Gifts of Life Insurance

Chasman, "Charitable Gifts of Life Insurance," 109 *Trusts & Estates* 891 (1970).

Alpert, "Gifts of Life Insurance in Florida," 45 *Fla. B. J.* 72 (Feb. 1971).

Creedon, "Lifetime Gifts of Life Insurance," 20 *Prac. Law.* 27 (1974).

Lane and Frantzreb, "Life Insurance for Endowment—Great Concept Or Booby Trap?," 21 *Fund Raising Man.* (No. 2) 47 (1990).

Luecke and Bauer, "Charitable Life Insurance—the Ideal Deferred Gift," 21 *Fund Raising Man.* (No. 2) 41 (1990).

Murdich, "IRS Ruling Denies Deduction of Charitable Gifts of Life Insurance," 3 *J. Tax. Exempt Orgs.* 26 (Summer 1991).

Chapter 17   Establishing and Maintaining a Planned Giving Program

Schultz, "Ask Before You Buy—Planned Gifts Software Questions," 16 *Fund Raising Man.* (No. 12) 40 (1976).

Bell, "Identify Super Donors Through Direct Mail," 11 *Fund Raising Man.* (No. 6) 36 (1980).

Collier, "Use 'Selling Technique' To Generate Planned Gifts," 11 *Fund Raising Man.* (No. 6) 28 (1980).

Sinclaire, Jr., "Tap All Sources in Search for Major Gifts," 11 *Fund Raising Man.* (No. 6) 14 (1980).

Cruickshank, "Good Management Requires A Director of *Planning and Development*," XVII *Phil. Mon.* (No. 8) 16 (1984).

Lamport, Jr., "Psychological Dimensions: Fund Raising or Friendship Building," XVII *Phil. Mon.* (No. 7) 33 (1984).

Stewart, "How To Qualify Planned Gift Leads Promptly," XVII *Phil. Mon.* (No. 3) 33 (1984).

Stewart, "A Training Aid to Help Volunteers Qualify Gift Leads," XVII *Phil. Mon.* (No. 4) 33 (1984).

Sharpe, "Today's Planned Giving Executive: A New Breed," 16 *Fund Raising Man.* (No. 12) 34 (1986).

Sinclaire, Jr., "Avoiding Pitfalls and Pratfalls in Planned Giving Programs," 16 *Fund Raising Man.* (No. 12) 44 (1986).

Caswell, "How to Market Planned Giving," 17 *Fund Raising Man.* (No. 12) 56 (1987).

Schultz, "Four Steps to Closing a Major Planned Gift," 17 *Fund Raising Man.* 44 (1987).

White, "Planned Giving and Computers," 17 *Fund Raising Man.* (No. 12) 24 (1987).

Zieger, "How A Bequest Program Succeeded," 17 *Fund Raising Man.* (No. 12) (1987).

Converse, "Planned Giving Adds Stability to a Program," 18 *Fund Raising Man.* (No. 12) 48 (1988).

Field, "A New Way of Looking At Planned Giving," 18 *Fund Raising Man.* (No. 12) 55 (1988).

Leeseberg, "Anatomy of a Gift," 18 *Fund Raising Man.* (No. 12) 60 (1988).

Moerschbaecher, "Ethics in Planned Giving," 18 *Fund Raising Man.* (No. 12) 62 (1988).

Converse, "Think of the Possibilities!," 21 *Fund Raising Man.* (No. 12) 54 (1991).

Moran, "Warning: Think Before You Begin A Planned-Giving Program," 21 *Fund Raising Man.* (No. 12) 43 (1991).

Moran, "Where The Real Money Is In Planned Giving," 22 *Fund Raising Man.* (No. 5) 38 (1991).

Schmeling, "Integrating Planned Giving," 21 *Fund Raising Man.* (No. 12) 38 (1991).

Wildern, "Planned Giving: Keeping The Balance," 21 *Fund Raising Man.* (No. 12) 50 (1991).

Table of Cases

703

Table of IRS Revenue Rulings and Revenue Procedures

Revenue Rulings	Pages	Revenue Rulings	Pages	Revenue Rulings	Pages
68-69	181	77-491	281	92-57	375
68-113	342	78-38	169, 170, 173	92-58	564
68-174	173	78-84	138	92-107	433
69-80	524	78-85	137	92-108	435
69-90	121	78-95	148	93-8	435
69-93	166	78-105	390, 402, 416		
69-545	137, 144	78-152	281	Revenue Procedures	Pages
70-323	121	78-181	175		
70-452	280	75-189	109		
70-519	345	78-303	450	82-23	568
71-135	345	78-309	143	82-61	346
71-216	169	79-81	416, 418	88-3	428
72-194	360	79-249	360	88-53	428
72-395	410	79-368	394, 406	88-54	428
73-571	372	79-428	387, 400	89-20	410
73-597	345	80-38	394, 407	89-21	410
73-610	373	80-69	352	90-12	563
74-39	405	80-77	117, 121	90-30	410
74-149	403	80-104	398	90-31	410
74-224	143	80-123	374, 410	90-32	410
74-246	121	80-200	138	91-3	410, 428
74-241	447	80-233	352	92-94	537

Table of IRS Private Letter Rulings, Technical Advice Memoranda, and General Counsel Memoranda

The following privately issued pronouncements from the Internal Revenue Service, referenced to indicate the extent of IRS activity in a particular area and/or to reflect the thinking of the IRS on a particular topic, are coordinated to footnotes of individual chapters. (IRC § 6110(j)(3) states that these determinations are not to be used or cited as precedent.)

Citations are to IRS private letter rulings, technical advice memoranda, and general counsel memoranda directly pertinent to the material discussed. Seven-number items are private latter rulings and technical advice memoranda; five-number items are general counsel memoranda.

Chapter 4 The Fundamental Definitions

Footnote

102	8620017, 8709069, 8733007, 8810048, 9141011
104	8607037, 8608039, 8617120, 8625056, 8645030, 8645031, 8645032, 8611041, 8647072, 8651031, 8701008, 8713028, 8717020, 8720018, 8721008, 8721063, 8722033, 8740009, 8743007, 8803058, 8806040, 8816063, 8823033, 8828058, 8830073, 8835020, 8837084, 8838052, 8844028, 8844029, 8847061, 9017014, 9018007, 9022008, 9033050, 9041060, 9045045, 9131056, 9136008, 9138010
105	8615069, 8622026
108	8705041 (withdrawn (8826012) but not retroactively (8836040)), 8705078, 8730059

Footnote

146	9252023
170	8601093, 8604053, 8609060, 8616090, 8616012, 8616014, 8616089, 8617062, 8621049, 8643046, 8649022, 8712008, 8736021, 8736022, 8806029, 9023033, 9143038, 9216006
177	8601043, 8602011, 8603026, 8603032, 8603033, 8603037, 8604008, 8604034, 8604053, 8605009, 8605017, 8606016, 8606043, 8606046, 8607109, 8608034, 8609057, 8609064, 8609065, 8610019, 8610020, 8610026, 8610030, 8610067, 8611017, 8611062, 8613006 (re 7842062), 8613016, 8613030, 8614015, 8614023, 8616013, 8617036, 8618013, 8618015, 8618016, 8618028, 8618037, 8620026, 8621005, 8621032, 8622009, 8622027, 8622037, 8623020, 8624013, 8625030, 8625032, 8625043, 8626099, 8628016, 8629016, 8629055, 8630012, 8631015, 8631024, 8631034, 8632026, 8633032, 8633045, 8634010, 8634017, 8634024, 8634044, 8636027, 8636048, 8636050, 8636099, 8637071, 8637073, 8637079, 8637084, 8638021, 8638037, 8638058, 8639015, 8639025, 8639027, 8641040, 8642076, 8642095, 8643058, 8644013, 8644014, 8644042–8644044, 8644063, 8644064, 8644069, 8645039, 8645048, 8645058, 8647007, 8647008, 8647027, 8649041, 8649059, 8650029, 8650031, 8650050, 8650064, 8651030, 8651063, 8651073, 8652041, 8652069, 8701035, 8701039, 8702011, 8702018, 8702038–8702041, 8702044, 8703024, 8703029, 8704011, 8704031, 8704032, 8705023, 8705024, 8706027, 8706029, 8706046, 8706054, 8707023, 8707052, 8708009, 8708019, 8708026, 8708047, 8708062, 8709017, 8709031, 8709041, 8709050, 8709057, 8709059, 8710040, 8710041, 8712029, 8712037, 8712038, 8713014, 8713017, 8713063–8713065, 8714040, 8715024, 8715025, 8715034, 8715043, 8720035, 8721007, 8721024, 8722044, 8722071, 8722105, 8723015, 8723020, 8723040, 8724011, 8724012, 8724032, 8725023, 8727022, 8727023, 8727029, 8727032, 8727034–8727036, 8727038–8727040, 8727053, 8727067, 8729015, 8729017, 8729031, 8729032, 8730027, 8730030–8730032, 8730066, 8731050, 8731051, 8731061, 8731062, 8732026, 8733016, 8733026, 8735027, 8737012, 8737088, 8739021, 8739022, 8740016, 8740018, 8742023, 8743006, 8743066, 8744039, 8745015, 8748063, 8749052, 8750012, 8752012, 8753009, 8801004, 8801016, 8803028, 8803073, 8804032, 8805022, 8805036, 8805037, 8805055, 8806045, 8807014, 8807020, 8807021, 8808013, 8808021, 8808039, 8808043, 8808079, 8809036–8809039, 8809045, 8809048, 8809058, 8810037, 8811012, 8811013, 8816058,

Footnote

8816059, 8817021–8817024, 8818021, 8819014, 8819021,
8819023–8819025, 8819035, 8820037, 8820065, 8821007,
8821014, 8821019, 8822022, 8822023, 8823019, 8823020,
8823031, 8823047, 8825074, 8825075, 8826031, 8828036,
8828038, 8828040, 8828042, 8828053, 8830085, 8836018,
8836022, 8836029, 8837037, 8837038, 8837041, 8838032,
8838065, 8839023, 8839064, 8841049, 8841051, 8844034,
8845016, 8646035, 8847027–8847029, 8847046, 8847069,
8849068, 8850019–8850023, 8852008, 8903041, 8903042,
8903050, 8903064, 8903069, 8904009, 8906046, 8907013,
8909042, 8909058, 9001058, 9002048, 9004010, 9005066,
9006010, 9008012, 9008044, 9008046, 9009018, 9009019,
9009040, 9009047, 9009048, 9012052, 9012056, 9014033,
9015025, 9015027, 9016015, 9016016, 9016068, 9016069,
9018015, 9018041, 9019016, 9019035, 9019043, 9020024,
9021018, 9021044, 9022014, 9022049, 9023013, 9023031,
9023033, 9024030, 9024033, 9025008, 9027023, 9028001,
9029006, 9031004, 9032020, 9032029, 9033009, 9034011,
9034035, 9035043, 9040048, 9042009, 9042056, 9043025,
9043038, 9044048, 9045042, 9048006, 9048050, 9051013,
9052054, 9104034, 9106008, 9110047, 9127030, 9132043,
9133012, 9134014, 9138024, 9253038

Chapter 12   Gifts to Pooled Income Funds

64

8601046, 8603031, 8603043, 8603045, 8603055, 8603068,
8604052, 8604071, 8607014, 8607036, 8609056, 8609058,
8609066–8609068, 8610021, 8611033, 8611051, 8611061,
8613021, 8614017, 8615012, 8615016, 8615017, 8615019,
8615020, 8615029, 8617009, 8617020, 8617021, 8618014,
8618029, 8618038, 8620009, 8620032, 8621031, 8621045,
8621046, 8621051, 8621053, 8622008, 8622014, 8622035,
8623014, 8624027, 8624030, 8624036, 8624057, 8625021,
8625024, 8627026, 8627028, 8627031, 8629017, 8629034,
8630077, 8631020, 8632015, 8633033, 8634042, 8634043,
8634047, 8637094, 8638018, 8638064, 8641043, 8642048,
8643063, 8647009, 8647014, 8648065, 8648067, 8649047,
8649048, 8650032, 8650034, 8650036, 8652060, 8652062,
8702042, 8702043, 8703035, 8703063, 8703070, 8704012,
8704013, 8704016, 8705020, 8705028, 8706017, 8706026,
8706047, 8706056, 8706064, 8707048, 8707053, 8708010,
8708034, 8709040, 8710036, 8710038, 8710042, 8710048,
8710069, 8710070, 8712015, 8712016, 8712030–8712032,
8712040, 8713050, 8713079, 8714041, 8715015, 8715016,

Footnote

8715028, 8718033, 8718052, 8720036, 8720064, 8721051,
8721054, 8721064, 8722018, 8722055, 8722058, 8723014,
8724016, 8724031, 8725059, 8727052, 8729007, 8729033,
8729046, 8730015, 8730028, 8730034, 8731006, 8731018,
8731019, 8731049, 8732032, 8737051, 8737066, 8739028,
8739029, 8741013, 8741031, 8741056, 8742024, 8743036,
8743040, 8743042, 8744008, 8744037, 8745009, 8745020,
8747063, 8753010, 8801023, 8803027, 8803032, 8803036,
8803037, 8803039, 8804041, 8804074, 8804076, 8805027,
8805030, 8805031, 8805039, 8805040, 8807019, 8807068,
8807069, 8807077, 8808020, 8808022, 8808024, 8809046,
8809054, 8809056, 8810025, 8810038, 8810063, 8810083,
8811014, 8811022, 8811035, 8811042, 8812030, 8812053,
8812056, 8815007, 8815039, 8816049, 8817035, 8817067,
8817068, 8818014–8818016, 8818018, 8818020, 8818024,
8819031, 8819036, 8820011, 8820025, 8820038, 8820042,
8821010, 8821011, 8821013, 8821016, 8821031–8821038,
8821040–8821043, 8821045, 8821048–8821052, 8821055,
8822007, 8823046, 8823048, 8823055, 8823080, 8823083,
8823090, 8825072, 8825076, 8828037, 8828039, 8828044,
8828052, 8830028, 8834035, 8834036, 8834038, 8834049,
8834053, 8834058, 8836021, 8836043, 8836044, 8837032,
8837040, 8837051, 8838031, 8839055–8839057, 8839063,
8839074, 8839086, 8845013, 8846026, 8846027, 8846034,
8846036, 8847022, 8847031, 8847057, 8847058, 8847062,
8849063, 8849065, 8849066, 8903067, 8903070, 8904013,
8904055, 8904056, 8906019, 8909015, 8909033, 8911038,
9002042, 9128023

72   9248017

82   8712046, 8713044–8713048, 8736008, 8752048, 8803042,
8823082, 8828068, 8830042, 8830044–8830045, 8831023–
8831024, 8838033, 9026017, 9027036, 9029053, 9030041–
9030042

Chapter 13   Charitable Gift Annuities

28   9042043

Chapter 15   Gifts by Means of Charitable Lead trusts

15   8736020

Chapter 18   International Giving by Individuals During Lifetime

19   9250041

Table of IRS Private Determinations Cited in Text

Private Letter Rulings and Technical Advice Memoranda	Pages	Private Letter Rulings and Technical Advice Memoranda	Pages
7802001	178	9015049	298
7842062	408	9037021	131
7938001	513	9110016	473
8015017	441	9118012	118
8110016	444	9119011	118
8202137	444	9143030	400
8204220	447	9147007	124, 577
8333019	448	9147040	475
8420003	177	9204036	403
8526015	298	9205031	401
8535019	448	9243043	345
8536061	409		
8601033	407	**General Counsel Memoranda**	**Pages**
8601041	426		
86080420	115	35319	501
8616020	427	37444	500, 502
8618051	178	39664	325
8706011	170	39877	118
8745013	371		
8748001	514		
8822935	392		
8832003	557		
8930001	184		
9004030	115		

Index

719

gift definition and, 107, 108, 109–110
gifts of property subject to debt, 296–297
income definition, 56
tax-exempt organizations and, 11
unrelated business income rules, 156
U.S.–Sweden Estate and Gift Tax Treaty, 521–522
U.S. tax system, *see* Federal tax system
Unitrust interests, contributions of, 337–338
Universal life insurance, described, 470
Universities, 8, 23, 144, 156–157, 294, 561, 578, 589
Unreimbursed expenses, gifts of, 343–347
Units, pooled income fund, 93–94, 419–420
Unrelated business income:
    charitable gift annuities and, 441
    definition, 159–160
Unrelated business income rules, 155–163
    exempted activities, 160–162
    exempted income, 162–163
    overview of, 155–163
    regularly carried on, definition of, 158–159
    trade or business, definition of, 157–158
    unrelated business definition, 159–160
    unrelated business taxable income definition, 160
Unrelated business taxable income definition, unrelated business income rules, 160
Unrelated debt-financed income:
    charitable gift annuities and, 441–443
    charitable remainder trusts and, 394
    life insurance gifts and, 481–482
Unrelated use property, property gifts, 189–192
Unusual grants, 149, 151
Use of property, gifts of, 340–341, 528

Vacation homes, 442
Valuation:
    appraisal requirements, 549–556
    art works, 290–293
    charitable lead trusts, 459
    conservation purposes, 323
    contributions in trust gifts, 338–339
    gain and, 57–58
    gems, 293–295

generation skipping transfer tax, 274
gifts of inventory, amount of reduction, 308–310
gift taxes, 254
gross estate, 268
inventory, 54–56
life insurance gifts, 471
money, gifts of, 179–180
penalties for misstatement, 363–365
pooled income funds, planned giving concept, 93–94
property gifts, 351–355
Valuation dates, 387
Valuation tables, 407–408, 425–426, 434–435, 455
Veterans' organizations:
    charitable organization definition and, 132
    in general, 8, 23, 31, 33, 223, 257, 599
    unrelated business income rules, exempted activities, 162
Voluntarism:
    creativity and, 17–18
    public policy and, 12, 13–15
Voluntary employees' beneficiary associations, 23, 31, 33
Volunteer labor, 125
Volunteers:
    planned giving program implementation, 487–488
    services, gifts of, 341–342

Wages and salaries:
    gain and, 56
    independent sector profile, 28
Wealth:
    estate and gift tax and, 248
    gain and, 56–57
    income contrasted, 42
    property and, 52
Wills, *see also* Estates
    charitable lead trusts, 462
    contests, 281–282
    planned gifts and, 79
    remainder interests, 280–282
Written statement requirement, inventory gifts, 306–307

Year-of-inclusion rules, 397